Secrets My Mother Kept

Kath Hardy

Kath Hardy grew up on a council estate in Dagenham in the 1950s and 60s, the second youngest of ten children. She was a teacher for more than 30 years, before becoming an education advisor. She now lives in Suffolk with her husband, and has two grown-up children.

KATH HARDY

Secrets
My Mother Kept

HODDER &
STOUGHTON

First published in Great Britain in 2013 by Hodder & Stoughton
An Hachette UK company

1

A CIP catalogue record for this title is available from the British Library

Hardback ISBN 978 1 444 77944 8
Paperback ISBN 978 1 444 76325 6
Ebook ISBN 978 1 444 76326 3

Typeset by Hewer Text UK Ltd, Edinburgh
Printed and bound by CPI Group (UK) Ltd, Croydon, CR0 4YY

Hodder & Stoughton policy is to use papers that are natural, renewable
and recyclable products and made from wood grown in sustainable
forests. The logging and manufacturing processes are expected to
conform to the environmental regulations of the country of origin.

Hodder & Stoughton Ltd
338 Euston Road
London NW1 3BH

www.hodder.co.uk

To Mum and Aunty, the towering forces in my life, who both in their own way shaped me into the person I am today.

Contents

Prologue

I remember wishing it wasn't so cold, but at least the sun shone through the breaks in the clouds.

'The sun shines on the righteous,' Aunty used to say.

It was four weeks since Mum had died. Standing still and straight next to my siblings, I thought of those who were missing: Marge, Marion's identical twin, and Mary, a year older, both in Australia with their families; my secret sister Sheila in the Isle of Man . . .

The priest stood next to the grave and said the prayers of internment in a soft clear voice. Mum was cremated soon after she died and now we were burying her ashes on the small family plot, next to her mother and father and older sister 'Aunty'. The only marker was a small plain wooden cross and the plot was overgrown with rough grass. I wished we had decided to scatter her ashes somewhere beautiful and not in that barren East London graveyard with its dilapidated statues and neglected monuments.

No one was crying except for me, and I wasn't crying for Mum, I was crying for myself.

I had begun to notice the changes in Mum during my weekly visits. She had lost weight, and was shrunken and grey. She had never had many wrinkles, but now her eyes were old and tired, and although she was only seventy-three, she looked frail and ill.

'Kath,' she said softly as I took her up a cup of tea, 'I need to clear out the cupboard in here.'

I looked at her lying in that bed and, to my shame, felt angry. In a few weeks I was having an operation – a serious one. It was my turn to be ill now; I needed her to look after me. Why was she talking about tidying the cupboard? It was blocked in by the wardrobe and no one had opened it in years.

'Mum, can you drink this?' I offered her the cup, but she turned her head away. Mum's bed was in the box room. I had slept most of my childhood nights in that room. First my sister Mary and I had slept together in a big double bed that took up most of the room. Once Mary had left home I shared the same bed with Mum. I used to dread the rare occasions when I was told to change the sheets because I didn't like to see the black speckles of mould that bloomed where the sheets touched the damp walls. There was a large air vent in the external wall but Mum covered it in plastic bags to stop the draughts and I guess that was why the walls were always running with moisture. The bedroom window looked out over our street, Valence Avenue. It was one of the main through routes in Dagenham. It was lined with tall horse chestnut trees, which we would scramble under every autumn searching for conkers.

Inside, the paintwork was peeling, and there was never any carpet on the floor, so when I got out of bed in the mornings my toes would freeze. As well as a double bed there was an old 1930s-style wardrobe and dressing table that had been donated by a well-meaning relative, and squeezed into the remaining space. These held a strange mixture of my things and Mum's and smelt of mothballs and damp. I still dream about that smell, and that room.

After Mary had left home she would sometimes send little presents home for Margaret and me. A pair of socks, a bar of soap, a flannel – small things, but I treasured them. We didn't really have things of our own, so I would squirrel these treasures away in my drawer of the dressing table. I never used any of them – they were far too special to use – I just got them out to touch and look at from time to time. There was no light bulb attached to the fitting that dangled from the centre of the ceiling because Mum couldn't afford to replace it. Consequently home-work had to be done sitting at the top of the stairs under the landing light. Downstairs was always much too noisy and busy and there was never any room for books.

As I stood in that room as an adult, it seemed to me that for all the happy memories, the walls were permeated with secret sorrows.

I hadn't got round to sorting out the cupboard while Mum was alive, but several months after the funeral I agreed to help my older sister Josie clear Mum's room. She and our sister Pat had never married and still lived in our old childhood home.

We began to sort through all the assorted junk and paraphernalia. Josie was looking hot and flushed, and I was worried about her.

'Are you sure you're okay, Josie?' I asked. 'We can stop for a rest if you like.'

She shook her head.' No, I'm fine.'

Her hair was fine like Mum's had been, but she dyed the grey. Josie had always been a very neat person, and was usually well groomed and conscious of her appearance. Her fingernails were always manicured and her hair perfectly styled. The one thing she had never been able to control was her weight, and it was this that was now making her breathless.

Cobwebs dangled from the top and sides of the cupboard, and my mind spun back fourteen years to when I had not long been at college, and my jewellery box mysteriously disappeared from the dressing table. Patrick, my then boyfriend, had bought me some large gold hoop earrings for my twenty-first birthday, a gold ingot pendant and some pretty gold and silver bangles. When I had questioned Mum about it she told me she had put the box in the cupboard to keep them safe. At the time I'd believed her totally, and it was only later that I realised that she must have sold them. Still, I watched closely as Josie groped about in the cupboard.

'What's this?'

She reached to the back of the shelf and pulled out a dusty old bag full of yellowing envelopes. They were all written in the same unfamiliar sloping hand, all with different postmarks, some dated from before I was born, but all addressed to me, Kathleen Stevens. I swallowed as I realised that she'd found something far more precious than that old jewellery box. Something that would have the potential to change my life; to help unravel the mysteries that had dogged it.

I

The Mummy Lady

Thinking back now, my memories of Dagenham began towards the end of the 1950s. I remember a patch of blue sky and someone singing 'Lulla Lulla Lullaby' in a soft, sweet, sad voice. I don't know how old I was, or who was singing, but the melody, though simple, was haunting. Rationing had ended several years before, and food was plentiful for those who could afford to buy it. However we were poor. Crushingly poor. We lived in the same house that our grandparents had moved to in the 1920s, but Dagenham had already begun a downward slide. The once well-kept red brick houses were starting to deteriorate, and many of the original tenants had moved on.

I don't suppose growing up as the second youngest in a single-parent family of ten is ever a bowl of cherries. Trying to do that as a Catholic in 1950s Dagenham was even harder. Pat was the oldest sister I knew, and I loved her to bits. She had shiny black hair and twinkling brown eyes that I could see through her glasses. To me she was all powerful; her strong arms kept me safe and she knew the answers to all my questions. Well, nearly all. I remember her taking me on a special visit one day. I suppose I must have been about three and my only younger sibling, Margaret, would have been about eighteen months old.

As Pat carried me, I wriggled in her arms. I could walk perfectly well; I wasn't a baby! The building we approached was tall, grey and forbidding. I decided to hang on to Pat after all. As we entered through the big doors there was a man who talked to us and then sent us towards the stone stairs. Pat carried me up them and I wondered where we were going. We had to wait with a lot of other people for the bell to ring so Pat took me over to the window to look out. I saw Margaret waiting outside with my other sister Josie; suddenly she looked up from my sister's arms with such a sad look on her face. I felt very important to be the one who was allowed inside.

The bell rang and we moved through the big swing doors. There were chairs and little tables, all empty and waiting. The doors at the other end of the big room opened and the ladies came in.

'There's Mummy,' whispered Pat, and walked over to the lady.

She kissed me on the cheek and gave me a sweetie. 'Hello darling,' she cooed, as Pat handed her an envelope. A tall man came over. He had a funny hat and he took the envelope from the Mummy lady, opened it, looked at it and then gave it back. She and Pat talked while I looked around at the other ladies and their visitors. Then the Mummy lady stroked my face and suggested, 'Why don't you run and say hello? They might have something nice for you,' and being a compliant child I slipped off Pat's lap and did as I was told.

''Ello sweetheart,' one lady said. She looked quite scary and big, with red raw hands and face, but she gave me a sweet so I took it and hurried on. Most of them were sitting at their own little tables, but others were dressed all the same in jackets with shiny buttons on them, and stood around the walls of the room watching everyone like nosey birds. Some of the ladies gave me a sweet, others just patted my head and some spoke to me, but I didn't go near the standing-up ones. I carried on without uttering a sound, just walked solemnly round to each in turn, round the big room with its shiny floor and cream painted walls and its unfamiliar smell.

Years later, Aunty used to stir her tea, look at the bubbles and say, 'Secrets and lies go to the sides and money stays in the middle,' and she would look slyly over at my mum, who would pretend she hadn't heard.

Our council house had been new when my grandparents had moved there in 1926. Granddad died before I was born and

Granny died when I was three, so I don't really remember either of them. I grew up in that house with my mum, two brothers and six sisters and Mum's older sister Edie, or 'Aunty' as we always called her. Strictly we were a family of ten children, but we never counted Sheila. Sheila was the oldest and had gone with her dad when he and Mum had split up during the war. I had never met her, and the only reason I knew she existed was because Aunty would sometimes say to my sister Pat, 'You're just like your sister Sheila.' Pat never answered and would just look away.

Aunty and Mum didn't talk to each other except through us.

Even though they were sitting in the same room as each other it'd be 'Tell your mother I'm going out!' or 'Ask Aunty if she wants a cup of tea.' The only direct communication they had was during ferocious arguments – the kind that makes your insides feel like they're falling out. Sometimes Aunty would throw things. She was smaller than Mum, with a thick head of tight curly hair that had been black, but was increasingly grey as the years passed. She would periodically have it permed at the hairdressers round the corner, and would come home looking like a poodle. She rarely washed her hair between times, preferring to rub olive oil into her head. She said it helped with her 'screws' which is what she called her arthritis. Her eyes were a deeper blue than Mum's but they still sparkled. Sometimes they sparked with mischief, as she loved to irritate people, especially Mum. We were never allowed to use bad language, even 'bum' was considered a swear word, but Aunty took great joy in flaunting that rule. If she was just in a playful mood she would talk about burps and farts, but when she was in a temper about something the language would get a lot more colourful!

One day we were sitting at the table and Aunty was shouting from the scullery. She came in like a whirlwind and turning towards Mum screeched, 'I don't care what yer bloody well say, I know what's been going on,' and she slung the teapot full of scalding tea on to the table where it landed, spewing out the hot liquid all over poor Mary.

'There was money in me drawer, and now it's gone!' she continued, spitting the words out, while we children looked on, open-mouthed.

I wasn't very old before I began to understand that lots of things about me were different from other girls and boys I knew.

Our mum was different from other children's mums. She was a lot older and spoke differently. Her voice always sounded posh. She had grey hair and was overweight, and her clothes were old and poor quality. She also smoked a lot, although this was the one thing she had in common with many women at that time. She would send us across the road to the shop to get ten Olivia when she had a bit of money or five Player's Weights when she was hard up.

Mum often had a bottle of PLJ by her bed: Pure Lemon Juice, guaranteed to make you slim. I realise now how desperate she was to recapture her youthful good looks. Though we sometimes only had boiled potatoes for dinner, or a big suet pudding with golden syrup if we were lucky, she would have her PLJ and her cigarettes.

She inhabited a fantasy world for much of the time – one where she was as young and beautiful and glamorous as any film star. The secrets and lies that dominated my childhood were the smokescreen that made her life bearable.

School

As we got older we all knew that there were things we were never allowed to talk about, and questions we weren't allowed to ask. There were so many things we didn't understand.

My younger sister Margaret was always the shy one. She was tiny with huge brown eyes like chocolate drops fringed with thick black lashes. We both had our hair cut in a pudding-basin style, although hers was black and mine was brown, and we shared the same bumpy nose. We used to whisper to each other about secret things. She would ask me, 'Where is our dad?'

I told her he died in the war because I didn't really know. I was the big sister and it was my job to boss her around, know all the answers and to always look after her, so I made things up.

Mum wasn't well when I was due to start school so I had started at the nearby state primary school instead of the catholic school all my siblings had attended. At the time I didn't question the decision, but many years later I was to discover the shocking reasons why it had been made.

From the age of six I had to move to St Vincent Roman Catholic primary school so that I could prepare for my First Holy Communion. There were two infant classes and four junior classes in our school, which was built as a long corridor with classrooms leading off. Everything seemed to be painted the same sickly green colour. There was also a hall, which was used for PE and school dinners, and an office where the headmaster sat. The playground was concrete and seemed very big and frightening. At break times there would be hundreds of children racing round, kicking footballs, playing two balls against the walls, skipping, doing handstands and headstands, shouting and running and roaring. My favourite game was Two Balls. We had special rhymes that we sang as we played: 'One two three and a downsey, four five six and a downsey, seven eight nine and a downsey, ten and a downsey, drop the ball.' And then the next girl would take over. And the rhyme would begin again. We would repeat this over and over replacing 'downsey' with 'over' or 'under' and changing the way we threw the balls to match the words. Skipping was another game I enjoyed. Two girls would hold one end each of a long rope and they would turn it, each of the other children taking turns to run in and skip. There was also French skipping which was quite complicated and involved double ropes and jumping in and out skilfully; this was far trickier and took lots of practice to become proficient.

Margaret and I didn't usually stay for school dinners, preferring to walk the fifteen minutes home. We always hoped that Mum would let us stay off for the afternoon, and she often did. We liked to have soup for lunch – always Heinz from a tin.

Once a fortnight it would be family allowance day. Mum would call out to us, 'Come on you two; we've got to go to the Post Office.'

We would run to join her, and holding a hand each she would whisk us over the road to the shops.

'If you stand and wait nicely,' she would say, 'we'll go and get same bananas and some rolls from the bakers and have banana rolls for lunch.' We would squirm with anticipation, and once the 8 shillings was collected, make our way to collect the promised feast. We didn't usually go back to school on family allowance day. If it was hot then we would sometimes be allowed a frozen Jubbly, an icy prism of orange heaven, and very occasionally Mum would also buy us a tiny box of Cadbury's Milk Tray chocolates, with a few nestled inside.

Some of the other children took packed lunches and others had free dinners. My older sisters had had free dinners, but when Margaret and I started at St Vincent's, Marge had pleaded on our behalf. 'Don't make them have free dinners. They're disgusting, and everyone knows you get free dinners because the teacher calls it out.'

Mum had given in; she was always softer with Margaret and I than with the others.

I thought the children that took packed lunches were the luckiest. They had a little box or bag and inside their mum would have packed the things that they liked: a little sandwich, a sausage roll, an apple and sometimes a slice of cake. But there were some children who just brought a plastic bread bag with the toast crusts left over from their breakfast. I didn't envy them.

We grew to hate school. It was an unfriendly place and most of the teachers were very strict and shouted a lot. We didn't go to school that often. Although Mum did her best to persuade us to go, we also did our best to persuade her to let us stay at home. Usually we won.

When I moved into the juniors we had a young Irish teacher who had some modern ideas. One day he brought in a tape recorder. He told us that we were going to come out to the front of the class to read our writing and he was going to record us on to the tape so that we could listen to ourselves. I felt quietly confident. I was one of the best readers in the class and even though my work was untidy I usually got at least 8/10 for my writing. I had been really careful with my writing today as I had something especially exciting to write about. I listened patiently as each child's turn came and went. When it was my turn I carried my workbook up to the front and stood next to the teacher nervously. He pushed the button on the tape recorder and nodded at me to begin. I began to read, but unfortunately had a bad cold. I didn't have a hanky and so tried to control the snot running down my nose by sniffing it back up every minute or so. Some of the children began to giggle but I didn't take any notice I was concentrating so hard on reading my writing carefully. When we had all finished our recordings were played back for us to listen to. Mine sounded awful . . .

'My cat Tiddy' sniff, 'has got 4' sniff 'kittens', sniff. 'Me and my' sniff 'sister look' sniff 'after them' sniff. 'We' sniff 'are going' sniff 'to keep one' sniff 'when it is grown' sniff 'up but' sniff 'the other one' sniff 'will' sniff 'go to a new' sniff 'home' sniff. The result of my runny nose had been exaggerated by the tape resulting in an explosion of laughter from the whole class including my teacher. I wanted to disappear! It would be a very long time before I could read out loud again.

Mum thought that children who played out in the street were 'guttersnipes', but she did let us walk to and from school on our own. My friends Hannah and Jane would sometimes knock for me on the way.

There were still some old bombsites near us, and a favourite game would be clambering through them to see what we could find. Today Hannah had another idea.

'Let's play "Knock Down Ginger".' She turned to Jane. 'You go and knock on the door and we'll hide here.'

Jane did as she was told, while Hannah and I ducked down behind the fence. As soon as she had knocked, Jane flew back down the path and joined us to watch and wait. After a minute or two, a lady with a baby in her arms opened the door and peered out while we crouched down laughing our heads off. This was a game that we played often, but sometimes the person who opened the door would catch sight of us and shout out and occasionally even chase us along the road.

More scary than that was the Milk Float Game.

The horse-drawn milk floats of my sisters' childhood had now disappeared and been replaced with electric versions. These could pick up a fair bit of speed on a straight road. We would wait for the milkman to get on board and then run behind.

'Jump!' we would encourage each other, and we would leap onto the back of the float and hang there for a free ride.

When I return to Dagenham now to visit my sister, who still lives in our house, I sometimes walk around the familiar streets remembering the games and the children that I played them with. I also remember the stark mixture of tension, fear, excitement and fun that was part of my childhood, and it helps me to understand and make sense of my life now – despite all the unanswered questions.

3

A New Friend

The most popular girl in my class was called Christine. She had short brown bobbed hair with a ribbon tied round it, and was always dressed in clean clothes. I was desperate for her to be my best friend.

'Christine is coming round to play!' I announced proudly. Mum just lifted her eyes to heaven. I looked around me. I wanted Christine to play in our back garden with me but was acutely aware that it was completely overgrown. It didn't seem to matter when Margaret and I played out there. In fact it made it more exciting, as we had very fertile imaginations. One of our favourite games was being explorers. We would play until the summer sun set red and gold over Mr Stan's corrugated garden shed, and I'd nudge Margaret and say, 'Look! Aurora borealis!' I must have heard about the northern lights from the television or from my sisters. Either way, I knew they were something exciting!

The only flowers that were visible in the garden were a few white flag irises and a big bushy pink dog rose, remnants of our grandfather's days. Most of the space was now covered in a dense layer of weeds and grass, almost as tall as we were. The thick scratchy heads of couch grass were difficult to cut with a pair of old blunt scissors, but that was all I had. I needed to 'tidy up' the garden before Christine came to play and so knelt down and slowly began to cut. My sister Marge came out into the garden.

'What are you up to?' she asked, watching me with a curious expression.

'Gardening.'

'Why?'

'Because my friend is coming to play.'

Marge smirked, 'You'll be lucky!' and she went back inside laughing. The sun was hot on my back but I didn't mind. I must have stayed there for a long time, because I remember how the grass and stones began to cut into my knees, and how my fingers ached from working the scissors.

Marge was right – Christine never did come to play. She told me her dad had forbidden her to come.

'He says I'm not allowed round your house cos he knows your dad. He works with him at Ford's.'

This was a bolt out of the blue for me. *My* dad?

I met her words with silence. I was used to not knowing things, used to things not making sense, and I was also used to keeping quiet. I just stared back, swallowing the disappointment and trying not to care.

Margaret and I continued to enjoy our garden throughout the summer, and played lots of pretend games, building homes with the sheets on the line, draping chairs with old bits of cloth, and using them as 'Indian tepees'. Other favourite games involved steeping flower petals in water to make perfume, and collecting stones and grass to make a 'dinner' from anything else we could find. There was one time when we took this a little too far. Mum had said we couldn't have a bath because she couldn't afford the gas. Bath time was usually only once a week on a Sunday and we would use each other's water. By the time it got to our turn it was an interesting grey colour. On this day we had decided we wanted our own bath. We whispered to each other in the garden, and then proceeded to plaster our faces, arms and legs with as much mud as we could find.

'Have I got much on my face?' I asked Margaret.

'No, I can't see much,' she lied, so I layered even more of the brown-grey mixture across my cheeks.

Mum came out to call us in for bed and let out a screech.

'You naughty girls!' she shouted, and bent down to take the slipper off her foot. Our mum never smacked us, but in that second we saw such frustration and anger that our instincts told us to run. How well I remember diving up the stairs with Margaret a step behind me, followed closely by Mum, slipper in hand. We ran into the bathroom and slid the lock across and stood inside breathing heavily, our hearts racing.

'Come out of there now, you naughty girls!' Mum said angrily. But we stayed where we were. It seemed like an eternity until we heard her going back downstairs but in reality it probably took no more than a minute or two for her anger to subside and for her to see the funny side. We got our bath that night. Mum sometimes bought us Matey bubble bath when she had some money. We loved it and would sit in the bath for an age, playing with the suds until our fingers and toes were as wrinkled as prunes. That would only be in the summer time, because the bathroom in our house was painfully cold in the winter. Margaret and I usually had our bath together, and I can remember our sister Mary trying to persuade us to get out of the barely warm water onto the freezing floor.

'If you don't get out soon the witch will get you,' she warned.

'I don't believe you,' I retorted, 'there's no such thing as witches.'

'There is!' Mary continued, lowering her voice. 'She lives under the bath, look you can see her peeping out now.'

Margaret and I jumped out of the water like flying fish, to be grabbed roughly and rubbed dry by our impatient, shivering sister. For a very long time that witch haunted my bathroom visits, and having to go to the toilet with the 'witch' waiting to pop her head out from under the bath was terrifying.

During the harshest winters Aunty would go the oil shop round the corner to our house and buy paraffin for the tiny stove that she would put in the bathroom to stop the pipes from freezing. The smell was acrid and permeated the whole house but it did take the chill off the air upstairs. The only room that was heated in the winter was what we called the kitchen but which in effect was our living room.

I mentioned being different; the rooms in our house were certainly called different names from those in my friends' houses. They had a kitchen instead of a scullery, and their living room was what we called the kitchen. When Granny and Granddad had moved to our house when it was newly built, that was indeed what the rooms were used for. The scullery had been where the laundry was done. There had been a huge copper for heating the water, a Butler sink perched on two enormous stone pillars and a mangle for squeezing the water out of the clothes before they were hung on the line to dry. The cooking was done in the kitchen on a black lead range. Although this changed over the years, the rooms retained their past names like ghosts.

Most of the families around us were relatively poor but the homes of my friends were usually clean and tidy and most important of all they were warm. One particularly icy winter morning I went to knock for my friend Hannah who lived across the road so that we could walk to school together. Margaret was staying at home but I wanted to go to school because our class were putting on a play called *Alice in Wonderland*. Our new young teacher had cleverly said that I could play the part of the Red Queen and say, 'Off with her head!'

'But,' she said, 'you will have to be sure to come to school every day so that you can practise . . .'

Hannah's mum glanced at her watch when she opened the door to me, but welcomed me warmly. 'Come on in and wait, Hannah is just having her toast.' She led me into their little kitchen and as I entered I was hit by the smell of the bread toasting under the grill. Hannah sat at the little table with her clean clothes on waiting for her toast and tea.

'Would you like some toast, dear?' asked her mum.

I took in the scene before me: the simply furnished but cosy room, the clean table, the fresh toast being placed on Hannah's plate, its delicious smell wafting across to where I stood watching. We never had breakfast. Mum wasn't usually up before school time, so I had just got myself dressed and come out as usual.

I looked solemnly at Hannah's mum and shook my head. 'No, thank you.' We had been taught to be polite, but I really don't know why I refused her kind offer, when what I wanted most in the world at that moment was to be Hannah with her fresh buttered toast, her hot cup of tea, her school socks warming above the oven and her mum, smiling.

Our primary school wasn't very far but it took us about fifteen minutes to walk there. The route took us up past the local corner shops at the junction of Becontree Avenue across into Haydon Road and we would then come out at the top where the C of E church was opposite the Catholic church that neighboured our school. There was a good selection of local shops then. We had two greengrocers, butchers, post office, bakery, two sweet shops and a newsagents. There was also a fish and chip shop, an oil shop and a grocers on the corner and next to that our favourite shop of all: the toy shop. Margaret and I were often sent on errands to the shops as soon as we were deemed old enough, which was when I was about seven.

We passed the greengrocers just opposite our house on our way to school. They ran a raffle every month, so when a customer shopped with them they would give them a raffle ticket. The monthly prize was always a lovely big basket of fruit and vegetables. I don't know whether my mum was extremely lucky, or the lady who owned the shop was very kind, all I do know is that we seemed to regularly win that basket of fruit and vegetables and it made a big contribution to our larder!

That wasn't the only contribution the greengrocers made to our family, but unfortunately the other was less welcome. Although we rarely had breakfast, we would occasionally get a penny for an apple to eat on the way to school. On one particular day when we went into the shop the lady said very kindly to me, 'Just wait there a minute.' She went out to the back of the shop and returned with a warm, damp flannel and then proceeded to wash my face and neck. I was outraged! I attempted to pull away but she held me fast as I wriggled.

'Just hold on – there that's better,' she said.

I was so angry and embarrassed! The poor woman

undoubtedly meant well and I was probably filthy, but it was a while before I ventured into that shop again.

The one shop I really didn't like going in was the corner shop The lady and man who ran it were always very unfriendly to us, and would follow us round, watching us carefully. It was the beginning of the supermarket era and although there were still certain things which you had to ask for, like cheese, butter, bacon and eggs, many things were displayed on the shelves for you to choose from.

It was only years later that I learned why those shopkeepers were so suspicious of us and the reasons were to shock me to the core.

4

Outings and Weddings

Although my primary school was pretty old and dilapidated, I do remember some things with great happiness and nostalgia.

One morning after Miss Jones had taken the register she said she had something to tell us. We looked at each other in anticipation.

'Children, next Monday we are going to High Beech for the day.' Some of the boys made silly noises, while we girls just smiled at each other happily.

I smiled along with the others but wasn't really sure what or where 'High Beech' was, but it must be something good.

'You will all need a packed lunch, and there will be orange squash available for you to drink,' carried on our teacher, 'but we will also have to learn some special rules to make sure we have a good time.'

I couldn't wait to get home that afternoon, so that I could tell Margaret and Mum about going on an outing.

'Can I come?' asked Margaret hopefully. She was off school again and had been helping Mum put the washing on the line. We both liked helping Mum with the washing, even though it was hard work. We didn't have a washing machine, so Mum would fill the big Butler sink full of hot water from the ascot that hung on the scullery wall. It was a gas water heater and I hated it because when you turned the tap on it made a really loud booming sound as the pilot light ignited the gas. This had taken the place of the old copper that had heated the water when my sisters and brothers had been young. Then Mum would pour in the Omo powder. It had a very strong odour and was a bright blue colour, but it made lots of bubbles, and had a nicer smell than the bar of soap Mum used to have to grate into the water. Sometimes I was allowed to stand on a chair and rub the clothes up and down the glass and wood washing board, which had thick ridges in it to help get the clothes clean. Once the clothes were washed and rinsed, the task of trying to remove as much water as possible from them began, so they would dry quicker. There was a big old mangle which Mum would pull out from the corner, and Margaret and I would feed the clothes through while Mum turned the handle. This then pushed the rollers round and squeezed the water out from the clothes. The only problem was that if you were not extremely careful your fingers could get 'mangled' along with the clothes, which we learnt to our cost was very painful!

Pegging the clothes on the line was the best bit of all, particularly if it was a windy day. We would take the basket into the garden and Mum would let the line down so we could reach. We would then be allowed to peg the smaller things out ourselves, but needed Mum's help with things like sheets.

Today though, I had been too late to help. The washing had been done and Mum and Margaret were just finishing putting it on the line.

'You can't come, because it's only for juniors,' I said to Margaret. I felt guilty when I saw her face fall. 'Don't worry. Your class will go on an outing too.'

Margaret and I sat in the kitchen in front of the television and Mum switched it on so that we could see *Watch with Mother* (although 'Mother' rarely sat with us). Every day of the week had a different show and we each had our favourite. Mine was *Picture Book* on a Monday and Margaret's was *The Woodentops* which was on Friday; we quite liked *Andy Pandy* though, and of course there was *The Flower Pot Men* and *Rag, Tag and Bobtail.*

Although Mum occasionally walked us to the park in Goodmayes, we didn't go out very often. So when I thought about our school trip, back came all my usual anxiety about having the right kind of lunch, the right kind of clothes and whether I would need the toilet. I would guess that over the next

few days Miss Jones told the class about where we were going
and what we might see, but I stayed at home for the rest of the
week planning for the outing. I had to make sure that everything
was ready.

On Saturday Mum took us to the shops in Green Lane.

'Do you want cheese spread or Spam for your sandwiches?'
she asked. I wanted cheese spread, I never did like the sweaty,
bland flavour of Spam. I was also allowed to choose a special
cake from the baker's and on Sunday evening helped Pat to
pack my lunch up in some greaseproof paper ready for the
morning.

Bright and early on Monday I was beside myself with a
mixture of happy anticipation and growing dread, especially
when I arrived at school to see a big coach parked outside. As I
went in to class, Christine turned to me. 'Where's your coat?' she
asked. 'Miss Jones said we have to bring a coat in case it rains, so
you probably won't be allowed to come.' I looked anxiously
around to see if anyone else had forgotten their coat, but no, even
though it was May I was the only one in just a cardigan.

To my utter relief a boy called Stephen burst into class. He
went straight to the teacher and said, 'My mum says to tell you
I ain't got a coat.'

Miss Jones turned to him, 'Don't worry, Stephen. The sun is
shining; I don't think it is going to rain today so hopefully we
won't need our coats.'

With that, I let out an inward sigh of relief and let myself
enjoy the day – a day of dappled sunlight, warm orange squash
and the sort of wild freedom that would never pass a health and
safety checklist!

Later that year my Godmother Julie had announced that she
was getting married and I was to be a bridesmaid. Julie was the
same age as my sister Pat and they were very close friends. She
was an only child and her Mum was my Aunty Maggie, one of
my mum's older sisters.

One Saturday as the time of the wedding drew nearer, Julie
came over to pick me up. 'We are going to get you fitted for your

dress today'. I was a quiet, shy and subdued child, so I didn't dare to ask the questions that were buzzing round in my head. Would my dress trail along the floor like a princess's? What colour would it be and would I wear a tiara?

Julie's friend was making my dress and my tummy did somersaults as we approached her front door. I hadn't had any breakfast and it was well past lunchtime. Julie didn't realise that I hadn't eaten, and as we went inside the house I began to feel headachy and nauseous.

'Come on then' said Julie kindly. 'Jump up on the chair so we can get you measured.' I tried to do as I was told but I wobbled and nearly fell.

'What's the matter with you then' said Julie's friend catching me with one hand.

'Oh she's probably over excited' said Julie oblivious to the fact that I was dizzy with hunger.

My dress was made from shiny pale green satin and had little puffed sleeves. It sat just above my knees, and had a flouncy petticoat, which wasn't particularly flattering as my legs were rather short and quite plump!

A few weeks later Julie arrived to take me shoe shopping.

'We're taking you to meet Carol the other bridesmaid and you can get your shoes together,' Julie told me as she picked me up.

Carol? I thought, who is Carol? No one had mentioned another bridesmaid.

'You can get to know each other and have a little play.'

We drove for what seemed like an age and finally arrived in Hayes where Carol lived. Her Mum welcomed us in and said kindly 'Carol, why don't you take Kathleen up to your room to play while Mummy and Julie have a chat, we'll call you down for lunch when it's ready.'

Carol had a room all of her own and didn't have to share it with anyone. I looked around me in wonder. It was the most beautiful room I had ever seen. It had pink flowery wallpaper and clean crisp white paintwork. At the window hung curtains full of white daisies like the ones I had seen growing in the park, but best of all, there on the floor, was the fluffiest, pinkest, softest rug I had ever seen! It was glorious, and I wanted to sit on it forever and run my fingers and toes through it.

'Do you want to play babies? Or we can play with my dolls house? She pointed to the shelf at one side of the room. I looked at the toys on the shelves, the assortment of teddy bears on her bed and at the rows of books neatly stacked on a tiny bookcase, and thought that she must be the luckiest little girl in the whole world.

After lunch we walked to the shoe shop. My eyes fell on a pair of shoes that sparkled. They were covered in glitter and sequins. I crunched up my eyes and wished with all my might, but at the same time was too timid to make my preferences known to the grown ups.

'I think these ones will look best next to the green' said Carol's Mum picking up a pair of dull cream satin shoes that had a small bow on the front, but Carol said 'Oh no please Mummy, the sparkly ones are the nicest, please, please, please.' The adults exchanged looks and smiled. Julie picked up the sparkling shoes and said 'Do you know Carol I think you're right, the sparkly ones are definitely the best, do you like them Kathleen?' I nodded so vigorously that my head almost left my shoulders and I couldn't stop myself from smiling broadly.

I knew then that wishes could come true. With my new green satin dress, sparkling starlight shoes, shiny flicked up hair and green feather headband, I would look like a princess and this time when people looked at me, they would be thinking I looked beautiful.

5

Michael

From the end of the Second World War to the early 60s, all young men were conscripted into the armed forces, as long as they passed a medical examination. My oldest brother Michael was no exception. He was called up for National Service when I was about three so I don't really remember him much before he was in the army. It would not be the first time he had been away from home. In fact, as I later discovered, he was already a veteran at living apart from our family.

As the second oldest in the family, he had been born just before the outbreak of war. He was a very beautiful baby with golden curls and a chubby face, but did not have a particularly happy childhood. Mum had already given birth to Sheila a year before, so they were very close in age. Mum and Ron Coates, their dad, had a house around the corner from Granny and Granddad. It was still on the Becontree Estate but was a bit smaller than mum's childhood home. Things started to go badly wrong. They were both quite young, still in their twenties when Mum became pregnant for the third time. War broke out and Ron was working long hours at Ford, and Mum was lonely.

Aunty told us many years later that Ron Coates was a 'womaniser', but we never knew if that was true. It was while Mum was pregnant with their fourth child, Josie, that they finally separated. Michael was five at the time. Today the idea of a single parent bringing up children alone doesn't surprise, shock or horrify anyone, but in 1942 in a Catholic community Mum was stigmatised.

★　　★　　★

After Michael's ten weeks basic training for National Service, he was shipped over to Gibraltar – 'the Rock', as it was known then. He was just over nineteen years old and had already been bringing a wage home. He was trying to help to keep the ever-growing family's head above water. Now all that had changed and he wasn't sure what chaos and calamity he would come back to. Despite his worries about Mum and us, he loved army life and soon metamorphosed from a chubby, shy, anxious teenager into a tall, slim, confident young man. After he had been in Gibraltar for about two years his letters home started mentioning a Spanish girl named Isobel. He sent us photos of her. She was so beautiful; with her dark hair and smouldering eyes, she was the most exotic looking person we had ever seen. Then another letter from him arrived.

'Your brother's getting married,' I overheard Mum telling Pat and Josie. They were in their late teens and had been working since they left school at fifteen.

I was so excited but wasn't sure exactly what it meant.

'Is our brother really getting married?' I asked Pat.

She nodded.

I knew all about weddings since I had been a bridesmaid.

'And will he be coming home now?' I added. The only memories I had of Michael at that time were as a brief visitor when he had occasionally come home on leave.

Pat gave me a look. 'I don't think so; not yet,' she said and changed the subject quickly.

They were married in Isobel's home village near to Malaga but none of our family were able to attend. The fare to Spain would have been as out of reach to us then as a flight to the moon would be now! They did send photos though, and when I looked at them I thought they were like characters from the pictures.

In the same year that Michael and Isobel got married, our class began to be 'prepared' for our First Holy Communion. This meant learning lots of things by heart, which I was quite good at. It also meant making our first confession. We had to confess our sins first so that we would be free from sin when we went to receive Jesus in the communion bread and wine. The problem was we were only six or seven. We didn't have any sins to confess so we made them up. We knew that telling lies, being unkind to our sisters and brothers, swearing and murder were all very bad sins so we confessed them. Apart from murder that is; I don't think any of us confessed to that one!

When the big day came we lined up in the church pew and knelt down to remember our sins and to pray for forgiveness. When it was my turn to go into the confessional box I was quite excited. I pulled the door that was already slightly ajar and slipped in. I could remember the words we had to say to the priest who was in the other side of the box. He couldn't see me and I couldn't see him.

'Bless me Father for I have sinned. This is my first confession,' I began.

The priest said some prayers and then asked me what I had done.

'I have lied, I smacked my sister and I was cheeky to my mum.'

None of this was true, of course, but I had to say something and these sins sounded along the right kind of lines.

The priest forgave me. 'Say two Hail Mary's and one Our Father and don't sin again.'

I left the confession box feeling ten feet tall. I was a forgiven sinner at last!

I was to make my Holy Communion in June. For Catholics, making your first Holy Communion is really important. For a start you get a new white dress and a veil and everyone looks at you and gives you presents. I was so excited.

However, the question of my dress was posing some problems for my family. One afternoon Margaret and I were looking through a big thick catalogue imagining the clothes we were going to buy.

'That white one's nice. And it's not too . . .'

Mum looked over our shoulders. 'Hmm. We'll have to wait and see.'

I bit my lip. What would I do if I didn't have a communion dress? It wasn't mentioned again for a while so I tried not to think about it. Then one day a letter arrived from Michael. That afternoon after school Mum had some news for me. My dress was on its way! Michael's new wife was a dressmaker, and a Catholic as well, so understood the importance of the occasion. She was going to make my dress!

Over the next few weeks she made me a beautiful, simple white dress that she hand stitched and embroidered. It wasn't fancy or frilly, but was made from fine white cotton with narrow white ribbon threaded through it across the bodice, round the sleeves and the hem. It also had a little Peter Pan collar, which I loved. She also made a replica dress for my little sister Margaret to wear so that we would look alike. But Margaret wasn't having a veil; that was special for me.

The day it arrived in the post, carefully packaged in tissue paper, my fingers were trembling with excitement.

Once I had made my Holy Communion it meant that I was old enough to walk in the May processions. These were very big events where all of the little girls and boys who had made their first Holy Communion would process through the streets along with the older children. All would be dressed in white and many of the girls would wear a little veil. I wore mine and felt so proud as we walked past the houses. People would come to their gates and stand watching us as we walked and sang hymns to Mary the Queen of Heaven and Queen of the May. There was very little traffic on the roads in those days so we must have been quite a spectacle.

Afterwards I carefully put the dress away. We didn't get many new clothes. Aunty sometimes bought us a few bits and pieces home from Plessey's where she worked. I think they must have 'fallen off the back of a lorry' and were sold on the factory floor. The other major source of our clothes was a kindly woman called Mickey. She worked in the United Dairies depot near to our house and sometimes Mum would say to Mary or one of the twins, 'Go into the dairy will you? Mickey's got some things for you.'

Mickey worked in the servery. That was the office section in the dairy that kept a record of the milk and other things that the milkmen would take out on their daily delivery rounds. Every now and again she'd send word to Mum that she had some things for us. One day Marge, Marion and Mary were sent into the diary and returned with a suitcase.

'That's huge!' I exclaimed, excitement rising. 'What's inside?'

Marge flung it open. 'Don't touch, you two,' she said bossily. 'We'll tell you which things will fit you.'

We ignored her and descended upon its contents, trying to push our way through the big girls' arms.

'A bra!' Mary said, shoving Marion out of the way. Marion was always the less confident of the twins and I could see the disappointment on her face. Marge picked up a yellow jumper that was probably a few sizes too big. As she held it against her, Mum said 'Just wait a minute, will you? Don't forget Pat and Jo might like some of those things.' Unfortunately most of the clothes were too big for Margaret and me, so we lost interest quite quickly and just looked over occasionally while the contents of the suitcase were shared between our sisters. We had the last laugh though because when our older sisters were at school and work, we would put on their clothes and bounce on the old iron bedstead singing at the top of our voices!

I do remember one Easter having a new little suit to wear. Margaret and I had one each. They each had a pleated skirt and a little matching jacket. We thought we were marvellous when we wore them to Mass on Easter Sunday. Mum told us that she had bought them but that we had to say thank you to Aunty, as she wanted us to think that she had got them for us. Poor Aunty, you can probably guess who actually paid the money for them.

6

The 'Special News' Day

Later that year, Mum told us some 'special' news. It was a damp chilly autumn and some of the luckier children at our school had gone hop picking. Our family never went. Mum said it was 'common' and looked down her nose at those who went, but Margaret and I were always envious at this time of year. All that time off school playing in the sunny hop fields!

It was Monday and Margaret and I had just started to walk home from school for lunch when we spied Mum across the road waiting for us with her headscarf tied tightly round her head and her big black bag over her arm. She never went anywhere without her bag. She even took it up to bed with her at night, and when she was sitting in her chair by the fireplace it would sit firmly at her feet. No one was ever allowed to look inside. Strangely it seemed almost malevolent lying on the floor next to her, daring us to peep inside. I didn't know at the time what Mum kept in there, but knowing now, that feeling makes sense.

'You will never guess what,' Mum said with a huge smile on her face. I looked at Margaret, as her huge brown eyes got bigger.

'What? What? What?!' we screeched. We were quite used to 'exciting news'. I think, looking back, that Mum may have had marginal bipolar as she would swing between extreme highs and lows with a ferocious regularity. Today was going to be a high.

'We've won the pools!' she exclaimed, beaming at us. Mum did the pools religiously every week. She would sit in front of the television on Saturday afternoons with the pools form in front of her, ticking things off in response to the monotonous voice of the commentator 'Arsenal 1, Chelsea 1; Wolverhampton Wanderers 0, Crystal Palace 1 . . .'

'No school for you this afternoon – we're going to see Aunty Maggie to tell her all about it.' We jumped up and down, clapping our hands. This day was getting better and better! Off we walked, Mum holding one of our hands in each of hers, swinging us along Becontree Avenue to the bus stop in Bennetts Castle Lane. The 145 or the 148 would take us to Aunty Maggie's house in Seven Kings. She lived there with her husband George, a small kindly man who worked at Plessey's with Aunty.

We had to sit upstairs on the bus so that Mum could have a cigarette. I raced to the empty front seat and Margaret followed. This was always our favourite place as we could pretend we were driving the bus. Today as the bus started to move I noticed the first few raindrops splattering onto the windows. We spent the whole journey talking about what we were going to do with all of the money we had. Pat and Josie could give up work, we would all have new clothes, and I could have a party and invite all the girls at school. By the time we got to Seven Kings it was pouring with rain. Our coats were quite old and poor quality but Mum had a battered old umbrella that the three of us huddled under to keep dry as we walked to Aunty Maggie's house.

'Don't jump in the puddles,' Mum said cheerfully, 'your feet will get soaking,' but we slyly splashed just the same, giggling together either side of Mum.

Aunty Maggie and Uncle George had bought their own house in a neat Victorian terrace on a quiet road. I knew that house well. I often came to stay for a few days and would be given my own room to sleep in. Every time my Aunty Maggie would take me to the big cupboard in the kitchen and when she opened the door inside would be an array of neatly stacked clothes including various quilted dressing gowns, or house coats as they were often called then, which had belonged to Julie. I would be given one to wear and then allowed to bring it home with me. Once I got home the 'housecoat' always seemed to vanish. I don't know where they went, but next time I came to stay I would be given another one. They had a dog called Trixie, who was a cross between a border collie and a few other things, and pretty snappy. Aunty Maggie and Uncle George were constantly warning me not to put my face too near her but I never listened. Margaret and I had no fear of dogs. We had always had a dog and whatever dog we had it was always called Pongo. The Pongo we had at the time was getting very old. She had a chronic skin condition that meant her hair fell out in huge clumps and my sister Pat would have to smear a foul smelling green sticky ointment over her back. The sight of the green slimy ointment together with the potent smell of wintergreen always turned my stomach.

In the front room at Aunty Maggie's there was a piano and a glass cabinet that held all of their treasures. There were small china animals, a tiny teapot ornament and a variety of knick-knacks that they had collected over the years from seaside holidays. I was sometimes allowed to play with them as long as I was careful.

On the 'exciting news' day we arrived rather damp and chilly at Aunty Maggie's front door. We knocked and waited, listening to Trixie barking and flinging herself at the door. When the door opened Aunty Maggie was standing looking a little surprised to see us.

'Flo – what are you doing here? Why aren't the children at school?'

'They're not very well,' Mum replied as we were ushered into the tiny back room that was warmed by a black coal-fired stove.

'A bit daft to bring them out in the rain then,' muttered Aunty Maggie, as she took our coats and gave them a good shake. 'I'll put the kettle on.'

Why wasn't Aunty Maggie happy to see us? She would soon cheer up when she heard we had won the pools. Perhaps Mum would buy her something special. On the bus Mum had pointed out the house we would be moving to. It was very large and we would all be able to have a bedroom each. There was a big garden with lots of flowers at the back and Margaret and I would have a bike. And I was definitely going to be allowed to get a horse. In fact I could probably have two! This had been my dream forever. I loved horses. I had once been allowed to have a ride at the funfair on a Shetland pony and had fallen hopelessly in love with it. Since then I had been horse mad. I painted and drew horses continually, longed for a *Pony Annual* every Christmas and played horses in the garden with Margaret. We had a stable each where we kept them. My favourite was a golden palomino named Champion. We would build jumps for us to ride the horses over. I almost always had a clear round, but Margaret often got faults for knocking the jumps down. The horses were in reality just sticks, but to us they each had a name, colour and personality and we loved them – so much so that once when my brother Peter had come out into the garden to play with us and had accidentally broken one of the sticks, I was heartbroken. I cried my eyes out while Peter tried to console me.

'It's only a stick,' he said. Little did he know that he had just killed Blaze, my second favourite horse!

This time it would be different. I was going to get a real horse now. I couldn't wait. The excitement was running off my skin like the raindrops. Margaret and I were given a biscuit and a drink of milk while Mum and Aunty Maggie had their tea.

'Yes, eight draws – all came up,' Mum said happily to Aunty Maggie. 'Only problem is that we won't get the money for a while. It takes time you see, to get it sorted out.'

I looked up and saw a strange look cross my auntie's face. She didn't look very pleased at our good fortune. In fact, she looked rather resigned and serious.

'I haven't got any spare money Flo,' she said firmly.

Mum's face took on the pinched look that I had seen before. It usually meant she was going into one of her moods. Her eyes would change too, and become more distant and worried looking. 'Just until the winnings come through,' she said, but Aunty Maggie was shaking her head.

She went over to the mantelpiece and took down one of several tins. Each was labelled differently: 'electric', 'gas', 'fares' and so on. The one that she reached for said 'food'. She took it off the shelf and handed Mum some money from inside.

'I don't want it back, Flo, but I haven't got any more.' She then went over to the kitchen cupboard and filled a bag with an assortment of tins and packets. These she also handed over to Mum.

Mum looked down sadly as she took the bag. 'Time to go,' she called to us and home we went.

Through the years of my childhood Aunty Maggie was a stoic support for Mum and us and I don't know what we would have done without her.

By the time we got home that afternoon, Mum's mood had changed. She hadn't said much on the bus, but instead had looked out of the window as if she could see something we couldn't. She didn't talk about winning the pools anymore that day, so neither did we.

I would see that sad, faraway look often on my Mum's face throughout my childhood, but it wasn't until I was a mother myself that I actually saw her cry.

7

Overcrowding

One day Mum told us that Michael was coming home!

'Is he going to live at our house?' I asked.

'Yes and he's bringing Isobel with him.'

'Is Isobel our sister?' Margaret whispered to me.

'No, she got married to Michael,' I said knowledgably, 'and guess what? She's going to have a baby!' At this news Margaret jumped up and down; she always loved playing babies best of all. I didn't let her play that game often because I thought it was boring. I liked action games where we would explore unknown territories or come across a band of renegade Indians.

'Will the baby live here as well?' she asked excitedly.

'Yes in yours and Josie's room.'

Margaret's look of excitement now became one of perplexity. 'But where will we sleep?'

I was relishing my superior knowledge now and took great pains to explain what was going to happen. The only reason I knew was that I had overheard an argument the night before between Aunty and Mum. I had crept out of bed to go to the toilet and had heard Mum talking downstairs.

'Tell your aunt that we're going to have to move the settee round to the other side so we can open it our more easily.'

I heard Aunty sniff loudly.

Then I heard Pat's voice saying: 'Michael and Isobel will need the back bedroom.'

'What are you talking about?' Aunty spat back.

My stomach lurched.

'Tell your aunt that Kathleen and Margaret are going to sleep in the bed settee with me.' Mum's voice had taken on a prim and proper air now.

I heard something being slammed down hard.

Aunty's voice got louder. 'I'm bloody well fed up with this!' She was shouting now. 'How am I supposed to get ready for work in the mornings with them all 'anging round the place?'

'Well they're coming here and that's that,' Mum retorted. She didn't often challenge Aunty. Aunty had a ferocious temper and we seemed to spend our lives avoiding awakening it. I was frightened by Mum's tone of voice and the fact that she wasn't backing down.

'Well you can sodding well *all* get out then,' Aunty retorted. 'And good riddance. P'raps I'll get a bit of peace then!' I heard a noise of something landing with a crash. Marion, Marge and Mary had all crept out of the bedroom they shared with Aunty. We huddled silently on the landing listening to the commotion below. I held my breath, hoping Aunty would calm down and stop shouting at Mum. Aunty slammed out of the room and stamped up the stairs; we slunk in the bathroom doorway as she charged into her bedroom. It was then that I noticed little Margaret had crept out to join us and was standing trembling, hanging on to my arm.

'It's all right,' I whispered, 'they've finished now.'

I always had to pretend to be brave for Margaret's sake. I was the big sister. I would always look after her, even when inside I was quaking with my own fears.

Mum got her way that time. Michael and Isobel did come to live with us for a while until their first daughter Vicky was born and they were given an army flat in Woolwich. How we all fitted into that house is completely beyond me now: Michael and Isobel in the back bedroom, Aunty, Marion, Marge and Mary in the big bedroom, Peter in the box room, Mum, Margaret and I on the bed settee in the kitchen and Pat in the front room. Poor Josie had to sleep in the tiny narrow hallway on a camp bed covered with coats as there were no spare blankets.

I needed the toilet one night, and was gently trying to squeeze past her little bed. As I began to make my way upstairs I stopped.

'Do you like sleeping out here?' I asked her innocently. 'Don't you feel cold?'

'No, not really.' She laughed. 'Well, maybe just a little bit – go on up you go.'

I stood watching her for a moment, then feeling the draughty fingers of cold from the front door chill my legs and feet, ran to the toilet as fast as I could before hurrying back to the warmth of my bed, and Margaret and Mum, my living hot-water bottles.

Of course that was before the Peter problem happened.

Mum was always exasperated by Peter. He refused to conform and follow the rules like the rest of us. He often teased us younger children.

'Give me your hand,' he commanded.

I trustingly obeyed.

'Here's the tree,' he pointed to my upturned palm, 'see here are the swings' (pointing to the base of my thumb) 'and look,' he spat into my hand, 'there's the pond!'

I screamed. 'Yuk! You're disgusting!'

'Peter, what are you doing to those children?' Mum would shout.

He'd just laugh as he ran out of the door.

Another time Mum had ordered him to take me for a walk. I don't know how old I was, but must have been quite young.

'Now make sure you keep an eye on her, and don't let her wander off,' Mum instructed. 'Now why are you taking your bike?' she shouted after us as Peter led me down the path. 'Don't you go putting her on the crossbar, she might fall!'

As soon as we were round the corner and out of sight, Peter lifted me up onto the crossbar.

'But Mummy says you're not to.'

'Oh don't worry about that,' Peter said and off we flew. As the wind blew into my face and I screamed with joy, I loved my brother even more than before.

I didn't understand why, but it seemed that Mum had not lived in Valence Avenue much when he, Mary, Marge and Marion had been little children. Certainly she never held, kissed or cuddled any of these 'middle' children the way she did Margaret and me. Life in our house was always chaotic, and she would send them out at any opportunity. Occasionally they would be made to take Margaret and I along. I clearly remember their annoyance when they had to take us to Sunday Mass, and can remember wondering why they didn't want us to go with them.

Peter was always going missing. He would disappear for days sometimes, even when he was still quite young. 'He's gone to find his father in Ireland,' Aunty would say, and Mum would ignore her and look the other way.

Aunty had always favoured Peter, probably because Mum had left him in the care of her and Granny from when he was quite small. He was like her own child, and she certainly treated him differently from the rest of us. She would always stick up for him against Mum and take his side in any conflict, and there was plenty of opportunity for that.

Now he had grown up from a scruffy bedraggled little boy into a handsome young man with a pretty large local female following. One Friday afternoon when Peter was about seventeen, there had been a flurry of activity all day. As Catholics, we were not allowed to eat meat on Friday so if Mum had enough money we would sometimes have fish and chips for dinner. This usually meant that Aunty would have fish and chips and the rest of us would share several bags of chips and maybe a wally or two – a large pickled gherkin – or a piece of cod roe. On this particular Friday I remember Mary, Marge and Marion were already home from school and we were waiting for my older sisters Pat and Josie to get back from work.

'Put the kettle on, the girls will be home soon,' was a familiar refrain from my mum. You could almost set your watch by it, twenty past five every weekday. Today though there was something different. Mum seemed agitated, and we had been made to 'clean up'. Those two simple words always struck dread into our hearts. Clearing up was not easy in our house. There were too many people and too much furniture and there was far too little space. Over time the house had become more and more cluttered, which resulted in it becoming more and more untidy and ultimately very dirty. We had a large settee across the corner in the kitchen. This was quite old and had become saggy with constant use. To make it more comfortable, Mum would pile newspaper under the seat cushions. These would periodically slide out on to the floor and have to be pushed back under. There was also a gap at the back of the settee where it crossed the corner. We thought this was extremely useful, as whenever we had to tidy up the kitchen we children would just throw everything behind the settee into the yawning gap. The problem was that every now and again the gap filled up and began to overflow. That morning Mum had suddenly announced, 'We'll have to pull out the settee.' That struck terror into our hearts. I hated those times. You never knew what you were going to find. There would be some old friends of course, like the odd toy that had been lost, or a friendly forgotten sweet still in its sticky paper bag, but mostly there would be less welcome finds, such as pieces of mouldy food, crusts of bread, dirty clothes and other items of detritus that had accumulated. Worst of all, though, were the silverfish. These little creatures seemed always to be present. They sound so pretty, don't they? But I hated them. They would slither so quickly that I would just catch them out of the corner of my eye, them and their friends the woodlice. The room was eventually tidied and cleaned to Mum's satisfaction. Pat and Jo had arrived home, tea had been made and poured, but there was a tense atmosphere in the house, which wasn't helped by Aunty's arrival at six. An air of expectancy hung over everyone. We were hungry but didn't dare to mention food. Suddenly there was a loud knock on the door.

As Mum stomped out to answer it, Pat turned her chair, which was directly in front of the television, so that her back was set to the rest of the room. Josie hovered around getting out cups and saucers that I didn't even know existed. Plates of sandwiches appeared, which was also very unusual. The only sandwiches I remember having were those that we took when we went on outings, which were usually sweaty and soggy. Mum came through the door leading a woman and a man, closely followed by Peter and his girlfriend Linda.

'Go and play you two,' said Mum, shushing Margaret and me out of the room, 'Marge, take them upstairs will you? And Marion, you go too.' We dutifully did as we were told until we got to the top of the stairs, where Marion and Marge stopped and knelt down to try to listen.

'You two go in the bedroom,' said Marion.

'But I want to hear!' I grumbled.

'Go in the bedroom and shut up,' said Marge. 'Mum will tell you off if she catches you listening.'

'Well, you're listening too!' I said as I was bundled roughly through the doorway. It was no good though, once in the bedroom it became impossible to hear what was going on downstairs. The man and woman seemed to stay for ages, but it was probably no more than half an hour. We didn't get any visitors at our house, apart from family and the tally men, so this was very unusual.

It wasn't long after this that Peter and Linda got married in a register office. Linda had their first daughter six months later. They were still both just seventeen years old when they moved with their new baby into the box room, which now made eight adults, five children and two babies living in a three-bedroom house with just one tiny scullery for cooking and laundry, one kitchen to live and eat in and one toilet and bathroom between us.

8

Feast or Famine

Food played a big part in my childhood. Mum definitely signed up to the feast or famine philosophy of eating. She was a good cook and could conjure up amazing meals within our limited means when she was in the mood. Roast breast of lamb was a favourite, and I learnt to cook this for the family from a very young age when Mum was unwell and unable to come down-stairs. I would run up and down to the bedroom picking up instructions from Mum. 'If it's getting too brown turn the gas down to number 5' or 'put the potatoes into the oven now and turn the gas up to 7.' This would go on throughout the cooking period so that the dinner was all ready by the time Aunty came home from work at six o'clock. Of course my cooking generated a lot of washing up. That was supposed to be Margaret's job, but inevitably as she was only a little girl it built up and the scullery was always a complete mess by the time dinner was served out. Pots, pans, dishes, plates, spoons would spill out of the old Butler sink, over the wooden draining board and on to the cupboard shelf. All surfaces would be covered in a mound of clutter that was always left to the twins to deal with later.

Another more unusual favourite was curry. Now I know that curry is commonplace right across the country today, but in the late 1950s and early 60s it was considered a very exotic dish and none of the other families I knew ate it. I suppose the reason we did was because our Granny was born in India, where her father was stationed. He had fled Ireland to escape from the potato famine in the 1850s and spent the majority of his life serving in the British army. We had curry usually once a week, cooked in a huge metal pot on the gas stove. The memory of the smell of curry powder frying with onion and meat still makes my taste buds tingle. Mum would throw in copious amounts of chopped up vegetables, and leave it to simmer for most of the afternoon. The aroma would fill the house and Margaret and I would stare longingly at the bubbling concoction, desperate for it to be ready, mouths watering, tummies rumbling. We would often have it cold for breakfast the next day, when it seemed to taste even better.

Marion, Marge and Mary did most of the household jobs when I was very young. Pat and Josie were absolved as they went to work and earned wages. Aunty never did household chores for the same reason and Margaret and I were too young to do them properly, although we liked to try.

Over the years we all learnt to cook. Mum taught us how to behead and gut mackerel, scrape the scales off the skin, and dip it in white flour ready for frying; how to rub flour and fat together to make smooth creamy-coloured pastry, used to top rich-smelling beef and kidney pies. We would help Mum to concoct aromatic stews and soups, my favourite being a rich salty pea and ham soup. Those were the good times of course, when there was enough money, but there were also too many days when there was no money at all. Those were the days when we ate a plate of boiled potatoes, or a bowl of porridge, or a lump of suet pudding for our dinner. Once, when there was no money for the gas meter, my sisters had to cook the porridge in a big pot on the coal fire.

'I don't want it,' I cried, pushing the bowl away and refusing to eat the sooty grey slush that it contained.

'Don't be silly,' Marion said, crossly. It had been a long day and Mum was in bed ill. The ice was starting to form inside the windows upstairs; it was a bitterly cold winter and the only warm room was the kitchen, with the coal fire scorching the knickers drying in front of it. They were poked through the wire of the fireguard, and the rest of the wet clothes hung from the picture rail that ran around the walls. There was a damp feel to the air and it must have stunk of coal and cigarette smoke, but you don't notice the smell when you live with it. As a teacher I could always tell which children lived in families with smokers. Their book bags always had that same smell.

Mum had been unwell and so the twins had been kept off school to look after us. We must have been a handful, especially along with all the other household duties they would have been required to do.

Seeing my sulky face, Marge tried an alternative tactic. 'Don't be silly. Don't you know that porridge is best when it's cooked on the fire?'

I began to consider this information.

They ate their porridge with manic enthusiasm. 'Mmmm yummy! This is sooo nice,' Marion mumbled through mouthfuls of thick porridge.

'I want some!' I said, reaching out for my bowl and wolfing down the whole lot. The problem was from that day onwards I always refused to eat porridge unless it was cooked on the fire, which exasperated my family on many occasions.

The gas and electric meters were hungry monsters in our house. Mum would feed them with shillings whenever she could but they were never satisfied and cold food and darkness were their cries for more. Every three months the electric man or the gasman would come to empty the meter. This was a bit of a red-letter day as because of the way the meters were calibrated households always overpaid, so there would usually be a sizable rebate to come. Margaret and I would wait expectantly in the kitchen while the meter was emptied. Then there would be a knock on the kitchen door that would indicate the gas or electric man was ready to go. Outside in the scullery, underneath where the gas and electricity meters were screwed to the wall, would be a pile of shilling coins sparkling with promise. This would definitely be a banana roll day if we were lucky!

Of course there were also the desperate days when the meter would have been broken into and there would be no money inside. This happened more than once, and I can remember the meter man questioning Mum sharply. We never knew how those bad people got in to take the money, or how they managed to break into the meter without Mum knowing.

We had no fridge when I was a child. Perishable foods, meat, fish tended to be bought on the day they were going to be used, or certainly not long before that. Items such as eggs, cheese and milk would be stored in the huge larder, which was built into the wall next to the front door. It had stone walls and was very dark with just a tiny ventilation grill at the back. Food did keep quite well for most of the year but in the summer Mum would try to keep the milk cool by putting it in a bowl of cold water. When Isobel came to live at our house the occupants of the larder slowly began to change. The smells were different now. Strange-looking sausages appeared and were hung in there. These added a new aroma, rich and spicy. Isobel showed Margaret and I how to eat melon, even sucking the seeds, splitting them with our teeth to chew out the insides. She also made tortilla with potatoes and eggs, turning these simple ingredients into a feast of flavour, which we devoured with relish.

The house was even more chaotic now than it had been before. Meal times were complicated, and sleeping arrangements were even more so. We now shared the bed settee with Mum in the kitchen, which meant that we stayed up very late every night. When the bed was put down, Margaret and I would snuggle up on each side of Mum. I remember so clearly how Mum would unfold her arms so we could rest our heads there. She always did this even when I shared her bed as an older child in the box room. It must have made her arms ache, but she never moved me away.

One bonus of having both Michael and Isobel and Peter and Linda living with us was that they both had tiny babies. Once they were born, Vicky in December and Carolyn in January, my brothers' search for a place of their own began in earnest. This meant that Margaret and I spent even longer periods of time away from school. We were allowed to play with the cast-off bottles, dummies, nappies and other baby paraphernalia. Mum even showed us how to 'swaddle' our dolls in some old material she found for us. Margaret was in her element.

Soon after the babies were born, my brothers both managed to find flats of their own. Michael was given an army flat in Woolwich and Peter found a small flat on the ground floor of a converted house not far from my Aunty Maggie in Seven Kings. Mum would often take us to visit them but most often we went to see Michael, or rather Isobel and baby Vicky. The journey from Dagenham to Woolwich seemed never ending. We would walk to the bus stop to catch the 62 and then get the 106 from Barking. For me, the journey was fraught with danger. Would people look at us? Would they say something horrible to Mum? Would they shout at us and would Mum have to shout at them? There had already been so many times in my young life where exactly that had happened. Everything could turn on a sixpence, and happiness could descend into chaos with a single look, word or action.

There was one time when Margaret and I had been playing happily upstairs. Mum was just about to serve up dinner. It was one of the 'plenty' days. We were having meat pudding. The savoury smells from downstairs were wafting up to us and our tummies were getting excited at the thought of the feast to come. Aunty, Pat and Jo were home and Marion and Marge were doing their homework on their laps at the top of the stairs, under the landing light.

'Shush,' Marion complained to us. She always had the hardest homework as she'd won a scholarship to a very posh grammar school in Hackney called St Victoire's. When the time had come for her to start she still hadn't got her special grey uniform and the tailored stripy blazer that was a requirement. The girls who were there on a scholarship had been sent grant cheques to pay for their uniform, and so they were to collect them direct from the school office. When her first day came she was called with the group of three other scholarship girls to go and collect it. When she came forward the lady looked down through her glasses at the label on top of the neatly folded pile.

'I'm sorry, dear,' she said kindly but with a knowing look in her eye, 'I'm afraid you can't take yours today; it hasn't been paid for yet.' Marion slunk back to class with a dreadful dawning awareness that tomorrow she would be the only girl in the class with the wrong clothes. When she came home and told us, Mum was furious.

'What do you mean she wouldn't let you have your uniform?' she said angrily. 'Just you wait; I'll write you a letter.'

It had taken more than a letter, Mum made many visits to the school and many protestations to the head teacher before the school accepted that the grant cheque had never arrived and Marion was allowed her uniform.

Today she had brought it home, and so was determined that this was a new start. Tomorrow she would look like the other girls, she would have done all of her homework and she would be able to walk into school without feeling that everyone was looking at her. She had even saved her bus fare by walking the three miles from the station so that she could buy some celebration sweets on the way home. It was going to be a good day.

Suddenly there was a sharp, loud *bang bang* at the front door. When Mum opened it the shouting started.

'I want me bleeding money!'

I recognised the man from next door. Margaret and I sat huddled together on the stairs, terrified. Mum was soon joined by Aunty and Pat and they all began to shout together. Then the man's wife Vera arrived on the doorstep.

'You promised! It's been over free bleeding weeks naw!' she bellowed and began swinging for Mum. The noise reached a crescendo and suddenly Mum pitched forward, clutching her chest.

Aunty let out a cry. 'Flo, oh no! Flo are you awright?' Pat supported Mum, who looked as though she was going to pass out, but the shouting carried on. I wanted to run to Mum, but was holding tightly on to Margaret who was now crying.

'It's all right. It's all right. It's all right,' I kept repeating, while I rocked back and forth, feeling as though my limbs were turning to liquid, and my tummy sinking in on itself. Aunty gave a huge push and managed to slam the door on the man and woman.

'Flo, Florrie,' she kept repeating as Mum slowly started to recover herself. Aunty was panicking as she always did. 'Paddy, get the doctor! Flo, Flo, oh my gawd, you awright Flo?'

Pat calmly led Mum into the kitchen, sat her down and then went to put the kettle on. We stayed on the stairs trembling for a while and then crept down and peeped into the kitchen; seeing Mum sitting on her usual chair by the side of the fire, we rushed over to cuddle her. Marion and Marge had stayed at the top of the stairs but now made their way quietly down, their eyes big and round. No one enjoyed their meat pudding that night.

9

Margaret

Margaret had stopped eating. She was getting thinner and thinner and deep black rings appeared underneath her eyes. Mum was beside herself with worry.

'Come on now, have a drop of tomato soup just for me.' Margaret turned her head away. Nothing anyone offered her could tempt her to eat. She was six years old but looked about four as she began to shrink and disappear before us. Her eyes, always big, now took on the appearance of dark brown saucers set in her bleached white face. Her hair had always been much darker than mine, and this seemed to exaggerate her sunken features.

Mum took her to see Dr Stanton. We sat in the crowded waiting room with its cream-coloured, sterile walls. The chairs were hard and were lined up close together in rows so that there wasn't enough room to move between them easily without having to push past people. I kept close to Mum but noticed one of the girls from my class at school just across the other side of the room with her mum. She had a big handkerchief held to her nose and kept coughing. We seemed to be there for ages when at last the voice that had been calling the patients one by one suddenly called out 'Margaret Stevens', so Mum got up and we walked towards the doctor's room. As we passed by the girl from my class, she said in a loud voice, 'Why is your sister called Margaret Stevens instead of Margaret Coates?'

As Mum pulled me forward, I turned and whispered, 'That's our special doctor's name.'

I thought everyone had a special name they used just for when they visited the doctor's; that was what Mum had told us. I wondered why this girl looked at me in such a quizzical manner.

Mum knocked on the door and we went into the room where the doctor sat smoking a cigarette.

'Now then, what's the matter with you, young lady, worrying your Mummy like this?'

Margaret just stared down at the floor. She attempted to bury her head in Mum's ample bosom but Mum turned her back towards the doctor again so he could examine her.

'Well young lady, you look fine to me.' The doctor smiled at Mum. 'I think she just needs fattening up!'

'But she won't eat, Doctor. She just turns her nose up at everything I give her.'

'Well let's give her a tonic and some Senokot granules in case she's constipated – that can sometimes affect children in this way. If she's not any better by next week bring her back.' We left the surgery and walked slowly home.

Margaret wasn't any better next week. Mum had duly cajoled and encouraged her to take the Senokot granules, which had to be mixed with water to make a muddy brown liquid drink. As Margaret would try to swallow it down she would retch and splutter. It was awful to watch and quite often I would hide away with my eyes screwed shut and my hands over my ears so that I didn't have to listen.

Today Mum had bought a special 'variety pack' of cereals to tempt her. This was made up of eight individual packs and was, Mum said, very expensive. Margaret pecked at a bowl of Ricicles, but she didn't really eat very much at all. I sat opposite her at the square wooden table, eating my cereal with enthusiasm, scraping up the last of the milk with my spoon. The kitchen wasn't a large room but it was stuffed with furniture. Apart from the big old wooden table there was a settee and three armchairs: one for Aunty, one for Mum and one for Pat. They had wooden arms and legs and there was a huge, ornate sideboard across one corner. Fitted carpets were still considered a luxury and our kitchen floor was covered in oil cloth, which was a bit like linoleum or vinyl flooring. I was always fascinated by the multitude of tiny circular indentations that were made by the stilettos my older sisters wore, and would sometimes trace their shape with my fingers. There was also a big rectangular grey rug in the middle of the floor which, even though it was quite threadbare and worn, made the room feel warmer. Today, as it was winter, wet washing was hung around the room to dry. Margaret's spoon dropped onto the table suddenly and it was as though she didn't have the energy to pick it back up. Mum stood up and carried her over to the settee – it was too cold for her to go upstairs. She tucked a coat over her, and put a shovel full of coal on the fire.

I was lonely without Margaret to play with. We were only eighteen months apart in age and had always been very close, but now that she was ill I began to be a more solitary child. I had always enjoyed reading, and would find books around the house – often unreturned remnants of my siblings' library visits. The whole family were now blacklisted, so although Margaret and I were sometimes taken to the library, we could never join or take books out.

I don't ever remember learning to read; I just seemed to be able to do it one day. I do know that I was reading quite well before I started school so must only have been about four or five. Books were very important in my life. There were plenty around the house, even though many of them were for adults.

When Margaret was first ill she wasn't yet able to read, so that became my job. Over the years I became adept at reading and sharing books with her. I wasn't scared or nervous when I read aloud to Margaret in the little bedroom she now shared with Josie. It was really quite cosy in there. Josie had stuck lots of posters of Elvis Presley on the walls and she kept the room tidy. Mum sometimes even lit a little fire in the fireplace on the coldest days if we had enough coal. We read the Katy books, *Little Women* and *Jo's Boys*; we devoured quantities of Enid Blyton and cried over *Black Beauty*. We explored some old poetry books that we found, and I sang the words to old songs and tunes that we half remembered. I would like to pretend that I did all of this because I was such a kind sister, but that wasn't the truth. I did it because I was tormented with jealousy. Margaret was the centre of attention. She was tiny, vulnerable and listless and so my Mum, Aunty and all of my sisters did their best to cheer her up. This meant that she got special little treats, one of which was a box of chocolate kittens each individually wrapped, which I coveted. I longed to be 'special' and wished many times that it was me that was ill, but I hid my feelings from everyone. The best way for me to get the attention I craved was to be the kind big sister. So I was.

Margaret was ill for several years. Over that time she had periods when she seemed to get better for a while, and things would be almost back to normal. We would play out in the garden again and get up to our usual mischief, but then she would suddenly go back downhill and slip back into a state of decline. Her body took on the appearance of an undernourished waif and Aunty would joke, 'Don't stand behind the lamppost or we won't see you.'

We started calling her 'Maggie Aggie Baggy Pants' and that name stuck with her until adulthood.

When you live with someone and see them every day you aren't always aware of their decline but looking back at photos it is clear that she was shrinking away. The doctor couldn't find anything wrong with her and I suppose these days she may have been diagnosed with an eating disorder or a more general 'failure to thrive'. The causes and symptoms were varied and sometimes vague, but for Margaret I believe it was a kind of saddening.

10

A Family Christmas

It would soon be Christmas. The preparations were always very exciting. Mum would buy us some little 'make your own' Christmas cards which we would spend hours colouring and spreading with glue and glitter. We would make one each for everyone in the family, taking great care with each of them and carefully writing: 'To . . . Merry Christmas from Kathleen and Margaret xxx'. We were also allowed to make paper chains from strips of paper – long looping strings of colour to hang around the walls and from the ceiling. Then the most exciting day would arrive and Pat would go to the market near where she worked in Poplar to get the Christmas tree. It would be placed in the same corner every year and we would cover it in all the old decorations. We would sing Christmas carols, and Mum would let us dance around the room like angels, and act out the Christmas story for our sisters.

On Christmas Eve the greengrocer would deliver a big box of fruit and vegetables which would include things we rarely saw other than at Christmas. There would be tangerines, oranges, grapes and bananas, all in copious quantities. The smell of the oranges would drive us wild but there was a strict rule that nothing could be tasted until Christmas morning. One year I gave way to my greed and crept downstairs to where the fruit box was standing in the passage and took a tangerine. It was the sweetest fruit that I have ever tasted, but the guilt that followed the eating was very bitter indeed and it was a sin I never confessed but certainly never repeated!

On this particular Christmas morning my excitement was uncontrollable. As my eyes snapped open it was still dark outside. Mum never went to bed on Christmas Eve. She always dozed in her armchair so that she could keep an eye on the turkey and the Christmas candle that had to be lit at midnight and would burn for twenty-four hours.

Margaret had joined me in bed with her pillowcase and we emptied them with gusto. We looked longingly at the sweets and fruit, but didn't eat any. We would be going to Christmas Morning Mass soon and we weren't allowed to eat before receiving Holy Communion. Mum never came to Mass but Aunty did. She attended every Sunday but would sit the other side of the church from us children. Perhaps she needed the peace!

Our tummies would rumble all through Christmas Mass, but we knew that Mum would have slipped some Quality Street into our pockets to eat on the way home and this always got us through.

We always had turkey, and the smell of it roasting in the oven when we got back from Mass sent our taste buds into overdrive. When Pat picked it up from the butchers there was always a concern that it wouldn't fit in the oven. We had to have a big bird as there were so many of us to feed and it usually weighed about 27 or 28lb. We would hold our breath while Mum covered it in streaky bacon rashers to keep it moist and slid it carefully into the oven. There was always a sigh of relief to see it actually fit! She would never cook the stuffing inside. We always had Paxo sage and onion and it would be cooked in a separate dish on Christmas Day. Christmas dinner was the only day in the year that I can remember us all sitting down together to eat. This was a huge logistical feat. The big table would be pulled into the centre of the room and we would have a tablecloth! The armchairs and settee around the edges would be joined by additional chairs retrieved from around the house. Mum would usually sit at the head of the table near the kitchen door so that she could get in and out to the scullery where the cooking was done. The rest of us would fit where we could. There was always a rush not to sit in front of the coal fire, as you would start to feel your back scorching halfway through the meal. We had crackers on the table which would be pulled early on so that we could don the paper hats from inside. Pat would always carve the turkey before we sat to eat, and the dog would sit hopefully next to her. We would watch as she carved perfect thin slices of meat, licking the juices from her fingers and occasionally throwing Pongo a piece of the meat as she cut. Josie would put our plates in front of us and then the sliced turkey would be brought in on a dish by Mum joined by a huge tray of crispy roasted potatoes and parsnips. Of course there were always copious quantities of brussels, peas and carrots and a huge jug full to the brim with Bisto gravy. Mum always made her own Christmas pudding, which we would set alight with a drop of Aunty's brandy. Mum never drank alcohol and neither did the rest of us, except for Aunty. At Christmas we did have non alcoholic ginger wine though, which was hot and spicy and singed our throats and was Mum's special favourite.

That year, after the Queen's speech, Pat and Jo announced that they had devised a game called 'The Tomb of Tutankhamun'. We were ushered out of the kitchen into the hallway.

'Stay there and no peeping,' Josie said.

We heard screams and laughter as one by one my big sisters disappeared into the room. Then it went eerily quiet. Margaret and I wriggled with anticipation. It was my turn to go in next. I crept fearfully through the door. The room was dark. The curtains had been closed and the light was off. There was a white sheet draped over one corner of the room and Mum, Aunty and my sisters were sitting round it. Suddenly I heard a voice which sounded a bit like Josie but deeper and much, much scarier.

'This is the tomb of Tutankhamun.' I shivered. 'You must follow the light and bow down and worship him. Go to the white sheet and say three times – "I bow to the tomb of Tutankhamun." '

I giggled nervously. Marge pushed me forward towards the sheet. I followed the light, which was in reality a torch held by one of my sisters behind the sheet. I bowed once and my sisters helped me to say the words. I did the same again and then on the third bow as I lifted my head and continued to follow the light to the top of the sheet, an arm sprang out from behind clutching a big wet sponge which was thrust into my face. I screamed loudly and jumped back to fits of uproarious laughter!

Goodness knows what poor Margaret was thinking when she heard this outside, knowing it was her turn next. I just remember feeling very glad that my turn was over and I would now get to be one of the watchers when she came through the door. Being the older sister had some consolations.

Over the years that game would be repeated every time there was a new addition to the family. Mary, Marge and Marion's boyfriends all had to endure this initiation to the Coates family.

Aunty, Mum and the Empty House

'Who's been going through my drawers?' Aunty shouted down. She had just got in from work early as it was a Thursday and she was clearly in one of her worse moods. She had stamped straight up the stairs when she arrived and was now banging around in the bedroom she shared with Marge and Marion. Since Michael and Peter and their wives had found flats of their own, the house was a bit less crowded. Mary and I shared a double bed in the box room, Margaret was in the back bedroom with Josie, and Pat had the front room downstairs all to herself. Mum still slept on the bed settee in the kitchen. She looked a bit worried now and raised her eyes to heaven. While she put the kettle on, we sat quietly, holding our breath to see what would happen next.

Aunty stomped down the stairs.

'Ask your aunt if she wants a cup of tea,' said Mum.

'I don't want no bloody tea – someone's been in my drawers again,' she shouted. She plonked herself down on her chair in the far corner near the window and crossed her legs. I watched nervously as her leg begin to swing agitatedly. This was always a sign that we were in for a stormy time.

Mum went out to the scullery to make the tea, throwing the words over her shoulder: 'No one's been in anyone's drawers.'

Aunty sniffed loudly, which was another sign that she was very cross. Today was rent day. Every fortnight the council man would come to collect the rent. When Granny had died the tenancy had been passed to Aunty as the eldest daughter in the house. This was very lucky for us as it meant that we at least always had a roof over our heads. Aunty had realised long ago that if she were to keep it that way she would need to find a way of paying the rent, as she knew if she left it for Mum to do, the money would disappear before the rent man arrived. Her solution was to give it to one of her friends who lived several houses along. Her name was Mrs Timberlick and we sometimes went with Aunty the night before rent day to take the money along. Mrs Timberlick's house was easy to recognise. Although most of the houses in Valence Avenue were very similar, it was the gardens that set them apart. Mrs Timberlick's had the most beautiful hydrangea bushes tumbling over her front garden, all around the gate and up the path – bluey pink balls of petals which bobbed about when the wind blew through them.

Sadly Aunty's fears for the rent money were well founded. Mum had a habit of acquiring money when she was desperate, and not worrying too much where it came from. There had been many incidents over the years that had caused arguments and tears in the family, and they were almost always about money. Every Monday before Peter had got married, Mum would take Peter's only suit to the pawn shop. She would get a few pennies for it and then she wouldn't give poor Peter the pawn ticket until he had handed over the majority of his wages on a Friday, after which he would then have to go and redeem it before he could go out with his friends at the weekend. It would drive him mad with anger and there were bitter arguments between him and Mum which often ended with Mum threatening him with a saucepan or some other kitchen implement. Peter was so annoyed once that he put a bolt and padlock on his bedroom door, but that didn't really help as it soon got mysteriously broken off.

The pawn shop was in Green Lane, which was about twenty minutes' walk away. The entrance to the pawn shop was down a short alleyway, which was quite dark, almost as though it were hiding its secrets. It had a sign outside with three balls hanging, which fascinated me. Mum would usually leave us waiting outside while she went in, but occasionally we would be allowed inside. It seemed to be full of objects of every shape and size, including big piles of clothes all laying on top of each other. It also had a musky, mothball kind of smell which stung my nose and made me want to sneeze. I always wondered how the man could see what he was doing as it was so gloomy in there. I don't think Mum ever got very much for the suit, but when you have a huge family of mouths to feed every little bit extra helps.

Mum was always looking for ways to get more money. Although she was able to claim social security, it wasn't a huge amount, and it certainly didn't allow for any extras. When the lady came from the social, Margaret and I were always sent upstairs. We would desperately try to hear what was being said, but we never knew what took place during those meetings.

Many of the items of furniture around the house had mysteriously disappeared over the years. One by one anything that was worth anything had been sold. Granny would have been sad to see her piano disappear from the front room, which used to be the parlour. Aunty Rene, one of Mum's older sisters, had been a really accomplished pianist and the whole family had nice singing voices. Of course in days before television singing around the piano had been a favourite family occupation, but that was all finished now. The piano had long gone, along with the wind-up gramophone and the pretty china that had belonged to Granny.

The only things left were bits and pieces of furniture that we had been given or found. Mum never really bought anything for herself except for her cigarettes. Her clothes were always poor quality and old, and her shoes were worn and usually in need of repair. She wore slippers most of the time, and if she went out would wear a headscarf tied tightly under her chin. By the time my memories began, the constant worry and stress that must have made up her life had started to take their toll, and she looked older than her years. Her hair was silvery grey and had begun to thin, but her skin was still as soft as a baby's. I can remember as an adult stroking her arm when she was near the end of her life, and wondering at its smoothness.

One of the ways that Mum managed to provide the things she thought we needed was to get things on 'tick'. This in effect meant buying from a door-to-door salesman, who would encourage Mum to 'have now pay later'. Over the years these debts grew to mammoth proportions, and the weekly problem of deciding who she could pay this week must have been a constant pressure on her. Occasionally there would be a knock at the door and there would be a man with a parcel that would always contain some unnecessary item that we would rush to unwrap. At the time, Margaret and I thought it was wonderful. Looking back, it must have been a kind of addiction for Mum, or an antidote to the dreary monotony and tedium of her life. She always wanted to give us things, to be the gift giver, the supplier of everything wonderful and exciting. The sad thing was that she didn't need to buy anyone's adoration, loyalty and love. She got that for free.

When Mum was cornered by her worries, and I suppose overwhelmed by the trap her life had become, she would sometimes tip over into flight mode. The first time I remember it happening was when she had just got back from the phone box over the road. We didn't have a phone in the house until I was a teenager, but my Mum's sisters did. Aunty often took us with her when she went to phone Aunt Maggie. She would sometimes make us wait outside, but more often we were allowed to squeeze in with her. She would dial the number saying 'RIP rest in peace' and laugh. It was ages before we worked out the reason for this was that Aunty Maggie's code was Rippleway which was abbreviated to RIP. She seemed to talk for an age, and Margaret and I would jiggle and wiggle about getting more and more restless. What did she have to talk about that took so long? Sometimes she would joke to Aunt Mag, 'They're laughing at me these two – saucy monkeys.'

When she was in a good mood she might placate us with the promise of some penny sweets from the sweetshop next to the phone box. There was an exciting array to choose from and we would spend an age on using up our thruppence.

Once Mum came out from the phone box very upset.

'Someone has taken my purse,' she wailed. 'We'll have to go to the Police Station,' and off we trundled to Chadwell Heath.

She was crying desperately as we went inside.

'My purse has been stolen,' she wept to the kindly police officer behind the desk. 'All of my food money was in it,' she continued, only stopping periodically to dab at her eyes, and bend to give us a cuddle, as we had 'caught' her distress and now stood crying too.

'All right madam, try to keep calm now,' the police officer said soothingly, 'then perhaps we can try to help you.'

'I went to phone my sister,' she told him, 'and must have mistakenly left my purse in the phone box, then when I went back,' here she burst into fresh tears, 'when I went back it had gone!'

The police officer lent forward and gave her a fresh hanky.

'There, there madam,' he said. 'Just leave it with us and we'll see what we can do.'

He wrote down the details and promised Mum that they would do their best to find the culprit, but Mum could not be consoled.

'You don't understand,' she whispered through her tears. 'That was all the money I had for the children's food. What am I going to do now?'

I don't know quite what happened next, but Mum was eventually handed an envelope, and she thanked the police officer profusely, and cheered up considerably as we walked all the way back home.

'You see,' she told us, 'the police are so kind, they always help you when you're in trouble.'

There were also times when she went to the phone box on her own. Once when she returned, her mood was black and bleak. She had that same look in her eyes again, the one that made her look like a different person, the look that took her away from us. Josie had got in from work and gone straight up to bed. She often did this; in fact she spent long periods of time in her room, listening to music on her little radio and writing stuff down in little notebooks. Pat was sitting in front of the television and Marge and Marion were trying to do their homework on the stairs before they were asked to help out. Mary had gone round to her friend Helen's house straight from school and Margaret and I were playing out in the garden. It was the beginning of the autumn and was starting to get dark and a bit chilly. Mum blew in through the front door and we heard her shouting at the twins: 'Where's Mary?'

'She's gone round to Helen's,' one of them answered.

'What on earth for? I need her here – Marion go round and get her now.'

'I can't Mum I've got to finish this homework for tomorrow.'

Mum stomped through to the back door. 'You two inside now,' she said roughly. We looked at each other; we weren't ready to stop playing so we just carried on. 'I said now!' she shouted. This was unusual; Mum rarely shouted at us and never with so little cause.

'Marion, Marge get down here,' she repeated, 'I want Mary home now.' The twins descended the stairs resentfully. They grumbled their way out of the house to walk the ten minutes round to Helen's house. By this time Margaret and I had come inside and were snivelling at having to leave our game. As they left, Mum walked into the kitchen and looked around her. Aunty wasn't yet home from work, the room was untidy and cold and there was no dinner cooking; the damp washing was hung around the walls as it had been raining earlier and she hadn't been able to put it on the line in the garden.

Pat murmured, 'Don't shout at the littluns. They're upset now.'

Mum spun round and snapped: 'I've had enough. I'm going out.'

'Where are you going?' Pat asked, shocked. Mum didn't usually go anywhere in the evenings unless it was to the phone box and she had just got back from there.

'I don't know, just out.'

Pat's face lost its colour. 'Why? What's wrong?'

Mum moved towards the door. 'I'm fed up, I'm fed up with all of it, and with the lot of you.'

Margaret ran to her and hung on to her coat. 'Mummy, don't go,' she cried, but Mum just shook her off and left, banging the front door behind her.

Margaret broke down in sobs, so I tried to comfort her. 'She'll be back soon,' I promised, but inside I was terrified of what might happen next. Pat went upstairs to talk to Josie and then the twins came back with Mary.

'What's happened?' asked Mary, at which I started crying along with Margaret, because I really didn't know.

Mum storming out become a recurrent theme throughout my childhood, and even though our experience showed us that she would usually return after a few hours, it didn't stop me feeling terrified that this time it would be different and she wouldn't come back. After all, I'd heard stories of how she'd disappeared for weeks at a time when my sisters were young. Sometimes Josie or Pat would go to look for her if she hadn't come back by nightfall. They would usually find her wandering around, or sometimes pretending to wait for a bus, just standing at the bus stop smoking and thinking. When she came back, she would be quiet and absent for a while, with that same faraway look in her eyes, but it never lasted long. She always did come back, because I guess by that time she didn't have anywhere else to go.

Mum didn't usually get up to see us off to school in the morning, but one summer morning she was up early and called to us to get out of bed.

'Come on you two, you have to go to school early today.'

We grumbled down the stairs; going to school was bad enough without having to get there early. As we reached the kitchen we were shocked to see Aunty still at home. She usually left for work at Plessey's at about 6.30 each morning so wasn't usually around by the time we rolled out of bed.

'Tell your Aunt that Julie is picking us up in the car at half past,' Mum said. We flicked our eyes at Aunty. We were so used to this way of theirs of talking through us children that we sometimes didn't even bother to repeat the words, because it was blatantly obvious that they had heard what each other were saying, but I was shocked. Mum and Aunty *never* went out together.

Aunty sniffed 'Tell your mother that I'm ready now,' and she went out into the passage to get her coat, even though it was promising to be a warm day. We were ushered out of the door even though it was only 8.15 and were left to wonder where they were going that was so important that they were going together – and with our Aunty Maggie's daughter Julie.

Margaret looked at me as we wandered slowly towards Becontree Avenue. 'Where is Mum going today?'

'I don't know. I expect they're going to Aunty Maggie's house.' I didn't really believe that was where they were going; social visiting wasn't something that Mum and Aunty ever did together, and anyway they would have gone on the bus, not been picked up in a car.

'They might be going to the shops,' Margaret suggested as we carried on walking. This again was highly unlikely, as the only shops Mum ever went to were the local ones, or occasionally to Green Lane. She rarely even went as far as Ilford or Barking and again she would have gone by bus. It was a puzzle.

School dragged on throughout that day. I was in junior 4 now and we were knee-deep in spelling tests, comprehension and maths, question after question, tables after tables. Outside the sun was shining, which only heightened our wish to escape. By playtime, when we were released from the confines of the classroom, it was as though the top had come off the pressure cooker. The boys in particular would go wild, tearing madly around the playground.

By the end of the day I had almost forgotten about the puzzle of Mum and Aunty's trip out, so when Margaret mentioned it on our way home, I didn't pay much attention. I was too busy thinking about the homework Miss E had given me, which I really didn't want to do. When we arrived at our front door we gave the usual family knock and waited for Mum to open the door as always.

No one came.

Margaret looked at me worriedly. 'Why isn't Mummy opening the door?'

I knocked again, louder this time, 'She might be upstairs,' I said, trying to hide my concern from Margaret as I always did. Still no reply. I knocked again, and this time we opened the letter box to look inside. Pongo was barking and jumping up at the door but there was no other movement. I waited for a few minutes and then tried once more.

'What shall we do?' Margaret started to cry.

'Don't worry, they'll be home soon.' But it felt strange and uncomfortable to be standing outside our own front door desperate to get in. Suddenly I had an inspiration. 'I know, we can go and knock at Mrs Timberlick's house.' Margaret agreed it was a good plan so off we walked. We opened the front gate and walked up the path. I knocked and waited. We heard a sound from inside and the door slowly opened. 'Hello my dears,' said Mrs Timberlick kindly. 'What's the matter?'

'No one's home,' I answered carefully. The kind old lady ushered us into the front parlour where she told us to sit ourselves down.

'Would you like a drink? Orange squash?' she offered, but we both declined politely even though we were incredibly thirsty. There we sat for what seemed like an age until finally Mrs Timberlick suggested we pop down to see if Mum was home. I held my breath as I knocked on the door and said a little prayer. My prayer was answered. There was Mum, distracted and upset, but not because of us. In fact she hardly seemed to be aware of us as we went inside. There was an air of sadness and silence and Aunty had very red eyes.

Our big sisters had all returned from work and so I went over to Marge and asked 'What's happened?' only to be told, 'Shh, Uncle John has died.' This sounded very sad, but I had never met Uncle John. He was Mum and Auntie's oldest brother and lived in Birmingham.

I had heard Aunty talk about him from time to time, but Mum always looked away or changed the subject when his name was mentioned, as though she were ashamed. We weren't allowed to ever show our feelings, or to talk about them either, so the rest of the evening was spent with very little being said, but a lot being felt by both Mum and Aunty. Every so often I would catch Aunty looking over at Mum with what looked like an angry look in her eyes.

It wasn't until many years later I found out why.

The Wages Mystery

When I was about seven my sister Mary got a job in the General Post Office (GPO). She was to be trained to be a telephonist. None of my sisters had been able to stay on at school past the age of fifteen as their wages were needed as a contribution to the household budget; none of them ever complained but it must have been hard. Mary was always very popular and attracted lots of attention from the local boys; she sometimes flirted back but she was never serious about any of them. Then she came home from work one day looking very excited and just a bit flushed.

'I've got a date,' I heard her whisper to Marge and Marion. There was only a year difference between Mary and the twins, so they often confided in each other.

'Who with?' Marion asked.

'A young bloke who works opposite me in London. He looks quite sweet.'

'What's his name?'

'Dave,' Mary replied a little dreamily.

Suddenly Marge put her hand over her mouth, 'Oh God, are you going to tell Mum?'

'Course not,' said Mary, 'she doesn't need to know. I'll tell her I'm going to the pictures with Helen.' Mary had been friends with Helen since primary school. She also came from a big Irish family, and Mary would often go round to her house to whisper and giggle about grown-up stuff.

'Do you think you'll get away with it?' asked Marion.

'I don't know but I'm going to try.'

I was outraged! How dare they do things that would upset

Mum? I wondered if I should tell Mum, but decided against it. It might make her go off again.

Mary and Dave began courting and Mum seemed to accept it quite well. This was very exciting for Margaret and I because Dave had a motorbike and sometimes he would drive it to our house from his parents' home in Leytonstone.

One night Mary told us that Dave had a surprise for us. When he knocked on the door, and Mary came running downstairs to open it, we peaked through the banisters to watch them. Dave looked up and said, 'Do you two want to come for a ride?'

We looked at each other in disbelief. *A ride?*

Mary laughed. 'Get your coats on then; it will feel cold.'

Mum shouted out from the kitchen: 'What are you doing?'

'We're just taking the littluns for a ride round the corner.'

'Oh no you're not,' Mum said firmly. 'They're too little; they might fall off.'

'It's okay, Mrs Coates,' Dave reassured her, 'I've put the side-car on.'

When we got outside it was dark and a bit windy, and a few drops of rain were starting to fall.

'In you go then,' said Dave as he opened the flap of the side-car. We clambered inside and squashed together as he zipped it up. It was very cosy, and smelt of petrol and grease. As Dave started the motorbike up, Mary climbed on the back and suddenly we were away! It was probably only about five or six minutes that we drove for but it was one of the most exciting things we had ever done. The bike was very bumpy and wobbly and as we turned the corners it felt like we were going to topple over on our side, but we loved it. When we got home we couldn't stop laughing and talking about it. Dave had suddenly become our hero, Mary was our favourite sister, and Mum was beginning to be won round – but that wasn't to last for long.

Being a GPO telephonist was a high-status job and Mary enjoyed it. She was taught how to work a 1A lamp switchboard, which was quite a complicated piece of equipment, but she was clever and quick to learn and she was also making lots of new friends. Mary had a sparkling personality and was always the centre of attention. She was both funny and kind to us younger children. The stories that she told us were always exciting and I can remember one time her sitting on the back doorstep with Margaret and I and telling us a story about fairies in the clouds and witches in the coal cellar. She also taught us to catch rain-drops in our mouths and to splash in puddles. Once she started getting serious with Dave she wasn't around quite so much, although Mum had very strict rules about courting. Mary had to be home by 9.30 p.m. if she saw Dave in the evening, which meant there was very little they could do other than go for a walk. Sometimes they hurried home from work so they could make the early showing at the pictures. This was tricky as it depended how long the film was as to whether they got home in time, and if they didn't there would be hell to pay! Mum would stand waiting at the front gate with her arms crossed and an angry look on her face. Mary decided it just wasn't worth it and so they often left before the film was over just to make sure they were back on time.

One day Mary had a very bad cold. She still went in to work, travelling on the train from Chadwell Heath into Liverpool Street station. It wasn't a long journey, but was stuffy and damp and by the time she got home that evening she was feeling worse. Mum told her she should stay at home the next day but Mary didn't want to. She had arranged to meet Dave at lunchtime, and was looking forward to seeing him, but Mum was insistent.

'You need to get rid of that cold otherwise it could turn to pneumonia.' Mum always worried about illness getting worse. I suppose she had experienced life before the welfare system and the National Health Service and knew that when little ailments were ignored they could progress into something much worse. She had lost her own little brother Peter when he was just two. He had caught diphtheria which was a terrible, and sadly common, disease before the vaccination was developed in the 40s. One day the poor little boy had a cold and a cough, then he developed a high temperature and within the week he began to struggle to breathe. He died not long after. At the time it wasn't only diphtheria that was to be feared, but also polio, tuberculosis and pneumonia. Things were better for our generation. Antibiotics were seen as the great cure-all and had almost eradicated the complications that had often accompanied childhood diseases such as measles, whooping cough, mumps and chicken pox. Those parents that had grown up in the pre-antibiotic age were still fearful at the mention of some of these diseases. I clearly remember Aunty's reaction when Mum brought me home from the doctors one day having been diagnosed with scarlet fever. Mum had managed to calm her down, repeating the doctor's reassurances, and Aunty was then further placated at the sight of the pink bottle of penicillin that had been prescribed.

Whenever Margaret or I were ill, Aunty would always go over the road to the greengrocers and buy us a huge shiny Jaffa orange, which was a very expensive and unusual treat. Mum would tuck us up on the settee and cover us with a coat or a blanket, cut the orange in quarters, and then give it to us to suck, one piece at a time. Being tucked up in front of the fire with orange juice trickling down our chins was almost as good for us as the penicillin.

Mary was older and her experiences of being ill were different. Mum had not been around for much of the time when she and the twins were small. They never knew where Mum went, only that she was often absent for long periods of time. She would come back to visit periodically, but they would view her as a visitor rather than a mother. Much later as adults we would be able to piece together her likely destinations and begin to understand why she went but for the young Mary, Marion and Marge, Granny and Aunty were the care-givers. Granny was an old lady by that time, and Aunty was out at work, so being home ill was a very different experience for them. For sixteen-year-old Mary, the prospect of being stuck at home with Mum, even with an orange for company, didn't compete with going to work and seeing her friends and meeting up with Dave, so she got up the next morning, got ready and went in to work. Mary's cold did indeed get worse. A lot worse. She developed a very severe throat and chest infection, which was slow to respond to the antibiotics she was prescribed. She ended up being off work for almost four weeks. At that time Mary was paid weekly, but as she was unwell, this was to be sent to her as a weekly postal order. The first Saturday came, but no postal order arrived.

'I don't understand,' said Mary, 'I'm sure that they are supposed to send it off on Friday – sorry Mum.' All of my working sisters gave Mum the majority of their wages. She desperately needed it to feed us and pay the weekly callers who continually harassed her for the money she owed. The girls would need to keep their fares of course, but after that and a shilling or two for an occasional pair of stockings, the rest went to Mum.

Mum reassured Mary, 'It's fine love, don't worry. I'm sure it will come on Monday.' Nothing came on Monday, nor the following three weeks.

'I expect you will get it in one go when you are back at work,' soothed Mum. Mary was so grateful that Mum wasn't angry. She knew that money was very scarce and didn't like letting Mum down like this. She planned to give Mum the money as soon as she was paid, and even thought how nice it would be that she would be able to give Mum a little extra as there would be three weeks' worth of fares and stocking money left over. When Mary finally recovered sufficiently to return to work, she was really excited. It would be good to see everyone again, especially Dave, who had brought round a bunch of flowers for her, even though he hadn't been allowed inside to see her. She got dressed carefully on Monday morning, backcombed her hair and even put on a little bit of a lipstick that she had managed to buy one week. The train journey to London felt fresh and new and Mary was feeling so much better, even though Mum had reminded her that the first thing she must do was to go and tell the wages people that she hadn't been paid for the four weeks she had been off sick. Mary arrived at work keen to return to her switchboard, but before she did she made her way to the wages office, and let them know about her wages not being sent. They looked puzzled but promised to look into it for her. Mary worked through the morning, and managed to find a few minutes to catch up with her friends.

'Dave has really missed you,' said Hannah. 'He keeps popping over trying to see if you are back yet.' They laughed together, Mary feeling happier by the minute.

At lunchtime she made her way over to the entrance of the building where Dave worked, hoping to catch sight of him as he went out to lunch. Suddenly there he was, beaming at her.

'Hiya,' he said, 'have you got time for a sandwich?'

'Yes, but I can't be too long, I need to go back to the wages office to see if they have managed to sort out my money.'

After a sandwich and a cup of tea, Mary left Dave with a promise of a date the following evening, and went to the wages office before starting her afternoon shift at the switchboard. She knocked on the door, and was asked to come in. The wages clerk was trying to smile and be helpful, but she was obviously uncomfortable about something.

'Mary, I'm really sorry but Mrs D wants to see you,' she said quietly, looking down at her shoes.

Mary was worried; had she done something wrong? Was she going to get the sack for being ill for so long? As Mary went through to Mrs D's office, she had a horrible feeling that something was not right.

'Hello Mary, are you feeling better now?' asked Mrs D kindly.

Mary nodded and waited.

'Mary, we are a little bit confused about your wages, dear,' Mrs D continued. 'Is there anyone else at home who might have signed for the postal orders? A brother maybe?'

Mary flushed. Peter was married now, and in his own flat, but she knew he would never take her wages anyway.

'No, not really,' she whispered, feeling a sinking dread. What was she going to tell Mum? If they were saying that the wages had been sent, there wouldn't be any extra money today, and

Mum was expecting it. What would she say? What would Mum do? She looked up at the kind but serious face of Mrs D.

'But I really need my money,' Mary continued. 'My mum needs it for food, and I haven't been able to give her any keep for four weeks now.'

Mrs D's look hardened, 'Mary, I am really sorry but I am afraid we are going to have to tell the police about this, because someone has taken your postal order, signed for it and cashed it every week.'

At this Mary started to cry, she didn't know what to do, but the thought of the police being told filled her with fear. What if they didn't believe her and took her to prison?

'Look dear,' said Mrs D, seeing Mary's obvious distress and confusion, 'why don't you go home and talk to your mum about it before we do anything else?'

Mary nodded and thanked her.

When she got home that evening, she was surprised that Mum didn't go mad.

She did look angry at first. 'Are you sure they said they were going to call the police?'

'Yes, I don't know what to do. Mrs D told me to talk to you about it.'

A strange look came over Mum's face and then she turned away to pick up her empty cup. Shrugging her shoulders, she said in a resigned voice, 'Well just leave it, then. It's not worth causing trouble over,' and walked into the scullery.

Mary was so very relieved; she was happy to let the matter drop.

A Family Holiday

Margaret's health had improved dramatically. The doctor had finally managed to have her referred to the London Jewish hospital in Stepney. The hospital had been founded in the middle of the nineteenth century to serve the growing Jewish immigrant population. This enabled their patients to adhere to the strict Jewish laws and traditions while being cared for. In 1947 the hospital was taken over by the newly formed National Health Service. I am not sure why Margaret was sent there, but through the years clues that have been revealed have shaped my suspicions.

Margaret was nearly nine by this time and had almost become resigned to being the sick member of the family. When Mum took her to the hospital Margaret was distraught.

'I don't want to go,' she wailed.

Although Mum must have been upset herself, she managed to hide it.

'It's only for a little while and when you come out you'll be all better.' This was wildly optimistic but Mum was always an expert at convincing people of the most unlikely outcomes.

'Can Kathleen stay with me then?' Margaret pleaded, her huge eyes taking on a pathetic desperate look. Mum didn't answer.

After Margaret had been weighed and measured the nurse called her colleague over to take her to the ward. Margaret clung on to Mum's arms as the nurse gently extracted her and led her towards the big doors. As she disappeared from our sight she was still crying for Mum. Today parents are encouraged to stay with their children when they are in hospital and being comforted by a loved one is recognised as being an essential part of recovery, but in the 60s this was not the case.

Margaret was subjected to a barrage of investigations including kidney tests, but they all came back clear, and the doctors became more and more perplexed. Finally they noticed that she had very enlarged tonsils and it was decided that these should be removed. I can still remember her crying silently after the operation because she was in so much pain, and the look of disgust on her face when the promised ice cream arrived in a flavour she wasn't expecting.

Whether it was the removal of her tonsils that triggered Margaret's improved health we will never know, but improve it did.

It was now only a week or so until the summer holidays. I was due to move to my secondary school in September and was very nervous. New situations always equated to anxiety. I was always fearful of not fitting in, being different from the others, not having the right clothes, shoes, things . . . I also knew that meeting new people meant answering difficult questions. Questions I never knew the answers to. The last few terms at primary school had not been easy for me. I was in the top group in my class, but did not attend regularly. Despite this my teacher was hopeful of me passing the 11-plus exam that all children took at that time to decide whether they would win a place at a local grammar school or would have to attend the secondary modern. I was also entered for a scholarship exam for the Ilford Ursuline Convent School, which took several scholarship students each year from its local community. My sister Pat had won a scholarship there and Mum was hopeful that I would do the same.

On the day that I attended for the exam at the Ursuline School I was very nervous. They had big girls there to show us where to go. Everything was quiet and clean and shiny. So shiny in fact that I slipped over. A kind nun in a long black habit came and helped me up.

'Hello,' she said, 'up you get. These floors are so slippery, aren't they?'

I scrambled to my feet, feeling very silly and embarrassed.

'What's your name?' she asked.

'Kathleen Coates,' I whispered back.

A look of recognition crossed her face. 'Ahh yes, your sisters came here didn't they?' I looked back puzzled. My sister Pat had come here but no one else.

'Yes, I remember them – Sheila and Patricia; lovely girls and very clever.'

I stared back and nodded. *Sheila*? My secret sister Sheila had come here?

'I'm sure you'll do well if you are as bright as they were,' she added.

I wasn't. I failed both the 11-plus and the entrance exam to the Ursuline, so secondary modern it was.

I remember going with my mum to the launderette shortly after the results had come. 'How did she get on then?' the lady had asked.

'Oh she passed both,' answered Mum, 'but I've decided to send her to the Sacred Heart Convent instead because I think she'll prefer it there.' I was very confused. Had I passed? I was sure I hadn't because when Mum opened the letter she was upset and I heard her telling Pat that I would have to go to the secondary school now with all the rough girls. I suddenly felt ashamed. Mum had lied to the lady because she was disappointed in me and didn't want everyone to know that I wasn't clever enough to go to grammar school. I was already a failure and I wasn't even eleven until August.

I was looking forward to the six weeks holiday though. That wonderful feeling of freedom, of not having somewhere you should go or be. When I arrived home from school Mum opened the door humming. This was a good sign. When we were staying off school with one of our 'mysterious' ailments she would often teach us songs, and sometimes sing while we danced around the room. We would dress up in old pieces of fabric draped around us and we would become graceful butterflies while she sang, '*Butterflies white, butterflies blue, butterflies golden and heliotrope too,*' and we would swoop around flapping our wings. I also loved to read poems from the books that were lying around the house and would sometimes try to match them to music and make up dances for us to do. There was one very mournful poem that I loved by Walter de la Mare:

> No breath of wind, no gleam of sun,
> Still the white snow whirls softly down

which I matched to the tune of 'Greensleeves'.

'Guess what?' Margaret said, flying to meet me as Mum opened the door. 'We're going on holiday!'

'What?'

'We're going on holiday!' she repeated louder this time in case I hadn't heard.

I dropped my school bag on the floor. 'Are we, Mum?' I asked, afraid to believe it. We had never been on holiday before – well, not in my memory. I had seen photos of myself holding hands with Pat and Josie as I tottered between them on a sandy beach when I must have been about a year old, but of course I didn't remember that. Something bad must have happened there because Mum never wanted to talk about it; I was only ever shown that photo furtively, when Mum wasn't around.

Now, nearly ten years later, here was Margaret telling me that we were going on holiday and Mum was nodding and smiling to confirm it.

'Where are we going? When are we going? Who's coming?' The questions came spilling out. Mum came and sat down in the kitchen on her chair and lit a cigarette, 'We are going at the end of July, which is in a few weeks, and we are going to a place called Ilfracombe.' That sounded like a funny name to us but it also sounded exotic and exciting. We started giggling. We were a pair of gigglers, at least that was what Mum called us. Usually it seemed to annoy her, but the more she told us off the more we giggled; it must have driven her mad. But not today; today she was in one of her good moods.

'We will all be going and Mary is staying here with Aunty to look after the cat.'

'Are we taking Pongo with us?' I asked worriedly. Pongo was supposed to be my dog. Old Pongo had died, but it wasn't long before Mum had brought home a new puppy. This one was black and white and I loved her. She was Pat's and mine, and I took my responsibility very seriously. That dog loved us back, and would always sit on Pat's lap when she was home from work, and I would squeeze next to them on the same chair. I was a bit too big to do that now, but I still adored playing with Pongo and she would rush to meet me when I got home from school.

'Yes, Pongo is coming with us,' Mum reassured me as she stroked the dog's head. 'We will get the train to London and then a coach all the way to Ilfracombe.' Margaret and I counted the days, desperate for the holiday to arrive. We talked endlessly about going and longed for time to pass until we got on the train. When we saw some battered old suitcases appear it began to feel more real.

On the Friday evening before we were due to leave, Marge, Marion, Pat and Josie had all arrived home from work. Margaret and I were beside ourselves with excitement, although mine was tempered by the dread that always accompanied anything new. Would people on the coach look at us? Would they say something to Mum?

We left for the station bright and early. Mum had arranged with Mary that she would leave her family allowance and benefits book with her so Mary could draw it out for the fortnight we were going to be away. Mary had agreed to 'loan' Mum the money in advance from her and Dave's savings so that we would have some money to take with us. Off we left for the station, dragging our heavy suitcases onto the 62 bus to Chadwell Heath station.

As we boarded the train I turned and looked around me. Something had to go wrong. This was all just too wonderful and exciting for words! 'I bet the train will break down,' I thought, 'or maybe it will crash and we won't get to the coach in time,'

but it didn't and we did. The journey seemed very long. The
coach was warm and stuffy, and when it stopped for people to
take a 'comfort' break and have a cup of tea we stayed on board.
There was no point in going into the café as we couldn't afford
to buy refreshments. Mum had made Spam sandwiches and
had filled bottles with orange squash for us while the older ones
had tea from a flask. As the journey was so long and the coach
was so hot, the sandwiches were sweaty and the juice was warm.
My head begin to throb and I felt a wave of nausea. I started to
feel panicked. What would I do if I needed to be sick? Everyone
on the coach would see. For the rest of the journey I was in
misery, my head banging furiously. I was trying desperately not
to be sick. In the end I managed to make it, but Pongo wasn't so
lucky. She vomited, but luckily Pat managed to catch it in her
sunhat! I don't think the other passengers on the coach were
very impressed and the smell was awful.

We were all relieved to arrive. The coach dropped us in the
centre of Ilfracombe and Mum got out the letter confirming our
holiday rental.

'Right, let's have a look now.' She read the directions out loud.

The house where we had hired a flat was at the top of a very
steep hill and the flat was at the top of a very tall house, so there
was a lot of climbing involved every time we went out, but we
didn't mind.

Margaret and I were given the bunk beds, her on the bottom
and me on the top. The beach was in walking distance, and we
went there almost every day. On the first day we passed a seaside
shop. It was glorious! Sun hats swung from its awning and buckets and spades tumbled out from its windows, along with shells,
paper windmills, wind breaks and all manner of exciting objects.
We were allowed to choose a bucket and spade each and a
sunhat.

'Can I have the red one?' I pleaded with Pat, as she reached
into her purse to find the money. Margaret pointed excitedly at
the yellow one and we were both delighted with our acquisitions.
We chose pink and blue sunhats that were cone-shaped with

pretty fringes all over. My heart skipped a beat when I saw the beach stretched before us for the first time.

'Oh look!' I shouted to no one in particular, pointing to the endless sand and white-topped waves. We had been on day trips to Southend before, but I had never seen such golden sand, so many tempting rockpools.

'Come on,' I said to Margaret, 'I'll race you,' and we tumbled along the sand towards the sea. The sun seemed to shine every day. We had ice creams and sticks of rock, and even had fish and chips, which we ate on the beach as we looked out at the seagulls swirling around us hungrily. We made good use of our new swimsuits and showed off the newly acquired skills that we had learnt from our weekly swimming lessons at school. In the evenings we would all go back down to the beach and play cricket. People would gather round to watch, and sometimes they would clap if one of us hit the ball a long way, or made an impressive catch. We must have looked the epitome of a big happy normal family. Looks can be deceiving.

14

Running Out of Money

The first week of our holiday whizzed past at speed, and everyone seemed to be happy for once. I had now moved to share the double bed with Marge, as I had fallen out of the top bunk on the first night we were there and had bruising all down my left side.

I had screamed my head off, but Pat said, 'Just go for a swim in the sea. Don't you know that salt water is healing?'

The flat we had rented for the fortnight was small, but clean and tidy. There was a table with enough chairs for us all to sit down at the same time, which was a real novelty. Mum would cook an evening meal for us after we had been at the beach all day and we were always ravenous by then. After dinner we would either play cards, snakes and ladders, draughts or sometimes Monopoly, which we had brought with us. We also went to the penny arcades a couple of times. This was a huge treat for us, and we had to decide whether to put the pennies in to see if we could get the silver balls into the right slots or whether to make the laughing policemen roar hysterically.

At night Josie told us ghost stories. She was very good at this, and could make all sorts of strange voices and noises. There is a very fine line between terror and delight and we enjoyed walking that line whenever Josie was in the mood to play with us, and would often go to bed trembling with fear and imaginings. We had watched a Punch and Judy show on the beach one day, and even at ten I remember feeling confused and unnerved by it. It was the one thing we did during that first week that I didn't enjoy. The strange guttural voice of the puppets, and the violent smacking just didn't seem right. Arguments, shouting, chaotic situations, violent outbursts and strange unfathomable, confusing secrets – it was just too close to the truth of my childhood, and ugly Mr Punch haunted my dreams for many years afterwards. But apart from that, I had a wonderful time; my sisters laughed and played around me and Mum was always smiling.

By the end of that first week things changed. There wasn't much food left and the money had run out. Mum had her family allowance and benefits book with her as she had forgotten to leave them for Mary, but she couldn't draw out the money until Tuesday. On Saturday we woke up and the sun had disappeared. Grey clouds had gathered, and with them came a change in everyone's mood. Margaret and I picked up on this and were starting to squabble. Most of our sisters didn't want to go to the beach because they said it was too cold and was going to rain, so we were just sitting in the small flat with nothing much to do except look out of the window hoping for sunshine.

Suddenly Pat jumped up and said, 'Come on you two, let's go for a walk with Pongo.' I put on my shoes eagerly but Margaret wanted to stay at home with Josie who had begun to make some little dolls for her out of a couple of wooden pegs she had found in a basket under the sink. Pat and I headed off towards the beach, but the clouds were getting blacker and it was soon obvious that it was going to rain. There was a loud clap of thunder and I let out a scream, then a jagged fork of lightning seemed to bounce off the sea.

It was really scary but Pat said, 'Oh it's all right, it's just God moving his furniture.' I didn't really believe her but it did make me feel better. By the time we got home we were both soaking wet and so was Pongo.

'Come here Pongo and I'll dry you,' said Pat, as she grabbed the towel from the bathroom and started to rub the dog's fur. Mum was sitting by the window looking out at the rain with that faraway look in her eyes. She almost changed into a different person at these times, and we would all normally instinctively know to adapt our behaviour. But today we were all irritable and hungry. We hadn't eaten since the night before and that had just been a plate of potatoes. Josie told Marion to put the kettle on for a cup of tea but she answered back: 'No! Why should I? It's always me has to make the tea, it's her turn,' and she gestured towards Marge. It was almost five o'clock. Marge got up and went out to make the tea without any fuss.

The room was unusually quiet but I broke the silence by asking, 'When is dinner going to be ready?'

Mum swivelled round and just looked at me crossly. 'There isn't any dinner.' She turned her back on us. I looked at my sisters who were all pretending that they hadn't heard. Margaret started to cry.

'Stop grizzling,' said Mum sharply, and went and got her coat. 'I'm going out.' With that she slammed the door behind her, stamped down the stairs and went out into the rain. Josie and Pat exchanged a look. Josie comforted Margaret, who by now was even more upset.

It was about half an hour later that Mum came back with another large bag of potatoes. 'Here,' she said, flinging them on to the table. 'Twins, come and peel these, and put them on to boil.' When they were cooked Josie brought them to the table and dished them out onto our plates. We had a good plateful each, but they didn't look very appetising sitting in their pale glory alone on our plates, with nothing more than a shake of salt to make them taste of anything. Still, at least we weren't going to bed hungry.

The next day was Sunday and Mum sent us to Mass at the local Catholic Church. Mum never came to Mass, even at home. When we came out she was there to meet us. 'We're going shopping,' she said, and we followed her to a small grocery shop on the corner of the road that was open on a Sunday. As we went inside we saw Mum hand over her family allowance book to the man.

'Right you are then,' he said, 'but only £1 worth.' Mum asked for potatoes, sausages, eggs, baked beans, lard, loaves of bread and margarine and various other items, which the grocer duly filled her bags with. Mum looked at the sweets and asked for two lollypops and then, hesitating, asked for ten Player's cigarettes. Mum lit up as soon as we left the shop and then we walked back up the tall hill, carrying the bag of shopping up the three flights of stairs to the little flat at the top. We were worn out by the time we got in; two days of nothing but boiled potatoes doesn't fill you with energy.

'Let's have sausages and chips for Sunday dinner,' Mum suggested, her enthusiasm returning, and we were very glad that it wasn't to be boiled potatoes again.

On Tuesday Mum retrieved her allowance book from the grocer's shop that also had a post office counter at the back, and drew out her money, paying the man back the money he had allowed her in advance. This didn't leave much to last for the rest of the week, so there wasn't any more ice cream or treats, but we still managed to have a good time and I certainly didn't want to come back home to Dagenham, even to see the cat and Aunty.

15

The Baker Boy

When we got home Dave was at our house with Mary.

'Mum, you forgot to leave your allowance book,' Mary said tremulously.

'Oh I know,' Mum answered, not meeting Mary's eyes but continuing to unpack the clothes ready for washing.

'Margaret must have put it in my bag before we left,' she said and carried the washing into the scullery. I watched Mary and Dave exchange looks, and when Mum returned it was Dave's turn to question her.

'Well, can we have it now? Only we need to get the money back into our savings,' he said firmly.

Mum turned to give him a withering look. 'Don't you speak to me like that,' she spat.

Mary started to cry. 'Mum, please; you know we need it for the wedding,' she pleaded.

'I know that, but you'll have to wait,' she said, turning to leave the room again. As she reached the door she stopped and looked them both in the face. 'And if you're not very careful there won't be any wedding,' and with that she flounced up the stairs.

Dave stood there and watched her go, muttering under his breath, 'Bloody hell.' When Mary started to cry again, he put his arm around her and led her out of the front door.

Aunty was in a bad mood all of the time and there wasn't anything to look forward to any more. We still had four weeks of the summer holiday to go but I knew that at the end of that time I was going to have to brave the new world of secondary school. I was becoming more self-aware and self-conscious. Puberty was just around the corner, and things were happening to my body that felt different and strange.

Mary had felt it her duty to tell me about periods. No one had ever told her and she was determined that I wasn't going to be as afraid as she was when she had thought she was bleeding to death! I was only about nine when she told me, and I had been so impressed with this knowledge that I had decided to pretend that I had one. She had shown me where she kept her Dr. Whites towels and told me that I could take one when the time came. I helped myself, and proudly told Josie that my period had started.

Josie looked shocked. 'How do you know about periods?'

When I said that Mary had told me she looked annoyed.

'You're too young for all that,' she said, but not unkindly. 'Show me the towel.'

I blanched; of course there was really nothing to show, but I went up into the toilet and, feeling a sense of panic, tried as hard as I could to scratch my finger. Finally managing to extract a pinprick of blood and blotting it onto the towel I proudly called down to Josie, 'You can come up now!'

When she saw the towel she smiled. 'Oh okay,' she said, going along with my deceit, 'but I think you might not have another one for quite a while.'

'No,' I agreed, 'I don't think I will.' Scratching my finger until it bled was not something I wanted to repeat any time soon.

By the end of that summer I was more self-conscious than ever. I had put on some weight, and I was beginning to get spots! I was not looking forward to the start of term.

Mum called me in from the garden about a week before school started.

'We need to get your uniform,' she said. 'Come on, we have to go to Lucilla's in Green Lane; that's the only place that stocks it.'

I knew that the uniform was maroon because my sister Marge had been transferred to the school for her last year of secondary education when it was first built. Marge's uniform was long gone, as she was seven years older than me. By the time it came for me to start at the Sacred Heart, she was almost eighteen and had started going out with Ron.

It had been strange how she and Ron had met. He was the young man who drove the baker's delivery van, and delivered bread and cakes all around where we lived. Mum had taken to having a loaf delivered every other day as it saved her going across to the baker's, and didn't cost any more. On this particular day Ron knocked as usual, although he was about half an hour later than normal.

'One sliced loaf,' he said passing the bread to Mum.

'Are you all right?' she asked. 'You look very white,' at which Ron started to sniff.

'I've had a bit of an accident,' he said. 'As I was turning at the top of Martin's Corner, this bloody great Rolls Royce went into the van.'

Mum put her hand to her mouth. 'Oh you poor thing!' Then she started to laugh. 'Fancy that, a Rolls Royce in Valence Avenue! Come in and I'll make you a cup of hot sweet tea.'

Mum led Ron into the kitchen where Margaret and I sat on the floor, our play suspended in disbelief. People didn't get invited into our house. Mum gestured towards the settee, and Ron sat himself down, feeling the cushion slip as he did so, and noticing the pile of newspapers beginning to slide out from underneath. As he tried to push them back under, we began to giggle.

'What are you two laughing at?' he said with a cheeky smile. He seemed very tall to us, and had thick bushy black hair but his eyes looked kind. Mum came back in from the scullery with a large, teaming mug of very hot, very sweet tea.

'Here you are.' She offered him the mug, and as he took it I saw an interesting new look cross Mum's face. Ron stayed and chatted for a while, and Mum told him she had twin seventeen-year-old daughters. When he came to collect the bread money on Saturday, it just so happened that the door was opened by Marge. Mum had taken Pat and Marion to Green Lane with her and left Marge looking after us two. Josie was up in bed as usual. Ron took Marge to the pictures that night and they had been together ever since.

Ron called Mum 'Mrs Lady'. He was so kind to us. Looking

back, I don't know how he put up with it really. Marge and he rarely got to go out on their own; most of the time they had to take either Mum or Margaret or me with them, and sometimes all three of us! We went stock car racing, and saw the cars smashing into each other – that was one of Mum's favourite outings. We also sometimes went to the Chinese restaurant in Ilford near to Plessey's where Marge had now joined Pat, Josie and Aunty working there. There we tasted new kinds of food that tickled our taste buds. My favourite were the fried banana fritters with syrup that were included in the price of the 'Set Menu'. Sometimes Ron just took us for a drive on a Sunday afternoon. Mum thought the world of him and I think he was also very fond of her, even though in later years she sometimes turned into the mother-in-law from hell!

Margaret and I also loved Ron. He was infinitely patient with us, and we must have cost him a fortune. One Saturday we started the Black Cat Café. I wrote out the menu:

egg on toast 6d,
beans on toast 6d,
bacon sandwich 9d,
tea 2d etc.

and then drew a big black cat at the bottom.

When Ron arrived at lunchtime I sidled over.

'This is the menu,' I said thrusting the carefully written list into his hand. He smiled at Marge, who raised her eyes to heaven. Mum was sitting in her usual chair, and Aunty was in the front garden. Poor Ron knew he didn't stand a chance.

'Okay then,' he said defeated. 'I'll have a bacon sandwich and a cup of tea please.' I bustled out to the scullery and prepared his meal for him. He duly paid his bill and was then allowed to take Marge out for the afternoon. The Black Cat Café was opened most weekends that year, and we extended our clientele to serve the rest of my sisters who were around on Saturday. It was a lucrative business for me the cook and Margaret my washer-upper, and kept us in sweets for quite some time.

16

Getting Ready for Big School

I was excited at the prospect of getting a new school uniform. We didn't have many new clothes and often wore things that had been passed down from our sisters or given to us by other people.

Pat and Josie had been saving money from their wages so that I could have the proper uniform. They were so kind. They hardly had any money left over after they had paid their fare and given Mum keep money, but they had carefully put by what little they could in preparation for this day.

The smell of Lucilla's made my eyes water. It was a strong, unpleasant chemical odour that permeated the whole shop. The smell reminded me of the dry cleaner's that my Aunty Maggie worked in. I had occasionally been allowed to help her, and she had given me a few pennies pocket money. I remember feeling very grown-up writing out the collection tickets for the customers until Aunty Maggie had told me off for not being neat enough, and for spelling things wrongly!

The sales assistant at Lucilla's ushered Mum and me into one corner and told me to take off my clothes. I really didn't want to as my underclothes left a lot to be desired and I was very aware that I was starting to grow 'bumps' on my chest. Mum just bundled me out of my things and I stood exposed to anyone who walked in. The lady looked me up and down.

'Hmm, what size do you want her to try?'

Mum looked at me and said, 'Big enough for her to grow into.' I knew what this meant; out from the rack of skirts came an enormous maroon box-pleated skirt with a strange sort of sliding zip that enabled you to tighten or loosen the waistband to fit.

'Try this,' she said, so dutifully I put it on. It was gigantic! Not only was the waist massive but it was so long that the hem almost touched the floor. I tried to protest, but I was shushed by Mum.

'No, that will be fine,' she said, and started to role the waist up to make the skirt fall just below my knee. I think I would have needed to grow to 6ft for it to ever fit properly! We also had to buy a special pair of PE knickers in the same colour, a stripy maroon and gold tie and a white blouse.

'Most people buy three blouses,' the lady said, 'then they can wash, dry and rotate them.' Mum said we just wanted one. Lucilla's was very expensive, and the lady spoke with a very posh voice, but Mum could talk in the same posh voice. In fact she did it better than the lady did. Aunty Maggie had knitted a maroon cardigan for me so there I was, all kitted out and ready for big school. Why then did I still feel that I would be different from the other girls? Why was I frightened that I wouldn't fit in?

As my first day of secondary school approached I got more and more worried. I didn't even know where the school was. Mum told me that there would be other girls at the bus stop in the same uniform, and that I should get off at the same stop as they did and follow them as they walked to school.

That first morning I got up very early. I'd had a bath the night before and washed my hair. It was quite long and very straight and was beginning to get greasy a day or so after being washed. I had borrowed some of Josie's foam rollers and had slept fitfully, because the plastic clips that fastened them had poked into my head throughout the night. My uniform was ready downstairs for me to put on so I crept down trying not to wake anyone. I wanted to be on my own for a while and that was always difficult in such a crowded home. Aunty had already left for work, and Mum was still asleep as I slid out of our bed. Pat and Josie always got up at 7.30 and caught the 8.20 bus so I had at least half an hour before anyone would be up. I went to the sink and splashed my face with cold water. We didn't have a basin in the bathroom, just a toilet and a bath, so we had to wash our face and hands at the scullery sink.

Aunty would have her early morning wash at that sink, and if you got up too early, you could be greeted by the sight of her in her many vests and baggy drawers, poised at the sink, flannel and soap in hand.

Today though she had already gone off to work so I had the scullery to myself. Then I heard a sound on the stairs.

'What are you doing?' whispered Margaret.

'Just having a wash,' I answered, inwardly annoyed that she had followed me downstairs.

'What time are you going?' she asked, joining me on the cold stone floor. Even in September the house could still be quite cold, particularly in the early morning.

'I don't really know, I'll watch out of the window about eight o'clock, I guess, and wait until some girls get to the bus stop.'

We only had one clock, and that always stood on the mantelpiece. It was an ugly 50s object but it did keep good time. Pat had bought me a watch when I was younger. She was often buying me little treats when she could afford them. When I was four I was playing in the garden, jumping over horse jumps that I had made out of bits and pieces I had found in the garden. When I stumbled and fell, dislocating my shoulder, it had been Pat that I cried for. It had been Pat that had to come home from work and taken me to the hospital to have it slotted back in, and it had been Pat who shouted at the doctors and nurses because they hadn't given me any anaesthetic. It was also Pat who took me to London Zoo and to see the Trooping of the Colour to celebrate the Queen's birthday as a treat for being brave. Unfortunately the watch from Pat hadn't worked for years, so now the clock was the only way to make sure I wasn't late for my first day at school. Pat and Josie got up at 7.30 as usual and while Pat had a cup of tea, Josie looked me up and down. 'Come here, Kathleen,' she said as she grabbed my arm and started to unroll my rolled up skirt.

'Look, if you fold it rather than roll it, it will sit flat and not make you look like you've got a spare tyre round your waist!' She showed me how to fold the waistband neatly.

'There,' she said, 'that's better, and what have you done to your hair? Pat, pass me my bag will you?' She took out a comb and tried to flatten the chaotic curls that surrounded my face and seemed to turn in a hundred different directions, giving me a kind of crazy unkempt look.

I wriggled. 'Oww!'

'Will you keep still? I can't do anything if you jiggle about.' She finally managed to tame my hair into a ponytail that hung untidily down my back. I didn't have a fringe so my broad forehead gave me the effect of having a dome-shaped head! I had practised doing my own tie up so that didn't look too bad, but the cardigan Aunty Maggie had knitted wasn't quite the right shape and had 'leg of mutton' sleeves that were extremely unflattering. The arms were also much too long and I had to roll up the cuffs so that they didn't cover my hands. Finally Josie was reasonably content with how I looked.

'Put your blazer on then,' she said. Now the blazer had been a big issue. Blazers were expensive. You could buy them more cheaply from a local shop but they didn't have the school badge on the pocket. However Lucilla's did stock the badges separately and you could buy these and sow them on to the cheaper blazer. Josie had done this for me, but although she had sewn very neat tidy stitches, it was still obvious that it wasn't the 'proper' badge. I donned my blazer, which had also been bought far too big for me so that it would last the whole time I was at the school. I looked ridiculous, but luckily I wasn't alone. I watched the 62 bus stop across the road from our house start to fill with girls of all shapes and sizes, mostly dressed in uniforms comically big for them – obviously, like mine, bought to last!

17

Little Anne

My first term at secondary school was almost worse than primary. I felt big and lumpy and ugly. My clothes felt uncomfortable and I didn't make many friends. I was put in 1B, which was the middle band, where I think the school placed all the children that they weren't quite sure what to do with. I was considered too bright to be in the C class but my non-attendance at primary meant they wouldn't chance putting me in the A class. So there I was in 1B with a strange assortment of other girls, none of whom I seemed to gel with. It wasn't long before I stopped going to school again. Mum would try to persuade me to go, but her heart wasn't really in it and I think she had too many other things on her mind. Consequently it wasn't long before I was demoted to 1C. Then something happened that changed everything.

I had been friends at primary school with my neighbours Jane and Hannah but they were in the year above me. They were already established at the school, but were kind to me and let me join with them and their friends at lunchtime when we were cast out into the playground to amble around for about an hour before being let back into class. One day in the spring term of my first year I was heading over to join Jane and Hannah's posse. One of the second-years stepped forward and said, 'I think you're in the same class as my sister Anne.'

'Am I?'

'Yes, her name is Anne McMahon.'

The girl's name was Miriam, and she took me over to where her sister Anne was standing surrounded by a group of other girls. Miriam pushed our way through the others and there I stood in front of a very small, neat and tidy girl with very blue eyes, a scattering of freckles across her nose and a perm that made her hair frizzy. I recognised her at once, as she was the most popular girl in our year.

'Anne, this girl is in your tutor group, her name is Kathleen Coates.' Anne looked at me for a few seconds and then must have decided that I was okay. For some completely obscure reason that I have never been able to fathom, Anne liked me.

'Do you want to play rounders at lunchtime?' she asked. I quickly agreed. I played rounders, cricket and all manner of other ball games with my sisters in our back garden, so was quite good at them. When the bell went for lunchtime, she came over to my desk.

'Are you sandwiches or school dinners?'

'Sandwiches,' I replied wondering if this was the right answer. It was.

'Do you want to come with us to eat them then?' she asked and as I nodded my head, she ushered me out of the classroom and down the stairs towards the back entrance of the school. There were a couple of girls who followed us, and a few more who were patiently waiting at the doorway. One girl, Joan, was very tall and thin; she smiled at me. We all left the building together and walked onto the grassy area where we were allowed to have our lunch. There was nowhere to sit except on the low walls that surrounded the building, which tended to fill up very quickly, so there were lots of groups of girls just sitting on the damp grass to eat. Although it was early spring, it was still quite cold and not very pleasant to be eating outside, but we weren't allowed to stay in for lunch except in the winter. Anne led us round the side of the building to where there were some dilapidated greenhouses. These were full of an assortment of old terracotta plant pots of various sizes, half-opened bags of compost and a few neglected gardening tools. Anne looked around us and slid the door of one of the greenhouses open, and we all piled in behind her. It was snug and warm, even if it did smell of old rotting vegetables and stale earth. Once we were inside we found something, anything, to sit on. I managed to perch on a broken piece of wooden staging and sat watching what the others were going to do. They started delving into their bags and bringing out an assortment of lunch boxes, packets and parcels. Anne and Joan both took flasks out of their bags and untwisted the lids. Joan had tea in hers, but Anne had a rich flavoursome-smelling soup. My mouth watered. Then Anne pulled out two chicken legs, which were a delicacy and quite expensive. She also had an iced bun, a bag of crisps and a Topic chocolate bar with peanuts in it. I had cheese-spread sandwiches and most of the others had something similar. Joan got out a huge bottle of lemonade, took a large swig and then proceeded to hand it round to everyone else to have a drink. I wasn't sure I liked the idea of this but felt obliged to take a drop. After we had eaten we went on to the playground at the back and chose rounders teams. My heart sunk at the thought. I was always the last to get chosen, but not this time. There were two teams, one led by Anne and one led by Joan.

Anne chose first of course.

'I'll have Kathleen,' she announced to my complete and utter amazement. I had never been chosen first for a team in my whole life; it was exhilarating, and I determined to play my heart out. When the two teams had been picked, Anne called the players around her. 'Right, I'll go backstop, you go on first base Kathleen, Teresa you bowl. The rest of you spread out, Jane on fourth, Maria on third and Sally right at the back cos you're a good thrower.'

Off we went. Backstop was a scary position to play, because you often got hit by either the bat or the ball, both of which could leave you with a nasty bump. But Anne was brave; she was never afraid of anything. My job on first base was to be ever alert to the batter and the backstop. If the batter missed the ball, the backstop would throw it as hard, as straight and as fast as possible to first base so that the batter would be out. What a responsibility!

We played. I managed to 'stump out' player after player from the opposing team, and each time I did so everyone cheered. By the time it was our turn to bat, they only had two rounders. We started to bat. Anne was a good batter, as were some of the others. When it was my turn to come forward I walked up in trepidation. Would I let everyone down? The hard round ball came hurtling towards me and I wanted to jump out of the way, but instead I held my nerve and hit with all my might. My team were shouting, 'Slog it! Slog it!' and I did. I ran like the blazes round the bases, getting a rounder to cheers from my team.

We won that game, and for the next few months lunchtimes followed that pattern every day, until the weather warmed up and we chose to sit on the grass in the sunshine instead and talk about stuff.

Anne had chosen me as her friend. She chose me. Me, out of all of the other girls that wanted to be her special friend, who followed her around and hero-worshipped her. It was me that she always looked for first thing in the morning when we got to school, me that she invited to her house to play, me that she told her secrets to. More strangely than all of that, it was my house that she always wanted to come to, my mum that she grew to love as a second mother, and my family that she chose to spend the holidays with. Anne really did change my life. She made me realise that I was worth something, and that I didn't need to always be afraid, especially if she was there with me. After that first game of rounders it was obvious that we were going to be friends for life.

Anne was always up to mischief. We began to build a gang of followers of which Anne was the leader and I was the undisputed deputy! The power was heady indeed. For the first time in my life other girls watched to see what I would do so they could copy me. They listened to what I had to say and took notice of me, and did what I wanted them to. This was a new experience for me, but not for Anne. She was the youngest in a family of six children. She was very small and petite for her age, and in fact had been in hospital for growth problems. Anne was spoilt by both her brothers and her sisters, and in particular by her dad, an amiable old Irishman who had such a broad accent I could never understand him. When he came home from work he would call out to her, 'Nan, Nan, cunya make ya da acuppata, darlinnow sweetart Nan?' and he was the one adult she would always look truly pleased to see.

I remember the day he passed his driving test.

'Dad's going to drive us to swimming,' Anne announced proudly. It was raining hard, and Barking pool was outdoors, but that wasn't going to stop us. We piled into his old Ford Anglia, swerving all over the road as he put his arm out through the window to wipe the rain off the windscreen because the wipers were broken. Anne's mum was very different. She would always make a big fuss of me when I called round insisting that I had a cup of tea and a piece of cake, but there was just something not quite comfortable about being in their house. It was a beautiful home with lovely things in it, which had been bought with the compensation money Anne's dad had received after an industrial accident. Before that they had lived in a council house on the some estate as us.

One day Anne said, 'Can you come around to my house straight from school today?'

'Okay, but why?'

'Wait and see,' she said running up the stairs two at a time with me trailing behind her. I knew Mum wouldn't be worried if I was late home as long as I was back before six, as she knew that I would sometimes go to the park with my new friends.

When Anne and I arrived at her house after school, we went up to the bedroom she shared with Miriam and there on the side was a record player.

'I've got some of my dad's old Irish records out,' she said pulling a huge 78 from its paper sleeve. 'It'll help us learn the words.'

'Why do we need to learn the words?'

'So we can sing to the old people, of course,' she answered incredulously, as though I should have been able to read her mind.

So that's what we did. I would love to be able to count the number of hours we spent listening to those old Irish rebel songs but it must have added up to whole days. We would often go swimming in Barking outdoor pool straight after school and then go back to Anne's where we would sit and sing along to those records, time and time again. We did learn the words and had great fun singing, even developing a strong Irish accent as we went along, but I never really thought we would actually go and sing to an audience of people.

Anne and I would usually meet at Becontree Station to walk to school together. We caught the 62 bus from opposite directions and both got off at Becontree. We would sometimes meet other girls and would all walk together to school. On this particular morning I got off the bus as usual and saw Anne waiting for me. She had a big grin on her face.

'Kathleen,' she started as I got off the bus, 'my sister has sorted out for us to sing on Friday night.'

'What!' I said, incredulous. 'You must be joking?'

'No, I'm not. We're singing at the Irish social club in Barking.' Anne smiled at me, and although I was terrified inside I knew that I would go and I knew that I would sing, because Anne wanted me to.

I had arranged to go round to Anne's house straight from school to get ready. My sister Josie had found an old green velvet corduroy dress at home that had a white lace collar and luckily it almost fitted me. When I took it out of my bag, Anne was delighted.

'You look like a real Irish girl in that,' she claimed, so off we went. We must have looked like a strange pair – me in my oversized green dress, looking clumsy and plain, and Anne, petite and pretty in her green Irish kilt and white jumper. We sang our hearts out that night! We sang 'Sean South of Garryowen', 'The Bold Fenian Men', 'Black Velvet Band', 'Spinning Wheel' but best loved of all was the song Anne sang as a solo, 'Danny Boy'. She held the notes so pure and true. By the time we finished there were few dry eyes in the hall and we withdrew to an intoxicating burst of applause.

Making a Stand

Although I was so much happier at school, things were tough for other members of the family. Isobel, my brother Michael's wife, was struggling to look after her baby Vicky, who was nearly eighteen months old, and now she was pregnant again. She couldn't read or write even in her own language and couldn't speak more than a few words of English. My brother Michael had become fluent in Spanish during the time he was in Gibraltar and so that was the language in which they communicated. Isobel was becoming more and more isolated and looking back she was probably also depressed. She came from a tiny rural village near to Malaga called San Roco, and had left behind her large close-knit family. Everything she knew and understood made no sense in her cold, bleak, adopted country. Michael worked long hours as he was now in the catering corps and was training hard to become a chef. They had a telephone but it was expensive to ring Spain, so she wasn't able to talk to anyone at home very often. The other servicemen's wives tried to be friendly but the language barrier hampered their friendships and so Isobel became more and more lonely. Mum came to the rescue.

'Mary, I want you to go and stay with Isobel until the baby's born,' she ordered. Mary was quite happy to do this; I suppose it was a kind of escape.

'All right Mum,' she said, 'I'll need to get my things packed up.' And so it was arranged.

This had the added benefit for Mum that she didn't need to feed Mary, although Mary was still obliged to send her 'keep' to mum every week. At first it seemed like a good arrangement.

Mary was happy staying with Michael and Isobel and Vicky, Mum still got her 'keep' money and Isobel had a willing helper in Mary during the long lonely evenings.

Unfortunately after a while things began to change. Marion and Marge were given the job of going up to wait outside Mary's work on a Friday so that she could hand over the majority of her wages to them to take home to Mum. At the same time she and Dave were desperately trying to save a few shillings here and there so that they could get married and try to find a flat of their own. Their savings had taken a dent after our holiday, and the 'misunderstanding' that had caused such an argument on our return. Saving was difficult, as after paying Mum her keep, Mary was only left with enough money for fares and the odd pair of stockings.

One day Michael saw Mary fishing in her purse for a spare few pennies.

'Why are you still sending Mum money? You live here now; just give me a few bob towards your food and stuff and you can keep the rest to save for the wedding.' This started Mary thinking; she had never questioned the fact that her wages in effect belonged to Mum, but now she wondered. Could she keep the money? Would it really be possible? She desperately wanted to get married as soon as possible, but that day seemed as far away as ever. Dave didn't earn a great deal, so between them their savings were growing very slowly. Mary made up her mind: she would do it!

The next Friday came and as Mary left the building where she worked, her heart was in her mouth. He knew Marion and Marge would be there waiting for her, and she also knew that if she was ever going to be able to get married she was going to have to stick to her guns. Although it was only five o'clock when she came out into the busy street, it was already beginning to get dark as winter had almost arrived. She saw Marion wave from across the street while Marge was looking in a shop window. 'Mary!' shouted Marion. 'Over here.' Mary slowly went to join them, a feeling of dread overwhelming her.

'Look,' she said, 'I'm really really sorry but I can't send any money this week.'

'Why not?' said Marge, who had now turned to join the conversation.

'I just can't afford it,' answered Mary quietly.

'Mum's going to go mad. What are we going to tell her?' asked Marion.

'Just tell her I can't afford it anymore.'

'Does that mean just this week or never?'

'Never,' said Mary with conviction. It was as though she had just made a very important decision, the first grown-up decision of her life apart from agreeing to marry Dave.

When Marge and Marion arrived back in Dagenham that evening, they were very withdrawn as they came into the house.

'What's wrong?' said Mum, who was always very astute at picking up on all our moods and vagaries.

The twins looked at each other but neither spoke.

'Come on, out with it,' said Mum, starting to get agitated.

'Mary said she can't afford to give you any more money,' blurted out Marge. Mum's face became red and then went a strange white colour.

'Right,' she said quietly, 'we'll see about that,' and she went out into the scullery to get the dinner out. Margaret's big brown eyes turned to me questioningly but I just carried on combing the dog.

The next morning was Saturday, so everyone was home. Mum told Pat that she was going to go over to Michael's.

'What, today?' asked Pat. Although Mum visited Michael's at least once a week, she rarely went on a Saturday as we were all home.

'Yes today,' she snapped back. 'Margaret, Kathleen, get your coats on.'

We ran to get our coats and join Mum as she left the house, and walked towards the bus stop. It was bitterly cold even though it was only November, so waiting for the bus seemed endless. Mum would always say, 'If I light a cigarette the bus is sure to come along,' so we would always be trying to encourage her to have one more, because we thought it was like a magic spell. The odd thing was that it did always seem to work – well almost always. At last the bus arrived and we boarded, heading upstairs as usual. Mum lit up her cigarette and Margaret and I settled into one of the seats nearby. The bus was quite crowded but we managed to find a seat together. Eventually after the usual changes and the trip across the river on the ferry we were almost at Michael's. By that time it must have been about midday and our tummies were grumbling loudly. We very rarely ate breakfast so we were still waiting for our first meal of the day. Michael and Isobel's flat was on the first floor and the stairs were on the exterior. It was an ugly 1950s block with concrete landings on each floor. Mum banged on the front door and we heard a baby crying. The door opened and there was Mary, looking as shocked as I had ever seen her.

'Oh,' she let out a little cry. Mum bustled us in through the door. Michael was sitting at the kitchen table with a large sandwich in front of him, Isobel sat opposite with Vicky on her lap and Mary's place was next to this, her half-eaten sandwich on a plate. Margaret and I looked at the food hungrily.

Michael got up. 'Mary, put the kettle on.'

Isobel watched over the top of Vicky's head, which was covered in golden curls.

'I'm hungry,' I whispered to Mum, tugging gently at her arm.

'Shush, wait a minute,' she answered.

Mary filled the kettle as Mum sat in the place she had vacated. She looked at Mary and said, 'You're coming home,' and as Mary tried to protest, Mum turned to Michael.

'If she's not home by Monday night, I'm informing the army that she's been living here for more than the allowed three months, and you'll be in deep trouble.'

With that she stood up, scraping the chair across the floor and grabbing our hands, dragged me and Margaret out of the door, both of us casting a longing, backwards look at the unfinished food on the table.

Mary didn't want to come home. She had tasted freedom, and glimpsed a different kind of life. Michael and Isobel were quite poor, and their flat was small and cheaply furnished, but for the first time in her life Mary had her own bedroom. She was allowed to go out with Dave a few nights a week or he would sit and watch television with them after Vicky had been put to bed. The only rules Mary had to follow were to help out Isobel with the washing up, keeps things tidy, and play with Vicky in the evenings before she was put to bed. It was quiet and uncrowded in the flat compared to our house, and she was allowed to see her friends without it causing an argument. She definitely wasn't going home. Michael came up with a solution. He had a friend who ran a pub down the road, and he let out a small room in the attic. Michael suggested that Mary live there and just come to the flat in the evenings for her meals and to keep Isobel company if Michael was working. That evening when Dave came round he was greeted by Mary sobbing her heart out.

'What's wrong love?' he asked putting his arm round her. When she told him the whole story he was horrified.

'There is no way you're living in a pub,' he said. 'My aunt's got a room; we'll see if you can live there.' But when they told Dave's mum, she immediately insisted that Mary move into the spare room until she and Dave were married.

Mum didn't say a word when she heard the news, but I could tell from the set of her lips that the battle was far from over.

19

Mary's Wedding

During the time Mary lived at Dave's parents' house, she would send us little gifts, which her old friend Helen would bring round. At first Mum didn't tell us who they were from, but one day we happened to be there when Helen knocked and heard her say she had brought us some things from Mary. Nothing was very expensive, sometimes a ribbon or a new slide for our hair, but I treasured those things because they were mine and only mine. One day after several months living at Dave's parents' house, Mary and Dave came to visit. It was the first time that we had seen them since the argument. It was a Saturday afternoon, and Pat had been to the shops in Green Lane to get a piece of meat from the butcher there, and had just got back, when there was a knock on the door. It was the family knock: rat-ta-tat-tat tat-tat. Mum was in the scullery getting the meat ready for our Sunday dinner and called out, 'Open the door, can you?'

Pat grumbled as she got up from her chair, which she had just positioned ready for the football results on the television. Margaret and I were playing on the floor with a pile of paper and pencils, Margaret drawing dollies and me drawing horses as usual.

'Oh,' said Pat when she opened the front door.

We heard Mary's voice: 'Hello Pat.'

We ran out into the passage and then stopped suddenly. We weren't sure if we were allowed to hug her or not.

Mum came out of the scullery with that pinched look on her face. 'Oh, what do you want?'

'We want to invite you all to the wedding,' Mary replied trying to smile.

'Wedding? What wedding? You're not twenty-one yet and you need my permission, and you needn't think I'm giving it either,' Mum answered, standing in front of poor Mary.

At this point Dave spoke up. 'Look, we just wanted to know how many of you lot want to come,' he said. 'My mum needs to know how many to cater for.'

Mum swung her stare in Dave's direction.

'Did you hear what I said? She needs permission and I'm not giving it.'

Mary starting to quietly cry and Dave put his arm around her.

'And you can stop that silly nonsense right now,' said Mum with her hands on her hips. I wasn't sure if she meant the crying or the comforting, so I watched Mary and Dave to see what would happen next.

Dave guided Mary back out of the house; they hadn't even got as far as the kitchen. As they left, he turned to Mum and said, 'We're getting married this October whatever happens. If you don't give your permission, we'll just have to ask Mary's dad,' and with that parting shot they walked back down the path to Dave's motorbike with Mary still crying and Mum wearing a look that was a mixture of anger, incredulity and shock. I was puzzled. Didn't Dave know that we didn't have a dad? What did he mean? The air was heavy with the coming storm, but strangely it never arrived.

I don't know what made Mum change her mind about giving Mary permission to get married, but she did.

This entailed a visit to the registrar. We went with Mary and Mum into a big building with shiny polished floors. Mum asked the lady behind a desk something and she pointed to the big swing doors. As we went through Mum turned to Mary: 'You wait outside with these two; I need to talk to the registrar first.' So we duly waited outside. After what seemed like hours, but was probably no more than twenty minutes, the door opened and Mary was called in while we sat outside swinging our legs and waiting. This process was to be repeated every time one of us was to get married, but it would be very many years after that we found out what Mum told those registrars.

A few weeks later, Mum called Margaret and I downstairs. We had been practising rolly pollies on the double bed that Margaret shared with Josie while listening to Dusty Springfield singing 'I Just Don't Know What to Do With Myself' on Josie's tiny transistor radio. I had done so many, so badly, that my neck was wobbling as though my head was going to fall off, so it was quite a relief to have a reason to stop. We ran downstairs to find Mum sitting in her chair by the fireplace with a strange look on her face. She was holding a letter in her hand.

'Do you and Margaret want to be Mary's bridesmaids?' she asked.

'Can we?' I asked. Margaret looked on hopefully.

'Yes of course you can, Mary's your sister! She's coming over on Saturday to take you out to get your dresses.' I was eleven years old and Margaret was almost ten. Of course I had already been a bridesmaid to my cousin Julie when I was seven, all dressed in green satin with a feathery headband and silver sparkling shoes, but Margaret had never been one and was very excited. Even now, almost fifty years later, whenever I hear that Dusty Springfield song I still think of rolly pollies and bridesmaid dresses!

My family were still not going to the wedding. Michael had been forbidden from giving Mary away but Peter had said he would do it despite what Mum had decreed and so that was the arrangement. Then suddenly, just a few weeks before the ceremony, Mum wrote to Mary and told her that the whole family would be going to the wedding after all! This caused all sorts of panic to Dave's mum and dad, who were not only planning the wedding with Mary and Dave but were also paying for much of it, but Mary was still happy that Mum and our sisters and brothers would all be there.

The day before the wedding, Margaret and I were taken to stay at Dave's house, so that we would able to go to the hairdressers early in the morning. Dave's house was a Victorian terraced house in Leytonstone in the East End of London and had no inside toilet, so we had to go through Dave's dad's lean-to if we needed to go. I remember the smell of geraniums and damp earth, and Mary telling us that if we needed the toilet in the night there was a 'pot' under the bed.

When we woke in the morning, Mary was already up.

'Come on, you two,' she said happily, 'we have to be at the hairdressers in half an hour.' We had never been to the hair-dressers before, and were full of excitement at the prospect. I just hoped desperately that my head wouldn't ache. I had devel-oped severe migraine headaches when I was about seven. I remember clearly the first time I had a bad attack. It was on the way back from a day trip to Southend with Aunty, Margaret and Marion. We had gone by train and on the return journey I had vomited all the way home and my head had felt as though it was ready to burst open. I was now constantly afraid of getting a 'bad head', as my Mum would call it. It always seemed to happen when I was excited, afraid, hot or hungry. Today was a potential 'bad head' day and even at eleven years old I feared it.

Once we were dressed, Mary walked us towards the hairdressers.

'What will they do to our hair?' I asked, skipping along beside Margaret, holding her hand.

'What would you like them to do? Do you want it curly?' I started to laugh, Margaret and I both had hair as straight as a poker!

Margaret started jumping up and down, 'Curly yes, curly!' When we arrived we were led into the salon. Mary was whisked off somewhere, and Margaret and I were left to the mercy of a very miserable-looking pair of hair stylists. They plonked us onto a chair next to each other and looked stonily at us.

'I don't know what she expects us to do with these two,' one of them muttered to her colleague. 'Look at this hair! Looks like it's been cut with a knife and fork.'

The other woman smirked in response, 'It looks like they've been dragged through a hedge backwards.'

Our hair was pulled and tugged and roughly fashioned into an upswept style that would have been more suited to a thirty-year-old. These women continued to talk over our heads as though we were invisible; they criticised our hair, the way we were dressed, and muttered and moaned the whole time. We emerged from the hairdressers resembling two miniature astronauts' wives and with all the morning's happiness now replaced with that familiar dread of being different, and not being good enough.

Apart from Peter arriving very late for the wedding – almost too late to give Mary away – the rest of the day went quite smoothly and we managed to have fun. In our yellow nylon flouncy dresses and with our upswept astronaut's wife hair we danced the night away! I have always loved a good family wedding. Even as an adult they remind me of so many happy times throughout my younger life when we would see all of our sisters and brothers together again, even long after they themselves were married and had their own children. Of course the only one who never came, who was never invited, was Sheila. She was the secret sister that I would never meet and never really know, and it was only after my son Sam was born that I found out why.

20

The Sewing Machine

With Mary and my brothers now married, that left only Pat, Josie, Marion and Marge bringing money into the home. Aunty always paid the rent, but food, gas and electric gobbled up the family's income and that was without the added stress of Mum's 'callers' who knocked for their money every week, and who were a persistent drain on Mum's purse. It must have been a constant juggling act for her, deciding who to pay what and when, but she was clever and astute and knew what she could get away with.

Josie was now working in London at an insurance company. She really liked her new job and was very well thought of, especially by the company secretary, Miss Pomfret. She told Josie that she had 'high hopes' for her; that she was a clever young lady and would go far as long as she continued to work hard. Then came the incident of the sewing machine.

Josie was keen on sewing but had to make everything by hand, which took a long time, especially as she didn't have much spare time after she had finished work and travelled home from London. She would go up to her room when she got home and not come down again until quite late in the evening, after everyone else had finished eating. Then she would get her dinner, and sit and eat it before she started her sewing.

She and Mary had started making their clothes some time ago when they realised that it was the only way they could keep themselves neat and tidy for work. Mary had also tried to make Margaret and I a few little things to wear, but now that she was married she wasn't able to do that so often, so the burden fell to Josie.

Mum said that Josie needed a sewing machine.

'I know, but there's no way I will be able to afford one,' said Jo. 'They cost a fortune.'

'I'll ask Mr Blanchflower if he can get us one,' suggested Mum.

Josie shook her head. 'Oh no, no don't. Please Mum, I'll make do.'

But the idea was planted in Mum's head now and within a few weeks an electric sewing machine had arrived. It was a big occasion. Shiny new items like that were not usually part of our life, so everyone was keen to 'play' with it, even though we all knew that it was Josie's. It was put in the front room where Pat slept, and was to be used in there, as there wasn't any space anywhere else to set it up.

Poor Josie was now responsible for the weekly repayments, which no doubt were charged at extortionate interest rates. It was a struggle, but Josie managed to find the extra money each week that Mum needed to pay the sewing machine off. After about six months it became clear that the sewing machine was a white elephant. Josie didn't really have time to use it much, and of course, even fabric was expensive, so slowly the machine became idle. Josie got more and more fed up and must have mentioned it at work.

'Why don't you sell it?' suggested one of the other girls in the office.

'Who to?' asked Josie despondently. 'I don't know anyone who could afford it.'

Miss Pomfret had overheard their conversation.

'If you really want to sell it, Josephine, then I would be very interested,' suggested Miss Pomfret kindly. 'I need to make the curtains for my new home, and have been thinking about getting one.'

That evening when she got home from work Josie told Mum what Miss Pomfret had offered.

'Hmm I think that would be a sensible idea,' said Mum thoughtfully. 'Yes, I think you should go ahead and sell it.'

The sewing machine was duly sold and poor Josie had to carry it into London on the train even though it was quite big and heavy. Josie gave the money from Miss Pomfret to Mum to finish paying for the sewing machine. She was so relieved to have the burden of the debt taken away and gave it no more thought.

A month or two after, Mary sent a dress for me that she had lovingly sewn by hand. Dave's Mum sometimes got off-cuts of a new fabric called 'Crimplene' and Mary had chosen some pale pink to make me a shift dress. It was gorgeous, and I loved it to bits! She hadn't had quite enough of the pink so had sewn a wide band of contrasting purple Crimplene around the hem and the sleeves. I tried it on and it was perfect! Mum made me stand on a chair while she looked on smiling. Then I saw Margaret looking on enviously.

'I'm sure Mary will make you a dress next time,' I said.

Mum looked at Margaret. 'I know,' she said, trying to cheer her up. 'We'll get Josie to make you one.' Then a strange look came over her face, and she was distracted and deep in thought until that evening. Josie was tired out from a long day at work when Mum told her about the dress for Margaret, so she didn't look very keen.

'I don't know, Mum, I haven't got much time at the moment,' she said, knowing that to sew it by hand would take hours of work.

'Well, why don't you ask that nice Miss Pomfret if you can borrow the sewing machine for a week or two? I'm sure she won't mind.'

Josie knew that Miss Pomfret would happily lend her the machine, as she had said so when she had bought it from her.

'Maybe,' she said, 'I'll have a think.'

'Oh please, please, please, Mo Mo,' said Margaret, using the pet name that she had for Josie. Josie couldn't refuse Margaret anything with her big brown eyes and sweet little face.

'Oh all right, I'll see what Miss Pomfret says.'

The sewing machine returned to our house the following week, and Josie took Margaret out on the Saturday morning to

Romford market to choose some material for her dress. She chose a dark purple velvet material, which Josie knew would be a nightmare to sew, but she let her have it anyway. It took a few weeks of the odd hour here and there before the dress was completed. Margaret tried it on.

'You look beautiful!' exclaimed Mum proudly, and indeed she did. Josie had made a good job of it, and the dress, although simple in design, looked really nice.

'I'll take the sewing machine back on Monday,' said Josie, pleased that the dress was finally finished.

'Oh okay, but I know Mary was wondering if she could borrow it to make a couple of bits. She works really fast so it would only be a week or so longer.' Josie agreed to check with Miss Pomfret to see if she minded. Miss Pomfret agreed that she could keep the sewing machine for as long as she wanted.

The next day Mum told Josie that Mary had collected the machine and would bring it back when she had finished with it in a week or so. Three weeks later it still hadn't been returned.

'Mum, can you ask Mary for the sewing machine? Miss Pomfret is taking a week's holiday and wants to make some curtains.'

Mum's face seemed to lose a bit of colour. I watched as she went into the scullery to put the kettle on. Something wasn't right.

'Mum, did you hear me?' called Josie after her.

'Yes, of course. I'll send her a letter and ask her to bring it back straight away.'

'Well, I suppose I could go over there at the end of the week and collect it on my way home,' offered Josie, but Mum came in with the teapot, shaking her head.

'No, no there's no need to do that; Mary can bring it over on Saturday. She wants to see the littluns anyway and Kathleen can show her how nice the dress she made her looks.'

When Saturday came, and Mary didn't arrive, Josie started to get anxious. She was sure Mary wouldn't intentionally let her down, and she began to wonder if Mum had forgotten to write the letter.

'Mum are you sure you wrote to Mary?' she asked.

Mum smiled.

'Oh yes, I forgot to tell you, she wrote back asking if she could keep it for another week, just to finish off some bits.'

Josie was annoyed. 'But I told you Miss Pomfret needs it back. She takes her week off from next Friday.'

Mum promised to go over to Mary's and collect the sewing machine herself on Monday to make sure Josie would have it to take back on Tuesday. Of course on Monday evening it still wasn't there. A dreadful realisation started to dawn on Josie. While she was drinking her tea she kept looking at Mum, who steadfastly refused to meet her eyes. Marion and Marge were washing up and Pat had the television on, but all the time I could feel the tension growing in the room.

Then suddenly Josie said, 'Mary hasn't got it has she?' almost in a whisper. When I looked at Mum I knew that was the truth. She got up and went out into the scullery and Josie followed her. 'You've given it back, haven't you? Mary never had it at all, did she? You've sent it back, back to Blanchflower!' We heard Josie's raised voice, and Mum's calm, quiet replies, but we didn't hear any more words.

Josie didn't go to work the next day, or the day after. She stayed in bed for almost a week, and we hardly saw her. Josie never went back to the job she had loved and to Miss Pomfret, one of the few people who had ever believed in her. Mum rang them to say she was leaving, and she never returned, not even to work out her notice or to say goodbye.

Mum's Good Luck

Marge and Ron were getting engaged and were going to have a big party! I was so excited. It meant that all of my sisters and brothers would be there and my aunts and uncles and cousins. Marge had to have a new dress, a special one for the party! The twins went shopping with Mum and when they came home they were carrying two dresses. The dresses were exactly the same except Marge's was white and Marion's was blue. They had a lacy bodice and a full flouncy net skirt, and Margaret and I fell in love with them. When we rushed forward to look, Mum said firmly, 'Don't touch, you'll make them dirty,' so we had to be satisfied with looking at them from a distance.

As the day of the party grew nearer, we got more and more excited. Marge and Ron had hired a hall in Ilford, and our brother Michael, who was now a fully trained chef in the army, was going to do the catering and make the cake.

Then we had some more exciting news. Over the past few weeks Mum had been in a competition. Every week she updated Marge and Ron with her progress.

'Only twenty people left in the draw now,' she said, and the next week: 'Only 10 people left now.'

The first prize was a car, and she was now in the last four. When Ron called round for Marge that evening, she asked him in for a cup of tea.

'You'll never guess what,' she started. 'I've only won that car!'

Margaret and I were amazed.

'Yes,' she continued, 'and I've decided that I am going to give it to you, Ron.' Marge stared ahead with an anxious look on her face.

'After all,' said Mum, 'you've been so good to me taking me and the littluns out; you deserve it.'

Ron didn't look as pleased as I thought he would. Didn't he realise he was going to get a nice brand new car?

Then Mum carried on. 'The only thing is I need to pay the £50 for the prize to be released and to pay the tax and other stuff before I can collect it for you.'

Marge still hadn't said anything, but Ron now replied. 'Where are you going to get that sort of money from?'

But Mum was ready with a solution. 'Well, I thought if you sold your car and gave me the money, I could pay to get the new car released for you,' she said smiling.

Ron didn't answer at first, but I saw him exchange a look with Marge.

'I don't think that's a very good idea,' he said. 'I'll wait until the car arrives before I sell my old one just in case anything goes wrong and then you can have whatever money I get for it.'

Mum looked disappointed, but nodded in agreement. I think something did go wrong because that car never did arrive.

Marge and Ron's engagement party was great fun. We had sausages on sticks, pineapple and cheese on sticks, little vol-au-vents filled with cream cheese, sandwiches and cakes. There was also lots of lemonade and cherryade and the grown-ups had beer and whisky. Aunty got a bit tipsy on the bottle of brandy Michael had brought her and danced with a plate on her head while Mum looked on disapprovingly. On Monday, after it was all over and the girls had gone back to work, Margaret and I crept up to the big bedroom that the twins shared with Aunty and quietly pulled open the cupboard door. There were the dresses! We slipped into them, me in the blue one and Margaret in the white, and then proceeded to bounce on the bed, giggling and laughing until we almost cried with the naughtiness of it.

I was twelve now and my friendship with Anne meant that school continued to be fun.

During our second year at school the headmistress, Sister Joan, told us there was going to be a school trip to Switzerland. It sounded wonderful. The trip would be by rail across Europe and because it would take so long there would be little 'couchettes' to sleep in on board the train. The final destination would by Lake Lugano, which was on the Swiss Italian border.

Anne was excited. 'I think we should go,' she said matter-of-factly as we left assembly. My heart sank. I knew the chances of me being able to go were about zero as the cost would be prohibitive. Several of the girls that we went around with were keen and so the talk from then on was of nothing else. The last date for putting your name down for a place was fast approaching.

Anne was continually on at me. 'Kathleen, will you go and get your name down or all the places will be gone,' she nagged, annoyed that I kept making excuses. The problem was not the 'putting my name down' – it was the £5 deposit that was the issue.

The only member of my family to ever go on a school trip was my sister Josie. She had been sponsored by her school to go to Luxembourg. They had paid all of the cost and even allocated her a small amount of spending money. Josie was always a very good scholar and I think that the school had recognised that she would not be able to take up the opportunity because of financial hardship so had awarded her the trip as a 'prize'. She had absolutely loved every moment of it, and it had sparked a love of travel in her that would last her whole life.

I got home one day after school feeling really fed up. We had been given the deadline of the next day to put our deposit down. Why was it that I couldn't go with my friends? It didn't seem fair. I was resigned to the fact that lack of money meant that I couldn't go horse riding with Anne and Jane on a Saturday, or ice skating, or even to the pictures in the holidays, but I could live with that. This was so much more, something really special that was so out of reach that I had to make myself stop thinking about it. They would all be talking about going all the time, and then when they came back they would be talking about what they had seen and done, and I would be left out of all of it. Different again, just like before, just like in primary school. When Pat and Josie got in from work I thrust the piece of paper with the information about the school trip in front of them. I hadn't bothered to mention it before because I knew it was hopeless.

Josie picked it up. 'What's this then?' she asked scanning the sheet of paper.

'The school trip in May,' I replied almost sullenly. 'The deposit has got to be paid tomorrow.'

'Why didn't you tell us before?' Josie exclaimed.

I shrugged and looked away. I guessed what was coming next. £5 was too much money, and where would they find the rest of the £22 to pay for the trip?

But Josie looked me straight in the eyes. 'Do you want to go?'

I nodded, amazed that she would even need to ask that question.

Then she looked at Pat. 'What do you think?'

Pat shrugged her shoulders.

Then Josie astonished me by saying, 'I'll ring the school from work tomorrow and ask if we can send the deposit next Monday after we get paid. I'm sure it will be fine.'

My mouth dropped open. Could it be true? Was this all it took? Did I just have to ask?'

Mum called out from the scullery. 'Ask your Aunt if she wants one or two chops on her dinner.'

'Tell yer mother I'll just 'ave one.'

And then we sat down around the kitchen and ate our dinner, while the whole time I was imagining sleeping on a train that was rushing through snow-topped mountains in a magical country called Switzerland.

22

The Trip to London

Goodness knows what level of hardship poor Pat and Josie had to endure to save the money for my trip, but save it they did. Every week I would take in a little bit more until just a week before we were due to go Josie gave me the final payment. I was ecstatic! Over the past few months Anne and I and the other girls had spent all of our time talking about the trip and I was beside myself with excitement. There were, however, a few blights on my happiness. One of these was the 'what to pack?' issue. Anne had no restrictions financially, so was keen to dictate what we would need.

'We'll have to have a soap bag with a flannel and soap, toothbrush and toothpaste and a nail file,' she announced. There were general nods of agreement, but inside I was beginning to panic. I was pretty sure I could get soap and a flannel but we had never had a toothbrush or toothpaste, although Aunty did soak her false teeth in Steradent. I was pretty sure that this wasn't what Anne meant. As for a nail file, I didn't even know what that was for! This was just the beginning, and just as I would manage to solve one problem, Anne would issue a decree regarding some other essential item that would need to be packed. My head spun. I couldn't ask Pat or Josie for help, as I knew that they were desperately saving any spare pennies to pay for my trip, and Mary was now married. Marge and Marion gave almost all of their wages to Mum and just had enough left over for their fare, and I would never have dared in a million years to ask Aunty for anything, so that just left Mum.

'Mum, I need some long white socks for the school trip,' I asked one day, 'and we can take a home dress to wear in the evenings.' Mum looked over at me while she was ironing on the kitchen table. When we were younger the iron had to be plugged into the light fitting as we didn't have wall sockets, and before that Granny and Mum had an old flat iron. It would have to be heated on the cooking range and then used before it cooled as there was no electricity in the house at that time. This was still out in the garden where Margaret and I had spent many happy hours playing at being grown-ups and 'doing the ironing'.

Now though, we were 'modern'. Not only had electric lighting replaced the old gas mantles which had sputtered and spattered their brightness across the room, filling it with a distinct smell, but we also now had a couple of sockets in the skirting board to plug things like the iron and the television into.

Mum paused from her ironing as though she were thinking things through and then said almost to herself, 'Mmm, you'll need some bits and pieces won't you,' and then carried on ironing. But the seed was sown.

The next day Mum said I wasn't to go to school. I wasn't too bothered, as I knew that Anne was going to a hospital appointment and wouldn't be there anyway. Margaret was off school with a 'cold' so she would be coming out with us. We walked over to the bus stop and caught the 62 to Chadwell Heath station. We got the train to Liverpool Street station which was usually about a half-hour journey, although because we got a slow train that stopped at all of the little stations it took more like an hour. I read the station names inside my head as we stopped, Goodmayes, Seven Kings, Ilford, Manor Park, Stratford, Maryland; on and on we went, seemingly forever. We arrived finally at Liverpool Street, where we got off and walked out into the East End of London. I hadn't been to London very often, although when Pat or Josie had a little spare money they would occasionally take the whole family out, buying each of us a 'Red Rover' bus pass. This pass allowed you to travel anywhere for about 4 shillings each all day, as long as it was 'off peak'. These were brilliant days when we would travel all over London, sometimes with a destination in mind such as Hampton Court or

Kew Gardens, which only cost a penny to get in, or sometimes we'd just jump on a bus and stay on until it reached its final destination and then get off and come back again!

Today though we were in an unfamiliar part of London. We walked around the back of the station towards a large building that looked a bit like a warehouse. When we pushed through the grubby exterior doors into the building it took on a miraculous transformation. It was a massive area that was immaculately clean, the floor shone with polish and there were bright lights illuminating the whole space. All along the walls stood racks of bright new clothes. Hundreds and hundreds of dresses, coats, suits, skirts, knitwear, all presented beautifully. I felt a surge of greed well up inside me. I wanted it all. I wanted to be able to wear lovely things that had never belonged to anyone else, and to look clean and smart and maybe even a little bit pretty. Margaret and I stayed close to Mum. As we walked in I felt eyes upon us, and realised that people were watching. That same old feeling of not being good enough, of Mum being older and fatter than other mums, of having grubby and old clothes, of being different, overwhelmed me and took away the excitement of the clothes, so that I just wished we could go home. Mum had different ideas though. She walked in confidently, approached one of the saleswomen and said, 'I'm one of Mr Blanchflower's customers,' and then proceeded to show the woman a piece of paper and a folded card. The look on the woman's face changed at once, and she nodded and directed Mum to a chair.

'What are you looking for today, madam?' the woman asked, with a smile on her lips but not in her eyes.

Mum answered in her 'special' voice: 'I want a dress each for these two and some shoes for Kathleen.' The lady then asked us to accompany her to the other side of the huge space where there were children's clothes and then left Mum and us alone to look.

I picked out a blue check dress with a white collar and a navy blue shiny ribbon tied in a bow both at the neck and at the sleeves. Margaret chose a plain black velvet dress that would have looked good on someone of thirty, but on a child of ten looked strangely sombre. Then I saw a jacket, it was white with blue trimmings.

'Oh look,' I said, picking it up and fingering it.

'Do you want that as well?' asked Mum.

I nodded enthusiastically. The jacket was duly put with the dresses. Then Mum selected a red skirt with a pretty purple pattern on it.

'What about this?' asked Mum, holding it up to me. Again I nodded, not daring to believe my luck. Mum became almost frenzied. There was a spark of excitement in her eyes, and she had a look about her that we had seen before. The saleswoman finally came back to join us and, seeing the pile of clothes that Mum had collected, went a little pale.

'Do you want to try *all* of these?' she asked, eyeing the assortment of dresses, skirts, jacket, underclothes, shoes and nightdresses. Mum nodded and I was ushered into a corner where the clothes were tried on me. In my eyes they all looked absolutely gorgeous! Margaret wouldn't try her two dresses on as she was too shy, so Mum held them against her and pronounced that they would be fine. The lady began to add up the prices. 'Am I really getting all these things?' I thought incredulously. Then the saleswoman said something too quietly to Mum and they exchanged a few more words that I couldn't hear.

Then the lady said, 'I'll tell you what we'll do. I'll telephone Mr Blanchflower and see what he says.' Mum nodded in agreement and the woman went over to the corner of the space where there was a kind of glass partition with a man sitting behind, head bent, writing with his nose almost on the paper. The saleswoman spoke to him briefly and then he picked up the phone.

It seemed like ages before the lady made her way back across the room smiling. 'Yes that's all fine, Mrs Stevens,' she said using our other special name. I was so happy – we had the best mum in the whole world! The things were then duly parcelled up and Mum had to fill in lots of forms, but luckily didn't have to pay any money. I was puzzled when we left for the station without the clothes.

'Why can't we bring them home with us?' I asked.

'Mr Blanchflower has to bring them because they're too heavy to carry on the train,' answered Mum, starting to get that other faraway look again. I would have been more than happy to have struggled to carry the precious cargo, but I knew there was no point arguing with Mum when she was like this, and anyway, she always made all the rules in our house.

23

A Foreign Adventure

Mr Blanchflower delivered the clothes the following week and he smiled as Mum signed a special piece of paper.

'17/6 Mrs Stevens, starting from next week.'

Mum nodded and smiled back, but after he had gone she told us not to tell Pat or Josie. We never questioned why. We were used to secrets; they were an intrinsic part of our lives. Mum squirrelled the parcels away at the back of the huge wardrobe in the bedroom that she and I shared, until the time came round for me to pack. The clothes suddenly appeared in a large bag that Mum told me to give to Josie. She was packing for me; she was always best at that sort of thing, and had come home from work a bit early to get it done. She lifted the bag that I gave her and my new clothes and the various other items spilled out. I saw the horrified look on her face.

'What's wrong?' I asked. 'Don't you like them? Are they the wrong things to take?' I was worried now, Josie was the only sister to have been on a school trip. If she thought the things were wrong then they must be.

She just shook her head without saying anything and continued to pack. Her lips were drawn tightly together, and when the case was finally packed she said, 'There you are, that's everything now,' without smiling, and put it on the floor of the bedroom and walked downstairs. I could hear her talking to Mum and their voices start to get louder. My stomach churned. I hated conflict, and I could tell by the tone of their voices that they were starting to argue. Josie stomped back upstairs into her bedroom and slammed the door shut, and I went down slowly, worried about the mood Mum would be in. Mum was sitting in

her chair by the fireplace and was smoking a cigarette and looking agitated.

'Shall I make you a cup of tea?' I asked trying to cheer her up.

She nodded and then added, 'Pat will be home soon, you can
make one for her too,' but she didn't mention Josie.

Josie wasn't talking to Mum. There was an awful atmosphere
in the house and we were all walking around on eggshells. Part
of me was glad that I was going away on my trip but part of me
was terrified that something bad would happen while I was
away. I couldn't sleep that night; everything was twirling around
inside my head. I knew Margaret was worried, and that I
wouldn't be here to look after her, and I knew that Josie was
angry about something and that Mum was in one of her downward spirals. Would there be a big argument while I was away?
Would Aunty throw things? Would Mum get ill? Would she still
be here when I got back? So by the time the morning came and
I walked across the road to the bus stop, I carried a heavy weight
inside my heart along with the heavy weight of my little case,
which I struggled to get on the bus on my own. I was still only
twelve years old, but felt as though the world was weighing
down on me.

The journey to Switzerland was magical, although parts of it
were a bit scary. We had little couchettes to sleep in and I was on
the top bunk. I was afraid that I would fall out, but managed to
get to sleep in the end, and remember so clearly the smell of the
air when I woke up. It was cleaner, fresher, colder and altogether
different from the air in Dagenham. Looking out of the windows
of the train we watched the scenery change, and saw mountains
topped with snow, even though it was late springtime. When we
arrived at long last at the hotel our excitement mounted. I shared
a room with Anne and little Lizzie M, who was in the first year.
We were very protective of her, and felt like the big girls. She
would clean her teeth and look in the mirror and say, 'I look like
Alfalfa,' and then laugh hysterically at her own joke.

Anne and I were two of the oldest girls on the trip, which was
a mixture of first and second year pupils. We assumed the role

of protector and guide to the first year's and thought we were very mature. It was probably our fault, however, that we were nearly all killed! Our teachers had told us that we were going for a mountain walk. It sounded like fun, the sun was shining, and we had eaten our continental breakfast of rolls, jam and unsalted butter. The hotel made us packed lunches which we had to carry ourselves, and off we set. For the first couple of hours every-one's spirits were very high. We knew we were going on a boat trip the next day to a place called Isola Bella, which sounded lovely. Then a bank of white cloud obscured the sun and the air turned colder quite suddenly. Anne and I were at the back of the very long and very straggly line of girls, which was beginning to slow more and more as the younger children got tired. The teachers were now a very long way ahead, and were completely out of our sight. We stopped to look at something, I can't remem-ber what, but by the time we tried to join the rest of the group we realised we didn't know which path to take. Some of the younger girls started whining, 'I'm tired, I want to go back,' but of course we didn't know which way back was. Then Anne had her 'good idea'.

'I know,' she said authoritatively, 'I'll climb up on to that ridge and will be able to see over the top of the trees and bushes to where the path is.'

I was less convinced at this but as always I deferred to Anne.

She duly climbed up on to the ridge and declared loudly, 'It's okay – I can see the pathway. It goes down through those bushes,' and she pointed to what seemed to me an unlikely route. But who was I to argue? One of the younger girls had started to cry and there were several others who were threatening to join them.

'Okay,' I replied. 'Let's go,' and I began to usher the group towards the tiny gap in the shrubbery which opened onto a narrow, steep track.

'Down here,' Anne shouted leading the way with confidence. I carried on at the rear of the group, desperately trying to encourage the others to keep up. I took their bags from them and carried them myself, as all the while the bushes got thicker and the track got steeper, until it was obvious that this couldn't possibly be the right way. Many of the younger girls were almost hysterical by now, as they slipped and slid downwards often losing their footing to be hauled back to their feet by Anne or me. Finally Anne called a halt. We sat everyone down and told them to eat their lunch. No one felt much like it but we insisted. We thought it would be good to have a rest and it would also make the bags lighter to carry. Anne then told me to stay with the others while she went to scout out a way back. After what seemed like a very long time she returned.

'Listen,' she whispered to me. 'I don't want to worry the others but we need to go back up. Just the other side of that slight ridge there is a steep drop. There is no way we can carry on this way.'

My heart sunk. It had been hard enough travelling downwards, but to go all the way back uphill was going to be horrendous! But there was no other way, so after picking everything back up we broke the news to the others that we would have to retrace our steps. They were not happy, but they didn't have much choice. They trusted us to keep them safe, and we were determined to do just that. It took us at least two hours to reach the proper pathway again, and it was with much relief and anger that we spied the teachers and the rest of the group standing at the top waiting for us and laughing. No one had been in the least bit worried or showed the slightest concern that we could have fallen off the mountainside!

Our next destination Isola Bella, or 'beautiful island', was just that. It was a tiny Italian island where there were no cars or buses, no traffic of any description apart from the odd donkey and a few cycles. We reached it by ferry and the first thing that struck me as we got off the boat was the silence and the freshness. It was spring and there was blossom everywhere. Beautiful flowers already tumbled out of the window boxes that seemed to hang on every wall. The houses were all painted white, and the Mediterranean light made them sparkle in the sun. The smells were intoxicating and assaulted our senses with a mixture of heady perfumes from the flowers and aromatic herbs and spices that flowed freely from the open windows as the inhabitants cooked their exotic food. Anne considered us to be the sophisticates of the group and suggested we left the main party to wander around. Our teacher had said we were allowed an hour to explore the island and that we would meet back at the ferry. So off we went, my friend Anne and I, walking through narrow cobbled streets that threaded backwards and forwards across the island like looped ribbons. Finally as we climbed down a sloping path that led towards the shore, we saw a tiny local bar. We went in, full of confidence and were directed towards a beautiful balcony that looked out to sea. It was such a clear blue that it hurt my eyes to look at it and made me think it couldn't be real. The sea in England never looked like this. A young waiter came over with a kind smile on his face, probably surprised at the youth of his customers.

I hesitated. 'Um, well . . .'

'Two Pepsis with ice and a slice of lemon please,' Anne ordered confidently.

It was the best drink I had ever tasted.

We left for England the next day and only then did I begin to wonder what I would find on my return, and whether or not all would be calm in the Coates household. When I got back to Barking station with Anne, her sister was waiting to meet her. She ran up, taking her case from her as they walked towards home. I, on the other hand, had no one to meet me. I knew that I would need to get the 62 bus, but didn't have any money. I'm sure that if Anne's sister had realised that I didn't have any way of getting home she would have given me the bus fare, but I was too ashamed to ask.

I stood at the bus stop outside the station and wondered what to do. We didn't have a phone so there was no way of ringing anyone, and I certainly didn't think I would be able to walk all the way home with my suitcase, which was now even heavier than when I left home, filled up now with the little bits and pieces I had bought as gifts for my family. I stood watching several buses come and go, knowing that they could take me home, take me to the family who I had missed desperately for the ten days I had been away. I came to the conclusion that the only way I could get home to them was to try to 'hop' my fare; that is to get on without paying and hope the conductor didn't notice. Sure enough when the next 62 arrived I got on. Luckily there were several people who got on with me, and the bus was already quite crowded. I sat down near the front next to an old lady and looked down at the ground when the conductor shouted, 'Any more fares? Any more fares please?' I felt hot and ashamed and looking down, almost held my breath the whole way home.

As the bus stop outside my house came into view, I started to relax a little and looked towards the platform where you could wait to get off. Again I was lucky, as there were three others getting off at the same stop and one of them rang the bell. On hearing this I quickly jumped up and hopped off the bus as soon as it stopped, without the conductor realising that I hadn't paid my fare, and quickly walked across the road, dragging my suit-case in both hands, feeling as though I were a hardened criminal now and carrying the burden of guilt that all Catholics are born with. I knocked on the front door and heard Pongo barking and Mum coming to open it.

'Hello,' I said, almost shyly. It seemed strange being back home, seeing Mum standing there. I felt as though I had been away forever. Mum stood back smiling; taking my case, she ushered me into the kitchen. She didn't hug or kiss me, and I didn't hug or kiss her. We just didn't do that sort of thing, but I knew she was pleased to see me.

'I'll make you a nice cup of tea,' she said as she bustled out into the scullery to put the kettle on. Margaret was sitting on the settee looking very happy, but everyone else was out at work. I looked around at my home. It was tidy but rather dishevelled and the air was permeated by the heavy smell of cigarettes, dog, and cooking fat that I had never really noticed before. The furniture was old and worn and there was only a threadbare rug on the floor. The walls, ceiling and net curtains that hung at the window were a dirty yellowish colour, stained from the nicotine of three heavy smokers, Mum, Pat and Aunty. At least the damp clothes were hanging on the line in the garden instead of around the walls, as the sun was shining. Pongo was jumping up at me, happy that I was home, and I could hear the kettle whistling as it began to boil. I knew then with a sudden intensity that this was where my family lived, where I belonged. Here was my home, and despite the fear and the secrets and the lies, I was glad to be back.

24

Visiting Mary

Mary had a baby boy! She and Dave had recently moved to a modern house on a new estate in a place called Rainham in Kent. Mum said we could go and visit them. It was coming up to the summer holidays and Margaret, Anne and I were going to spend two weeks with Mary and Dave, and we would be able to help with their new baby Tony. As the day to leave drew closer we started to get more and more excited. Mum packed some groceries in a bag and we put a few items of clothing together and they were loaded into Ron's car. He was going to drive us to Kent with Marge and Mum. We all squeezed into his little car and started off. It wasn't too far, but the difference in what we saw around us was amazing. As we left Dagenham behind us and drove through the tunnel, the houses spread out and the landscape became more and more rural. When we arrived, Mary showed us all around the house. It was very neat and clean but Mum didn't look very impressed.

'It's very small isn't it?' she noted, and I saw Mary's face fall.

'Are you staying for lunch?' Mary asked, but Mum shook her head.

'No, we need to be getting back, we'll have a cup of tea though.'

She seemed keen to be on her way and, after saying goodbye to us, left with Marge and Ron. Mary didn't seem that pleased to see us, although she was kind and showed us where we would sleep in a little bed settee all together like sardines.

It was going to be fun. 'We can have midnight feasts!' suggested Anne.

Of course what we didn't realise was that poor Mary and Dave were finding it hard to feed themselves and the thought of another three mouths to feed was very worrying for them. Mary encouraged us to go out every day, so we wandered along the country lanes, going into the farms to look at the animals. Most people were surprisingly kind and usually didn't mind us. One day we visited a pig farm. The smell clung to us, but then we spied an enclosure with a huge sow lying on her back and a multitude of piglets fighting to suckle from her.

'What are you up to over there?' we heard from the inside of a nearby barn. A heavily built bald-headed man emerged holding a pitchfork in his hand.

'You don't want to be getting too close to 'er,' he advised, 'she's got 'er young uns see, makes um a bit vicious.'

'Can we look round?' asked Anne.

'Yep if you like, but be careful, farms is dangerous places!' he added, smiling now. 'Does you want to hold one of the piglets?'

We all nodded our heads enthusiastically.

He passed us a piglet each to hold. They were so sweet!

'I as to watch 'er in case she rolls on 'em.' He bent to the side and picked up a lifeless purpley blue body. 'See,' he continued, 'this is wot can 'appen. Squashed 'im, poor little thing.'

We looked on in fascinated horror at the poor little stiff-legged piglet.

We would also play in the barns if we could get away with it, and Anne wasn't averse to relieving herself in the corner when necessary, which Margaret and I thought was outrageous!

The sun seemed to shine every day, and the lure of the petrol station on the main road, with its mini doughnut stall, was great, so quite soon the little bit of spending money we had was gone.

Margaret sent Mum a postcard saying: 'Dear Mum We haven't got any money but it doesn't matter Love Margaret X'

Anne decided that we needed to get a job. We walked round the lanes knocking at each house we came across to see if we could get one. One lady had us weeding her garden for the whole day. The sun was hot and we were thirsty, but she didn't even offer us a drink. By the end of the afternoon we were getting excited at the thought of how much we had earned. The lady came out into the garden and gave us a few final jobs to do. Then she pulled her purse from her pocket.

'You've really worked hard girls, and have got most of the weeds out – well done,' and then gave us 6d between us for our efforts! Luckily most people were a little more generous.

Not too long after that we heard that Mary and Dave were going to emigrate to Australia. There was a special offer that meant that they could go all the way to Australia for just £10! Australia – the other side of the world. At that time it was almost the same as saying goodbye to your family forever. The distance was so far and the cost of airfares was so high that the possibility of them coming back home or us going to visit was tiny. Emigration wasn't something new, of course. The potato famine in the 1850s resulted in the slow starvation and collapse of society in rural Ireland. Many families had no choice but to leave the land they loved, to search for work and be able to feed their families. The older people had little chance, but the younger men, and in some cases women, could find an escape. So my great grandfather had joined the British army and been sent to India. In Ireland when family members went away like this they would have a wake as it was thought to be like a death. I think we thought of Mary's going as something equally final, and I felt sad to think I would never see her again. When the time came for her to leave, Mum became quite withdrawn. The rift between them had healed over time. Although there had always been a lack of closeness between them, I think Mum felt the loss keenly.

I was growing up fast, and although life at home was still full of turmoil, my friends were very important to me. The poverty at home should have lessened. Pat, Josie, Marge and Marion were all working now and contributing the majority of their wage to the household budget. Mum still got her family allowance and benefits for Margaret and me and Aunty paid the rent. If Mum had been a manager, life might have been reasonably comfortable, but she wasn't. She had a desperate addiction to the highs of life, times when she would spend money we didn't have on things we didn't need, and couldn't afford. Of course the result of this were the mirror images: the desperate lows, times when there wasn't enough money for food and gas, times when we had to hide from the tally men who knocked on the door with a terrible regularity, week after week after week. It also meant that many necessities of life were absent.

The winter after Mary and Dave left was a particularly harsh one. Snow had begun to fall before Christmas and there was a bitter biting wind that cut through my thin coat as I waited for the bus to school every morning. It was just over a week until school finished for the holiday and as I jumped off the bus at Becontree Station I saw Anne and Jane standing on the other side of the road. I waved and crossed to meet them.

'We're just talking about going carol singing tonight,' said Anne, 'Mrs B's collecting for her son's school.' Mrs B was our needlework teacher, who we really liked. Unlike some of the other staff at the school, she took a genuine interest in us and although we were hopeless sewers she never gave up on us. She encouraged us to persevere and spent time helping us sort out our messes. Her son attended a 'special school' as he had a severe disability, and she often talked to us about the things they did there. Recently she had mentioned that they were collecting money to have a hydrotherapy pool installed.

'Are you coming?' asked Anne. 'We thought if we went round Barking we would get more money.' I knew this made sense, Barking was a much more affluent area than where I lived in Dagenham, but I would need bus fare so I hesitated.

'Oh come on, it'll be great. We can practise at lunchtime.'

I nodded my agreement and we talked about which carols we would sing as we walked to school. That evening I asked Pat if I could have some bus money. She always tried to help if she knew I really needed anything, even though she wouldn't have had much left after paying Mum and her fares. She gave me a handful of coins to cover the cost of my fare. It was freezing as I opened the door to go and meet Anne and the others. I waited for the 62 and shivered in my thin coat and plimsolls. The moisture had been drawn up through the canvas into my socks, almost to my knees, forming a dark grey watermark. I always wore plimsolls – they were the only footwear I had. In the summer this was fine, although my feet sometimes felt hot and sweaty, but in the winter months it was desperate. By the time I got to Barking station where we were meeting it had started to snow again. Anne and the others were already waiting for me outside the Wimpy Bar. Off we went, trailing around the long avenues opposite Barking Park where the posher houses were. We had worked out a routine. We would walk up the path of each house, sing a short carol and then knock. It was my job to speak when the door was opened as I had the nicest speaking voice, and was also the only one of us who could say 'hydro-therapeutic'! People were surprisingly generous, and probably just glad to give us a few coins to get rid of us so that they could close the door on the atrocious weather. Then we had a real stroke of luck. Suddenly we heard the sound of trumpet music. It was the Salvation Army carol singers. At first I thought that this was bad news, as they were much more impressive than our little group, but Anne knew better.

'Look I know what we can do, we can just follow them round and then knock and shake the box. People will think that we are collecting for them!' It was a brilliant scheme and by the end of the evening the collection box Mrs B had provided us with was full to bursting and we hadn't even had to sing!

25

Being Discovered

I think God invented puberty as a form of torture that would make sure we grow up with strength of character!

Mum was sympathetic. 'I've got you some special soap,' she would say and hand me a bar of Neutrogena soap, which all the advertisements said would miraculously cure spots. Of course the spots remained, my body started to change shape, and each month I would have to spend at least a day curled up in a ball with cramping pains in my stomach. Mum would make me a hot-water bottle, give me an aspirin and tuck me up on the settee. Although I was in pain, it was comforting, and oddly became something I almost looked forward to. Being warm, safe and cared for was a luxury and I revelled in it. Margaret was also growing up fast, but still hardly ever went to school. She was quiet and painfully shy, but I had told her as much as I knew about the birds and the bees, which really wasn't much at all.

We had a new teacher at school called Miss Leahy. She taught us maths and PE and was also our form teacher, and she was very different from any of the other teachers we had had before. Miss Leahy was Welsh, and was very athletic. She always wore trainers and leggings and bounced around the school with a calm, firm air of authority. No one dared cheek her or misbehave in any of her classes. No one except Anne, of course. Anne could get away with anything. Perhaps we were such good friends because I saw in her something of my mum. That same charisma, that sense of fun that drew people in and made them want to be near her, and also that same sense of underlying mischief. Anne had an effect on teachers as well as pupils – even on Miss Leahy.

Our popularity in school meant that we were given certain privileges. We didn't deserve them, and pushed the boundaries at any opportunity. I can remember the many tricks we played on unsuspecting teachers, the salt in their cups of tea, the whoopee cushions, the itching powder, but we seemed to survive each attack with a kind of invulnerability. Our reputation grew, and with it an intoxicating sense of power. Then Miss Leahy discovered my brain.

'Kathleen Coates, come out here and finish this problem please,' she'd say, and I would oblige. I had grown quite expert in concealing any signs of academic ability over the years, and had consequently become lazy. Miss Leahy must have spotted something in me, a moment when I let down my guard, a flash of underlying intelligence. And then there was no escape. During maths lessons she would pick me out to solve problems, to explain things to the rest of the class, to do 'special' work which I actually started to enjoy.

'What are you doing in the C class, Kathleen Coates?' she asked me one day. I was taken aback. She was the teacher; how should I know? I just shrugged my shoulders in answer and she raised her eyes. 'You, young lady, are wasting your brain and my time.'

Being noticed for intelligence was exciting and I began to feel that I was special in my own right, and not just as an extension of Anne. It felt strange, and it also felt good, but I knew I was walking a dangerous line. Then came parents' evening.

Miss Leahy asked if my mum was coming. Mum never came to parents' evening. What was the point? I was in the C class. No one came and that suited me fine, because it also meant that there was never any danger of me being moved to a higher stream. I was comfortable in my laziness, and I didn't want to leave Anne behind. But Miss Leahy was determined.

When I got home from school that afternoon, Mum was holding a letter in her hand.

'Your teacher wants to see me,' she said. 'You didn't tell me it was parents' evening next week.' I looked away, pretending my heart wasn't beating double fast.

'Yes, it's on Tuesday,' I answered in what I hoped was a disinterested way.

'I think Pat and I should go.'

My heart plummeted to my knees. *Oh God no.* Everyone would mistake Pat for my mum like they always did; everyone would think Mum was my gran. I would be so embarrassed.

'Oh don't bother,' I said. 'What's the point anyway?'

But Mum was adamant. I never found out exactly what was in that letter, but it must have been powerful stuff!

When Tuesday came around I wanted to die. Mum and Pat got their coats. They didn't have good clothes and they were both very overweight. There was never any money spare for hairdressers so they looked dishevelled and permanently untidy however hard they tried. Both Mum and Pat smoked heavily and the evidence was visible in their nicotine-stained fingers. Teenage years are painful for all sorts of reasons, but one of the most powerful is that need to be the same, to belong, not to be seen as different. Even though at school I had re-invented myself, the spectre of home always lurked, waiting to trip me up and remind me that I could never be quite like the other girls. And now everyone was going to discover my secret.

Parents' evening was held in the school hall and the teachers were positioned at various points around the walls. There were chairs placed nearby so that parents could sit and wait for their turn.

'Where is this Miss Leahy?' Mum asked as she scanned the sea of faces.

'Over there,' I muttered with my head down, dreading what was to come. As we walked across the hall I saw several girls looking at me, but they weren't in my class; in fact hardly any girls from the C classes were there. As we approached, Miss Leahy spotted me and called me over.

'Hello Kathleen, this must be your mum,' she said, extending her hand towards Pat. Mum stepped forward and took it.

'Good evening,' she said in her best voice. 'I'm Mrs Coates.' Mum was never intimidated by authority; she was a very intelligent and articulate woman and could hold her own with anyone.

Miss Leahy composed herself and asked Mum and Pat to take a seat. I stood by mortified. 'Kathleen is in the wrong class,' she began. 'She's a clever girl and has a mathematical brain. I would like her to move to the O-level class next year so that she can take her exams.'

Mum sat nodding, but I couldn't read her face.

Miss Leahy continued: 'I don't know why she's in 3C. She's clearly bright enough to take her GCEs but if she stays where she is she will only be able to take CSEs, which would be a real shame. It will mean lots of hard work, but Mrs Lobbit can give her extra maths lessons over the summer holidays to help get Kathleen ready.'

Mrs Lobbit was a young science and maths teacher who was very trendy and wore modern 60s clothes, short skirts and shift dresses. She had shiny straight hair that was cut at her shoulders in a style that made her look like Sandie Shaw and we all envied her.

Mum hesitated for a few minutes and then smiled at my teacher.

'Kath's not afraid of a little hard work.'

I gulped; this sounded serious.

26

The Halloween Party

Being in the O-level class was a culture shock to me. The girls I was with were focused on their work and the teachers expected homework to be completed on time, and to a high standard. I was halfway between being exhilarating and terrified but I managed to cope. My confidence levels had increased considerably since I was that timid little girl in primary school. By the time I left school I had managed to obtain a clutch of O-levels and was keen to get to work and earn some money.

I needed clothes to go out in and although the discos would usually let girls in for free, we still felt obliged to buy a drink once inside. We usually only ever had to buy that first drink because after that there would be some young man who would be only too happy to supply our drinks in the hope of a good-night kiss on the way home. I had discovered boys!

Mum always encouraged us to have dates. I think she was disappointed and felt a little bit guilty that Pat and Josie had never married, and was keen for the rest of us to find husbands. There had been a period of time when Mum had insisted that I accompany Marion to a series of dances and clubs because now that Marge was 'courting' she didn't have anyone to go with. I had hated it. There was a seven-year age difference between us and the kind of places that we went were beyond my maturity levels. Since Marion had met Geoff and started going steady, I was left to my own devices and the world was full of opportunities. Both Margaret and I had grown into attractive teenagers. Margaret had always been a pretty child but I felt as though I was the ugly duckling turned into a swan as we got more and more attention from the local boys. We both felt so grown up when that Christmas Mum bought us a record each.

Mine was 'Sugar Sugar' by the Archies and Margaret's was 'Tracy' by the Cuff Links and we played them incessantly. I can still remember all the words to both over forty years later.

Halloween was still a fairly low-key celebration, but was starting to gain favour as fashion and trends moved across from America. Margaret loved all things witchy.

'Shall we ask Mum if we can have a Halloween party?' she suggested.

I gave this some thought. 'Do you think she'll let us?' I was sceptical. We had never even had birthday parties when we were younger. In fact the only party in our house that I could remember was when Josie was twenty-one. Mum had invited all our aunties and uncles over, apart from those in Birmingham. We never saw much of Uncle John's family, and they were rarely mentioned in our house by Mum, although Aunty would sometimes say, 'It's a shame the Birmingham lot can't come,' and Mum would turn away without meeting Aunty's eyes.

Michael had made a cake for Josie with '21' written on it and as my birthday fell two days before Josie's, Mum told me the party was for me as well. Of course even though I was only nine I knew that this wasn't really true but I went along with it anyway. The overriding memory of that day was not the disappointment that Josie was the only one who got any presents, or that the cake only had her name on it, but the utter embarrassment of having Julie, my godmother, calling upstairs for me.

'Kathleen,' she called. 'Come on down so we can say Happy Birthday.'

I could see her standing at the bottom of the stairs looking up to where I was crouched behind the banisters. I think she thought I was upset because I was feeling left out, but the truth was that I couldn't find any clean clothes to wear.

'I'll come down in a minute,' I replied, panicking at the thought. Eventually I managed to find a heavy tartan kilt that someone must have donated to us. As it was the middle of a warm August it wasn't particularly comfortable, and I still remember that awful hot scratchy feeling of the rough wool on my bare legs.

So when Margaret made her suggestion about Halloween I was unconvinced.

'We can ask if you like,' I said and she nodded enthusiastically.

'You ask,' she said. 'You're the oldest.' I was just seventeen and we both worked in London in offices. Jobs were plentiful at that time, especially if you could speak nicely, were attractive, and could read and write well. We fulfilled all of these criteria, so had been in work since we left school – Margaret as soon as she was fifteen and me at sixteen. Just like our siblings before us, most of our wages went to Mum, who still had her tally men, or 'callers' as Aunty called them, who continued to bleed our family dry.

'All right, I'll ask, but if she says no I'm not asking again.'

To our complete shock and surprise Mum agreed at once.

'Oh yes, that's a good idea,' she said, her blue eyes twinkling, 'we can decorate the kitchen with witches and make some party food.' On the rare occasions when Mum had hosted family parties in the past, all of the furniture from the kitchen, including the television and settee, had been piled into the front room that Pat used as her bedroom, so that was what was arranged. We rolled up the rug in case people spilt drinks, and cleared a space in the middle of the room for dancing. There was also a table of party food, and all this in a room measuring about 14ft by 12ft!

'The boys can bring the drinks,' Mum said, 'otherwise it will cost too much.' We knew this wouldn't be a problem. I had met a boy called Patrick who was four years older than me, and he was bringing his friends. It was customary for boys to bring drinks to parties. It would usually be huge 7-pint cans of beer called 'Party Sevens' that had to be opened with a can opener and would often spray their contents all over the room and anyone standing close by. Occasionally they would bring a bottle of spirit or two, and there would sometimes be a few bottles of Babycham for the girls.

Margaret and I went over to the phone box to contact our friends, who all had phones in their homes by this time, and so it was arranged.

We bought black sugar paper from the shop across the road and cut out witchy shapes and stuck them on the walls with Sellotape. Mum helped us push the pineapple cubes and cheese onto the cocktail sticks.

'Look, we can stick them in the grapefruit to make hedge-hogs,' she suggested, really getting into the spirit of things now. Josie made vol-au-vents filled with cheese spread and fish paste, and we made some cheese sandwiches.

Aunty went around sniffing loudly. 'All this fuss,' she mumbled. 'Tell your Mother I'm going over to Aunty Mags's.'

I breathed a sigh of relief as she headed out the door. I always felt on edge when Aunty was around; she was still volatile, even in her sixties.

It was on that evening that Margaret met her future husband Tony.

The party was a huge success. We played records really loudly, and Mum came and knocked on the door to tell us to turn it down a bit.

'Oh don't worry about it,' Tony said, 'we can just make out we've done it.' He was always very confident and jokey.

Mum came back a few minutes later and knocked again. Tony pulled her into the room. 'Now then, let's have a dance.'

Across the other side of the room, I braced for an explosion.

'Oh you cheeky monkey!' Mum said, but to my utter amazement she was laughing as she did so.

By the time the party ended Tony had won her over, and Mum was on his side, encouraging Margaret to go out with him the following night.

Although she was only fifteen, Tony was obsessed by her. He was tall and dark and a real 'Jack the Lad' from Plaistow, East London, and most exciting of all he drove a Mini Cooper! He took her out almost every night, although Mum always insisted that we were home by 10.30 in the week and 11 p.m. at the weekend. Wednesday night we had to spend at home and tell our boyfriends that we were 'washing our hair'. They were the rules and woe betide us if we dared to break them, so Margaret never did. I, on the other hand, was a rebel. Perhaps it was Anne's influence, or just because I was the older sister, but I was always pushing the boundaries. Not long after Halloween I wanted to go to an 'all-night party' in London with Patrick. These were very trendy and most of my friends had been to one or more. It was considered a very grown-up thing to do.

Mum was adamant.

'No, definitely not,' she said, arms folded, when I asked her.

'But it's a Saturday night, and I don't have work in the morning,' I wheedled. 'Patrick will bring me home in the car, and I can lay in on Sunday.'

But there was no budging her. Mum had made up her mind.

'What if Margaret and Tony come?' I tried, thinking this might give me a chance.

Mum didn't answer for a few minutes. She went out into the scullery and put the kettle on. When she came back into the kitchen she made a suggestion. 'If Patrick and Tony dig up the front garden for Aunty and weed outside the front door, then you can go,' she announced. I couldn't believe my luck and went over to phone Patrick straight away. Of course he and Tony kept their side of the bargain and so did Mum, but it set a precedent. From then on our lives were all about bargaining. She used us as a kind of currency to get things done by the boys, which was rather inconvenient at times, but at least it meant that we got to do the things we wanted most of the time.

Marion and Marge were outraged.

'How come you're allowed to go out till past twelve? We had to be in at half nine at your age,' they complained, even though they were both married by this time. I just shrugged my shoulders and smirked.

Things didn't always work out so smoothly though. The one thing Mum didn't ever budge on was having one night in a week for supposed 'hair washing'.

'But I wash my hair every night!' I argued. I thought it was a stupid rule, more about Mum holding onto her control over us than anything else.

'I don't care what you do,' Mum shouted back. 'You're staying in tonight, and that's that!' and she stomped upstairs with a pile of dry washing. Normally I would have given in, but tonight Patrick wanted to take me out with his friend Jim and his girlfriend Sheena, who was one of my friends from school.

I phoned Patrick.

'I can't come tonight.'

'Why not?' he asked, with an edge to his voice. He was getting more and more fed up with having to placate Mum all the time just to be allowed to take me out.

'You know what she's like; she'll go mad if I don't stay in.'

He went quiet at the other end of the phone.

'Look, Jim and Sheena have taken a night off from their bar job to come to that new disco tonight. It will look really bad if we don't go.'

I loved dancing and in the 70s it was big business; every pub seemed to have a discotheque. They were all flashing lights, loud music and hormones.

I made a decision. 'Okay, I'll come. I don't know how, but just pick me up at eight. I'll be ready.'

Patrick was from an Irish Catholic family who also lived in Dagenham, although on another part of the Becontree estate. He was four years older than me and an apprentice printer. We had been going out for almost a year now. He was twenty-one and was quite tall, stocky and broad, with blue eyes and floppy brown hair. He was very ambitious, a real hard worker, and looking forward to completing his training. 'That's when I'll start earning really big money,' he would say, 'and I can buy you things like Tony buys Margaret.' The truth was, I didn't care at all about that, but Mum did.

'Have you seen that lovely gate bracelet that Tony bought Margaret?' she asked. 'Its 18-carat gold, you know.'

I knew all right, just like I knew about the ring, pendant, charm bracelet, watch and numerous other gifts that Tony could afford to shower on her.

'Tony's already finished his apprenticeship, Mum,' I would point out.

Still, Patrick felt it, and would say, 'One day, you'll see; one day soon I'll give you everything you ever wanted.'

Poor Patrick, he couldn't have got it more wrong.

After I'd rowed with Mum, Margaret would always ask: 'Why do you do it? Why don't you just get home on time / stay in one night a week / not wear your skirts so short? I don't get it.' Well, I didn't really know why either; I just felt that I was old enough to make up my own mind. I was almost eighteen so, as far as I was concerned, I could do what I liked.

That Wednesday I snuck upstairs to put on my make-up and get changed, while everyone was eating their dinner in front of the telly as usual. I put on my new white silky trouser suit. Margaret and I had a favourite shop near Barking Station that sold trendy clothes quite cheaply, and we also shopped in Petticoat Lane Market, so managed to stay fashionable on a very tight budget. I thought I was magnificent! I watched out of the bedroom window, and saw Patrick's little blue Ford Anglia pull up outside at 8 p.m. sharp. Flying downstairs, I burst out of the front door and shouted behind me, 'Bye Mum,' and I was gone. I knew I would have to pay but would worry about that later.

As I jumped in the car Patrick turned and said, 'Wow, you look gorgeous.' I was very slim now and I had lightened my long hair from mousey brown to a coppery blonde. Being attractive to boys was as intoxicating as having friends. In fact it made me feel even more powerful, and I loved to feel boys gazing after me when I walked into the room, even though I was still very innocent.

'What are you doing?' he laughed, as I wriggled out of my trousers. I pulled on my long white platform boots so that I could wear the tunic as an extremely short mini dress. I knew Mum would have gone ballistic if she had caught me!

'You can't go out like that,' he said, suddenly looking concerned.

'Why not? I wear hot pants!'

'That's different,' he said, looking more and more uncomfortable. 'Everyone will be looking at you.'

I smiled. That was exactly my intention.

27

My Secret Sister

We had the phone connected when I was about seventeen and it had been a revelation. No more going to the phone box! Aunty was wary of it at first but was getting more confident about using it to call Aunty Maggie and her other siblings. Mum loved it! She was always keen on gadgets of any kind and buying them on the 'never never' had contributed to the huge debts that she still carried around with her in that big black bag. Like a millstone around her neck it dragged her down and she never let it out of her sight.

Aunty was now retired from Plessey but had gone out and got herself a part-time job in Ilford in the café at Clark's bakery. Margaret and I would sometimes get the bus there on a Saturday to look at the shops.

'Come into me for your lunch,' Aunty would offer, and if we did she would always say, 'what do yer want? Welsh Rarebit?' and would scurry around and present it to us proudly.

'I don't want yer money,' she would say, waving us away, which was just as well as we never had any.

One day Josie and Pat were home from work, as they had both taken a few days holiday, and my brother Michael's middle daughter Sheila was staying at our house. She was only about eight, and loved her Nanny desperately, as did Michael's other two daughters, Vicky and Tricia. They would frequently argue about whose turn it was to come and stay, and the result was often that they all came. I dreaded those times. It wasn't because I didn't love them, just that our house was so crowded already that an additional three bodies made it almost unbearable, especially as they were lively young children. They had all inherited their mum and dad's good looks; they had Michael's colouring so their hair was blonde, but they had Isobel's huge eyes surrounded by dark thick lashes, although where hers were dark Spanish brown, theirs were a bright blue. It was Sheila who had won the fight this time and Pat and Josie were going to take her and Pongo to Valentines Park on the bus to feed the squirrels.

Just as they were getting ready to go, the phone started ringing. I was getting ready to go out with Patrick later that evening and Mum was in the middle of making tea, so Aunty, who had arrived home after her lunchtime shift, wandered out into the hall where the phone was perched on a little table and answered it. I ran down the stairs assuming it would be for me, and stopped short as I heard Aunty shouting into the receiver.

'Hello,' she said, putting on her posh voice. 'Who?' She was going quite deaf now and struggled to hear people on the telephone. 'Who is it? Oh my God!' A shocked smile sprang to her lips. 'Wait . . . Pat, it's your sister Sheila! Florrie, it's Sheila!'

Time stood still. No one moved. No one went towards Aunty in the hallway.

'Pat,' Aunty called again. 'It's your sister Sheila.' I caught sight of Josie and Pat who had been almost on the point of leaving, holding little Sheila's hand. She looked mystified, confused that there was another Sheila on the other end of the phone, and struggling to understand why everyone had suddenly stopped in their tracks.

Pat finally responded. 'I'm not talking to her.' She made to continue towards the door, but then Mum appeared from the scullery.

'It's Sheila,' repeated Aunty again, looking from one to the other, getting more and more agitated. Still no one moved to take the phone from Aunty; Mum bustled back into the scullery, so finally Aunty thrust the phone at Pat who listened for a while, occasionally making a mumbled response.

'I couldn't care less,' she said, 'we're not interested.' After another few minutes she hung the phone up and grabbed little Sheila's hand, muttering, 'Ron Coates is dead.'

With that they left, leaving Aunty, Mum and me lost for words until Mum said, 'Ask your Aunt if she wants a cup of tea.'

Aunty just sniffed, shook her head and, mumbling under her breath, turned away.

No one ever discussed that phone call. No one went to Ron Coates' funeral, no flowers were sent, no card of sympathy to Sheila, daughter, niece, sister, half-sister, was written. The hatred that his former wife and other children felt was still as raw as the day he had deserted them decades before.

It did stir Aunty's memories though. She started letting things slip out. Maybe it was because she was getting older and sometimes forgot the unwritten rules of secrecy, maybe she was being her mischievous self, or maybe she was starting to realise that we all had a right to know about our past. At first there were just occasional comments made when Mum was at the shops or had gone to see Michael.

'He was a terrible womaniser, yer know,' she would suddenly announce completely out of the blue. We would sit in silence. We knew that if we tried to pull any information from her she would shut up like a clam, but if we didn't respond it was almost as if she were talking to herself.

'She was big with Josie when 'e was messing around; 'e said Josie wasn't his,' she continued tutting. 'Wicked thing to say,' and then nothing. Margaret looked at me quizzically; we knew a little about our Mum's marriage to Ron Coates. We had even seen a faded sepia photo of their wedding day, Mum looking beautiful, young and happy, Ron Coates tall and thin and equally youthful, seemingly happy too. Their first three children, Sheila, Michael and Pat, had been born in quick succession with barely a year to eighteen months between them, and then she had got pregnant with Josie when Pat was just over a year old. They were still in their twenties and were soon going to have four children under six years old! Ron Coates left before Josie was born and that was when things for Mum must have started to spiral out of control.

The one thing Aunty would be drawn on was our sister Sheila. If Mum was out we would sometimes dare to broach the subject.

'Aunty, have you read any of Sheila's books?' we would ask, attempting innocence. We knew that she had because we had seen them in her bedroom, and we also knew that she was extremely proud that Sheila was a successful writer.

'Yes I 'ave,' she answered. 'They're a bit lovey-dovey for me, but she's a very clever girl, yer know.'

We chanced our luck. 'Why did she go and live with her dad?'

Aunty sniffed loudly. 'Make a cup of tea.'

I leapt up; perhaps she was in a talkative mood. I made the tea, and as Margaret and I sat with her in the kitchen we tried a bit more probing.

'Why don't Pat and Josie talk about Sheila?'

'Your mother was very good-looking, you know.' Aunty carried on sipping her tea. 'All the boys were after her. She could have had anyone, anyone, but she chose 'im.'

We stayed quiet.

'She should have ditched him as soon as 'e started mucking around. It was wicked what he did.' Sip, sip. 'Your poor sisters and little Michael, all of them crying they were, and hanging on to me and your Granny.' Sip sip. 'I still don't know why he did it.' Sip sip. 'Wicked.' There was a loud sniff and then silence.

We waited with baited breath.

'It wasn't her fault; she was only a child. Your mother went mad when she found out.' Sip, sip, sip.

What was she talking about? Who was only a child? Mum? Sheila?

'Who do you mean, Aunty?' I asked.

This was a mistake. Immediately she got up. 'I've got to do me garden,' she said, putting her tea down and picking up her little spade from the hallway as she went.

'Yer mother will be 'ome soon,' Aunty threw over her shoulder.

Margaret looked at me. 'What was she talking about?'

'I don't know, but I'm going to find out.'

'Oh yes, and just how are you going to do that?' Margaret asked.

'I don't know yet, but I am.'

I was sick of secrets, sick of mystery and sick of being treated as though I were still a child. I was eighteen now. It was my right to know, wasn't it?

Going to Work

I had been at work for over three years and had been employed in a variety of roles. I had been a receptionist, a telephonist, had worked in a typing pool, been a kind of secretary, and generally had a great time working to live rather than living to work. I had learnt early on that underachieving was a safe option. If you always took on jobs that were easy you could concentrate on the more important things in life like dancing, dating, wearing nice clothes and having fun with your friends. Margaret and I were still very close, and often went out in a foursome with our boyfriends, Tony and Patrick, and sometimes with bigger crowds as well. There always seemed to be someone who was having a party. It was the done thing to have a 'steady boyfriend' and it was also the done thing to get engaged and married young, so when Margaret told me that Tony wanted to get married I wasn't surprised.

'What do you think?' she asked me as we walked to the station, swishing her long black hair. We were both slim and pretty and loved fashionable clothes. We never had any difficulty attracting boys so were quite used to being called out to by any likely young man who fancied his chances.

'Do you like him?' I asked. I knew Margaret would listen to me, she always did, and I felt it was quite a responsibility.

'Yes I do like him; he's really kind and is always buying me presents.'

'Well if you want to get engaged, why don't you? You don't have to get married for a while.'

She nodded and smiled. I knew I had given her the answer she wanted, but wasn't sure if I had given her the answer she needed as a sixteen-year-old girl with her head in the clouds. They started saving for the wedding straight away, or rather Tony did. Margaret didn't earn enough to save and what spare cash she had went on clothes. Mum hadn't put up any objections to their marriage; in fact she seemed to be all in favour of it. They had saved up about £50, which at that time was quite a lot of money, in order to put a deposit down so that they could rent a flat of their own. Mum thought she might be able to help.

'I know this friend of Aunty Maggie's,' she told them one day. 'She wants to rent out the top floor of her house but she hasn't got the money to convert it.'

Tony's ears pricked up; he always liked the idea of a bargain.

'If you could give her the £50 she can put it towards having the building work done, and the money will act as your deposit.'

Margaret and Tony agreed and Tony went and withdrew the money and gave it to Mum. Three months later there was still no news of the flat. Tony asked Margaret about it.

'Has your Mum sorted that flat yet?' he asked.

She shook her head. 'No I don't think so.'

'Can you ask 'er about it then?' Tony suggested. After all, that £50 represented all of their savings.

But Margaret shook her head again emphatically. 'No, just be quiet and stop going on about it will you?'

Of course the flat never materialised and neither did the money. Tony complained to Margaret. 'I don't understand; where has the money gone then?'

Mum explained that the builder who was supposed to be doing the conversion had gone broke and had run off with this poor lady's life savings, including the £50 of theirs. Tony was angry and wanted to go round there to sort it out, but Margaret told him that it couldn't be helped, and so they started saving for the second time.

Margaret and I had never been short of male attention. One Christmas when I was working on the Thamesview Estate in an office attached to a small factory, I remember going to the local pub, the Volunteer, for an office party. The lads from the factory were all there as well, and by the end of the first hour I had a long row of drinks that had been bought for me lined up waiting for me to drink them. By the end of the afternoon I was so drunk I could hardly find my coat. I went back to the office and found my boss, Mrs Lovell, a kindly lady who was tall and elegant and had a beautiful speaking voice. I can still picture her amused look when I asked in a slurred voice, 'Ish it okay for me to go home now Mrs Lovel?' That was probably the sickest I have ever been!

Tony was a very jealous boyfriend, and wasn't happy that Margaret was also popular at work. She worked quite near to me at that time, and was the receptionist at a local firm. Her boss was considerably older than her, though probably still only about thirty, and was besotted by her. He was always asking her to go out with him, even though she told him she had a boyfriend. She was still only sixteen at the time and didn't have the sense not to tell Tony. Once she did, he went mad. 'What?' he roared. 'I'll kill him!'

Margaret realised she should have kept quiet, but it was too late. The next day when she got to work there was a note on her desk. She had been fired. Tony had got there first and had shared a few words with her boss!

Margaret and Tony were married when she was just seventeen and he was twenty-two. It seems insanely young now, but it wasn't particularly unusual for working-class families at that time. Mum and I went with Margaret to arrange for the registrar to attend the wedding. At that time Catholic priests were not allowed to conduct the legal side of weddings so the registrar had to be booked and would attend the church to complete the formalities in the side room.

As we arrived at the offices, Mum turned and said, 'You two wait there while I go in first and I'll call you when we're ready for you to come in.' Margaret duly sat and waited for the call and the process was concluded. This was a scene that was repeated prior to each of our weddings and it wasn't until after she'd died that we discovered what happened. Unbeknownst to us, she'd go in and claim that the bride's father died in Canada – a fairy-tale designed to explain our multiple names.

Margaret and Tony had a big Catholic white wedding but soon after she started to slip into a deep depression. It was this that prompted her to apply to become a trainee State Enrolled Nurse at Southend Hospital, which was to have a profound effect on the rest of her life, transforming her from a timid, compliant, shy young girl into a highly skilled and qualified nurse and a confident young woman.

29

New Opportunities

At the same time that Margaret was applying to become a nurse, I was getting restless and dissatisfied with my office job. I had lots of friends, a steady boyfriend, and a bit more money now, but I was bored. I decided I wanted to be a teacher without the slightest idea of what it would entail. I suppose I had always been the big sister to Margaret, always felt responsible for her, for calming things, keeping situations under control, but now that she was married it was as though a burden had been lifted and I wanted to spread my own wings. I had a friend at work that I often confided in and when I shared my thoughts she encouraged me.

'I think it's a great idea,' she said enthusiastically. 'You'd be a great teacher, I reckon.' I felt buoyed up by her confidence in me and when she came in to work a few days later with the name and address of a teacher training college that her cousin had gone to, I decided to take the plunge. It was called Digby Stuart and was in Roehampton, West London. It had the added advantage that it was only for women, as although I liked male attention I had gone to an all-girls convent school, so wasn't used to co-ed.

Patrick was sceptical. 'Why do you want to go all the way over there?' he asked. 'It'll take you at least an hour to get there each day.'

'I'm not going to live at home,' I told him. 'I'm going to stay at the college in the week.' That was not met with any enthusiasm from him, so when I found out shortly after applying that I was an O-level short of the admission requirements, he couldn't hide his pleasure.

'Oh well,' he said, 'it's probably for the best.' I was so angry inside – it might be best for him but it wasn't best for me! I decided then and there that whatever it took I was going to get into that college one day.

The following spring I applied to take my O-level Art as an external candidate at a local secondary school. It felt strange to be walking back into a school after all this time. When I arrived to sit the first paper, I had done no preparation whatsoever. It was art, wasn't it? And I had always been good at art. The lady in the office pointed me in the right direction and I walked into a big classroom with tables set up. I was wearing my white cheesecloth tunic top over my jeans and my blonde-streaked hair was hanging loose, so I walked in feeling nervous but suitably arty. There were examples of the pupils' work everywhere, paint pots laying around and a general buzz of creativity, and in the middle of it all stood a young man probably no more than four or five years older than me. He had long dark hair, kind eyes and stubble on his chin. To my surprise he was wearing a T-shirt and jeans. The teachers that I knew from my school days had been mostly nuns, and those that weren't were usually mature and sensibly dressed older women. We certainly were never taught by men, let alone attractive young men!

His eyes lit up when he saw me. 'Hi,' he said hurrying over to where I stood. 'Can I help?'

'I'm here to take the exam.'

With a broad smile he led me over to a vacant table. He was kindness itself and by the end of that first day I was beginning to feel more confident. There were three 'papers' to sit in all, arranged over three days. At the end of the third day, as I was about to leave, the young art teacher handed me a letter.

'Please read this when you get home,' he asked, smiling into my eyes. My heart gave a little skip and I smiled back. But as I walked out, I was painfully aware that I was wearing the solitaire diamond ring that Patrick had bought me when we had got engaged a few months before. It had been very expensive, but now that he had finished his apprenticeship money was more plentiful. We'd had a big party and my sister Pat had kissed me on the cheek for the first time ever. Patrick had been insistent that we got engaged when I told him I was determined to go to college. I suppose it was a kind of label saying 'Don't touch, already spoken for' but I didn't really mind too much. Usually I loved my ring, although it made my hand feel heavy. I liked all the gifts we had been given and being the centre of attention at the party; I even quite liked Patrick. We had got used to each other; he was kind and considerate and had accepted and been accepted by my family. His mum was a lovely, funny Irish lady, who I liked to believe was as fond of me as I was of her. Anyway Margaret had said it was about time we got engaged; after all she and Tony had already been married for over a year.

When I got back from that last exam I opened the letter.

'Dear Kathy,' it began. 'When I saw you for the first time a few weeks ago, I thought an angel had walked into my classroom.' I gulped as I continued to read. 'You looked so beautiful standing there, so scared and vulnerable, I just wanted to pick you up and run away with you, and look after you for ever. Please meet me so that we can talk. I promise nothing too heavy, just a chance to speak to you without a class full of kids watching us. Here is my phone number – please, please, please ring me . . .'

'What's that?' asked Mum, seeing me standing in the hallway with the letter in my hand.

I jumped. 'Oh nothing,' I said, looking guilty.

'Let me see then,' she continued. I held the letter downwards so she couldn't read it.

'No, it's nothing. Just embarrassing.'

'Don't be silly, let me have a look.' She held her hand out and I passed it to her reluctantly. She scanned the pages.

'Hmm, what are you going to do?'

'What do you mean? Nothing of course.'

'Why not? Don't you like him?' she asked.

'I'm engaged!' I retorted, shocked at her attitude.

'Yes, but you're not married are you?' she added, looking at me closer than she normally did.

I felt myself blushing; Mum never talked to us about this kind of thing. It felt uncomfortable and wrong but I didn't know why. I took the letter back and ran upstairs. I re-read it a few times that night before throwing it away, but I often thought of that young man and his kind eyes and wondered what might have happened if I had rung that number.

'I've got in!' I shouted, waving the official looking letter from West London. 'I've got a place for this September!' I was so excited. Mum looked over at me, and Pat smiled.

'That's good,' she said.

Mum added, 'You'd better ring your cousin Julie and tell her; she will be so pleased.'

When I had passed my Art O-level and re-applied for a place at the college I hadn't really thought through the implications if I was offered a place. Yes it was exciting, but the enormity of it suddenly dawned on me with a thud. I would be living away from home; I wouldn't be earning any money; I wouldn't know anyone; Patrick would be annoyed; but above all of these concerns was that same old doubt, that familiar feeling that I wouldn't be the same as the other girls, that I wouldn't be good enough.

Mum said we would need to apply for a grant, so we went together to Dagenham Town Hall at the Fiddlers to see about me getting one.

'Tie your hair back,' Mum said, when I came downstairs ready to go. 'You need to look smart and tidy.' I pulled my long blonde hair into a tight ponytail.

'Is this okay?' I asked, standing on my tiptoes trying to see in the mirror that hung on the kitchen wall. When Margaret and I were little, Mum, determined that we wouldn't be vain, would tell us, 'Don't look in the mirror, or you'll see the devil pop up behind you.'

It was years before I had the courage to look at my reflection, and even now, at nearly twenty, I almost expected to see horns, a hairy face and red eyes peering at me over my shoulder!

'Yes, that's better,' she said as we hurried out of the front door.

Aunty was in the garden as usual, fork in hand. The flowers that grew across the front of our house were magnificent now. There were several rose bushes that tumbled their way towards the privet hedge, and a mixture of colourful perennials that gave the impression of a cottage garden. Aunty had cultivated this completely on her own, and over the years it had become a solace for her when she needed to escape. She had gathered the plants together over time, not by buying them, but by bartering with friends and neighbours. When we were younger we would be embarrassed when she stopped outside a garden that she noticed looked particularly pretty and called out to ask if she could have a cutting. I don't believe anyone ever refused; in fact they would more often than not get into a deep, long-winded conversation about plants. She waved us off and turned back to her pruning.

The Town Hall was an imposing 1930s building – austere and forbidding. Mum wasn't daunted though; she knew how to handle authority. I, on the other hand, was feeling increasingly anxious. As we approached the reception desk, Mum handed the grant application to the man behind the desk.

'Oh yes,' he said, hardly looking up, 'you need to go down that corridor and take the first right through the double doors, then up the stairs and it's first door on the left.' He had lost me after the double doors, but Mum was sharp and led the way. When we got to the door marked 'Maintenance Grants', Mum turned to me.

'Now you wait out here while I go in and I'll call you if you need to come in.' I was more than happy to oblige and sat on a chair near the wall. Mum was in the room for about half an hour when the door opened.

'Come in for a moment please, Kathleen,' a kind-looking man asked.

'So, you are going to college to become a teacher?' he asked as he continued to write on the form in front of him. 'We just need you to sign this and then we can start the application process.'

As I bent to sign I noticed that the name on the form was Kathleen Stevens. I hesitated and glanced at Mum. 'What name should I sign?' I whispered to her. The man looked at me over the top of his glasses with his eyebrows raised.

'Your own name of course,' he said suspiciously.

I hesitated again, should I write Kathleen Coates or Kathleen Stevens? Mum just calmly indicated the place on the form and said quietly, 'There, that's where you sign, K Coates, on that line there.' I did as I was told and we handed the man the form and left for home, buzzing with anticipation.

30

The First Step

The day I was due to start college, Patrick drove me to Barking Station to get the District Line to Hammersmith. I had packed a small suitcase that Josie had lent to me; it was covered with stickers of all the exotic places she had visited. Josie had worked her way up over the years and now had an exciting job as the manager of the Travel Office at Plessey. It was an important position that carried with it power and influence, and her salary had increased to reflect the responsibility of her role. She got flown all over the world by airlines that were keen to secure business from such a big company, and stayed in hotels that had similar motives. It must have been bizarre for her to pack her bags and leave our increasingly dilapidated and dowdy council house in Dagenham and fly off to strange and unfamiliar destinations, often travelling business or first class, and all free of charge!

When Patrick kissed me goodbye, I noticed an unfamiliar look in his eyes. 'Are you sure you want to go?' he asked, holding on to me tightly.

'Yes – I think so,' I said, but actually I was starting to think that this wasn't such a good idea after all. I wanted to be a student, it felt like a trendy, modern thing to be, and I liked the excitement of the unknown, but as usual this was tempered with anxiety. As the train pulled out of the station I waved to Patrick, and watched as everything that was familiar and safe faded out of sight. I realised with a jolt that for the first time in my life I was going into the unknown alone.

The instructions for where to go were very easy to follow and I found my way to the bus garage in Hammersmith where I had to catch the 72 bus to Roehampton. I saw the buildings of the college and rang the bell to stop the bus, my stomach turning somersaults.

In the entrance hall of the college there were lots of young students, both male and female, milling about.

A lively young woman bustled up to me. 'Hello there,' she greeted me, smiling down at my case, 'and where have you flown in from?'

I looked at her, puzzled. 'Dagenham.'

'Oh,' she said, and I watched the interest leave her face. 'You have to sign in over there.' Pointing me in the direction of a wide table, she disappeared into the throng.

The registration process seemed endless. There were numerous queues to join, and a multitude of forms to fill in, and during that time I got chatting to some of the students around me.

'I thought this was an all-girls college,' I said to a girl called Gerry.

'It was, but this year they opened it up to boys as well. Great, isn't it?' She smiled mischievously. She was small and pretty with tightly curled blonde hair, and was from North London. We soon found that we had things in common. We both had steady boyfriends, and we were both slightly older than most of the other students as we had worked before coming to college. In a college that was predominantly full of affluent middle-class students, Gerry and I stuck out as coming from working-class backgrounds.

'What's your main subject?' she asked. Although we were training to be teachers we had to choose a main subject to study.

'Art,' I said confidently; it was the only thing that I felt I was any good at.

'Oh I'm geography, but we will be in lots of education lectures together.' So we palled up.

The college had found me approved lodgings in East Sheen, which was a short bus ride or long walk from the college. Most of the students that came from London or the surrounding areas were lodgers, as the campus rooms were reserved for those who came from further afield.

The first six weeks of college were set aside for an 'approach course', which was time given over to visiting each of the main subject departments to ensure that we had made the right choice. One of the first departments we went to was the drama department. The leading lecturer was a very old, very posh lady called Mrs Dalgliesh who terrified everyone. When Gerry and I bundled into the drama theatre we sat ourselves down towards the back. Neither of us were planning to do drama as a main subject so we thought we might be able to slide out before the end of the session. Mrs Dalgliesh stood up gracefully and with elegance.

'Good morning,' she enunciated perfectly with her rich deep voice. 'I know that you are all keen to hear about the endless possibilities that choosing drama can bring to you, but *what . . .* can you bring to drama?' She paused and looked around her dramatically, scanning our faces with her hooded eyes.

'You will all be familiar with our old friends Chekhov and Ibsen. The Greeks will no doubt conjure the ancient world for you, and some of you may even know Beckett and Pinter. Ah yes, I can see heads nodding.'

I didn't have a clue what or who she was talking about, so kept my eyes down. Being small had its advantages, I thought, as I slunk further into my chair.

Another lecturer stood up. He was a tall thin man with a smiling open face and a bright red cravat tied round his neck.

'Welcome,' he bellowed at us, throwing his voice at the walls so that it echoed back at us and extending his arms as though to enclose us in an embrace. 'Welcome my friends!' He introduced himself as Ted. 'Be prepared for a morning of exhilaration and creativity, my dear ones.'

He then proceeded to give us a tour of the drama department facilities including the green room, the stage, the lighting and sound box, the dressing rooms, and last but not least the room where the props were made. This was the place that I wanted to be! I was swept away by the electricity in the air, the sheer variety of experiences and the excitement of performance! Then I came back to earth with a bump. Mrs Dalgliesh was now addressing us again.

'You have tasted the intoxicating nectar that is drama and all that it could be for you but first . . .' (long pause) 'first we must see what you can offer the dramatic arts!'

We were handed out a copy of a play I had never heard of, 'A Doll's House' by Ibsen. We were given a few minutes to acquaint ourselves with the play and were then to read from it.

I felt prickles of sweat forming on the back of my neck, and my hands became clammy. Although I used to love reading aloud to Margaret, I hated public speaking. My eyes swam over the words as I desperately tried to make sense of them, and I listened with torment as one after the other we were asked to read Nora or Torvald.

Before long it was my turn. I stood as the others had done and took a deep breath. Pushing aside my nerves, I thought about Nora. Nora the wife, the doll, the caged songbird, the little squirrel. Nora the deceiver, the forger, the desperate and suicidal woman, and all I could think of was Mum and I read like I had never read before, with all of my emotion, all of my passion, and all of my suppressed anger stinging my lips.

When I stopped and looked up from the text all eyes were riveted on me and there was a hushed silence. I saw Liz sitting with her mouth open, and Gerry looking at me as though I were a stranger as Mrs Dalgliesh walked towards me, a look of rapture on her face.

'Oh my dear,' she whispered, 'that was wonderful,' and she reached over to hug me. I signed up for drama as my main subject there and then, leaving the safety of the art department to others.

Throughout my first year, every Friday afternoon I would leave college and my new life behind, get the 72 bus to Hammersmith station and travel back to Dagenham. It was a strange kind of dual existence. Patrick and I were engaged and planning a wedding while I was in Dagenham, and in Roehampton I was the young education and drama student, seduced by the theatre in all its guises. I loved it all, acting, producing, make-up, choreography, set design, lighting and sound, everything! I was also fascinated to be learning about learning, how children's minds and bodies develop, and what I as a teacher could do to help them. I walked around in a bright haze while I was away, only to return to the grim reality of 1970s Dagenham on my return. Mum was still desperately in debt despite Josie and Pat repeatedly giving her money to pay her 'callers' off. Within a few months more new things would surreptitiously appear and have to be paid for.

It was towards the end of my first year at college that things came to a head.

31

A Clean Slate

Josie made a decision. She wanted to help Mum, but first she needed to know how much was owed. She took a morning off work to try to get to the bottom of it.

'Mum, we have got to sort out this money,' she started. 'I'm going to pay off your callers. I'm sick of this constant worry and pressure.'

Mum turned to her and a nervous look swept across her face as though she knew what was coming next.

'But I need to know exactly how much you owe and who to.'

Mum looked away. 'Well, I'm not sure really,' she mumbled, busying herself by tidying around. 'Not much now.'

'Okay, if you give me all of your cards I'll work it out,' Josie offered.

'No no, that's okay. I think it's about £100.'

Although that was a considerable amount of money Josie wasn't stupid and wasn't going to be fobbed off. She knew Mum well and also knew not to believe her where money was concerned.

'I'm going to do this, Mum,' she insisted, 'and I'm going to do it once and for all, so you might as well hand over the cards to me now.'

Mum looked at her for a moment or two and then turned to me. 'You go and tidy upstairs while I talk to your sister.'

I did as I was asked and left them to it. There were no raised voices, and so I guessed that Mum had acquiesced. Josie was as stubborn as Mum was, and almost as scary when she wanted to be! She never told us how much she had to pay, but I know it took her over a year, using every spare penny she had, to finish them all completely. The relief when the last payment was handed over was enormous. Josie sent me over to the bakers to get half a dozen Belgian buns that day, delicious doughy concoctions filled with dried fruit and topped with a snowy white swirl of icing.

'Here's to the end of the tally men!' she said, raising her cup of tea and smiling. It was a celebration of determined endeavour, and Josie was justifiably proud of herself! As we ate the buns with steaming mugs of tea, there was a sense of a new era beginning.

Shortly after that momentous day, Mum got a letter from Marge and Ron who were now living in Australia close to Mary and Dave. 'Oh Marge is going to have another baby,' she read out to us. 'It's due in September.' Mum got a wistful look on her face. It was many years now since Mary had emigrated, and now that Marge had joined her it must have been sad for Mum, losing them both like that. Josie had joined Mum up to a special club for families of people who had emigrated as '£10 Poms', designed to help them save enough money to plan a visit. The cost seemed prohibitive to us, but we knew that Mum still dreamed about going to see her Australian grandchildren.

'I think I'll send her something for the baby,' Mum said, starting to smile. I didn't really give it much thought, but shortly after a large parcel appeared wrapped in brown paper.

'Oh. What's this?' I asked Mum. It had been pushed into my side of the dressing table in the bedroom she and I still shared when I was home from college.

'It's just something for Marge's new baby,' Mum answered casually, not meeting my eyes.

A niggling thought crept into my head. 'Mum, where did you get it from?'

She bustled out of the room. 'Oh I got it in Ilford. In Bodgers, I think it was.'

I was distracted at that moment by the phone ringing. It was my school friend Anne. She was off this weekend and wanted to know if Patrick and I would like to come over for a meal at her flat at Gants Hill. Like Margaret, Anne had just finished her nurse training at Barking Hospital. She had been going out with Tony V for a while now. He was such a sunny person, and seemed to suit Anne perfectly. He had been a merchant sailor when they first met, but Anne had encouraged him to become a fireman and that was what he did now. He was a handsome lad and had a great sense of humour. We always had fun when we went out in a foursome, so I readily agreed. By the time Pat and Josie got home that evening from work I had completely forgotten about the parcel.

At 5.25 p.m. exactly Mum put the kettle on, with the usual words, 'Oh nearly time for the girls to come home,' and bustled around in the scullery, preparing dinner. Aunty was sitting in the opposite corner to Mum where she always sat, and was reading *Bleak House*. She loved Dickens, and had a full set upstairs in her room, and would read them in rotation. I couldn't tell you how many times she'd read each book.

'Ask your aunt if she wants peas,' Mum called into the kitchen where we sat. Aunty was quite deaf now and hadn't heard, so I went and stood in front of her.

'Aunty, do you want peas?' I asked.

She looked up. 'What?'

'Do you want peas?' I tried again, louder this time.

'Aye? Peas? Oh yes, I'll 'ave a few.'

As I went to tell Mum Aunty's reply, I heard Pat and Josie arrive at the front door. Mum seemed agitated; it was quite warm in the scullery, and she seemed flustered, spilling some gravy.

'Oh damn!' she muttered crossly.

The girls took off their coats and made their way into the kitchen and Mum asked me to take the tea in.

There was a loud knock at the door.

Mum hurried to answer it, shouting out, 'It's just the man for the football money.' She still did the pools every week and a man collected the money every fortnight.

Pat and Josie were drinking their tea when Aunty put her book down and sniffed. 'It ain't football week; 'e came last Monday.'

Pat and Josie exchanged looks, and Josie got up and went towards the door. Mum was still talking to the man who stood there. We heard raised voices, the loudest of which was Josie's. I moved nearer the door so that I could hear what was going on and heard Mum saying, 'But it isn't much, only 10 shillings a week, and I can easily afford that,' and then Josie's reply, deep, clear, firm and menacing.

'I am telling you now, once and for all, that if you sell my mother one more thing you will never be paid for it. I have spent the last year clearing her debts and I don't intend to do it again. How much does she owe for it?'

A man's voice mumbled a reply and I jumped out of the way as Josie barged into the room, went to her handbag and took out a cheque book. She went back out into the hallway and shortly after we heard the door slam shut with a bang. Josie came back into the kitchen, her face red with anger and Mum turned back to the dinner. No one mentioned the incident, but Mum never got into debt again.

32

Mum's Job

I was luckier than many of my fellow students because I had office skills and experience that enabled me to get a holiday job in the city. This was a stroke of luck as despite having a full grant, money was still tight. Pat and Jo gave me £5 a month between them, which helped tremendously, but there always seemed to be another book to buy or play to see. Patrick always paid for me to go out when I was home, and even occasionally came up to East Sheen and took me out there, but my fare back to Dagenham every weekend made a hole in my finances, as did the teaching resources we needed to buy.

I managed to get temping work through an agency and was earning a reasonable amount of money. At the end of my first week I offered Mum some 'keep' money.

'No, I don't need it now,' she said proudly.

I was puzzled. 'Are you sure?'

'Definitely – I'm going to get a job.'

I thought I had misheard. 'Pardon? You're getting a job?' Mum hadn't worked outside the home since I was born, to my knowledge.

'Yes, I've applied for a job as a cook,' she offered settling herself down in her chair and lighting her cigarette. She inhaled deeply.

'Mum, no one is going to give you a job as a cook. You've never had a job before.' Mum was going to be sixty at the end of July but I didn't mention that.

'Don't be daft,' she said crossly, 'I worked for years before you were born. I was a silver-service waitress in London, you know.'

I did know, as it happened, because throughout our childhood she had conjured up an exciting life of restaurants and clubs in London, which Margaret and I would always try to persuade her to talk more about.

'But that was years ago,' I said more gently now, realising that I had upset her.

'All right, we'll see then.'

The conversation was closed.

When Pat and Josie arrived home later that evening they looked tired. I knew even then that they had given up their lives to make sure that we younger ones were safe, and to try to make sure that we had the chances that they had missed out on.

The next day I found another piece of the puzzle, although the jigsaw of my life was still far from complete.

It was Tuesday morning and my sisters had all left for work. Margaret was coming over to see me later that morning as she had a couple of days off. I knew she was really enjoying her nurses' training, but I also knew that she had to work long hours and that it was very hard work, so wasn't surprised to see her arrive with her pale skin looking even whiter than normal and her big brown eyes red with tiredness.

'What's wrong?' I asked as I opened the door to her.

'Something really embarrassing happened yesterday,' she whispered as she came in to the kitchen and sat herself down. 'Where's Mum?'

'You're not going to believe this,' I replied. 'She's got an interview!'

'What?'

'She's got an interview!' I repeated. 'In London – she's applied to be a cook for London Transport.'

Margaret just looked at me incredulously. 'But she's not a cook.'

'I know,' I said, 'but you know what she's like – she'll be able to convince them, I bet.'

Margaret shook her head in disbelief. 'But how will she manage it? All that travelling?'

'Do you want a cup of tea?' I went out to the scullery to put the kettle on. Margaret followed me, and stood playing with her long black hair as I switched on the gas.

'It was awful yesterday,' she started, chewing her lip. 'All of us new trainees had to go the classroom together for registration; there must have been about twenty-five of us, all sitting there, when our tutor came in.'

I listened as I poured the boiling water into the old stained tin teapot that we seemed to have had forever.

'She was going through our documents, and when she came to me she called out in a really loud voice "Margaret Butler?" And as I raised my hand she looked at me and said, "Oh yes, Margaret, can you please just explain why it is that you have two different maiden names?" Well I nearly died! I didn't know what to say, and just stammered that I wasn't sure – and then everyone was looking at me as if I were an idiot or something. It was so embarrassing!'

As we took our tea back into the kitchen, I was thinking hard. This was madness. We were both adults. Margaret was a married woman, for goodness' sake! And still we didn't know why we had different names, who our father was, and why no one ever mentioned our secret sister!

'Right, I think it's about time that we started asking some questions,' I said, sounding more confident than I really felt.

'You're not going to ask Mum?' said Margaret fearfully.

'No of course not, but perhaps we can try to find out from someone else.'

'But who?'

I paused. There had to be someone who would talk to us as adults; someone who would know the secrets. We sometimes snatched at nuggets of information from Aunty when she was in the mood, but she always stopped short of giving us complete answers. Even when we had directly asked her what she knew about our father, she had just sniffed loudly and said, 'I can't tell yer about your father without telling you about yer mother,' and then walked out of the room leaving us as ignorant as before.

But as I sat sipping my tea with Margaret I suddenly realised there was someone. It was so obvious now; there was someone who might be persuaded to tell us about our past, someone whose own mum, our dear Aunty Maggie, would have certainly been in our Mum's confidence – my godmother and cousin, Julie.

33

The Children's Home

Mum was going to be out for the whole day because she had to go to Baker Street for her interview, so I phoned up Marion and begged her to drive us over for a visit. As usual Julie was incredibly welcoming, and made a wonderful spread for our lunch. We managed to eat, although inside my stomach was flipping around. Sitting listening to Marion and Julie catching up, I knew that if I didn't take the plunge soon, I'd run out of time to accomplish my mission.

Julie asked me how college was.

'Oh it's really good. But, hard work.'

'And are you managing okay with money?'

'Oh yes – there's the grant, and Pat and Jo are so kind, helping out with everything.' I paused and then launched in. 'I wish Pat and Jo had been able to go to college or something; they're both miles cleverer than I am. Why do you think they didn't? Was it just the money?'

Julie looked at me and then at Marion. 'No, not only that,' she replied cautiously.

'What then?'

Julie paused, and was obviously considering whether or not she should continue, so I prompted her. 'We really want to know about what happened when they were little. Aunty has told us some things about their dad, Coates, and how wicked he was, but we'd like to hear what you know.'

Julie looked down. 'Hmmm, well I don't know whether he was wicked – not really. I was only the same age as Pat so I don't remember him much at all. But I do know what my mum told me.'

I sat still, almost afraid to move in case I broke the spell.

'They were only little. I think Pat was about six so that would make Michael seven, Sheila eight and poor little Josie only about four.'

I watched Marion and Margaret. We were all three of us sitting on the edge of our seats. Three grown women waiting to hear about the past, hoping desperately that it would help us to understand more about ourselves.

Julie went on. 'It was winter but probably wasn't very late, because Mum remembers that Dad wasn't home from work, but it was dark when the phone rang. I remember Mum talking to Dad about it once he got in. Aunty Edie had called from the phone box. She was really upset, almost hysterical.'

I was almost holding my breath. Marion lent nearer to me and put her hand on my shoulder. Margaret was sitting quite still but her big eyes were tightly fixed on Julie.

'There were two of them apparently. One was a policeman the other was a woman, probably from the social, I suppose. The children didn't want to go with them.'

'Go with them where?' I interjected and immediately regretted my interruption. I had learnt by now that the best way to get information was to wait for it to tumble from a person's mouth rather than trying to pull it out forcibly.

But this wasn't Aunty talking now, or Pat or Josie, and this wasn't Valence Avenue, so Julie continued.

'To the children's home.'

'Children's home? But why? Where was Mum?'

'I don't know the answer to that. I'm sorry but all I know is what my mum told me. She just kept saying to my dad, "I should have taken them; I should have taken them," over and over as he was trying to comfort her.

'They were all crying – the children were all crying and clinging on to Edie,' Mum told him. Apparently Aunty Edie swore at the policeman and at the woman. She shouted at them and tried to hang on to the children but the policeman held her arms down and kept apologising, but they were adamant that they had no choice. It was the law, they said, it was the law, as if that made it all right.

'The policeman got upset, but it wasn't really his fault. He couldn't have let them stay there, you see.'

'But why not?' asked Marion.

'Because their father had told them, told the social, that your mum wasn't there, and that Aunty Edie was out at work all day and that Granny was an old woman in her seventies. She was struggling to look after them you see, five little children all under eight, it was just too much.'

She stopped and looked round at the three of us. 'You didn't know any of this did you?' she asked, already guessing the answer.

We shook our heads and Marion said, 'No – we didn't know.'

'Julie,' I started warily. 'Do you know anything about our dad?'

Julie swivelled round to meet my eyes. Did I see pity there? Or was it just kindness? She paused before answering slowly, 'Whose dad?'

I looked at Marion and then at Margaret. 'Our dad,' I repeated.

'Do you mean yours or Marion's?'

'Stevens,' I replied, feeling more and more confused. Julie looked away towards the window. She had always been so close to Pat that I wonder if she felt maybe she was betraying too many secrets. She waited for a moment and then went on.

'Well Reg Stevens was a good man according to my mum; that's all I know. He was good to your mum, but just whose dad he was, I really can't say.'

'Can't say because you don't know or can't say because you don't want to tell us?' I asked, starting to muster some courage.

'Mum and Dad will be home any minute,' Julie murmured. Walking into her little kitchen she put on the kettle, and we knew it was time to go. Marion had to get back for the children anyway and Julie was determined to say no more.

On the way home there was a deep silence at first as we all tried to come to terms with what we had heard. It had been a strange day and we were left with more unanswered questions than before.

By the time we got home Mum was already back from London.

'Well, aren't you going to ask how I got on?'

With all that had happened today, Mum's first interview for at least twenty years had gone completely out of my mind. My hand flew to my mouth. 'Oh yes, yes, of course I am. What happened?'

'I am now the head cook at the Baker Street depot of London Transport,' she said proudly, sitting herself down in her worn old chair and kicking off her shoes. Margaret and I looked at each other in disbelief.

After all these years our mum could still manage to completely shock and surprise us! And then we both started laughing, almost hysterically, as Mum looked on completely bemused.

34

The Runaway Train

I would be having a big Catholic wedding as had all my siblings before me. The church and the hall for the wedding breakfast and regulation disco in the evening were booked for July at the end of my second year at teacher training college; I would be just twenty-one. For my final year I would continue my course as a married woman and have to commute into college daily by train and bus, which would probably take at least an hour and a half each way.

When I was at college it was as though I changed into a different person, and the two halves of my life were kept firmly apart. I still went home to Dagenham almost every weekend, and would resume my role as fiancée, daughter and sister, while at college I was a producer, actor, make-up artist and most importantly of all, soon-to-be teacher. The more I learnt about children, and the impact of external forces during their most formative years, the more I started to compare this with my own childhood. I wanted to know more. I started to have trouble sleeping and began to have vivid dreams that I didn't under-stand, and would wake up in a sweat, shivering.

Since our visit to Julie we'd got stuck, and hadn't been able to find anything else out about our past. Margaret was living in Canvey Island with Tony and was concentrating on her final exams, and my life was pulled between studying and wedding preparations. I was still desperate to know more about my child-hood, but just didn't seem to have the energy or time to continue to ask the questions. Some of the memories Margaret and I shared we never spoke about and they got buried in the baggage of day-to-day living. I tried to convince myself that it was easier that way, but inside I had a gnawing hunger to know more.

As the end of my second year approached the reality of the wedding started to dawn on me. I couldn't talk to anyone really. Margaret was desperate for me to be married like her, Anne's boyfriend Tony was great friends with Patrick, my friends at college all thought it was terribly grown-up and exciting, and Patrick's family were over the moon. It was only me that knew about my growing dread of being trapped. I kept remembering the first play I had read at college: Ibsen's 'A Doll's House', and how Nora's husband treated her, the heroine, almost as a pet. I couldn't help comparing the relationship I had with Patrick to theirs. He even had a pet name for me, 'Boo Boo', that made me cringe, but I tried desperately to be the girl he wanted me to be.

There was one girl called Rachael who was in the drama department too. She was slightly older than me and was considered to be very mature and intellectual. We happened to be travelling on the bus to Hammersmith station one Friday, and she started to ask me about the wedding.

'Are you all ready now?' she asked, making small talk. I guessed that weddings weren't on Rachael's agenda really, but she was a pleasant, friendly girl.

'Yes, everything is sorted out, I think,' I responded drearily.

'Well you don't sound very happy about it.' She smiled. 'Wedding nerves?'

'Mmm, I guess so.' I looked out of the window as the sun shone down hotly. 1976 had been the hottest summer on record so far, and the bus was very stuffy.

'Are you going on honeymoon?' she asked. I just wanted her to stop talking, or at least I wanted her to stop talking about the wedding. I could feel tears beginning to sting my eyes and didn't want to embarrass both of us on a crowded number 72 bus!

'Yes, we've booked two weeks in the Canary Islands.'

She started to laugh. 'The Canary Islands! That's going to be even hotter than here!'

I returned a watery smile. 'Mmm, I know.'

What I wanted to tell her was that I had a recurring dream that I would wake up in the sunshine and realise that I was

married and that my life was over. I wanted to tell her I was
terrified of being trapped, that I didn't know what love was, who
Patrick was and most importantly I didn't know yet who I was!
But I didn't know Rachael well enough to say those things to
her. She fumbled with her bag and then looked at me directly in
the eyes. I don't know what she saw there but it prompted her to
say in a slow and serious voice, 'You're really not happy about all
of this are you?'

I shook my head, and then the tears did begin to slide down
my cheeks. I left them there unchecked and looked away.

'Kath, you've got to do something!' she said, putting her arm
around my shoulder.

I was aware that other people on the bus were beginning to
look, so I quickly brushed my tears away and tried to smile. 'But
don't you see, I can't do anything? I'm trapped.'

'You're not trapped! No one can make you get married if you
don't want to.'

I tried to explain. 'It's like I'm on a train speeding out of
control, and the passengers are on board. The reception is
booked, dresses are bought, honeymoon booked and, worst of
all, everyone is really looking forward to a big Irish wedding –
everyone but me! And if I derail the train to stop it there will be
a massive crash, it will just leave too many casualties – don't you
see?'

She shrugged her shoulders. 'You're insane. Don't be bullied
into this.'

I knew she thought I was weak and probably stupid as well,
and I suppose I was, but I was used to looking after people,
calming conflicts not making them, and the last thing I wanted
to do at that moment was to cause an almighty explosion. No,
there was no choice. I would be getting married at the end of
July.

When I got home Mum was in the scullery washing up. We
had a fridge now and although it was very old it worked beautifully. Aunty Maggie had donated it to us when they moved to
Bishop's Stortford. It was a 1930s design so took up a lot of

space but the benefits it brought far outweighed the disadvantages. I was desperate for a cold drink so went straight into the tiny scullery to see if the new addition could provide one.

Mum looked up. 'Oh, you're earlier than I expected,' she said, smiling.

'So are you,' I answered, surprised to see her home from her cook's job in London.

'Oh Friday is POETS day.'

'What's that then?'

'POETS day!' she repeated, pleased that she had learnt a new saying from her colleagues. 'Push Off Early, Tomorrow's Saturday!'

She seemed really happy in this new job and had surprised the whole family, firstly by actually getting the job , and secondly by going to work three days a week, leaving home at about 5 a.m. and not usually returning until about 6.30 p.m. She was earning lots of money as well, and for the first time that I could remember she looked really, genuinely happy. How could I spoil that new state of happiness by turning everything on its head? No, I would just have to stick it out. I had got myself into this mess and now I would just have to put up with it. It wasn't that I didn't like Patrick or that he wasn't a really nice young man, but I just wasn't ready to be the person he needed me to be, and I wasn't sure that I ever would be.

'I've got my new hat for the wedding,' she said proudly. 'Josie got it for me in Ilford. It's a really good one – not cheap.' She dried her hands on her apron and led me into the kitchen. 'Look, here it is.' She plucked out a pretty blue hat covered with tight fabric flowers, and pulled it on to her head. 'What do you think?'

She looked so sweet. Although she was quite overweight and her hair was silvery white and rather thin, she still had a rosy bloom to her complexion, and bright twinkling eyes. She had kept her lovely soft skin and there were very few wrinkles on her face. She had some gentle laughter lines, but they suited her and she was sixty-one after all.

'Mum, you look gorgeous,' I smiled, and she smiled back and put the hat away in its bag, humming 'I'll Be Loving You Always' to herself. I walked upstairs to the bedroom we shared, and saw my dress hanging on the wardrobe door covered in plastic. My heart gave a lurch. At college I loved dressing up, I loved acting and becoming a different person from the real me, loved hiding behind the mask of theatre. On my wedding day in just a few weeks' time, I was going to have to give the best performance of my life.

35

My Wedding

The end of term and my second year at college arrived. We had a party to say goodbye to Mrs Dalgliesh, who was retiring. Typically of the drama department it was to be a 'Chekhovian moment' by the lake in the grounds of the college. The sun had shone brilliantly all day, and although it was 6 p.m. by the time we gathered together, it was a magnificent evening of soft breezes skimming off the lake, dragging the aroma of the musk roses and honeysuckle towards us as the bees droned soothingly. The trees were shaking their leaves gently, offering some welcome shade. I closed my eyes for a moment and imagined I was far away on my own and could do whatever I wanted, with no wedding, no honeymoon and no life mapped out in front of me. Then one of the other girls called out and the spell was broken. I came back to reality with a jolt.

I should have been happy, I reminded myself. My end of term production piece had been really successful. Our task had been to stage an excerpt from one of the plays we had read. We not only had to produce it but also had to cast it, set the scenes and make the props, light it and rehearse it. It was a tough challenge, but we had all relished it. I had decided on a scene from 'Waiting for Godot' by Samuel Beckett. There was something about the bizarre nature of the play, the strange conversations that the characters trapped themselves into, the hopelessness of their condition, that appealed to me. I decided to cast the characters of Vladimir and Estragon as clowns, and two of my fellow drama students consented to play them. They were brilliant; they listened to my every instruction, discussed it all with me and basically did a fantastic job. It was mainly down to their amazing interpretation that I was awarded an A−. *Why can't life just go on like this?* I thought. *Why does it have to change?*

As the term ended I collected my things together, packed my case and returned home to Dagenham, where preparations for the wedding were at full throttle.

'Aunty will press your dress,' Mum said. This had become a tradition in the family. 'Your aunt used to iron for the Prince of Wales,' Mum would tell us time and time again. 'The collars were terrible to press; she had to dip them in starch to make them stand up stiffly.' So Aunty would always be given the chore of pressing our wedding dresses before the big day. It was strange really because it was just about the only household job she ever did. When I was a child I remember Aunty always being placated, always being served dinner first, and having to walk round on tiptoe when she was home in case we disturbed or upset her. As she went to work every day, she was never expected to do any housework or cooking. As a matter of fact she was a terrible cook, although she did sometimes have a go. Bacon sandwiches were her speciality, and she would fry the bacon up, swimming in melted lard, until it was crispy and then slap it into the middle of two doorsteps of white bread and say, 'There you are. Yum yum, piggy's bum.' She had been known to try to cook a suet pudding but although we had eaten it because we were so hungry it had lain in our stomachs for ages, sitting there like a lead weight.

Apart from 'cooking', Aunty would occasionally have a bleaching frenzy. She would come home from work carrying bottles of the stuff, and then proceed to slosh it everywhere until the whole house smelt like a swimming pool.

'This place is filthy,' she would shout, bustling round with her bottles and cloths. 'We'll all be down with the fever!'

We came to dread the stinging smell that choked our throats and burned our nostrils which followed in her wake.

Now Aunty was nearing seventy and starting to slow down. She could still have an outburst of temper if provoked, but was more mellow now, so much so that Margaret and I thought she might just respond to a little probing. The week before the wedding, Mum had gone to work and so Tony agreed to drop Margaret off at our house in the morning. Aunty was already out in the garden even though it was early, and waved to Margaret as she got out of the little Mini.

''Ello Margaret,' she called affectionately, 'I'll make you a cup of tea.' She put down her spade and followed Margaret into the house. 'Kathleen, your sister's here,' she called out, and I came downstairs, trying to formulate a plan.

'I'll make the tea, Aunty,' I offered. Aunty made awful tea, and anyway I wanted to get her in a good mood. She sat down with Margaret in the kitchen and I could hear them chatting.

'Do you want some bacon? I'll make you a bacon sandwich,' she offered. 'No? What about some toast and jam then? Nothing? Look at you, all skin and bone; no wonder if you don't eat.'

I brought the tea in.

'Just like when you were little, an 'am bone with a frill on, that's what you are,' she joked. Margaret and I sat with Aunty as she drank her tea. Sip sip.

'Do you want to go and get a cake from the baker's?' she continued. 'Here, take some money.' She rummaged in her bag.

'No, it's okay Aunty. We don't want any cake, thank you.'

'I can leave me money around now, you know,' she continued. 'If I put this five pounds on the mantelpiece it would still be there tomorrow,' she continued, apparently amazed at this fact. Poor Aunty – we could only guess at the things she had put up with from Mum over the years.

'Your mother's got plenty of money now. Ah, but she's had an 'ard life, yer know.' She carried on drinking her tea: sip sip. We didn't answer; we knew the rules well.

'You might fink she's bad, but she only ever did what she did for you children.'

Aunty lapsed into silence, deep in thought. Margaret and I sat waiting when suddenly she continued. 'Your Uncle John loved 'er, you know. She was wrong to take advantage like that, and he never really forgave her.' Aunty sniffed loudly and continued. 'Ah well, it's a long time ago now and I suppose she didn't know what else to do.' We exchanged glances – what was all this about?

'Aunty Betty is coming to the wedding you know, and she's bringing Dot and George.' Aunty Betty was our Uncle John's widow, and we hadn't seen her since the last wedding. They had lived in Birmingham for the whole of my life, and had brought up their children there, but both Dot and George, our cousins, had visited on occasions. George was a lovely, funny young man, who had bought me a toy sewing machine once when he had arrived unexpectedly and found that it was my birthday.

Aunty now sat without saying another word and finished her tea. Sensing that she was about to go back to her garden I decided to take a chance.

'Aunty, what did she do to Uncle John?'

Aunty got up without meeting our eyes, sniffed loudly and said, 'The Lord makes work for idle hands.' Putting her cup down loudly on the table, she went back out of the front door to her precious garden.

On the morning of my wedding day I got up and went over to the hairdressers to have my hair styled with my sister Margaret. We were both going to wear our long hair loose. I had a little 'Juliet' cap with a beautiful lace veil, and my dress was a simple Empire line with scalloped, almost medieval, sleeves that draped gracefully. It was a delicate dress that suited my tiny frame, and I felt very special as I walked down the stairs out into the sunlight on my brother Michael's arm. It was the tradition at that time for all the neighbours to come out to their gates and see the bride off, and I felt a bit shy as we made our way to the shiny black car. I didn't say anything on the short journey to church, but my insides were twisted in knots. The sun was hot and the church felt cool and calming as I walked down the aisle to become a married woman. The church was full to bursting, and every head turned as I made my way towards the altar, clutching a bouquet of Madonna lilies, just like my mum had many years before me in this very same church. A shiver ran down my spine, despite the heat, and I looked to where Patrick waited, with his smart new suit and freshly cut hair, little knowing that the vows we were about to make would last for such a short time.

36

The First Cracks Appearing

After we got back from honeymoon, we set up home in Rainham. It was a sweet little house that was built at the turn of the century, with a long strip of garden at the back. Unfortunately it was perched right on the side of the A13, a busy dirty road running through Dagenham towards Ford's, and lorries thundered past relentlessly night and day.

Mum had been over before we got back, and had made sure that it was clean and dust free, even putting a bunch of flowers on the table. It was a lovely thought, and brightened my mood considerably. The weather in the Canary Islands had been intolerably hot, and I was keen to get back to England.

At that moment the phone rang. It was my school friend Anne, calling to tell me that she and her boyfriend had split up.

'Oh no! When did that happen?'

I could hear her hesitate. 'Actually, just before the wedding. We didn't want to tell you because we didn't want to spoil your day. So we just played along.'

As I tried my best to cheer her up, it was difficult to ignore the sick feeling of foreboding in my stomach.

My last year at college was the hardest. Being married was difficult in so many unexpected ways. Patrick didn't seem to realise that college was tough, especially in the final year. As a drama student, I was often working into the night and sometimes had to sleep on a friend's floor as it was too late to travel back to Rainham. Patrick was working nights for much of the time, and his job was very demanding, so he came home exhausted, slept and then got up expecting a cooked meal and a sympathetic ear.

What he got for much of the time was either a solitary evening or a distracted young wife whose thoughts were still in Roehampton, either in the drama theatre or in the education classes. I knew I was being unfair, but I also knew that this was important to me. I had my final exams soon and I was determined to pass.

Things struggled along, but we started to argue over trivial things. What we had both failed to realise was that we had grown in different directions. Just seeing each other at weekends for the last two years also meant that we didn't really know each other any more and now that we were in each other's company for much of the time, the cracks began to show.

My third year finally ended, and my exams were over. As I headed back to Rainham, having said goodbye to my college friends and a different way of life, I thought how strange it would be to be one person again instead of two.

'I've passed,' I announced as soon as Patrick arrived home from work. He looked tired and worn out, but still managed a broad smile.

'That's great news,' he said, giving me a hug. 'I'm starving, is there any breakfast?'

I turned away and went to cook some sausages, feeling hurt. I had worked for this moment for three years. I was a qualified teacher not just a housewife. But rather than picking a fight I served up the meal and chewed on a piece of toast, telling myself I was just being silly.

37

My First Teaching Job

It wasn't easy to get a teaching job the year I qualified, as there had been a review of teacher's pay scales the year before that had awarded a huge increase. This had prompted many teachers who had opted to leave the profession to return, and consequently there were very few jobs around. One of the girls from college, Maggie, had managed to get a job at an all-boys comprehensive in Stratford.

'I can put in a word for you if you like,' she offered kindly.

'But I'm middle-school trained, not secondary, and I'm planning on working in a primary school,' I replied. But then I started to think. It would be easy to travel to, I would have a ready-made friend, and at least I would be teaching.

'Okay,' I said. 'If you could, that would be great; thanks Maggie.'

The following week I was called for an interview at the school.

I knew that it was a boys' school and I also knew that I didn't want to look too young or attractive, so I pulled my long hair into a tight ponytail and twisted it into a bun at the back of my head. In a plain beige shirt dress, a touch of make-up and flat shoes I made my way to my first interview as a teacher.

The headmaster was a huge Scot with a broad body and a broader accent. He must have been about six foot tall and as he came to meet me at the door he extended his hand.

'Well halloo there, young lady. I hear that you would like a job in ma school?'

I looked at him as he stood there smiling down at me, and felt myself shrink even smaller than my five foot.

'Yes please,' I responded, smiling back even though I was quivering inside.

'Take a seat,' he said, but as I went to sit he stopped me and said, 'No, wait now, why doncha come and meet the lads first?' and he took my arm and guided me out of his office and into the dimly lit corridor that led to the rest of the school. He showed me round, and introduced me to some of the teachers. They all seemed very friendly, but the classrooms looked untidy and rather neglected. Then he took me into the sixth form common room. I looked about me; there was graffiti scrawled on one wall and half-full paper cups clustered on every surface, surrounded by discarded crisp packets. Several teenagers – some White, some Afro-Caribbean, all considerably taller than me – were lounging on the chairs eating crisps. They all stopped as we came in and looked at us with a smirk on their faces.

'Helloo boys,' the head said and turning to me continued, 'This young lady wants ta come and be a teacher here – whaddya think?'

They looked me up and down and one of them sucked his teeth and said, 'Na – I don't fink so!'

They all laughed and continued to chat amongst themselves. I wanted to die, but the head just grinned and led me back to his office where he promptly offered me the job!

When I rushed back to Dagenham to tell Mum, Pat and Josie were already home from work. Josie had eaten her dinner and gone up to her room as she usually did, so it was just Mum, Pat and Aunty sitting in front of the television. I bounced into the kitchen. 'I've got a job!' I announced, standing in front of the telly. 'It's a proper teaching job! And I'll be earning over £3,000 a year!'

Mum gave a watery smile but Pat just said, 'Mind out of the way, I'm watching this.'

I went into the scullery and put the kettle on.

I started at my new school in September and loved working there. The kids were great fun, and although it was extremely hard, the rewards were incredible. There was also a great sense of comradeship among the staff and we gave each other mutual support. When you needed someone to moan to, laugh with, or simply to talk to we were there for each other. As many of us were young teachers in our first jobs we had loads of energy and enthusiasm and working in a boys' comprehensive in East London at that time, we needed it!

It was here that I met two of the most important people in my life: my dear friend Sherry, and the man who would become pivotal to my future – Colin, remedial teacher, political animal, brave champion of the underdog, known as Mr Softy by the children and Superhero by the staff. The man who would change my life forever and turn it upside down.

That first term went by like lightning. I was learning so much, and often getting things wrong, but it was an incredible place to be. One day in mid-December, Maggie came over to me in the staffroom, and plonked herself down beside me.

'Are you coming to the cooks' Christmas party?' she asked, as she got out her sandwich.

'Oh I don't know. When is it?'

She munched through her lunch quickly; we always seemed to be in a hurry.

'It's on the last day of term after the kids have gone. Go on, it'll be a laugh,' she promised. 'Everyone is going.'

I couldn't think of a good reason to refuse, so I smiled. 'Oh okay then, if you insist.'

As I called the register the day before we broke up for the holiday, I noticed that there was some disturbance at the back of the classroom.

'What are you up to, Michael?' I asked, looking in the direction of the laughing.

'Nuffin Madam,' replied the little short blond boy who was always at the centre of any trouble. He was surrounded by Devon and the twins Melvin and Kelvin, big West Indian boys who liked a good joke.

I peered towards them. 'Come on, what are you doing? It's not Christmas yet you know.' I had grown very fond of my tutor group, even though it was made up of some of the most challenging boys in the school.

Michael came out to the front of the class. 'I've 'urt myself, Miss.' As he thrust his hand towards me I looked down and saw that his thumb was covered in blood.

'Oh no! What on earth have you done to yourself?' I asked, reaching out for his hand, at which he started to giggle. On closer inspection I realised the hurt thumb was a fake, and not a very good one at that.

'Oh, very funny,' I said, dropping my hand and sending him back to his seat. Then I had an idea. 'Tell you what, boys, shall we play a joke on Miss B?'

They were very keen! My friend Maggie had her classroom next door and it just so happened that she had a strong aversion to anything to do with blood. We made our plan. Kelvin would run into Maggie's room and ask her to help as there had been an accident. Meanwhile I would be holding Michael's wounded hand, getting hysterical.

Off he went; the rest of the class was silent, craning their necks to get a better view.

Maggie came rushing through the door. 'What's the matter? What's happened?

'It's his thumb!' I wailed. 'He caught it in the window.' I put on my most pathetic and desperate look.

Maggie took charge. 'It's all right boys,' she said firmly, 'go back to your seats.' She ushered the boys away and moved towards Michael and I. 'Let me see, Michael,' she said tentatively, moving towards the 'injured' hand.

Michael thrust his hand at her, moaning in mock pain, and as she went to look at it the 'severed' thumb flew off, at which she let out an almighty scream and the whole class erupted into uproarious laughter. Before we had a chance to recover, I glanced up to see the face of the headmaster looking through the window of the door. He came in.

'Is there something the matter, ladies?' he asked with a broad Scottish growl. 'Are these boys misbehaving?'

'Oh no, thank you,' I insisted, 'everything's just fine.' The head didn't say anything else but he must have known that we had been up to mischief, and I think I caught a sly smile cross his face as he turned and left the room.

We had a great time regaling our colleagues with the story during the party the next day, and it sounded even funnier after we had drunk copious quantities of alcohol! The party was great fun and I danced with lots of the other young teachers, all of us feeling the relief of finishing our first term without any major mishaps. By the time I went to catch the bus back to Rainham though my mood had changed. I didn't want to go back there, it didn't feel like home, and I didn't feel that I belonged in that house with my husband. I stood waiting for the bus, and realised that, unlike my colleagues, I wasn't glad it was the end of term. In fact I couldn't wait to get back to my boys and my friends in January.

38

Making a Decision

As the new term started, I decided to try to be more positive about my situation. It had been hard to pretend to everyone, including Patrick, that everything was fine, and that I was settling in to married life, but I had done my best.

Maggie was waiting for me when I arrived early on the first day back.

'Stuart is organising a skiing trip to Aviemore at the end of February,' she told me. 'Do you want to go? It will work out really cheap if we go as teachers with the kids, and we won't have to look after them during the day because they'll be having their skiing lessons.'

'Oh I don't know, Mags,' I replied. 'I'm not sure Patrick would like me going.'

'Oh come on – he doesn't own you, does he? It'll be fun.'

'Okay, I'll think about it,' I said, and went up to my classroom to get ready for the boys to arrive. What I hadn't told her was that I thought I might be pregnant. I was really depressed about it and hadn't told anyone, but I didn't think that skiing would be a good idea if I was. I made a deal with myself – if I was expecting then I wouldn't go, but if I wasn't then I would! The next week I found out that it was a false alarm, and so went straight away and put my name down for the trip. I wasn't ready to be pinned down just yet.

The trip was great fun, and the boys had a whale of a time. I learnt how exhilarating slicing through the snow can be, even though I was a complete beginner. On the first day all of us adult beginners were standing in a line on the nursery slopes.

'Now,' said our very patient instructor, 'I have taught you how to snowplough to stop, so we're going to have a go one at a time.'

Off we went. Debbie was first; around she went, heading back to the end of the line. Then it was Maggie's turn. She pushed off and we watched her go.

'No, no!' shouted the instructor. 'Turn! Turn!'

But Maggie wasn't able to turn, so she headed towards us at some speed and then proceeded to knock us down like skittles! Luckily no one was hurt and eventually we all got the hang of it and managed to negotiate the nursery slopes with some expertise by the time we had to go home.

Coming back to Rainham felt like a big anti-climax, and I realised with a jolt that I'd been dreading it.

Back at school, time flew by and before we knew it Easter was approaching. Things at home were not getting any better. It wasn't that we were constantly arguing, it was just that we wanted different things from our lives, and were beginning to resent each other for not being able to be the person we needed. I was getting so desperate that I confided in my friend Anne. I was shocked at her response.

'Kathleen, you two were never suited,' she said after I had tried to tell her how I felt.

'What do you mean?'

'You were never right for each other. I could have told you that years ago.'

'But I don't understand; why didn't you?' I returned angrily. The thought that it had been so obvious to someone else shook me to the core, especially as this person was my closest friend.

'Kathleen, it wasn't for me to tell you what you should do. I knew that you'd tell me to mind my own business.' She was right of course; although we were very close we had always respected each other's decisions.

I looked closely at Anne for the first time in ages, and noticed that she had worry lines beginning to appear on her smooth freckled skin, and that her eyes had lost their old sparkle.

'Do you still miss Tony?' I asked gently now, conscious of how caught up I'd been in my own problems.

'No,' she answered quietly, 'not really. We just weren't right for each other either. But I'm more worried about you now. What are you going to do?'

'Oh Anne, I don't want to hurt anyone, but I can't stand pretending to be happy anymore.'

'Then don't,' she said matter-of-factly. 'Just leave.'

'How can I leave? We're married!'

'So? Just because you're married doesn't mean that you have to put up with being miserable. Just get out and blow everyone else.'

I wiped my eyes and started to think that maybe Anne was right. Maybe I could just leave. What was the worst that could happen? We couldn't be any more unhappy than we were now, could we? What about my family; what would they think? And most of all, how could I tell Patrick? What would I say?

I made my mind up – I wouldn't tell him, I would write him a note!

My mind feverish with the thought of escape, I made plans. The first day of the half-term holiday was a Monday, and Patrick was back on day shifts for the next three months. After my conversation with Anne, I had decided that it would be best to leave as soon as possible even though I felt sick inside at the thought of it. I had packed a suitcase of clothes and belongings and had a couple of big bags full of my college books and other paraphernalia. As I was getting my things together, I couldn't help thinking what a terrible person I was, and how everyone would think I was crazy, cruel or both. I didn't cry; inside I was excited at the thought of freedom, even though this was tainted by the knowledge of the hurt I would be causing to Patrick by not having the courage to tell him to his face, and also what our families and friends would think of me and what I was doing. I tried to push these thoughts out of my mind and concentrate on the task in hand. I had written the note and kept it very short. I wasn't sure how to explain how I felt, so in the end I just told

Patrick that I had to leave because I knew we were both unhappy and it wasn't fair to carry on like this.

Propping the envelope on the mantelpiece I looked at my watch and saw that the minicab would be arriving any minute now. There was a sound of hooting outside and as I looked out I saw the car waiting for me. Grabbing my things, I stopped and looked round one last time, and in that split second I knew without a shadow of a doubt that I was doing the right thing, and with that I turned and walked out, shutting the door firmly behind me.

When the minicab driver saw me, he opened the car door and got out to take my bags. 'Blimey love,' he joked, 'wot you doing? Leavin yer 'usband?'

39

Telling Everyone

I arrived at Valence Avenue just before Pat and Josie were due home. I knew Mum would be there and I wanted the chance to talk to her before they arrived. When she opened the door to me she looked taken aback but just said, 'Oh,' and opened the door wider for me to come in. I dumped my things in the hallway and followed her into the kitchen.

'I've left Patrick.' I said it with defiance, expecting her to be angry.

'I thought so,' she replied coolly.

'I'm going to stay with Marion, but would like to stay here tonight if that's okay?'

'Yes, that's fine.' She lit her cigarette and inhaled deeply. 'Why are you going to Marion's?'

I hesitated before answering, not sure how to explain. 'Because he'll come here looking for me.' As I looked around me I couldn't help noticing the yellow nicotine stains that covered the walls and ceiling, the scratched paintwork and the worn, tired furnishings. There was no way I could ever come back here to live. Besides I couldn't cope with my family's endless disapproving looks.

Once Pat and Josie returned from work, their reaction was entirely as I had predicted. Pat said angrily, 'Why have you left? What's he done?'

'It's not like that,' I tried to explain. 'He hasn't *done* anything. We just don't get on, that's all.'

She looked away. 'Well I think you're terrible. You can't just leave. What will poor Patrick do?'

Josie walked into the scullery and banged around for a while before storming back in. 'Kathleen, I don't know what's going on, but it's not right you know – you're married now.'

'I know,' I responded, 'that's the trouble. I don't want to be married.'

'Well you should have thought of that before – it's a bit late now,' added Pat. 'You can't just change your mind.'

Suddenly and unexpectedly, Mum leapt to my defence.

'Keep your nose out of it, both of you,' she said sharply. 'It's none of your business.'

All three of us were taken aback and looked at Mum, who carried on as though nothing had happened.

'Now then, I thought we would have fish and chips tonight because I haven't cooked any dinner,' and with that she rummaged in her purse and thrust a pile of money on the table 'I'll have cod and chips, but wait until Aunty gets home and we'll see what she wants.' Then she went into the scullery to put the kettle on without a backward glance.

When Aunty arrived a few minutes later, the tea was on the table ready. 'Ask your Aunt what fish she wants,' Mum said.

Aunty looked up as she took off her jacket. 'Oh now, what shall I 'ave? A bit of cod roe? No, I'll have a nice wing of skate,' she said licking her lips exaggeratedly, 'and a wally.'

'I'll go over,' I volunteered, jumping up, glad of an excuse to escape the charged atmosphere.

'Ain't you going home to cook Patrick's dinner?' asked Aunty in all innocence.

We all looked anywhere but at each other until Mum said firmly, 'She's left him.'

Aunty tutted loudly. 'Well I don't know, bloody kids. You're just like your mother.' She sniffed loudly as I left for the chip shop, feeling like a naughty child.

Later that evening there was a loud knock at the door. We all stopped what we were doing and Mum got up. 'I'll go.'

My heart was beating fast as I sat rigid with anxiety.

From the kitchen we could hear muffled voices, but no one sounded angry. Then the door closed and Mum came back in.

'He said he didn't know where you were,' she announced.

'I left a note. He must have seen it.'

'Well, he said he didn't. Anyway, I told him you had left him, but that you weren't here.'

I could have kissed her. I knew I was being cowardly, but it had taken all the courage I could muster to get out of that house.

'Did he seem upset?' I asked quietly.

'Well he didn't look that pleased, but he wasn't angry. It almost seemed like he wasn't surprised.'

I nodded. That made sense. Patrick must have realised that it wasn't working between us, but maybe he was just too kind, or maybe too cowardly, to do anything about it. Maybe it was me that had been brave after all. That was a strange notion, one that I hadn't considered.

For now though I needed some time to gather my thoughts, and decide what I was going to do after I left Marion's. I didn't intend staying there for more than a few days, because I didn't think it would be fair. I had started to look for a little flat of my own, somewhere not too far from school that I could live in all by myself. It would be the first time that I had ever done that. All of my life I had shared a room with someone. Even at college there were other girls close by, and of course once I was married I had lived with Patrick. Although I was twenty-three now and an adult, I was still such a child. I wanted to know how I would cope on my own and whether or not I would be able to survive in the big world, standing on my own two feet. One thing was for sure – I was certainly going to try.

That night, as I crept into the bed that I had shared with my Mum for so many years, I stared up at the ceiling and the flaking paint and thought about the mess that I had got myself into. I glanced over at Mum and wondered about how she had felt all those years ago when her marriage to Ron Coates had ended. Had she left him or he her? I had never been sure. Aunty had said I was just like her.

I shivered. Maybe I was.

40

A New Flat and a New Romance

It wasn't long until I found myself a little bedsitter in Leytonstone, which was only a short bus ride from my school. I felt more grown-up now than I had ever done before, a real independent young woman. When I first lived there it felt strange to be on my own. I did have a phone, which was brilliant, and meant that if I felt lonely or nervous I would at least be able to phone someone for a chat, so was pleased when it rang about a week after I moved in.

'Kath?'

'Hello Mum,' I answered cheerfully, determined to be upbeat. 'Are you all okay?'

'Yes, we're fine. Aunty's gone over to see your Aunt Mag so she'll be gone all day.' Then she hesitated. 'Kathleen, you know that I have been through the same things as you; I know what it's like. You do know that don't you?' she said quietly.

It didn't sound like Mum at all really. All at once I felt her sadness, as though she were somehow able to transmit all her regrets, the disappointment her life had been, without saying very much at all.

'Mum, can I come over for a talk?' I almost whispered. I wanted to seize this moment. At last, this could be when it would end, a whole lifetime of secrets and mysteries. I could feel my heartbeat quicken, my hands go clammy and my head spin with possibilities. Mum wanted to tell me something, wanted to explain, I could sense it.

'Of course,' Mum said, speaking almost as quietly as I had. After I hung up I immediately phoned Margaret and told her what Mum had said.

'I'm going over there straight away,' I told her. 'If you want to come I'll see you there.'

I was in Valence Avenue within forty minutes, knocking on the door of my childhood home.

Mum answered, and looked almost shocked to see me.

'Oh, I didn't expect you to get here this quickly.'

'I know; I was lucky with the buses,' I answered, trying to keep my voice calm.

As we sat down with the tea Mum had made, I looked up at her.

'Mum,' I started, 'you know what you said on the phone . . .'

She looked away. That familiar faraway look came over her, a look that I hadn't seen for a while now, covering her face like a shroud.

'That was all a long time ago,' she said without meeting my eyes.

'But I just wanted to know . . .'

'It doesn't matter now; it's all too long ago. And anyway,' she said, picking up the clock from the mantelpiece and peering at it, 'Aunty will be home soon.' With those words her face closed up like the shutter of a camera and I knew that was all. There would be no talk. When Margaret arrived, about half an hour later, I caught her eye when Mum wasn't looking and gently shook my head. She knew what that meant without me needing to say a word. She knew that today would not be the day we would find any answers.

One of the problems with my new bedsit was the rent, which was very expensive, so that with bills, food, fares and other bits and pieces I was really struggling. By this point I'd made friends with one of the other teachers at the school. Her name was Sherry, short for Sheherazad, which better reflected her exotic looks. She was tall, slim and olive skinned, with a crown of raven curls, and she taught modern foreign languages. We were unlikely friends when I think about it and our backgrounds couldn't have been more different, but something drew us together. Years later I discovered that although her childhood was very different from mine we shared many things – among them a fear of desertion and a commitment to improving the lives of the children we taught.

Sherry shared a flat with an art teacher, Penny. It was a special teachers' flat. These were designated council properties put aside for teachers, to encourage them to take up positions in more challenging school districts.

Sherry approached me one morning. 'Penny's moving out of the flat at the end of term. Are you interested in taking over her room?'

'Oh yes please!' I responded with enthusiasm. 'But what's the rent?' When Sherry told me the cost, including all bills, I was even happier. In total I would be paying less than half what I was paying for the bedsit, and it was a lovely modern flat in a purpose-built block in Upton Park. It even had a rubbish chute!

I booked a date to move in and Colin – 'Mr Softy' – offered to help. He was about five years older than me, and very skinny with a crop of reddish blond hair and a small beard, both of which were badly cut, but I really liked him. He was funny and clever and kind, and was always ready to help out any of us newer teachers. Colin taught most of the remedial groups, which were the children that we would these days refer to as having a Special Educational Need (SEN), and he was always keen to try to find innovative ways to engage and motivate the boys and help them to see that education could help them to change their lives for the better. At that time many people had given up on these children, which infuriated Colin, and we teachers would often have discussions about the intolerable unfairness of the system, and what we could do to change things.

I arranged to move in with Sherry on the first day of the summer holidays and so Colin agreed to pick me and my belongings up in his car as I didn't drive.

He usually cycled to work from his teacher's flat in a tall tower block in Stratford, so I was surprised to see him arrive in an old Sunbeam Talbot car that he was in the process of renovating.

'This is a funny old car,' I said laughing as he pulled up and swung open the door. 'How old is it?'

'It was made in 1955, I think,' he answered, proudly stroking its aged paintwork.

'That's only a year younger than me,' I smiled, and Colin began to put my bags and boxes into the little boot. The car was painted British Racing Green, and had lovely curved bumpers and leather seats. Although it was quite rough around the edges I loved it! We loaded up the car and set off for my new flat share.

We started to chat about things and then he asked tentatively, 'Are you separated from your husband now?' I was a bit taken aback, as although it wasn't a secret, I hadn't broadcast the fact.

'Well, yes I am actually,' I stuttered. 'How did you know?'

'This is our school we're talking about here. Everyone knows everything – you should know that by now.'

'Hmm well, I didn't think it was such a big deal really,' I answered irritated. I didn't like the idea of being the topic of people's conversations.

'It is to me,' he said softly. I wasn't sure I had heard him correctly, so didn't comment.

'What I mean is,' he continued, 'that it's a big deal to me, because if you are separated from your husband, I for one am very glad. I mean very, very glad.'

I looked at him as he stared fixedly ahead at the road. I hadn't really thought of him like that. Although we had been good friends since I started at the school, our friendship hadn't had any romantic connotations.

My heart was starting to somersault, and I felt awkward suddenly. This was a sensation I hadn't expected. Once we had unloaded the car and I had sorted a few things away, Sherry asked if we would like to go out with her and her boyfriend, who confusingly was also called Colin, and also taught at the same school as us. There was a Labour Party Social being held that evening in East Ham.

Colin looked at me. 'I'd love to go. What about you?'

I nodded.

The evening was great fun and included a fish and chip supper that I couldn't eat because I felt funny inside and strangely confused. Many of the teachers from school were there, and I was very conscious of being smiled at and whispered about. It was all very good-natured but still very embarrassing! As Colin walked me back to the car he put his arm around my shoulder for the first time and I felt a warm, unexpected glow of happiness.

From that night on Colin and I started to 'go out'. He turned my life upside down and inside out and I felt as though he had given me back my wings and I could fly wherever I wanted to. We talked endlessly – about school, the children, politics, our families, books we had read, plays we had seen. We just seemed to slot together, as though we had always known each other, and every time I saw him my stomach did flip-flops! One day, later in the holiday, Colin came round to see me full of excitement.

'I've seen an advert for a holiday cottage in Devon,' he said with a big smile on his face. 'It's for hire next week because they've had a cancellation – shall we go?' It sounded perfect so I agreed, and during that holiday in that tiny cob cottage deep in the Devon countryside, I think we both realised that we had fallen in love.

Colin and Sherry became great friends with my Colin and I, and although we didn't know it at that time, they went on to help us survive the most traumatic time of our lives.

41

Babies and Other Mysteries

Sherry was desperate to have a baby. She and her Colin had been trying for quite some time, but so far they had not been successful. They bought a beautiful old four-storey Georgian house in Hackney to renovate ready for their longed for family and kept themselves busy between that and teaching. At about the same time Colin and I bought a house in Ilford. It was a very smart little Edwardian house that had been 'done up' really well by the previous owners, so it was extremely comfortable to live in if a little boring. I was almost twenty-six and Colin thirty-one when we decided that the time was right for us to also think about babies.

I had a real dread of marriage though, and was quite hung up about it. My first marriage had been a big mistake, and I now associated weddings with deceit and hypocrisy. My family had taken ages to come to terms with what I had done. Margaret and Tony hardly spoke to me for a while, and Pat and Josie were extremely disapproving, although since Mum had told them to mind their own business they didn't say much. Aunty had made her feelings known right from the start, and whenever I visited the house and she was there, she felt it her duty to point out my shortcomings.

'Where you livin' now?' she would ask, knowing full well the answer.

Mum would say, 'She's just living with Colin, because he's got a nice house with plenty of rooms,' as though anyone really believed that fiction.

I had taken Colin to meet Mum with a real sense of anxiety, but she had been fine, although I could see she was watching us like a hawk. She had told everyone in the family that I had left Patrick because he beat me, which couldn't have been further from the truth, but I suppose she felt she had to justify my actions.

The idea of having a baby before you got married at that time was still a little unconventional, especially for a Catholic family in Dagenham, so when I eventually became pregnant we had a problem.

I was adamant at first.

'No, I really don't think it's a good idea,' I said when Colin broached the subject of weddings. 'There's no point. We're happy as we are, aren't we?'

'Yes we are, but it just feels strange.'

'What feels strange?' I asked.

'Well, when I introduce you to someone, or talk to someone about you, I don't know how to describe you. I say "my girl-friend" – but you're so much more than that, it just doesn't sound right.' He hesitated. 'And also we won't know what to call the baby. Whose name will the poor little thing have, eh?'

I laughed, and gave in. 'As long as it's just us,' I said. 'No big wedding, and no white dress!'

'Definitely!' he agreed. He wasn't the sort of person who liked a lot of fuss.

We booked the register office for 2 January without telling anyone at first but we knew we would need witnesses. 'Do you want to ask your sister Margaret?' Colin suggested.

'No, I don't think that's a good idea. She won't want to do it anyway. I think we should ask Sherry and Colin.'

So it was decided.

Colin and Sherry agreed at once, congratulating us heartily. I felt sad for Sherry because she was still not pregnant, and had dreaded telling her about our baby, but she had been really lovely and happy for us.

In the end I decided I would ask Margaret and her husband Tony if they would like to come to the wedding. When I told her about it, Margaret went quiet for a while and then said, 'Oh I'm sorry but we can't make it that day. We'll be at Tony's mum and dad's.'

I tried to hide my disappointment. 'Don't worry, we just thought you might like to come – it's no big deal really. It will be just a little wedding.' I asked her not to tell anyone else about it and hung up, trying hard not to be hurt.

The day of our wedding was bitterly cold and windy. It was the middle of winter and the landscape looked bleak. We'd moved house recently, and were now living in a modern house on a small estate in Frindsbury, Kent. It was very rural, which was why we liked it. Colin had grown up in Balham, South London, and we had both spent our lives dreaming of an escape to the countryside. This was our first stab at it. As we both still worked in East London it was quite a commute, and being in the early stages of pregnancy didn't make it any easier.

We hadn't told anyone about the wedding except for Margaret, not even Colin's widowed mum. He was an only child and, looking back, I can't believe we kept it from her. She had been so kind and accepting of me, even though she hadn't liked the fact that we were living 'in sin'. Still, I was afraid. I couldn't bear the thought of this wedding being anything like my first, with all the relatives and uncomfortable associations. So in the end just the four of us drove to Chatham Register Office on that cold January day.

When I went over to Mum's the next week I told her our news.

'Oh,' she said, 'I knew you'd get married again.'

Margaret now had a little girl called Emma, who was the sweetest little thing I had ever seen, and was pregnant with her second baby. I hoped that now I was expecting too we would be able to regain some of the closeness that seemed to have diminished over the last couple of years, so I wanted to tell her before the rest of the family.

Margaret was ecstatic. 'That's great! What date are you due?'

When I told her the end of June we laughed, realising that our babies would be born just two months apart.

We made an arrangement to meet at Mum's the following Saturday so that we could go shopping in Ilford. We both wanted a Moses basket and Margaret had seen one in Boots that was really pretty. When we got to Mum's she was in a happy mood. She had retired from her job about six months before, but still had plenty of spending money. Pat, Josie and Aunty paid for everything between them so Mum had her pension to spend in any way she liked.

Pat came in with a plate piled high with bacon sandwiches.

'Here you are,' she said plonking the plate down on the table. 'You must be hungry.'

'Oooh thanks,' I said and as I helped myself the phone rang.

'Who's that?' Mum asked. Both she and Aunty would always say that whenever anyone phoned, as though the other people in the room had some kind of sixth sense and could tell without answering it!

Pat walked out into the hallway and then called out to Mum. 'It's Mary, quick!'

Mum pulled herself out of the chair and hurried to the phone.

Phone calls to and from Australia were very expensive at that time. I tried to listen as I munched my way through the tasty food, but couldn't really hear what was going on. When Mum finally came back into the room she was beaming. 'Mary's coming over!' she announced happily. We were all so excited. It was about seven years since we had seen her and now she was coming home.

Mary's first visit home was joyfully anticipated by all of us. Of course over the years we had kept in touch by letter and the rare phone call, but it wasn't the same as being able to see and talk to her. It was almost like old times again, with nearly all of us together again. When it was my turn to have Mary to stay with me, I was over the moon with excitement.

'Where do you want me to put my case?' she asked, bundling through the door.

'Just chuck it down anywhere,' I answered, ushering her in, and giving her a whistle-stop tour of our little home.

'It's funny you live in Kent now,' she said, looking out of the window over the playing fields of the school next door. 'It's where me and Dave started out.'

Over the next few days we talked endlessly about everything, but inevitably it wasn't long before we got to talking about Mum and her secrets. When Mary had left for Australia I had still been a young teenager, but now I was an adult and I wanted to hear what Mary knew.

'I know some things,' she offered, 'mostly from cousin Dot; although Julie will talk about stuff if you get her in the right mood.'

'Yes I know,' I said. 'We got her talking one day, and she told us about Pat, Michael and Josie going into the children's home.'

'Hmm, yes, well, that was about the time I was born, I think; but do you know why Mum wasn't there?'

'No. Do you?'

'Yes, I do. Well, I think I do – you see Josie and I have talked, but she was only little so she doesn't remember everything that clearly.'

I was on the edge of my seat when Colin came in with tea. 'There you are,' he said, placing the hot mugs of tea in front of us. 'Shall I put some dinner on?'

'Yes please, anything will do,' I said hurriedly, and thankfully he left us to continue our conversation.

'Well,' said Mary, 'the thing is . . .' She stopped and looked at me for a minute. 'The thing is . . . did you know that I was born in prison?'

'What? What do you mean?'

'What I said,' she repeated. 'I was born in prison – well not literally in prison, but Mum was in prison when I was born.'

'In prison for what?' I asked incredulously. 'What had she done?'

'She had committed bigamy. She was in prison because she had married Reg Stevens, my dad, while she was still married to Ron Coates.'

'Oh God,' I said, 'poor Mum! But why did she do it?'

'Who knows? Things were different then. Remember it wasn't long after the end of the war; everything was still muddled up and confused.'

'What? You mean she didn't know she was still married?'

'No – of course she knew, but she didn't care, I suppose. Perhaps she just thought she deserved a bit of happiness.'

I was taken aback by this revelation, but I was totally unprepared for the next.

'That was the first time,' Mary continued slowly, her eyes sliding away from my face now, as though she wasn't sure whether to continue or not.

'First time what?' I asked, frightened that she was going to stop, just as all of the other people I had asked did.

'The first time she was in prison,' she continued, still averting her eyes. 'Do you think we should help Colin with the dinner?'

'No! Blow the dinner – tell me what you mean!'

'Okay,' she said quietly. 'If you want to know, I'll tell you all I can, but I don't know everything.'

I waited while she sipped her tea, and then, swallowing hard, she carried on.

42

More Secrets Revealed

'I think Mum must have met Reg Stevens when she was working as a waitress in London. At least that's what Dot was told,' Mary said, thoughtfully. 'Apparently he adored her, fell head over heels for her, but he never knew she was already married.'

'But how did she hide it? What about the children? Where were they? Sheila must only have been about eight, and the others were younger. Who was looking after them?' I asked, my head starting to ache with that old familiar pain.

'Well Granny was still alive, and Aunty lived there as well, so I suppose it must have been them.'

'But Granny would have been in her seventies . . . Wait, that's when they were taken into the children's home, wasn't it? How could Coates do that to his own children?'

'I don't know, but of course we only know one side of the story.'

'What about Peter? Who was his dad?' I asked. 'Ron Coates or Reg Stevens?'

'I don't think it was either of them. I'm not sure anyone knows the truth about that, apart from Mum.'

'But you said she was in prison again. What was that for?' I asked, greedy for more information now, despite the throbbing in my head and sick feeling in my stomach.

'Well, it was when you were about two and a half, not long after Margaret was born,' Mary said, watching me closely for a reaction. I tried to hide my shock, but then distant memories began to surface.

'The big building,' I said suddenly interrupting her. 'The

big building where I went to visit her – I thought it was a hospital!'

Mary shook her head. 'No – it wasn't a hospital,' she said sadly.

'Oh God, poor Mum. How did she bear it? But what was she in prison for that time? I don't understand.'

'Slow down! We have to go back a few years,' Mary said, twisting her hands in her lap. 'So I was a little baby when she got out the first time, and Mum took me with her to stay with Uncle John in Birmingham.'

'Oh yes.' Again a memory flashed in my head. 'Aunty said something about that, but she wouldn't tell us any details, just that Mum did something bad to Uncle John.'

'Yes it was something bad all right. She went up to stay with Uncle John and Aunty Betty. Dot was only young, about eight I think, the same age as Pat.' Mary stopped speaking, and looked at the floor.

'Go on,' I encouraged, 'I'm a big girl now.'

'Okay, well Uncle John had his own painting and decorating company, so Mum offered to do his accounts for him. She's very clever, you know.'

I nodded.

'After a while, Uncle John started getting some complaints about overdue bills, payments that went missing, invoices that were returned as unpaid, that kind of thing.'

'Oh God no,' I said slapping my hand over my mouth, I could guess where this was heading.

'Well, she was basically cooking the books.'

'Not her own brother's business!' I said, knowing that I wasn't as surprised as I should have been.

'Yep that's right. He ended up so much in debt that he had to be declared bankrupt; he lost everything, and basically had to start all over again.'

'Oh poor Uncle John. No wonder we hardly ever saw him.'

'Yep, Aunty Betty found it very hard to forgive Mum, but that's not all.' She hesitated.

'Go on!'

'After she had swindled him out of his money, Uncle John told her to go back to London, but the money was all spent, so he even had to pay her fare.'

'No . . .'

'But apparently before she left, Reg Stevens arrived in his navy uniform, desperately looking for her, and persuaded her to go back with him.'

'So is he definitely your dad then?' I asked.

'Well yes, I'm pretty sure he is, and Marion and Marge's.'

'But not mine and Margaret's?' I asked, already knowing the answer.

'No, I don't think so.'

'Even though his name is on our birth certificates?'

Mary nodded.

'So who is our dad?' I asked. 'And what about the second prison sentence? What was it for?'

Mary shrugged her shoulders, 'I'm really sorry, but that is something that I'm afraid I don't have the answers to.'

43

Scary Situations

By the time we heard Mum had been taken into hospital, Margaret and I were both quite heavily pregnant.

'It's nothing to worry about,' said Pat when she phoned me. 'They're just taking her in for some tests, but she's fine.'

'Well she can't be fine if she's having tests,' I replied. I was feeling really tired now and work was becoming more and more of a strain.

Pat reassured me that Mum was soon going to be discharged and that I shouldn't worry, and it was easy to be convinced, as things were quite hectic in my life at that moment.

Colin and I had both moved on from the school where we had met. Colin was working at a Special School and I was now working at an IT centre. It had nothing to do with information technology though! The IT stood for Intermediate Treatment and it was run jointly by Education and Social Services for young offenders, as a last stop before borstal. It was set up in a big old Victorian house in East London where there were a group of us – some teachers, some social workers – trying to keep about fifteen youngsters out of trouble, and hopefully teach them something as well! They were a good bunch, but could be very challenging. Many of them had been through a traumatic childhood, and had been offending for many years: TDA (taking and driving away), theft, burglary etc. We all grew very fond of them, although their behaviour could be exasperating, inconsistent and frighteningly volatile.

When they found out I was expecting a baby they became very protective. We would often take them for outings into the countryside and they would be so kind and caring, helping me down the steps of the minibus with such tenderness.

Then there were the other times.

I was almost at the point of going on maternity leave and the Easter holiday was fast approaching. It was hot that year, although it was only March, and my 'bump' seemed enormous! So much so that the hospital had sent me for an ultrasound scan to see if I was having twins. I was feeling very uncomfortable and clumsy, and so when Rob, the head of the centre, suggested taking the kids swimming, I opted to stay behind in the house with anyone that wasn't going. Although we were fond of our charges, we were also realistic. Experience had taught us that if any of the kids opted to stay at the house it was usually in the hope of stealing some of the contents.

Freddy was fifteen. Despite his skinhead hair and bovver boots he could be the sweetest boy going. He was the apple of his mum's eye, and she would always iron a sharp crease in his jeans in an effort to make him look presentable.

He wasn't pleased when he realised I was still there after the others had left.

'Why ain't you f***ing gone, Kath?'

Using strong language was commonplace among the kids there – it wasn't meant to be an insult – and they always called us by our first names. We tried to make the centre as much like a home from home as possible. These youngsters had pushed against authority most of their lives, and if we were going to get anywhere with them we had to take a different approach.

'I don't feel up to it, Fred.'

'You don't f***ing trust us, do ya?' he said petulantly, pushing a chair out of his way.

'That's got nothing to do with it, Fred. You know we can't leave you in the house on your own.'

Steve and Tommy were there as well. Steve was a tall, broad boy, and was usually quite sensible, but Tommy had a history of aggressive behaviour and I was obviously thwarting some plan the three of them had hatched.

'F***ing 'ell, Kath,' Freddie started to shout, getting into a temper now. 'You lot, yer aw the f***ing same; yer say ya f***ing trust us but ya f***ing don't, not really.'

I could see that the situation was starting to get out of hand and was very aware that I was on my own, heavily pregnant and facing three very angry young offenders. I tried to think how I could defuse the situation,

'Look, why don't we just have a cup of tea? Then we can cook some dinner for when the others get back. They'll be starving.'

I started to turn towards the kitchen area, when suddenly Freddie said, 'I don't f***ing believe it. This is a load of bollocks!' and pulling his hand from behind his back I watched, almost in slow motion, as a sledgehammer hurtled towards me. It clattered in front of me, hitting the table with an almighty bang, and the three boys, including Freddie who had thrown it, stared with a shocked look on their faces as I stood motionless in front of them.

Tommy broke the silence. 'That's f***ing out of order Fred; totally f***ing out of order.'

Fred turned and slammed upstairs, shouting, 'Oh f*** off, why don't ya? Bollocks to the lot of ya.'

Steve and Tommy came over to me.

'You awright, Kath?' Steve asked quietly.

'Yes I'm fine, thanks both of you.' I eased myself down into one of the room's comfortable armchairs.

'He didn't mean to hurt ya, yer know Kath,' Steve continued. 'He's jus' annoyed cos ya didn't go and leave us 'ere.'

'I know, I know Steve, but he could have really hurt someone,' I said, feeling quite shaken now it was over.

'I'w make ya a cup of tea Kath, awright?' offered Tommy, and I nodded my thanks, glad that I only had a few more weeks to go before I would be at home waiting for the arrival of my baby.

44

A Bittersweet Birth

When Mum came out of hospital she seemed more subdued than usual. Margaret began to wonder if there was something serious wrong, but Pat reassured us that although Mum had been diagnosed with type 2 diabetes, there was nothing to worry about. She had been to the diabetic clinic and seen the nurse, and now knew how to adjust her diet to deal with it.

Mary had gone back to Australia a few months ago and we all missed her, but we kept both of our 'Australian' sisters updated regarding Mum's health problems. I suppose when you have a family as big as ours there's always someone missing, but we felt the loss of Marge and Mary all the time, even though it had been many years since they had emigrated.

Margaret had her baby, another beautiful little girl they named Rebecca. She was the model of Margaret as a baby – a shock of very dark black hair and enormous eyes fringed with curling black lashes.

I waited impatiently for the arrival of our baby. It had been a hot spring and was now becoming an even hotter summer.

'I wish this baby would hurry up and arrive. I feel like a lump in this heat,' I moaned to poor Colin as he kissed me goodbye before leaving for work.

The summer holidays were approaching when my due date, 21 June, came and went.

Colin suggested calling the baby Titania if it was a girl, after the fairy in 'Midsummer Night's Dream'.

'I hope you're joking,' I said laughing. I wanted a little boy and I already had a name in mind . . .

On Monday night as I was trying my best to relax and stay

cool, I felt a twinge. Within a few minutes my waters had broken and I was in the first stages of labour. We travelled to the hospital in Chatham by ambulance, as it was quite a long distance, and our baby boy was born at 10.45 the next morning. He had a head full of wispy red-blond hair that glinted in the light and eyes the colour of bluebells. He was beautiful, and we called him Sam, just as I'd planned.

When I was offered a postpartum cup of tea, I drank it thankfully, smiling and still fuzzy-headed from the Pethidine and the gas and air I had taken. I didn't really take much notice when the midwife took the baby, and used a suction tube on him. I knew that babies often swallow mucus during the birth. I still wasn't alarmed when she took him out of the room saying, 'I'm just going to get baby checked by the paediatrician. Nothing to worry about.' This was my first baby after all, and I assumed that this was all perfectly routine.

When she returned a while later without Sam I began to feel anxious.

'Is he all right?' I asked, expecting to be reassured.

'I'm afraid that he might have a little problem,' the midwife answered kindly, not meeting my eyes. 'Doctor just needs to do a few tests, and then he'll come and talk to you.'

My head sprang up from the bed, 'What do you mean a little problem?' I whispered, not wanting to hear the answer. Colin held my hand tightly, a look of real concern crossing his face.

'Let's just wait for the doctor, shall we? Then he can explain,' and with that she left us clinging on to each other, terrified that the tiny bundle we had held and stroked a moment ago wasn't coming back.

After what seemed like an age, the doctor arrived with a nurse who we hadn't seen before. They came in, and as I looked at their faces I knew that this wasn't going to be good news.

'Mr and Mrs Hardy, good afternoon,' the doctor began. 'Now I'm afraid that your baby has a few problems.'

My mind was going into overdrive now. A minute ago it had been a little problem; now it was 'a few' problems.

'Let me explain,' he continued. 'Baby's windpipe and food tube are joined, and that needs sorting out.'

Colin and I exchanged looks and I saw my fear reflected in his eyes.

'How?' Colin asked. 'How can it be sorted out?'

'Well, Baby will need to have an operation to separate the two. The condition is called tracheoesophageal fistula or TOF for short,' the doctor said, speaking slowly as though we were stupid and wouldn't understand. I sat and stared at him, trying to make my muddled head focus.

'When?' Colin asked.

'As soon as possible,' the doctor replied. 'We will need to transfer him to London today. The ambulance has been ordered, and the operation will be done either tonight or very early tomorrow morning.'

I knew I was going to cry then, and sniffed back the tears as Colin put his arm around me.

'Can we go with him?' he asked.

The doctor gave me a pitying look 'You can,' he indicated to Colin, 'but I'm afraid your wife will need to stay here until the midwife signs her off. We need to look after Mum too, don't we?'

I felt patronised by the doctor but I knew that he was trying to be kind.

'But I want to go too,' I said, the tears becoming heavier as I spoke.

The nurse then came forward and took both my hands.

'Look now, you have had a rough labour and you're exhausted. You need to get your strength back for when Baby comes home from hospital.'

'He's *not* Baby,' I almost shouted. 'He's called Sam!'

'All right then,' continued the nurse calmly, 'then Sam will need you to be fit and well when he comes home. We'll get the midwife to get you stitched up and then she can assess when she thinks you will be well enough to travel to London.'

I gave in and then hated myself for doing so. I was weak from a long labour, and had been torn badly so needed a lot of stitches.

I felt nauseous from the drugs, and from the news that we had just been given, and there was a familiar dull ache beginning behind my eyes. The doctor arranged for me to be wheeled down to Special Baby Care to see my Sam one more time before he left. He was in an incubator now and there were tubes everywhere. He was too fragile for a last cuddle.

Then he went off to London in an ambulance with his daddy, leaving me behind.

45

The Terrible Fear

I was put in a side room. When Colin came back to see me after Sam had been operated on we sat and cried together, our arms around each other, clinging on desperately but not saying a word.

No one else came near me except for the occasional midwife. I had been stitched and cleaned up, and they had offered me food that I couldn't eat, conversation I couldn't take part in, and kindness I wasn't interested in; then I was left alone. The other mums probably assumed that my baby had died, so they would creep past my door, and sneek a pitying glance, but never come in to talk to me. Colin was back and forwards between Chatham and London to see Sam, and my family stayed away. I felt abandoned. No one sent me a baby card, there were no excited congratulations, and the doctors still refused to let me out of hospital.

Then Mum arrived. She came bustling into the ward looking dishevelled and determined, and I've never been so glad to see her. She brought me grapes. I probably would have laughed any other time, but instead I only just managed not to cry. Mum never liked overt expressions of emotion, and crying was always referred to as 'being silly', so I kept my tears in check.

'Hello love,' she said. 'Where's Colin?'

'He's gone up to the hospital to see Sam,' I answered. Saying our baby's name was still hard. It didn't sound real; it was as though I was talking about a stranger, someone I didn't know.

'When will you go up there with him?' Mum asked, moving the things around on my bedside cupboard, keeping busy.

'Well, I haven't seen the midwife today yet. She should be round any minute now; hopefully she'll be able to tell me.'

Mum shuffled her feet and fidgeted about. I could tell she felt awkward, didn't know what to say.

'How did you get here?' I asked, as though I really cared.

'Bus and train and then another bus.' She had always been resourceful, and she was comfortable travelling on public transport even though Pat had passed her driving test many years before and had a nice car now.

We continued to talk about other unimportant things, until she suddenly said, 'You won't lose him, you know.' She looked at me directly and I believed her; despite all of my fears, I believed what she was saying. At that moment the midwife arrived and Mum said her goodbyes and shuffled out of the room back to Dagenham without a backwards glance.

It was two weeks before I was able to join Sam at the hospital in London. Although I was allowed a tiny room of my own that I shared with him and his little incubator, the walls were glass and the lights were on all night. I was desperately trying to feed him myself. It was difficult, as my milk had almost dried up by then, but somehow we managed. It was the neonatal ward for very sick babies, many of whom died while we were there, so it was not a very happy place.

By the time we were discharged, and allowed to take our baby home, I was terrified. I didn't feel like he belonged to me at all, and I was also afraid that I wouldn't know how to care for him, that I would get it wrong. The truth was that I was still afraid he was going to die.

It was on the day of the royal wedding of Charles and Diana that we had our first outing as a family. Colin wanted to take Sam to see his mum, who still lived in their family home in Balham. It was a Victorian terraced house, old-fashioned and dilapidated, with flaking paint outside. Inside was always neat and tidy though, with a huge aspidistra taking pride of place in the middle of the front room. Throughout the journey I'd been on edge. When we arrived we found that Colin's mum had, as usual, put on an enormous spread.

'I've just made a few things,' she said, indicating the vast array of sandwiches, pastries and cakes that were laid out on the ironing board. The table itself was already heaving with two places set for a huge roast dinner.

'I've had mine already,' she said. She always ate before we arrived. I think she was either shy, or wanted to free herself up to run around after us, despite our protests. Colin's mum Beat (short for Beatrice) was now in her late seventies, but she was very active and independent. She ushered us in but didn't attempt to take the baby. I think she was probably a bit scared, as were most people.

'How are you, Kathy?' she asked, busying herself with the preparations.

'I'm fine,' I lied, smiling back.

'Let's have a look at the little chap then.' She pulled back the shawl that the baby was wrapped in. 'Oh, he's a lovely little fellow, aren't you?' she said, stroking his face gently.

Sam opened his big blue eyes, and gazed at her earnestly. He was beginning to squirm around looking for food, so I decamped into the front room and sat in the armchair to feed him. For the first couple of minutes he was fine, drinking greedily, then suddenly he stopped and pulled back with a jerk. As I looked down I realised with horror that he was motionless and didn't appear to be breathing. Shaking him, I shouted for Colin, who was still in the other room chatting to his mum.

'Quick, he's stopped breathing! He's stopped breathing!' I screamed in panic. They both appeared at the door and rushed in, Colin grabbed the baby and banged his back, while all the while Sam was getting bluer and bluer. I was in a state of complete breakdown at this point, shivering and crying, with Colin's mum desperately trying to calm me down and phone for the ambulance at the same time. Finally Colin turned Sam on to his front and gently gave mouth-to-nose/mouth resuscitation. It worked. Sam gave a few short gasps, and then began to breathe normally again, so that by the time the ambulance arrived just a few minutes later he was calm and so were we. It had seemed as though hours had passed, but in fact it had all happened in a few short minutes. We were taken to hospital so that the doctors could check Sam, and were kept in overnight. It didn't happen again and the doctors assured us that it was probably just a normal choking accident that could happen to any baby.

I knew better.

Over the next few weeks the same thing happened again and again. The pattern was set. I would be feeding him, he would gasp, stop breathing, turn blue and then come round after resuscitation and be fine by the time the ambulance arrived. Thank God that Colin was on school holidays. I could never have coped alone, and worst of all I knew the doctors didn't believe us.

'They think we're making it up,' I complained to Colin, as once again the ambulance had arrived to find Sam breathing normally. 'They think I'm paranoid, I know they do.' I was so upset and frustrated the tears slid down my cheeks. 'I can't bear it. If he's going to die then I just wish he would; I can't go on like this.' I dropped my head into my hands crying, ashamed that I could say those words. But I meant them. The misery of holding my baby in my arms only to have his life threatened time and time again, with no one taking any notice . . . it was intolerable.

Then it happened in hospital.

Sam's consultant had finally admitted him to Great Ormond Street to do some checks. For the first day he was fine, and then they put a special tube through his nose and asked me to feed him as usual. As soon as I began to feed him, he made the now familiar gasp, stopped breathing and began to turn blue. I rushed out of our little room with him still in my arms and called for help. The nurse took one look at him and shouted to her colleague, 'Press for the crash team!' and then everything burst into life around me, Sam was whisked away and I was ushered out of the room and restrained by a nurse, all the while knowing what was happening to my baby.

I was almost glad. At last they believed me.

46

Finding Sam

Sam had a second operation, which thankfully solved the problem of his breathing. It was a new beginning for us as a family, but as I brought him home, he still felt like someone else's baby. I was afraid to love him.

My friend Sherry had got pregnant about six months after me and had now had a baby boy of her own called Tom. Colin and I were desperately trying to sell our house in Kent so that we could move nearer to our friends and family. We needed their support so badly. Finally our house sold and we were faced with the problem of finding a new home fast.

My sister Margaret had seen a little cottage for sale in a village about twenty minutes from where she and Tony now lived. The problem was it was a wreck and in need of total refurbishment. Our friends Sherry and Colin came up with an answer.

'Come and live here with us, lass, while you do up the cottage,' suggested Colin B in his broad Geordie accent. 'That way you and Sherry can help each other with the bairns, and the hospital is only about twenty minutes away. It's a win win.'

We agreed before they had time to change their minds!

One morning we had just put the babies down for their morning nap and were looking forward to a coffee.

'I'll put the kettle on,' Sherry offered, and I settled myself down at the big wooden kitchen table with a pile of post. As I flicked through the letters I picked out one addressed to me that was postmarked from the Isle of Man. My heart beat fast as I held it tightly in my hand.

'What's wrong, Kathy?' Sherry asked, and I suddenly realised I had frozen and was staring at the envelope.

'I've got a letter. I think it might be from my sister.'

'Oh, which one?' asked Sherry, pouring the hot water into the percolator. She wiped her slim hands on the front of her dungarees, and sat on the chair opposite mine.

I swallowed heavily. 'Sheila.'

'Sheila? I don't remember you mentioning Sheila. Which one is she again?'

I wanted to rip open the letter and devour its contents, but I was almost scared to read it.

'Well, it's kind of a long story,' I said, 'but if you're interested . . .?'

Sherry nodded slowly. 'Only if you want to tell it.'

I closed my eyes for a minute, took a drink of my coffee and began to fill her in. About the split. About Sheila choosing to live with her father and blanking Pat in the playground when they were both at the Ursuline. About the others being sent to children's homes.

'Poor little things!' murmured Sherry.

'They never talk about what happened there . . . but they were very unhappy. Anyway, Margaret and I wanted to know about Sheila, so we wrote to her publishers to get her address. She writes romances, you know.'

'Look, why don't you take it upstairs to read?' Sherry suggested. 'I need to go and get a few bits of shopping anyway. Do you mind listening out for Tom?'

I agreed readily, relieved that I was being given the chance to be on my own. I wasn't sure what the envelope contained, but whatever it was I wanted to have some time to think about it.

Once Sherry had left, I plucked up the courage to slide my finger under the flap of the envelope and open it up. I held the sheets of paper in my hand and began to read.

The letter told of Sheila's life, as a journalist, author and mother of five. She asked about us, what we did, whether or not we had children, a kind of easy-going letter that you might write to a long-lost acquaintance, not a sister – not even a secret one.

I sighed, and sat down to reply. This time I would dig a little deeper.

I tried again and again, but every letter I got back was the same: friendly and interesting, but giving nothing away.

During the months that we stayed at Sherry and Colin's, I still felt removed from Sam. It was a strange feeling, a detached, arm's length kind of relationship that I had with him. I would hold him, I played with him, I kissed and cuddled him, but it wasn't quite right, and I'm sure he sensed it too. Then not long before we moved into our little cottage things changed. We had taken Sam to hospital for an overnight stay as the consultant was worried that he had seen something that might mean yet another operation. Colin and I had been so worried, but we had got the phone call early that morning to say that there was nothing to worry about; it must just have been a shadow on the X-ray. When we arrived to pick Sam up, weak with relief, something strange happened.

Colin and I walked into the ward just as the children were being given breakfast. Sam was sitting on a tiny chair, still with a drip in his arm, tucking into a mashed up bowl of Weetabix with a serious yet determined look on his tiny round face. I looked at him, his big blue eyes, his red-blond hair, and suddenly my heart gave a lurch. All the love that I had kept in check, all the tenderness, swam over me and I almost drowned in the warmth of it. I felt such a surge of powerful love that I had to hug him. As I bent down I stroked his soft little face, I breathed in the sweet smell of him, and whispered in his ear, 'Mummy's here now.' He turned towards me and gave me a huge smile. It was as though he knew that his mummy was really here now, that things were going to be different from now on, and indeed they were. Sam was mine now and I was his; we had found each other at last.

47

Talking to Aunty

Margaret had not long had her third baby, and everyone had come for the baptism. They called her Elizabeth Edith, which seems like fate now because she would be the last baby that Aunty Edie would hold.

Aunty was becoming more and more fragile, although she still retained her sense of fun. 'Come out, Jimmy Green!' she would say with a mischievous smile when she accidentally passed wind. Her hair was quite grey now, but still thick and curly. She had never been as overweight as Mum, but more recently she appeared to have shrunk into herself.

The day after the baptism Aunty and I were invited to lunch at Margaret's house. As it was an unusually warm day for April, Margaret suggested we sit in the garden.

She placed baby Lizzie in Aunty's arms for a cuddle.

'Ooh, she's the model of yer mother,' Aunty said, rocking the baby back and forth. 'Hello my darling,' she cooed gently.

Lizzie gazed up at Aunty, spellbound.

'*Little girl you're crying, I know why you're blue,*' sung Aunty, softly rocking the baby in her arms.

The sun was shining, and the smell of lilacs was heavy in the air. Feeling warm and lazy like a cat, I felt myself starting to drift off to sleep.

Margaret broke the silence suddenly. 'Aunty, can I ask you something? Do you know who our dad is?'

I jerked awake with a start. Surely I must have dreamt that?

Aunty carried on singing:

Better go to sleep, now, little girl you've had a busy day.
You've been playing soldiers, the battle has been won,
The enemy is out of sight
Come now, little soldier,
Put away your gun, the war is over for tonight.

'Aunty,' she repeated, louder this time, in case the old lady hadn't heard, 'if you know, please tell us.'

Aunty stopped and looked down at Lizzie. 'You'd better put 'er to bed; she's gone fast asleep.'

Margaret took the baby gently and laid her on her lap.

'Did you hear me Aunty?' she continued, refusing to let it go.

'Yes I 'eard yer,' Aunty answered, irritated, 'I've told yer before, I can't tell yer about yer father without telling yer about yer mother.'

'Please Aunty,' I joined in now, 'we really have a right to know,' but Aunty just looked away towards where the other children were playing at the end of the garden.

'Be careful now,' she called out to them as a clod of mud flew up in the air. 'Mind yer 'eads.'

Margaret and I exchanged an exasperated look, when suddenly Aunty continued. 'He was good to 'er, 'e was,' she said, refusing to meet our eyes. 'He would 'ave stuck to 'er like shit to a blanket, if she adn't dun wot she did.'

We sat bolt upright now, hardly daring to move, knowing from experience that the slightest distraction could stop the conversation dead.

'Jewish 'e was, so kind, always 'elped 'er out, money, flowers, whatever she wanted. But then when it all stopped, she couldn't manage, you see, that's why she 'ad to do it, and they took 'er away again.

'I said to your Granny more than once, "I can't stand no more; either she goes or I go," and do yer know what yer Gran used to say? She said "She's going nowhere." I knew then, see, that she couldn't turn 'er out, not with all you children, so I just 'ad to put up with it.

'Anyway,' she added, 'yer mother was always 'er favourite. It was always Florrie that she wanted.'

Aunty gazed into the space around her, seemingly gathering her thoughts and then continued. 'She was determined not to die till yer mother got out, yer see, but as soon as she came back home, your Gran gave up. You must 'ave been about the same age as Becky and Sam are now, maybe a bit older.

'Anyway, where's me cup of tea? I feel like me throat's been cut,' and with that Lizzie woke, and Margaret fed her out there in the garden, with the children playing, the sun shining, and one more little piece of the jigsaw falling into place.

48

A Sudden Death

Later that summer we went with Pat, Josie and Mum to Crewkerne in Somerset for a week's holiday during the May half-term.

We were staying in a lovely old stone cottage, complete with leaded windows, and exposed beams, surrounded by the most beautiful cottage garden, spilling over with flowers. 'Aunty would love it here,' I said to Colin, while we watched Sam playing with Mr Lion, his favourite plastic ride-on toy.

'Perhaps we should try to take her some cuttings?'

We decided to take Sam for a walk in the nearby woods, and set off promising to be back by dinner time, leaving Mum and my sisters to enjoy the garden in peace. The trees were almost in full leaf, and when the sun shone through their branches it sent dappled drops of light sweeping across the forest floor.

As we walked, we talked about Mum. I had always shared everything with Colin, and he knew as much as I did about my past; we didn't believe in secrets. He also knew that there was a deep, burning need in me to know who my father was, to understand my Mum and make sense of my muddled memories.

'I really find it hard to understand why you can't just ask her outright,' he said, not for the first time.

'You know what she's like; she wouldn't answer me, or she would pretend she hadn't heard, like she did to Mary when she plucked up the courage to ask.'

My sisters and I had laughed when Mary had told us that Mum had just said, 'Yes, I will have another cup of tea,' when she had asked about her dad. We all knew the rules, and what to expect if we tried to flout them.

'There's just no point,' I continued, watching Sam weave in and out of the trees.

'Mummy, can we have a dog like Aunty Pat's?' he asked.

Pat and Sam were best friends and adored each other. She spoilt him terribly. He could do no wrong in her eyes, and the feeling was mutual.

'One day maybe,' I said absentmindedly.

'But surely if you tell her how important it is to you to know, surely then she would have to tell you?'

'I don't want to upset her.' I knew how hard it must be for Colin to understand the complexities of the relationships in our family. Nothing was as straightforward as it seemed.

'Well then, what about Pat or Josie? You're not telling me that they don't know more than they're saying.'

I just shrugged. It was like an itch that I couldn't scratch; every now and then the ignorance, the secrets, became intolerable.

We carried on walking in silence, both lost in thought, with Sam running up every now and then to show us an interesting stone, or a bug that he had spied crawling through the undergrowth.

When we approached the cottage, Mum was standing outside smoking a cigarette and leaning on the door frame. She looked strangely distracted.

Sam ran up to her. 'Nanny, I got you some flowers!' He thrust a handful of daisies towards her.

She bent down and took them and patted his head. 'Go in and find Aunty Pat.' When he was out of earshot she drew deeply on her cigarette and said in a flat, unemotional voice, 'Aunty's dead.'

The breath was sucked out of my body as I tried to comprehend what she was saying. 'What?'

I hadn't realised how much I had loved Aunty until that moment. I had been so preoccupied with myself and my own little family, that I had failed to notice her continued decline, had ignored the way she had looked when Geoff had picked her up to go and stay with Marion just a few days ago.

'She knew she was never going to come home again,' I cried bitterly to Colin later that night. 'I saw her looking around, like she was trying to fix it all in her head, take it with her: her chair in the corner, the old photos on the wall, her precious garden . . . all of her memories . . . and all I could think about was that I wished she would hurry up and go so she wouldn't wake Sam up as she left!'

Colin held me close and tried to comfort me but it was no good. I pulled away and curled up on the bed in a tight ball. Aunty was gone and I was inconsolable. I had never once told her that I loved her.

I cried myself quietly to sleep that night, and dreamed of an old lady with a mischievous smile and a sparkle in her blue eyes, who swore more than she should, had a fiery temper, threw teapots, liked a drop of brandy, sang and danced, loved her garden and our children who sometimes played in it, but most of all a woman who gave up her own life so that she could keep us all together and safe. She had been loyal to Mum to the end, never betraying her secrets.

They say that you go through stages of grief. At first comes the overwhelming desolation, then the next stage: anger.

'I don't understand,' I said through tightly drawn lips. 'Why didn't the doctor resuscitate her?'

Me, Margaret and Marion had met up at Mum's to help arrange the funeral, and had taken the children for a walk to Goodmayes Park.

It was worse for Marion. Aunty had been staying with her when she was taken ill.

'She knew she was dying,' she explained. 'She just kept saying, "Let me go, let me go." She was ready; she knew it was her time.'

The three of us watched the children run towards the lake where the swans were gliding across the sparkling water. How could the sun shine so brightly amid so much grief? Aunty loved the park, and she would sometimes walk through there on her way home from Mass on Sundays. For all the swearing she had been a devout woman, never missing a service.

I turned away and called to the children, 'Don't go too near the water.'

'Do you remember Aunty telling us that a swan would break your arm if you went near its babies?' Marion asked smiling.

It felt strange to be walking in the park that had been such a big part of our childhood. The memories of happier visits crowded in. The cricket matches we had all played, the races we had run.

We stopped to admire the beds of flowers, and then Marion said, 'All she had was her old rosary beads and a little miraculous medal that she always pinned to her vest.'

'Oh poor Aunty,' Margaret said starting to cry again.

'The ambulance man gave them to me. He shouldn't really have taken her from my house, you know, she was already dead, but when he realised that Cathy and David were upstairs asleep he took pity on us, I suppose.

'Mum must be upset,' I said, to reassure myself as much as anything. 'Aunty has been part of her life for so long. I mean, I know they argued, but I think they loved each other, don't you?'

'I think Mum finds it hard to feel sadness; in fact I think she finds it hard to show love,' said Marion.

'But she must realise what Aunty gave up because of her?' I said. 'That must mean something?'

'Of course it must!' Margaret added with conviction.

'Well, I suppose she loved Aunty in her own way, but she didn't exactly show it did she?'

'I don't know, I never really thought about it,' I admitted.

'Well,' Marion said, 'I certainly don't think she has ever loved me.'

It was Margaret who broke the silence.

'Of course Mum loves us,' she said. 'She's the best mum in the world.'

Marion looked at us carefully. 'Yes, I think you're probably right. She does love you two, but I don't think she has ever loved me, or Marge and Mary.' Her eyes slid away from ours as she continued. 'What you two still don't understand is that she was never there when we were small. In fact I remember her coming to see us in Valence Avenue once, and we didn't even know who she was. Aunty said to us, "Come and give your mother a cuddle," and we just looked at this stranger standing there. We didn't know her at all.'

'Where was she then?' I asked. 'Not prison again?' Margaret gave me a look. It felt a little disloyal to say the words aloud, but we both needed to find out the truth.

'No, not that time. Who knows? It might have been London or Southend or anywhere. I don't suppose we will ever know now Aunty is gone. Mum had another life, a secret life wherever she was, and it didn't include us, her ever-expanding brood of children, that's for sure.' Marion hesitated, and then went on, 'And when she finally did come back to Valence Ave to live, she used to send us to bed you know, we had to be upstairs by half six even when we were older, just to get us out of the way. You never had that, you and Margaret; you were always the favourites, the babies. We just got sent to bed without any dinner, just bread and jam for our tea. How do you think that made us feel? Loved? No, I don't think so.'

As we walked back to the house in silence, my mind was in turmoil. If Margaret and I could find out where Mum used to disappear to and with who, we might just be able to solve the questions that eternally tormented us: the identity of our father, and why we had never known him. Then I remembered Aunty and the loss hit me again like a slap. What did any of it matter anyway? The person who had stood up for us, who had been beside Mum through all of it, that person was dead, and then I remembered a saying my friend Anne had often used: 'You never miss the water till the well runs dry,' and I smiled. Aunty would have appreciated that.

49

Josephine

By the time Sam was three and a half, Colin and I had plucked up the courage to try for another baby. I was frightened. I knew that Sam's condition wasn't thought to be hereditary, but that didn't completely reassure me. Margaret was expecting her fourth baby and I knew that if I didn't have one soon, I never would. I wanted desperately to know what it would be like to have a 'normal' baby with no problems. I wanted to be able to enjoy the excitement and happiness that other women felt after they gave birth, without the crushing terror that had accompanied my experience and followed me throughout the first year of Sam's life. Within a couple of months I was expecting. When I told Margaret she was overjoyed.

'That's great,' she said, 'they'll be born about the same time apart as Becky and Sam.'

I was devastated when I miscarried my baby at twelve weeks. There didn't appear to be any cause; I was just told to try again in a few months. Depression began to overwhelm me. I couldn't believe I would ever have a healthy baby. When Margaret gave birth to her fourth daughter she called her Faye, the name that I had picked out for our baby. The name suited her completely. She was tiny and fragile, with fine wisps of black hair, and enormous blue eyes. When I visited Margaret in hospital I looked down at the baby enviously.

'She's beautiful,' I murmured, stroking her pale skin.

Within a month of Faye being born I found out that I was pregnant again.

The doctor was very cautious. 'Bed rest!' he advised sternly. 'Bed rest and lots of good food!' The hospital had now identified that I had a fibroid, and it was that which they thought may have caused my previous miscarriage. Colin was very strict with me, but I put my foot down when he suggested that I might use a bedpan!

'I hope you're joking?' I said, 'Because that is not going to happen!' But I did rest. I wanted this baby desperately and I wasn't taking any chances this time.

About six weeks before my baby was due, I was watching a new comedy series, *Blackadder*, which I thought was hilarious. As I watched I felt a few minor contractions. When I told Colin, he was worried.

'Why don't you ring Margaret and ask what she thinks?' he suggested.

'Oh for goodness sake, it is just practice contractions, I think they're called "Braxton Hicks",' I said, but I rang Margaret anyway just to be sure.

'How bad are they?' she asked.

'Well, I suppose they're quite painful,' I replied as I paced up and down our tiny living room.

'And how frequent are they?'

'About every five minutes or so, I suppose.'

'I think you should ring the hospital,' she advised, 'just to make sure.'

Luckily our cottage was immediately opposite the hospital that I was booked in to have the baby, because when I rang they insisted that I come in immediately.

'Okay,' I said, 'I'll walk over with my husband.'

I couldn't believe it when they insisted that he drove me. It was literally as far to our driveway as it was to the hospital, but Colin insisted we do as we were told, so I climbed into the car for the thirty-second journey!

After chauffeuring me, Colin drove Sam to my mum's. By the time he arrived home later that night the phone was ringing to tell him that if he wanted to see his baby born he had better get over there quickly. Our baby girl was born as Colin walked into the delivery room. I heard the midwife say to her assistant,

'Thank goodness, her airways are clear,' and I knew that my baby was going to be all right even though she had been in such a hurry to get here. She had arrived six weeks early and was the most beautiful baby ever. She was tiny, weighing just 4lb 10oz, but was perfect, with the same red-gold hair as her brother and the same enormous blue eyes. She was like a baby doll and I fell in love with her immediately. Unlike my previous delivery, I felt really well and was out of bed by the time Colin arrived the next morning with Sam.

'Be careful,' he said. 'Do you think you should be out of bed already?'

I laughed. 'I'm fine. Look Sam,' I said, calling him over, 'here's your baby sister.'

Sam peered into the cot. 'What's her name, Mummy?'

I looked at Colin over our two little ones' heads. We hadn't had a chance to decide yet, but in my heart I knew what kind of little girl my baby would be. She would be strong, fiery and creative, just like my favourite heroine in *Little Women*, and just like her Aunty Josie.

'Shall we call her Josephine?' I suggested to Sam and Colin. They nodded their agreement. 'What second name shall we give her?' I asked Sam, 'You can choose if you like.'

Sam gave it no more than a couple of seconds thought and then suggested firmly, 'Jet Plane – I think we should call her Josephine Jet Plane.'

Colin and I exchanged a smile; we might have to persuade Sam to think of a slightly more conventional name. Later that morning we agreed on Kate – Josephine Kate, our perfect baby daughter!

Jo, as we called her, was indeed a perfect, contented baby. She was easy to feed, slept well, and was a peach of a baby, always smiling and happy. Those early days as a family of four were some of the happiest of my life.

50

Trying to Hold On

By this point, Margaret and Marion lived with their families just around the corner, so we saw lots of each other.

Marion had decided to train to be a teacher and was now attending a local teacher training college.

Mum had not been very encouraging to poor Marion.

'You'll make a terrible teacher,' she said when Marion told her. 'You don't even like children.'

Marion was hurt and upset. 'I don't understand why she's always so horrible to me,' she said later that evening when she popped in for a cup of tea. 'It's as though she always has to put me down, make me feel useless.'

'I'm sure she doesn't mean to be hurtful,' I assured her. Mum had been just as dismissive of Marge when she had decided to go into nursing, telling her that she wouldn't be any good because she was afraid of blood. 'Perhaps she's just trying to protect you, in case it doesn't work out.'

Marion took a gulp of tea. 'Yes, maybe, though I think we both know that's not the real reason,' and with that she left for home.

I knew that Mum was funny about some things. She liked to be able to boast about us to other people, but she would always remind us, 'Don't tell the devil too much of your mind,' as though she was always expecting the worst to happen. It is strange how you retain an irrational fear for your whole life, and the worry that something bad was waiting just around the corner was something that we all still carried with us.

I had another miscarriage shortly after Jo's first birthday, and had been very upset, but we knew we were lucky to have two lovely children, and so were able to put it behind us the best that we could.

By the time Jo was three, we had decided we would definitely like another baby. I had always wanted a big family, and was envious of Margaret's growing brood. I needed to catch up! I was feeling very tired, and Margaret persuaded me to go to the doctors to get checked out first.

The doctor's surgery was small, and the doctor that I saw was the only member of the practice. He was a kind man, but unfortunately had a rather insensitive bedside manner. When he examined me he smiled. 'Ah Mrs Hardy, you are pregnant! About three months at least I should think.'

'I can't be,' I replied. I knew that I wasn't expecting a baby, I wasn't an idiot.

'Well I'm afraid you can be, and I think you are,' he stated matter-of-factly. 'What makes you so sure that you're not?'

'Because I have been having periods, heavy ones,' I told him, 'and anyway, I don't feel pregnant.'

The doctor looked perplexed, and then called his nurse into the consulting room.

'Feel this,' he indicated to her.

She felt around. 'Mmm yes,' she said nodding.

'Do you feel the lump?' he asked her. I felt my insides turning to water. A lump? A hot prickly sweat broke out on my neck and hands.

'Yes, yes I can,' she murmured, palpating my abdomen.

'It's enormous,' the doctor continued, talking to the nurse over me, as though I was invisible, 'the size of a melon!'

'Well Mrs Hardy,' he said, as though he had just noticed that I was there, 'you have a very large lump in your womb, and we need to get it checked out as soon as possible. I'll get you referred to the hospital immediately.'

'So this is it,' I thought to myself. 'I knew things were too good to be true. I've got cancer and I'm going to die.' The faces of my two children came into my mind. How could I leave them? How would Colin cope on his own with two young children? The negative thoughts swam around inside my head, panic spiralling out of control. As I drove down the country lane close to our cottage, I considered driving into a ditch. For a few seconds, in my mind that was an actual possibility. I just didn't want to have to face up to it.

Then I remembered the doctors speculating about me having fibroids. I desperately clung on to the possibility that the lump was something like that – something fixable.

I shuddered to myself as I turned my key in the door and heard Sam and Jo calling out, 'Mummy's home! Daddy – Mummy's home!' My heart did a somersault as I thought, 'Yes, but for how long?'

I went into a downward spiral of depression, worse even than the months after Sam was born. I suppose that I had never really fully recovered. People didn't expect me to be depressed. I wasn't 'that sort' of person, whatever that means. When the social worker used to wander round the neonatal ward that Sam was in as a baby, she would often go up to the other mothers and ask them if they were OK. I knew that many of them were given counselling and other types of support, but she would look at me reading my book as I sat next to Sam's cot, and say 'You're fine aren't you, Mrs Hardy,' as a statement, not a question, and every time she said it I would smile at her and nod my head.

'Yes thank you.' I would say. 'Absolutely fine,' when inside I was falling apart. Oh the lies we learn to tell to protect ourselves from ourselves. My drama training came in handy, here. I was still a good actress;, no one knew how shattered and damaged I was inside.

It was the same now. I hid my terrors from almost everyone, but Colin knew. I cried myself to sleep some nights while I was waiting to go into hospital.

The consultant had been kind.

'Mrs Hardy, without opening you up and having a good old poke around, we can't be sure whether it is a fibroid or something a bit more troublesome,' he told me. Then he hesitated before going on. 'You have two children, don't you?'

I nodded fearfully.

'Well I want you to have a good think about whether your family is complete,' he went on. He was a tall slim man with kind eyes, and he was looking at me now questioningly. 'Because that will help us to decide what to do next'.

I wasn't sure what he meant.

'I don't understand,' I said. 'Can you explain please?'

'Of course,' he said obligingly. He lent forward and took my hand. 'I am almost certain this is just a fibroid,' he started by saying, 'but there is a small chance that it is something more sinister that we will have to deal with promptly.' I knew what he meant now.

'If it is just a fibroid, I can do a myomectomy, which means that you will keep your womb, and can continue to have more babies if you want – although I have to tell you that the fibroid will probably grow back and you will have to go through the operation again at some stage in the future. If your family is complete, then I can just whip out your womb once and for all, and "Bob's your uncle," no more problems.' He smiled. It sounded so easy. He patted my hand, 'You have a chat to your husband outside and let me know before you leave,' and with that he ushered me to the door.

Colin was waiting patiently outside. I wasn't crying when I joined him, but my hands were trembling. He put his arm around me.

'Are you OK?' he asked. 'What did he say?'

I told him that I had a choice: have a myomectomy, which would leave my womb intact but meant that I might have similar problems in the future, or undergo a full hysterectomy. Of course, if the lump turned out to be malignant my choices would be narrowed even further.

'I think you should just have it finished and done with,' Colin said, his blue eyes searching my face. 'We've got two children now, our little boy and our little girl.'

I gave him a watery smile.

'Sam was born ill; Jo was born early. I'm not sure I want us to take any more chances. Perhaps we are only meant to have two children,' he said carefully, watching for my reaction.

I nodded reluctantly, feeling worn down by it all. The most important thing was to be around for Sam and Jo as long as possible. I felt as though I had this malevolent growth inside me, and I just wanted it gone, to be able to get on with my life if I could.

That evening after the children were in bed, Colin and I went out into the garden. He put his arms around me as we looked at the sky. The smell from the early lilac blooms swam around us and the stars were very bright. 'Look,' he said, pointing upwards, 'it's funny isn't it? The light that we are seeing now was shining thousands if not millions of years ago. It makes you feel very small and unimportant, doesn't it?'

I snuggled into him, strangely comforted by the thought that we were just small dots in a vast picture.

I returned to that moment many times over the weeks while I waited to be called in to hospital.

51

Mum's Illness

'Kathleen, will you help me clear out the cupboard in my room?' Mum asked softly watching me with her blue eyes that had faded now to grey. I had popped round with some fresh scones, to find her ill in bed. With her wispy white hair spread across her pillow she looked older than her seventy-three years.

Mum had asked me about the cupboard several times over the past few months. Surely she didn't feel up to it at the moment? It was becoming an obsession with her.

'Mum, I can't do it tonight,' I said, 'the kids will be wanting their dinner.' She looked away and I thought I saw tears in her eyes. 'Are you all right, Mum?'

She nodded sadly, 'Yes, but I'm not well, Kath,' she whispered.

I stroked her head; it still felt alien to kiss her, but I did. 'I know. I'll come back at the weekend,' I promised, packing up my things. 'I'd better get going. You never know what the traffic will be like.'

I looked back from the doorway, and saw Mum, a shadow of herself, melting into the bedclothes.

'Try to eat something, Mum; you won't get better unless you do,' and with that I left Valence Avenue and drove our little 2CV back to the cottage, Sam and Jo squabbling in the back over the Matchbox cars that Pat had bought them, my thoughts back on myself and my own fears. I pushed Mum out of my mind. I would worry about her after my operation, I thought. I couldn't worry about everything at once.

The next morning I got the letter through with the date for my operation. As I opened the envelope my hands shook. I gave it to Colin when he got home. 'I have to go in on the 7th May,' I said flatly. I was trying hard to hide my emotions.

'Good,' he said, 'it will be over and done with and you will feel better'.

I nodded. 'I hope so.'

Mum continued to struggle to eat, so shortly after my visit she was taken into hospital.

Margaret and I met outside at visiting time and walked to the ward together. We saw Mum propped half up in bed looking very frail.

'Mum,' I said kissing her lightly on the cheek. 'How are you feeling?'

She just looked at me with a faraway look in her eyes.

Margaret gave her a kiss and held her hand.

'Oh Margy.' Mum said softly, and her eyes took on a wistful look.

'Have the doctors been round yet?' Margaret asked, her nurse's training kicking in. 'I'd like to have a word with them.'

Mum shook her head. 'No they've been round already today.' She spoke so quietly I could hardly hear.

Margaret turned to me, 'I'm just going to see if I can have a chat with the nurse,' she said, and I stayed with Mum, holding her hand and stroking her arm. Although she had lost all the plumpness from her body, her skin was still soft as silk. 'Don't worry,' I joked, 'Margaret will get you sorted out, you know what she's like.'

Mum tried to smile, but I could see that she was very weak, and I was getting worried.

The staff nurse was talking to Margaret, and I watched them out of the corner of my eye trying desperately to get a sense of their discussion from their faces. Margaret glanced over at Mum and I and then turned back and continued talking to the nurse. She came back with a thin smile on her lips. She looked paler than usual, but had a slight red flush to her cheeks.

'Everything all right?' I asked as brightly as I could.

She nodded unconvincingly. 'Yes fine. Let's grab a drink.' She looked at Mum, who was starting to close her eyes, and whispered, 'Mum, we're going to get a cup of tea. Do you want us to bring you anything back?'

Mum shook her head almost imperceptibly and drifted off to sleep.

The hospital café was starkly lit and almost empty.

'Why is it that hospitals always have the same sticky, antiseptic smell?' I asked, stirring the grey liquid.

'Mum's kidneys are failing,' Margaret blurted out.

'Is it to do with her diabetes?' I knew that she had been warned over the years to control her diet more carefully, but she had never been very good at being told what to do, and this had resulted in her being put on insulin a while ago.

Margaret nodded. 'I would have thought so. The doctors want to run some more tests.'

'Does that mean they'll be keeping her in for a while longer then?'

Margaret looked down at the remains of her coffee. 'Kathleen, I don't think Mum will be coming home for a good while yet.'

'Well I must admit that's a relief. At least now she's getting the attention she needs, and it will get sorted once and for all.'

Margaret just gave me a strange look and pushed herself upright. 'Sorry, but I've got to go and pick up the kids. Can you say goodbye to Mum for me?'

I nodded, swigged down my horrible coffee and tried to put on a cheerful face for Mum's sake.

52

Falling Apart

The following week was busy. I was desperately trying to get everything ready for my impending hospital stay, and I was also aware that I would be incapacitated for a while after the operation. That was going to be tricky to manage with two young children. None of this was helped by my secret conviction that I was never going to come home again, and the deep, debilitating depression that was beginning to overwhelm me.

I went upstairs to make sure that Sam had not thrown his school uniform on the floor again. He was almost eight and had recently had a growth spurt, so looked even skinnier than usual. His hair had lost its red tinge very soon after he was born and was now a pale golden blond, the same as his sister's. Sam had always been boisterous and lively, and Jo emulated him – she was a real tomboy, and wanted to be with her brother and her cousins at every opportunity. They were always together, the six of them, running around outside, climbing, making dens, playing at pirates, racing drivers, explorers, anything where they could let their imaginations fly. We were so lucky to live out here, with a wild garden ripe for exploration.

Just then the telephone rang and I heard Colin's key in the door. As the kids ran to meet him, I picked it up.

'Oh Kath, is Colin with you?

My stomach lurched. I tried to speak but my throat felt tight, so that I had to cough before I could respond.

'Pat?' I didn't want her to say anything else then. Until I heard the words, life would be the same.

'It's Mum,' she said, 'I'm sorry, she died this afternoon.'

And there it was – boom – the explosion that rocked my core. The floor beneath my feet shifted, and I involuntarily sat down on the bed, hands shaking, barely able to hold the phone.

'Kathleen?' Pat said. 'Kath, are you all right?' I could hear the concern in her voice, but couldn't answer at first. Why wasn't I crying? My eyes stung with the unshed tears.

'Why didn't you call me?' I asked. 'Why didn't you phone?'

'The hospital didn't let us know until after,' she said, her voice heavy with sadness, 'Josie and I had been up to see her this morning, but she slipped into a coma after we left.'

'Who was with her?' I wailed. 'When she died, who was with her?'

Pat didn't answer at first but then said, 'The nurse held her hand; she went in her sleep. She didn't know anything about it.'

Then the next explosion happened, this time it was more like a powerful thud. My mum, our darling mum, had died alone, with just the nurse to see her out of this world. Not one of her ten children there with her to hold her hand, to stroke her silky soft skin, to touch her wispy white hair, to kiss her cheek, to say goodbye. None of us . . . none of us.

Then the tears came, sliding slowly down my cheeks at first, and then the wracking sobs that hurt my chest and throat with a welcome pain. I wanted to hurt. *I wasn't there . . . I wasn't there . . .*

Colin was standing watching me from the doorway, not knowing what to say or do. He was never very good at emotions. 'Just like Mum,' I thought as he came over and tried to comfort me. Sam and Jo had crept into the room now and were peeping round the door at us.

They didn't ask what was wrong. Children have a knack of knowing when not to speak, when words would be out of place. There were a lot of tears then. A week full of them. All of us, desperate that we hadn't been able to say goodbye, angry that we had been cheated of our chance to tell her we loved her, that despite everything, anything that she had ever done, we adored her. Those tears were full of regret, of unsaid words and unasked questions. Mum was dead, and there was an empty space in our hearts where she had once lived. The finality felt too much to bear, and it plunged me even deeper into depression. My world started to crumble and there was nothing I could to do to halt the disintegration.

I had lost my way, and I didn't believe that I would ever find it again. The world had shifted, and didn't make any sense any more; nothing did.

Then there was the funeral.

It was a strange ceremony, so different from Aunty's; a solemn and desperate day. My mum's remaining siblings were there, as were our cousins. My dear friend Anne, who had loved my mum as her own, came and we clung together to withstand the tempest that was blowing through our family. But I took no comfort from it. I was surer now than ever that it would be my children's turn to grieve soon, to feel this same bereft sorrow, because I knew that I was not going to survive my operation, and I would never be there to see them grow up. So I cried my tears with my brothers and sisters, but I cried them for me, not for Mum, and the guilt made it even harder to bear.

53

Saying Goodbye

I looked at the letters I had written before placing them in a box covered in paper flowers. 'These are for you,' I told Colin, the night before I was due to go into hospital.

'What is it?'

'Letters for the children,' I explained, feeling the tears that had become as familiar as old friends to me slip down my cheeks, 'and one for you.'

'Oh Kathy,' he said, taking the box hesitantly, 'you're going to be fine, I just know you are.'

I looked away. 'Please make sure you don't lose them,' I asked plaintively, 'and remember to look after my babies, give them an exciting life, do lots of wonderful things with them, and be patient – they're only little you know'.

I tiptoed into their rooms, Jo's first. It was a blue room. She had chosen the colour herself and had been very clear about what she wanted. She was only three, and still had tiny plump baby hands and feet, but had a strong personality. She was my little fighter and I gently stroked her cheek, and bent to kiss her. Her hair was a little damp still from her bath, and had formed tiny tight curls that stuck to her baby soft skin. She was beautiful, so perfect, like a little doll, and I tried to pour my love into her so that it would sustain her after I was gone.

Then I moved into Sam's room. On the shelf above his bed were the beginnings of his football trophy collection. He loved football just like his dad and played it at every opportunity. I looked down at his sleeping frame, and remembered the heartache of his babyhood. It wasn't fair, I thought, that he was going to be unhappy again. Hadn't he had to go through enough? I bent and kissed his cheek, and he stirred.

'Mummy?' he said sleepily.

'Shhh, go to sleep now,' I whispered, and crept out of the room without looking back.

The apple blossom was out on the trees in the garden as we drove off towards the hospital. I couldn't help wondering if I'd ever see it again. As if he'd read my thoughts, Colin's hand searched for mine as we drove, and we continued the journey in a silence that said more than any words could.

Margaret worked as a theatre nurse in the hospital where I was to be admitted. Although of course she was not allowed to be involved with my operation, she made sure she was there as I started to come round in the recovery room. It was her huge brown eyes peering above a white mask that I saw before anything else when I first opened my eyes.

'It hurts so much,' I muttered through my anaesthetic-induced confusion.

'Of course it does!' she said matter-of-factly. 'What did you expect?' But I was still very glad to see her there. It just seemed right somehow.

My recovery went well, and I was elated when the doctor told me that it was just 'a fibroid the size of a melon!'

The elation didn't last. I couldn't shift my conviction that there was something badly wrong with me and that I was going to die. I didn't realise that I was in the grip of an all-consuming depression.

My friend Anne came over to stay while Colin took the children for a short break camping, and my other friend also called Anne came over too. Each assumed very different but equally essential roles. Anne M tiny, funny and matter-of-fact made me laugh even though it hurt, and Anne D tall, slim, sensitive and kind, cleaned the house and made us food. After a few days I thought I could see a glimmer of hope, but it took more than six months of careful care from my new wonderful GP, and my dear family and friends, before I felt that life might just be worth living after all, and I was strong enough to confront the ghosts in Valence Avenue.

The leaves on the trees which lined Valence Avenue were in full leaf, helping to disguise the growing dilapidation. As our car drew up, I felt a deep sadness and loss that the person who had been a constant presence in this house would no longer be there. I gathered up my new-found strength and opened the car door, waving goodbye to Colin. I wanted to be on my own so that Josie and I could make a start on clearing Mum's room.

I knocked on the front door with the usual family knock, and waited, a host of memories crowding into my head. Aunty's once beautiful front garden had been paved over now so that Pat could park her car, and it made me feel sad that the flowers she had loved were gone forever. The door swung open after a while, and Josie stood there looking rather dishevelled.

'Oh there you are. I wondered where you'd got to.'

As I came in I felt an oppressive weight bearing down on me. I could feel Mum there even after all this time. The house looked different to when I was a child. Pat and Josie had bought it from the council with Aunty before she had died, so at least they had that security now. They had put in a fitted kitchen, complete with a new fridge and an automatic washing machine. The coal fire was gone, replaced with gas, there was fitted carpet every-where now and a new three-piece suite with reclining chairs. Upstairs had a new bathroom, 'fully tiled' as Mum had boasted, and complete with a washbasin and shower over the bath.

Although I almost resented the changes, I was glad that Mum had enjoyed her 'mod cons' for a while at least before she died. She had never been sentimental about the past, and had been greedy for the new world, including all the gadgets that went with it.

'Come on then,' I said, 'let's get started,' and we climbed the stairs to the landing. As I got to the top I stopped under the painting of the Sacred Heart of Jesus which hung there, looking down at us. It had been there for as long as I could remember, and I had prayed in front of it many times as a frightened child. I said a prayer now, for Aunty and for Mum.

Mum's old room, the box room, didn't look very different from when I had last seen it, not long before Mum died. Colin had helped Pat and Josie to move most of Mum's things to the front room downstairs, so that she wouldn't need to climb up and down the stairs. The wardrobe that blocked the built-in cupboard over the stairwell was still in the same place it had been when I was a child. There was a layer of dust over everything, and I ran my finger along the top of the dressing table that held so many childhood memories. This had been where I stored my treasures. The little things that had been so important to me then. All gone now. Josie and I manoeuvred the dressing table towards the bedroom door, and then began to inch the wardrobe out of the way of the cupboard door so that we could open it.

'God, this weighs a ton,' I complained.

'Are you sure you're all right to do this, Kath?' Josie asked. It wasn't much more than six months after my hysterectomy, but I felt fine.

'I'm okay,' I said, 'anyway, we're nearly done now,' and with a final push and a shower of dust, the solid wooden piece of furniture moved, and the cupboard door, with its original brass catch painted closed, stood revealed in front of us ready to be opened.

Despite the sad circumstances, I felt an odd shiver of anticipation.

54

The Letters

We opened the stiff cupboard door to a musty smell of age. Inside piled high and draped with cobwebs were boxes, mostly empty, some faded photos in broken frames and a few old bags. Josie's face was red with the exertion of moving the furniture, and tiny beads of sweat covered her forehead.

'Why don't you let me do the rest?' I offered but she shook her head.

'Don't be daft; I'm fine.'

There was a layer of thick greasy dust everywhere, and when Josie reached in and picked up an old black patent bag, it scattered and stuck to her fingers. The bag was now cracked and worn with age and smelt of damp and darkness, but was strangely familiar. As she looked inside she made a little sound of surprise and a knowing look crossed her face. 'I think you should have these,' she said flatly.

'What are they?'

She just held out the tattered bag and carried on sorting through the cupboard, not even glancing in my direction. As I peered inside I saw it was stuffed with faded old envelopes. They were yellowed with age and were all different shapes and sizes. There was even a card, like the ones you attach to a bunch of flowers, all addressed to me. Or at least all addressed to Kathleen Stevens, which is the name on my birth certificate, but not the name I'd grown up with. The postmarks were wrong too. One envelope was dated December 1953 but I wasn't even born until August 1954.

'They're Mum's letters from Thomas. I don't know much more than that, but I think you need to read them.'

'But I don't understand . . .' I started to say. Josie just looked away and carried on with the sorting.

My hand shook slightly as I slipped them into my own bag, and turned back to the filthy cupboard.

'Why don't you put them in date order before you start to read them?' Colin suggested, as I settled myself at our kitchen table later that evening. We had got the children to bed earlier than usual, so now at last I could concentrate on the letters.

'This looks like the earliest.' I held the envelope in my hand and turned it over; it was yellow and had a slight brown tinge to the edges. The writing was confident and sloping and it was addressed to Mrs Kathleen Stevens, as they all were. The postmark was Paddington W2 and it was dated 27 Dec 1953, the year before I was born. It looked as though it had been handled many times because of its worn appearance and crumpled feel. We slotted the rest in place. Seventeen letters altogether, starting around the time of my conception and continuing through to after I was born in August '54, and then stopping dead in July 1955 when Mum must have been three months pregnant with Margaret. I looked up at Colin, and saw the look of sudden realisation mirrored in his eyes. These letters could hold the answers that I had been searching for my whole life.

Mrs Kathleen Stevens. These letters weren't addressed to me at all. How could they be? They were written to Mum.

Although it was early winter and quite cold, I felt a rush of heat course through my body as I gently teased the thin paper from the first envelope and began to read:

27th December, '53

Dear Kathleen

I have something very important I would like to see you about, concerning your present. Could you arrange to see me for certain on Thursday next at 6.30 at Seven Kings. I am going to Newcastle on Monday morning, but I shall be back early on

Thursday. Will you answer this letter by return of post so that I will receive it in good time and please try not to disappoint me again. I have been telephoning you all over the weekend, but you have not been there. I do hope you are now quite better. Whatever happens do please answer this letter and do try and come on Thursday

T

I am enclosing a stamped addressed envelope and paper to make it easy for you

'T must be Thomas,' I said to Colin, trying to control the catch in my voice. 'Josie said they were his letters to Mum, but she didn't know any more.'

'And you believed her?' Colin asked incredulously.

'Yes, I believed her.' I was stung by his suspicions. 'Why would she lie?'

'Well let's face it, your family are not exactly known for their honesty and openness are they?' he said bluntly, 'and anyway, why did she give them to you? It must have been pretty obvious by their age that they were written before you were around.'

'I don't know,' I reflected. 'Maybe she had her suspicions, but wasn't sure about who Thomas might be.' I added, 'I think we both know what these letters could be hinting at . . .'

'Hinting is right; that's quite a leap to make. Open the next one.'

My hands shook as I picked up the next letter.

It felt strange to feel the whisper of past words brush against my face as I continued to read:

30th April '54

Dear Kathleen,

Thanks ever so much for your very nice letter, which I appreci-ated far more than I can tell you. I am so glad you have decided to consider your doctor's advice over the weekend and sincerely hope you will decide wisely. I should very much like to come up and see you, either at your house, or the hospital, and will endeavour to cheer you up when I come. I hope you will be your old self again (or young self, I should say)

    I am enclosing £2 which you will have no difficulty in getting cashed.

    I am looking forward to hearing from you again, so I am enclosing a stamped addressed envelope and paper, and perhaps you will be able to drop me a few lines letting me know how you are getting along, and when I shall be able to see you again.

    Hoping sincerely you are now feeling very much better

    With my very best wishes and lots of luck

T

'Well, he certainly seems keen, whoever he is,' Colin said. 'What do you think was wrong with her?'

'My guess is probably just pregnancy. She would have been about five months gone by this date.'

'Do you think he knew? He doesn't refer to any baby, does he?'

'Maybe he did,' Colin said. 'Remember we're talking about the 50s. People were more sensitive to that kind of thing, you know, less open about pregnancy and things.'

The rest of the letters were along the same vein. Thomas desperate to see 'Kathleen' and often being disappointed, promises of telephone calls sometimes kept by her and sometimes not, cheques enclosed, and even mention of visits to films and a trade show.

'Well there's nothing so far to give much away,' I remarked, feeling increasingly despondent.

'Isn't that the Disney emblem? On the envelope?'

I shrugged, too tired to think any more. I wasn't sure what I was expecting, but I knew for sure what I was hoping for – some clear, unequivocal evidence that T or Thomas as he sometimes signed himself, was more to Mum than a pen pal!

I picked up the letter that was sent 8 August 1954, a week before I was born – one of the longer letters in the set.

Sunday 8 August '54

My Dear Kathleen,

I was more than delighted to receive your letter on Saturday morning, and was so glad you received your flowers etc. okay.

You really must have gone through an awful time, being still so weak. I am looking forward so much to phoning Bridie on Monday morning to know whether you will be able to come away. I am hoping I shall not have another disappointment. It has happened so often.

It seems, and is, ages since I saw you, and I am looking forward so much to doing so. I am sure it will do you more good than harm if you could come away, as the change, after being in bed for so long, would act like a tonic, so I hope you will do your best to be strong enough to come. Bridie has kept me well informed of your health the whole time, and it has been marvellous of her to come and take my calls every time I have phoned up. You too, must have found her a great help and I am sure she has looked after you well. Tell her I am very grateful, and thank her very much for all she has done.

Well my dear, I must close now, hoping to be able to see you on Monday and wishing you the very best of luck and good wishes

Thomas

There was also a little card from a bouquet of flowers which was sent at the same time saying:

Very much looking forward to seeing you on Monday quite well

Thomas

'That's strange,' I commented. 'That letter and card are dated a week before I was born. Mum would have been heavily pregnant. Surely he wouldn't have expected her to go away with him?'

Colin rubbed his head: 'What do you mean?'

'Well she wouldn't have been up to it I wouldn't have thought, would you? Unless he didn't know . . .'

This was not as easy or straightforward as I had hoped it was going to be. It was like trying to complete a jigsaw without having the picture to follow.

'But you could have been premature,' Colin suggested. 'She was an older mum after all and she had already had eight children.'

'Yes, I suppose that could account for why she was so unwell.' I shook my head, trying to clear my muddled thoughts. 'It's all so odd. These letters have been in that cupboard for a very long time by the look of them. It was just chance that Josie and I happened to find them . . .' Then it struck me like a blow. It hadn't been chance. Mum had wanted to show them to me before she had died. It was like a sudden bolt of lightning. How many times had Mum asked me to help her sort out that cupboard? Four? Five? Maybe more. Were these letters the real focus of her obsession? I knew the answer instinctively. Of course! Mum had known she was dying, and she had wanted to tell me about Thomas before it was too late.

'But you don't know any of this for sure,' Colin tried to reason with me.

'I know,' I said, 'but it's all starting to make sense. The pieces are falling into place.' Then a terrible realisation hit me, and I laid my head on the table and cried, hot angry tears of frustration.

I had denied Mum that last chance to unburden herself, to tell me about the man who was mine and Margaret's father, whoever he was. And so I had missed my chance again. How could I hope to understand the messages hidden in these few hastily written lines? Too late again, too late . . .

55

Trying to Make Sense

Colin had tried to persuade me to leave the rest of the letters until the morning, but I couldn't. I greedily sucked the words from the pages, not just once, but several times. Reading and re-reading, until Thomas's words swam around my head. I had even begun to answer the letters, trying to guess what was in the replies that Mum had clearly sent. 'I'm going mad,' I thought, 'I need to stop.' But it was out of my control now. By the time the children woke up in the morning I hadn't even been to bed. Colin came downstairs and looked at me.

'You look awful,' he said. 'Why don't you try to get some sleep now, and I'll take the kids out?'

'No!' I almost shouted, 'I'm going over to Margaret's. She needs to see these too.'

By the time I arrived Margaret was already up and about. Her children were also early risers, and so they had eaten breakfast and were upstairs playing.

'Well,' she said as soon as I got there, 'what's all this about?'

I pulled the letters from a folder I had carefully filed them in.

'Josie and I found these in Mum's cupboard yesterday when we were clearing it out, but I don't think it was an accident. I think I was meant to find them.'

'Meant by who?' Margaret asked puzzled, obviously surprised.

'Mum,' I stated flatly.

It was only just starting to get light, even though it was nearly nine, as we sat to read the letters together. I hated those long dark winter mornings and evenings. They seemed to cast an air of depression and a loss of hope. There was still a slight smell of hot buttered toast floating from the kitchen, and I suddenly felt ravenous, and realised that I hadn't eaten since yesterday lunchtime.

'Can I make myself some toast while you carry on reading?' I asked, knowing that I could probably recite the contents of each and every one of Thomas's letters by heart.

Margaret nodded without looking up. She was being drawn in just as I had been.

'The last letter talks about a holiday,' she said finally. 'What holiday was that?' 'Listen . . .' she started to read aloud,

Friday 1st July '55

My dear Kathleen,

I am sending you a cheque as promised for £5.
    I do so hope you will have a very lovely time away and enjoy a nice rest. I also hope the weather will keep nice and fine for you my dear. I will look forward to having a letter from you so that I receive it in good time to meet you.
    With my every good wish for a very nice holiday

Lots of luck

Thomas

'That was written about six months before I was born,' she said, chewing her lip, 'and that's the last one, right?'

'Yes, there are no more after that. Well, none that we know of.'

'But why?' she continued, 'he was obviously expecting to meet her either on the holiday itself or when she got back, so why do the letters stop so abruptly?'

'I think that we need to talk to Pat and Josie,' I said firmly, 'It's time we got some proper answers.'

Pat and Josie had come to visit me most Saturdays since Mum had died. They enjoyed the children's company and in the better weather Josie would bring her watercolours to paint in the garden. The next Saturday they were due to come over, I made sure that Margaret would be at my house so we could tackle them together.

It was almost March and the garden was starting to stir into life. The snowdrops had almost finished, and the bluebells hadn't yet arrived, but daffodils were bursting into life all over the place. Their sunny yellow heads made me feel more optimistic somehow, and I was determined that I would find out just what my sisters really knew about that time 35 years before. Pat was fourteen and Josie twelve when I was born, and they would have been eighteen months older than that when Margaret arrived. They hadn't been young children, they must have seen things, heard things. They must remember something.

I heard Pat's car draw up in the driveway. 'Aunty Pat's here,' Sam shouted, galloping out to meet her, as usual excited at the prospect of seeing his favourite Aunty. When he was about six he had come home after a weekend at Mum's and announced 'Mummy, it's not that I don't love you and Daddy, but I think I would have a better life if I lived at Aunty Pat's house.'

We had all laughed over it, and things hadn't really changed since Mum died. He still adored his Aunty Pat. She could converse with him about all his favourite things, football, cricket, tennis, in fact sports of any kind, and was also very knowledgeable.

I really didn't want the children around while I talked to my sisters, so had arranged for them to go with Tony to the local country park for a spring picnic with Margaret's four girls.

'Can I see Aunty Pat first?' Sam had pleaded when I shared the plan with him.

'Yes, of course, she can help you pack the picnic things,' and so he had been placated.

'Look Aunty Pat,' he said as soon as she opened the car door, 'we've got a picnic basket ready to pack, and you can help me pack it up with stuff.'

Pat laughed at his enthusiasm, and allowed herself to be led into the kitchen saying 'Isn't it a bit chilly for a picnic?'

'They'll be fine,' I reassured her smiling. 'It's not like they'll be sitting still for long if I know them.'

Tony arrived with Margaret and the girls and Sam and Jo bundled into his car excitedly, while Margaret made her escape and came in to join Pat, Josie and me.

'Hello Marg,' said Josie. Margaret had always been her favourite, and I had always been Pat's.

'Are you staying for lunch?' she asked.

'I hope so!' Margaret answered, sitting herself down on the sofa with a sigh. Neither of us got much time to ourselves without the children, so this was a rare treat, despite the serious purpose.

As soon as we had eaten, I made a cup of tea, and then produced the black folder containing the letters.

'What's that?' asked Pat innocently. I looked at her and felt sad. Her hair was going grey even though she was not quite fifty, and she was quite overweight, just as Josie was, and this had the effect of making them look older than they were. When she was very young Pat had been very pretty and a keen sportswoman but had started smoking heavily in her teens, which had put an end to all that. She was such a kind person, never seeing any bad in anyone, never judging, and here I was, about to try to force her to spill all her secrets, and I felt a stab of guilt. What was it that Aunty had always said 'I can't tell you about your father without telling you about your mother.' Her words rang in my ears, but I had to go on now.

''They're some letters that Josie and I found in Mum's cupboard,' I said.

Josie's eyes slunk away; she had recognised them.

'What letters?' Pat asked.

Josie cleared her throat. 'They're letters that Thomas sent to Mum.'

Pat was taken aback. 'Thomas? Thomas who?' I was surprised to see that she looked as though she didn't have a clue who we were talking about.

'Thomas, the man that used to be so kind to Mum,' Josie explained.

Pat went quiet. That was always her defence. She didn't attempt to look at them, in fact her face closed down completely, giving nothing away.

'One of them talks about a holiday,' I carried on, determined. 'It's dated July 1955. Do you remember it?'

Her face relaxed and she smiled. ' Oh yes of course, that was the Isle of Wight. We went there when you were still a baby, just learning to walk. I'm sure you've seen a photo? I'm holding your hand as you're trying to walk along the beach.'

'Oh I'd love to see it,' I answered, and then continued ' Who went?'

'We all did,' Pat said. 'Granny, Me, Josie, Mary and the twins, and Peter of course and you, but it was before Margaret was born.'

'Oh right, and where did we stay?'

'We were camping, Granny and us had a tent together and Mum had one on her own the other side of the campsite.'

This sounded puzzling. Why was Mum's tent so far away? But I couldn't ask – not yet, anyway. Even now we knew if we wanted to find things out it was best not to be too obvious.

'So you don't remember any Thomas?' I asked her pointedly, and she shook her head.

'Don't you remember anything about when I was born?' I asked.

'Look Kathleen, all I remember is a man coming to visit Mum just after you had been born. She was in bed and told me to take the baby downstairs. He came in a big posh car and had a dark coat and hat. He seemed really nice and I remember he gave me 10 shillings! That was a lot of money then which is probably why I remember.'

'And . . .?' I prompted.

'And nothing,' she said, 'I'm afraid that's all. I don't know if he was this Thomas, but from what Josie says I suppose he probably was.'

'Was Mum pleased to see him?'

'I don't know really, I think so, I can't remember.'

'Please try,' I pleaded. 'Did he know there was a baby, did he know I existed?'

Pat didn't look at me. She was getting more and more uncomfortable, but I wouldn't let it go.

'Do you think he was my dad?' I asked outright.

There was a long silence. I could tell Margaret thought I had gone too far, but I didn't care.

'Kath, I don't know who your Dad was, I really don't. I'm sorry.'

I looked across at Margaret whose face betrayed the same disappointment as mine, because the sad thing was, I knew Pat was telling the truth.

56

The Scandal

A few years after Mum died, I had a strange conversation with my niece Sheila. She was my brother Michael's middle daughter and was now married with two children of her own. We had often talked about Mum, and the many secrets that still lay buried, but recently she and her older sister Vicky had become more and more curious. They knew some details of course, but they were muddled about others, and wanted to try to get a clearer picture of why their dad had been put in a children's home, and what had happened there that made him refuse to ever talk about it.

When the phone rang I was out in the garden pegging the washing on the line. Colin called from the back door. 'It's Sheila on the phone.'

I pegged the last towel onto the line, and bent to pick up the washing basket. It was a glorious warm day, full of the promise of the long summer holidays. 'Tell her I'm just coming,' I shouted across the lawn. Sam had thrown his bike down casually, and wandered off to do something else, and I almost tripped over it. 'Damn bike,' I muttered to myself as I hurried towards the house.

Colin thrust the phone into my hands. 'Hi Sheila,' I said distractedly, mentally trying to tick off the list of things I still needed to do.

'I've got some news,' she blurted out. Sheila was ten years younger than me, but despite that we got on very well.

'What news?'

'Vicky and I have been to Valence Library,' she said, barely able to contain her excitement, 'and we've found Nan.'

'What do you mean you've "found her"?' I asked.

'We went there to see if we could find out about Nan going to prison for bigamy. We thought if we could find the date then we could see if it would help us trace which children's home Dad was in and for how long.

'Well we found her in the *Dagenham Post* all right, but not when we expected to. The date of the articles we found is years later.

I started to pay attention. 'How many years later?'

'Hold on,' she said, 'I'll read it to you.'

Waitress appears on £458 fraud charge

A 41-year-old waitress, Florence Catherine Stevens of Valence Avenue, Dagenham, appeared at Stratford Court on Wednesday charged with obtaining credit over £298 from Mr A F— by false pretence or by means of fraud other than false pretence. She was also accused of similar offences of obtaining £135 and £25 by false pretence with intent to defraud. All the money was from Mr A F—.

Stevens was remanded on bail until 19th September.

'What year was it?' I asked slowly, guessing the answer.

'1956,' Sheila replied.

I held the phone in my hand and said almost to myself, 'the year Margaret was born . . . the September after the letters from Thomas stopped.'

'Yes that's right, but there's more,' she continued.

'Go on.'

'Well, there's another article from the same newspaper. Listen to this one . . .'

Mother of ten gets 18 months for fraud

Mrs Florence Catherine Stevens, 41, mother of ten children, of Valence Avenue, Dagenham, was sentenced to 18 months imprisonment at Essex Quarter sessions Appeal

Court on Thursday for obtaining credit by fraud and money by false pretences.

'This is one of the most extraordinary instances of gullibility it is possible to imagine,' said Miss Nina Collins, prosecuting.

The charges related to groceries and money, totalling £433, which had been obtained from a Dagenham grocer Mr A F— of whom Mrs Stevens had been a customer.

Disguised Voice

Miss Collins said that Mrs Stevens assumed a series of poses, disguised her voice over the telephone, and led the grocer to believe she was a highly paid member of the Walt Disney Film Corporation.

She assumed various identities over the phone at varying times such as Mrs Roy Disney, Roy Disney himself, and attorney to the Walt Disney Corporation.

She persuaded the grocer that he was going to get a contract to supply groceries to the corporation and in that belief he supplied her with groceries and about £122 in money.

At the time she was friendly with an executive of the Walt Disney Corporation and she led Mr F— to believe she was to receive a substantial sum under a will.

Wild Extravagance

Miss Collins said that in that belief the grocer indulged in wild extravagances including the purchase of houses and a car. Evidence was given that Mrs Stevens at the time of her arrest was receiving national assistance and family allowances. Mrs Stevens' legal representative said she was trying hard and loyally to look after her family and temptation came her way. He added, 'She saw this opportunity of getting something for her children and having started the snowball continued. What she did was out of need and necessity.'

I was stunned, but it made perfect sense.

'It was Thomas!' I said. 'He was the Walt Disney executive – don't you see? It all fits, the Disney emblem on one of the envelopes, the different places the letters were posted from, the cheques that he was always sending her, the money she had probably grown to rely on ...'

'Yes, but why?' Sheila broke in, 'If Thomas was giving her money, why did she need to steal it?'

'Because he stopped! Something happened that made him break off contact with her, stop the letters, the money, disappear from her life, something that we don't know about yet. And because she was desperate, I suppose, because she saw the opportunity, like the solicitor said, and it just snowballed.'

We both stood at our phones, silent for a moment now, our minds teeming.

'There is another one; this time it says much the same things except it also refers to her "two previous convictions", one for bigamy, and one ...' Sheila paused. 'One for trying to kill herself.'

This time I let the silence grow and lengthen. Maybe some secrets were best left untold.

57

Fragments of a Memory

I arrived at Margaret's house and Tony opened the door.

'Marion's not here yet,' he said, 'but Sheila is out in the garden with Margaret having a coffee, do you want one?'

I nodded my thanks and wandered outside. Sheila and Margaret were deep in conversation as I approached to join them.

'Hello you two,' I said. 'Whew it's hot out here.'

'We can go inside if you'd rather,' offered Margaret, but I sat myself down at the patio table with them, making sure I positioned my chair in the shade. I still got migraines, and the sun was one of my triggers.

'I've brought the letters round, so we can have another look, just to see if they give up any clues as to what happened.' I placed the black folder on the table and sighed at the same time.

'What's wrong?' asked Sheila concerned.

'Oh I don't know, I suppose I'm just tired of it all. We seem to get so far but then every time we think we're getting close to cracking it, it peters out, another dead end.'

Margaret sipped her coffee and said, 'Look, this newspaper stuff is really helpful. We can write to the home office now we have a date; they might be able to give us details of her previous convictions and get exact dates for them.'

'Yes,' I said, 'but how is that going to help us find out if Thomas was our father? I think we're just going round in circles.'

Marion suddenly appeared at the doorway carrying a tray with two cups of coffee. She was wearing a bright yellow T-shirt which was attracting tiny black thrips.

'Tony made me bring these out,' she joked. 'He said he didn't want to interrupt the witches' coven!' and then she stopped abruptly as she picked up on the air of despondency that had settled over us. For once, no one laughed. 'What's up?' she asked, setting the tray down on the table, and brushing at the flies.

'Sometimes I just wonder why we bother,' I said flatly, slumping back in the chair and watching the swifts swoop in circles.

'Marion caught me watching them. 'They never stop, you know,' she said. 'They never rest, they fly round and round apparently in circles, gathering up the insects they need to survive, and that's how it's got to be with us – we've got to keep going, keep looking, keep gathering.'.

Now I laughed out loud, 'You're beginning to sound a bit preachy,' I said good-naturedly, and reached for my coffee. At that moment there was a loud clap of thunder and the heavens opened. We all jumped up and ran for the door, screaming and laughing as the rain thrashed down ferociously. I grabbed the folder of letters and held it close, and Sheila clasped the newspaper photocopies that she had brought with her and we went inside to go through it all over again.

'OK so, we know that Mum had been in prison,' Marion said, 'but I found something else out last week when we went to see Pat and Josie. Pat had taken the dogs for a walk so I managed to corner Josie on her own.'

We all turned towards her in expectation.

'Mum had electric shock treatment, the first time she was in. I think it was quite commonly used for people with depression.'

'Depression?' I asked.

'Why do you think she had depression?'

'Josie told me that she tried to kill herself, but she wasn't sure when, she thinks it was either when she was arrested for bigamy, or maybe before that during the split with Ron Coates.'

'Does Josie think she really was depressed?'

We all knew that Mum had fantasised about a range of illnesses over the years, to manipulate sympathy, and also to try to get money on some occasions.

'Yes, I think she does, and then when I was talking on the

phone to Marge in Australia about it last night, she told me something else.'

She stopped for a moment. It was so quiet we could hear the soft murmur of the children playing upstairs.

I broke the silence, 'What did she tell you?' There was something stirring in my memory, fragments of forgotten moments, a frightening, half-remembered day from long ago.

'She wasn't sure if she should tell you, but I told her you had the right to know. She told me about the time it happened again,' Marion continued 'when she and Josie came back and found . . . the time when you and Margaret were still only little.'

Margaret and I looked at each other and there was a sudden shock of realisation.

'Yes,' I said, 'I think I remember.'

Margaret started to cry. 'I thought it was a dream, a horrible, scary dream,' she sobbed.

Sheila put her arm around her. 'Don't cry Marg,' she comforted. 'She must have been desperate if she was prepared to leave you two'.

'No, you don't understand,' I said. 'She wasn't going to leave us, she was taking us with her.'

No one spoke, and Margaret carried on crying, more quietly now. It wasn't that we had forgotten that day many years before, just that we had chosen not to remember it. Sheila looked more shocked than I had ever seen her, as the colour bled from her face. There was a look of disbelief and horror in her eyes that made me feel ashamed.

'She was ill, she must have been,' Sheila said now, trying to justify the unjustifiable.

I nodded, the one thing that was becoming clearer the more we found out, the more we remembered, was that Mum must have been very ill indeed, not physically, but mentally.

We sat quietly for a few minutes and then Marion pulled an A4 writing pad from her bag. 'I've started to make a timeline,' she said, 'of all the things we know, and I have put question marks where we don't.'

We pored over her work, the four of us, making a few changes here and there as we all chipped in with what we remembered. It took us a few hours, but what we had in front of us for the first time ever, was a sequence of events and information that we hoped would help us to make sense of what we already knew, and help us see what questions we still needed to find the answers to. Whether we would ever be able to do that remained to be seen.

58

A Double Death

As the new millennium approached, I stood next to my husband and daughter on Parliament Hill in Hampstead, surrounded by an eruption of colour and noise.

'I wonder where Sam is now?' I shouted to Colin, trying to be heard above the chaos of celebration. 'Do you think he's all right?' There was a little bit of me that was worried, desperately hoping he was somewhere safe with his friends. At the same time I knew that I had to learn to let go, after all he was nearly nineteen!

'He's probably having a great time. Don't worry!'

By the time we got back home from Sherry's the next day, my teenaged son was lying fast asleep in bed. It was a relief to know that the world hadn't ended with the old century; Sam and Jo were safe and sound and life suddenly felt full of new beginnings.

I was teaching at a local infant school at the time, and enjoying every minute. It was Marion who had first introduced me to the head teacher, and she had initially offered me a temporary job-share. It wasn't long since my Mum's death and the blackest period of my depression, and I was still feeling very vulnerable.

'Come on Kath,' Marion encouraged me. 'It will be good for you, and it's only two days a week.' I had been persuaded to accept because everyone told me it would help, and they were right. The temporary part-time job had now become permanent and full time. It wouldn't be too great an exaggeration to say that the children at that school helped save my life, and I loved working there. Everyone was so friendly and supportive that before long the term that I had originally signed up for became a year, and then another, and before I noticed it I had been at the school for almost ten years and become the deputy head teacher!

Perhaps Mum was right about the devil, or else our run of luck had just been too good to last. First Colin's feisty, independent mum took a turn for the worse. And then I got a call from Pat.

'Oh Kath . . .' she started, clearly very distressed.

'What is it?' I asked, 'What's happened? Are you all right?'

There was a brief moment of silence until she gathered herself together and was able to continue.

'It's . . . Well first I had a phone call from Sarah, our sister Sheila's daughter in the Isle of Man. Sheila's died.'

I gave a sharp intake of breath. I had never met Sheila. The correspondence that we had exchanged many years before had petered out once I had started to ask questions that she didn't want to answer. Now I'd lost a sister I never really knew.

'Oh no. What happened? How old was she?'

Pat sniffed heavily. 'You don't understand, Kath,' she said. 'I phoned Michael to tell him, and Vicky answered the phone. She was hysterical. At the exact moment I rang, the paramedics were trying at restart Michael's heart.' At this point her control gave way and she sobbed.

I was dumbstruck, trying desperately to process the information she had just given me. Sheila *and* Michael?

'They've taken him to the hospital now, but oh Kath, they don't think he's going to make it.'

Then it sank in. I was not just losing an unknown sister, a hazy image conjured from photographs in magazines, a television programme and a few letters, but maybe also Michael, the brother who'd remembered us all those years when he was far away in Spain, sending us parcels and letters. The dear big brother who we might never see again.

'Oh God,' I said crying down the phone. 'What shall we do?'

'There's nothing we can do. Just wait and pray.'

So that was what we did. We waited and we prayed, but our prayers weren't answered. Our brother Michael died on the same day as our sister Sheila, hundreds of miles apart, not having spoken to each other for nearly sixty years and neither of them reaching their sixty-fifth birthday.

59

A New Home and a New Sadness

Over the next few years my depression came and went. It usually manifested itself through symptoms of illness. It would always be so real, so palpable, that even my GP would send me for various tests, just to make sure. There was the pain in my side that came and went, the lump in my throat, the panic attacks that would debilitate me, turning me into a quivering wreck, with clammy hands, palpitations, sweats . . . and all the while I managed to hide it. Teaching helped because I would never let the children be affected, and I never took time off. Being with the children made me focus on them instead of me, and for the most part I managed to keep my depression hidden. I tried a range of antidepressants, cognitive behavioural therapy, counselling – I was so desperate to conquer this curse I would try anything.

My sisters Pat and Josie were both retired now, and living in the same house in Dagenham that we had all grown up in. They continued to come and visit me every Saturday, and I like to think that they thought of our cottage as a second home. We had thought about moving further into the countryside, but although Sam was now at university, Jo was still at school in Brentwood, so we decided we should wait.

As the years flew by we were lucky enough to be able to build a new house next to our cottage, it was big and modern, and easy to live in at first, but I soon started feeling restless.

'Shall we move?' I half joked to Colin, one Saturday morning.

'OK then,' he replied to my amazement.

'Did you hear what I said, I said shall we move?' I repeated.

Colin laughed, 'I knew you would get fed up living here,' he said, 'it's too finished isn't it? Too perfect.'

'Do you feel the same then?'

'Well let's put it this way, I have never really been that keen on this house, it's too big for us now that Sam and Jo have moved out, and anyway, we want to move to the country at some point don't we?'

'Yes! Let's do it!' I exclaimed enthusiastically.

Within a week the house was up for sale, and we were looking for a new home in rural tranquillity.

We found a beautiful old house in a picturesque village in Suffolk. It felt like a fresh start, but not for long.

When Colin's wonderful mother passed away shortly afterwards, I was convinced that our family had had its share of bad news. I was wrong.

Like Mum, Josie had been diagnosed with type 2 diabetes. She had been in and out of hospital a few times over the years, so we weren't unduly worried at first when Margaret phoned to say she'd been admitted. The hospital ran some tests and then she was discharged once again, but it wasn't long before she was taken in again as an emergency.

'She looks really bad,' Margaret warned me.

We arranged to meet at the hospital the next morning, only to find that Josie had been moved to intensive care. She looked yellow and could barely open her eyes. With her fine wispy hair spread across the pillow, she reminded me so strongly of Mum that I shivered.

She was connected to all manner of machines that whirred and clicked quietly in the background and there were the remnants of tears on her cheek. I reached for a tissue from my bag and gently wiped them away.

'Don't worry,' I told her. 'I'm sure they'll get you sorted soon.'

'Kath, I've spoken to the consultant,' she started, and then hesitated before going on. 'He's told me that they won't resuscitate me.'

'What?'

'He said that there would be no point, that I would need someone to look after me all the time; that I will never be able to go home.'

I was shocked and confused. She started to cry quietly again.

'Don't worry, if you need to be looked after then I'll look after you.' I was crying myself now. 'We'll sell the house and buy one that has a little annex for you and Pat to live in. Would you like that?'

She nodded and gave a little smile.

'I'll look after you, silly,' I said again, smiling through my tears, knowing in my heart that I might not be given that chance.

Marge flew over from Australia and she, Marion, Margaret and I stood vigil with my poor sister Josie while she slowly slipped away. We were determined that, unlike Mum, she wouldn't die alone.

We slept on chairs in the room she had been moved to for her last few days, taking turns to rub her legs, stroke her forehead and talk quietly with her. Her nieces and nephews all came to visit, bringing laughter, life and ice-lollies into that little room. We crossed our fingers that Mary would make it in time from Australia, and still Pat wouldn't come. She couldn't bear to say goodbye to the sister who had been by her side throughout her life. The sister she had looked out for in the children's home all those years before, who had been the backbone of our family through so many difficult times. It was she and Pat together who had kept us safe and fed, who had looked out for us, always putting our needs before their own, and now Josie was about to leave us and Pat would be alone.

The morning Mary was due to arrive at Heathrow Josie died quietly, knowing that she was a much loved sister and auntie and that she would be leaving an unfillable hole in all our lives. Mary was distraught when she arrived at Valence Avenue no more than an hour after Josie had died.

Each of our children wrote out a memory of their Aunty Josie. Sam's was her love of travel, which he caught from her; Jo's was of collapsed summer puddings and fairy dolls made from pegs. We cried as we read them, my sisters and I, and after the funeral we gently placed them with the flowers.

60

Finding Thomas

The first couple of years after Josie died were hard for all of us, but the loss also made me appreciate how lucky I was.

'Gem keeping you out of trouble?' I joked with Sam. I had gone up to London to meet him for lunch. He was now living in Hampstead with his partner, a beautiful, clever Australian girl who he had met while working at a political think tank.

'Just about.' My handsome son was almost thirty now, but with the same cheeky grin and sandy blond hair and his grandmother's charismatic personality. 'Look Mum, can I ask you something?'

'Of course.'

'Mum, I've done something that I hope you won't be annoyed about.'

'What's wrong?' I asked nervously. 'What is it you've done?'

He laughed then. 'Sorry, I didn't mean to worry you. It's just that, well, I know that you have always been unhappy because you don't know who your dad is, and I got to thinking about it a few weeks ago, and I thought how I would hate it if I didn't know my father.'

'Sam, what are you talking about?'

'Well, I decided to see if I could help, and I've found out a few things.'

I sat back in my seat. How could my son know anything that I didn't about my past? Who could have told him anything new, after all this time?

'So I rang round a few people, and finally contacted a genealogist. She's been doing some digging and I think we've found him.'

'Found who?'

'Thomas,' he replied. 'Thomas Bartholomew, the man that you think is your dad.'

My hands and head tingled as I felt a hot flush of excitement and trepidation flood over me. The jacket that I was wearing over my new blue dress suddenly felt intolerably hot. I started to take it off, trying to process what Sam had said.

'But I don't understand. How do you know his surname?'

'Well,' he continued, smiling with satisfaction, 'you know your letters – or should I say your mum's letters – well I thought I saw something on one of the envelopes. It was just a trace of a surname, under the label that was stuck over it, he must have re-used it you see'.

'Slow down Sam', I said. 'What do you mean?'

'Listen Mum', he spoke more slowly now, 'I was looking through the letters last time I came over, and saw that one of the envelopes had been re-used. There was a label stuck over the original address. I managed to peel it off.' He laughed again. 'It wasn't easy, I kept thinking that you'd kill me if I tore it!'

'So what was underneath then?'

'His name is Thomas Bartholomew, and his address is Ralph Court in Paddington.'

How could I not have noticed? How many times must I have read and re-read those letters? And not just me, my sisters as well . . .

'I suppose you were more concerned with the letters than the envelopes,' he said seeming to read my mind, 'it was just chance really that I noticed.'

'Thomas Bartholomew.' I played with the name on my tongue. 'So what about the genealogist? Where does she come into this?'

'Well I showed her the name and address, and she did some research, and she came up with a few bits of information. Are you ready for this, Mum?'

I nodded, transfixed.

'Well, I'm afraid he's dead,' Sam started. 'He died in 1960

and I've got his death certificate.' He thrust a brown envelope across the table. 'He was a widower with one son. He definitely worked for a film company, because it's on his death certificate.'

It all fitted. I sat in that busy pub, with people coming and going around me, and thought about a man that I had never, would never, know. A man who might be my father, whose name was Thomas Bartholomew, and who had written so many letters to a woman that he must have cared deeply for.

'1960,' I said eventually, 'so I would only have been five or six when he died.' I suddenly felt relief. All through my life I had imagined that time was running out. That if only I could find him soon, I would be able to ask him the unanswered questions. Now I realised that would never have been possible. I was just a little girl when he died, and I was glad that I wouldn't have to torture myself any more.

'Are you okay, Mum?' Sam asked, and I realised that I hadn't said anything for a while, and was just staring into space.

'Sorry Sam,' I said. 'I'm fine, really. Of course I'm not annoyed and thank you.' I picked up the brown envelope on the table. 'Do you have the name of this genealogist? I think I'd like to speak to her.'

61

Fitting the Jigsaw Together

Over the next few months, with the help of the genealogist, I was gradually beginning to fit the jigsaw of my mum's life together, piece by piece – but there were still some important gaps.

When Marion phoned me and told me that Marge was coming over for another visit it seemed like perfect timing. I was almost ready to share my findings with my sisters.

'I know you've got a lot to tell us,' said Marge, when we were curled up in my living room, 'but I've got some more things as well.' She sat back and tucked her legs under her to get more comfortable.

'Okay,' I began, 'let's start from the beginning. We know Mum married Ron Coates in 1937 when she was just twenty-one and already expecting their first baby, Sheila.'

'Yep, Sheila was born later that year,' added Marion.

'And during the five years they were together they had four children.'

'Just a year or so between each of them,' Marge said.

'And don't forget that Mum was evacuated with Sheila, Michael and Pat. They went to that Lord's house in Somerset,' said Margaret. 'Mum herself told me about that, said how she had been told off for feeding the hunting dogs or something.'

'Yes, I remember that too, and it must have been about that time that things started to go wrong between them,' I continued, 'and we still don't know who Peter's dad was.'

'Aunty always used to say that Peter had gone to find his father in Ireland every time he ran away,' interrupted Marion.

'Hmm, well maybe, but Peter was born a couple of years after Josie, so he definitely wasn't Ron Coates' child.'

'Okay, carry on,' said Marge.

'Well as far as we can tell it was after she had Peter that she went off to London.'

'Yep, to be a waitress.'

'That's when she met yours and Mary's dad,' I said looking towards the twins.

Reg Stevens – the man whose name was written on all of us younger children's birth certificates. I had begun to feel sorry for him the more I found out. Uncle George, my mum's younger brother, had always told us what a nice man Reg was, a kind and gentle Yorkshire man who had fallen head over heels in love with Mum.

I picked up a tiny black and white photo and passed it to my sisters.

'She was so pretty wasn't she?' I said. 'A real Irish Rose.'

The photo showed a beautiful young woman with dark hair, and although we couldn't see the colour of her eyes, we could see the sparkle.

'She could charm the birds out of the trees,' said Marge, wryly sipping her tea.

Marion shook her head. 'It was more than that though. Everyone, men and women alike, were drawn to her. She was so good at listening; made people feel that they were important and had something to say that was worth hearing. Everyone except us, of course,' she added, glancing over at her twin with a pinched, hurt look on her face.

'It was almost as though she was capable of hypnotising them,' I said.

'We didn't need a genealogist to figure that one out,' Marge said with a little laugh.

'No, I know,' I continued, 'but there are some things that she has helped me to find out. For example I have a copy of Mum and Reg Stevens's bigamous marriage certificate.' I took the envelope and handed it to Marge.

'They were married in Sheffield!' she exclaimed.

I nodded. 'Yep, and look at the name!'

'Kathleen Francis Coates – widow!' Marge looked across at me. 'She used a fake name – your name!'

'Well it wasn't my name then; it was nine years before I was born.'

'And her age – look: she says she was twenty-six, but in 1945 she was thirty!'

My sisters all wore the same shocked look on their faces. Mum had always been so good at lying, and here it was in front of us, proof that she was well practised even then.

'But why lie about her age?' Margaret asked.

'Well have another look,' I said. 'Reg was only twenty-six, so perhaps she felt it was a good idea to become the same age as him.'

We sat in silence considering the document in front of us. Had this been the start of the downward spiral of Mum's life? Just when she thought she was getting a second chance at happiness? Or had the descent into misery started long before, when she married Ron Coates?

'So she married Reg, just before the end of the war,' Marion stated, 'and Mary was born about a year later.'

'Yes, but by that time, her bigamy had been discovered, and she was in prison. Holloway we think, as Mary was born in St Mary's Hospital, Paddington. You know they gave her electric shock therapy?'

'Oh God, poor Mum,' said Margaret, letting the tears flow freely now. I got up and got a box of tissues from the table and pulled one out to give her.

'I think we might need a few more of those before you go home tonight,' I said smiling thinly.

'So do you think Reg knew anything about her other family?' asked Marion, looking intently at the certificate in front of her.

'No, I doubt it. She already had five children, but she kept that well hidden. I don't believe he knew anything about her other life. He was a young sailor, just back from the war, and to him she was a single waitress who was fun to be with and had a reckless enthusiasm for life – a shining girl. Someone worth coming home for.'

'When she got out of prison that first time, that must have been when she went up to Birmingham, to Uncle John's?' Margaret added. She was starting to look more and more tired as the evening wore on. She had never been much of a drinker, and the glass of wine she'd drunk had obviously already affected her.

'Yes, I think maybe she was hiding from Reg, because he came to find her. Remember what Dot told us? I supposed she was ashamed . . .' I sipped my wine, and its heat warmed me. 'And then she went back with him, but obviously not for long.'

'Long enough for her to get pregnant with me and Marge,' Marion interjected forcefully, 'and then she must have just dumped us at Valence Avenue with Granny and Aunty and the others. But why?'

'Well reading between the lines, I'm guessing that she either met someone else, and was messing Reg around, or of course he could have found out about her other family. He wouldn't have left her otherwise.'

'Unless something happened to him,' Margaret said.

'I'm guessing she was still waitressing in London when she met Thomas all those years later.'

'Well she certainly wasn't at home with us. Until that day she turned up out of the blue.' Marge took another gulp of wine and I filled up her glass, emptying the bottle.

'I think I'll open another one,' I said and went into the kitchen.

I could hear Marion now. 'Yes I remember that too, it was weird, we just stood looking at her. It wasn't long after that Kath was born.' The twins would have been seven and Mary eight when I arrived. 'And do you remember telling our teacher at school that we had a baby sister?'

'Yes, and feeling really upset because she just raised her eyebrows and said, "Not another one!" ' replied Marge. We all laughed, as I refilled our glasses.

A silence descended for a few minutes. It was as though we were trying to ready ourselves for the next part of Mum's story – the part when Mum must have lost all hope; when she felt like it was time for her to give up.

'The letters start the December before I was born, and stop the July before Margaret was born. It would be an unlikely coincidence if he wasn't our dad,' I said.

Margaret was silent. We all knew that we would never know for certain.

'But why did they stop?' Margaret spoke now suddenly. 'Why did they stop before I was born? What happened?'

Marion and Marge exchanged looks, and then Marge broke the silence.

'We were on holiday in the Isle of Wight,' she started. 'Granny was there, we shared a tent with her, Pat, Josie, Peter and Mary, all of us in the one tent with you – except for Mum.'

Their eyes met again and Marge went on. 'You were only about a year old, just starting to walk,' she continued. 'Mum had her own tent the other side of the campsite, we didn't see much of her.'

'There was nothing to eat, I remember that,' said Marion joining in now. 'We had to pick blackberries and Granny cooked them up for us to eat.'

'And then the lady came,' said Marge.

'What lady?' I asked. Why hadn't I heard any of this before?

'We don't know; she was very smart, I do remember that,' said Marion.

'Yes and she asked where our auntie was,' said Marge, 'so I told her, "She's not our auntie, she's our mummy." I suppose I was proud that I had a mummy now.'

Their words jangled around in my head. What did it all mean?

'When we got home from that holiday things got harder than ever,' Marion carried on. 'Money was very scarce. I suppose looking back now it was because Thomas had stopped sending any more cheques. Mum was suddenly around all of the time, but always seemed to want us out of the way – especially us,

Mary and Peter. We still loved her and wanted to please her however we could.'

Marion was getting upset now, and the emotions in the room were growing.

Was Thomas with Mum in that tent? It didn't seem likely, but it was possible. Who was the mysterious woman who came looking for Mum? Could she have been Thomas's wife? His sister?

'The fraud, that's when she was convicted of fraud and sent to prison again,' I said. They nodded.

'She must have been desperate,' Marge said, watching our reactions. 'She had come to rely on the money from Thomas, it helped feed us, kept her in cigarettes, kept her sane, knowing that there was still someone who cared so much about her, even though by that time her looks were starting to fade . . .'

'So she used the fact that the grocer had cashed cheques for her over a couple of years,' I said, the pieces fitting together more snugly now.

'And Thomas worked for Walt Disney – she would maybe have had letters from him with their letter heading . . . who knows how she managed to convince that poor gullible grocer that she was Roy Disney's wife! It beggars belief, but she did,' Marge finished.

We sat looking at each other.

Did Thomas even know I existed? And Margaret, did he know about her? Were we his children? Or was there always someone else?

I picked out the last remaining sheet of information that the genealogist had given me. I held Thomas's death certificate for a moment and then, trembling, handed it to Margaret.

'I was five and you were three when he died.'

A look of realisation washed over her face. 'Oh no,' she murmured quietly.

I nodded. 'The scary day,' I said and we cried quietly together, each of us swamped by our own memories of that day so many years before. The day we'd chosen to forget for so long.

62

Hidden Truths

When the knock came Mum was startled, her eyes flying towards the front door.

'Come on, quickly!' she hissed through almost closed lips, bending down and grabbing our hands. We got as far as the doorway when we heard a scraping noise; someone was pushing at the tall rusty gate that led round the side of the house to the back garden.

'Come on – run now!' she said pulling us forward and bending down low, so that we fell towards the stairs.

'Come on – up here!' Positioning us halfway up the staircase, she held her finger up to her mouth. It was a tally man, and he was trying to get in the back door while we were crouched out of sight.

Mum was rigid with anxiety, and hung on to us in case we moved and gave ourselves away. 'Don't worry,' she whispered, 'he will go soon if we keep quiet and pretend we're statues.'

We froze, hardly daring to draw breath and wanting desperately to move or cough. There was a loud knocking at the back door and then at the kitchen window. He was banging so hard I thought the glass would break and he would come jumping through all covered in blood. I tried saying some prayers in my head but couldn't remember the words. We waited for what seemed like an age until we heard the back gate clang shut as though he had swung it in temper.

Mum let out a soft sigh. 'Wait there while I peep out of the window.' She slid down the stairs and into the front room, then called to us, 'Come on you two, the coast is clear!'

We followed her back into the kitchen, and watched as she sat and lit a cigarette. Her pale blue eyes had taken on that other look, the one which made us feel like she was being pulled away from us. As she sat in her chair by the fireplace, looking much older than her forty-five years, she told us a story about a bear.

'There was once a bear and he was a friendly bear but had no friends. He was a cuddly bear but had no one to cuddle. He was a kind bear but had no one to be kind to. He was a loveable bear but had no one to love. He was a lonely and desperate bear.'

As she continued we were rapt, listening to her words spoken in a soft voice, drawing us into this other world of longing as we sat at her feet.

'One day as the bear wandered through the forest looking for the things he could never find, he heard something. It sounded like crying, so he followed the sound. Behind a big old gnarled oak tree, with roots that reached deep under the ground, the bear saw that a trickle of water was bubbling and gurgling and forming into a stream, which flowed away into a wide river, which rushed towards the sea.

'He wondered where all the water was coming from, and for a while he puzzled to himself. Then suddenly he realised what the water was and as he looked up he saw the whole world crying. Crying for those who had no friends, no one to cuddle, no one to be kind to and no one to love and to love them back.'

Mum's eyes misted over as she continued the story, not looking at us at all now.

'The bear became sadder and sadder as he stopped and watched, and as he stood there he grew more and more tired out with feeling so sad. So tired that his arms ached, and his head hurt, and he couldn't keep awake, so he lay down next to the trickle of water and the oak tree and fell fast asleep. And as he slept he had a wonderful dream. In the bear's dream he had friends, lots of them, and they cuddled him and were kind to him and loved him, and he loved them back, and he was so happy not to have to worry any more, so he decided that he would stay in his dream forever and never wake up again.'

As we listened Mum's eyes grew brighter, and towards the end of the story she seemed to have cheered up.

'What happened to the bear next?' I asked.

'Well he stayed in his lovely dream, of course,' said Mum smiling.

'But wasn't he sad not to wake up again?'

'No,' said Mum, 'of course not! He had all the friends, cuddles and love that he needed now in his special dream place.'

With that she got up and picked up a worn old green cushion from the settee. It had a smooth, grey sheen on it from many years of use and it had never been washed.

Mum took the cushion out into the scullery and opened the oven door. As we followed her, she smiled at us.

'Come on,' she said, 'let's go and find the bear's special dream place.'

We giggled, excited to be acting out the story, and tiptoed after her.

'Lay your heads on the cushion,' she said. 'It's nice and cosy in there.' And she placed the cushion in the oven.

We did as she asked, and I can remember the feel of the cushion on my skin, and the smell of our dog Pongo's special ointment, from where he had lain on it a hundred times. I saw the stone pillars that cradled the big Butler sink where Margaret and I would stand on a chair to help Mummy wash up or sometimes float orange-peel boats. I looked at the pile of pans under the sink, the fat congealed inside them that smelt of stale, long-past meals. Then I smelt another smell. A smell that I didn't recognise at all and that choked my throat and made me feel sick. Margaret tried to sit up, but Mum said, 'Shh now, try to go to sleep. We will all hold hands and we will all go together to the dream place.'

It was quiet apart from a strange kind of hissing sound, but I didn't like the smell, so Mum sung to us:

> Lulla lulla lulla lulla bye bye
> Do you want the moon to play with?
> Or the stars to run away with?
> They'll come if you don't cry . . .

I felt sleepy and started to close my eyes when suddenly the silence was broken. I heard a key in the front door, and my sisters Josie and Marge came in.

I sat up. 'Josie's home,' I said sleepily, rubbing my eyes.

Everything changed. Where there had been silence and stillness there was now shouting and movement.

'Open the window!' Josie bellowed as she attacked the back door, pushing it open wide. A blast of cold air blew in as Marge pushed at the scullery window, which was stuck tight through years of over-painting. I didn't like the banging as Marge tried to force it open, and I put my hands over my ears as the old bottles and soap dish and jugs that stood on the window ledge were knocked skittering into the sink.

Margaret was awake now and was desperately trying to cling on to Mum as she walked slowly away. I sat on the scullery floor, crying from the shock of it all, with Josie and Marge staring on in silence. All the while I could hear Margaret wailing 'Mummy! Mummy!' and not getting any reply.

63

Missing Pieces

My life has been so full of confusion, so full of an all-consuming need to find out who Mum really was, and why she behaved in the way that she did, who my father was and why he abandoned us. I have found some of the answers, but still have many left to ponder over.

I am not sure if Mum ever loved Ron Coates or Reg Stevens. In fact I am not sure that she ever loved any man, although I like to think that she cared for Thomas. Surely she wouldn't have kept his letters all those years if she hadn't? Or is this just something that I want so badly to believe – that out of all of them, the one that she really loved was my father. Margaret and I knew we were always special to Mum. Perhaps that was because we reminded her of our father. Or maybe it was because by the time we came along she was beginning to realise that the men in her life came and went, but her children would always love her with a fierce adoration, not only until she died, but beyond.

I still have many things I want to know. Was Thomas Bartholomew really our dad? Why did she keep his letters for all those years? Did the news of his death when I was only five years old trigger her desperate attempt to finally escape from the bleakness of her life?

The genealogist has left Margaret and I with a tantalising thread to hang on to, but I don't know whether or not I will ever have the courage to use it. You see Thomas had a son, and we know his name, and that we could find him. But how do you ask a man who probably doesn't even know you ever existed if he's your brother? How many memories would it hurt or destroy?

★   ★   ★

Will we ever look into the past again? I'm not sure, but we are determined to find out whether or not we are full siblings, my little sister Margaret and I, and a DNA test should be able to tell us that.

I went to visit my brother Peter not long ago.

'If you had to use one word to describe your childhood, what would it be?' he asked.

I had no hesitation in answering: 'Fear.' The fear that our darling Mummy would leave us; that someone, anyone, would hurt her or that she would be unhappy, or be disappointed in me. The fear that I was different, wasn't good enough, would mess things up. But most of all the fear that I carried with me for so long that I will never truly know the name of my father, and why he deserted us so long ago. As I have written this book I have come to a startling realisation that this is no longer true.

Depression is devious; it has no morals. It will lay in wait for you, and be there ready to pounce when you are least expecting it. It slides into your mind, and corrupts your body with darkness, leaving you struggling and panicked, desperate and desolate. I have learnt to fight back – not on my own, but with the love and loyalty of my wonderful family and the laughter and enduring support of my dear friends without whom I couldn't survive.

Over the years I spent as a teacher I came into contact with many troubled families. What I have come to realise is that the greatest gifts we can give children are love and self belief, because with these comes an enduring tenacity and strength of spirit that will allow them to be ready to stand up to the world proudly, to fight their corner, to know that they are worth something. Family and friends are what make that possible, and I am so glad that I have been given so many of those wonderful people in my life.

I have many failings, faults and weaknesses that I am ashamed of, but there are also things of which I am proud. I still ache with longing to know who my father was, but this is soothed by a kind of calm acceptance. I have at last managed to exorcise my ghosts. Does it really matter whose blood flows in my veins? After all I am still Kathleen, my mother's daughter. I am the sister, the aunty, the wife and mother, the friend . . . despite my past, or perhaps because of it. All of these are what I was able to be with the love of my family and friends. I have at last found a sense of peace and I dedicate this book to you all as a token of my gratitude, and of course to you Mum with thanks for those sunny days when we sang and danced and ate banana rolls.

Acknowledgements

I have only been able to write this book with the love and encouragement of my family and friends to support me. Thank you to my sisters Pat, Mary, Marge, Marion and Margaret, and my niece Sheila – all of whom showed immense patience and kindness, reassuring me along the journey. To my dear husband Colin and our children Sam and Jo (and Gem of course!) thank you for always believing in me and keeping me going when I faltered (and for the copious cups of tea and coffee!). I send my grateful thanks to my friends, Anne and Anne and Sherry – and especially my dear 'partner in crime' Karen who helped me to believe in myself, and my wonderful boss lady Liz who read my work with enthusiasm and made me believe that I had a story to tell. I would also like to thank both my editor Fenella for her kindness, patience and support and Women and Home for the opportunity they have given me.

Nourishing Your Daughter

*Nourish
yourself!
too!*

Nourishing Your Daughter

Help Your Child
Develop a Healthy Relationship with
Food and Her Body

Carol Beck

A Perigee Book

A Perigee Book
Published by The Berkley Publishing Group
A division of Penguin Putnam Inc.
375 Hudson Street
New York, New York 10014

First edition: September 2001

Published simultaneously in Canada.

Visit our website at
www.penguinputnam.com

Library of Congress Cataloging-in-Publication Data

Beck, Carol
Nourishing your daughter: help your child develop a healthy
relationship with food and her body / by Carol Beck
p.   cm.
Included bibliographical references.
ISBN 0-399-52707-9
1. Teenage girls—Nutrition.   2. Teenage girls—Mental health.
3. Eating disorders in adolescence—Prevention.   4. Parent
and child—Psychological aspects.   I. Title.

RJ506.E18 B43 2001
616.85'2605'08352—dc21

00-068476

Printed in the United States of America

10   9   8   7   6   5   4   3   2   1

Contents

Contents

Acknowledgments

To my clients, both daughters and parents, for taking the risk of sharing your real selves with me. I am so blessed.

To Nan for years of rewarding professional partnership and your unfailing patience, encouragement, and on-the-mark suggestions.

To Susan A-C for your constant clarity, truth, love, laughter, and velvet glove.

To Keneth for your outstanding ability and patience to transcribe my scribbles and arrows through literally thousands of pages to organized chapters.

To Michael for your willingness to spend hours and hours sharing with me both your love and your uniquely creative way of thinking about the world.

To Mark. You are truly an angel.

To Janet and Sheree for being the pros that you are.

To Amy and Jack for telling me I knew what others could really use and that I should write about it.

To Sherry for your shoulders to cry on when I felt like giving up.

To Peggy for only encouragement and support while putting up with months of one-sided friendship as I wrote this.

To Susan M. for taking time away from your untiring commitment to spreading healthy self-care to girls to review my book.

To Dawn H. for your willingness to share all you have learned through your family's recovery path so others might be helped.

To Mom and Dad for your gift of a lifetime of being a daughter.

Introduction

Help! I don't know what to say. What do I do? Am I doing the right thing? Oh, no, I wonder if our reaction just set her up to struggle more. All I know to do is what my parents did. Is there another way? How can I know what I don't know?

These fears, concerns, and questions are just a few of the most common worries I hear from parents of teens. Most every parent wants to see their daughter develop a healthy relationship to food and body image, but how to do this is cause for lots of concern and worry. This book is an easy-to-read guide that gives specific tools, techniques, and examples of ways to effectively help your teenage daughter through any struggles she has with weight and, hopefully, prevent eating disorders before they start. If your daughter has been diagnosed with an eating disorder, some of the suggestions in this book may not be a recommended part of her treatment plan. If that is the case, please follow her already established treatment.

Each chapter begins with a situation common to young girls, such as snacking, sneak eating, shopping for clothes, gaining weight, and so on. A brief discussion explains the dynamics behind the behavior, then concludes with specific answers to commonly asked questions and suggestions about how to handle that situation. The background information and techniques are designed to give you confidence that you can handle her struggles in a healthy way. Using these suggestions does not guarantee that your daughter will never develop an eating disorder. She may still struggle, but both you and she will be more aware of the situation and confident about handling it.

Not about Perfection

It's hard to try new things, and even harder to try them in such an emotionally charged area as weight and eating. It can be terrifying to bring up topics that might cause conflict or hurt feelings. Often, fear prevents us from bringing up difficult issues because, even if we do, once the issue is out in the open we don't know how to handle it and seem to make the situation even worse. This book covers many anticipated difficulties, and presents specific suggestions on how to word difficult conversations about many of the topics you will encounter concerning food and weight with your daughter.

You will make mistakes—make a mess, say the wrong thing, make her mad. That's normal and healthy. If you can, try to laugh at these errors and keep experimenting. It's important to use a very light touch with yourself and your daughter as you practice new ways of handling weight and eating struggles. After all, these issues have been around for generations. You can't expect to cure them in one generation. But you can start to make a difference by trying new ways of approaching your daughter about food and weight.

About Nourishment

It's easy to get bogged down in the "shoulds" and "should nots" of nutrition and health. And it's even harder for your daughter to avoid that trap. Throughout this book, when food and weight are discussed, what we are talking about is how you can help your daughter nourish herself—physically, emotionally, and spiritually—how you can help her set aside time to do so, and how you can help her feel important and special enough that she deserves to be nourished.

For women in this society, preteen and teen years are the age when many begin to sacrifice themselves, their likes and dislikes, their needs and desires, and begin to focus more on what their friends, schools, activities, and so on want, need, and expect of them. And that's just the beginning. As women become adults with families of their own, they sacrifice even more of themselves to care for others. Is it any wonder many women struggle with food and weight? Beginning in girlhood, they gradually lose sight of themselves, their likes and dislikes, their needs and desires, what nourishes them (as well as how to do that), and replace it with responsibilities for marriage, children, aging parents, communities and churches, work, friends, and neighbors.

Setting aside time to plan, prepare, and eat a nourishing meal often just feels like one more stressor. Many try to make up for this lack of attention and time by under- or overeating.

The techniques in this book are designed to help prevent your daughter from falling into this pattern. Use the tools and suggestions to help you help her stay in relationship with herself, her wants and needs, her body, and her food in a way that nourishes her physically, emotionally, and spiritually.

Following is a list of the basic patterns that are covered in more detail and applied to specific situations throughout the chapters.

1. Trust your instincts. If you're concerned, trust that and bring it up.

2. Find one-on-one time to discuss food and weight concerns.

3. Start the conversations with a sentence about you and your feelings. For example, "*I'm concerned* that you aren't eating much at dinner."

4. Use specific information. For example, "I'm concerned *that you aren't eating much at dinner.*"

5. Stay curious. For example, "I'm wondering what your thoughts are about that."

6. Mirror her. For example, "It sounds like you're really upset. I can understand that."

7. Use the questions "Are you hungry?" and "What are you hungry for?" to help her use her own body signals to determine food choices and amounts.

8. Ask for help from professionals. Nutritionists and therapists are invaluable resources for new, different, healthy ways of handling problem areas.

9. Look at yourself—honestly. Are you struggling with issues similar to your daughter's? If so, get help for youself *before* you try to help her.

10. The goal is to *be with* your daughter as she feels, experiments, questions, and struggles to develop a healthy relationship with herself, her body, and her food.

The information in these chapters will not make you the perfect parent who always has the right response so your daughter never

has to worry or struggle with weight and eating. Often, what adults say and do to try to make the pain go away for their daughters is based more in their desire to avoid feeling their own pain, fear, and uncomfortableness as they listen to and watch her. I challenge you to step into your own uncomfortable feelings and tolerate them. Use the techniques in the following chapters to experience sitting with your daughter while she struggles and hurts. This is really a hard one for most of us: Be on her team and support her in the midst of her pain and worrying, and solve problems with her, not for her. These shared experiences are some of the most precious, intimate, loving times you and your daughter can share. If you try to fix her or to make the situation go away, she misses out on the opportunity to develop a deep relationship with herself and her own feelings, and you miss the joy of sharing the growing-up process with her. So relax, explore, experiment, laugh, and enjoy.

Experiment

Struggles are opportunities to learn and grow. This book will reassure you that you are handling these difficulties as healthily as you can. In discussing these issues, I speak from my experiences of being a daughter and working for more than twenty years on high school and college campuses and in private practice with teens and adults struggling with their food, eating, and weight. I am not a child psychologist. The suggestions in this book are ideas and reactions that my clients and I have experimented with and found successful. I share them with you not because I believe they are *the* right way but to present options that may alter how you respond to your daughter now. I know most of us would much rather have someone tell us what will work so we don't have to face the unknowns of trial and error. But, because there is no one right way, these ideas are here to give you a place to start to try something different. See what feels right for you—

even if it feels awkward at first. You may discover that it will be more effective in the long run. Also, ask others—teachers, therapists, friends, relatives—what they have tried and test these out as well.

While experimenting with different ways to help girls through adolescence and face the difficulties they encounter as a result of society's expectations about weight, body image, and self-worth, you may also discover what can be a rewarding experience of healing for yourself.

Don't be surprised if you find yourself using these insights to more confidently and comfortably relate to yourself, your son and his struggles, your spouse or partner, friends, and coworkers. The ideas presented here are really methods of developing open, honest, compassionate connections and relationships.

As you read through and try some of the different suggestions, notice what goes on inside of you. You can use this time of struggle for your daughter to discover parts of yourself that you've long buried and tried to forget. As a result, you will get another chance to notice your relationship with yourself and food and try some new techniques that might be a more pleasurable, healthful match for your own body. In the process, you help your daughter.

This book is not a source for diet plans, menus, or recipes. There are many other resources available for that information. Instead, this book focuses on helping you and your daughter develop a new relationship with herself and food.

How to Use This Book

While it is not necessary to read the book from start to finish, I encourage you to review the first section to become aware of the basics that I'll refer to in later sections. Throughout the book, you will see some of the common issues that girls have with food and weight, such as control, power, doubts about being good enough, and the question "Must I *earn* love and acceptance by having a certain appearance and weighing a certain amount?" I wrote and organized this book to be a quick, easy-to-use, concise, and substantive guide for you. Each chapter addresses common situations that adolescent girls struggle with. It puts the topic into perspective, follows with an example of how a parent handled a similar situation, and then presents specific responses and actions that you can try. You might also share this book or a particular chapter with your daughter and use it as a tool for discussion about some new ways of relating to food and weight.

It is my hope that perhaps these girls, the next generation of adult women, will be spared the time, money, effort, and sense of failure that so many women have spent on these issues, and that they will grow up in a family environment that acknowledges the difficulties they face as a result of society's expectations about body image. They need support and guidance to help them develop a sense of value and self-worth separate from their appearance.

Part I

The Science of Adolescent Eating

Chapter 1

What's Normal Eating for Girls in Puberty?

One of the most common questions I hear is, What is normal eating for girls in puberty? The difficulty with answering it is, every girl is unique: her body's size, shape, and metabolism, the timing and amount of her growth spurt, when she's hungry, how much she is hungry for, and what foods are most satisfying to her. Also unique is the degree to which she is comfortable being a part of the family routine, how much independence she desires, what her friends are doing and not doing, her degree of interest in foods and cooking, her health, and her activities.

The bottom line is this. During adolescence she will almost always change what have been her normal eating patterns. This is the time for her to begin experimenting with food choices and patterns and this is the period when her body goes through tremendous changes too. So expect change. Expect upheaval of routines. Expect experimenting.

All these "normal" changes and experimenting are the source of

ern for parents. Most of these changes result in us losing varying
egrees of control over our daughters' eating and that is scary. It is
normal for parents to worry and to be concerned about these changes.

Grayson was sixteen years old and had just got her driver's license. With
the new freedom this gave her, she was away from home most afternoons
and evenings. Her mother called me, concerned because Grayson was gaining weight and complained almost daily of being tired. Her mother was
scared Grayson wasn't eating the foods she needed for her health and energy
and that she was creating a weight problem she would have to battle for the
rest of her life. But, every time they talked about her mother's concerns,
Grayson would become very angry and tell her to quit controlling her and her
food. Grayson agreed to come in to see me for two visits. We did a metabolic
test so she would know how many calories her body burned at rest during a
day and talked about some ideas for eating at the fast-food places that she
and her friends liked to visit. (Metabolic tests are available through some hospitals' wellness centers or pulmonary departments.) She could choose
whether or not to use this information about her body and its fuel needs. In
addition, she and her mother set up a schedule where Grayson would eat at
home with the family four nights a week. Her mother would make sure these
meals were a healthy balance of all the nutrients Grayson needed. The other
three nights she could be out with her friends. When I last heard, Grayson had
made some changes, was feeling less tired, and had stopped gaining weight.

Grayson's mother faced some of the most common fears parents
face when letting go of control over their daughters' eating. "Will
she get the nutrients that her body needs for health?" "How do I
know if her eating patterns are just normal experimenting or the
beginning of a lifelong struggle with weight?" "Is this the beginning
stage of an eating disorder?"

The transition from you making decisions about meals and
healthy eating for your daughter to her knowing what feels right for

her involves watching her experiment, make mistakes, fail, and try foods and patterns that you don't agree with until she begins to find her own way, her own rhythm of healthy self-care. It's only natural that you would be tempted to reduce your anxiety by stepping in and telling her what she needs to do. But, she needs practice using her own body's sensations to determine her own style of healthy eating rather than feeding herself based on your direction. Following are some suggestions for you to use during this often difficult time.

■ Normal, healthy eating:

- *Varies from person to person.* Because our tastes, bodies, activities, and emotions, are different, our bodies require different foods to feel nourished.
- *Is cyclical.* Weekly, monthly, and annual cycles, even life cycles, change our body's need for and responses to food.
- *Is imperfect.* We won't always choose absolutely "healthy" foods. We won't always feel that our bodies are perfectly balanced.
- *Is rhythmic.* We feel pleasantly full after a meal and pleasantly hungry before the next.
- *Includes a wide variety of foods.*
- *Is free of obsession.* It acknowledges that our compulsions are due to biochemical or emotional reasons and any over- or undereating is a clue to begin looking further as an opportunity for learning.
- *Is nourishing to the body and spirit.*
- *Feels good.*
- *Is an essential component of self-care.* We nurture ourselves with the foods we need and enjoy in the amounts we require.

■ Talk with your daughter about what seems to be going on with her eating. A good formula to use to start these conversations is to tell her about your experience in this situation, stay curious, listen to her experience, then put your heads together to come up with

some creative solutions. For example, Grayson's mother might say, "When you talk about being tired so much lately, I'm scared you might not be getting the nutrients that you need and I'm worried that you are gaining weight. I'm wondering what your thoughts are about that." Listen and stay curious—even if she gets mad. Expect resistance. It's her job description at this age for healthy autonomy. However, many girls will not resist and will instead try to reassure you that everything is fine. Trust your instincts and stay focused on specific behaviors or situations that concern you. Grayson might respond, "Get off my back. You can't tell me what to eat. Quit trying to control my weight." Grayson's mother might respond, "It sounds like you're really mad. Tell me more." By staying curious and staying with Grayson while she shares feelings, they could be a team to solve problems about Grayson's eating, rather than adversaries. Another girl might respond with reassurance instead. "Oh, Mom, everything is fine, I just got tired the other day from studying for all those tests and haven't caught up on my sleep. I'm OK." Be careful with these kinds of responses. Because it's what you want to hear, it's easy to let your concerns drop. Don't. Stay focused on the specifics you are concerned about. For example, "It sounds like you aren't worried about feeling tired. I've noticed you've been tired for a while, even before your test. I'm concerned and think we need to come up with some ways to help you get more energy. Any ideas?" Using this formula takes practice but it is one of the most effective tools for working through problems with food and weight issues with your daughter.

■ Fortunately, most fast-food places, where groups of friends tend to hang together and eat, offer foods that are good sources of protein and carbohydrates and do supply some of the basic nutrients our bodies need. The foods are usually really high in fat and such

restaurants don't have many vegetable or fruit options, but experimenting and exploring means that for periods of time, your daughter's eating will not be ideal. This is normal. During these phases, be sure you have a variety of fruits and vegetables and low-fat options at home that are easily and readily available for her to pick up and eat. You may want to get some suggestions and ideas for these foods from a nutritionist. Be sure to include these items in the family meals that she eats at home. If healthy foods are regulars at home, you don't need to worry as much about what she eats when she is out.

- Altering the balance of independence and control can be renegotiated after a period of time. For example, Grayson and her mother came up with a schedule where she was free to hang out and eat with friends for a certain number of nights a week and would eat family meals on certain other nights. They then renegotiated this balance during summer break and again in the fall when school started again.

- Be open to including some new foods into the family routine that she might like to try, keeping different foods from what is the norm in the house and serving different menus at family meals. This does not mean catering to her every whim—just be open to trying some of her new preferences. Her likes and dislikes will change as she goes through this stage. While it can seem like a hassle, it is normal.

- Another very helpful tool is offering a couple of visits to a nutritionist. Most teens are much more open to listening to suggestions from people other than their parents. This is a part of their normal push toward autonomy. If they have seen a nutritionist, you know they have at least been exposed to information about how to feed their body well. Of course, they still have a choice whether they apply the information or not.

■ Many girls will experiment with vegetarianism during their teen years. This approach to eating can easily supply all the nutrients they need for health, if they are careful to include meat substitutes for their protein sources and include enough fats to supply their body with the necessary essential fatty acids and energy. Some examples of nonmeat proteins are: soy products (there are usually many different varieties of these in both the freezer and produce sections of the grocery stores), tofu, tempeh, nuts and seeds, beans, eggs, and dairy products. In my experience, most girls eating vegetarian include these nonmeat proteins in their diets, but not in enough quantities to supply all their protein needs. In addition, making these changes in protein sources often reduces the amount of fat in their diet and rarely do they add fats from other sources to replace what is lost. Visiting with a nutritionist or attending a class on how to be a vegetarian can help your daughter determine amounts of protein, fats, and calories that her body needs for health.

■ Dieting and restricting calories is very normal for girls during this period. So don't be surprised if your daughter begins to count calories, eat smaller servings than usual, talk about fat grams, and complain about foods you prepare that have fat in them. These situations are usually good opportunities to invite her to go grocery shopping with you and help prepare meals so her calorie and fat concerns can be incorporated in the daily routine. Again, remember, this is normal. Let her try out this new way of thinking about food and eating. And, using the formula we discussed above for talking with her, make sure you don't let her run the entire household's eating with her experimenting.

■ Experiments and exploring usually last for days or weeks, sometimes a few months. For the most part, health will not be impacted for the long term in that period of time. So a good rule of thumb is to allow just about anything your daughter would like to try with

her food for that short period of time. Take notice and talk about it as we discussed in the second point above, but, in general, don't intervene. After a few months, if you still have concerns, it's time to step in and begin putting your heads together, as I mentioned above, to alter the pattern toward a more healthy alternative.

To avoid turning a conversation into a verbal war, use the techniques below to keep the dialogue with your daughter open.

Daughter Says	Healing Responses	Not Helpful Responses
Get off my back. You can't tell me what to eat.	It sounds like you're mad. Tell me more.	I'm not on your back. Just listen.
Quit trying to control my weight.	I can hear that you feel controlled, help me understand that.	I'm not controlling your weight but if you aren't going to do something, I will.
I'm fine. Don't worry.	I understand you don't want me to worry but I'm concerned about _____ and we need to address it in some way. What are some of your ideas?	OK. I'm glad you think everything is fine.

These healthy responses often feel stiff and awkward to both parents and daughters at first, but keep trying them. With time, you'll develop your own style of wording them and be able to respond with ease even in emotionally charged interactions. And, emotionally charged interactions about food and eating are normal and to be expected as your daughter begins to experiment and change her eating patterns as she decides what is right for her.

Chapter 2

Your Daughter's Intuitive Sense about Food

Remember your infant daughter's cries at three A.M. calling you to feed her? Remember when you would prepare a meal and your toddler ate a few bites of just what she wanted and left everything else on her plate? These memories are perfect examples of your daughter's intuitive eating in action.

Your daughter felt sensations that her body sent to her brain which told her that she needed food and how much. She listened, trusted, and acted on those signals without a second thought. She was in perfect harmony with her intuitive eater—that part of all of us that knows instinctively what our body needs, how much, and when.

Inside versus Outside Control

But as our daughters grow up, they must adapt to the bigger world around them. She is hungry but Dad isn't home from work so dinner will be served when he gets home. She is hungry but her lunch

period at school isn't until one P.M. so she just has to wait. She isn't hungry when the family stopped by the drive-through to eat, but you knew she would be hungry later so you asked her to eat. Then, she is still hungry although she has finished her plate and there aren't any seconds. She isn't hungry but the family rule is to clean your plate, so she does. She noticed that when she eats breakfast she gets hungrier during the morning than when she doesn't eat breakfast. But you know breakfast is healthy, so she eats a bowl of cereal. In many ways our daughters override their own intuitive eater and begin to listen and act on other stimuli. She will eat when it's convenient for herself or others. In time, her food choices are what other people think she should or should not eat. She begins to eat only what she believes will make her body the size she wants it to be. She eats only when it fits her schedule and how much she has time to swallow rather than what her body really needs.

Certainly, the world and our families would be in complete chaos if all of us ate only according to our intuitive eater with no regard for our other responsibilities, schedules, and so on. However, we should not disregard our intuitive eater and replace it with decisions about what we eat based solely on outside influences. Balance is required and you can help your daughter learn to listen to, trust, and act on her intuitive eater *and* adapt to the world around her. Rarely will she be able to do this successfully without your help and encouragement.

Adolescents, like most of us, are strongly influenced by what their peers do and by what magazines and television shows suggest. They are involved in extracurricular activities, all of which seem much more important than what their body is telling them, such as, "Am I hungry, what do I need, and how much?" As a result, adolescence is that stage of life in which the intuitive eater starts to get covered up, lost, and eventually buried. The result is usually a struggle with weight and health as an adult. However, when your daughter learns to notice these body signals and respect and act on them, she can still

go out with friends, be involved in activities, etc. and develop a skill to carry with her as an adult.

Ellen was a twelve-year-old struggling with her eating and class schedule. She started school at 8:15 A.M. Her assigned lunch period was at 10:30. When she ate her regular breakfast of cereal, milk, and juice, she wasn't very hungry for lunch during her assigned period. So, she usually ate salad and some crackers. Then at 1:00 P.M., right when she attended PE class, she felt hungry, weak, and often dizzy. By the time she got home she was starving and would usually want lots of cookies, crackers, or cereal—and she'd eat so much she wouldn't be hungry for her family dinner. When she came to see me, I validated for her and her mom how difficult her school schedule made eating.

We began to problem-solve using her body signals. She discovered she rarely felt hungry in the morning, so we experimented by reducing what she ate at breakfast to just enough cereal, milk, and juice that she felt hungry at 10:30 lunch period. Then she wanted a full lunch. She started taking a sandwich, some chips, and fruit from home and bought a dessert and drink at school. This seemed to fuel her through PE so she felt energetic rather than dizzy and weak. She needed a snack after school but since she wasn't starving she ate much less quantity. This helped her feel good through the afternoon but hungry again at dinnertime. Ellen began to use her body signals as the basis for each change in food she tried.

Here's how to encourage your daughter's natural wisdom about what, how much, and when to eat:

■ Take a moment to remember your eating as a child and adolescent. Do you remember your intuitive eater? What situations can you identify that encouraged you to override your intuitive eater? Is your intuitive eater still a factor in your decisions about food, or was it buried over time? How can you know? Notice

what your body signals to you about hunger, fullness, and what foods would be satisfying at each meal.

Some Examples of Body Signals

hunger	stuffed feeling	sluggishness
satisfied feeling	aching head	irritability
shakiness	dizziness	light-headedness
energetic feeling	weakness	recurring thoughts
sleepiness	growling stomach	about food
alertness	nausea	calmness
		mouth watering

■ Be an example for your daughter. Focus on incorporating *your* intuitive eater into *your* food decisions. In other words, use the signals your body sends you to determine if you are hungry, what you are hungry for, and how much food would satisfy you. Don't be surprised if your communication system is rusty and out of practice. Just notice. Talk about your body signals as you balance them with your other responsibilities and schedules. This gives your daughter opportunities to see you juggling work and self-care. It doesn't have to be the perfect balance. She just needs to see you trying.

■ Avoid using information from books, magazines, talk shows, etc. as the authority on what is right for you and your daughter. These can be used as helpful tools for you and your daughter *if* you notice your intuitive eater in action. For example, after experimenting with a new way of eating that she read about in a magazine, encourage her to notice: "That felt really satisfying," or, "I'm still hungry," or, "That lasted thirty minutes and I'm already hungry again," or, "That kept me satisfied and not thinking about food for three or four hours."

- Encourage your daughter to make food decisions whenever possible, based on her body signals. If you're concerned that she's eating too much or too little, avoid telling her what you think. Ask her to focus inside her body and trust what her body is telling her.

- Help her problem-solve, by scheduling her meals and snacks not just to fit her schedule but also to respect her intuitive eater's signals.

Recognizing her body signals, and using them to make her decisions about food, is the most important way your daughter can learn to feed herself well and avoid struggling with weight as she grows up. With your encouragement, she will learn to trust these intuitive signs even when friends and others might disagree.

Chapter 3

What Influences Your Daughter's Food Choices?

Because so many factors influence eating, it is very easy to get lost in all the questions. Here are just a few of the most common ones.

What is everybody else eating?

What do people expect me to eat?

Do I want to do what they expect?

Do I want to rebel?

What are my favorite flavors?

What foods make me feel satisfied?

How can I eat this and feel good afterward?

Is it time for lunch?

How long has it been since I ate last?

When will I get to eat again?

Do I feel hungry?

How hungry am I?

What do my parents keep around the house?

What do my parents prepare for me?

What do I like to prepare for myself?

What do I know how to cook?

What time of year is it?

How hot or cold is it outside?

What do my friends want to do?

What foods soothe me?

Where do my friends like to eat?

What do they usually eat?

What can I afford?

What time of day am I hungriest or feel "out of control"?

Whom do I enjoy eating with?

What do "they" eat?

When do "they" eat?

Where do "they" eat?

What time does my class schedule and after-school schedule leave for eating?

What combination of textures, temperatures, shapes, and colors of food do I feel most satisfied with?

What mood am I in?

Do I have choices?

Have I been given an ultimatum?

Guide Her Inside

These questions address feelings which impact what, when, how much, where, and why we eat. The more clearly we can state questions such as these and identify the factors which impact our eating in every situation, the more easily we can identify the information we need to make healthy and satisfying choices of food to eat at each moment.

The two most powerful questions you can ask your daughter are, "Are you hungry?" and "What are you hungry for?" Begin any interaction or conversation you have with your daughter about food, meal plans, menus, or concerns about eating with these questions. It keeps you curious and, most important, it guides her into her own experiences, body sensations, feelings, and thoughts to answer them.

When you ask your daughter, "Are you hungry?" it gives her practice going inside herself, using her body sensations to learn what it is telling her it needs, and experiencing how her body feels when she acts on those signals. Don't forget to practice asking yourself the same question. This question helps you to distinguish between different types of hunger: head hunger for a particular texture, flavor, or temperature; physical hunger for a certain volume of food and a certain combination of food choices to satisfy physical hunger; and emotional and spiritual hunger for something to soothe

us when we're lonely, sad, scared, and so on. If she continues answering the question "Am I hungry?" first, she will find it much easier to sift through all of the other variables that can impact her food choices.

Katie was seventeen and had been battling her weight since she was five or six years old. As we began to work together, she chose to write down what she ate for several days, and next to each meal she made a note about some of the factors she used to make her choices. As we looked over them together, Katie began to see certain patterns. Her choices for breakfast during the week were primarily chosen for speed and ease of eating in the car but didn't hold her long enough. Her choices at lunch were whatever she could find that cost less than four dollars at whatever drive-through her friends chose. So, sometimes she felt satisfied, sometimes not. Her snack after school was based on whatever was in the cabinets—no thought about crunchy, salty, sweet, smooth, cold, or hot. Her dinner choices were determined by what was planned for the rest of the family, rather than how hungry she was or what she was hungry for. Her snacks after dinner were usually smooth and creamy and she usually wanted them when she got stuck on some homework problem or just got bored working on homework. She identified that she wasn't hungry for food but wanted a break, an escape of some kind that required no brain power, like calling a friend or listening to music. What an eye-opener for her! Once she saw which variables had the most impact on her choices, she then could experiment with adding some others from the list at the beginning of this chapter and combining them in different ways. Over a period of several weeks, she played with using some different combinations and felt much more in control with her food and found that she felt more satisfied after eating than she did before.

You and your daughter might enjoy doing a similar kind of experiment. Each of you answers the questions for yourself and then shares and discusses. You can use the list of questions at the begin-

ning of this chapter as a guide to identify some of the most common factors influencing your food choices at a particular meal. Don't be afraid to add your own if you have a reason that isn't on the list. Remember to notice each time if the questions "Am I hungry?" and, if so, "What am I hungry for?" were addressed. If not, plug them in and see what happens. Sometimes, it feels overwhelming to experiment with which factors influence food choices. A nutritionist can help you and your daughter sort through these factors with more ease if it feels too unwieldy. You can find nutritionists at local hospitals or through a referral from your doctor. They also are listed in the Yellow Pages under "Dietitian" or "Nutritionist." Because there are many different specialties, be sure to ask them about their experience working with intuitive eating and adolescents.

Many different factors influence what we choose to eat in any given situation. Recognizing which factors she uses most often can help your daughter determine if there might be others, such as her own intuitive body signals, that might make eating well easier for her.

Chapter 4

Different Kinds of Hunger

"Are you hungry?" and "What are you hungry for?" are the two most powerful questions to ensure that you and your daughter nourish yourselves well.

"Are you hungry?" seems to be a very simple question to answer—for infants, toddlers, and young children. They enjoy an easy trust with their hunger signals and rarely, if ever, question them. Interestingly enough, these years when they are most connected to their intuitive eater are the years that we adults worry the most. Kids go through food jags, refuse to eat, create chaos as they see food more as a fascinating toy than as something to eat, or devise very particular rituals about the order of eating, no mixtures, or only mixtures, and so on. My mother loves to tell the story of when I was a young girl and ate only bologna for years, yet I was healthy and grew up to be a nutritionist. So trust that your daughter's tastes will shift and change as she grows, even if she seems stuck at this moment.

Focus on Body Signals

Children get through these very normal spells of what we usually think of as "weird" or "picky" eating. What you want to do is help your daughter keep this connection to her own body's signals about hunger through the teen years. Using the two questions "Are you hungry?" and "What are you hungry for?" is the most effective way to help her do that. These questions help both you and your daughter stay focused on her body signals for her decisions about when, what, and how much she will eat. This focus on her own body's needs and wants greatly improves the odds of her nourishing herself well, enjoying what she's eating, and maintaining a healthy weight.

What are you hungry for? There are three major types of hunger that need consideration as you and your daughter begin to answer this question.

Head Hunger

What will satisfy my eyes, nose, and mouth? What temperature, texture, flavor, color, or shape do I want? Do I want something cool and creamy? Sweet? Hot and spicy? Crunchy and salty? Start with texture, temperature, and flavor to begin to answer this question. Most of us feel most satisfied when we eat a variety of these attributes within a meal and within a day.

Leaving head hunger out of the decision-making process about food is one of the biggest reasons for gaining weight and why restrictive diets fail. Most weight loss diets do not consider the importance of head hunger. Indeed, they expect us to be satisfied with lots of cold, crunchy fruits, vegetables, and salads! Our intuitive sense recognizes that soft, smooth, and hot foods are missing in our daily intake, and it reminds us to choose these food attributes to

better satisfy our natural desires and balance. In response, we begin to dream of hot rolls, macaroni and cheese, warm peach cobbler, and so on, and we often binge on them to make up for the absence of those temperatures, textures, and flavors.

In response to this basic human drive for a variety of textures, temperatures, flavors, colors, and shapes in our food, you can store a wide variety of these foods in the kitchen and consider these attributes as you plan meals. It is hard to satisfy everyone's needs in the family for these varieties given that most of us eat different lunches during the day. As a result, everyone may need a different balance of these factors to satisfy their own unique head hunger. Let each member add to or substitute easy, quick items to the menu to take care of their individual needs. *Do not cook different foods for each person.* Simply have some quick, easy staples with different textures and flavors on hand from which to choose. Some ideas are yogurt, different types of crackers, dried fruit, frozen fruit, cups of soup, peanut butter, hard-boiled eggs, or individual cans of corn, peas, chili, and so on.

Sasha is an eleven-year-old who feels sad about her body size and she wants to do something about her eating. Each time she visits her doctor he weighs her and tells Sasha and her mother that she needs to do something about her weight. She is feeling discouraged and so is her mother. They tried to follow a low-calorie diet, but Sasha started getting mad when her mother suggested she drink a diet shake for breakfast, eat carrots and celery after school instead of cookies, and order the chicken sandwich without fries when the family went to a fast-food restaurant for dinner. Once they both understood the impact that different types of hunger have on food choices, and on feeling satisfied with food, Sasha began to plan options for her problem times taking these hungers into account. She decided to continue using the diet shake in the morning since she enjoyed the cool, creamy texture, and it also helped prevent her from feeling really hungry at lunch when she

might overeat candy to try to fill up. She asked her mother to buy a variety of things at the grocery store each week to have on hand for snacks. And she asked her mother to remind her, when she gets home from school, to use the two questions, "Am I hungry?" and, if so, "What am I hungry for?" to decide if she will snack, what she will snack on, and how much.

Physical Hunger

Each of us has a unique set of body signals that lets us know if we need food and if so what kind and how much. Luckily, we all start our lives knowing this intuitively. We need no lessons. As we mentioned before, just help your daughter be familiar with her particular cues. It really helps if you can identify yours, too. Some of the most common cues are weakness, headache, stomach churns, mouth watering, sleepiness, crankiness, and being tired.

Many diet plans encourage eating only when you are physically hungry. I have found this to be helpful in general. But when, based on your experiences and body signals, you recognize that you can anticipate being hungry at a time when you can't eat, it is a good time to override this rule.

Sasha experienced no hunger pangs in the mornings on schooldays. But if she didn't eat, she would begin to get stomachaches and headaches and couldn't concentrate very well by midmorning. Her school had a rule of no eating between classes or during classes. By the time she got to lunch, she ate large quantities of candy to try to turn off her hunger signals. So, using her hunger signals from later in the morning, Sasha decided to drink her shake before school, even though she didn't feel hungry then. As a result, she started feeling her body sensations telling her she was hungry much closer to her lunch period.

Emotional and Spiritual Hunger

What are you hungry for? Many times the answer to this question is not a particular food. Your daughter may want someone to listen about her day when she gets home from school. She may want hugs and reassurance when she has had a fight with her girlfriend. She may want time alone out in nature to balance being inside in class all day. She may just need to zone out, listening to music as a break from studying after dinner. Asking the question "What are you hungry for?" helps her to begin considering all the ways that she wants and needs to be fed in order to feel balanced and satisfied.

Sasha discovered she wanted a combination of things after school. She wanted to talk about her day and any stressful things going on for her and she wanted time alone doing nothing. Once she identified this combination, she and her mother devised a routine for her to get both. She tells her mother whether she wants to talk first or her mom asks her what are you hungry for—support or alone time. They then discuss what else is on the schedule that evening to plan around. So, they make sure they have both support and alone time worked in before bed. In addition, she felt physically hungry after school and used her body signals to choose foods to satisfy that part of her hunger.

If girls don't know to consider their head hungers, their physical hungers, and their emotional and spiritual hungers, they will often substitute food to try to compensate for the lack of nourishment.

As you can see, most of us, like Sasha, might have one kind of hunger or a combination of all three at one time. The most important thing to remember is that there are three different kinds. So when you and your daughter ask the questions "Am I hungry?" and "What am I hungry for?" be sure to check for head, physical, emotional/spiritual hunger or some combination of them.

Chapter 5

The Link Between Food and Pleasure

Hunger: to yearn; a strong desire for anything; experiencing weakness, pain, or other discomfort from lack of something.

What are you truly hungry for in life? What is your greatest longing? I'm not talking about what you wish for your daughter or what you wish for your spouse. Focus on you. What is *your* greatest longing? Not considering the question "What am I truly hungry for *in life?*" is at the base of most people's struggle with food. And, as a parent, if you are willing to face that question for yourself, then it's very likely your daughter will believe she has permission to address her greatest longings as well. As a result, she will struggle less with weight and food.

It is human and healthy to want pleasure. I also believe it is healthy to make sure you get pleasure. The more we deprive ourselves of pleasure, the more our desire intensifies for it and the more unruly and unmanageable our food choices become in response. Food is a very popular substitute for the lack of pleasure in broader

and deeper areas of our life. Food is convenient, eating can be done alone, and it doesn't usually impact anyone with consequences but ourselves. But food only satisfies physical hunger, not emotional and spiritual hunger, no matter how it feels at first.

Elizabeth, a fourteen-year-old freshman in high school, struggled with pleasure. When she first talked to me, television, listening to her stereo, and eating were the only things she allowed herself to do for pleasure. Anything else was just too scary. As we worked together over several weeks, she began to notice a link. She began to identify her pleasure needs, and when they weren't satisfied, she ate instead. She started identifying some wishes: I wish I could be in the school play. I wish I could play soccer. I wish somebody would call me and talk to me outside of school. I wish I could wear red. This recognition was the first step in her progress toward feeling in control with her food. We started exploring and working with her fears about doing some of these things. Her eating habits shifted. Just recognizing that pleasure is a required part of her life, and that she could learn to engage in some of those pleasures, helped ease the hopelessness she felt about her overeating. As she moves on and tries some of her pleasure wishes, I expect her eating to be even less of an issue. But we are taking it slowly and are gradually letting her integrate the courage and skills to be able to act on her pleasure needs and wants.

Pleasure Overrides

How many subtle ways do you override your pleasure on a daily basis? Consider something as simple as going to the bathroom when you need to, rather than holding it until you finish your duties. Do you eat meals when you are truly hungry? Do you choose foods that satisfy you? Go to bed when you are sleepy? Say no to an invitation with people you don't enjoy being with? Work at a job you truly enjoy? Rest when you are tired? Ask for attention or a hug when you

need reassurance? Wear clothes and shoes that are comfortable and that you like? Make love when and how you most enjoy it? Take time to play? We have daily opportunities to give ourselves pleasure. But most of us override our need for pleasure in every arena of life—our relationships, our food, our jobs, our balance of time spent working and playing, and so on. Pleasure is often suppressed because of fear. What will people think? I'll be a bad parent if I do things for *my* pleasure. I don't deserve pleasure. I don't have time, and so on.

Honor Your Instinct

How do you help your daughter satisfy her hunger for pleasure? You must teach her that pleasure in every arena of life is required for her to be whole and healthy. You must teach her to honor her own instincts about what is pleasurable for her and to help her learn to balance what gives her pleasure with her responsibilities for self-care, family, school, and community.

- The first step to accomplishing this is for you to take an inventory of *your* pleasure. Make a list of those activities and experiences you do that don't bring you pleasure and make a list of those things that do bring you pleasure. Look for the subtle things as well as the more obvious. This is not an exercise you need to share with your daughter. This is for you to identify the balance of pleasure and responsibilities that you model for your daughter. Choose one item that you would like to change. Then, see if your daughter might be interested in doing a similar list.

Things That Might Not Bring You Pleasure	Things That Might Bring You Pleasure
cleaning house	listening to my CDs
getting up at six A.M.	red roses
working on Saturday	weekends off
going shopping alone	hugs
filling the car with gas	wearing purple
having the TV on all the time	having my hair washed
brown curtains in the den	driving by myself
sister living so far away	riding horses or motorcycles
having to smile when I don't feel like it	laughing with my spouse
dinner parties	staying up late after everyone else has gone to bed

■ Think about ways that you might have fun on a regular basis. Adults in our society have very few options to play if we follow our cultural norms. Eating out, getting together for drinks, and inviting people over for dinner are *the* most common outlets for adults to play and they all involve food. What are other ways you could incorporate more fun/pleasure and some ways that don't involve food? Be an example for your daughter of an adult having fun without needing food. Most of us allow ourselves a long weekend or a vacation once a year, but humans need pleasure daily. You may want to talk about this as a family or start out by discussing it as a couple, and then get the rest of the family's ideas.

▪ Notice if you ever eat and then get angry at yourself for doing it. These are usually times when you substituted food for something you really wanted. As you become more aware of this as a pattern, you may want to help your daughter use this same technique if she is struggling with eating in these situations.

▪ Include pleasurable foods throughout your week *without* using them as a substitute for pleasure you're missing somewhere else. Most of us who struggle with allowing ourselves pleasure have difficulty giving ourselves permission to include pleasurable foods in our regular pattern of eating without guilt. Yet, if we do this in balance with other healthy foods, the emotional charge that builds up around these pleasurable foods often minimizes. It is very rewarding to begin the process of separating your longing and hunger for pleasure from pleasurable foods. This separation allows you to enjoy both pleasurable activities and pleasurable foods and not have to overuse food to make up for something lacking elsewhere.

▪ Consider pleasure as you decide what to eat at meals. Think about what textures, what temperatures, what taste combinations would sound satisfying and pleasurable as you decide what to eat at a meal. Eating something cold, creamy, and sweet when you are really wanting something warm, crunchy, and salty or vice versa is usually unsatisfying and often is a setup to overeat. Remember head hunger is one of the big three types of hunger we need to satisfy daily.

▪ Plan family meals with everyone's pleasure foods getting a turn. This is also a way to reduce complaining when you serve something they don't like. They know their pleasure foods will be included at another meal that week.

When it comes to food, and life, many parents get bogged down in all the responsibilities and the "doing" that making a living and having a family require. It's easy to forget to even think about fun and pleasure, much less actually make time to enjoy it. It takes effort to make some pleasure a regular part of daily life and daily meals. And, it takes reassurance and encouragement from you for your daughter to learn to balance "pleasure" foods with "healthy" foods as well as fun with her responsibilities.

Chapter 6

The Role of Food in Moods

I'm sure we all have had the experience of feeling body signals such as "cranky" when we get overly hungry or sleepy and lethargic after eating a large holiday dinner. These experiences are examples of how food impacts mood. Components of the food we eat impact brain chemistry, and as concentrations of different brain chemicals change, our moods alter. In reality, this is a very complex system which scientists and researchers are trying to better understand. But the findings from this research give us some incredibly helpful clues to understanding our own body signals, hunger patterns, and moods.

Food Component	Brain Chemical	Body Signals
sugar, starches *examples: beans, potatoes, bread, desserts*	serotonin	sleepy calm relaxed

Food Component	Brain Chemical	Body Signals
fat *examples: olives,* *butter, avocados, nuts*	endorphin	euphoria reduced pain relaxed
protein *examples: beef, eggs,* *tofu, fish, poultry*	dopamine	energetic alert productive clear thinking

As you can see from this chart, food has components which impact particular brain chemicals. As these chemicals are released in the brain, they cause specific moods, sensations, and feelings along with influencing appetite for various foods. After eating a meal that is a good match for us, each of these chemicals would be released in proportions that would balance our moods and sensations.

Sylvia is exploring these concepts, so let's use her experiments as an example.

Sylvia is twelve years old. Her mother is a vegetarian, her brothers are big meat eaters, her grandparents on both sides are overweight, her friends at school are starting to not eat lunch and to eat rice cakes instead. She wanted to work with me to figure out what foods are the right match for her. She began by recording what she ate for a few days and what sensations she felt in her body before and after each time she ate. We then reviewed her notes and used the brain chemical chart above to help her recognize that the sensations she recorded were perfect descriptions of brain chemicals shifting in her body.

Foods for Calmness

Several of the dinner meals Sylvia recorded contained just vegetables. One meal was a salad with lettuce, spinach, tomatoes, carrots, broccoli, cauliflower, and pea pods. Another meal contained green beans, coleslaw, asparagus, and sliced tomatoes. Her notes from those evenings listed irritable, stressed, can't concentrate, angry, couldn't go to sleep, and hungry. When serotonin is low, we feel nervous, irritable, stressed, and hungry for starches and sugars such as breads, cereals, crackers, or desserts. If we include starches and sugars in our meals, serotonin levels rise and, almost immediately, we have calm, more satisfied sensations.

Sylvia experimented with this piece of information first. She added a potato and a roll to her vegetable dinners and recorded her sensations again. She described much less anxiety and stress but found she became sleepy before she finished her homework. She recognized these sensations as her body's signals from having higher serotonin levels in her brain.

Protein and Alertness

After reviewing the chart, she noticed that by adding some protein, her brain would release dopamine and she would have some alertness and concentration to balance with her calm, relaxed state. So she repeated her vegetable meal, adding a potato and roll for serotonin's calming effect and a handful of grated cheese on her potato to give her body a protein source. It only took one try and she knew that was the right balance for her. Dopamine, another brain chemical, rises in response to eating proteins such as beef, pork, fish, chicken, turkey, cheese, eggs, tofu, or tempeh. Meals that include enough of these foods help most of us feel alert, energetic, and productive. This is especially important for your daughter to consider

as she plans her breakfasts and lunches. Enough protein in those meals helps her stay awake and focused during her classes and especially helps before tests.

Fats for "Just Right" Meals

Sylvia then played with how much fat would give her just the right satisfied feeling after her meals. She experimented by adding just a broiled chicken breast for protein and didn't feel satisfied. She felt dull and heavy when she ordered fried shrimp at a restaurant. So she tried adding different amounts of fat somewhere between fat-free and deep-fried. She noticed that when she added certain amounts of fats along with her starches and proteins she would record "just right" on her notes. One of her "just right" meals was her salad meal with leftover rice tossed in it, black beans (both starches), grated cheese (protein), olives, and salad dressing for her fats. Another "just right" meal was spaghetti (noodles for her starch; meat sauce and grated cheese for her protein) with salad and dressing (for fat) and ice cream (sugar and fat) for dessert.

"Just right" is a great descriptor for when endorphins are released in the brain and balanced with serotonin and dopamine. As you can see from the chart, endorphin levels are raised when fat is included in a meal. Exercise is another way endorphin levels rise. Exercise releases fat from within the body and, in response, endorphin concentrations rise and we usually feel less stressed and often describe it as "feeling good."

Authority over Her Own Body

Noticing what we eat and its impact on brain chemicals is usually an easy and helpful activity to do with your daughter. It opens up the science behind the mystery of moods and hunger and what is

right for her own body. And it encourages her to practice using her own body as the source for what she needs to know about satisfying her body's food needs. The authority over her food choices is her own body, not someone else's ideas or a diet plan. I encourage you to play with this as well, especially if you have experimented with lots of different diet plans through the years. Many diet plans encourage you to disconnect from exploring and noticing your own body's reactions to foods, different combinations of foods, and their impact on your body's brain chemistry, moods, and body sensations.

For just a few days, play with different meal combinations, track your body's reactions, compare them to the brain chemical chart, and see what you come up with. This is often a fun project to do along with your daughter. Like Sylvia, you may want to notice what happens in your body after a meal with no starches (corn, crackers, yams, cornbread, and so on) or half your normal serving of starches. Then experiment by adding starches to that same meal and notice what changes happen in your body. Do the same thing with protein (tuna, steak, ham, milk, cottage cheese, soy, and so on). You may want to try a meal with double your normal portion of meat and notice what signals you get. Try a meal with half the portion you usually eat and notice the signals. Do the same with fats (olive oil, salad dressing, sour cream, bacon, and so on). Sometimes, your results can be confusing and you and your daughter might like some guidance from a nutritionist to interpret your results.

By starting to recognize body signals as linked to certain brain chemicals and food components, your daughter can begin to trust that her intuitive signals are giving her very clear suggestions about which foods in which combinations are a good match for her body. As she practices using this new connection to her self, she will build a confidence and knowledge about herself and her own body which will protect her from future struggles with weight.

Chapter 7

Some Thoughts about Exercise

Serena is thirteen years old and has come in to talk with me because her body seems to be changing and she is scared. As part of my initial meeting with her, she talks about her activities through the week. She attends PE class three times a week but describes her experiences there as boring and too organized. She plays on a soccer team in the spring along with her whole group of friends and plays a match almost every weekend during the season. She seems to love being outside and with her friends. Her family has a membership at the YMCA and her parents go at least three times a week in the evenings along with Serena and her two brothers. She'll usually swim with her mother, while her dad lifts weights and the boys play basketball or lift with their dad. Sometimes, if some of her friends are there, she'll go upstairs and use the treadmills or stationary bikes and talk with her friends on the machines next to her. She describes exercise as an ordinary part of her week, and part of her and her family's routine.

Being active gives you many benefits. But being active does not ensure that you will be thin. That is especially true for preteen and teenage girls. Activity and movement during these years establishes healthy patterns that they enjoy and will carry with them through their adult life. It is not about losing weight. If you require your daughter to perform a certain number of minutes of exercise each week to achieve a nice body shape, you will encourage her to develop a reward/punishment dynamic connected to exercise that she will often battle for her entire adult life.

There are a variety of reward/punishment scenarios but each seems to have a common thread: I exercise because I'm not "good" enough at the size I am. I have to force myself to exercise because I'm "bad" since I'm not the "right" size. Exercise is the punishment if you eat something you like but that wasn't fat-free or on your diet. The reward is, if you exercise often enough and long enough, you can eat foods that you like.

Physical exercise positively impacts mental, physical, and emotional outlook if it is *not* done as punishment for a wrong body size. Encouraging your daughter to experience these benefits while she is young encourages her to carry these patterns into adulthood regardless of her size and weight.

Exercise changes brain chemistry such that a girl will feel more content within herself, more calm, more able to handle whatever stress she is going through. As girls experience this, they are less compelled to overeat to try to change brain chemistry in response to stress.

Exercise, depending on what she chooses to be active in, can give girls a chance to simply enjoy and have fun or experience positive aspects of her body such as strength, endurance, skill, agility, flexibility, and so on without the requirement of reaching a certain weight.

Exercise alters brain waves such that girls will often come up with creative solutions to problems. You and your daughter can benefit from this aspect of exercise. The next time you or your daughter are trying to figure something out like a school project, theme for a term paper, or how to handle a girlfriend problem, get up or go out and move around. Often a solution will pop into your mind. It's amazing how well this works.

Exercise is an activity that reinforces the idea that we are worth the time and energy it takes. Making time to move indicates that we are important enough to stop our other activities and responsibilities for others and do something for ourselves. In our society, women especially are trained and expected to care for others first, rarely setting aside time to nurture themselves. Setting aside time for activity and movement yourself and encouraging her to do so, too, will teach your daughter how to achieve a different, healthier balance. It will teach her the importance of setting aside time and energy for herself as well as for others when she is young enough for it to become a habit.

Exercise, depending on what we choose, often gives us an opportunity to socialize and interact with people interested in similar things. This is especially helpful for shy girls who have trouble making friends. Clients, who in the past have been lonely in the afternoon after school and struggled with snacking, find that they have a common interest with others when they begin to take dance or soccer, for example. They then begin to build a connection with other girls, which, in time, leads to friendships and activities after school rather than loneliness, eating, and weight gain.

Exercise strengthens muscles and, as a result, creates and maintains a higher metabolic rate than inactivity does. Components of the foods your daughter eats are burned and converted into energy by metabolic pathways in muscle cells. So the more muscle she has, the more metabolic pathways she has available to burn food and fat.

The higher your daughter's metabolism, the more energy she has available and the easier it is for her to maintain a healthy weight.

If your daughter doesn't eat enough food to supply her body's needs for fuel and energy, then her body will begin to break down her muscles and use them as a substitute for food to provide the fuel and energy she needs for life. When her body is forced to use her muscles for fuel, then the metabolic pathways in those muscles are destroyed and her metabolism is slowed. When this happens, it is easier for the foods she eats to be stored as fat rather than burned for her energy needs. The bottom line: Exercise helps keep our daughters' metabolisms burning at a healthy rate if, and only if, she eats the foods she needs in the proportions and amounts that fuel her body well.

Exercise regulates appetite as a result of building more muscle. The more muscle cells a girl has, the more capacity she has to store carbohydrates, which she can then use for energy between meals. Also, exercise impacts brain chemistry to reduce the appetite for eating fat. You and your daughter might want to experiment with this. On days you exercise, notice how your appetite for fatty foods might differ from on days that you don't exercise. It is usually quite noticeable, especially when your body is in the habit of exercising regularly.

Below are some suggestions that can help you and your daughter explore what kinds of activity she enjoys and some ways to help her get started if she isn't involved already.

- Examine your own likes and dislikes about exercise. If either of you as parents are caught in the reward/punishment cycle of exercise then be very cautious about what you say about activity to your daughter and how you say it. This might be a great opportunity for you to reevaluate if that cycle is working for you and maybe experiment with some new approaches to exercise while you encourage your daughter to experiment as well.

■ Explore different exercise possibilities as a family project. This reinforces that activity is an important and pleasurable part of family life rather than something your daughter needs to do because she is the wrong weight. This might mean family nights at the YMCA like Serena's. It could be day trips on the weekend to nearby parks for a hike or swimming at a lake. Depending on the season, it could be snowball fights in the backyard or gardening and mulching in the spring, or maybe a vacation snorkeling or skiing. It doesn't have to be expensive, just active. The goal is to have fun family time.

■ Remember to speak from your experience and to stay curious as you discuss options and ideas about exercise. For example, "I'd like to find some fun ways to move and I'm wondering if you have any ideas about that. Let's put our heads together and come up with some new fun things we can do that will be active."

■ Help your daughter think through some of the options that help her identify what kinds of activities "feed" her or are most enjoyable to her. Most of the failures people experience around exercise are a result of not listening to their own intuitive sense about what feels right to them and what nourishes them.

Here are some options your daughter may want to consider if and when she explores exercise:

■ Does she enjoy being alone on a solitary walk in the neighborhood, or with others in a class or a team?

■ Does she like competitive activities or not? And, if so, a team sport or one-on-one sport like tennis or badminton?

■ Does she love the outdoors or would she rather be inside, unaffected by the weather?

- Does she enjoy quiet, serene experiences like yoga or swimming, or does she love the energetic hip hop of a jazz dance class?

- Does she wake up early and feel energetic and ready to move or does she like to stay up late, wide-eyed and energetic, into the night? This can really help determine when the most enjoyable time of day is for her body to move.

- Does she want to incorporate a spiritual aspect into her movement with martial arts, tai chi, or yoga?

- Does she like variety and want to do different things throughout the week and vary it weekly, or does she relax when she has a routine and love the comfort of knowing what she will do each time?

- Be sure to consider your role in her planning and experimenting, too. Try to stay in that curious, creative place as you discuss the logistics that would be required to do some of the ideas she would like to try. Will she need a ride? Will you be available at that time? Does the expense fit the family budget?

Just remember to keep it fun and experiment. One of the ways you'll know which exercises are a good match are to identify those that feel boring or even horrible. The failures play an important role in experimenting. So start small. Do an introductory class just to get the feel before you sign up. Collect brochures from different clubs or gyms and then go to just watch once or twice. The idea is to help your daughter notice how movement can "feed" her by giving her time to come up with solutions to problems, a chance to be with friends, practice setting aside time to do something fun for herself, and in the process be strong and healthy.

Chapter 8

Dieting: A Rite of Passage

Purchasing her first bra, experiencing her first period, and going out on her first date are all rites of passage for a young girl. However, one important event is missing from this list—her first diet. A girl's first diet has definitely become one more addition to a girl's rite of passage into womanhood. An adolescent girl starts noticing her body—its size and shape, focusing on particular parts (especially those where females store fat—hips, thighs, stomach, breasts, backs of the upper arms)—and then begins to compare hers with the bodies of others. Hers invariably comes up lacking and the first diet begins. The first diet is experienced by virtually all females in our culture as they move through adolescence, and it can simply be a rite of passage or it can become a lifelong struggle with food and body size.

What can you do as a parent to support your daughter through this passage and to help her move through it with the least harm to her health and esteem?

- Even before she moves into this stage, set up a family environment that values her and all females for who they are, and not for how they look. This is not easy. Parents trying to influence their daughter in this way are going against the social and cultural image and information that bombard her every day. So we can't expect success here too quickly, but if we don't try it, our daughters will have no one to support their internal value.

- Recognize that the first diet represents her asking, "Am I good enough? Will people, especially peers, accept me and like me? Can I be who I really am and fit into this culture, this world? Must I mold myself to fit what others want me to be—not just in terms of body size and shape but my interests, opinions, ideas, dreams, talents, and so on?" The belief is this: If I look "right," then I'll be accepted and loved. The overriding message is that if she doesn't fit the norm (whatever that is for the population she wants to fit in to), then she'll start changing, altering, molding, pretending, hiding—absolutely anything it takes to be loved and accepted. During this passage, it is imperative for your daughter to *know* she is accepted and loved by you no matter what her size, shape, or appearance may be. As she's talking about calories and fat grams, and hips and thighs, be sure to look past these issues to what is underneath her concerns—acceptance for who she is.

- Ask your daughter about her concerns behind the calorie restrictions, counting fat grams, and dieting. When you approach the subject, it's likely she will simply focus on her body—its size and shape. Listen to her. And stay curious. This gives her a chance to talk about whom she wishes she could be, about how that would make her life different, and about what she feels is missing in her life now.

Daughter Says	Healing Responses	Not Helpful Responses
I want to lose ten pounds.	If you could lose ten pounds, what do you wish would happen?	You don't need to lose any weight. You are just right
	How would your life differ from what it is now if you lost ten pounds?	
	Who do you hope would notice your new size and how would that feel?	

As you help her focus on the underlying issues behind her first diet, use this opportunity to help her practice caring for her body in a healthy way—helping her to clarify some of the misconceptions about how her body works. Some of the most common components of a first diet include these three erroneous beliefs:

Myth #1: Exercising harder and more often raises metabolism and burns more fat. *Truth:* This is only true if her body has been fed with enough calories to supply the fuel it needs for exercise. Many clients simply believe that eating fewer calories and exercising to burn more calories is all that it takes to burn fat. This is not the case. Metabolism occurs in muscle cells. Metabolism is the word to describe how a body converts food into energy. Therefore, eating sufficient protein at each meal throughout the day is essential to making sure your metabolic rate burns at its peak. Also, muscle cells require carbohydrates for them to burn fat efficiently. So if your daughter is exercising more and going hungry, her body will not burn fat as efficiently. In the long term this pattern will lower her metabolic rate, making it harder to lose weight.

Myth #2: Avoid all fatty foods and desserts to lose weight. *Truth:* Not eating any "pleasure" foods *always* backfires. If we deprive ourselves of fat and its pleasure, we will eventually feel so deprived that we will give up and eat some—usually a lot. Then we feel guilty that we didn't have enough willpower to keep restricting, so we try depriving again, only to give in again, and the cycle begins: diet, give up, feel guilty, try again, over and over for the rest of our lives. One way to avoid this cycle is to keep both healthy and higher-fat pleasurable foods in the house and serve a mixture of low-fat and higher-fat foods throughout the day and the week. This enables your daughter to experience balancing health and pleasure.

Myth #3: Hunger pains are a good sign that your body is getting thin. *Truth:* Hunger signals flare up when a body has run out of available fuel to burn for energy. The belief is, "If I tolerate this hunger or just drink water in response, my body will burn fat for the fuel it needs." Before your body burns fat it first breaks down muscle tissue and in the process, it destroys metabolic pathways. If this hunger pattern lasts for days your body will shift into creating ketones from fat stores to try to slow down the muscle being broken down. But ketones are only formed when large amounts of muscle are deteriorating. So tolerating hunger signals without feeding them actually slows metabolism and makes it easier to gain fat once you don't restrict anymore and return to eating normally. Feeding the hunger actually keeps metabolism high and helps to burn calories.

Popular diets such as the many varieties of high-protein or high-carbohydrate diets out there are not designed or recommended for adolescents. Teens have nutrient and calorie needs which differ from adults. Even more importantly, none of these diet plans are designed especially for her. To develop a lasting, healthy eating pattern and maintain a healthy weight, adults and teens need to be guided inside themselves with questions like, "Are you hungry? What are you hungry for?" rather than told to follow recommendations which

fail to take into account their own bodies' signals, likes and dislikes, hunger patterns, and intuitive sense about head hunger, physical hunger, and emotional/spiritual hunger. Certainly, in some cases, teens must follow diets prescribed for particular medical conditions. These food plans are often very difficult to follow and teens will often struggle to comply, rebel, and worry about how "different" from their peers they must be. I strongly encourage teens involved in these special medical procedures to work with a therapist to help handle these intensified worries and struggles.

You are the most effective tool to help her through this rite of passage. Model for her, be who you really are, whether others accept that or not, eat a balance of healthy and pleasurable foods regularly throughout the day, and incorporate regular pleasurable exercise which is fueled by your food intake.

Most diets are a cover for fears about if she's good enough, whether she has to look a certain way to be accepted, and other such worries—not the calories you hear her talking about. These concerns are a normal part of adolescence so don't be surprised when your daughter begins to "diet."

Part II

Meals, Snacks, and Cooking

Chapter 9

What to Say and Do about Family Meals

Several scenes concerning family meals are described again and again in my office.

My mother prepares gourmet organic vegetarian meals each night with candlelight and soothing music. None of my friends have to do this. Why can't my mom be like everyone else's and just let me eat on my way to the activities for the night and quit making such a big deal out of family dinners?

We get quizzed about our day as soon as we sit down and everybody starts arguing. I hate it and can't wait until it's over.

We never eat together as a family. We all just grab something on our way to wherever and never really get full. We pretty much eat all night until we go to sleep. I hate it. I wish we'd have healthy meals.

It's awful at mealtime in our house. My parents always cook these healthy meals and I'm sick of it. I just want something that we all like rather than these diet meals.

My parents don't think about health at all. They keep feeding us these fast, filling meals. I hate it. Why can't they cook healthily?

I relate all these scenarios to make one major point. There is no one right way to feed your family. And, no matter what you do, someone is bound to complain and want to do something different. The nature of adolescence is to rebel and to resist and it's often over food and meals. Food choices, food likes and dislikes, the amounts eaten, and the times eaten are all ways that teenagers can and do exert independence and control.

At the same time, the table is an important place to experience being together as a family and to learn the importance of setting aside time out of a day to nourish ourselves. The importance of family meals is not simply to satisfy physical hunger. As M. F. K. Fisher writes in her book *Dubious Honors*, "Hunger is more than a problem of belly and guts . . . the satisfying of it can and must and does nourish the spirit as well as the body." Children raised with regularly scheduled mealtimes seem to continue the pattern into adulthood of making time on a regular basis to feed themselves. As a result, they seem to have a less difficult time maintaining a healthy weight and they struggle less with setting aside time to nourish themselves. So, how can you balance the need to teach your daughter the importance of family meals while at the same time give your daughter the freedom and independence she wants and needs, *and* not overload yourself with unrealistic expectations about family meals?

- Develop the pattern of family meals when children are quite young. This models a pattern of setting aside a regular time to

nourish themselves and gives them the opportunity to experience a balance of time to take care of themselves, as well as an opportunity to take time out from other activities.

■ Include family meals as just one activity you do as a family. There are numerous other fun activities you can do as a family. Watching certain TV shows together, going on family outings and hikes, or going to the gym can be pleasurable without being dramatic or expensive. If she rebels or resists family meals, remember to stay curious. "I miss having you eat with us as a family. What are your thoughts about that?" Then listen to her response and put your heads together to come up with options. The two of you may determine that she does other activities with the family but isn't hungry when the family eats. Or, you and she may identify that she wants to eat with her friends more often so you can negotiate a minimum number of family meals a week. Just stay curious and creative. Be willing to experiment with some different ways to handle her involvement in family activities—including mealtimes. You can always reevaluate in a few weeks and renegotiate.

■ Use family meals as a time to enjoy. This is a time to share some laughs from the day and hear about activities and what's happening in each other's lives. This isn't a good time to argue, fight, discipline, or problem-solve. Say something like, "Let's make sure to set aside some time after dinner to talk more about that," or, "If you need to argue about that, make sure you take some time later and hash that out. During our meal is not the time." If mealtimes continually turn into conflict and you keep having to set boundaries, use it as a signal for setting aside time for frequent and regular family meetings. This sets up time and space to bring up problems and conflict without linking it to food.

■ If regular family meals are inconvenient, don't try to do it every day. But set up certain days of the week that everyone knows are scheduled family mealtimes. These may need to be renegotiated as seasons change.

■ We usually think of family meals as dinner. But they don't have to be. Maybe weekend breakfasts work best in your house, or a combination of weekend and midweek breakfasts and dinners would be better. Which meals and which days doesn't matter. What's important is that everyone understands that there are certain times and days that are set aside for family meals.

■ Let everyone have input on what they want for meals. Every family meal won't necessarily be liked by everyone, but everyone at least knows that they will like the one they asked for. In addition, it's a relief to have help coming up with ideas so you aren't always having to come up with what to serve. Keep an idea list on the refrigerator so when people think of meal items they'd like, they can put it on the list. You can use this as the basis for a grocery list. The list is also a great way to reduce complaints. When you hear complaints, tell them to instead put some ideas of what they want on the list.

■ Avoid preparing more than one menu at a mealtime. Some of my clients stopped doing family meals because they were just too exhausted preparing four and five different menus because every member of the family liked something different. Getting input from all family members about their favorite meals and foods helps reduce this difficulty. In addition, you as parents might want to set an age over which if they don't like what is being served they are allowed to prepare their own foods as long as they still sit down and eat as part of the family. This gives the older adolescents some extra freedom but also an added responsibility.

- Negotiate who makes the family meals. This is usually welcomed if family members have suggested meal items on the list that they can be responsible for preparing. When family members take turns planning and preparing a meal, they are much less likely to complain about meals that others prepare since they have personally experienced how much work goes into preparing a meal and have experienced being on the receiving end of complaints for meals they have prepared. A regular family meal is much easier if different people are responsible for preparing different meals, or at least different parts of each meal. It's usually asking too much for just one person to prepare all family meals. In addition, I strongly encourage parents to give their children (both boys and girls) and adolescents experience choosing the menu for family meals, preparing the items, and cleaning up afterward. People who have no experience doing this in their youth have a very difficult time nourishing themselves well as adults and often struggle with their weight.

- Remember, family meals don't always have to be prepared at home. Bring home foods from "take-out" restaurants. Order something delivered. Go out to a restaurant—just do it together.

The bottom line: Eating together as a family is important. Which meals are family meals, when, what's served, and how often are all options to be designed around what works best for your family.

Chapter 10

The Importance of Cooking

Renee is a very busy sixteen-year-old, taking piano, volunteering, working part-time, going out with friends, and maintaining an A average. Over the past year she has steadily lost weight and complained of being tired. Her dad was very concerned and made an appointment. We started exploring by having her ask questions of herself: Am I important enough to set aside time for me? Is it embarrassing to make time to feed myself? What will my friends think or say? Is nurturing myself a good enough excuse to say no to other activities? As Renee grapples with these questions, she is experimenting with a schedule of family meals three nights a week and cooking one night a week with her dad for a three-month trial. Her dad loves it. Renee is still deciding how she feels about it.

Setting aside time to feed ourselves well is a powerful example of self-respect and honor. And preparing these meals is an opportunity to offer to ourselves energy, focus, creativity, thought, and care. Traditionally, cooking has been an integral part of how women were

taught to care for others. It's important to teach your daughter that cooking is also an integral part of caring for herself. This type of "nurturing ritual" reflects back to us that we have value, we are important, and we are worth spending time on and giving nourishment to. In our busy lives we often feel forced to give up preparing meals for ourselves in order to make time to fulfill our responsibilities to others. The teen years are when most of us begin this shift from nurturing ourselves to, instead, focusing on others.

You can help your daughter develop the ability to balance her self-care with her interest and involvement in others. One healthy and fun way is to involve her in preparing family meals.

- Use interest in baking as a signal for you that it's time to help her broaden her cooking experiences. Most girls begin their kitchen experiences with baking—following a recipe, using measuring devices, safely using the oven, and cleaning up. This gives her the satisfaction of creating something tasty as well as learning to handle the disappointments of failed cooking projects. Consider sharing with her some funny stories about failures you've experienced in the kitchen. If you're like me, you've had some real whoppers. One of my favorite flops was a "so sorry" cake, as my family named it. My dad and I got up very early and tried to bake a cake and ice it for Mother's Day. The cake never rose in the middle—just the sides—and as we attempted to frost it, big chunks of cake tore off and spread around with the frosting. It was a mess, but what fun memories I have of Dad and me laughing about it. Stories of your mistakes will help your daughter to normalize the cooking mistakes that she will definitely experience at some point and will help her laugh at them rather than avoid cooking to try to avoid failures.

- Ask her to help you prepare meals. Girls (and boys) who are responsible for meal preparation while at home adapt to fending

for themselves later in life with ease. Decide together which part of the family meal is her responsibility. She needs experience preparing meats, fish, and chicken as well as vegetables and starches, such as noodles, rice, potatoes. Her tasks can be as simple as boiling water for the minute rice, placing fish on the broiler pan, opening the package of salad, or washing the lettuce and tearing it into bite-size pieces.

If cooking is something you just don't do, consider setting up one time a week that you go ahead and cook—just so she can have the experience. Preparing something easy and quick is fine. It doesn't have to be a four-course meal. Think about using salad greens in the bags, seasoning packets that you just add meat or chicken to. It's not what you prepare that's important. It's that you took time out of your busy schedule to prepare food for yourself and her and that you share that experience with her. If you try it, you may be surprised at how fun it can be when you don't set up expectations that it needs to be fancy and complicated.

■ Set up prep time as special, fun, one-on-one time. Preparing meals together is often a time your daughter will talk and share herself with you. Consider not answering phones and keeping TVs and radios off. Try scheduling ahead of time with your daughter which meals during the week would be most convenient for her to help with and what she'd like to prepare. Be sure to include at least one dish she especially enjoys. Remember, this time is for fun so don't worry if it's not perfect nutrition. There's time for that at other meals. Don't feel pressure to do this every night. At times, when you are just too tired or hurried, invite her to sit in the kitchen with you while you microwave frozen entrees or open packages of take-out. Watching you prepare these types of quick, easy meals gives her ideas she will use later when she's tired or hurried.

■ Include her in planning what foods to have for family meals. Encourage her to notice what sensations happen in her body after eating certain meal combinations. Which combinations give her a feeling of satisfaction? Which set her up to be hungry later? What are her favorite combinations? Notice your body sensations after meals and share your discoveries with her. Meals that combine protein-rich foods, such as meats, fish, beans, and tofu, with starches and fats usually take care of hunger best. Help her notice that a variety of textures, temperatures, flavors, and colors usually create the most satisfaction and pleasure. She might want to compare her sensations after two different meals: for example, fast-food hamburger and french fries (mostly soft, hot, savory, and brown) versus spaghetti and meatballs, salad, and garlic bread (soft and crunchy, cold and hot, spicy and bland, and reds and greens and tans).

■ Take her grocery shopping with you. The basics—meat, dairy, produce, and breads—are usually around the outer edges of the store. Knowing this layout will help her spend less time and effort grocery shopping. You may want to introduce her to health food stores or small specialty groceries first. These are usually smaller and easier to maneuver through than supermarkets. Give her a chance to practice determining which fruits and vegetables are ripe or which fish is fresh. Sometimes the best way is to let her make mistakes and notice the looks, smells, and feels that she'll remember for next time.

■ Encourage her to attend some cooking courses, if she's interested. These give her a chance to try a broad range of different foods and cooking methods that you may not be familiar with. This is an especially good idea if cooking is something you'd rather not do much of. Consider taking a course together.

When it comes to knowing how to nourish herself well and feeling comfortable and competent to prepare the foods that do that, your daughter's middle and high school years are invaluable. Help her practice. The key word here is practice—not demand, insist, or require, but practice.

Don't be surprised if she resists or rebels against preparing meals. Remember, resisting is a normal, healthy pattern for adolescents. Just use your three-step tool. Tell about you, stay curious, and problem-solve together. "I'd like you to get some experience grocery shopping and cooking and I'm worried that you're not getting those experiences. What are your thoughts about this?" Listen. Then problem-solve and negotiate how often, what time, what would make it more fun for her, and so on. These sorts of conversations are usually great sources of creative options. She may want to invite a friend to go with you both as you grocery shop. What about inviting friends to the meal she prepares? She may be angry if her brothers aren't expected to do cooking responsibilities, but she is. If that is the case, rethink that requirement. She has a good point. Both men and women need experience with nourishing themselves well. If she's involved in lots of after-school activities, she may come home too late and too tired to help. Which days would work? What about weekends? Be flexible and creative.

The purpose of involving her in food preparation is to give her the experience of nourishing herself well and learning ways to balance that with other interests, and to link food preparation with fun, creativity, and pleasure as much as possible.

Chapter 11

Help with Breakfast Conflicts

She can't hit the snooze button another time—only twenty minutes and school begins. Shower, throw on jeans and T-shirt, out the door. Second period begins and her stomach is rumbling. By the end of the period she has a headache. She grabs a diet soda between classes and forgets about hunger for another half hour. Then it's back again. Thank goodness, an early lunch period today—pizza, french fries, candy bar. Still hungry. She worries about eating so much, grateful that at least she hadn't eaten any calories for breakfast. Her dad worries that she skips breakfast and doesn't know what to say when she complains about no willpower at night when she snacks while studying. Both come into my office, frustrated and scared.

Breakfast is the most argued-about meal of the day. Often parents, concerned about nutrient intake, desperately negotiate for downing at least a glass of milk or a bowl of cereal. Many times, daughters argue for the comfort, convenience, efficiency, fewer calories, and more sleep that results from skipping breakfast. So, in some homes,

mornings begin with a fight that nobody seems to win—to eat or not to eat breakfast.

DAUGHTER: I just don't have time for breakfast. No way am I going to get up any earlier than I absolutely have to. Research is clear that sleeping late in adolescence is very common and probably important for proper development. So, the time crunch is a given when planning breakfast. Offering some options that can be eaten in transit usually helps this dilemma much more successfully than attempting to get the alarm clock set earlier. Keep some quick, easy foods on hand to grab as she goes out the door.

Some Quick, Easy Foods		
granola bars	fresh or dried fruit	cups of yogurt
protein bars	low-fat hot dogs	sandwiches
toaster waffles	or deli meats	leftover slices of
	string cheese	pizza

DAUGHTER: I'm not hungry. I've always heard it's healthy to eat only when you're hungry. So I don't eat breakfast. Noticing your body signals, such as hunger or lack of hunger, and honoring those signals are important methods to balance the right amount of food with the energy needs of your body. Taking some of the quick foods listed above to eat as a snack at midmorning break when she finally feels hungry seems to work really well. If a midmorning snack isn't an option because many schools have rules against eating between or during classes, eating something for breakfast, even though not feeling the hunger signal, is a healthy alternative. If she doesn't, she will probably overeat at lunch and after school in response to getting overly hungry in the morning. Drinking something for an early breakfast is

another idea to consider. Sometimes drinking is easier than chewing and swallowing when she's really not hungry, but needs to fuel her body now in anticipation of hunger happening at a time she can't eat.

Some Breakfasts to Drink		
instant breakfast	a can of vegetable juice	a glass of milk
a smoothie		a protein shake
(yogurt and fruit/juice)		

DAUGHTER: When I eat in the morning, I feel more hungry than when I just skip breakfast. For some, eating a bowl of cereal or a bagel actually makes them more hungry than if they don't eat. If you or your daughter is one of these people, trust it and honor your body's response. It's telling you that starches such as cereal are not a good match for your body in the morning. Often, eating protein such as eggs or meat rather than toast or cereal will be more satisfying and not trigger hunger. Experiment.

PARENT: Breakfast fuels your brain. You need to eat something to think clearly and do well on tests. Study after study reinforces that hungry students do not perform as well on tests. Hungry students retain less information and have a more difficult time grasping complex ideas. Again, have plenty of quick-to-grab foods around (listed above) to make eating something as easy as possible in the morning.

PARENT: If she wants to control her weight, she needs to eat breakfast. Metabolism is the physical and chemical processes which our bodies' cells perform to supply our bodies' energy needs. Just to breathe, get out of bed in the morning, sleep, sit, work, walk around, talk, and everything else our bodies do to perform daily life requires

energy. Our bodies' metabolic processes convert the food we eat into this energy that our bodies then use for all its functions.

A healthy metabolism is one that burns food to create energy at a rate that fuels our body well for any functions it needs to perform. When metabolism is working well, we feel energetic and in balance.

But, our eating patterns impact this system. Hunger is a signal that your body needs food to burn for its energy needs. If you don't give it the food it needs, it will break down your body's muscle cells and burn them to provide the energy it needs. If your body has to break down its own cells to supply energy, very often it begins to slow down the rate it burns and not supply you with as much energy. This is called a slower metabolic rate or "lowered metabolism."

Skipping meals and following restrictive diet plans cause this slowing of metabolism. Eating in response to hunger helps metabolism to run at peak because it stays supplied with food to burn for all its energy needs.

So, eating something in the morning keeps metabolism burning at peak throughout the morning. This high metabolic rate supplies her with lots of energy to do life through the morning and helps her control her weight.

However, the most important link between weight and eating breakfast shows up much later in the day. Cravings, binges, and overeating at midafternoon and night are directly linked with eating too little food earlier in the day. Remember, eating causes changes in brain chemicals which in turn switches off appetite for more food. So, eating calories at breakfast often leads to a desire for fewer calories from snacks and cravings later.

PARENT: You need energy to run on all day. Eat something or you'll get run-down and get sick. Food is *the* energy supply for the body. The body burns energy throughout the night fast and, without breakfast, begins breaking down its own muscle in the morning hours to try to fuel its

energy needs in the absence of food. This process weakens the immune system and our body's natural ability to protect it from colds and flu.

It's no wonder that breakfast is such a source of conflict for many of us. If you and your daughter argue about breakfast, begin by having some of the quick, easy options handy—even if you consider them junk compared to what you'd like her to eat in the morning. Then, stay curious and help her experiment to come up with an alternative that feels like a good match for her body.

Consider Lunch

Everybody has heard the adage, Breakfast is the most important meal of the day. I think we need to be realistic—it may be, it may not be—but the bottom line is most girls struggle to get anything down in the morning, whether as a result of there not being enough time, it being too early to swallow much, or her trying not to eat. Lunch at school then becomes an extremely important meal because breakfast is usually far from ideal.

For most girls there are only a few options: pack and carry lunch from home or buy at school or some combination of those two. Encourage your daughter to use her body signals to decide what works best for her and experiment with some different combinations to find a good match. Help her identify some of the difficulties she faces concerning lunch. Not enough time to get through the line and eat is often a problem. Does she have friends to sit with? If she buys her lunch, does it contain the amounts and combination of foods that makes her body feel satisfied? Is what she eats holding her through the afternoon until she can get a snack?

Many parents are concerned about the fat content of school lunches. I think it's much more important for girls to eat to be well fueled through the afternoon than avoid eating because it's prepared with too much fat. In fact, the girls that skip school lunches,

saying they just don't contain healthy foods, usually end up eating higher-fat foods later on in the afternoon in response to being deprived. So be sure to help your daughter see the big picture.

If you and she decide she will take foods from home, consider going shopping together to identify some new, interesting foods that she might want to try. Your daughter needs fuel for her body to be well nourished throughout the school day. So, if breakfast is not ideal, try focusing on lunch and see if that helps.

Most importantly, stay flexible. Both you and your daughter should keep experimenting. Use any conflicts you have as a chance to stay creative and keep trying until she finds which foods work best for her in the morning as well as for lunch.

Chapter 12

What about Junk Food?

I don't like that food anymore. I know it has always been my favorite but not anymore.

I'm not hungry. I just ate with my friends, so I'm skipping dinner tonight.

I don't have time for breakfasts anymore. I'm staying out later so I want to sleep later.

No way do I want that. Only kids eat those.

I can't take my lunch. None of my friends do.

I can't eat in the cafeteria. None of my friends do.

Food choice is one of the most popular and important symbols of independence and autonomy used by adolescents. Parenting an adolescent girl concerning her food choices is one of the most challenging arenas to balance health and structure with respect and autonomy.

Too much structure and too many rules can create a power struggle which is often followed with eating disorder behaviors. Too little structure and too few rules can cause her health and energy to suffer and eating disorder behaviors may follow. As such, parents walk a very fine line, requiring thought, discussion, and creativity.

Junk Is Cool

Girls will often choose to eat candies, gums, chips, and drinks with the wildest colors, flavors, textures, and packages that can be imagined, items that we adults simply label as junk. However, your daughter's friends are eating them and therefore, to your daughter, these foods are cool. And, the thinking goes, if they eat cool foods then they will be cool. And, if they are cool, they believe they will be liked, popular, and accepted by their peers.

Family Meals Are Embarrassing

Almost everyone eats meals with their families, but no adolescent wants their friends to know that they do. Eating foods like casseroles, vegetables, and milk with siblings and parents is not cool; in fact, to quote one of my clients, "It's just too embarrassing." It projects the image of being a nerd, under a parent's control, and simply not hip.

Your role as parents is to help your daughter balance these two opposing views about food. "Junk food" serves as a password into the popular set of their peer culture. "Family foods" represent health and dependence. Certainly, these descriptions of foods are sweeping generalities and each girl will approach this cultural pull toward different foods with varying degrees of intensity. In fact, some girls follow a very different approach to junk food—refusing to eat any—choosing only the most healthy, nutritious foods. Whichever extreme your daughter chooses, the junk food route or the perfect

health route, the bottom line is the same. She misses out on experiencing a comfortable balance of health and pleasure with food. The important point for you as parents to realize is that your daughter is experiencing this pull to some degree, and you have an opportunity to help her address this part of her transition into adulthood with creativity and balance.

Following are some hints for you to use during your daughter's delicate dance with health and freedom as it relates to food.

- Let her know that you are aware of the two "worlds" she lives in as it relates to food. Tell her you want to support her in developing her independence and autonomy regarding food while making sure she stays healthy and strong.

- Set a structure of what you expect in your world (at home) that is clearly defined and is designed with her other world in mind. Some points within that structure might include:

  1. Set a minimum number of family meals she needs to be a part of every week. The older and more mature she gets, the fewer meals she is required to attend. Remember, research shows that when teenagers eat family meals, they have fewer problems with delinquency and eating disorders.

  2. She needs to be responsible for preparing at least one family meal each week. She plans the menu and cooks it, but you set a structure of what components it must include, such as meat, starch, vegetable, salad, and dessert.

  3. Let her know how much of her "other world" foods you are willing to purchase as part of the family groceries, and clearly define what she needs to be financially responsible for purchasing.

  4. Decide if you are going to provide her money for her to purchase these "other" foods for herself or if you expect her to pay for those out of her allowance or part-time job income.

These are just suggestions. The most important point is that boundaries and structure such as these are discussed and clearly defined so everybody knows what is expected. Don't discuss and negotiate these boundaries and expectations at mealtime. These discussions often uncover lots of emotions and need space and time separate from mealtime to work them through. Remember to use the approach of staying curious and telling your daughter your concerns.

Daughter Says	Healing Responses	Not Helpful Responses
I'm not hungry.	It seems like your tastes are changing lately and I just want us to talk about that. What do you think?	You're eating so much junk food lately. You'd better watch it.
I don't want any dinner.	I know you enjoy snacking with your friends after school. I want us to think through how to balance that and your health needs. Any thoughts?	The snacks you eat with your friends aren't good for you.
	I'm concerned that you might be hungry at different times now than when we usually eat dinner. What have you noticed?	You're not eating your dinner. You need to stop snacking so much.

Daughter Says	Healing Responses	Not Helpful Responses
	I'd like to set up some balance for the week so you and I can count on and plan family meals certain nights and certain snack foods to be in the house. What ideas do you have?	You're required to eat dinner with the family. And I'm not going to keep snacks in the house that aren't healthy for us.

- One of the biggest concerns about "junk" foods for many of the parents I work with is whether to have it in the house or not. I always encourage parents to include "junk" in the house except when dealing with a daughter's eating disorder. Then we individualize the plan around her recovery. It is important that normal, healthy adolescent girls be given opportunities to use their hunger signals, acknowledge their need for pleasure, and practice developing a healthy relationship with sweets and snacks. If these foods are restricted at home, many girls will eat more forbidden foods away from home, sneak them, or crave them just because they aren't "allowed." So consider normalizing "junk" by keeping some in the house routinely.

- Be open to renegotiate the boundaries and structures about food as your daughter matures and becomes increasingly responsible about including healthy "family" type foods in her eating with friends or vice versa.

- Respect your daughter's need to experiment with these two "food cultures." Let her have fun. You can join in by trying some of her "cool foods." Laugh with her about them if she feels comfortable with that. But be careful not to shame her. Share with her

some of the ones you remember from when you were an adolescent.

■ Share this chapter with her and let her know you'd like to know if she is experiencing conflicts between eating at home and eating with friends, if she has any thoughts about it, and what she thinks. Listen for what she has to say. Often teenagers will tell you what they want to say at the end of a conversation. Try to stay in listening mode and wait.

Your willingness to relax and enjoy this stage of your daughter's path to nourishing herself well can build a very strong bond between the two of you. If you let her know you recognize her balancing act between freedom to choose "junk" food and the need to eat healthy "family" foods, then she can see that you honor her need for more independence from the family and, at the same time, are there, at home, making sure the structure and foods she needs are there for her to feel safe as she takes these risks into adulthood.

Chapter 13

How to Handle Snacking

Bethany describes it like this: My two best friends and I love to hang out after school. We meet at different houses on different days and eat different snacks at each. At one house, everything is "healthy," like pretzels, no-fat fruit candy, and orange juice. At another, it's leftovers from the night before, with chips and sodas. At another house, we go to the convenience store for whatever we're in the mood for. But I'm not hungry for dinner after I snack. Mom's getting mad that I'm eating so little for dinner and doesn't want me snacking after school but that's when I'm hungry.

To determine your role as a parent in situations involving snacks, consider the following points. You can discover ways to help your daughter balance the fun and freedom of snacking and the health and nutritional needs she has as an adolescent.

Opportunity to Practice Listening to Her Body

To snack or not to snack? How much? When? What? Who decides for whom? Each of these questions gives your daughter a chance to practice using her body signals to determine if and when she chooses to snack, on what, and how much. A girl who uses these signals to make snack choices rarely has to worry about her choices causing havoc with her weight or her nutritional needs. Review the examples of body signals on page 13 to help your daughter practice identifying her unique signals.

If you are concerned about your daughter's snacking, start by asking yourself, Are you using your body signals to determine your snack decisions? And are you modeling for your daughter how to include snacks in the day without sacrificing your health and weight? Doing this will help you more comfortably encourage and remind her to use her body signals to make snack choices by using the questions "Am I hungry? What am I hungry for? How do I feel?"

Snacks, Often a Source of Conflict

All of us oversnack once in a while, and most girls will periodically eat too much candy or chips and then skip the next meal. Talk to your daughter if such a pattern is happening regularly. Ask her if she's noticed this pattern and let her know you're concerned. Talk about the difference between once-in-a-while versus daily. Negotiate.

But, watch out when you want to control her snacking. When parents step in and dictate if, when, and how much their daughter can snack, it usually backfires. The more you try to control, the more she will tend to resist. At this point, you and she are no longer a team, creatively problem-solving together. Instead, it feels like war and she will see you as the enemy rather than her ally.

In addition, this kind of restricting prevents her from using her body signals to figure out her food needs. So keep a variety of snack foods (sweets, proteins, starches, fruits, and vegetables) available and shift your focus from trying to control her snacks to helping her use her body signals to ask herself the questions "Am I hungry?" and "What am I hungry for?" If she finds these difficult to answer, you and she may want to review the different hungers in chapter 4.

Snacks, a Part of Friendships

Young girls bond after school—hanging out, snacking, and talking. I encourage you to support your daughter in this teenage experience by having snacks available. This does not mean that she and her friends should have free rein of the kitchen. Ask your daughter what snacks she would like to have available to offer her friends. Depending on her age, talk with her about the money you are willing to spend on these and, if she is old enough to have her own money and spending choices, what she and her friends will need to be responsible for. Let her know which foods are off-limits as snacks. These may be leftovers you are planning to use for dinner or expensive items. Together, set boundaries about what volume of snack foods she can feel free to offer each week. Both of you then know what the other expects. Talking and listening is the crucial point here.

Snacks Supply Needed Fuel

Snacks often supply teens with needed nutrients and calories. The body stores fuel and nutrients to last about four or five hours. With lunch periods at school often ranging from ten A.M. to two P.M., afternoon snacks are an essential part of most girls' fuel needs. I encourage afternoon snacks even for girls concerned with weight gain. My

reasoning: If they are hungry at midafternoon and don't snack, in response they often overeat at dinner and later at night.

If, however, she seems to be snacking throughout the day, it's often a signal that she isn't eating enough at meals and/or isn't eating a healthy proportion of protein, carbohydrates, and fat that her body needs to satisfy her fuel needs. A meal that fuels her well will satisfy her for four to five hours. If she snacks more often than that, go back to the basic questions about hunger. Encourage her to notice her body signals. And she may want to experiment with different amounts of proteins, starches, and fats at her meals to see if she can fuel herself for a longer period of time.

Satisfying snacks can be more than carrots or fruit. Carrots and fruit don't control hunger as effectively as more substantial snacks that include combinations of protein, carbohydrates, and fat, which alter brain chemistry and, as a result, turn off hunger.

Snack Ideas

fruit smoothies made in the blender with fruit, milk, and a dollop of peanut butter

soup

muffin or cupcake

leftover pizza or English muffin pizza

dried fruit and nuts

a sandwich or half of one, depending on how much she wants or needs to satisfy hunger

chili

popcorn

pizza

toaster waffles with fruit

cereal and milk

cookies or granola bars and milk

cheese and crackers

leftover entrees

nachos

trail mix

yogurt

Candy, cakes, and other sweets are fun and, let's face it, they taste good. I encourage families to keep sweets in the house so daughters can practice using their body signals to determine what, how much,

and when to eat them. Again, if sweets aren't on the shelves in the house just like other foods, girls see them as special and off-limits. This is a perfect setup for sneak eating and binging.

Snacks are another way your daughter can show her independence. It is important to honor that, while setting boundaries to safeguard her health, and to discuss with her how to balance these two important concerns.

Part III

The Family's Role

Chapter 14

What Is My Daughter's Responsibility Concerning Food and Eating?

Alex is a forty-two-year-old mother of three. Her oldest child, Ashley, is fourteen years old. Alex came to see me for help with the family meals. Alex has struggled with her own weight all her life. She has been diligent with making sure healthy foods for her family are in the house and meals are available every evening. Most of the time she tries to cook, but two or three times a week, she picks up food on the way home from work. At least one evening on weekends, she and her husband go out for dinner without the children. For the past several months, Ashley and her parents have been arguing and fighting over what, when, and how much Ashley eats. Alex saw these conflicts as a warning sign that something needed to change but she wasn't sure what to do differently. She came into my office to explore what she could expect from Ashley concerning her own food.

Changes in Food Patterns Follow Changes in Age

Alex, because of her past struggles with eating and weight, was aware that the conflict she was having with Ashley was telling her something important. As their relationship shifted, with Ashley getting older and more autonomous, the system they had always used about food and meals and eating was bound to need some changes. So don't be surprised when your family's routine around food starts falling apart. It is very normal and a sign of growth. And, it gives you a chance to create a new way of interacting with food. Sometimes it takes just a small tweak for everyone to be more comfortable. At other times it takes a complete overhaul. Both adjustments are very normal and, in fact, can be fun depending on how parents handle it.

Up until the teen years, parents have been completely responsible for the family's eating: planning what to serve, grocery shopping, deciding when meals would happen, preparing it, serving, cleaning up, and putting up with everyone's comments about it. Now that you have a teenage daughter, you can begin to let go of some of the responsibilities about food you have shouldered all of these years and hand them off to her. At first, most parents are quite uncomfortable letting go of the control. If you're concerned that your daughter won't do it right and her health might suffer, please know you aren't alone, and then do it anyway. Passing the baton about her eating on to her *at this young age* is essential for her to learn how to nourish herself well through adulthood.

Put Your Heads Together and Create

This shift of responsibility can happen gradually and needs to be done as a team with your daughter. Remember, your role is to say what is going on for you and to stay curious. So, as your daughter enters the teen years, put your heads together and get creative. A good place to

start these shifts is wherever the two of you are having conflict about food, meals, or eating (no breakfast, snacking, or skipping dinner, for example). Tell her your feelings about these conflicts and that you'd like to hear her ideas on how you and she might reorganize how eating is handled in your home and experiment with different approaches.

Don't forget to have some fun with this. There is no one right answer on how meals and eating should be organized. Just keep in mind, at the base of any plan you create, your daughter is responsible for answering the following three questions: "Am I hungry?", "What am I hungry for?" and, "How much do I need to feel satisfied?" There are lots of different options to address her answers to these questions, depending on your family system, such as what you as parents are comfortable with, how old your daughter is, and what both of you would like to try. Below is a list of some ideas that my clients, both daughters and parents, have tried and enjoyed. But, don't feel limited to these suggestions. Feel free to come up with your own. Just remember, as parents, you are responsible for making sure food is available and meals are planned, prepared, and cleaned up. This doesn't mean you have to do these tasks, just that you are responsible for making sure these are taken care of.

■ Your daughter is responsible for letting you know what foods she likes, what foods she would like to have available in the house, and when she needs more from the store. Keep a blank sheet of paper on the refrigerator for anyone to add whatever foods sound good to them for the next week or so. Then, pull ideas from this list as grocery shopping is done and meals are planned. Most families that have tried this have absolutely loved an organized, regular system of input into food and meals. Daughters love it because it allows them more control over what is served. Their ideas are considered and used as a base for the family's food. Parents are usually very leery of this approach. They are concerned

that she will ask for loads of junk food and outlandish, too expensive, unhealthy items. It's a valid fear. Usually at the beginning of using this communication system, girls will often go wild, especially if there has been a lot of conflict in the food realm. Usually this behavior calms down after the first few weeks of excitement and newfound freedom. If it doesn't, you and she can put your heads together again and reevaluate your thoughts and concerns.

▪ In earlier chapters I discussed family meals and cooking responsibilities. But it's important to consider your daughter's responsibility regarding family meals. She is responsible for being there for meals that you have planned with her. And, she is responsible for discussing and making plans ahead of time with you about when family meals are most convenient for her and any changes she would like to make concerning them. As she gets older, you may want to be more flexible with the number of family meals she needs to attend. The two of you may want to experiment with a system where she skips family meals and eats with her friends or in her room by herself, if she chooses, a certain number of times a week. As she gets older, her choices at mealtimes are another option. If she would like different foods than the rest of the family is having, you may want to experiment with her by preparing what she would like for a certain number of times a week. Again, these are situations where there is often a lot of fear on the parents' part as you give up some of your control and order and give your daughter more freedom and autonomy. However, parents usually look back on these shifts as a relief, ultimately burdened with much less worry, much less conflict, and much less work around food.

▪ It is your daughter's responsibility to identify what foods, in what amounts, in which combinations, and at what times nourish her best. You can help her by reminding her to ask herself the three basic questions: Am I hungry? What am I hungry for? Have I had enough

to satisfy myself? But, for the most part, your daughter will like to figure this out on her own, for herself. This may mean she tries some foods and eating patterns that don't seem very healthy to you. Let her explore. For the most part, she won't experiment much longer than a few weeks and rarely will anything hurt her in the long term from these short-term trials. You may want to offer to pay for cooking classes or health or nutrition classes. Girls are often interested in these and they tend to learn a lot. It's more fun to learn what is healthy for them from someone other than their parents. Making an appointment for her to visit with a nutritionist is another option girls often enjoy if they are curious and searching for answers.

■ It is your daughter's responsibility to learn how to plan and prepare meals that nourish her, and to clean up afterward. This book is especially about daughters, but as an aside, I believe this is equally imperative for sons as well. As I work with more and more clients, I see both men and women struggling with nourishing themselves well as adults when they had no practice preparing and feeding themselves in childhood. It's important to devise some regular routine for your daughter to be involved in these responsibilities. This can be really fun. Dads and daughters can shop for groceries together. Moms and daughters can cook together. Daughters can prepare the meal for the family once a week, maybe Sunday breakfast or dinner. If she isn't old enough to cook much on her own, set up one part of the meal that is her responsibility. Again, plan this with your daughter. Say what you feel is important and stay curious about her thoughts and concerns. Be creative and see how much fun you and your daughter can have as you let go of control and encourage her to take responsibility for her eating. There is not a set age to start this process. Trust your instincts, and invite her into the kitchen and experiment in little ways gradually over time.

Chapter 15

Parental Responsibility for Your Daughter's Eating

As daughters develop more independence through their teen years, parents often struggle with a difficult juggling act between taking care of their daughter's health and allowing them the control, power, and fun to experiment with their own ways of nourishing themselves.

Following are the basics of a parent's responsibility around healthy eating for their daughter.

- Address any food and weight struggles that you personally have. See a nutritionist or counselor and begin to work through the issues that make eating an area of concern for you. Without taking this step, you may unknowingly hand down your baggage about weight and food to your daughter.

- Have a variety of foods available in the house for meals and snacks. The planning, preparing, serving, and cleaning up after these meals is your responsibility as the parent. But this does *not*

mean you have to actually do all of these all of the time. You simply are responsible for making sure they are done. I encourage families to work out a schedule for grocery shopping, meal planning, meal preparation, and cleanup so everyone takes turns helping to feed the family, depending on their age and capabilities.

■ You are not responsible for serving what your daughter likes at every meal or for preparing her something else when she doesn't like it. If she doesn't eat what is served once in a while, that is quite normal. If it is a pattern every day, talk to her about it, but not at mealtime. Take time separate from mealtime and explore. The important thing is to give voice to what is going on.

Daughter Says	Healing Responses	Not Helpful Responses
I don't want any. I don't like that.	I'm concerned that you seem to eat very little at dinner. Help me understand what's going on.	You don't eat what I fix for meals. I'll cook anything for you if you'll eat.

■ Watch out trying to control the quantity of what your daughter eats. She is responsible for how much she eats unless the amounts are causing health concerns. Even then, let her experiment for a couple of weeks or so. Then, if you're still worried, take the approach of staying curious and letting her know your concerns and begin to suggest some changes that the two of you can come up with together.

■ Remember to keep you and your daughter's concerns confidential about her weight or body size. She needs to trust that you won't talk about her at work or with your friends. If you plan to

discuss your concerns about her weight with others, let her know who it will be with—for example, your spouse, doctor, or therapist—and make sure they hear her need for confidentiality.

- Make sure to take one-on-one time, rather than mealtime, to explore any conflicts, concerns, or discipline. Set a boundary that these issues will not be addressed during mealtimes. This reinforces the concept that feeding ourselves is associated with nourishment, replenishment, and calmness. People raised with conflict at mealtimes often find it difficult to feed themselves well and often avoid setting aside time for meals.

- Use any explosions of anger and arguments between you and your daughter about meals, food, and eating as a signal that the shift between dependence and autonomy is probably in flux. Remember that this is a normal and healthy transition. Rarely is it without conflict, anger, and discomfort.

Daughter Says	Healing Responses	Not Helpful Responses
I don't want that and you can't make me.	I've noticed we seem to be fighting more and more about food. I'd like us to explore what is going on and to see if we can come up with some new ways to try that might work better for us. What are your thoughts about that?	As long as you're in my house, you will eat what I serve.
	I can tell you don't like _____. Let's make sure we plan some meals with what you like in the next	It doesn't matter if you don't like eating _____ for dinner. We all do things we don't like.

Daughter Says	Healing Responses	Not Helpful Responses
	week so we all have a turn liking dinner. What are some things you're wanting? Be sure to put those on the list on the refrigerator so we'll remember and get what we need at the store.	
	What is something quick and easy we could keep in the house that you could substitute when we have this dish again?	

■ Experiment. Allow her to try some new ways to take care of her food needs. Make sure everybody is clear that this is an experiment with a specific time period such as the next month or the next two weeks. This creates a safety net. At the end of the trial period set up some more one-on-one time to explore and fine-tune the new approach. If it doesn't seem to be working, discuss how she could do it differently and ask if there is another way that you can support or help her. Stay curious. As a parent, you want to encourage her in this shift toward more independence, but not to the detriment of her health. It might take trying several different scenarios before something feels like it could work. Just remember to keep setting up the safety net of a trial period and stay curious about other possibilities.

■ If you have tried exploring different options and they are just not working, and her health is impacted, it is time for you to set a boundary. "I have to be responsible for your health. We have tried

a number of ways to take care of your eating and none of them are working, so this is what we need to do." This is a great time to consider bringing a therapist, nutritionist, and/or physician in to offer some new ideas to try and/or help identify if an eating disorder may be starting. Having health professionals on your team is reassuring for most parents and teens alike. Use them for support, reassurance, and guidance to work through this transition into more independence for your daughter. They can usually suggest ways of altering the family systems around food and help you through the conflicts that often erupt when experimenting with these. They also can work with you to develop boundaries that are most effective. You may want to give her a time period of several months within which she is expected to attend these appointments. The professionals can help you and her determine when to reevaluate. If she follows through, then you could offer to try experimenting again. She may react angrily to getting some outside help, but stay firm. You gave her a chance to try doing it differently and you said you'd be willing to reconsider in the future. Setting boundaries such as this, as you know, are usually uncomfortable, but they supply her with an important structure that she needs in order to feel safe and loved. Many of my clients with eating disorders tell me quite often how grateful they were that their parents required them to see a professional but they also share that they would never have let on that was the case at the time. Their "job description" at adolescence is to resist, rebel, and push against anything their parents suggest.

Chapter 16

Dad's Role in Eating and Weight Issues

Jonathan and Teckla came in to see me and were concerned about the weight of their daughter Sara. Sara had just started high school. She had been "big" all of her life, according to them, but this past year Sara was gaining weight very rapidly and they were scared. As we talked, Jonathan shared some of his experiences about being "big" as far back as he could remember, and his memories of being teased in high school, and how guys avoided dating "big" girls. He desperately wanted to help Sara not have to repeat his experiences or be excluded from dating because of her size. Sara was willing to work with me for a period of time, and to learn some new ways of taking care of herself. Jonathan has been working with a counselor regularly and he plans to continue. Jonathan, Teckla, and Sara worked together on setting up some new structures and schedules to experiment with some new patterns at home and on weekends.

Recognizing how your own experiences can impact your daughter is a powerful and often terrifying awareness, especially as it

relates to weight. Fortunately, Jonathan's willingness to seek help and talk about his experiences with weight has given Sara an opportunity to learn some new and different ways of relating to her body size.

Fear Comes Out as Control

Parents must be brutally honest with themselves anytime they feel a *desperateness* about protecting their daughter from repeating their own patterns. It is understandable to want your daughter to be happy and safe and to not have to endure the painful experiences that you did. And it is uncomfortable, sometimes unbearable, to watch her go through painful situations. But be very cautious when you feel desperate about your daughter's weight issues. Most of us, when we feel desperate, begin trying to control their painful situations. This causes even more pain, and begins a power struggle with our daughters in the arena where we most want to prevent it, and, in the long term, it never solves or prevents the problem.

Feeling desperate tells you something about yourself. It is a signal for you to seek help and it is an opportunity for you, as a parent, to understand yourself in a different way. Then, with the help of a professional, such as a therapist or a minister or rabbi, you can determine how you might be able to help and support your daughter in handling whatever the difficult situation might be in a way that gives her an opportunity to explore and decide for herself how to make different choices than you might want.

The Impact of Dad's Words

A dad's smallest comment—one he probably won't even remember saying—speaks volumes to his daughter. A girl's first understanding of how men think and feel and react is from watching and listening

to her father. The power fathers have to impact their daughter's beliefs about women, women's bodies, how they can expect to relate to other men in their life, and how they may think that men relate to them can be downright scary. Because of the power girls give fathers, fathers can play an enormous role in helping their daughters to feel comfortable and confidant with themselves and their bodies.

Most of the men that I work with don't realize how influential they are in their daughters' view of themselves and how they fit in the world. And, for the most part, they have had no reason to stop and think much about how their thoughts and beliefs about women and women's bodies might influence their daughters.

How Dad Views Women

Dads, you may want to put into words what you may have never considered before about your view of women. Here are some questions, just to get you thinking. Spend some time alone with these and then open up a discussion with your spouse, friend, minister, or therapist—get input about their experiences and what they may have noticed. How do you view women? What do you notice first about a woman? What type of women are you attracted to? What body size and shapes do you notice and which do you think are most attractive? Which do you dislike the most? What women do you enjoy being around? What size women did you date? What size women do you view as undatable? What do you talk to women about? What comments, either to yourself or others, do you make about women and their bodies while watching television or a movie? What have been your experiences with women of different sizes and shapes—your mother, grandmothers, sisters, bosses, employees, neighbors?

Time spent exploring your own experiences, beliefs, thoughts, and attitudes about women's bodies is absolutely invaluable in setting up

a healthy environment for your daughter to develop, grow, and create habits that nourish and nurture her body and her view of her body. When you are aware of your own beliefs and prejudices, you are then in a position of choosing what beliefs you would like or wouldn't like to share and teach to your daughter. If you aren't proud of some of your attitudes, it doesn't mean you are bad. I believe that knowing yourself in this way is the single most important thing you can do to help your daughter develop a healthy relationship with her own body. Understanding the beliefs you share may help her cope better when she runs into similar beliefs and prejudices in others.

A daughter doesn't always make it easy on her dad. She wears a new outfit and wants to know what you think. Or she tells you she thinks she's fat and wants to know what you think. What do you say? As we've talked about in each difficult situation, the best thing to do is to speak from your own experience and to stay curious.

Daughter Says	Healing Responses	Not Helpful Responses
Do you like my new outfit?	I really like how that color highlights your eyes. Did you notice that? or I don't really like that very much. What do you think?	Yes, or No.
Do you think I'm fat?	I've noticed you seem to be changing in size. What are you thinking about that? or I don't think you look fat, I like how you look. Tell me more about what you're thinking.	Yes, or No.

It's usually healthiest for your daughter that you do not comment about her appearance in sexual terms, such as, "Wow, the guys are really going to like that," or, "You look really sexy in that."

Healthy Interactions

You may want to notice any comments throughout the next few weeks that you make to your daughter. What are most of your interactions about? Many daughter and dad interactions concern her appearance, such as, "Well, don't you look pretty today," or around her performance of some kind—"That was a great goal in your soccer game today," or, "Congratulations on that A on your test." None of these comments are bad. In fact, she wants and needs your recognition for her achievements as well as her appearance. But, try to give some attention to and interact with her about other things too. What about wishes, dreams, worries, daily life, and friends? Try setting up some one-on-one time with her on a regular basis. The two of you, together, decide what you want to do. It can be as simple as riding in the car somewhere together. Go out for breakfast on Saturday, just the two of you, or consider cooking a meal or working in the yard. The whole idea is about you just being with her. Some of the best interactions I've experienced in my practice are between dads and daughters when they play "what if" with each other. "What if you won a million dollars, what would you do with it?" "What if you could travel to any country in the world, where would you choose to go?" Questions like these give both of you a chance to not just answer the questions but to talk about everything else that is involved in making a decision. It makes for stimulating, enlightening, fun, and playful conversations.

Dads play such a unique and important role in a daughter's ability to learn to nourish herself well. Many fathers have been the

one girls go to when they have a concern or problem they need to have "fixed." In the food and weight arena, be careful that you don't try to fix it by telling her what she should do. Instead, be a male figure with whom she can interact and practice expressing herself.

Chapter 17

Mom's Unique Role in Eating and Weight Issues

Cynthia is a single mother. Her oldest daughter, Jennifer, is eleven years old and she's beginning to make comments about her body and to notice her clothes more than she has in the past. Cynthia struggled with anorexia as a young adult and she feels confused when she tries to respond to Jennifer about weight and eating issues. Cynthia and I put our heads together and began to explore some ways she could try creating a healthy environment around food for Jennifer through her teen years.

Cynthia is smart to recognize that any struggles she has with her body size and her eating will spill over into Jennifer's life unless Cynthia addresses them first. Daughters are like sponges when it comes to many things, especially about eating and body size. Jennifer has a very high probability of creating habits through her teen years that copy what she sees and hears Cynthia doing. So, moms, if you are uncomfortable with eating certain foods, you struggle with cravings or try to restrict, or you struggle with your weight

and have difficulty finding clothes to fit (whether too little or too big), this is a great opportunity to work with a nutritionist or counselor to help you feel more at peace around food and your body. To find a good one, ask your doctor or your minister or rabbi for a referral. Nutrition counselors are also listed in the Yellow Pages. Just be sure to interview them to see if you are comfortable with them and their style. Also, ask about their experiences working with your type of issues. As you become more comfortable in the food arena, then you can become a healthy influence for your daughter.

Ideas, thoughts, opinions, and beliefs about body size and shape are multigenerational. What you were taught about women's bodies as a young girl is usually passed down to your daughter many times without you even realizing it. Moms, think back and try to put some words to what you learned about women's bodies as a young girl. Here are some questions, just to get you thinking. Spend some time alone with these and then consider discussing your responses with other women to help get their perspective too. What did you think about your mother's body while you were growing up? What kinds of things do you remember seeing her do to take care of herself when you were growing up? Do you remember hearing her say any comments or phrases about her body? What messages did you get from your mother about your body? What messages did you get from your mother about food and eating? How about your grandmother? What comments about food and weight did your father say to your mother? To you? How do those comments impact your view of your body size and shape today?

Time and effort spent exploring your experiences about eating and weight helps make thoughts and beliefs about these more conscious. This then gives you the opportunity to choose which ones you would like to encourage your daughter to use as a foundation for building her view of herself, food, eating, size, and shape. This

clarity also gives you a chance to discard any unhealthy ideas about eating and weight that have been passed down for generations.

■ Let your daughter hear when you are hungry, see you sit down to meals in response to your body signals of hunger, and eat meals in quantities that satisfy your hunger. Through the generations, girls have gotten the impression that to be feminine means to order salads and other "light" fare, to eat very small portions, not to finish what is on your plate, to never have seconds, and if you have dessert to eat just a bite or two and feign being full, even if you are ravenous. During your daughter's preteen and teen years, it is very likely that she will be surrounded with peers who are dieting, restricting, and ignoring their hunger signals. She needs models of women eating responsibly and healthfully to satisfy their hunger.

Daughter Says	Healing Responses	Not Helpful Responses
Nobody eats like that anymore. Everybody at school is on the _____ diet.	Everybody is different. We all don't have the same needs. How does it feel when your friends eat differently from what your body tells you works for you?	You don't have to do what everybody else does. If everybody jumped off a cliff, would you?

■ As you prepare meals at home and when eating out, choose a variety of foods. When your daughter notices you eating meats, starches, vegetables, fruits, and desserts, she learns that women eat a variety of foods to be healthy.

■ If you are struggling with binging and overeating, be honest with your daughter about that. She doesn't need to know specific

details. Tell her that you struggle with this and you're getting help (and make sure you are). This is a wonderful example for her that she doesn't have to be perfect around her food and weight—just honest about it. Let her know you will help her find a professional to work with if she needs it. Be very careful about trying to help her yourself if you struggle with weight. Parents tend to overcontrol when trying to fix their daughters out of fear that they can't fix themselves.

■ Share your worries and concerns about your body and its shape and size with your partner, a trusted friend, a nutritionist, or a counselor. Protect your daughter from needing to soothe or comfort you about your weight.

■ Encourage individual approaches to food. Deciding to diet together with your daughter must be handled very carefully. Each body needs its unique amount of food, timing of food, and combinations of food that work best for its particular metabolic rate, exercise, and genetic makeup. Rarely do both a mother and a daughter have needs similar enough to be on the same diet plan. So, encourage your daughter to listen to her own body signals about which meal combinations are most satisfying for her, when she gets hungry, and how much food she needs to eat at that time, and so on.

■ Purchase clothes that are comfortable and fit you well, and encourage her to do the same. Wearing clothes that are too small sends the message that you ought to be smaller and the size you are now is not good enough. Honor your body's need for comfort no matter what its size. In addition, wearing too tight or too small of a size suggests you deserve discomfort and pain because of your size. Whatever the size, you and she deserve to feel free to move and breathe comfortably.

■ Spend time interacting with your daughter about aspects of life other than clothes, food, meals, weight, and body size. Give her time to discuss those concerns if she needs and wants to, but set up other situations that allow the two of you to connect over joint charity projects or garden projects, creative projects, school, or athletics, and so on.

■ Notice how you respond to comments about your body from other people, and help your daughter create some responses for her to use. As women, we often are in social situations that require us to respond in some manner to a comment about our appearance, whether we like it or not. For example, "You're looking lovely tonight," or, "You look like you've lost weight." There is no one right response to comments such as these. What is important is that we help our daughters learn some responses to remarks such as, "My, you've grown so much since I've seen you last," or "You are turning into such a woman" so they can handle this attention about their bodies as comfortably as possible. My suggestion is to keep it simple and honest, such as, "Thank you. Anything interesting going on with you lately?" or "Thanks, let me tell you about the play I have a part in at school," or something of interest going on in her life.

■ Be involved in what you enjoy doing, regardless of your size, and encourage your daughter to do the same. If she likes volleyball but is too big to move with enough speed to make the A team, find a church league or YWCA and encourage her to play. If you love to dance, then dance, even if it is in your own living room. Let your daughter see you involved in life and your interests. Encourage your daughter to do the same. One of the most healthy tools for controlling weight is to feed ourselves in nonfood ways. Many women avoid doing what they love out of shame of their body until they lose weight. The opposite seems to work best. If

you do what you love, it feeds you in ways that food never can, and as a result, it often helps you feel more in control with food.

Mom, your daughter will more than likely develop a pattern of nourishing herself based on what she's seen you do. This creates lots of anxiety and pressure. Consider using this pattern to explore your weight issues with a professional so that you can share your growing and healing with your daughter as she grows and develops.

Chapter 18

Eating Strategies During Joint Custody

Mom, Dad doesn't keep any food but snacks in his house. I'm so hungry when I'm over there.

Dad, Mom doesn't eat regular meals, so I just snack the whole time I'm there. It's awful.

Mom, Dad's wife cooks with lots of fat and I'm gaining weight from staying over there.

Dad, Mom eats all this diet food, all these salads, I can't ever get full.

Mom, Dad and his wife eat vegetarian. Why can't we eat that way?

Dad, Mom and her husband eat out all the time and don't care if I eat desserts. Why do you make such a big deal out of it?

If you are a parent of a daughter sharing joint custody with your ex-spouse, I'm sure you've heard one of these complaints and strug-

gled with what to say and what to do to resolve these concerns. Following are some of the approaches my clients (daughters, dads, and moms), have used to make eating in two different households comfortable and healthy for their daughters.

- Most important, don't ignore your daughter's complaints about food, eating, and meals. She needs to be heard even if nothing can be done. Let her know that you understand how difficult it is for her to adapt to two different households and two different approaches to food.

- In response to her complaints, DO NOT COMMISERATE WITH HER. Using her complaints as ammunition to prove to her that your ex is a bad person is often interpreted as permission to use food choices and eating as a manipulative tool. When your daughter starts playing these sorts of power games with either of you about eating, she is stepping into the beginnings of an eating disorder.

- Discuss with her what, if anything, she would like you to do to help her handle this concern. Do not jump in and try to fix it. Ask her if she would like you to help and, if so, how. She may simply want to complain and be heard.

- Before taking any action about the situation at the ex's house, explore with her what you can do differently in your own household that would help her address her eating needs more comfortably. Making sure healthy meals are available at your home is the most important consideration and one which you have the ability to control. Sometimes, this is the only and best way to balance unhealthy eating at your ex's.

- When she stays at your home, as the parent, you are responsible for supplying a variety of healthy foods in your home to feed her

three meals a day (two, if she eats lunch at school) and snacks. And you are responsible for seeing that meals are available at regular times, even if that means using a delivery service, take-out, or foods prepared ahead of time. However, expect her to take turns along with other family members to complete these responsibilities.

■ As often as possible, eat meals with your daughter when she is staying with you. Research has shown, eating as a family reduces the frequency of eating disorders and delinquency.

■ After having worked with your daughter about food and eating at your house, then it's time to address her experiences at your ex's. If you don't have a communicative relationship with your ex, expect to feel extremely frustrated and angry about not being able to control what your ex does about your daughter's eating. Talk about this anger and frustration with a trusted friend, therapist, or minister or rabbi so that you are not venting these on your daughter.

Sometimes, it is easy to confide in your daughter as you would a trusted friend, but doing so sets up a dynamic between you and her that can unbalance the relationship of parent and daughter and can change it to an unhealthy version of friend to friend. Although confiding in your daughter about your anger toward an ex, or your fears about being lonely, or your concerns about finances or your job, for example, might seem comfortable and natural, it will frequently cause your daughter to take on your concerns as hers. When this happens, your daughter may not bring her concerns to you to protect you from having more problems. This shift in focus from her own concerns is often very subtle and happens gradually. Struggles with her food and body very often grow out of this situation without you even noticing. Your daughter needs you to listen to *her* concerns, focus on *her* feelings, and be *her* ally to problem-solve.

Daughter Says	Healing Responses	Not Helpful Responses
Mom, Dad doesn't keep any food but snacks in his house. I'm so hungry when I'm over there.	It sounds like you're really upset about going hungry at your dad's. Tell me more.	Just make him take you to the store. This sounds just like him.
Dad, Mom doesn't eat regular meals, so I just snack the whole time I'm there. It's awful.	It sounds like you're struggling with not getting meals at your mom's. I'm glad you said something. I wonder if we can come up with some ways you can handle that?	I'll just make your meals to take with you from now on.
Mom, Dad's wife cooks with lots of fat and I'm gaining weight from staying over there.	It sounds like you're scared about gaining weight. Tell me more about that.	Your dad always did like fatty foods. I hate that you have to deal with this.
Dad, Mom eats all this diet food, all these salads, I can't ever get full.	It sounds like you're frustrated about Mom dieting. Let's put our heads together and see if we can come up with some things to help.	I get so sick of your mom doing this to you.
Mom, Dad and his wife eat vegetarian. Why can't we eat that way?	I'm glad you're enjoying that. Let's think about a vegetarian meal or two that we can try in the next week or so. Would you like to cook it with me since I don't usually eat this way?	Because I'm not vegetarian and neither are you.

Daughter Says	Healing Responses	Not Helpful Responses
Dad, Mom and her husband eat out all the time and don't care if I eat desserts. Why do you make such a big deal out of it?	I'm glad you're having fun eating desserts with them. Tell me about some of your favorites.	We've been over this before. I'm not talking about it again.

■ Depending on the relationship you have with your ex, your daughter and you have a couple of options to consider. One, ask your ex for specific changes that would help your daughter have a more comfortable eating environment. Remember, she decides if she wants you to speak for her, or if she will speak for herself (except in negligent or abusive situations where the environment she is exposed to needs to be addressed through legal means). If she decides to speak for herself, help her think through how she might word her requests and which requests are most important. If there is no response to this request, consider having your daughter carry the foods she needs or wants with her from your home.

Be careful about competing with your ex in the food arena. It's very rare that a daughter living in two different environments won't use things they like about the food in one household to try to make you feel guilty and, in response, you may offer something to try to be as well liked as the other parent. If she seems to be using this technique, let her know you heard what she really likes about the food at your ex's household, but that you are not comfortable doing that in your house. Feeling guilty, scared, and/or angry about this competition is very normal. Just don't vent it on your daughter.

Chapter 19

Siblings' Role in Eating and Weight Issues

Megan is a twelve-year-old who got teased at school for her weight. She came home and e-mailed her sister, Emily, who is away at college, about what happened. Emily wrote back about her experiences with teasing and agreed with Megan about how much it hurts. Then she talked about how her friends at college are all different sizes and shapes, how everybody wears different styles of clothes, and how she and her friends are involved in theater productions, a mural project at a local school, and charitable projects around town with a big group of students and adults from the community. She shared with Megan that she is beginning to see that the world is filled with interesting people of all different looks and styles and weights and heights. Emily's e-mail did wonders for Megan. It gave her hope. It gave her encouragement. And it gave her a different way of seeing the world through somebody else's experiences—somebody who she trusts and loves and who isn't an authority figure.

Siblings can have such an impact on how your daughter feels about her body. We all know there are so many different sibling

relationships, all with varying degrees of closeness and competition that depend on variables such as age differences, interests, personalities, birth order, genetic body type, height, weight, and so on. One might be labeled the "smart one" while the other is the "pretty one." One thinks of herself as the "artsy one," while another sees herself as the "athletic one." Some are inseparable while others are constantly at each other's throats. The only constant: Each child is constantly exploring and experimenting with who she is, how she fits into the world, what she likes, what she doesn't, what she feels about her self and her body, how she takes care of it, what others think about her, and how she compares to others. Each child is unique and yet is often wondering, "Am I good enough? Will people like me? How can I make sure?"

In my practice, I have heard an amazing array of stories about siblings' words and actions affecting our daughters' thoughts, feelings, and beliefs about their bodies and what they eat. Siblings seem to have an incredible influence on how we see ourselves. I've listed below some of the more common interactions or patterns between siblings that often influence weight and eating.

■ Let your mind wander back over your childhood and teenage years. Notice any memories you have about your siblings and make note of any experiences that relate especially to what you looked like, your height, your weight, what you ate, or how much you ate. What is the common theme? Were you accepted, encouraged, and supported or were you criticized, ridiculed, and teased? Somewhere in between? How are your thoughts and choices today about food and your body influenced by comments from your siblings back when you were a teen? Are your siblings still making comments about your body and eating patterns even as an adult? Are they helpful? Do they discourage you? How do you handle them? Depending on your relation-

ships and your comfort level, you may want to talk to your siblings about your thoughts and memories as they relate to your weight and body and eating. This would be a great opportunity to let your siblings know how much you appreciate how they encouraged you, and so on. Many parents find it very helpful to talk to a professional counselor or minister about any painful memories that may come up. Counseling certainly can't change the past, but it can help change what we think about the past. As a parent, you have an opportunity to understand and clear any patterns that you now have that might have their roots in how you defended yourself from your brothers and sisters when you were young. In addition, it gives you a broader base of understanding to handle any situations going on between your children.

■ One of the most difficult situations to handle is when one daughter fits society's definition of beautiful—tall and thin—and another daughter is short and weighs more than what society calls normal. This difference usually causes fear, guilt, and anger in both girls. Set up alone time with each of your daughters, talk together about these differences, and listen to how each daughter feels about herself. Then consider all of you talking about it together. Simply putting voice to and honoring their feelings about their differences are incredibly healing tools in these situations.

Daughter Says	Healing Responses	Not Helpful Responses
I'm scared Sister will be hurt when I wear these new pants because she doesn't wear styles like this because of her weight.	I'm so glad you told me. Tell me more about your fear. What are you afraid will happen?	Don't worry about it. She'll get over it.

Daughter Says	Healing Responses	Not Helpful Responses
I hate that Sister is so tall and thin. She gets to wear all the cute clothes.	That really is hard, isn't it? Tell me more about what happens for you when she does that.	It's not her fault she's that size. You shouldn't be mad at her.
I feel so guilty that I'm hurting her/hating her.	I can really understand that. Tell me more.	You don't have to feel that.

- Often, an underlying belief our daughters may have about tall and thin women is that if we looked like that, people would like us more and we would feel less lonely, hurt, and unsure of ourselves. One of the most healing gifts siblings can give each other is honesty about this belief that we rarely put into words. If the tall and thin sister would share with the other when situations come up, such as, "I'm afraid that Jim doesn't like me," it can help each of them realize that we, as humans, each have fears and dreams and problems no matter what our body sizes may be.

- Sharing clothes between sisters is an area that can be great fun and can also cause tremendous competition for the thinnest body and smallest size. I suggest parents minimize this issue by encouraging each daughter to have a basic wardrobe of her own choosing—her colors, her styles, and her size based on her uniqueness.

- Brothers can play an important role in helping their sisters learn how to interact with males and learn what role, if any, their bodies play in that. Brothers and their friends, interacting with their sisters, help them see themselves as being so much more than just their bodies. In addition, a girl can learn from her brother that males worry about their looks and are unsure whether people like

them, too, just like she worries. This awareness gives both siblings the opportunity to interact with the opposite sex on a human level without regard to their body size and weight.

■ Brothers often use teasing as a way to make a connection with their sisters. And, often during the teen years, bodies are a popular topic for teasing. Set up clear guidelines that teasing should be about something fun. If it hurts, it is not teasing. See chapter 29 to review some ideas about this.

Sibling relationships give girls many situations from which to learn, experiment, and practice how to relate and interact with others out in the world. If you can help your daughter develop the strength and confidence to effectively take care of herself around her siblings, she will more comfortably address situations she encounters outside of the family.

Chapter 20

What to Do if <u>You</u> Struggle with Food and Weight

"I know what to do. I just don't do it."

If you have heard yourself say these words then this chapter is for you. It will help you to begin to put into place a way out of your own struggle with food. Then, you can more comfortably and confidently guide your daughter through any concerns she may have about food. What is something about food and weight that you struggle with? Several things may come to mind but for now just pick one to consider as you read through this chapter.

Overwhelming and Confusing Nutrition Information

There seem to be more and more new healthy food items available in the grocery store, more and more new exercise approaches to maintain health, and more and more information about health and weight available in newspapers, magazines, books, and on the radio and television. Yet, most of us are struggling more and more with

our weight and trying to eat and exercise healthily. In fact, these products and recommendations about nutrition and health that are available seem to cause more confusion, especially when many sources of information seem to recommend conflicting advice. Also, we're exposed to so many suggestions for healthy living that, even if they don't conflict, it feels as though we would have to quit our jobs and work full-time on our healthy lifestyle to be able to follow all the recommendations we'd like. How do we figure out what is right for us? No scientific study, article, book, magazine, or television or radio show can know what foods, eaten in what amounts, and at what times are the best match for your particular body. No wonder so many of us feel overwhelmed, want to give up, and end up struggling.

The Missing Piece

Knowledge about food, nutrition, and health from outside of ourselves is only half the information we need. Knowledge from within our own bodies is the missing piece that, in conjunction with nutrition facts and research, allows us to truly know what is right for us. Our bodies send us this knowledge from within by way of our intuition or body signals. Then, if we listen to those body signals and trust they are telling us something important and useful, we can use the knowledge from outside of ourselves to begin to interpret what those signals might mean. This blending of knowledge from within and without gives us an incredible ability to stop struggling with food and to feel in balance with our eating and health.

Sandra is a forty-two-year-old mother of eleven-year-old twins and works at a local law firm in research. She describes her struggle with food and weight as hopeless. Sandra has experimented with lots of different diet programs and eating patterns only to end up struggling with her midafternoon

cravings for candy, donuts, French fries, or chips. Her pattern is this: try to hold off succumbing to the craving for as long as she can, finally give in, feel guilty and ashamed afterward, and vow she will do better tomorrow, only to repeat the same pattern. Or crave, give in, feel guilty and ashamed afterward, decide to punish herself by going without dinner that night and breakfast the next morning, only to end up craving and giving in again, then feeling like such a failure that she decides to give up and binges all evening after she gets off work until she finally falls asleep. The next day, she starts the struggle over again.

Redefine Failure

When we struggle and fail with food, our intuition is trying to talk to us, but we usually feel so guilty, angry, frustrated, and hopeless, the last thing we would think to do is get curious and search for knowledge from within. But, our body is trying to tell us something we need to know. Feeling like a failure about eating is a signal that your intuition was probably not included in the blend of knowledge you used to decide about eating in this situation or for a meal or two previously. All of us struggle with food and eating and weight if we use only knowledge from outside of ourselves. To avoid the struggle and to be at peace with food requires *both* knowledge from inside our own bodies and knowledge from nutrition research.

Sandra decided to experiment with a different way of using her afternoon failures. She decided it was worth the risk because what she was doing now wasn't working and she couldn't imagine anything being worse. So, when she repeated her pattern again, she added another step after feeling guilty and ashamed and asked the question, "What is this telling me?" and got curious. She then experimented with four points that her intuition might be telling her.

Four Intuitive Signals

First, signals from your five senses tell you intuitively what foods you need to satisfy your head hunger. These signals about head hunger are usually one of the easiest intuitive signals to begin with. So, anytime you feel a desire to overeat or feel like a failure about what you just ate, start with these. Head hunger is a natural hunger for a variety of flavors, textures, temperatures, colors, and scents. Sandra noticed when she tried to eat a "healthy" lunch according to her knowledge from outside of herself, she would choose a salad with lettuce and vegetables, maybe some tuna or chicken on top, and a diet dressing. By midafternoon, her body would send her a craving signal. She noticed when she ate this lunch, she would usually crave donuts or French fries. She got curious and started looking for what her intuition might be telling her. Her first reaction, without thinking too much, was her lunch was mostly cold and crunchy and her craving was for warm and soft. Her knowledge from within, her intuition, was telling her to do something different to satisfy her head hunger. The signal from her intuition may be telling her she needs a different blend of textures and temperatures at her meals earlier in the day. One day she tried adding a warm yeast roll to her salad lunch. Another day she added a bowl of lentil soup. Another day she had a baked potato with her salad. She noticed on days she added these warm, soft foods that her craving in the afternoon was much less intense.

Second, her cravings at midafternoon may be signaling her about her physical hunger needs. Physical hunger is an intuitive knowing of what kinds of foods and in what amounts your body needs to be well fueled. Sandra wondered if her intuition was possibly telling her that she needed a different combination of foods or different amounts. Her intuition might be signaling that her unique physical hunger needs were not being met with her lunch of salad. Because

she craved donuts and French fries (carbohydrates and fats), she decided it might be telling her she needed more carbohydrate and fats in her meals earlier in the day. When she tried adding butter to her potato or roll, she felt much better in midafternoon. On days she had the lentil soup, she tried using a regular salad dressing on her salad instead of fat-free and that seemed to ease her craving some.

Third, her intuitive signal of craving may be telling her about an emotional hunger. What was she feeling? Whenever Sandra ate a salad lunch she would always feel proud of herself for being so good, based on her knowledge from outside of herself, but she never felt satisfied afterward and usually felt deprived. Here again her intuition is telling her important information. Just salad for lunch doesn't satisfy her emotional hunger for pleasure. As she started exploring some other additions like soups, potatoes, rolls and butter she felt more satisfied.

Fourth, how might this craving be signaling her about a spiritual hunger? What did she long to do in midafternoon that she wasn't able to do? She came up with quite a list. Take a nap, be home when her kids got home from school, talk to a friend rather than constantly reading files and research, and be outside instead of in her office. Addressing these spiritual hungers was going to take some work. She couldn't just change her lunch and have these addressed. But, she did take these longings seriously and began to explore how she might be able to address these important needs, longings, and hungers. She still hasn't decided how she plans to take care of her spiritual hungers, but she is committed to looking at options and making some changes when it feels right.

Sandra didn't have to know the answer right away to ease her struggle with food and afternoon cravings. She only had to listen to the craving, honor that it was telling her something important, and experiment with some different ways she might want to feed her various hungers. Using these four intuitive signals gives her a pat-

tern or tool to use the next time she runs into a struggle with food. As she practices with this pattern in response to her own eating, she models a pattern her twins can use to listen and respond to their intuitive signals about food as well. If you hear your daughter expressing that she feels like a failure about some situation with food, help her use these four signals as a tool to learn from the situation, connect more deeply to her body's needs, and practice nourishing herself well. As you practice this pattern for yourself, you will more easily and confidently be able to guide your daughter. Plus, most parents feel relief by using these tools with their daughters. They don't have to know what's wrong. They don't have to handle her panic at her failure. They don't have to know what to say—they can listen, use these tools, and explore.

Don't be afraid to ask for some professional help yourself in using these tools, practicing applying them, problem-solving what they might be saying that you're hungry for, and supporting and/or guiding you through making changes that will help you feed the hungers in your life. The more comfortable and confident you are at using these tools, the more help you will be teaching your daughter to use them. Following this pattern of identifying your hungers and addressing them can be enjoyable. Many people are amazed and relieved when they don't have to fight food anymore and actually get to feed their hungers with foods and other things that they have always wanted in their lives. It may sound scary, but the payoffs are worth the risk: turning your struggle with food into a life pattern that nourishes your greatest longings and teaches your daughter a way to nourish herself so that she may not have to repeat your struggles.

The more comfortable you are using your four signals to help you through struggles with food, the more you can effectively guide your daughter away from a lifetime of struggles with her weight. Replacing failure with curiosity is one of the most powerful tools for her to use to nourish herself well.

Chapter 21

How to Be Your Daughter's Advocate

"Guys only like really thin girls," say her friends at school.

A magazine article discusses the heights and weights of fashion models.

"Come on, have a second helping," says a relative to your daughter at a family gathering.

"You're getting a little chunky, aren't you?" her grandmother says during a family visit to relatives.

"You must lose ten pounds if you want to dance in the recital," says the dance instructor.

"Watch those pounds, you're getting awfully close to the weight limit," says the cheerleader advisor.

"You eat all the time. What a pig!" says her brother.

The audience jeers and laughs at an overweight person in a movie the family is watching.

We could fill pages with all the situations where your daughter is confronted with comments, judgments, and expectations about her body, its size, or her eating. With family members, teachers, advisors, friends, boyfriends, movies, magazines, television, and books, she is absolutely surrounded with subtle and not so subtle messages about what a woman's body and weight should be or how she should eat. Because everyone seems to have an opinion about her body and/or what she eats, she begins to recognize that she is, and always will be, judged by others about these matters. As a result, she concludes that other people know better than she about her food and her body. Sadly, this process of acculturating girls into a lifetime of judgment and self-doubt begins much younger than adolescence and usually is deeply imbedded in her thinking by the teen years. But, with your help and encouragement, she will learn that she has the power and the right to make decisions about her own body.

Alone, she will have a very difficult time not caving in to the attitudes which surround her. She needs an advocate. She needs an adult, a parent (ideally both parents), to support, filter, clarify, discuss, explore, model, edit, protect, stand up for, and question whatever or whoever tells her how to be in her body. Below are specific ways you can be your daughter's advocate.

■ Avoid judging your daughter's body and food choices. If she asks for your opinion about her body, which I am sure she will, use that as a time to help her see you are not there to tell her what is right for her. Help her to determine for herself how she should look by not telling her what you think she should look like.

■ Discuss with your daughter how to check in with her own body and determine from that what seems right for her, even if it differs from what others say. Let her know how difficult doing this

can be so she will know that she will probably struggle with making her own decisions and won't always do it perfectly.

- One of the major ways your daughter begins to develop her beliefs about her own power is through her body experiences: Does she have any power? What does power mean as it relates to her body and eating? Does she have the right to have power? How can she handle power? In what ways does she give her power away to others? What criteria, if any, does she use to determine whom she chooses to obey about her body?

- She will usually mimic how her mother handles power. So, as your daughter's advocate, begin by looking at how *you* might give *your* power away, how *you* are impacted by society's expectations about women's bodies, and how *you* choose to respond to messages and judgments about *your* body. Do you struggle to look as thin as you think others think you should be? Do you wear clothes and shoes that others think you should wear even if you're uncomfortable in them? Do you choose foods so others won't comment about what you eat? These are some of the ways we, as women, have been taught to give our power away. Begin to notice how you do this as well.

- Share with her some of your experiences where others have influenced what you did about your body and food. Help her to know that each of us within our culture is affected by this and not just her.

- Discuss with her how you might be an advocate for her. For example, in the situations listed at the start of the chapter, you could offer (remember, she can say no to your offer) to: back her up when she says, "No, thank you" about food when a relative doesn't respect that. Ask relatives not to make judgments about your daughter's body and food. Call teachers, advisors, and/or

coaches and discuss your concerns if you feel that they set up unhealthy or unrealistic weight and/or eating goals for your daughter. Set limits within the family about teasing as it relates to bodies and food. Talk frankly as a family about movies, books, and magazine articles that set up judgments about food and bodies. Discuss with her the difficulties and disadvantages of trying to please others by looking a certain way.

Plan Ahead, behind the Scenes

Simply let her know you are on her team. If she's uncomfortable with you acting in her defense, you can still be a very helpful advocate behind the scenes. Put your heads together before she goes somewhere that she might encounter comments about her body or what she eats and come up with some responses she could use or actions she could take. Having a plan helps ease some of the stress in these situations. Encourage her to talk about situations that come up that she hadn't anticipated so you can help her have a plan to prevent stress next time. Clearly state that you support her taking care of herself in these ways. It's scary when others might respond in anger or call her rude when she doesn't do what they want her to do with food. It's easier to tolerate these responses when she knows you are her advocate and will back her up.

It is so hard for teens, and adults, to stay confident and focused on what is right for them when surrounded with many different opinions and suggestions from others. You can be a safe haven for her. You can be one person she knows will trust, encourage, support, and defend the wisdom of her connection to her own body signals and intuition. She needs you as her advocate.

Chapter 22

How to Handle Holiday Eating

The holidays mean "diet" or more accurately "diet failure" for so many of us, adults and daughters alike. Instead of looking forward to months of joyous celebrations, we go to war with the holiday season and all the temptations to eat and feel out of control with our food.

Halloween begins this annual fight between our desire to celebrate and our anxiety about what we should or should not eat, and our struggle to maintain a healthy weight. The battle continues on for months into Thanksgiving, through Christmas, New Year's, and even into Valentine's Day, with most of us coming out in the spring feeling disappointed about our weight and frustrated at our failed attempts to juggle pleasure and health.

Samantha was seventeen years old and had been working with me for about a year. She was gaining confidence and trust that if she would eat using her body's hunger and fullness signals, she would feel satisfied and her body would stay a healthy size. But when the family visited her dad's par-

ents for family gatherings, she would dread it, beg to stay home, and eventually come home angry and frustrated. She described the gatherings as a big food fest. As she walked in the door, one of the relatives would comment on her weight since the last time they saw her. Food was out on all the counters and one meal was served a day. The rest of the day, people grazed and snacked. She felt overwhelmed, out of control, and when she chose to not eat until she felt hungry, people would notice, tease her, offer her food, and act hurt and mad that she didn't want what they were offering. They would warn her that she was being rude and ungrateful to her grandparents since they had gone to such trouble to fix the food.

We decided to invite Samantha's parents to one of our meetings and to talk about what to do. As we discussed it, both of her parents realized that relatives were doing similar behaviors with them, too, but they were so used to it they just put up with it, never realizing its impact on Samantha. So Samantha asked them for some specific ways they could help. Together, they worked out how Samantha could respond when people commented about her weight as she walks in, saying, for example, "I really don't want to talk about my size or weight, Aunt." The parents agreed to back her up. If the aunt still continued after she stated that, the parents would say, "Samantha asked you not to talk about that and I'd like you to honor her request." Then, Samantha told her parents she wanted to say "no, thank you" to offers of food, but needed their help when people tried to override her response. She asked them to step in at that point by saying, "She said, 'No, thank you.' Please don't ask her again." They've all worked hard on trying these new things and are making it easier for Samantha, but it has not been easy. Her aunt and some of the other relatives are angry and impatient with this new approach.

Family gatherings with lots of relatives and lots of food can be stressful—especially for young girls.

Using Her Voice

Holidays are often command performances for our daughters, i.e., they don't have much choice about whether they will attend, how long they will stay, or what they'd like to do while they're there. As a result, they often feel frustrated, powerless, angry, and guilty. In response to these strong feelings, they will often overeat to soothe themselves and, then, feel guilty and mad at themselves for overeating. I think many adults struggle with a similar pattern. We participate in many holiday rituals and activities because we are expected to do so by family, friends, coworkers, and so on. When we fulfill these sorts of obligations, rarely do we feel nurtured or "fed" and often end up eating to soothe our anger and frustration. In contrast, choosing to be involved with people we truly enjoy being with and activities in which we truly want to participate, nurtures, satisfies, and actually "feeds" us by changing brain chemistry without using food.

Samantha and her parents began to set aside time to talk about her feelings prior to each gathering and periodically throughout their visit. Setting aside this time to talk gives girls permission to voice anger and teaches them to use their voice to communicate strong feelings rather than to use food and simply cope. In addition, it's a good time to begin to discuss compromises and problem-solve specific worries that either of you may have.

Set aside time for you and your daughter to talk about the holidays both before you make plans and during the events. Ask her about any worries or concerns she may have about going places or any part of being there. Remember to stay curious and listen. Ask if she would like you to help problem-solve any of her worries with her. It may be enough for her just to talk about them. As you do this, don't be surprised if you begin to identify that you have similar worries, anxieties, and concerns. If you do, it makes problem-solving even more fun.

Samantha and her parents began to pick and choose which family gatherings they wanted to attend rather than going just because they always had. In addition, they are experimenting with some new ways to celebrate and create new traditions for themselves.

It's Not about Willpower

One of the most popular and painful pitfalls of the holidays for both girls and adults is dieting between parties. Restricting intake of food and eating only nonfat foods changes brain chemistry to set up a bigger appetite for more fatty foods to attempt to bring the body back in balance. This drive for more food and especially fatty foods is a natural, healthy response to deprivation and extreme dieting. Samantha found herself in this trap as she tried to stay healthy through the holidays. In reality, she was feeling more out of control with food at the parties, not less. The most effective way to bypass the trap is to add fats back into meals during the week and include desserts once in a while. This bypass allows the body to stay more in balance and seems to help normalize desserts. As a result, party food can be fun and pleasurable rather than the enemy.

Encourage your daughter to follow her regular, healthy structure of eating between parties rather than to diet and restrict. Be a model for her by doing the same thing yourself. Holidays do offer extra temptations of food that make this time of year hard to eat healthily. But when her body is well fueled from regular meals prior to the party, she can more easily choose foods that she wants in portions that are a good match for her body.

Plan Ahead for Self-Care

Routine self-care is harder throughout the holidays because most of us aren't on a normal schedule. This lack of structure is often very

stressful for young girls. Reassure her that it is unrealistic to expect the kind of self-care structure that she follows routinely to happen during the holidays. Then help her plan alternatives, such as how to set up the alone time she needs while at the relatives' houses. Plan ahead some time for her to be alone with you. Work out a way to help her schedule some exercise around other events.

We are all juggling more during the holidays, so encourage her to keep it simple but keep self-care a priority. Time for herself can be as simple as a walk around the block, going shopping, seeing a movie—anything that gives her a break from interacting with others and time to focus on herself and her needs.

Losing Body Signals

When eating with others, most of us, both adults and adolescents, focus on topics of conversation, lose track of our own body signals about hunger and fullness, and end up eating more than we want. It takes lots of practice to balance conversations while at the same time noticing our own signals telling us what textures, temperatures, flavors, and volume of food our bodies want and need. Keep it simple by asking the questions "Am I hungry?" and "What am I hungry for?" Samantha and her parents created a code word to help each other remember to ask themselves those questions while attending parties.

In addition, we often feel pressure to eat what others offer at family gatherings. Food is one of the ways family and friends show love. Sometimes this kind of love turns into either pressure to eat what others would like us to eat, or hurt and angry feelings if we respond with, "No, thank you." This is especially true for teens. Samantha struggled with this. She felt pressure to have a serving of each dish her aunts made so she wouldn't hurt their feelings—even if she didn't really like it or want it.

As you and your daughter talk and plan before the next family gathering, encourage her to choose foods using her own body signals rather than just to avoid reactions from others. Ask her how you can help her do this. Do not assume she wants you to say something to anyone. Often, just talking about it ahead of time is enough to reassure her that you support her making her own decisions about her food. If she does want you to help, plan together what she could say and what you will say, when, and how you will say it.

Like Samantha, you and your family can begin to develop a new and different relationship with the holidays and with food by taking some time to review what in the past has not "fed" you and by exploring some new methods to enjoy and to celebrate rather than going to war with your body and food during this holiday season.

Part IV

Helping Your Daughter:
What to Say and Do

Chapter 23

When She Uses the Bathroom Scale

In *Full and Fulfilled: The Science of Eating to Your Soul's Satisfaction*, my coauthor and I discuss this ritual, typical for most adolescents (and many adults):

1. Wake up, get out of bed, go to the bathroom.

2. Get naked.

3. Stand on the scale.

4. Start a mental tape. Choose one or more of the following:

   - Why did I eat that yesterday? I am so big and feel so heavy.
   - How could that extra ounce of chicken put three pounds on me?
   - I'll never be thin enough. I'm hopeless.
   - I am so ugly I shouldn't go out of the house.

- Wow! I pigged out all weekend and I'm down two pounds. I ought to pig out all the time.
- I lost a pound. Big whoop! At this rate it'll take me until I'm ninety to be the size I want.
- No wonder I don't have a boyfriend/girlfriend/good marriage. Why would anyone in their right mind be attracted to someone this size?

5. Step off the scale.

6. Feel bad about yourself and repeat these internal messages over and over all through the day.

7. Decide to eat absolutely no pleasurable foods that day, or better yet, plan to avoid eating all day, or just give up totally and binge.

Does the ritual have a familiar ring to it? For most of us, we've done it for so many years that it seems as normal as brushing our teeth. And yet, if we think about it, what an unpleasant and even traumatic start to our day. Is your daughter already engaging in this ritual? Before it becomes a lifelong pattern for her, let's take a look at whether scale trauma is something she can avoid.

- Understand the reasons behind using the scale. The scale is usually a tool to evaluate herself as being "good enough" or "pretty enough." Many girls believe that the number will tell her whether her size is small enough for her to be well liked. During adolescence, when concerns about popularity, sex appeal, and appearance begin to be major issues, girls will often use the scale more than once a day.

- Weighing replaces body signals for hunger and fullness. People often seem to eat in response to weighing no matter what the

number is—rather than in response to their body's signals of hunger or fullness. If they *gain* weight: "I'm a failure." If they *maintain* weight: "All this work and no results? I'm a failure." If they *lose* weight: "Is that all I lost? I'm such a failure." And, in response, people will usually restrict their food intake to the point that they're hungry all of the time, or give up and overeat or binge on all of the foods they've been trying to avoid in order to lose weight. In my experience, weighing is one of the most consistently demotivating tools people can use to eat healthily and to maintain a healthy weight.

■ The scale cannot tell you if you are losing fat. It is unable to differentiate muscle weight from fat weight. Most girls will interpret any fluctuation in weight to be a loss or gain in fat. This is not the case. Instead, any fluctuations in weight throughout the day or even over a course of several days are changes in muscle weight, stored carbohydrates, or fluid. One pound of either muscle or carbohydrate contains 500 calories. A pound of water contains zero calories. Compare that to one pound of fat, which contains 3,500 calories. This means to lose one pound of *fat*, you must burn off 3,500 calories. This is absolutely impossible to do in a week, over a weekend, in a day, or, much less, overnight.

Katie is a sixteen-year-old athlete. She is on the swim team and diving team at her school and, as a result, she has either two hours of practice every day after school or a meet where she competes with other schools. She was feeling tired and wanted to work on her nutrition to give her peak energy and endurance for her sport but she and her coach both wanted to make sure she could eat for peak performance without gaining weight. We set up a food plan based on her metabolic rate and activity level. She followed it religiously for two weeks. She felt more energetic, her times were good, she wasn't as exhausted at the end of practice, and her clothes fit the same or

looser. Then, the team had their biweekly weigh-ins and she found she had gained two pounds. She stopped following her plan. She started weighing each morning before her first meal and then ate smaller and smaller meals the rest of the day trying to figure a way that her weight wouldn't go up after a meal or a glass of water. For each weigh-in since then, she has met the criteria for weight but she binges after each one due to intense hunger and fights these cravings every night after practice. Her times have increased and her endurance has deteriorated. Katie is really struggling. We continue to meet and explore how bodies work and how weight differs from fat. Katie's parents offered to take the scales from each of the different bathrooms in the house and store them in the attic. Katie's mom realized she was also using the scale daily to determine what she would eat, and as a result of Katie's struggles, she has begun looking at her own weight concerns and is working to break her routine of the scale ritual as well.

If you or your daughter would like to break the scale ritual, consider using body signals to replace it on a daily basis—like energy level, amount of time spent thinking about life rather than what to eat or not to eat, how clothes fit, and so on. Another option is to use the scale only once every couple of weeks or once a month in order to give the body the time it takes to lose a pound of fat. Use body signals for a daily check-in. Combining weight with a body composition measurement allows you to know what fluctuations in weight come from muscle changes and which come from fat. Body composition tests are available at most gyms and recreation centers for a small fee.

If the scale ritual is something your daughter is starting to do, consider the following:

- Are you, as parents, following the scale ritual? If so, consider stopping in an effort to encourage your daughter not to get started.

- Consider holding a family meeting and discussing some of the points discussed in this chapter.

- Regularly comment to your daughter about the many ways she's "good enough." This helps to minimize her need to search for validation using her body and the scale. Remember, stay curious. Maybe "I've noticed you're weighing yourself more often than usual for the past couple of weeks. I wanted to check and see what your thoughts are about that." Remember, rarely is weight at the root of this scale ritual, but rather doubts about her being good enough, pretty enough, or popular enough, i.e., "Am I good enough to be liked and accepted just as I am, or do I need to change in some way to deserve acceptance?"

- Give your daughter the opportunity to talk about how the scale affects her life.

- As a family, decide to store the scale away for a trial period of a month or six weeks and then meet and reevaluate your decision.

- Have a family ceremony of throwing the scale off the back porch (some of my clients did this and had great fun) or something equally as dramatic.

After using the scale, most teens, like Katie, fill their day with self-hate, disappointment, and hopelessness about their food and weight. Trying some new markers, such as body signals, often eases their struggle to nourish themselves and, most importantly, strengthens the connection they have to their own body's intuitive sense.

Chapter 24

When She Loses Weight

Don't be surprised if your daughter begins to look thinner as she moves through puberty. Growth spurts use any stored energy, or fat, available on a girl's body in addition to her daily intake of calories and nutrients to build new bones and tissues. This drop in fat is in direct opposition to the normal preteen *gaining* of fat in anticipation of this growth spurt. So, through adolescence, a girl's body composition often fluctuates radically in response to her changes in height. Obviously, these dramatic shifts are often quite scary and worrisome to girls as well as to their parents. What's happening? What's normal? What should we look for? When should we become concerned that she is getting thinner? How do we know if this is the beginning of an eating disorder, or a natural physical change in her size, or just a symptom of her reacting to all these changes with the "rite of passage" of adolescent dieting and rebellion concerning food?

Emily is a perfect example of this dilemma. She is fourteen, and grew one inch this past year, but at her last pediatrician appointment she had not gained any weight. Because her older sister struggles with an eating disorder, the doctor, her parents, and Emily wanted to be extra careful and decided to send her to me for an evaluation. She talked about her daily schedule of activities and meals. Daily, she explored her body signals that she was aware of about hunger, energy, and fullness. She reviewed any reactions or comments she received from friends, teachers, and family members. Finally, we came up with a few changes that she was willing to try that could help her gain some additional pounds to reach a more comfortable weight for her new height.

Let's walk through some suggestions for handling a situation like this with as much comfort and ease as possible.

- Find some one-on-one time in order to discuss any comments about her body. You may first notice she is thinner when she is hanging out with friends or clothes shopping or at a family meal. Simply make a mental note and bring it up privately with her later. Finding private time to talk with her sends a signal to take this conversation seriously, that you honor her feelings about her body's changes, and she may be very sensitive about these issues.

- Before you say anything to your daughter, check in with yourself. What are you feeling in response to this? How is any of this about you? Are you too thin or too heavy? Is it OK for you to be thin but not her? Are you envious of her thinness and uncomfortable about your weight as a result? If any of these questions cause a reaction for you as you read them, you may want to talk to a nutritionist, minister, or counselor about your concerns before you talk with your daughter about her size.

■ Bring up your concerns by speaking from your own experience, and by maintaining an attitude of curiosity. For example, "I'm worried about your weight," or "I'm concerned how thin you look lately. I'm wondering if you've been thinking about this?" Or, "What are your thoughts about your weight? I've noticed you don't seem to be eating as much lately, is that right?" "I noticed in the past few weeks you say you are really hungry when you get home from school. What do you think that's about?" Then listen and, most important, stay curious. This is about letting her know your concerns and exploring with her what might be happening.

Daughter Says	Healing Responses	Not Helpful Responses
[No comments about the changes going on.]	I'm concerned how thin you look lately. I'm wondering what your thoughts about that are.	You are losing too much weight. You need to eat more.
	How would you like me to help?	I'm going to make these foods for you from now on so you won't keep losing weight.
	I'm worried that I haven't seen you doing the changes we talked about. What's going on for you about that?	You haven't done what you said you would.

■ Wait a week or so to actually do any problem-solving about her weight, unless *she* brings up some specific changes that she would like to try. Waiting to problem-solve gives her time to think and to notice the concerns you brought up, and possibly alter

some patterns on her own if she'd like. Then, bring it up again and begin to discuss some possible options. "I wonder if you've been thinking about our talk about your weight? What do you think?" Let her come up with her ideas for change. And offer any you would like for her to consider.

■ Ask her, "How can I support you in problem-solving this?" or "How would you like me to help?" Discuss specific situations that came up during the exploring that are difficult. For example, Emily asked her dad if he would cook her eggs in the morning while he was cooking his since she had been drinking only juice in the morning. Emily asked her mom to make sure healthy snacks were available in the kitchen when she got home from school and to join her at the counter in the kitchen to snack and talk after school because she came home hungry most afternoons. Emily's parents agreed to not say anything like, "You haven't eaten enough," or try to press her into eating.

■ Set up a period of time to experiment with the changes you've discussed, and then meet and explore again. It is imperative that you as the parents make sure this next meeting actually takes place. With busy schedules it is easy to get lost in the daily routine. But, following through on these regular reevaluations ensures that a concern about weight loss does not gradually grow into a more serious eating disorder that no one notices until it's too late. A trial period of a couple of weeks saves you from bringing up your concerns on a daily basis, which often sounds like nagging to your daughter. It also organizes the problem-solving such that you and she are in this project together rather than you against her and her eating patterns at each meal. Remember to speak from your own experience and stay curious. Perhaps, "I've been enjoying our snack time after school. How is that working for you?" "We talked about you eating eggs in the morning but I

haven't seen you doing that and I'm worried." Or "What are you thinking about the changes we talked about?" These kinds of comments and curiosity set up a perfect environment for more problem-solving. Be sure to ask specifically, "What else could I do to support you in this?" You may find out that eggs made her nauseous in the morning but she'd like to try a protein shake. Or she wasn't snacking because she was taking more in her lunch and was not as hungry in the afternoon. Consider setting up more reevaluation meetings. If things seem to be improving, set one up in a longer period of time.

▪ These meetings are also a good time to bring up new concerns you've noticed. She may have followed through on the food changes she had planned, but in response, is now exercising twice as long or eating much smaller servings at dinner. These types of trade-outs are signals of more serious concerns. It is important to state them again from your experience and with curiosity.

Even though weight fluctuations and body changes are normal during the teen years, the patterns that may be influencing these changes need your attention. Be sure to talk with your daughter about the changes you notice and stay attentive to reevaluating these patterns together on a regular basis.

Chapter 25

When She Gains Weight

Your daughter is gaining weight. What should you do? Should you say something? Should you ignore it, not make it a big deal, and hope she'll grow out of it? Should you have her see a professional? Should you help her find a diet program? Should you help her to accept herself whatever size she is? Of course you want to protect your daughter from the teasing, ridicule, and social ostracizing that often comes with weighing more than others do. At the same time, you want her to feel good about herself whether she fits society's size requirements or not. You fear that this may lead to the first of many diets and the beginning of a lifetime battle with her weight. It often feels like a no-win situation.

FOCUS ON REASONS, NOT THE WEIGHT. Recognize that there are many reasons for gaining weight. The place to start when deciding what to do is to review some of the reasons.

■ Is there truly a medical reason? Certain medications or a hormonal imbalance may cause weight gain. However, in my practice, I have found this to be rare. So I usually suggest that parents explore other possibilities as well as checking with their daughter's physician and including her physician as part of her team of advocates.

■ Is she eating to cope? A much more common reason for gaining weight comes from eating larger quantities of food than the body needs, especially foods with lots of fat or a fat and sugar combination. These foods cause changes in a body's chemistry which make people feel calm, sedated, less stressed, sometimes even numb. Eating these foods may be helping your daughter cope with feeling lonely, scared, anxious, overwhelmed, or unsafe but may cause weight gain. She may feel like, "Nobody understands me, I'm not smart enough, cute enough, or popular enough and I don't know what to do with all of these feelings so I'll eat to try to forget about them." As I'm sure you know, these kinds of thoughts and feelings are normal parts of being human—especially in adolescence. Where can she learn how to handle these emotions in healthy, responsible ways? Most adults don't have the benefit of a teacher to help them figure these issues out. They make up coping techniques like avoiding, pretending, or acting out in some way. For your daughter, consider giving her a chance to see a therapist for a period of time—not because she's in crisis or mentally ill, but to simply learn about and explore her self, her feelings, and techniques to care for herself in other ways. Consider seeing a therapist yourself to explore similar things about you.

■ Is she eating to fit in with friends? You might have experienced times when you felt more comfortable eating what, when, and the amount that others with you were eating. Teens are even more

likely to eat to fit in and be accepted. Just being aware of this is sometimes enough for her to recognize that her gain is not out of control but based on some concrete change in her routine and that she has choices about how she might like to alter this variable—or not. The most effective tool to address this issue is for her to use her questions "Am I hungry?" and "What am I hungry for?" Often the answer is no, not hungry for food but hungry for company and time with friends in a group.

- Is alcohol involved? Alcohol is often overlooked as a source of weight gain. Many teens choose to drink alcohol. Although alcohol contains no fats, it is converted by the body to sugars and fats. So, if a teen makes no changes in her food but adds alcohol, often she will gain weight. Remember, just stay curious.

- Is she maturing? Another very common reason for gaining weight is the natural maturing process. Hips, buttocks, thighs, and breasts get larger and softer. It's a fact of life for women. Yet, if you've never experienced these changes before, it just feels like "I'm getting fat." Give her the freedom to express her concern about this. Don't hurry in to fix it. Just listen. Then you might use the opportunity to talk about how normal these changes are for women. Let her react to this. Don't be surprised if she responds really strongly. I've found most girls want to hear this fact of life and at the same time want to rebel against these same normal female changes. Again, give her the freedom to express this revolt if she needs to. Usually this rebellion about her body changes is a cover for her fear about growing up and the expectations she feels about being a woman that she hasn't had to face as a little girl— sexually, financially, socially, in every way. You might respond with "It sounds like you're feeling scared about all these changes. I can understand that. Tell me more."

■ Does she exercise? As parents, I'm sure you've felt the need to be more active in order to control your weight. The same is often a problem for teens.

■ Is she trying to be too healthy by restricting her fat intake to mostly fat-free foods? Bodies require a certain amount of fat from foods for the most efficient appetite control. Without it, we seem to feel an insatiable appetite and often end up overeating or binging in response.

Diets Don't Address Reasons

As you can see from the reasons listed above, *simply putting your daughter on a diet would not be addressing the possible reasons for the weight gain.* You may be tempted to try such things as limiting what foods are kept in the house to only fat-free or low-fat, controlling the quantities of food she eats, having regular weigh-ins, or rewarding her with money, new clothes, cars, and so on for weight loss. None of these are effective long-term. Most important, at the root of these techniques, you are trying to manipulate and control your daughter's food choices and eating patterns. If you do that, your daughter will miss another opportunity to explore and practice using her own body signals to determine her food choices. These control techniques are so tempting, but remember, when you want to control your daughter's eating patterns it's a message to yourself that you are scared—for her and probably for yourself.

Jessica just turned fourteen and gained weight over the past year. She and her mom decided to sign up for a local diet program. For three months they both followed the food plan they received. They both were to eat a certain number of grams of fat per day, exercise for forty-five minutes six days a week, and avoid sweets, and they had very limited choices of starches

and vegetables. Her mother loved it. She didn't have to think about food. She developed certain meals that fit her plan, followed those, and felt like her food was in control. Jessica, however, hated the monotony, felt deprived and restricted, seemed to constantly be going off the program, and felt guilty that she wasn't staying on it and hopeless that she could ever lose without following such a restrictive plan.

Many creative ways that we attempt to "motivate" people to diet may work for a few days, but then it's back to what they were doing before, with the added ingredient of feeling ashamed and even more of a failure. This is the point where girls often start eating in secret— trying to hide that they just can't follow the diet. This then doubles the shame and tends to speed up the process of gaining. She has now added self-hate to the mix. The lifelong struggle of dieting and gaining, dieting and gaining begins. After looking past the weight to try to understand the reasons that may be playing a role, what else can you do?

Take a look at yourself. Review the above reasons with yourself, instead of your teen, in mind, no matter what your weight may be. Amazingly, focusing on your healing and helping yourself is *the* most effective technique to help your daughter stop gaining and to prevent her from establishing a lifelong pattern of struggling with her weight.

Listen, listen, listen. Let your daughter know that she is important to you no matter what her size. Let her know that she can tell you what and how she feels about her body and try to hear her without jumping in and trying to fix it. Keep in mind some of the possible reasons for the weight gain that we just discussed, such as eating to cope with worries, eating to fit in with friends, body changes without any changes in eating patterns, or reacting to trying to diet. If your daughter wants to work on some of the reasons for her weight gain, help her to find a professional who works with that particular reason

and specializes in working with adolescents. Avoid signing her up for a diet program. Most programs specialize in adults and focus on food and pounds lost rather than the reasons for the weight gain. Maybe you could share this chapter with her if she seems open to it.

Of course it's difficult to watch your daughter gain more weight than you think is healthy for her. It's even more difficult for parents to address their concerns without sounding critical and judgmental. Just remember, focus on the reasons, not the weight, and stay curious.

Chapter 26

When She Says She Looks Fat and Ugly

Gail's mom called me and was feeling confused, scared, hopeless, and desperate. Gail has gained weight over the past year and the night before, her mom had found Gail crying in her room. They had a long talk and Gail finally told her how fat and ugly she felt. Her mom, overweight most of her life, had been trying hard to have Gail not repeat the patterns that she grew up with, but now wonders if it was all in vain. She doesn't know what to do to help Gail.

Think for a minute. Have you ever described yourself as fat and ugly? If so, can you remember the situation, what was going on, who was involved, how you felt, whom you told? Have you ever had a friend tell you she was fat and ugly? How did you respond? How did you feel?

I like to think of the terms *fat* and *ugly* as code words. When your daughter shares her feelings of being fat and ugly with you, stop what you are doing and think. She is talking in the language of her body, trying to communicate something much deeper—with her

emotions that she may not be able to put into words. Fat and ugly almost always mean something happened, in response to which she feels unlovable, unpopular, or bad, and scared she can't do anything about changing this situation—she probably feels it's hopeless.

Daughter Says	Healing Responses	Not Helpful Responses
I am so fat and ugly.	It sounds like you're upset. Tell me more.	Oh, no, you're not. I think you're beautiful.
		I've noticed you've been eating more snacks lately. Maybe you need to cut back some on your calories.
I don't want to talk about it.	When you'd like to talk, let me know. I'd like to know more about what you're feeling.	I can't help you if you won't tell me.
I can't fit in any of my clothes anymore. I am so fat and ugly.	I bet that feels really bad. Tell me more.	Don't worry. Let's just go shopping and get you some new clothes.

- One of the most healing responses to shared feelings of fat and ugly is simply, "Tell me more." Sit down with her and give her a quiet space and time to speak. This lets her know she has your attention, you hear her, you are interested, and you are taking her seriously.

- Avoid responding with a quick, "Oh, no, you're not. I think you're beautiful." As parents, we often think this, but it relates to her at the body level and I believe she is usually trying to tell us something much deeper inside of her and she needs our help.

■ If she chooses to not tell you more at the time, use this interaction as a step toward future discussions. Don't force her to tell you more if she doesn't want to. Say something like, "When you'd like to talk about it let me know. I'd really like to know more about what you're feeling."

■ If she does start talking, don't be surprised if she keeps talking about her body and using code words at the beginning. As she does this, listen for the feelings about the words more than the actual content of the words. Let her know you hear those feelings and understand. For example, "I just feel really ugly and fat. None of my jeans fit and I want to wear a skirt Friday night and they're all too small. I just can't believe how fat and ugly I am. How did I get this way?" To respond to her, try a technique called mirroring. "It sounds like you're really upset. I can understand how awful that must feel." At these times, rarely does she really want you to answer any of her questions or suggest ways to handle the Friday night skirt problem. I treat all questions in the midst of these kinds of talks as rhetorical and just mirror the feelings that seem to be communicated around them until we get to the deeper core of the conversation.

■ Avoid fixing or problem-solving anything she is sharing with you. Your goal is to help her go deeper into her feelings and share those with you. It's very tempting to give suggestions like, "Well, let's go get you some new jeans that fit," or, "Did you try your blue skirt? That one always fit looser on you." *Don't do it.* Suggestions like these often get an angry response because she's at step one, which is feeling upset. She needs time to get to problem-solving. If she feels heard and understood about that then she will be ready to hear possible solutions. Let her lead into step two. If you're uncomfortable discussing feelings or feel scared about what to do with them, that's very normal and understandable.

Recognize it and find a therapist to help you and your daughter learn how to "do" feelings with more confidence.

■ Don't be surprised if, as you keep mirroring her feelings about her body, she shifts over into her concern about a friendship at school, or her fear about a guy, or her worry about a situation or some combination of stresses. These worries are the precious part of your daughter which is hidden under the code words. These are the problems that she needs you on her team to handle. Remember to stay curious and follow her into problem-solving, rather than leading.

■ Sometimes simply talking about her worries can make them manageable and less significant. At other times, you and she can put your heads together for some creative problem-solving. Another option is to find a professional counselor or therapist that specializes in teens who can help your daughter and/or you as a family to make some changes. Again, don't wait for a crisis. Counselors and therapists offer many healthy ideas for handling everyday life with much greater ease than we often think is possible.

■ After you've identified the emotions under fat and ugly, if she is then still concerned about being overweight and wants to explore some different eating and exercise patterns, you can guide her in a variety of ways, as discussed in earlier chapters.

■ As usual, daughters can be good teachers for parents. If you feel fat and ugly and you haven't gone deeper than your code words, I encourage you to explore your feelings too and serve as a model for your daughter.

Getting clear about the feelings hidden under fat and ugly give you and your daughter information about what's really going on. From there, simply give her your attention. Here's your chance to share her inner world with her.

Chapter 27

When You Comment on Her Appearance

"My daughter is so beautiful." Surely you have heard yourself say this.

Before reading any further, grab some paper and a pen and write a description of your daughter. Describe her to someone who doesn't know her, as if you were introducing her. Simply make a list of words which come to mind—don't think hard on this.

When you finish, notice how many of your words on the list are about her appearance, such as her hair length, hair color, height, body size, distinguishing features, eye color, and so on. Notice if any of the words describe her appearance as cute, beautiful, petite, muscular, chubby, fashionable, neat, and so on. How many words on your list are about her as a person, with no link at all to her body or about what she wears? Perhaps adventurous, curious, creative, funny, studious, theatrical, kind, generous, shy, and so on.

Recognize Her Value beyond Looks

If you're like most of us, more than half of your list describes your daughter's looks. Thinking your daughter is beautiful and giving her compliments about her appearance is healthy and helpful. I encourage you to do it. However, *focusing* on her appearance can frequently become a problem for her because, in our society, girls are reared with their appearance being the first thing we notice, the first thing we describe, and a major factor in whom we label them to be—how we value them as a person. This is what I call "society's beauty trap."

Our sons are beautiful. Have you ever heard anyone say this? Sounds odd, doesn't it? Our sons are athletic. Our sons are industrious. Our sons are adventurous. Rarely, in this society, do we describe our sons primarily by their appearance. Sons are not raised with our equating their appearance with their value. Certainly, we notice men's appearances. Certainly, men care how they look. But, in general, a man's appearance is one of many attributes used to determine his value and what he may accomplish.

This difference, viewing women first by their appearance and men by their character, is one of the primary roots of the large number of eating disorders in this country. As a parent, you can begin to help your daughter to recognize her value and worth as being separate from her looks. What you say and do at home has much to do with whether your daughter gets caught in society's beauty trap, or if she develops a core of recognition that she is much more than her appearance. This core belief will serve her well as she goes out into society and faces other people's assumptions that her value and appearance are synonymous. Sadly to say, this foundation you give your daughter doesn't protect her from having to cope with society's expectations. The most you can hope for is that she will find it easier to balance these expectations with her knowledge of her true value.

Shifting Beauty Standards

What makes society's trap even more harmful and difficult to handle is that society changes its definition of attractiveness over time. The beauty standard by which our daughters (and moms too) are evaluated constantly shifts. As women work harder and harder, eating more and more carefully, exercising more and more dutifully, critiquing their bodies with more and more detail to look like the current standard of beauty, the standard shifts. They constantly work to meet a constantly moving definition of beauty. They are trapped. They can only fail. If they believe they must look like society's current beauty standard to have value, then they must spend time, energy, and dollars transforming their natural bodies to fit the latest look, only to find when they get there, that the latest look is no longer the *latest* look. Then, they start over, spending their lives molding their bodies, missing the mark, forever chasing what they believe they need in order to have value.

Remember the Twiggy period of beauty? All women needed to be flat-chested, bone thin, and have no hips to be considered attractive. During the Marilyn Monroe period the exact opposite was valued as beautiful—curvy, buxom, virtually the opposite of Twiggy in every way. Women who looked like Marilyn during the Twiggy period felt self-conscious, unattractive, and they worked to alter their natural curves. During the Marilyn period, roles were reversed. These cycles continue today.

The point is that if you teach your daughter that her appearance is a major part of her value, but society's standards for beauty continually change, then your daughter is trapped; she is set up to believe that she must keep running, but have little hope of ever crossing the finish line.

What can you as parents do to create a family culture where your daughter will know that she is wonderful no matter how she looks?

Is it possible to protect her from being caught in society's beauty trap?

Below is a list of ideas which my clients, both daughters and parents, and I have developed over time to help create an environment at home where daughters can absorb and recognize that they are so much more than their appearance.

■ Parents, start noticing situations where society equates a female's worth with her appearance. Over the next few days, listen and watch people introduce and describe other people. Notice if you hear more words about looks and appearances when people describe women than when they describe men. Notice this as you listen to friends, watch TV, and read magazines. An example on television is when a host introduces a woman guest as the beautiful or lovely Ms.——, and will often make some comment about their clothes. Notice whether the announcer makes any comment about the looks of men or evaluates their appearance. Usually, the introduction is something like the talented and witty Mr.——.

■ Start listening and watching for these same inequities in what you say and what your spouse and the rest of the family say. (It's important at this point to try not necessarily to do anything about any of this—just notice.) This exercise isn't to try to make you feel guilty or bad, but to bring to your attention to how much most of us in society do it without even thinking.

■ Think back to how your parents described and introduced you. Do you remember any common themes, if not specific words? It might be interesting for you to discuss this with your spouse, your daughter, or a friend and compare experiences and realizations.

- Start practicing taking people seriously, especially females, for what they say, feel, and do—*not* for how they look. Most people's reaction to this one is, "Well, of course, I already do that." That is not my experience. Most of us have an extremely difficult time *not* using first impressions and dress to give us a read on people, especially women. We often use looks as a major factor in deciding if we want to spend time with people, or if we will respect or trust what they say.

- Try to ignore body shape as an indicator of a person's personality or value. Avoid using phrases like fat slob, lazy pig, thunder thighs, and thin as a rail.

- Avoid criticizing your own body. Work at describing yourself in terms that are separate from your looks, size, and appearance.

- Encourage your daughter to develop interests and involvement in activities which don't emphasize appearance. Some examples: outdoor adventures, music, art, astronomy, pets, and so on.

- Ask your daughter to think of a woman she admires and what qualities, besides appearance, she admires in this woman.

- Ask your daughter if she has noticed how society equates her appearance and her value. If she is open and interested, discuss her experiences with this and how it makes her feel. Maybe share with her what you have noticed and some of your experiences. Keep the dialogue open and stay curious.

Have patience with yourself as you practice. Remember, you're bucking society on this issue. Keep trying even if it doesn't seem to make any difference. Your daughter deserves to have at least one place, home, where she experiences being appreciated for being her—no matter her appearance.

Chapter 28

When She Asks for Diet Advice

I heard margarine is bad for you, should I not eat it?

Maybe I should become a vegetarian—what do you think?

I want to lose ten pounds—will you help me?

Do you think I need to eat more protein?

Do you think I need to eat more fiber?

How much fat should I have with each meal?

Both daughters and parents wonder about what's healthy to eat. Nutrition studies seem to bring up more questions rather than give us concrete answers. In fact, we are given so much information about nutrition we stay confused and overwhelmed most of the time. One article will suggest we do the exact opposite of another. As parents, you're expected to help your daughter make some sense of

all this information, but it is just as confusing to adults as it is to adolescents.

Monica, a seventeen-year-old "health nut," as she calls herself, describes her eating patterns like this: "There are more and more fat-free products on the market, more and more health and fitness magazines and newsletters to read about food and nutrition, and more and more new exercise videos and equipment to use to stay lean. But I seem to just keep getting fatter and fatter, and working harder and harder at trying to eat healthily. I eat 'good' until I feel so deprived. I can't stand it anymore and then I eat what I want but feel guilty and like a failure, so I go back to being 'good' and then repeat the whole pattern again."

I call this the bounce. This bounce pattern of eating usually begins at around eight, nine, or ten years old as girls start to override their own body's wisdom about what to eat, when to eat, and how much to eat. Once they've replaced much of their natural instincts with rules and suggestions from others, the struggle with weight and diets begins, often lasting throughout adulthood.

When your daughter has a question about nutrition, prevent the bounce by interpreting her question as a request to explore an area about her own body and eating that she hasn't figured out yet. You do not have to have the answer for the question and even if you think you do, hold your tongue. The answer you have is what you figured out is right for you. Her own body's wisdom is the most accurate source of answers for her questions. But you can be a wonderful source of guidance for her to explore and find her own answers.

- First and most important, if you are performing the bounce pattern, use the tools to begin recovering your own body's wisdom that you probably started overriding when you were younger.

Reconnecting to a long-lost part of yourself usually is very rewarding and offers you answers and hope that the constant bounce between diet and nondiet can never supply. As you become familiar with exploring your own intuitive eater, you will model for your daughter how she can do the same. This is often enough to prevent her from experiencing a lifetime of struggles with diet and weight.

■ "Good question. Let's think about some ways you can explore that and figure out an answer." This is a sample response to any of her questions about eating specific foods. Don't be surprised if her response to that is something like "I don't know how to do that, just tell me."

■ It is hard for most of us to tolerate the anxiety of staying in that "I don't know" space. I encourage you to stay there by not answering her question and encouraging your daughter to stay there so she can begin to get answers that she is searching for. Say something like "I know this probably seems like it would be so much easier if I just told you or you just did what the book says, but nobody knows what is right for your body but you." Nutrition facts about vitamins, minerals, proteins, carbohydrates, and fats give her important information she needs to know. But the other equally important half of the equation for eating healthily requires her to go inside and listen to her own body's wisdom about which combinations of foods, in what proportions, at what times, and in what amounts nourish her best. Remember to listen to her as she complains about how hard this seems. Don't fix it. Just let her know you understand.

■ Help her experiment by giving her some signals to watch for. For example, "You might want to try noticing how your body feels for a couple of days. Do you notice any different sensations? Are

you more energetic, more sleepy, more full, more hungry, spending more time thinking about food, spending less time thinking about food, and what else do you notice that is different?" Help her connect how these reactions relate to what she's eating, amounts, and timing. She may want to keep notes about what she's eating for a few meals as she's noticing these reactions.

■ If she doesn't notice anything, it could mean a couple of different things. One, she didn't make a big enough change to make the effects noticeable. If this is the case, you might want to help her set up a more obvious test. For example, she may be exploring eating more protein, and experimenting by adding a glass of milk to her usual routine. It may not be a big enough change. Try adding a restaurant-size portion of fish at a meal in which she usually doesn't include protein and see if any signals are more obvious. A second possibility is that she isn't used to reading her signals so she doesn't notice them. You might suggest that she keep notes about any physical sensations she experiences between meals. This often helps her to focus on her body in ways she might be unaccustomed to. Third, her body may need to experience the change for more days in a row to feel a difference. I recommend initially testing changes for two days. If no responses turn up, experimenting for a week will usually show something.

■ This exploring process can be fun and rewarding, but can also get complicated and unwieldy. A nutritionist can help her clarify what she discovers.

Asking for diet advice is one more part of her exploring what's right for her. Lead her back to her own body's signals each time she asks. This response helps her gain increasingly more confidence and assurance that she can find answers within.

Chapter 29

When She Is Teased about Her Weight

Stephanie is a thirteen-year-old with two brothers, one older and one younger. Her mother called me in response to a very emotional talk that she and Stephanie had. The family has always been one to tease and play and laugh a lot. Since Stephanie turned thirteen and her body is changing, it hasn't been as fun for her. Instead, it makes her cry, stay in her room more than usual, and avoid her brothers and their friends at all costs. Stephanie hears oinking noises when she walks by her brothers. She gets laughed at about her portion sizes at family meals. She gets teased if her snacks are part of a diet specially designed for fat people. Her nickname in the family has been Soupy since childhood, but now it seems to have changed to Tubby. This teasing at home affects her at school too. She has two really close friends, but when she is not with them, she avoids eye contact with others, tries to hide and not be noticed, and is coming home with stomachaches from stress.

Our female bodies, from the time we are children to fully mature women, are truly mysterious blends of unfamiliar growing parts

along with seemingly awkward, not growing sections. I don't know a one of us who wasn't sensitive about some part of our looks as we grew through puberty. It is normal, healthy, and certainly not unexpected for bodies at this age to store extra fat for the energy that is needed to fuel a growth spurt during puberty.

This stage is when so much of our struggle with body image begins. This is when we begin to cope with people noticing our body changes and often judging who we are based on our body shape or lack thereof. This is the age when we are very unsure of who we are or how we fit into the bigger world. This is the age when your daughter will begin to want to be more independent and yet doesn't have much practice handling conflict, difficulties, teasing, and such. As a result, your daughter will observe people around her and may use their reactions and responses to fill in the blanks about who she is and how she is valued. When she is surrounded by others who tell her she isn't normal, doesn't fit, or is bad, ugly, or someone to laugh at, she stores that information inside of her as if it were true. She begins to build her view of her body, her personality, and future interactions with people based on what she believes is true from these comments.

As a parent, you can help her develop a more balanced, whole picture of who she is. You can create a safe place for her to talk about and think through what she is hearing from others, and you can teach her some healthy and effective responses to unpleasant situations that she can begin to experiment with.

- First and most important, if either parent is teasing your daughter about anything regarding her body size or shape—stop!

- Even if she doesn't seem to mind the teasing, or she teases about herself with you—stop. Teasing about herself and showing no reaction to your teasing are often techniques to cover or to make light of deep hurts inside.

- Avoid teasing or making critical comments about body size, weight, and appearances of friends, TV characters, family, and acquaintances. When girls hear you ridiculing others behind their back, they often assume you think and say the same of them behind their backs.

- Assume that any criticism (whether teasing or not) said about her body may be interpreted as fact by her. As I listen to women's stories in my practice, I no longer am surprised that most people remember exact quotes of what their siblings, doctors, dance teachers, coaches, parents, grandparents, and friends have said about their bodies back when they were Stephanie's age and even younger. In various subtle and not so subtle ways, their lives continue to be impacted today by these comments.

- Consider *all* of the ways that you value your daughter, and tell them to her as you notice them. In this way you offer her validation and recognition of all the parts of herself that you value and love and want her to know about. This helps her to recognize that she is so much more than just her physical appearance. Some examples might be: her love of animals, her favorite color fuchsia, how she curls up next to you watching TV, her chatter in the morning, her sensitivity to others' hurting, or her tenacity when practicing the violin.

- Be sure to compliment her on her physical appearance when you notice something you like. Tell her when you really like how a dress fits her, or when a certain color blouse highlights her hair. These positive comments about her physical appearance are very important mirrors for her, as long as they are balanced with comments about her whole being.

- Begin to listen to your family in a new way. Teasing is fun when it is about playful things, not personal things. Often, teasing will be

such a normal part of everyday life, we grow accustomed to it and don't even notice if some of it has a cruel edge to it. If you hear teasing that is hurtful, don't ignore it.

■ Depending on the family dynamics, there are a variety of options to try to change any hurtful teasing patterns you notice. Talk with each individual who is teasing and discuss your concerns with them. Ask them to stop teasing about her body and possibly ask them to read this chapter to help them recognize the significance of what they are doing. A family meeting is another option. Discuss the teasing and each person's feelings and reactions to it. From this discussion, come up with some solutions together as a family. Or see a counselor or minister to help you, as a family, change the pattern of teasing about appearances.

■ Often teasing is a person's way of connecting, or showing love and attention that has no ill intent. However, it still hurts and impacts on a girl's beliefs about her body. This is often the case with brothers who feel awkward and are uncomfortable showing affection in other ways. As parents, help her brothers identify what teasing is playful and what is hurtful. Make it clear that teasing about their sister's body is not fun and is off-limits.

■ Rarely will your daughter tell you about teasing and painful situations without some alone time. Make sure you are setting up situations where each parent will have some one-on-one time with your daughter. Recognize opportunities that exist between the two of you, such as riding in the car, cooking dinner together, going for a walk at a park, or weeding in the garden. Be willing to not talk about yourself or others and give her space to talk about herself. You may want to say something like, "What's the latest?" Then be quiet. If she doesn't respond or says, "What do you mean?" don't pump. Try, "Well, I've noticed you seem stressed

about something, and when you want to talk, I'd like to hear about what's going on with you." Then just listen. Be careful not to jump in with your opinion about what she's saying. In response to anything she brings up, a good healthy response is simply, "Tell me more." Her immediate reaction to that question might be, "I don't know." But if you just give her a minute she'll usually be able to put some more ideas together that she needs to share and you need to know. Once she starts sharing, use expressions like, "Hmm, that must really hurt. I can understand how you would feel like that." Expressions like that let her know you are listening, concerned, and open to hear more. Stay curious. Don't attempt to fix anything here.

- Ask her, "What part of what you are being teased about are you concerned is true?" Then listen. Asking a question such as this helps her open up to what her feelings are in a way that you and she can then begin to problem-solve. Remember, most of us think teasing is funny if it doesn't sound accurate to us. If the teasing is about something we are ashamed of and believe is true, it hurts instead.

- After you help your daughter identify the part she believes is true, then explore some tools she might use the next time she is teased. One of the most effective responses to teasing rarely comes naturally. When she is teased about being overweight, for example, and can own the 5 percent that is true in what they say, they rarely will repeat the teasing. "Yes, I do have a weight problem. It's true." She might want to add at the end something like "I really don't like to talk to you about it."

Daughter Says	Healing Responses	Not Helpful Responses
I feel awful when they make fun of my _____ at school.	I know that must really hurt. Tell me more.	Just consider the source. Don't let them get to you.
	What part of what they are saying are you afraid may be true?	

It's never pleasant to hear your daughter was teased about her weight. However, your willingness to listen, make changes within the family system, if need be, and help her to respond in healthy ways can help ease her pain.

Chapter 30

When She Shops for Clothes

Buying a bathing suit for summer vacation.

Needing new shorts for spring.

Looking for new jeans for football games.

Finding new outfits for the first day of school.

Wanting a long dress. Prom is coming up.

Before each of these shopping trips, many girls will start worrying about their body size and, in response, restrict their food. The plan: fitting into the smallest size possible. Smaller is better. Smaller is prettier. Smaller is more popular. Smaller is more accepted and loved. Smaller is more feminine. Or at least, these are the messages our society sends to us and our daughters.

Looking in the dressing room mirror.

Being watched by salespeople and friends as she tries on outfits that don't fit or don't look good.

Finding the "hip" outfits only in sizes smaller than she wears; having to settle for "old lady" styles.

Needing a larger size than on the last shopping trip.

During shopping trips, girls will judge their bodies with incredibly critical eyes and start focusing on certain parts of their bodies, deciding some parts, usually their hips and thighs, are ugly, too big, too fat, and need to be cut off, exercised off, and dieted off. In general, many girls will go into self-hate and react to these shopping experiences in extremes, either restricting their food or overexercising or both.

Leslie is thirteen years old. She hates her body. She describes it like this: "My breasts are huge. My hips and thighs are so fat. Nothing cute even comes close to fitting me. The only trash that would fit me is old lady polyester. I refuse to go to those big lady specialty shops. I wear men's T-shirts, black, and some giant jeans I found at an outlet mall. I'm sick of it. We're going to the beach for spring break and I can't wear a bathing suit, but I can't wear black and jeans either. I just want to stay home but my parents won't let me. I hate my body. I hate that I have to eat. I can't seem to lose anything. And, if I do lose, it's never enough to fit into the cute outfits."

What is hard about this situation is Leslie is right. She has every right to be furious and frustrated. For the most part, manufacturers don't sell cute, youthful, hip outfits for teenagers in large sizes. So, the first thing Leslie needs is to be heard about her anger and hate and told something like, "You have every right to be mad." Second, her parents can help her redirect that anger toward stores and man-

ufacturers where it belongs rather than on herself. Third, her parents can help her address any food and eating issues that she might want to look at to help her maintain a healthy weight for her. What is difficult at this point is that a healthy weight for Leslie is larger than junior sizes. That is just a fact. No matter how hard she works at dieting and exercising she will not fit in them. Her parents and I are supporting her as she expresses her anger and she works at trying not to "use" food in response to her self-hate. Also, she has begun to explore some large-size catalog possibilities that are advertised in some magazines for large women. Most important, she is getting enough support about this issue that she is not as tempted to cycle into a starvation diet out of desperation only to end up binging and feeling terrible about herself.

Shopping for clothes, especially bathing suits, is a very common trigger for both girls and parents to begin the diet/fail/hate cycle once again. Shopping can trigger evaluation and judgment about our size, which in turn may trigger self-hate, which in response sets up a new decision to diet and exercise. For most people this means going hungry until they feel so deprived they break down and eat what they really want. This then triggers them to feel guilty that they broke their diet, they get mad at their failure to stick to it, and then they go back on their diet with even stricter restrictions until they can't stand the deprivation anymore, and then overeat on something pleasurable again. Then the pattern repeats over and over. As a result of this pattern, they don't lose the weight, but instead hate themselves with even more intensity the next time they go clothes shopping.

Below are some suggestions to help make clothes shopping a pleasant experience for your daughter, and if not, how you can help her cope in healthy ways.

■ Take a look at your own experiences clothes shopping. How do

you respond to your own shopping trips? Do you come home hating yourself and determine to punish yourself by restricting your food and overexercising? If so, this might be an area to consider working with a counselor or nutritionist. Your response to shopping, sizes of clothes, and your body is a model for your daughter.

- If you accompany your daughter shopping for clothes, encourage her to purchase outfits that are comfortable and fit her well. Avoid the approach of saying, "Why don't you buy it and just lose about five pounds so it will fit better?" The idea is to help her accept who she is right now, even if she is working on making changes.

- Avoid commenting about a style being slimming or making her look thin. What that statement really says is she is not good enough or pretty enough as she is, but she needs to be thinner. Instead, buy clothes because the style and color are what she likes and are comfortable. This is an easy place to slip into punishing ourselves in response to size: buying clothes that fit uncomfortably tight, that bind us so we can't move and breathe freely and easily, or outfits that cover us so much we feel overheated. We deserve to feel comfortable whatever our size.

- Avoid making any value judgments about her body, its size, or its shape. If the outfit looks bad to you, criticize the clothing manufacturer, the material, the color, the design. Remind your daughter that sizes vary depending on the manufacturer. The size on the label is not an accurate reflection of her body size.

- If she starts criticizing her body, listen to her and let her know you care about her no matter what her size. For every negative thing she says, encourage her to say three positive things about herself. This is a time when *she* needs to identify these positives about *herself*. At this point, it is not helpful for you to offer positives about her.

- If she decides to alter her eating and exercise in response to a clothes shopping trip, help her do this in a manner that is taking care of her rather than punitive, i.e., eating regular meals, not going hungry, eating a variety of foods, and exercising moderately. Responding in this way avoids the diet/fail/hate cycle, which does not result in long-term maintenance of a healthy weight.

Clothes shopping can be a traumatic experience for adults and teens alike. Your willingness to try some new responses when she begins to criticize herself can be a tremendous help.

Chapter 31

When She Smokes for Weight Loss

I would rather die than be fat.

I would rather die than look like this.

I have heard these statements more times than I can remember from girls who smoke in order to lose weight. These girls know about the long-term consequences of smoking, but they believe the short-term benefit of losing weight is too attractive to pass up. When a girl chooses to put her health at risk to stay at her current body size, I think we can assume two things:

She feels unacceptable at her current weight or size. She is operating on a belief system that says something like, "If I could lose weight, then I would be accepted, loved, happy, or popular, which I don't feel at this size and never will feel at this size."

Don't get bogged down in what weight she wants to be or believes she needs to be. Instead, stay focused on what she is long-

ing for—to feel accepted, loved, popular, and so on. One very effective tool to explore this issue is to ask her, "If you were the weight you want to be, how would you be different, what would you feel more comfortable doing, what would you be willing to say that you don't now?" The answers are usually the hidden jewels that parents and others can then help her with. She may respond, "I'd go to parties without being scared that people wouldn't like me. I would know what to say when boys talked to me. I would wear bright colored clothes." These answers indicate that she is feeling shy, scared, and awkward about attracting attention and believes that people who are a smaller size don't struggle with these unpleasant feelings.

She feels hopeless that there is anything else she can do to change her body to look the way she wants. She believes she has tried everything that has worked for others and nothing works for her.

My response to this is, "We can't know what we don't know." All she can know at this point are the strategies that family and friends have used or what she reads in books—eat less food and exercise more. But which foods should she eat less of, how much less, how often should she eat, what proportions of what types of foods and at what times are best for her body, what exercise would burn fat best for her, how much exercise would be balanced with her food intake, what time of day would be the most effective? Once she sees there is information about her body and how food works in it that she hasn't tried yet, she has hope.

Girls use smoking as a diet aid because food and feelings are linked. Listening to girls and helping them explore the feelings that drive them to smoke is important. Bleak as those feelings may be, they are the important "talking points" you need, to give a girl the opportunity to achieve peace with her body size and with food.

Food, Feelings, and Cigarettes

One factor that makes smoking hard to talk about with girls who use it as a diet aid is that it works. Smoking seems to increase metabolic rate. All else being equal, smokers seem to burn more calories on a daily basis than they would as nonsmokers. Smoking reduces appetite for food, too. It reduces the intensity of taste sensations in the mouth, making food less appealing and satisfying. As a result, girls who smoke tend to eat less volume of food than they would if they didn't smoke.

Many girls (and many adults) use certain foods as a drug to dull intense feelings. Foods high in sugar and fats change a person's brain chemistry in ways that ease anxiety, anger, or excitement. Substitute a cigarette in place of food, and you get the same soothing feelings, but without weight gain. It may help you to think of a girl's smoking as a screen for her feelings. The key is to understand what the smoking masks, what distress it signals, and help her with those.

Getting Help

If your daughter is using cigarettes for weight control, express your confidence that she can learn to make healthy decisions and there is another way. Then, get her the help she needs:

- If you use smoking as a diet aid, get professional help from a nutritionist before you say anything to your daughter about her smoking. You may want to explore for yourself how you believe life would be different if you were another weight just as we suggested for your daughter above.

- Take her behavior seriously. Interpret it as a sign of hopelessness about her weight.

■ Help her develop other ways of dealing with intense feelings. Often, this involves listening to information about very uncomfortable situations that you may not know how to help her with. If you don't know, help her find a therapist or counselor who can teach her some new tools. Avoid saying she shouldn't feel like that or arguing with her about her belief system.

■ Seek out sound nutritional information for her about weight control. Remember that if a girl is using cigarettes, she needs a much more specialized approach than routine diet plans and programs.

Part V

Understanding Eating Disorders

Chapter 32

Food as a Drug

Scared. Excited. Nervous. Worried. Mad. Embarrassed. Surprised. Tired. Sad. Bored. What do you do to handle all of these ups and downs of life? And what, then, is your daughter learning about handling her emotions?

Good or bad, up or down, or simply bored, many of us have learned to use a variety of substances or activities for temporary relief. Prescription medication, sex, alcohol, television, work, tobacco, computers, shopping, recreational drugs, busyness, spending money, exercise, and over- or undereating are some of the most common ways people try to make feelings more manageable. And, they work. They all, in fact, change the body's chemistry, relieving the intensity of feelings for a period of time. Therein lies the problem. They all offer temporary relief, then the feeling returns and the pattern is repeated again and again: substance, temporary relief, substance, temporary relief. Without meaning to, we have developed an addiction to satisfy our hunger for relief.

Kathryn is a fourteen-year-old. She is in her freshman year of high school and is gaining weight. She is scared, anxious, excited, and nervous. She only knows one or two girls from the past year at her middle school, neither of them very well. She wants people to like her and want to be her friend. She wants guys to notice her, but if they do, she's scared. She wants her body to look sexy and thin. And she wants to be able to eat whatever she wants when she's hanging with old friends in her neighborhood. She feels awkward exercising and would much rather do something "fun" than work out. She's mad at herself because she doesn't go to exercise class at the gym where her parents belong. She wishes she could eat like the models talk about in her teen magazines. She wants to be in the school play and photography club but she is too nervous. Kathryn has many feelings. And she doesn't like talking to her parents—"It's just not cool." Her parents noticed her reluctance. They asked if she'd like to talk to someone else regularly and so they set that up for her. Kathryn needed an outlet for everything that was going on inside of her. As she began to feel safe there, discussing life and her feelings, she found she snacked less in the afternoons, ate smaller portions at meals, and still ate with her friends, but not as much. Her weight gain slowed.

Food, a Gateway Drug

Using food, whether over- or undereating, often serves as the first drug-of-choice for adolescents and it is often the gateway through which girls move on to abusing other substances or addictions and begin their lifelong struggle with food and their weight. To "use" food simply means she eats food, thinks about food, or refuses food to substitute, replace, or pretend that she's not feeling uncomfortable or scared. She eats food not for nourishment and in response to body signals but, instead, the way people use drugs.

Chocolate and Brain Chemistry

Foods cause very powerful responses in our brains. Specifically, eating starches and sugars causes brain chemistry changes which literally make us feel calmer and more relaxed. Eating fats causes different changes in brain chemistry which help us feel even more relaxed and even euphoric. Put the sugar and fat in chocolate together with other chemicals in cocoa and we get a brain chemical change—a triple whammy of feeling calm, relaxed, euphoric. No wonder so many of us and our daughters choose chocolate when we want relief from feelings. It gives us relief, physically, by changing brain chemistry. In addition it tastes good, so we satisfy our hunger for relief and at the same time satisfy our hunger for pleasure—*for a short time.*

Food, an Avoidance Tool

Food, or more specifically over- and undereating, can satisfy a hunger for relief from feelings in another way. If your daughter is gaining or losing weight, she can focus on changes in her body and think about what she needs to eat or not eat whenever she needs relief from feeling her emotions about other areas of her life—situations she may feel powerless to do anything about. She instead substitutes thinking and feeling about food and her body rather than having feelings which she can't figure out. For example, "Do people like me? Do guys think I'm pretty? What do I say when I meet somebody I like? I wish my hips weren't so big. What can I do? I'm scared about that book report. One of my girlfriends isn't talking to me. What did I do? I'm mad and embarrassed that Mom and Dad won't let me go Friday night. I'm worried about my parents fighting. I'm scared about Dad's heart attack," and so on.

Suggestions

"Using" foods in these ways are potentially dangerous "fixes" to satisfy a girl's hunger for relief. To help your daughter learn to handle her feelings without addictions, consider the following suggestions:

■ Begin with the questions "Am I hungry?" and "What am I hungry for?" These questions are very powerful tools to begin to determine if your daughter is "using" food. Watch for answers like, "No, I just want something," or "I don't know what I'm hungry for." These answers are usually good signals that physical hunger isn't present. Start looking for feelings rather than food.

■ Notice if you use any substances or activities to satisfy your hunger for relief. If you don't have a safe place to feel all your feelings and talk about them, find a place. Your daughter needs you to model this for her.

■ Healthy ways to handle feelings are to feel them and to talk about them with someone who is safe. Encourage your daughter to feel *everything* she's feeling and give her a safe place to talk about all of these. Use comments such as, "Hmm. Oh, that must be hard. Tell me more." Stay curious. This means you must tolerate the feelings that you start to have as you listen to her. You can run into trouble when she feels things you don't like, don't approve of, wish she didn't feel, or are uncomfortable about feeling for yourself. To avoid feeling your discomfort in response to her feelings, it's easy to jump in with phrases like, "You're just being silly, that's life; oh, it won't be that bad; you don't need to feel like that; go do something to take your mind off of it." When this happens, she may turn to other activities or substances to get relief since she knows not to talk about those things with you. This does not make her feelings go away. She just starts pretending she doesn't

feel them anymore and begins to use activities or substances for relief. So, if you aren't comfortable listening to *all* her feelings, help her to find a responsible adult who will. And even if you are able and willing, she might be more comfortable problem-solving with an adult other than a parent, such as a teacher, a counselor, a minister, or a trusted friend.

Daughter Says	Healing Responses	Not Helpful Responses
I'm feeling so _____	It sounds like you're really feeling a lot. Tell me more.	You don't need to feel like that.
		It's not that bad. Don't be silly. You don't have to feel that.
		Find something to do to take your mind off of it.

Food is a necessary and pleasurable part of your daughter's life. She cannot avoid food later if she starts to "use" it for relief, as she can cigarettes or alcohol. So, learning healthy tools and techniques for handling emotions is one of the most precious gifts you can give her.

Chapter 33

All about Sneak Eating

Packages of candy and chips hidden in her drawer.

A noticeable weight gain but you never see her eat.

No appetite at mealtimes.

Ice cream disappears overnight.

Wrappers stashed under the bed.

A bag of chocolate chips disappears from the pantry.

Sneak eating is defined as choosing different foods when eating alone than when eating with others and/or eating a larger quantity of food when alone than around others. Sneak eating is very common in both parents and daughters.

Fear of Being Real

Most of us live our lives behind masks, appearing competent, sure of ourselves, mature, responsible, and in control, when, in reality, behind the masks we are frightened, unsure, and anxious. One way we reinforce the mask is that when we eat in front of others, we choose foods so as not to attract attention, but to appear comfortable, healthy, and competent. When we are alone, it is often the only place we are free to take our masks off—admit we're not who we pretend to be—and eat what and how much we really want. It is a time we can be completely self-centered, not have to think about anyone else, and can then focus totally on ourselves.

This unmasked reality (or our real, vulnerable self) is hidden out of fear: afraid our real self isn't good enough, wouldn't fit in, is not acceptable, or would be criticized, ridiculed, or shamed if anybody knew it existed.

Food and its relation to brain chemistry adds another interesting twist to this dynamic. Eating sugars and starches causes greater concentrations of serotonin, a brain chemical, in the body. This change in serotonin concentration makes us feel relaxed, calm, less stressed, and sleepy, all of which most people find very soothing. In addition, eating fat changes endorphin (another brain chemical) levels, which causes another dose of calming, less stress, and even a bit of euphoria. So, instinctively, when we unmask and feel anxious, frightened, not good enough, lonely, and so on, we know eating sugars, starches, and fats such as cookies, candies, ice cream, donuts, or crackers will soothe us by altering our body chemistry.

Most of us who are hiding our real selves and eating in response hate that we can't live up to our masks. We hate that we eat in response to feelings, even if it makes us feel better at the time, and we hate that we can't seem to find any way to change this pattern. Therein lies the difficulty. Sneak eating at its root is not about food.

Instead, it is an indicator, a symbol of some real needs that we are usually afraid to admit we have, afraid that we aren't supposed to have, and afraid that we don't know any other way of addressing.

Tiffany is an eleven-year-old gymnast. Her mother used to teach dance, is very health conscious, and works at keeping her weight the same as when she danced. When she made the appointment for Tiffany, she was concerned that Tiffany seemed to be gaining weight and was having some difficulty with her gymnastic maneuvers as a result. As we explored Tiffany's food and exercise routine, we discovered the following. One, she had grown an inch in height in the past year and seemed to be in a growth spurt. Weight gain and changes in balance are a natural result of these. Two, she was burned out on gymnastics but didn't want to disappoint her mother. So, instead of saying she'd like to take a break, she ate healthy food when her mother was around, but ate lots of what she called "fun" foods when alone or out with her friends, figuring if she had difficulty with the moves due to her size, she would have a good excuse to quit gymnastics. Luckily, her mother, based on her own experience with food issues in dance, quickly saw the developing pattern. She would suggest various diet options for Tiffany to try but each one was a failure. She also realized something else was going on but didn't quite know what. She trusted her instinct about this and sought additional help. It only took a few weeks of appointments to clear up the situation. Tiffany told her mother she wanted to quit gymnastics and each of them talked about their fears and disappointments about that. Tiffany used her voice to communicate rather than using food to tell her mom she wanted to quit. With the change in her workout schedule she then decided to explore what foods and how much would be a good match for her growing body.

What can you do as parents if you think your daughter may be sneak eating?

- Recognize that sneak eating indicates a healthy, natural, human longing to be real without the frightening consequences we expect or believe will happen.

- Before addressing your daughter's sneak eating, be honest about whether you, or your spouse, are doing any sneak eating or sneak drinking. If so, talk about it with your family. Bring it out in the open. Seek professional help to learn less destructive ways to address the needs and longings of the unmasked you that trigger the secret behaviors.

- Only after making sure you and your spouse are not doing any secret eating yourselves, talk with your daughter about the specific signs that you have seen that make you think she is sneak eating. Do not invade your daughter's privacy. Do not search through her drawers or under her bed. However, say something about any wrappers or missing food you notice. Do not pretend you don't notice or avoid saying something because it is uncomfortable. But be very careful that your intent, your tone of voice, and the words you choose don't attack her. It's easy in this situation to start accusing and come up with a variety of controlling devices to stop it. Remember, when adults want to control, it's about their own fear. Tolerate your fear and stay curious so you and she can problem-solve this together as a team. Sneak eating is simply a red flag that tells you she's struggling with who she is and if it is OK to be the real her. Try saying things like, "I found candy wrappers behind the curtains in the living room. I'm curious about what's going on." Consider giving her this chapter to read as a first step in bringing it out in the open.

- Be sure you have a support system where you can vent your frustration and anger about this situation so you don't take it out on your daughter. It is normal and natural for you to feel fear, frus-

tration, impatience, and anger when you discover your daughter is sneak eating. It is not helpful or appropriate for you to vent these at your daughter. However, be sure to honor her need for confidentiality about her sneak eating. She does not need to hear comments about herself from neighbors or friends whose parents heard about it from you.

■ Sometimes we adults unconsciously encourage sneak eating by setting up rules about food that restrict which foods she can eat, when she can eat, and how she can eat. These rules seem to be designed to help daughters eat healthily but instead often set up sneak eating as a way to rebel against this imposed control. The questions "Are you hungry?" "What are you hungry for?" and "How much will satisfy?" are more effective tools for her to confidently and comfortably use her own body signals to choose foods which balance well with her body.

Chapter 34

Some Ideas for Handling Eating Disorders

Your daughter asks you if she looks fat in a new outfit.

She stops eating her normal snacks when she gets home from school.

She orders the light entree instead of her favorite when the family eats out.

One day she counts calories and eats only nonfat foods and the next she eats pizza and brownies.

Are these signs of eating disorders? No, not by themselves. The answer to what indicates an eating disorder is not a clear-cut one. That is what makes eating disorders so difficult to identify and work with. The exact same behavior could be a sign of an eating disorder in one girl and not in another. The same behavior occurring for a short period of time or infrequently could be just a new concern about how she looks but over time be considered a signal of an eating disorder.

Here are some statistics that might help put eating disorders into perspective. Eighty-one percent of ten-year-old children are afraid of being fat, according to the Eating Disorder Referral and Information Center (EDRIC). And, according to the *Healthy Weight Journal* (May/June 1999), during adolescence the average healthy weight gain for girls is twenty-two pounds. So, you can see how a girl's struggle with eating, food, and weight might come about. She already thinks she's fat before her body even begins its natural shift in size, shape, and weight to a woman's body during puberty. As a result, 91 percent of girls diet by the time they reach college and 95 percent of dieters regain their lost weight in one to five years (EDRIC). What these numbers tell me is that diets fail. And diets fail because the underlying causes for the weight gain (concerning self-worth, value, attractiveness, body image, desirability, loveableness) and lack of tools and support for dealing with their own feelings about these concerns (whether scared, sad, mad, guilty, or confused) are rarely addressed. Sadder still is that 55 percent of these dieters go on to pathological dieting and eating disorders.

The National Association of Anorexia Nervosa and Associated Disorders (ANAD) states that 86 percent of eating disorders begin by the age of twenty. And 46 percent of these eating disorders last from six to fifteen years with only 50 percent reported being cured. As I write these statistics, I think about how much of life girls sacrifice fighting their bodies and how much of their energy and focus is spent on eating and not eating. You can help minimize these struggles for your daughter by exploring and practicing with some of the tools and techniques we've discussed in this book. Your willingness to experiment with some new ways of handling situations that come up in your daughter's everyday life will help her develop a healthy relationship with her body and her eating.

If you're worried that your daughter might have an eating disorder, start by focusing on whether your daughter is struggling with

food, weight, or her body size. It is much more useful to identify whether your daughter is fighting with her food and her body. Watch for the following signs to help you determine whether there is something to be concerned about.

1. How much time each day does she spend thinking about what she has eaten and will eat or won't eat, or what she will wear or not be able to fit in?

2. How is her life impacted by her concerns about her food and weight? Has she stopped going to certain events because she feels too fat in the outfits she would usually wear there? Does she avoid situations where friends or family would be eating? Is she sneaking food? Is she only eating food she prepares? Is she never letting anyone see her eat? Is she eating only in her room?

3. How much of her conversations with others are about food, recipes, menus, calories, fat, weight, or her looks? Is she answering questions about her life and what she's feeling with how fat she feels, or how ugly she feels, to the exclusion of being scared, mad, nervous, sad, and so on?

4. Is she spending most of her free time cooking, baking, reviewing recipes, and cleaning the kitchen?

5. Is she refusing to talk about food or her weight even though you have noticed a distinct change—a loss or a gain?

6. Is she using the scale to determine what she eats that day, what she wears that day, where she will or will not go that day, and so on?

7. Does she go to the bathroom after each time she eats? Does she use an isolated bathroom? Is she taking showers fre-

quently throughout the day? These are often signs of vomiting, laxative abuse, or diuretic abuse.

8. Is she spending more and more time exercising? Is she choosing to exercise rather than doing other activities with friends, family, or school?

9. Is she developing very specific rituals that she believes she must follow, such as what she eats, the order that she eats foods within a meal, the plate she uses, and so on?

10. Are you finding empty wrappers of food hidden throughout the house? Are packages of food from the pantry or freezer disappearing overnight?

11. Is she severely limiting her food choices by skipping meals, eating primarily fruits and vegetables, or describing herself as a vegetarian but not substituting other proteins for meats in her daily intake?

These are some of the most common distress signals about food. If any of these signs describe your daughter's behavior, I encourage you to schedule an appointment with her physician, a nutritionist, or a therapist to ask for their help in determining a plan of action. Remember, it is not important for you as parents to be able to discern if your daughter has an eating disorder. It is important that you watch for signs of your daughter struggling with food and weight.

Interestingly enough, these food-related signs to watch for lead us to think that eating disorders are primarily about food, weight, and body size. However, these signs are a cover. Eating disorders are about power, control, feeling emotions that are often uncomfortable and scary, finding a voice to say things that are difficult to discuss, and not knowing how to handle issues such as these. The struggle

with food is just a tool to try to avoid these other issues that daughters don't know how to handle effectively. So, parents, don't fight the food patterns. Rather, see them as a symptom of a girl struggling with issues that she can't put into words. Therefore, counseling needs to be an integral part of the help your daughter receives if she is struggling with weight and eating issues.

If you see some of the signs listed above in your daughter then consider the following:

- There are lots of good books, organizations, and Web sites that offer more information than I discuss here to help you better understand eating disorders and find the counseling and other support services that you and your daughter will need to effectively cope with her struggle with food, weight, and the underlying issues. (See the resources section on page 195.)

- Do not confront her with, "I think you have an eating disorder." Remember, she is usually feeling lots of emotions, especially fear, and confronting her makes her situation more scary. Because it is so scary, she will probably react in anger and not agree with you anyway. Often, in response, she may go further underground with any behaviors that she thinks you might notice. Instead, use the technique we've discussed throughout. Begin with yourself. "I'm concerned that it seems like you are struggling with your weight." Then, stay curious. "I'm wondering what your thoughts are about this." Then, just listen.

- If she gets mad and says there is no problem, you may want to try something like, "It sounds like you're feeling mad, tell me more about that." Listen. Then, put your heads together and problem-solve. Remember, using this technique helps you stay on her team and the two of you, together, address the problem, rather than setting up a "she against you" scenario.

- If she refuses to discuss her concerns as we suggested above, bring up very specific behaviors that you have noticed and, again, try the same format. For example, "I've noticed that the box of laxatives in the bathroom is empty and I'm concerned." Or, "I've noticed that you are exercising two hours a day and I'm concerned." Then stay curious, listen, and problem-solve as a team.

- It is tempting to search her room, look through her purse or backpack, read her journal, and so on to try to find evidence of her struggle. Don't do it! Your honesty and her trust in you are an essential foundation of your teamwork with her to work through eating and weight issues. Trust your intuition. If you think she's struggling, then talk about it and schedule an evaluation with a doctor, nutritionist, or therapist to get a professional opinion.

- Notice when you are tempted to set up rules to try to control her eating behaviors. When you want to control your daughter's eating, it is usually a good sign that you are scared—often terrified— that she is in trouble and you don't know what to do. As a result, you may come up with a solution to try to ease your own terror. Rarely is it effective and helpful for your daughter. And trying to control instead of building an alliance with your daughter sets you up as an adversary against which your daughter can fight.

- Your daughter will sometimes ask you to help her control her eating by confronting her when she wants to eat something she is trying to avoid, or hiding food from her, or not letting her have certain food items. In your desire to do something, you will probably agree to "help," only to see that over time your "help" sets up fights and sneaking and anything but the alliance with your daughter that you wanted. If you step in and try to control at this point, even if your intention is to help, you are encouraging her to depend on you to make her eating decisions and prevent her from

connecting to her own body and learning to feed and care for herself. Instead, agree to help and then suggest some other possibilities.

- Often, the least threatening step to begin to address any struggles that she has with food or weight is a visit to a nutritionist. This usually sounds attractive to her since nutritionists are a resource with specific answers to food and weight questions, which is what she feels safest focusing on at this point. Remember, though, the food and weight issues are only a cover for other seemingly unruly emotions she doesn't know how to handle. As your daughter and the nutritionist develop rapport, the nutritionist can then serve as a referral source to counselors, physicians, and psychiatrists who specialize in eating disorders for you and your family.

- Avoid diet and weight loss programs. They are *not* designed for an eating disordered population. They only reinforce the problem. Nor are they usually designed to address an adolescent's nutritional needs.

- Be open to looking at what role you might play in her struggle with food. Consider participating in some family therapy to identify problem areas and create some new ways to interrelate.

Chapter 35

Words of Hope and Encouragement

All of your daughter's questions, worries, and struggles with eating and weight are simply a sign that she is concerned and interested in learning and creating her way of answering the following questions: Who is she? What are her feelings and how can she communicate in a way that others will understand and respond to? How can she balance being true to herself and being a part of the community around her, and what does she have that will bring meaning to herself and the world around her? She is becoming her own creative being, but she only has the experience of how others around her have handled issues and situations to use for information. Rarely does that provide enough of the right mix of healthy options for her to choose who she is. Getting help for her eating and weight issues introduces her to new pathways offering much broader possibilities of relating to the world and how she might create her own "dance" in it.

We all play as if counting calories and obsessing about pounds and so on are the goals rather than simply the gateway into discov-

ering something much bigger and better that can usually only be seen in hindsight.

Eating disorders and struggles with food are outward signs of a girl's inward calling to heal, expand, create, explore, grow, and change. If we respond to her concerns and struggles with this in mind we don't have to feel as threatened or terrified. If we can, instead, respond by encouraging her in this creative journey she is starting, we not only have the tremendous joy of sharing the excitement of her discoveries about herself with her but we also have the opportunity to open doors into our own creative journeys. Maybe then we can begin exploring how we would like to redesign ourselves, who we truly want to be, and what our unique "dance" is as well.

I am not saying that this journey may not have tremendous pain, fear, confusion, and upheaval. I am only saying that these feelings are an integral part of a growth path. As you and your daughter encounter these feelings, sometimes it is easier to cope with them and the changes that may result by recognizing them as the feelings surrounding death and loss required for new birth and new growth to occur.

As she cycles through these struggles, she has the opportunity to develop and design her own unique style for nourishing herself in more ways than just with food. And, as her parent and teammate through her process, you too have a chance to review and redesign your own connection to yourself, your body, and its physical, emotional, and spiritual needs.

In the next few pages, I list Web sites, books, newsletters, and phone numbers for resources you might find useful as you continue on this journey of nourishing your daughter and yourself. Stay curious, experiment, make mistakes, laugh, cry, and keep trying. This path through food and weight issues into connection with our real selves is a very powerful and healing one. It leads to daughters who are comfortable and capable of taking good care of themselves and are confident sharing their unique gifts with the rest of the world.

Resources

Other Books by the Author

Full and Fulfilled: The Science of Eating to Your Soul's Satisfaction, Nan Allison, M.S., R.D., L.D.N., and Carol Beck. An easy-to-read, step-by-step guide to intuitive eating.

Newsletters

Daughters. 1-888-849-8476.

AmericanGirl.com. Fantastic resource for parents. Concise, how-to articles and columns about a wide range of topics you handle with your daughters ten to sixteen years of age.

Web Sites

www.focusas.com/adolescence.htm. A great site to link to everything about teens.

www.bodypositive.com. A unique and very helpful site concerned with

body acceptance. Easy-to-use worksheets about listening to your own body.

www.aboutface.org. Creative, colorful, very easy to maneuver site about the impact of advertising on body image. I found it fascinating.

www.youngwomenshealth.org. A good source of helpful information and convenient links.

www.wholefamily.com. This site focuses on family relationships from each member's perspective. They have a newsletter available and interactive questions.

www.health.org/gpower/girlarea/bodywise/index.htm. Long address, but worth the work. All about nutrition and healthy attitudes about food for girls, and it is part of the Girl Power web site, which provides a broader spectrum of information for girls.

www.eatright.org. This is the site for the American Dietetic Association. It has basic nutrition information and can help you locate a registered dietitian in your area.

Books

Nourishing Wisdom: A Mind/Body Approach to Nutrition and Well-Being, by Marc David. An excellent book to begin to recognize food and eating as part of a daily nourishing ritual.

Making Peace with Food: A Step-by-Step Guide to Freedom from Diet/Weight Conflict, by Susan Kano. A guide through most of the major hurdles people face that keep them from being at peace with their food.

Women's Bodies, Women's Wisdom: Creating Physical and Emotional Health and Healing, by Christiane Northrup, M.D. A very informative and helpful resource linking emotional and spiritual components to the physical body.

The Beauty Myth: How Images of Beauty Are Used Against Women, by Naomi Wolf. Fascinating book, full of information about the impact of society on our beliefs about our body. Lots of "Ahahs!" in this one.

Preventing Childhood Eating Problems: A Practical, Positive Approach to Raising Children Free of Food and Weight Conflicts. by Jane R. Hirschmann, C.S.W., and Lela Zaphiropoulous, C.S.W. The subtitle is a perfect description of this short, easy-to-read book.

Eating on the Run, by Evelyn Tribole, M.S., R.D. Quick and easy snack ideas.

Feed Your Soul: A Cookbook That Nourishes Body, Mind, and Spirit, by George Fowler and Jeff Lehr. A cookbook with interesting, creative recipes and quotes and affirmations encouraging the physical, emotional, and spiritual connections to being truly nourished.

Professional Organizations to Help You Locate a Referral in Your Area

Find a Dietitian. 1-800-877-1600, ext. 5000, or *www.eatright.org*

APA Psychologist Referral System. 1-800-964-2000

National Association of Social Workers. 1-800-638-8799

American Psychiatric Association. 202-682-6000 or www.psych.org/public_info/index.html

Directors' Shakespeare

approaches to
Twelfth Night

by
Bill Alexander
John Barton
John Caird
Terry Hands

edited by
Michael Billington

$$\frac{\begin{array}{c}N\\H\end{array}}{B}$$

NICK HERN BOOKS
A division of Walker Books Limited

A Nick Hern Book

Approaches to Twelfth Night
first published in 1990 by Nick Hern Books
a division of Walker Books Limited
87 Vauxhall Walk, London SE11 5HJ

Text Editor: Simon Trussler

British Library Cataloguing in Publication Data
Approaches to Twelfth Night — (RSC Directors Shakespeare)
I. Billington, Michael
II. Series
822.33
ISBN 1 85459 007 3

Typeset by L. Anderson Typesetting
Woodchurch, Kent TN26 3TB

Printed and bound in Great Britain
by Biddles Limited, Guildford and Kings Lynn

Contents

Preface

Most books about Shakespeare focus on textual analysis rather than practical performance. I see the two disciplines as complementary rather than antithetical: the plays are there to be studied and seen, experienced and enjoyed in the theatre. Indeed, one good thing, of many, about the evolution of the Royal Shakespeare Company over the past three decades is that it has helped to bring the worlds of academe and the theatre into closer contact. It has certainly helped to make the plays of Shakespeare more readily available to a nationwide audience.

About eighteen months ago Nick Hern approached me with the idea for a series of books that would tap the collective knowledge of RSC directors about Shakespeare's plays. The books would be based on extensive discussions with the directors about the problems each play poses. They would focus on the practical questions of interpretation, characterisation, and design. They would be aimed both at the general reader and at students, theatregoers, and those about to embark on a production of the play in question. We put the idea to Genista McIntosh, the RSC's General Administrator, who both readily endorsed it and secured the willing co-operation of the RSC directorate.

The end result was that I sat down with Terry Hands, John Barton, Bill Alexander, and John Caird to discuss their several approaches to *Twelfth Night*. We had two marathon, day-long talk-sessions interrupted only by coffee and sandwiches. No punches were pulled. No areas were taboo. Nothing was declared off-limits. I then went away and edited the transcript and added a stage-history which attempts to put the productions under discussion into the broader context of how *Twelfth Night* has fared in the British theatre over nearly four centuries.

The book is a genuinely joint venture that could not have come into existence without the enthusiastic co-operation of the directors themselves. I also hope it fills a real need and preserves, in print, the working knowledge of a band of Shakespearean directors. Theatre is naturally ephemeral; but it seems a pity that

so much experience of the practicalities of staging Shakespeare should not somehow be recorded.

I can only add my personal thanks to everyone involved, both at Nick Hern Books and the RSC, and say that all of us have every intention of exploring further plays along the same lines. Given Shakespeare's prodigious output, it is a process that should see us all through into the next century.

Michael Billington
January 1990

Twelfth Night: a Stage History

Twelfth Night may be Shakespeare's most perfect comedy. It is also one of the hardest to bring off in the theatre because of its sheer kaleidoscopic range of moods. It contains some of Shakespeare's most lyrical writing about love. It also contains scenes, such as the baiting of the confined Malvolio, that to a modern sensibility seem extremely cruel. It is about the impact of truth upon fantasy and about the journey of discovery undertaken by Orsino, Olivia, and Malvolio. At the same time it is about the cyclical nature not only of the seasons but of human life itself. It takes place in the imaginary world of Illyria. Yet it also exists in the concrete world of the Elephant (an inn in Southwark), Mistress Mall's picture, the spinsters and the knitters in the sun. To realise the play's complexities and contradictions required, suggested John Russell Brown, five years' study or a repeated return to its problems in a succession of productions. Even for the fortunate directors of the RSC, it is usually a matter of months rather than years of study, six weeks' rehearsal, and a chance to get it right (or not) on one specific occasion.

Looking back over the history of *Twelfth Night* in the British theatre (and abroad) two things are immediately apparent. One is the way different characters become, at different times, the pivot of the play. Some productions belong to Malvolio: others to Viola. But, in conversation, the quartet of RSC directors suggests that Sir Toby is the motor that drives the plot and Feste the character who determines the mood. One has also seen productions where either Olivia or Sir Andrew emerges as the dominant character. It is Shakespeare's most Chekhovian play in that the attention is shared by half-a-dozen characters any one of whom may emerge as the most individually arresting. But stage history also indicates there is a constant debate about how the play should be staged. Does Illyria yield up its secrets to realism or to the imagination? Between the archaeologically exact terraced gardens of Beerbohm Tree at one end of the scale and the neo-Elizabethan simplicity of

William Poël at the other there seems to be an infinite number of options. The debate still continues.

When was *Twelfth Night* first performed? In a book published in 1954, *The First Night of Twelfth Night*, Leslie Hotson plumps assertively for 6 January 1601. We know that a Court play was performed in Whitehall that night. We know that the Lord Chamberlain, Hunsdon, was ordered to provide a play that, amongst other things, had 'greate variety of Musicke and dances.' We also know that the guest of honour at the Court revels on that specific Twelfth Night was the Italian Duke Virginio Orsino. In Hotson's argument, Shakespeare's play becomes a topical comedy run up to please both the Queen and a visiting grandee; though since Shakespeare's Orsino is something of a deluded narcissist, it may be just as well that the Italian Duke spoke no English. But Professor Hotson pushes the argument much further and suggests that the arena staging adopted for the Great Chamber at Whitehall was the model for all Elizabethan theatres. He posits a production of *Twelfth Night* with the spectators on tiered benches 'all Round abowte' and 'on every side' and with a couple of tents to represent Olivia's and Orsino's houses. This is, in fact, theatre-in-the-round. But although it makes sense to suggest this is how Shakespeare's play was first presented in a hall ninety feet long, it is presumptuous to argue that this was therefore the model for all Elizabethan theatres.

Hotson's theories are speculative. But we do know, for a fact, that *Twelfth Night* was played in the Middle Temple Hall at the Inns of Court on 2 February 1602, because a barrister who was present, John Manningham, recorded the event in his diary:

> At our feast we had a play called *Twelfth Night* or *What You Will*; much like *The Comedy of Errors* or *Menaechmi* in Plautus, but most like and near to that in Italian called *Inganni*. A good practice in it to make the steward believe his lady widow was in love with him, by counterfeiting a letter as from his lady in general terms, telling him what she liked best in him, and prescribing his gesture in smiling, his apparel, etc. And when he came to practise, making him believe they took him to be mad.

What is significant about Manningham's account — apart from getting a minor point in the plot wrong by making Olivia a widow — is that the play is both associated with a 'feast' or revels and that it is Malvolio who sticks most firmly in his mind. Today

Twelfth Night is so regularly performed that it has lost any association with a specific event, but it is worth recalling that it had its origins in revelry and was presumably seen as a celebratory comedy. Manningham also does not simply seize on Malvolio but sees the other characters' pretence that he is mad as a good joke. I am not for a moment suggesting that we should attempt to recapture that ethos today but Manningham's observations may come as a salutary corrective to those actors and directors who seek to transform the play into Malvolio's Tragedy.

You could say, in fact, that the Malvolios of this world got their revenge in 1642 when Parliament issued the 'First Ordinance Against Stage Plays and Interludes' which ordered that 'public stage plays shall cease to be foreborne', that the theatres should be pulled down and that 'players shall be taken as rogues'. The savagery of those decrees is a reminder that Shakespeare, in satirising the Puritan spirit, was harpooning something that was philistine, pleasure-killing and destructive.

After the Restoration, *Twelfth Night* (in common with many of Shakespeare's plays) was interfered with by Sir William Davenant, which puts in perspective Samuel Pepys's comment in 1662: 'But a silly play and not related at all to the name of that day.' It wasn't, in fact, until the next century that Shakespeare's text began to be performed in anything like the original version. The Irish actor, Charles Macklin (whose Shylock drew from Alexander Pope the memorable couplet 'This is the Jew that Shakespeare drew') started the vogue for authenticity with a revival at Drury Lane in 1741: himself as Malvolio, Hannah Pritchard as Viola.

Macklin's success, and the growing influence of women on the theatre, firmly established *Twelfth Night*'s popularity: between 1741 and 1819 it was rarely out of the bill at either Drury Lane or Covent Garden which then enjoyed a monopoly on legitimate drama. But the most vivid account of an eighteenth-century *Twelfth Night* is provided by Charles Lamb in his graphic description, in *Some of the Old Actors*, of a 1780s revival. Robert Bensley's Malvolio, he said, came near to being the perfect Don Quixote. And Dora Jordan as Viola obviously had the precious ability to make the lines appear new-minted. 'When', wrote Lamb, 'she had declared her sister's history to be a "blank" and that she had "never told her love", there was a pause as if the story had ended — and then the "worm in the bud" came up as a new suggestion — and the heightened image of "Patience" still followed after that, as by some growing (and not mechanical)

process, thought springing up after thought, I would almost say as they were watered by her tears.' That could be a description of Judi Dench almost 200 years later. The foppish comedian, James William Dodd, also brought all his skill to Ague-Cheek. 'You could see', wrote Lamb, 'the first dawn of an idea stealing over his countenance, climbing up little by little, with a painful process, till it cleared up at last to the fullness of a twilight conception — its highest meridian. . . . A glimmer of understanding would appear in a corner of his eye, and for lack of fuel go out again. A part of his forehead would catch a little intelligence, and be a long time in communicating it to the remainder.' That's great criticism: vivid, descriptive and exact.

In the nineteenth-century, *Twelfth Night* was rarely off the London stage: Samuel Phelps staged it at Sadler's Wells in 1848, Charles Kean and Robert Keeley opened the new Princess's Theatre with it in 1850, the Royal Theatre of Saxe-Meiningen (ancestor of our modern ensembles) imported it to Drury Lane in 1881. That makes it all the odder that when Henry Irving staged the play at the Lyceum in 1884 he had apparently never seen it acted before. *Twelfth Night* was also one of Irving's most marked failures as both actor and producer. Part of the problem was his own Malvolio which, rising to the ungovernable vehemence of a Shylock in his final line, was short on comedy. Ellen Terry, playing Viola, also had the misfortune to go through the first night with her arm in a sling and had to play many of her scenes sitting down. But the real problem was that the sets, designed by Hawes Craven, smothered the play in a decorative romanticism. Orsino reclined on a velvet couch, tasselled in gold, while behind him in a dim mysterious alcove, dark with painted glass, minstrels played their seductive melodies. And, in the final scene, the spreading portico of Olivia's house was flanked with branching palms beside a blue sea while guards, pages and courtiers stood picturesquely by. It was difficult for Shakespeare's comedy to survive such overweighted, picture-book literalism.

But the late Victorian and Edwardian era seems to have oscillated between the extremes of spectacle and simplicity. The American manager and distortionist, Augustin Daly, in 1894 frantically rearranged the text in order to meet the demands of scenic realism. His version at Daly's theatre in London began with the arrival of Sebastian and Antonio, proceeded to the star-entrance of Viola (Ada Rehan) and then went on to play the first and fourth scenes of the first Act, featuring Orsino, so that the sea-coast could give way to a fantastically elaborate ducal palace.

Those who complain about modern excesses of 'directors' theatre' would sometimes do well to look back in the archives and see what happened in the days of managerial domination. If Daly's approach was absurd, Herbert Beerbohm Tree's at Her Majesty's in 1901 wasn't much better. He had Malvolio followed everywhere by four miniature stewards. And, seeking verisimilitude, his designer copied Olivia's garden from a picture in *Country Life*. According to a contemporary critic: 'It extended terrace by terrace to the extreme back of the stage with real grass, real box hedges, real paths, fountains, and descending steps. I never saw anything like it for beauty and vraiesemblance. The actors were literally in an Italian garden.' The only problem is that the characters weren't, and the set 'was perforce used for many of the Shakespearean episodes for which it was inappropriate'.

Irving, Daly, and Tree went to one extreme: William Poël to another. In 1894 he founded the Elizabethan Stage Society 'to give practical effect to the principle that Shakespeare should be accorded the build of stage for which he designed his plays'. Shaw, seeing their *Twelfth Night* at Burlington Hall in 1895, admitted that the amateur cast was rank bad ('The clown made no pretence of understanding a single sentence he uttered: it sufficed for him that he *was* a clown'). But he welcomed the prominence the platform stage gave to the actor, applauded the use of Elizabethan music played on viol, lute, and viola de gamba, and suggested that Irving and others might come down and have a look at what they could do 'on the sort of stage which helped Burbage to become famous'. Max Beerbohm (who in a letter to Florence Kahn later wrote that 'poor William Poël's honoured name is a guarantee of badness') was less persuaded. Seeing the Elizabethan Stage Society's *Twelfth Night* at the Royal Court in 1903, he made the perfectly fair point that Shakespeare wrote at a time when scenic production was in its infancy and was conscious of its limitations. 'We', wrote Beerbohm, 'have developed that science and it is only when Shakespeare's plays are produced with due regard to this development that they seem to us living works of art.' Beerbohm, *pace* Sam Wanamaker and his projected Globe Theatre of today, was right: one cannot simply turn one's back on the present. But surely there had to be some way of presenting Shakespeare — and the opal-like comedy of *Twelfth Night* in particular — that was neither scenically top-heavy nor filled with an owlish solemnity and detachment.

There was; and it came, at long last, in Granville Barker's legendary production which opened at the Savoy on 15 November

1912. This, by all accounts, was Shakespeare as we understand it today. Norman Wilkinson's black-and-silver setting, evoking a half-Italianised Elizabethan court, combined beauty with intimacy: there was a formal garden with a great staircase right and left, with drop curtains and a small inner tapestry set for the carousal. The verse was spoken with lightness, speed, and dexterity. 'It goes slick but not too fast,' wrote *The Times*. 'It is a most agreeable sensation to feel that for once you are listening to Shakespeare as he wrote.'

But, above all, Granville Barker got rid of all the false accretions of stage tradition and sought for the essential truth of character. Lillah McCarthy's Viola was praised for not 'making fun of the equivocations due to her disguise'. Writing to Granville Barker shortly after the premiere, John Masefield said: 'Lillah often got the most exquisite effects with a sort of clear uplifting that carried us away, and I believe that the women scenes were never once allowed to drop to the dreamy and emotional; they were always high, clear and ringing, coming out of a passionate mood.' Arthur Whitby's Sir Toby was not simply an eructating sot but a gentleman with, in Robert Speaight's phrase, 'the beaming roundness of a full moon'. Henry Ainley's Malvolio was a Puritan prig who flamed up in fury on 'I'll be revenged on the whole pack of you.' But, most significantly of all, Granville Barker broke with tradition by treating Feste (Hayden Coffin) not as the conventional hop-skip-and-jump youthful jester but as a sad, mature man through whom ran what the director himself called 'that vein of irony which is so often the mark of one of life's self-acknowledged failures'. Coffin was, in fact, a musical comedy performer who nineteen years before had starred in George Edwardes's production of *A Gaiety Girl*, and presumably brought with him just that touch of frayed melancholia you often find in veterans of the popular stage past their prime. It was also a mark of Granville Barker's precision that the part of Fabian was not tossed away but played as an elderly respected family retainer. Modern Shakespeare production, one feels, began with Granville Barker's *Twelfth Night*.

Barker also greatly admired a production of the play by a director who shared something of his own idealism, intellectual refinement, and preoccupation with text: Jacques Copeau. Copeau's French-language version opened at the Théâtre du Vieux-Colombier on 15 May 1914, with Copeau himself as Malvolio, Louis Jouvet as Ague-Cheek, Suzanne Bing as Viola, and Duncan Grant designing the costumes. Copeau's avowed aim

was to bring 'true beauty and poetry' back to the French stage and in this production he seemed to have succeeded handsomely. According to Robert Speaight, the play was presented in curtains with stylised trees and simple cubes for seating. Viola was clad in white doublet with thin black stripes, Ague-Cheek in sky-blue top hat, Feste in pink and blue and a red cap shaped like the claws of a lobster. Reviewing the production in *The Observer* when it was revived in 1921, Granville Barker noted several flaws (far too bright costumes for Olivia and a household in mourning), but declared that the French actors spoke Shakespeare better in French than English actors spoke him in English: they had 'precision, variety, clarity and, above all, passion'. What Copeau achieved was also something that, before Barker, few English productions had ever realised was possible in Shakespeare: a quicksilver fluency. You sense that most clearly from Copeau's own description of the opening scenes:

> While the Duke, followed by his gentlemen, slipped into the shadows on the left, Viola emerged from the other side in a different light, veiled in pink and holding a palm leaf in her hand. So, right from the beginning, the comedy discovered its rhythm and began to trace its winding pattern. Hardly had the grave and slightly melancholy voice finished speaking than a woman's voice — Suzanne's — clear and bell-like, transported us elsewhere without the slightest jolt. 'What country friends, is this?' 'This is Illyria, lady.'

How many productions, even today, achieve that crucial ability to dissolve one scene meltingly into the next?

For both Granville Barker and Copeau the text had the sanctity of a musical score: something to be viewed in its entirety rather than as a collection of parts. Reading about the various productions in London and Stratford in the inter-war years, one gets the feeling that the play once again simply became an occasion for some memorable individual performances. Indeed William Bridges-Adams who ran the Shakespeare Festival in Stratford-upon-Avon from 1919 to 1934 (in both the old and new theatres), rejected many of Barker's innovations in Shakespearean production, including the use of a brilliant white light which he described as 'germ free'. Strange liberties were also taken with the text in between-the-wars productions. At Stratford, Bridges-Adams cut the prison-scene, thereby softening the play's cruelty. At London's New Theatre in 1932 (where James Agate said of

Jean Forbes-Robertson's Viola that the character's 'steel-true and blade-straight quality, her sticking to the spirit as well as the letter, of Orsino's instructions can never have been conveyed better'), the director, Robert Atkins, gave the last verse of 'The wind and the rain' to Olivia. Donald Wolfit, in his touring production first seen in 1937, suggested that Malvolio enjoyed a last-minute return to Olivia's favour.

But the lesson taught by Granville Barker — that any Shakespeare play, and *Twelfth Night* most particularly, requires some controlling directorial vision — took a long time to sink in. Between 1918 and 1939, it is hard to trace one single production that commanded universal respect. What one got instead was a string of notable performances. Edith Evans's Viola at the Old Vic in 1932 was admired by some, though J. C. Trewin felt that 'Her Viola sounded oddly heartless. This was the Restoration shipwrecked upon the Illyrian coast.' Tyrone Guthrie did what he called 'a baddish, immature' production at the Old Vic in 1937 with Jessica Tandy doubling Viola and Sebastian, and Laurence Olivier playing Sir Toby, in the words of one critic, 'like a veteran Skye-terrier, ears pricked for mischief'. Copeau's nephew, Michel Saint-Denis, also staged the play at the Phoenix in 1938, in what many thought was a fussy, overloaded production that prettified Illyria in the manner of a fancy-dress ball. Its chief glories were Peggy Ashcroft's Viola, full of charm, warmth, and wit, and Michael Redgrave's Ague-Cheek based, in part, on that of Louis Jouvet: not so much a fool as a man whose intelligence was, for a whim, deliberately fantasticated. The temptation of lead actors is always to go for Malvolio. Ague-Cheek, however, is the part that often yields up the most surprising comedy.

The critic W.A. Darlington once said that there is a perfect production of *Twelfth Night* laid up for us in heaven. What is fascinating is how hard it was, post-Barker, to come by the perfect one on earth. Time and again, one finds one aspect of the play emphasised at the expense of another: usually prankish comedy at the expense of delicate melancholy. When *Twelfth Night* was chosen to re-open the Old Vic on 14 November 1950, it was given a production by Hugh Hunt filled with *commedia dell'arte* fussiness; there was a chorus of boys in beards and girls in urchin cuts rounding off each scene with skipping dances, clapping of hands, smacking of knees, and lots of hurraying. Only Peggy Ashcroft, playing Viola again after a gap of eleven years, gave the production real distinction. She was much praised for her rapt stillness in the scene where Orsino talks of love and Feste sings

'Come away Death.' She also showed the true Shakespearean actress's ability to focus on a particular moment and give it an unswerving truth. When Viola (in the guise of Cesario) is confronted by Sebastian, who asks 'What countryman? What name? What parentage?', there was a long, charged, beautifully held pause before she quietly breathed 'Of Messaline'. How rarely since then has one seen an actress seize on the pure poetry of that moment.

In the immediate post-war years at Stratford, productions of the play once again seemed to miss the mark. In 1947 Walter Hudd directed a revival that transposed the first and second scenes of the play (something Kenneth Branagh did forty years later at the Riverside Studios): a pointless reversal that completely ignores the first scene's announcement of the play's major themes. In 1955 Sir John Gielgud directed a Stratford production starring Sir Laurence Olivier as Malvolio and Vivien Leigh as Viola. Gielgud himself has written: 'Somehow the production did not work, I don't know why. . . . It is so difficult to combine the romance of the play with the cruelty of the jokes against Malvolio, jokes which are in any case archaic and difficult. The different elements in the play are hard to balance properly.' My own chief memory of that production is of Olivier's Malvolio: a bumptious arriviste with faintly Hebraic appearance and an insecurity over pronunciation. When Olivier came to 'Cast thy humble slough' in the reading of the letter he agonised endlessly over whether it should be 'sluff' to rhyme with 'cuff' or 'slow' to rhyme with 'cow'. He also rocked back and forth on a bench in the garden with such ecstasy that at one point he fell over backwards. If one had to sum up his performance in a word it would be 'camp'; and it was redeemed only by the whiplash fury he revealed in Malvolio's exit line which introduced a note of Lear-like revenge into Illyria.

But in 1958 (two years before he officially took over as director of what soon became the Royal Shakespeare Company) Peter Hall created a production at Stratford that solved many of the play's problems. Most directors of *Twelfth Night* see the play as made up of a romantic half and a comic half. Hall's genius was to see that these divisions were not watertight: that the romance was invaded by high-spirited fun and the comedy by a grave melancholy. Hall's most radical decision was to cast Geraldine McEwan — in her mid-twenties and best known as a delightful West End ingenue — as Olivia. Stage tradition always had insisted that Olivia was a grave, mature woman. Ms McEwan presented her as a pouting, giggling, squealing *poseuse*, affecting a love for her dead brother

that she didn't really feel and bored to death with acting the role of the great lady. Erotically stirred by Cesario, she threw herself on her knees in front of him (her) on 'Nor wit nor reason can my passion hide'. And when Sebastian later responded to her overtures, she entered mischievously beckoning with her fore-finger to a priest. There were those at the time who resented this drastic re-evaluation of the character. John Wain wrote in *The Observer* that Olivia was 'played as a kittenish typist on holiday from a City office. . . . It isn't her (Ms McEwan's) fault that Shakespeare made Olivia a countess full of authority and aristocratic hauteur.' But is the Olivia who rushes so speedily to the altar with Sebastian ('Blame not this haste of mine') all that full of aristocratic hauteur? And isn't there something suspect about her reported determination to 'water once a day her chamber round with eye-offending brine'? But if Hall tapped a new vein of comedy in Olivia, he also (possibly less originally) unearthed a sweet melancholia in Ague-Cheek. Richard Johnson played him, in Mr. Wain's description, as 'a paranoid manic-depressive strongly reminiscent at times of Lucky in *Waiting For Godot*'. In his long flaxen wig, Mr. Johnson looked like a lachrymose spaniel: he was the eternal, dogged trier who wants to be a great blade and a roaring lover but who can never quite make it. I recall still Mr. Johnson's look of wan hopelessness as, having claimed to be a very dog at a catch, he was squeezed out by Sir Toby and Feste.

Hall's ability to merge, rather than separate, the play's romantic-comic elements was also embodied in Dorothy Tutin's Viola. For a start, in her Caroline pageboy, 'And when did you last see my Father?' costume, Ms Tutin made a thoroughly convincing Cesario and cut through all the academic arguments about the oddity of the Shakespearean boy-girl heroine. But she also balanced a genuine amusement at the confusion created by her disguise ('Poor lady' was done in a mischievous drawl that got a big laugh) with a lyrical sense of passion. Her 'Ay but I know . . .' to Orsino was a soaring cry from the heart halted just in time and brought down in the vocal scale to a more moderate 'Too well what love women to men may owe'.

The design by Lila de Nobili, a distinguished Italian painter who had worked with Visconti at La Scala, Milan, also suffused Hall's production in a warm romantic glow without ever becom-ing cumbersome or heavy. I cannot better Robert Speaight's description of it: 'Peter Hall's Caroline *Twelfth Night* was a rich symphony in russet, designed by Lila de Nobili. The cavaliers

were gathered round Orsino in a panelled hall out of Nash's *English Mansions*, and just as this gave way to the cloud-capped towers of a transitory Adriatic, so these quickly dissolved into an English garden and Sir Toby Belch enjoying an obviously continental breakfast.' But the gauzy romanticism of the design was offset by touches of realism: when Viola clambered ashore in Illyria after the shipwreck she had the wet-wigged, drowned-rat look of someone extremely happy to have at last reached *terra firma*.

Such a production was too good to die; and in 1960 Hall revived it at Stratford as part of his opening season devoted to exploring the range of Shakespearean comedy. By then, there had been some major cast-changes, proving how much the delicate balance of this particular play depends upon the right match of ingredients. In place of Geraldine McEwan, Barbara Barnett now played Olivia: a good but immature actress who mistakenly tried to ape the cooing vanity of her predecessor without her spontaneous sense of the ridiculous. Ian Richardson capably replaced Richard Johnson as Ague-Cheek without quite achieving his exquisite hangdog mournfulness. But two of the other new arrivals greatly strengthened the production. Eric Porter's Malvolio was logical, precise, outwardly rational, and rather like a civil servant trying to master a difficult brief in his reading of the letter. He also kept the comedy within bounds, conveying the constriction of the cross-garters by thrusting all his weight onto one foot; and in the famous last line he exuded a wronged dignity rather than tragic suffering. But possibly the greatest gain of all was Max Adrian's Feste. Hall followed Granville Barker in casting a mature actor for the role, and one equipped with a peculiar gift for sardonic sadness, well caught by Alan Pryce-Jones in *The Observer*: 'It would be possible to make a case for Feste as the ancestor of the modern anti-hero — a resounding tinkler, a caretaker, a mad mother all rolled into one. Not an inflection is lost by Mr. Adrian, who not only speaks his lines with singular distinction but conveys the psychological subtlety of a character whom it is easy to dismiss as a mere clown. In fact, Feste is much the most interesting character in the comedy; he provides in his own person the interplay of light and shadow which makes it memorable.'

But it is worth recalling that *Twelfth Night* is a play that it is hard to get exactly right first time; and even Hall's production only achieved a mellow perfection when it transferred to the Aldwych in December 1960 with a cast that combined the best of

the two seasons' work. McEwan and Johnson returned, Porter and Adrian stayed, and at the centre of it all was Tutin's enchanting boy-girl Viola, eyes glowing with mischief at the thought, 'Heaven forbid my outside hath not charmed her'. It is fascinating to note that even now, thirty years on, Hall is contemplating a return to this most Mozartian of comedies.

A first-rate production like Hall's is, whatever directors may say, a hard act to follow: so it proved when the RSC next turned to the play in June 1966. It was directed by Clifford Williams, who four years previously had given the company one of its most spectacular early triumphs with a production of *The Comedy of Errors* run up in a hurry to give Paul Scofield extra time to work on *King Lear*. It might have seemed the magic could work again. Once again we had a comedy about twins separated by shipwreck and mistaken for each other. Once again we had a coolly austere set by Sally Jacobs, consisting of an elegant row of Roman arches topped by a minstrels' gallery. There was even Diana Rigg, from the cast of Williams's *Comedy of Errors*, to lend her beauty and intelligence to the role of Viola. But somehow, on the first night at any rate and in spite of a front-rank cast (Alan Howard, Estelle Kohler, Brewster Mason, Norman Rodway, David Warner), the ingredients failed to mix. Where Mr. Williams's *Comedy of Errors* worked because of its dazzling uniformity of style, his *Twelfth Night* didn't because the rich individuality of the characters was only half-realised.

But out of *Twelfth Night*, like Africa, there is always something new. On this occasion, it was one memorable piece of business and one original performance. The classic bit of business came when Maria said of Malvolio, 'He will come to her in yellow stockings and 'tis a colour she abhors', at which point everyone looked at Ague-Cheek dressed from head to toe in vilest yellow. And the one genuinely finished performance came from Ian Holm as Malvolio, expertly described by Ronald Bryden: 'He plays him as Olivia's sergeant-major, a small dapper disciplinarian with NCO vowels, who knows his authority resides only in his rank. Under it he combines the odd sexlessness of the military bachelor (brought from his bed by Toby's carousing, he appears in a nightcap which conceals paper curlers) with the frail petulance of a middle-aged child. For no obvious reason he's made up in the likeness of the Droeshout portrait of the Bard, but the irrelevant joke somehow fits. Holm convinces you that this is the face of self-made, middle-class Elizabethan industriousness.'

Outside the context of the RSC, *Twelfth Night* was inevitably

seized on in the sixties as a high camp hymn to unisex: the most celebrated example was a New York musical, *Your Own Thing*, which pre-dated *Hair* by three months and which used the framework of Shakespeare's play to advocate an unbuttoned sexual liberality. It played in London at the Comedy Theatre in 1969, but was overshadowed by the much more melodious and free-spirited *Hair*. It was John Barton, however, who returned to Shakespearean basics with a legendary production that opened at Stratford in August 1969, moved to the Aldwych the following year, and was revived again at Stratford in 1971. The casting underwent a number of permutations and combinations, but the constant factors were Judi Dench's Viola, Donald Sinden's Malvolio, and Emrys James's Feste: those and John Barton's unremitting exploration of text and sub-text, his detailed exploration of character, and his well-nigh perfect achievement of the balance between comedy and tears. It was the most Chekhovian *Twelfth Night* most of us had ever seen.

Barton's production was staged in the context of a season devoted primarily to Shakespeare's late plays for which the designer, Christopher Morley, devised an enveloping white box. He modified this, however, for *Twelfth Night*, as J. W. Lambert indicated in *The Sunday Times*: 'Christopher Morley has set this play in a long receding wattle tunnel decorated by four stately, flickering candlesticks but lit from the outside, sometimes a sombre twilit umber, sometimes soaring into sunburst brilliance. No bright colours are allowed in Stephanie Howard's costumes, though a pleasing muslin flutter invades Lisa Harrow's fresh young Olivia as she emerges from the comfortable certainties of mourning into the perilous playground of desire. But the essential furniture is all a silvery white, including the shrubbery.'

The depth of perspective afforded by the tunnel was brilliantly used. At the beginning of the second scene, doors at the far end were thrown open and Judi Dench's Viola appeared in a swirl of smoke, moved slowly downstage and became, in J. C. Trewin's words, 'a figure entering a world of fantasy and uttering suddenly that romantic line, "What country friends is this?" "It is Illyria lady"; and Illyria is the country of a dream.' It was a strong contrast with Peter Hall's much more realistic entry for Viola, gratefully arriving on some distant Adriatic shore. But Barton also used the long perspective to great comic effect for the entrance of Donald Sinden's Malvolio. He entered down through the slatted tunnel practising behaviour to his own shadow, loftily extending his hand and giving curt orders in dumbshow. Before he had

spoken a word, we realised that Malvolio was in the grip of his own fantasy.

But the real secret of Barton's production was that the characters were presented with all their contradictions intact and endowed with a wealth of detail. Judi Dench's Viola, for instance, in her wooing of Olivia on Orsino's behalf was more ironic than impassioned on 'Make me a willow cabin at your gate'. But the comedy gave way to something deeper in the short scene where Malvolio catches up with her to give her Olivia's ring: innocent astonishment was replaced by tremulous self-doubt on 'Disguise, I see thou art a wickedness Wherein the pregnant enemy does much'. And, yet again, this gave way to the anguish of unspoken love as she bit her lip while watching the effect of Feste's 'Come away, come away, death' on Orsino. But this was not a performance made up of momentary effects. J. W. Lambert again got it right when he wrote: 'Miss Dench manages to be sturdy, steadfast and — if the word doesn't sound absurd — spiritual at the same time; not least in her tiny scene with the Fool and his tabor, where bickering upon a bench they seem to discover in each other the same bewildered hard-pressed love of life.'

For a description of Donald Sinden's Malvolio, I commend you to the actor's own chapter in his book *Laughter in the Second Act* (Hodder and Stoughton). It offers a vivid account of the way an actor builds up a character partly by creating an imaginary biography for him and partly by seeking visual inspiration in the outside world: in this case, it was Graham Sutherland's portrait of Somerset Maugham with its turned-down mouth, its thinning hair, and its vaguely jaundiced look. Sinden also records mild disputes with John Barton about the propriety of Malvolio's responding to Olivia's injunction, 'Run after that same peevish messenger', by himself repeating the word 'Run'. Barton disapproved and asked Sinden to leave the gag out on nights when fellow-scholars were known to be in front. But Sinden is also fascinating on how he reconciled his detailed characterisation with his ability to address the audience directly. I have never, in fact, seen a Malvolio make more of the letter-reading scene simply by acknowledging our response to his words. I recall even now Sinden on 'These be her very C's, her U's and her T's; and thus makes she her great P's', shooting a lock of mock-reproof to the gallery at its burst of unseemly laughter. Sinden managed to play the house without, in any degree, diminishing his ability to play the character.

But Barton's most intriguing innovation in this production was his upgrading of the ages of the characters. The Viola and the

Olivia (Lisa Harrow) were both young. But Bill Fraser's Sir Toby was an ageing, far-gone Falstaff with a touch of melancholy defeat about him. Barrie Ingham's Sir Andrew was a hapless Scot, beadily scrambling for the smallest coin in his sporran or proffering unwanted posies to Olivia: hearing that she couldn't abide anything yellow, he quietly and sadly concealed the little bunch of primroses with which he had been hoping to woo her and thereafter carried only pink flowers. The age of Sir Toby and Sir Andrew lent extraordinary poignancy to Feste's delivery of 'O Mistress mine': the two of them sat listening to the song in a state of rheumy-eyed retrospection while Feste watched them with tender irony. And by playing Maria (first Brenda Bruce, later Elizabeth Spriggs) as a fiftyish governess rather than a pert serving-maid, Barton deepened the sense of pathos: one recalls this Maria lurking in a door's shadow to look back anxiously at Sir Toby draining one more tankard.

Barton invested *Twelfth Night* with psychological detail without depriving it of its magic. Indeed, J.C. Trewin picked out a revealing example of the way Barton's immaculate sense of detail enriched the production. Trewin highlighted 'the passage when, as Sebastian comes downstage with "This is the air, that is the glorious sun", we hear faintly, from underground, the baffled sobbing of Malvolio.' This gift for allowing the mood of one scene to linger into the next is not only the mark of a great director. It is also the surest way to realise *Twelfth Night* to the full and to give us the play in all its emotional complexity.

'Everyone is connected to everyone else,' Ronald Bryden wrote of Barton's production, citing as an example Olivia's troubled glance after Malvolio thrust his chain of office into her hands and stumbled away. The exact opposite was true of the next RSC revival directed by Peter Gill in 1974. The dominant image on the back wall of William Dudley's bare set was of Narcissus gazing down into his pool, and we were presented with a group of characters all intoxicated with their own reflections. The function of Viola and Sebastian, as Irving Wardle noted in *The Times*, was 'to put them through an Ovidian obstacle course from which they learn to turn away from their mirror and form real attachments'.

All very well in theory; but, in practice, it led to a somewhat cold, unfeeling production, short on comedy and lacking that dense network of relationships one found in the Barton production. It was hard, for instance, to imagine Patricia Hayes's busy-bee Maria forming any attachment to David Waller's gruff, free-loading Sir Toby. And although Frank Thornton's Sir Andrew

(elaborating on a now familiar RSC joke by wearing in his hat a yellow feather — the colour Olivia abhorred) was a rather good dejected White Knight with no will of his own, he seemed to have no particular interest in Olivia. Even the late John Price's Orsino, lying back on cushions fondling whichever favourite happened to be nearest, was simply a variation on the theme of romantic narcissism. Self-love may have been the theme, but what one missed was a particularised sense of Illyria, once excellently described by Hugh Leonard as 'a fairyland with back streets'.

As so often in a moderate *Twelfth Night*, one was left admiring one single performance: in this case, Nicol Williamson's Malvolio. While not being in the same class as Sinden's, it was founded on a combination of innate loneliness and emotional pain. His snarling, peremptory dismissal of Ron Pember's cockney Feste for once justified the plot against him. In the garden-scene, he cut a sadly ridiculous figure as he distended his mouth into grotesque shapes in an attempt to make the cryptic letters form a meaningful word. And in the final scene he tore Maria's epistle into miniscule fragments before departing to his own permanent private hell. Malvolio was the greatest narcissist of the lot; and the only one who finally resisted cure.

But although the production was based on a sound logical principle, it lacked lyricism and laughter. Mr. Gill made his name as a director with his meticulously realistic productions of three plays by D. H. Lawrence. But instead of applying the same kind of detail to Shakespeare, he stripped the action of social context and human warmth. It was a modest production rather than an indifferent one; but it suggested again that the dreamlike environment of Illyria needs to be realised on stage with a fierce particularity without going to the absurd lengths of the Victorian hyper-realists.

The play came round again in 1979 in a production by Terry Hands: an Anglicised reworking of a version he had originally created for the Comédie Française. Some found it extravagantly original: others (myself included) thought it tended to underscore things that should rise easily from the text. Thus Mr. Hands had Geoffrey Hutchings's turnip-faced Feste (who, incidentally, was on stage throughout) repeat the line 'Youth's a stuff will not endure' at the end of the drinking-scene lest we had missed the point. But the production was blessedly funny and offered a drastic re-interpretation of one particular role. Visually, Mr. Hands's (and the designer John Napier's) chief conceit was to take the title literally. The evening began in midwinter with snow underfoot, bare, silvery branches, frosted crates serving as both

seats and as lanterns when illuminated from within, and with a blurred, watery full moon above. Only after the interval did daffodils begin to peer and trees to blossom. As Garry O'Connor pointed out in *The Financial Times*, 'all very effective and decorous but it does ignore the necessity that Act Three Scenes One and Two (in which Viola returns to the proxy wooing of Olivia and Sir Andrew is dissuaded from returning home) must follow a matter of hours only after the previous scene.' The time-scheme of *Twelfth Night* is, in fact, a crucial matter to be explored in discussion.

But Mr. Hands's boldest stroke was to capitalise on the youthfulness of his Olivia (Kate Nicholls) by emphasising that she was smitten hip and thigh with love for Cesario. It is a mark of how much Shakespearean production had changed that back in 1955 Maxine Audley, in the prettified Gielgud production, followed stage-tradition by playing Olivia as a serene, mature beauty: Kate Nicholls was more like an Angela Brazil head-girl discovering the giddy delights of young love. Benedict Nightingale in the *New Statesman* approved mightily and described vividly:

> She has no sooner swept on stage than she has thrown aside her mourning veil to reveal a lavish auburn mane that at once justifies her overweening vanity and gives due warning of her torrid temperament. Before long this pre-Raphaelite beauty is proclaiming her loves and hates with a flamboyance that must be audible halfway across Illyria, and enthusiastically matching voice with movement and gesture. She flirtatiously rubs up against Malvolio, flings aside the wretched Ague-Cheek, and proceeds to astonish Cesario-Viola with the physical frankness of her unruly emotions. 'To one of your receiving enough is shown,' she cries, and promptly disproves her own words by leaping at her, cuddling her, and pursuing her pell-mell through the garden. At one moment of high excitement she seems actually to be trying to rape her, and at another she blunders into and very nearly knocks flat one of the spindly, woebegone trees that cower onstage, like crones in a gymnasium. It is as if defloration were not enough: this rampaging lady will be satisfied with nothing short of deforestation.

But in addition to a rampaging, headstrong Olivia, there was a Viola from Cherie Lunghi full of wit and feeling. In her first scene, where she was shivering, barefoot and palpably shipwrecked, you actually saw her slowly forming the idea of

appearing as 'an eunuch' to Orsino as if in love with the notion of him before she had seen him. And later, as they listened to Feste's 'Come away, come away, death', she wrapped him protectively in her cloak while gazing at him with enslaved intensity. John Woodvine's Malvolio was also extremely funny. For once it seemed entirely plausible that he should fall into the waiting trap since Olivia frequently nuzzled and caressed him and treated him as a useful platonic escort. Mr. Woodvine also went the whole hog by appearing not just in yellow-stockings but in a saffron body-stocking with bulging codpiece, which he periodically flashed, and in a ringleted hairdo that Harpo Marx would not have disowned. It may not have had the precise social placement of Sinden's performance, but it undeniably worked. The originality of this production, however, was that it put Olivia and Viola right at the very centre of the play, and seemed a further exploration of the idea which Shakespeare offered a couple of years earlier in *As You Like It* that 'Love is merely a madness'.

If Terry Hands's production was full of the wild exuberance of young love, John Caird's 1983 RSC revival was widely perceived to be dark, autumnal, and melancholic. Partly this was because of Robin Don's outdoor setting, apparently inspired by Giorgione's *La Tempesta* in the Academy at Venice and well described by Michael Coveney in *The Financial Times*: 'The play is set on a neo-classical exterior with Illyria a cliff-top retreat where the waves beat against a distant shore and a jutting, craggy knoll pushes out and away into the sky. A great gnarled tree dominates the stage. To the left, we see the neglected pillars and wrought-iron gates of Olivia's fortress. To the right, a chapel with a flickering candle by the door.' Never before had we been made so aware of the elements in a production of *Twelfth Night*. What is more, the permanent set managed to accommodate the play's various shifts of locale. Orsino's court was encamped on the craggy knoll. The below-stairs revels were out in the open as night gave way to dawn. The gulling of Malvolio was observed by his persecutors entwined in the branches of the overhanging tree. The Sir Topaz scene was played with Feste addressing his victim down a well. Obviously the alfresco setting made for a few textual oddities (such as Olivia's reported request to Malvolio to turn the nocturnal revellers 'out of doors') but the success of the production depended very much on its creation of a complete and plausible Illyrian world. Ilona Sekacz's music, filling Illyria with waterwashed sounds, also brought the play closer to *The Tempest* than the inland pastoral world of *As You Like It*.

Inside this fantasy-world, however, there was a strong sense of emotional reality: something Mr. Caird may possibly have inherited from the production of *Peter Pan* that he had earlier co-directed with Trevor Nunn. Gemma Jones, for instance, made Maria a social-climbing gentlewoman, conscious of her status in Olivia's household, but also thrilled to be in the company of John Thaw's acerbic bully of a Sir Toby and raptly determined to become Lady Belch. You could even see the precise moment (her fierce bellow at Malvolio — 'Go shake your ears') when she decided to burn her boats in Olivia's household and throw in her lot with the opposition. The same care was invested in the Viola-Olivia relationship. Unlike some previous Violas, Zoë Wanamaker was not tickled or amused to discover her own sexual drawing-power, but palpably troubled both by Olivia's declaration of love and by her own equivocal response to it: a contemporary female equivalent of the sexual ambiguity inherent in any Elizabethan production when two boys were thrown into close emotional contact. Without going quite as far as Mr. Hands's Olivia, Sarah Berger was also young, vehement, and quick to strike twelve, as when she intervened in Sir Toby's attack on Cesario by raining fierce blows on the back of her sottish cousin.

'Brooding' was the word Giles Gordon used to describe Mr. Caird's treatment of the play, but the comedy, where appropriate, was given due measure. The late Emrys James was always a full-blooded actor and his Malvolio was character-istically robust. One thing about the character has become increasingly clear over the years. If Malvolio is no more than an uppish steward, then the plot against him leaves behind a sour taste. If, however, he is genuinely threatening, the machinations of Maria and the rest have some motive. Emrys James realised that, making him an obstreperous, finger-wagging tyrant who genuinely deserved a moral lesson. But Mr. James (Feste in the Barton production) had also learned something from Sinden's technique of acknowledging the audience: in this case, Mr. James whipped himself into a state of erotic fervour while reading the letter, which he then proceeded to brandish at the front stalls in a state of sheer disbelief. The comedy in Mr. Caird's production was there (not least in Daniel Massey's goofy, limp-stockinged Ague-Cheek, constantly looking on at the witty folk in dazed incomprehension) but it derived from character and served as a counterpoint to the autumnal setting.

Four years later the play came round again at Stratford-upon-Avon in Bill Alexander's production: a highly enjoyable one that

raised many fascinating questions. The determining feature was Kit Surrey's geographically precise set: a sun-kissed, white-walled, travel-brochure Greek island full of shadowy ginnels and exotic arches. This was an Illyria that existed as a real place on the map. But, in dispensing with such traditional features as a ring of box-trees for Olivia's garden, Mr. Alexander had to come up with new solutions to old problems: thus in the gulling of Malvolio the malevolent jokers were not placed immediately behind the uppity steward but peered at him through overhead windows. Some, such as Michael Coveney, welcomed the jettisoning of generations of hackneyed stage-business. Others, such as Stanley Wells in *Shakespeare Survey 41*, debated the wisdom of relocating that particular scene: 'Much of the scene's comedy', wrote Professor Wells, 'derives from the tension between Malvolio's self-absorption and the danger that they (Sir Toby, Sir Andrew, and Fabian) will burst into it with their outraged reactions to his presumptions. Placing them in windows where they had little freedom of movement upset the balance of the scene, throwing too much emphasis on Malvolio's fantasies, too little on the tricksters who had stimulated them.'

But in Stratford-on-Avon, where Antony Sher played the part, Malvolio's fantasies were very much at the heart of the production. Mr. Sher and Mr. Alexander had worked together twice before, on *Richard III* and (earlier in the same season) *The Merchant of Venice*: the result, on each occasion, had been a crucial redefinition of the central character. The intention here, quite clearly, was to push both the comedy and tragedy of Malvolio to its utmost limits: opinions varied wildly on how far the device succeeded, but it was certainly an audacious experiment.

In the early scenes, Mr. Sher was outrageously funny. He came on looking like a bug-eyed Archbishop Makarios dressed in black from his fez to his gaiters. You could see that he was totally enslaved by Olivia by the way he rushed off to rinse her tear-stained handkerchief under the village pump and by his unnerving habit of popping up from behind walls like a private eye every time she cried 'What ho'. In the cross-gartered scene he even turned the linings of his pockets and hat inside out to show that they too were yellow.

The real controversy centred on the final scenes, which Mr. Sher played as if Malvolio had been driven out of his wits: in the prison-scene he was tethered to a stake by a halter and he was last seen essaying cross-gartered high kicks as if totally deranged.

Stanley Wells made the point that 'If Malvolio has a tragedy, it is not that he goes mad but that he remains irremediably sane.' But, for Charles Osborne in *The Daily Telegraph*, Mr. Sher remained 'the most charismatic Malvolio I have seen since Donald Sinden and Laurence Olivier'.

But the production was not sheer Sher. Harriet Walter's Viola had a gentle erotic melancholy: I also retain an image of her, at the moment of Sebastian's reappearance, standing with hands flattened against the wall, like a knife-thrower's apprentice, in stunned disbelief. David Bradley's Ague-Cheek was also far and away the best since Richard Johnson's in Peter Hall's production. Mr. Bradley's mournful, spaniel eyes and long, lean body, tapering down to spindle shanks in bedraggled green stockings, induced laughter every time he came on stage. He also combined the manic with the depressive. During the midnight revels he suddenly went wild and started jumping vehemently up and down on the spot as if treading invisible grapes. But when urged later by Roger Allam's strong, bullying Sir Toby (Hardy to his Laurel), he vaguely demurred and limped off to his cubiculo, only to crawl back seconds later to fulfil his role of eternal whipping-boy. A brilliant performance in a production that (as often happens) matured between Stratford and London, and that raised many important questions. To what extent is Illyria a state of mind or a real Mediterranean locale? And how much is the play Malvolio's tragedy or simply a turning-point in Shakespearean comedy in which, for the first time, the merry fooling is pervaded by a sense of loss?

It is a measure of the extent to which new young companies capable of performing Shakespeare are springing up that in the same year (1987) as Mr. Alexander's production opened in Stratford, two other versions of *Twelfth Night* were seen in London. Diversity is good — but both of the rival productions raised fundamental questions about the staging of Shakespeare and the extent to which liberties may be taken with the text.

Declan Donnellan's production for Cheek by Jowl, which arrived in London at the Donmar Warehouse after a long provincial tour, was by far the more irreverent of the two. It began with Viola's arrival in Illyria. It treated Ague-Cheek as, in Michael Ratcliffe's phrase, 'a tumescent jack-rabbit from the boondocks of Middle America', and gave the saxophone-playing Maria a Brooklyn twang. It had Orsino petting Cesario as heavily and unequivocally as Olivia did. It showed the gay Antonio at the last striking up a liaison with Feste. And, most controversially, it

had the midnight revellers singing a drunken, bellowed version of 'My Way'. How one reacted was a matter of choice. For Michael Ratcliffe in *The Observer*, 'This was a *Twelfth Night* for those who have never seen the play before and those who thought they never wanted to see it again.' For Peter Kemp in *The Independent*: 'Self-indulgence — mocked in *Twelfth Night* — is pandered to in this production. The cast strain to seem cute and street-wise. But, for all their contortions in search of "sophistication", clod-hopping callowness prevails.'

Kenneth Branagh directed a much more sober and intelligent production for the Renaissance Theatre Company at the Riverside Studios. I felt there were some mistakes. The snow-flaked Victorian Christmas setting swathed the production in a misleading prettiness. Some of the darker areas of the play went unexplored: the Sir Toby was simply a bland buffoon and the Maria a neat lady's maid with little hint of admiration for a drunken sot. And, once again, the order of the first two scenes was reversed, which implied a certain tone-deafness to Shakespeare's musical statement of his themes.

But, elsewhere, Mr. Branagh showed a sensitivity to the play's shifting mood and combined a first-rate Malvolio (Richard Briers) with a sense of ensemble. The Victorian setting helped to give social precision to a Malvolio whom Mr. Briers played as a frockcoated, wildly ambitious fanatic: a combination of Mr. Murdstone and Samuel Smiles. For once his ambitions had more to do with class than sex. In the box-tree scene, Mr. Briers skirted the usual innuendoes to stress his dream of being '*Count* Malvolio'; and at his next sighting of Sir Toby he extended to him an outflung hand like a Richard the Third who had been boning up on Self-Help. It was a star performance without being a stage-hogging one, and was nicely balanced by Anton Lesser's shaggy-locked Feste, Frances Barber's clear-spoken Viola, and Caroline Langrishe's Olivia, who combined aristocratic beauty with clear hints that she could not wait to get her hands on Orsino's boy-emissary.

Looking back over its stage history, what is clear is that *Twelfth Night* is now and always has been an extremely elusive play. It rarely fails to afford pleasure or to yield a batch of memorable performances. But, equally, it is difficult to achieve what Stanley Wells calls 'the transmuting alchemy' that unlocks its ambivalent darkness and resonant comedy. In company with four RSC directors, who have had practical experience of working on the play, it now seems sensible to take up some of the questions

the play poses. How does one achieve a balance between the play's light and dark aspects? How much of the mood of a production is determined by the casting and, specifically, the age of the actors involved? How far can one go in treating the play as a realistic picture of a particular society? Is there any one character who determines the tone of a production? How does one embody Illyria on stage? Obviously there is no single, right or wrong answer to these or multifarious other questions. Each production throws up its own solutions. But only by addressing the questions with skilled practitioners can one begin to get to the heart of this most haunting, beautiful, and opal-like of all Shakespeare's comedies.

What Kind of Play?

Michael Billington John Russell Brown wrote in 1961 that *Twelfth Night* 'might have been designed for an age when each director must make his name and register his mark'. In other words, it's a play of infinite possibilities. But the key question seems to me how much one regards it as a festive piece of saturnalia, written for a very specific occasion, and how much as a dark comedy about impermanence and pain. And I wondered when you were first thinking about the play, was it the light or the dark side of *Twelfth Night* that you were looking at most?

John Barton: I suppose every director has to decide, or feel, which way he wants to tip the balance, and sometimes it's very much pushed one way, sometimes another. So my main wish was to keep what I thought might be a right balance, because it's not as simple as just seeing the play at one or other of those polarities. It's so full of contradictions and different elements that it's hard to bring them *all* out; and usually, I think, a production, either through casting or design or what happens in rehearsal, tends to iron them out. I certainly had in mind that simple 'either/or', but very soon I stopped defining it just in those terms. I thought that the area of magic fairyland was terribly important. Equally I thought that the sea in the background was as basic as the idea of a festive comedy or a dark comedy, because it's got something of the romantic quality of people being washed up on shore and drowned — people finding one another — which connects it more with the late plays. But then the trouble with saying 'Is is a late play, or a middle play, or whatever?' is that these are labels invented in a rather desperate attempt to define something that has already happened. And I'd rather look at it the other way round, trying to find out and bring out what's in it rather than to label it.

Michael Billington Terry, can you find any label that applies to *Twelfth Night* or is it, as John implies, a play that almost defies categorisation?

Terry Hands I agree with John. I don't think it helps to see the

play in terms of festive or dark. If we're talking about a comedy, then in Shakespeare's terms we're talking about a play which concerns itself with marriage and the approach to that, and whether, in each case, it's good or it's bad. It appears to be potentially optimistic in the case of two couples.

Michael Billington   Which two?

Terry Hands   Olivia and Sebastian, and Viola and Orsino: it looks as though they've got a chance. Whereas you feel the Belch-Maria marriage hasn't. So, in that case, it seems bound to be a play examining relationships and the way to the state of marriage. Therefore, there are bound to be melancholy aspects and there are bound to be optimistic aspects.

Certainly, what I got from John's production was what seemed to me to be, through his use of the sea, which I stole, very much that sense of timelessness and therefore of a natural order of things. And I suppose my own feelings were about winter and spring, and that *Twelfth Night* meant just that — the sixth of January, the moment when you take down the decorations and Christmas is over. The festive moment has passed, and this is now the cruellest point of the year. The old leaves are going to come off the trees, but the young ones are going to come through strongly, and the oldies are going to be humiliated and lost. *But* you feel that the cycle will continue, the wind and the rain, that it will start all over again.

So the melancholy of it, plus the madness, those two things, defy a simple categorisation of 'Yes, it is festive' or, 'No, it's not festive'. It was the feeling I had very strongly that this would go on and on. Just like the seasons happen again, so these moments would happen again. The spring would come again for the youngsters and leaves would drop off the trees for the old ones. And so I saw it as a natural cycle, and within the womb of the sea. That all seemed to fit the play.

Michael Billington   The fact is, though, that the title implies that the play was written for a celebratory occasion, and there is evidence showing that it was performed on certain festive occasions, as at Middle Temple Hall in 1602. . . .

John Caird   There is evidence that it was a play Shakespeare thought about for a very long time and then wrote very quickly. That's what I've always felt about it. But the full title is *Twelfth*

Night, or What You Will. And I can imagine somebody coming to Shakespeare, who has written a play to be performed for the first time on Twelfth Night, and saying, 'Well, what are you going to call it?' and him saying, '*Twelfth Night* — or what you will, I don't care.' And somebody says, 'Bill, that's a wonderful title. Call it that.'

Bill Alexander   I'd go a little further. I think that for me, when I was studying the play, the title was a kind of distraction. I'd often read things which said that the title *Twelfth Night* meant that it was a revels play. I don't actually see anything in the play which suggests that. It is a comedy dealing with all the things that Shakespeare deals with in comedy: justice, love, madness, the truth of love between people. I myself subscribe to the view that it was originally called *What You Will* because that title fits in very well with *As You Like It*, *Much Ado about Nothing*, *Measure for Measure*. That kind of title was very common for Shakespeare writing that kind of play.

The theory that I enjoyed reading was that because there was another play called *What You Will* written around about the same time, he quickly had to think of another title so as not to clash; and because they found they were performing it for the first time for a particular Twelfth Night celebration, he said, 'Oh well, we'd better call it *Twelfth Night* then, as that's when we're going to be doing it.' So I don't find the title helpful, in fact I find it quite distracting because it can give you a focus to do with that particular point of the year, to do with Terry Hands's winter and the end of festivities, that I don't find in the play. I have never seen it as a 'revels' comedy, whatever that means, or felt that its themes particularly tie up with the time of the year.

Seasons, Months, and Days

John Barton   I agree with all those comments, and I think the confusion is in the title, as Bill says, because it was performed on a Twelfth Night occasion and it got the title that way. I agree that there's the area in it that Terry describes, the winter-to-spring theme, but of course that isn't connected with Twelfth Night. *That's* connected with the end of February and Lent, right back to the return of Persephone in Greek mythology. So it's nothing to do with Twelfth Night, but the title suggests it is, and I nearly went very wrong because of that, because for a long time I couldn't get

3

away from an absolute conviction that the play had to end with the taking down of decorations from a Christmas tree. I took weeks before rejecting that, because I saw it didn't work for the play, though it seemed a wonderful idea when I had it.

Michael Billington Since we're onto the subject of the seasons, could we talk about the seasons in which you chose to set your productions? Terry, I remember you went for a very clear, very sharp distinction, didn't you? The first act of your production was wintry, chill, cold — the second act was spring. That was deduced from the text? Or from the mood of the text?

Terry Hands Both. I agree with John. I don't think you actually have to be as visual or as certain as that. John set it indoors and it was this wonderful candlelit world. I set it outdoors, and therefore in outdoor terms had to make some point about that. I took it very much that Twelfth Night marked the end of the revels, and that there were a group of people who wanted them to continue — specifically Toby Belch and Sir Andrew. But this was the beginning of the tough part of the winter, and Malvolio would be in charge. So yes, I did begin it with snow, and everybody at that point seems to have failed. There's no more revelry, there are to be no more cakes and ale. Olivia is in mourning for her brother. There's the disaster of the shipwreck which has thrown the girl up on the beach. Orsino is in the middle of this dying-fall feeling of fantasy. Feste is a failed fool. You're at the bleakest point of the year. And there's a battle which takes place between those who in their different ways are insistent upon that, the Malvolios and the Belches, while at the same time there are the beginnings of new life. But Shakespeare's time scheme is never the same as our own — and here there are double time schemes, triple time schemes. I certainly felt that, as it were, the first daffodils of spring were the yellow stockings.

Michael Billington But while you, Terry, went for two contrasted seasons, Bill, your production was the most recent, and you went for one season, the summer season?

Bill Alexander Very much so. I went for one season, but different times of the day within it. Terry is quite right to point out the double time schemes in the play, which one of these days someone's going to write an absolutely definitive, wonderful essay about.

4

Michael Billington Could you explain briefly what you mean by a 'double time scheme'?

Bill Alexander Well, perhaps the best example is between the last part of *Henry VI* and the beginning of *Richard III*, when clearly an awful lot has happened between Edward IV coming to the throne and the beginning of the following play. And yet in one of his early speeches Richard refers to the young Prince Edward, 'who some three months since I killed in my angry mood at Tewkesbury'. Yet actually sixteen years of history have elapsed. And in *Twelfth Night* there is no particular evidence of the passing of a particular number of weeks or a particular number of months, right? The sense of it, for me, is of events happening within a few days.

John Caird No, there is precise information.

Bill Alexander There is precise information, but it's precisely *contradictory* information, which is why there's a *triple* time scheme. I define the time schemes as, first, what your sense of time is; second, what information you're actually given; and third, how that information internally contradicts itself. A few days have passed between Viola becoming Cesario, right? And then three months are said to have passed at the end on the reappearance of Antonio.

John Caird But the double time scale is three days and three months, precisely. If you look through the play, it's very clear that whenever a night-time scene happens, the next morning something else has happened and you've moved on. But Shakespeare makes you feel that a lot more time is passing because the events are so momentous. So by the time you get to the end of the play, with Orsino saying, 'For these three months he has been with me', you are not in the least bit surprised, because it does feel like Viola's travail in love has lasted for three months. But the triple time scale is, of course, that the play takes almost precisely three hours to perform. So you're dealing with three hours, three days, and three months — a fascinating reverberation.

Bill Alexander That's right, and that's why in production, to get a double sense of time, you have to feel that enough time has passed to make the events believable. But what I tried to do within that was to give the shape of morning, midday, and evening,

roughly twice over. That's how I felt it in terms of times of day, although on another level, you feel three months have gone by.

John Barton The trouble is that the technical label 'double time' creates rather than defines problems, because it's in most of Shakespeare, and in many other Elizabethan and Jacobean plays. They didn't think twice about it, they didn't need to label it, and nobody raised any questions. The questions actually that the director now has to handle are very often in explaining it to the actors, because if the actors study their text and say, 'But it says there and it says there', they find they're affected, and it actually becomes difficult for them. But they are inventing a problem which Shakespeare doesn't know exists.

John Caird Well, I think that the seasons are irrelevant to this play, because they're not in the text.

Michael Billington 'More matter for a May morning?'

John Caird Well, think about it. If you read *As You Like It*, the sea is not mentioned once. Not once. And that's astonishing: it's a very long play, it's got masses and masses of natural imagery in it, but the sea is not once mentioned. Yet as John has pointed out, the sea is mentioned in *Twelfth Night*, fifty to sixty times. It's a constant image. And as with all his plays, Shakespeare is working from his own palette of vocabulary and imagery. He chose the particular things he wanted to write about and to tell the story through. And he doesn't concentrate on the seasons at all. He mentions a month here and he mentions something that you could associate with seasons elsewhere, but he's much more concerned with the sea.

Now the sea is something which in England anyway is seasonal to a certain extent, but actually has its own life. It can be stormy and aggressive in the middle of winter — or in the middle of summer. It can be calm in the middle of summer, it can be calm in the middle of winter. It is beyond the seasons. It is something that has an absolute danger and an infinite number of possibilities within it.

And so, I felt that Shakespeare simply wasn't interested in the turning of the seasons. In *As You Like It*, it is of absolute importance, when two little boys come out and sing about the spring, at that particular moment in the play. He's handing it to you on a plate. That doesn't mean that the whole of *As You Like It*

up until that moment has to be about winter. That's rather a dogged, schematic way of looking at it. But it's very clear that from the very beginning of the play he's constantly on about the seasons, about how forbidding nature can be in the winter and how much more wonderful it is in the summer, and how spring is regenerative and all that.

So in *Twelfth Night* I went for the prevailing notion of the sea. Terry said he stole the 'sea' idea from John. I think we all stole it from Shakespeare! The sea is so prevalent in the text, you just can't avoid it. And once you've concentrated on the sea image, the seasonal thing becomes less important. And actually, Terry, although you did say you concentrated on it, I think it wasn't as important as a lot of other very interesting things about your production.

John Barton   I don't think the seasons matter in the sense that, as John has said, to make a basically winter or spring decision is perfectly possible and not wrong, but it's not insisted on in the way that it is in *As You Like It*, or in *The Winter's Tale*. If I had to name the season I went for, I suppose it was autumn — not in calendar terms but in terms of casting and the age of the various people. I was very conscious of people being older or younger than usual, and what their middle age was like. And I looked at it that way, if that is a seasonal way.

Michael Billington   Autumnal in mood, in fact, rather than in specific setting?

John Barton   Autumnal in mood, but I thought that somewhere inside that there was an autumnal scene and a spring scene and a wintry scene — not necessarily in a conscious way, particularly as one did it with a permanent set and changed it very minimally. It was to do with mood rather than calendar.

Terry Hands   I would agree with John entirely. Where we're getting into a muddle is about the manifestation of the seasons in terms of décor. Just as you would say that *Merry Wives* is an autumnal play, the same is absolutely true of *Twelfth Night*. You don't in any way have to manifest that in terms of the design, though, if you don't feel like it. I personally think that the matter of the May morning has swept us on to that point, and that lines like 'this is very midsummer madness' are ambiguous. I mean, you can either stress it, 'This is midsummer *madness*', in which

7

case we know we're in midsummer. Or you can say, 'This is midsummer madness', and it might be the longest night of the year.

As John says, it's a question of the journey taken by the characters, which is an emotional journey. And that's really where the time schemes come in. All that Shakespeare was concerned about, I feel, is that certain characters were living their lives at a rate of intensity which would take say, a couple of days, and other characters were living their emotional lives at an intensity that would take a couple of weeks. That's all he was concerned about.

So John had the spring and he had the summer, but there were no physical manifestations. It so happens I allowed the snow to melt, the yellow stockings were the first daffodils, and the revelling in the night was an attempt to put Christmas back together — to put their Christmas tree back up. And Malvolio comes down and says, 'No, it's over, it's stopped.' Not only has it stopped, it's bad luck to continue.

What is Illyria?

Michael Billington We're on now to the crucial question which seems to be fundamental to the play, of how you make Illyria manifest on stage. One commentator says, 'The play is set in the limitless and immortal land of dreams', but obviously for stage purposes you've got to be absolutely precise about where you are. I'd like to talk about the contrasting decisions you took. Both John Barton and you, Terry Hands, went for quite a bare stage, with fairly minimal scenery, while both John Caird and Bill Alexander were much more detailed, even archaeologically exact. John Caird, you gave us, or rather your designer Robin Don did, a very precise rocky, craggy, rough piece of coast. Bill, you went for a Greek island. How were all these decisions taken?

John Barton Well, I thought through a lot of possibilities about making it a very specific ambience, and because in the end I couldn't find one that felt right, I ended up by doing the play on a stage rather than a set. That's one of the basic decisions one always has to make. Sometimes one feels very strongly that one's got to create a domestic world of great precision, and sometimes one fears that.

And I suppose it has to do with the whole question, 'What is Illyria?' I mean, even the word 'Illyria' resonates on a romantic

and mysterious level. It's a strange word, and I wanted to get that element of strangeness where it was relevant, so I made Viola coming out of the sea, or Sebastian and Viola meeting, those 'places' in the play, as magical, romantic, *Illyrian* in that sense, as I could. And, on the other hand, the mad, Feste and Malvolio side of the play, which is so strong in places, that had to be brought out as well.

One of the reasons why in the end I didn't try and define it locally, which I had rather wanted to do, was because I thought it would pin down and unify the mood too much, whereas I wanted to stress the extraordinary contradictions and contrasts of feeling — like the writing of the letter, and the scenes between Orsino and Viola. So in the end that is what I was groping for, but the solution that I worked with grew out of Chris Morley as designer responding to my worries about the alternatives.

Michael Billington   Terry, what do you feel about Illyria? Defining Illyria — how precise do you have to be?

Terry Hands   Well, I don't believe you have to be scenically precise at all. The place is defined by the characters and the journey they undertake. It's also defined by where you play it: both John and I felt that it was a chamber play, that you only have fourteen people on that stage and you're not required to have any more. *Othello* is a chamber play, with six characters, or even fewer, and if you're doing it in a very big theatre, then you have to define a chamber within that. So also with *Twelfth Night*.

Now that means some reduction of the space. You can do that either by having a great deal of scenery, by actually filling the space up with things, or you can do as John did. He used the white boxes Chris Morley designed for Stratford in 1969. There was this huge white box which was really designed for the season of late plays which do require great kind of cinemascope spaces.

John put his willow cabin in this: the production was all set inside a willow cabin, which effectively reduced the space. It allowed us to concentrate on the performers in a chamber within a bigger space, and we followed the journey of their emotions. In my case, again I used a platform — an outdoor solution with some little box trees, which again reduced the space but enabled the story to flow. That was filling up the middle air, which you've always got to worry about when you're working on a proscenium stage.

John Barton Terry's put his finger on one of the crucial problems that we all have with Shakespeare, which is the question of labelling the plays in terms of 'chamber' or 'epic'. Some plays require the one, some the other, and some require a mixture of the two. I felt about *Twelfth Night*, where there was this huge white box which clad the whole space of the theatre, that I needed to make it more domestic. But the chamber that we made was all done with skeletal frames and gauze, so that at times it could be lit to show a mysterious world beyond. I wanted to do that because I thought that was a way of suggesting magic and the sea and the world outside that they'd come from.

Michael Billington John Caird, your decision was different, wasn't it? You gave us a very large, stage-filling coastline.

John Caird Terry has defined the problem: of course it's a chamber play, but the difficulty that we have at the RSC is that we have to do Shakespeare's chamber plays in a theatre that is designed on the Victorian principles of epic pictorial theatre, with a huge great big picture-frame on one side of the building and lots of seats on the other. That was one of the things that affected my decision about how to design the play. We had had two or three years of minimalism in that space — most productions were in one way or the other taking the square-footage floor measurement of The Other Place theatre, and putting that in one way or another on top of the main house stage. We kept doing it. John, you did several productions — *Love's Labour Lost*, *Hamlet*, *The Merchant* — where you put the Other Place dimensions into the main theatre, and other directors did exactly the same thing, because we had all been so regenerated by working at The Other Place and by seeing each other's work there. And I felt strongly that the need now was somehow to come clean about the way the big theatre was built, and what the people who built it meant when they built it.

Another reason for doing what I did was that I felt that one of the great difficulties of the play is the scene you mentioned, the box-tree scene — people hiding in a tree, *the* box-tree, not *a* box-tree. And it seemed to me that a design solution that provided for the great comic scene of the play in a literal way, but had not sort of broadcast itself as a solution from the beginning, would be a good thing.

I also talked to the designer about the tree being in some way representative of the more traditional ancestral things in the play.

You know, people talk about fathers and being old, and the rebirth of some characters, and the feeling that this is a play that is taking a slice out of a long history of people's lives.

Michael Billington So it's the tree as metaphor?

John Caird The tree as metaphor. I said to the designer, 'I want the sea to be very present. I want the feeling of the sea just rumbling away there all the time, to be there.' And what Robin Don did was to find a seafan, only about this high, to stick on the model. The tree was actually made out of something which grew under the sea, because that was the other world. These were the ingredients that I gave to the designer, and he came up with something rather different from what we saw initially. But we talked about it and slowly it took the form you then saw. It was very naturalistic.

'How do you define Illyria?' is a slightly different question. As John says, it's a very mysterious place. It is romantic — that part of the play that's to do with danger and death, and with being shipwrecked, and Shakespeare suggesting that if you go on a voyage you might run into trouble. If you go on a journey to anywhere, you can get thrown up on the shore and have your world turned upside down.

But the other thing he's saying is that if you set sail from England on your way to Illyria and you finally get there, you find you are back in England. At least half the play is like an *Alice in Wonderland* version of England — it's all Toby Belch, Malvolio, Andrew Ague-Cheek and Feste. Probably well over three-quarters of the play is like a Lewis Carroll version of an English country house. It's not Illyria at all.

A Displaced Englishness?

Michael Billington That's true in Shakespearean comedy in general though, isn't it? You're always coming back to England whether you're nominally in Athens or wherever? But Bill, your decision was different again, wasn't it — to go for a geographically specific Illyria?

Bill Alexander The question that faces us all with all of Shakespeare's plays is: do you go for the design solutions that are stage solutions, that basically are there to underline and serve

conceptual and subtextual elements in the play; or do you go for the kind of solutions that create a recognisable social ambience against which people's behaviour can be explained and set in relief?

I chose the latter in my production, and the particular ambience I chose was based on the fact that I worked out the voyage that Sebastian and Viola were on. We know they come from Messaline, right? That's probably Marseilles, down there on the south coast of France. And they obviously had not intended to go to Illyria, otherwise why did they not know where they were? They were probably on their way to Venice, I reckoned, which would be a natural place to get caught up in a hurricane and swept onto the Illyrian coast, which is a perfectly real place in what is now northern Greece or Yugoslavia.

So, I decided to make the radical but really unexceptional decision that Illyria is precisely where Illyria really was. Now Shakespeare probably knew it was there, but he almost certainly had never been there, and probably didn't know much about it except the fact that it was hottish. Because one of the things he does is to write all the time about the manners and behavioural patterns of the people that he knows around him. And therefore you can say that everything that happens in the play is English. So why does he choose to set it abroad — unlike, say, Jonson in most of his plays, which are set in London against a very realistic background? I think he does it for its compression value: it's almost like saying that when people are displaced, their characteristics become heightened in some way. It enables us to look at the ways in which we behave and relate to each other under a sort of microscope. There's an intensification of human behaviour.

I also think that *Twelfth Night* is a very realistic play in the timbre of its dialogue, in the aspects of human behaviour that it's exploring, in the whole feel of it. And therefore I wanted to put it in the context of a naturalistic world: so I chose a place that was recognisable to any member of a modern British audience who had been on holiday to Greece.

But at the back of my mind there was the fact that you have to account for behaviour. You have to account for the relationship between love and madness in the play. And although I never hoped that anyone in the audience would actually get this, I almost saw the people as essentially English, but living in a climate that didn't suit them — a climate that actually brought out elements of madness in them, particularly Malvolio. Malvolio is a classic case of an Englishman who should not have gone out in the midday

sun. The things that Malvolio believes about himself and is made to believe are quite extraordinary, and they always tend towards a critique of a particular kind of vanity in human behaviour that can, if uncontrolled, lead to madness. Olivia says, as Terry's pointed out, 'This is very midsummer madness', what's going on here. It's the madness of an individual who has blinkered himself to the realities of his situation, his personality, and the aspirations that he can have. Therefore, when it comes to the point where he's been through the yellow stockings scene and people are about to come on stage and tell him that he's mad, he is going over everything that has just happened as if it confirms his aspirations and what he believes. Whereas what the audience can quite clearly see is that the evidence contradicts him, if he'd only listen with a sane and rational mind to it. It's a classic case of someone hearing only what they want to hear.

I wanted to intensify that, by setting the play in a hot country where the heat gets to people, but modifying the mood by using the different times of day — very early in the morning, very late at night, the middle of the afternoon, and so on — to try to catch those emotional colours that are in the play. So I thought, well, I will set it in Illyria — in a recognisable Illyria, rather than a con-ceptualised theatrical Illyria, or an Illyria that actually represents some kind of mysterious Englishness. It's one of the really nitty-gritty problems in the play actually, how to set it, and what you call Illyria.

Naturalism and Its Limits

Michael Billington Can I just pick up one word you used, which is 'realistic'. You say it's a realistic play, a naturalistic play?

Bill Alexander It's a very naturalistic play.

Terry Hands I would challenge that. Every event that takes place in the play is extraordinarily heightened. And not only are there two different time-schemes, there are two different life-schemes, it seems to me, going on as well. You get a Belch, Ague-Cheek world which does seem rather naturalistic: they do get drunk and they do get tired and they do get cold and upset, and they seem to go through quite natural sets of behaviour patterns. Feste, on the other hand, like the sun, shines equally in both

13

camps. Once he is in one, he walks straight out and into the other — he's got there in a second, though it's supposed to be miles away.

Then you've got twins. You've got people who believe in those two twins. I agree with Bill about the difficulty and I suppose that's why John and I were going for a very free world, poetic and dreamlike. And it *is* very difficult, because I would also wonder whether our solutions, John, which were very bare, would be acceptable today. We were working at a time when people were very interested in listening and watching what happened in those terms, whereas I remember we took a decision in 1981 that the RSC should and needed to go into spectacle. Whether or not an audience would now want to see a willow cabin or a simple platform, I'm not at all sure.

John Barton It's not necessarily a comment on the *result* of what Bill did, but one could ask about what he's said, aren't you falling into about four or five of the naturalistic fallacies? My personal view is that one of the richnesses and traps in Shakespeare is that he keeps moving within a play from using naturalism, which he perhaps invented in England, to using the poetic or the surreal or anything that he feels he wants at a given moment. If you say, 'That play is naturalistic and I will do it that way', you limit the richness of the play. I know I've fallen into that trap. It's very easy for a director to do for the best of reasons.

The thinking that, geographically, they set out from Marseilles and hit Illyria when they're aiming for Venice is a *total* imposition on the way the Elizabethans would think. Shakespeare in his comedies, the Elizabethans in all their comedies, are tremendously arbitrary and virtually never go into any social detail about abroad. They just didn't think in this way, which is an imposition. Now sometimes, and very occasionally, it might be a totally valid imposition and come off totally, like Bill's daring with *The Merry Wives* . . .

Michael Billington Or your own in *Much Ado about Nothing*, which was naturalistically conceived?

John Barton Yes, I think it may have worked for that, but it probably didn't work when I did it with *Othello*. It's very difficult to know until you've tried. I'm not against it necessarily, but it's a very dangerous question. I think such a production will gain pluses in the bits that are written very naturalistically, but maybe it'll lose

something in the bits that are poetic or the bits that are way out. What I think is dangerous is to say that the *whole* of the text of *Twelfth Night* is written naturalistically.

Terry Hands I was going to ask if we could maybe not use the word 'naturalism'. If you're doing *Much Ado* you've got to have Messina because it's a social context play. *Merry Wives* is a social context play. But I've never really felt that *Twelfth Night* was. I've always felt it was, if you like, poetical.

Bill Alexander I don't necessarily disagree with that at all. In fact, all I'm trying to do is explain *why* I made the decisions that I made — not to defend them, but just to talk about them. I think *Twelfth Night* is a very peculiar blend of the realistic and the poetic, and it's quite unusual in that sense.

I was at pains not to make it overly realistic. That set could have been far, far more naturalistic. In fact, if you look at it and start thinking about it, you know it's not a naturalistic set at all. Where are the fishing nets, where are the front doors, where are all those elements of street life that you would get in a tiny fishing village on the Illyrian coast?

That to me would have been going too far in terms of the imposition of a social context. But I wanted there to be about the feel of it something that was quite general, and therefore supportive of many different things that one could explore in it. I wanted the set to be capable of being seen as different places at different times, depending on how you lit it, and, indeed, sometimes interior and sometimes exterior.

John Caird I've a similar feeling to Bill, because I think, just as one mustn't confuse naturalism with — what's the term you just used?

Terry Hands Social context.

John Caird Social context, one must also not confuse naturalism with scenery. I mean, you quite rightly said that my production was very scenic. You're aware of the sea and there's a bloody great tree in the middle of the stage. But actually there wasn't anything else.

Michael Billington There was a door to Olivia's house, wasn't there?

John Caird There was a door to Olivia's house, yes. But it could also have been a door into a garden or it could have been just a door. But there wasn't a lot of naturalistic clutter that the actors would have to use and which perverts the text, and I think there wasn't in Bill's production either. What they were doing was coming on and sitting down or standing up and getting on with the scene in exactly the same way as they would do on John's bare stage or Terry's stage. And if you wanted props or things, you could bring them on into that situation just as well as you could in any other situation. Interestingly enough, my production, which some people thought to be intensely naturalistic because it was all set in one place and had a consistent reality about it because of its scenic content, led one critic to say that 'The trouble with this is it made nonsense of the kitchen scene!' Thus proving that naturalism is in the eye of the beholder!

Michael Billington Which kitchen scene?

John Caird Which kitchen scene indeed! It completely foxed me.

John Barton I think that this arises quite naturally from what Bill said, and poses for me some of the basic questions one has to ask about how one does Shakespeare and designs the plays. The truth is that sometimes one pushes it a bit one way and sometimes another. But I suppose what I feel is that it is much easier to put naturalistic elements into something not too naturalistic than it is to release something poetic in a play which is highly socially organised and naturalistic. That, I think, is where I went wrong with *Othello*. The theory was that I wanted to build a mundane world around a mythical figure, but actually I reduced his stature as a result.

Secondly, I feel that we're talking of it all as though it were defined by its setting. But my sort of gut feeling about doing Shakespeare, and certainly *Twelfth Night*, is that in the end the most important design element is actually the props, however few or many, as much as the scenery, and that it's perfectly possible to have the most austere of settings, in which you get the naturalistic life and the social density through the props. They set up a way of working that the actors have, and give the play its naturalistic roots. To me, that is as important as what the set is.

Michael Billington I was really trying to pursue what seemed to

be two very different views of the play — as a 'fairy tale', which was the word John Barton used at the beginning of the discussion, and as a 'naturalistic' piece, by Bill's definition. Is *Twelfth Night* more a mixture of those two than any other Shakespeare play?

John Caird I would stick very closely by John's description of the play as having significantly different moods from one scene to another. I'd like to go back, Michael, to your earlier question about how much it is a festive play and how much it is a dark play, because it's very patently both. You can't say that it's a festive comedy, because if you read the text carefully and analyse the words that Shakespeare's using, in every scene there are words like 'death', 'decay', 'die', 'drown', 'pestilence', 'hanging' — consistently in every scene, there is dark, dark imagery, even in the scenes which are famous for being broadly comic.

And my theory is that one of the ways of tackling the play, which I found the most useful, is to accept, as John says, that there are major differences in tone from scene to scene, and to get at the comedy by going through the darkness of the play. As soon as you play it for comedy, it falls to pieces. What you've got to do is go for the passions of the people, whether they are inherently comic and you have an inherently comic actor playing them, or inherently dark and you have an inherently pathetic actor playing them. Whichever you choose, the comedy releases itself when you get at the dark, serious intentions of the characters. And it's a paradox, but it's then much, much funnier. It explodes with laughter at the end if you take the dark themes of the play really seriously.

Emergence of the Themes

Michael Billington I'm sure we'll come onto that more as we talk about individual characters. But John, you've brought up the language of the play: could we talk a little bit about the text of *Twelfth Night*? John Barton, is it a play that poses any textual problems? Is it a play that you need to edit or cut?

John Barton I can't really remember now! I think I cut very minimally. Almost always one does make tiny, verbal alterations which either help an actor or remove something that is unviable or unclear. I don't remember anything more than such minor, routine changes. The only substantial alteration I can remember was

altering the song I had them singing in the drunk scene, into which Malvolio erupts, to 'The Twelve Days of Christmas'.

What I did feel very strongly, both in thinking about it and in rehearsal, was the huge difference between the prose and the main verse scenes. I found that the prose scenes sort of leapt off the ground as soon as you put them into rehearsal with the actors. That was in the nature of the writing, and — agreeing with Bill — there is something that is esentially naturalistic about the play which is unlocked in doing it with the actors.

I had to think much more about how to release the strength and intensify the poetic passages, for the simple reason that the prose mechanism and the comic mechanism is very powerful indeed in the theatre. Therefore you are left with these huge problems, such as how to make the audience really listen and be moved by the big Orsino-Viola scene when it's sandwiched between wonderful comic scenes. The audience go along with the comic part and think this fellow who's brooding about love is rather a bore.

Michael Billington   You say that's one of the problems. Do you know what the solution is?

John Barton   Well, I think that my own solution was that the passions and feelings and psychology in it, which are deep, can only be released by terrific work on the text and the poetry — a kind of work that wouldn't obtain for nine-tenths of the rest of the play. But I know I thought more about that; how does the opening scene work, how to do Orsino's first speech? It's those areas I found much more challenging and difficult.

Michael Billington   Isn't one of the strange things about *Twelfth Night*, though, that the division between the comic scenes and the romantic scenes is not at all sharp or clear? What seems to happen is that the comedy invades the romance, doesn't it? And the darkness invades the comedy. That's what makes the play so mysterious, isn't it?

John Caird   There's an interesting touchstone for all this. It is that many directors, when they first look at *Twelfth Night*, are tempted to reverse the order of the first two scenes. And it's a trap. It's a trap because it *is* the correct chronological order, but by doing it you create a naturalistic, over-simple chronology which denies what Shakespeare is doing on a very deep level. He's using the first scene partly to set up Orsino, and Orsino being in love,

and partly as a massive minor chord. He's saying, 'This play is about this great big theme', and all the imagery that he uses is introduced somewhere in that first very short scene. All the images of *sea*, *madness*, *love*, and *death*, which are the four main strands of thematic material in the play, are in that scene, and they reverberate right through the rest of the action.

Michael Billington So you've got to stick to Shakespeare's order of the scenes?

John Caird If you don't, I think you diminish the play.

Terry Hands I would agree with that. It actually is a play which begins with two prologues, isn't it? The key one is the first scene. Out onto the stage comes a man who says 'I'm terribly in love and I haven't got anybody', and then out onto the stage comes a girl who says 'I'm totally alone and I don't know where to go'. Supposing we were to see no scenery and we were Martians, we'd still have an idea of where the play was headed, wouldn't we?

John Caird But it's wonderfully disguised, isn't it? Just reading it, it's absolutely wonderful. 'If music be the food of *love* play on' — music is another great theme in the play — 'Give me excess of it that surfeiting The appetite may sicken and so *die*. That strain again! It had a *dying* fall. O, it came o'er my ear like the sweet sound That breathes upon a bank of violets, Stealing and giving odour. Enough, no more! 'Tis not so sweet now as it was before'. 'Oh, spirit of *love*' (again) 'how quick and fresh art thou, That notwithstanding thy capacity receiveth as the *sea*' — another theme introduced — 'Nought enters there of what validity and pitch soe'er But falls into abatement and low price Even in a minute. So, full of shapes is fancy That it alone is high fantastical.' You end with the madness theme.

Michael Billington So, all the major themes are being planted there?

John Caird In fifteen lines. It's fantastic.

Terry Hands Doesn't it also bring us back to this business of presentation? The purer you have your man and his statement and the girl, and her own statement, the better for the listening process. Because if you have a shipwreck and you've got forty battered

Victorian sailors coming up out of the sea and hauling things in, and mouth-to-mouth resuscitation going on at the back of the stage and all the rest of it, are you actually going to follow what is in fact a psychological and philosophical journey? Even if you take something like a shipwreck, it has a psychological and a philosophical significance as well as an actuality. We know the Elizabethans placed a lot of stress on the sea as being regenerative and a womb-like place. We also know that Viola comes up out of the sea, having lost her parents and now she's lost her brother as well. But we could also say, well, it's a girl who's fourteen years old, who is now cast abroad on the process of life. . . .

Bill Alexander The sea was an important metaphor for the Elizabethans because a lot more of them spent a lot more of their time on it than we do. I'd agree with everything you say, Terry, but the sea was a metaphor with a very realistic base to it. All Shakespeare's plays that deal with the sea would have spoken through that imagery to people's hopes and fears and sense of themselves as living on an island from which their fellows went out exploring the world, with a tremendous resonance.

Topical References — and Rhythms

Michael Billington Can I ask another question about the language of the play? It is a very topical play, full of obvious topical allusions, and I wondered how you cope with these when you're directing the play? Take Sir Toby's 'Are they like to take dust like Mistress Mall's picture?' None of us knows what Mistress Mall's picture is. Or 'The lady of the Strachey who married the yeoman of the wardrobe.' What do you do about lines like that?

Bill Alexander Two examples of what it is I think you do. 'Are they like to take dust like Mistress Mall's picture' is so topical that it is probably utterly unintelligible, and therefore you have to think very hard about retaining it. But the second, which is also unquestionably topical, has nevertheless about it a universal comprehensibility, right? 'The lady of the Strachey who married the yeoman of the wardrobe', you know exactly what that means.

John Caird Class difference.

Bill Alexander Absolutely. Even if you don't know the

particular reference. That's how you estimate those topical things all the time.

John Caird   There were people in Shakespeare's audience who didn't understand that reference either. . . .

Terry Hands   I think this is a bit like, say, David Hare's *The Secret Rapture*. There are one or two references in it, like 'Of course, I can't offer you a job, I'm a Conservative', which are just like 'The lady of the Strachey' for today.

John Caird   Or 'I had as lief be a Brownist as a politician.'

Terry Hands   Those are little jokes which meant more to an audience of the time.

Michael Billington   Yes, but do you have in any way to try and explain those references visually, by business?

John Barton   My personal view is that one has got to look at each of them *ad hoc*. 'I had as lief be a Brownist as a politician' works because of the word 'politician'. It actually works *better* probably than it would have done in Shakespeare's day. If it's something of impalpable density, sometimes the actor can relish it and make it funny because it's dense. Sometimes it's just a nuisance. One might do something about it. I think you've got to look at individual cases.

Bill Alexander   Yes. If it's impalpably dense, you can relish it in a way that says something about the character. But the awful trap is to play it as a joke *about* the line not being comprehensible. That is absolutely deathly.

John Caird   Shakespeare knew very well how many of those jokes would live and how many of them would die. He was far too clever a playwright not to know that. And it's very interesting that most of the dead jokes are in a particular part of the play — almost as if once he got onto the idea of having topical jokes, he couldn't stop or didn't want to stop, he wanted to mine a richer vein of topical comedy. And they happen all to be at the only part of the play where we nearly always find there's a rhythmic problem.

Mainly, *Twelfth Night* is a play of almost perfect rhythm: if you just play the rhythms in the text and the rhythm from one scene to

another, it all comes right for you in rehearsal. It's miraculous to work on in rehearsal, the way it motors itself along. But in Act III, Scenes ii and iv, you have major problems. The first is the scene where Ague-Cheek is deciding to leave but is persuaded not to by Sir Toby. And the second is the yellow stockings scene, right the way through to the duel and that huge, great, long 'more matter for a May morning' scene.

Rhythmically speaking, the problem happens because Belch goes on and on and on. And every actor who's ever played Belch says that when he first took on the job, he thought that with a name like that character, and with the stage history of the play, and photographs he's seen of other actors who've played it, he thought he was taking on the funniest part in Shakespeare. But within three weeks of rehearsal, he realised that the other characters get all the laughs, and constantly he's being undercut by Ague-Cheek or Malvolio or Feste.

And in that particular part of the play, he's incredibly prolix. He's got these great long speeches just when what you most want is for Ague-Cheek to meet Cesario and have a duel. Or just when what you most want is actually to see Malvolio in his yellow stockings, or for Ague-Cheek to go and write the letter. And I think that it might not be coincidental that the very place where Shakespeare put a lot of topical jokes is the place where you do need a few snips, when you actually get to performance.

The Order of the Scenes

John Barton Yes, John's somehow jogged my memory. I completely agree that it's a difficult area of the play, where the tension goes, for the reasons John's given. In any Shakespeare play, somewhere along the line there are danger areas, or difficult areas — not just difficult scenes, but bits where you feel or you know that you may lose your audience. And I do remember now I did make one drastic change which I'd completely forgotten about. I transposed a whole scene in the middle of the play — the first scene where Sebastian and Antonio appear. It goes in the text from the end of Olivia falling in love with Viola to Antonio and Sebastian in Act II, Scene i, then Malvolio comes in with the ring in Act II, Scene ii, and then it goes into the drunk scene. And some time in rehearsal, I experimented, and I moved the Antonio-Sebastian scene to after the ring scene and the Viola soliloquy, because I felt that where it came it seemed a minor, boring scene

of two rather boring characters turning up in the middle of the action.

I got the two pluses that the momentum of Malvolio following with the ring happened *immediately* after Olivia had sent him off, and that Viola ended the scene by saying, 'O time, thou must untangle this, not I. It is too hard a knot for me t'untie.' And immediately the knot, as it were, came on. So it worked.

Michael Billington We are into an ethical question though, aren't we? I mean, you talk about Sebastian and Antonio presumably as two minor and slightly boring characters. . . .

John Barton No, I'm talking in terms of the audience's concentration.

Michael Billington Yes, except that it's a short scene they have, isn't it, Act II, Scene i? But what it is about, surely, is very much what the play is about: relationships, fidelity, gratitude, trust?

John Barton The point is that it is a very difficult scene because it is palpably exposition, it is written on a mundane level of setting up plot. It doesn't tell you much about the feel of those characters. The actors playing it know that they're sandwiched between two jolly good scenes, and they're not easy with that. But it's also an important scene because it introduces two new characters and tells us Sebastian is alive. And I thought, 'How does one make it a major scene?' Particularly since you're going to be jumping from your major actors playing Malvolio and Viola to your supporting actors. There is a theatre problem there.

Michael Billington But doesn't Shakespeare set up a rhythm that you do have to observe? If the scene is put by Shakespeare in that position, then there must be some good reason for it?

John Barton You start on that assumption, yes. But if you find that it's not working, or that the losses are more than the gains, then you do question it. Sometimes you solve it and sometimes you don't. And sometimes it is entirely to do with 'I don't think those two actors are going to bring it off!' I felt that it was such an important scene that it needed air time, it mustn't be rushed. But the actors felt at first that, because of the rhythm of the play, they'd got to rattle it off and get off the stage as soon as possible. That was worse. But when one moved it, it was able to breathe.

Terry Hands It's the pragmatism of being into previews, finding you've got a chunk that isn't working, and having to find a way out. But it doesn't necessarily mean that John would want to prescribe that change for ever after: it was just something that solved a problem he had at that time. I mean, we're also talking about a different period of acting. We're talking about the 'sixties, and in my case the 'seventies, which was quite different in acting terms from the 'eighties.

There again, it's a question of asking, what is the tempo up to that point? What is the weight of the scene? Personally I would risk keeping it in the original order because I don't think *Twelfth Night* is a problem play in terms of its structure, in the way that I believe *Hamlet* is. But we've also talked about the jokes of the period and things like that, and I think one ought to say, really, you check them out mainly on the previews, don't you?

John Barton There are three points to be made, aren't there? One is that we know that technically text is text. Inevitably there were experimental transpositions in Shakespeare's theatre: The placing of 'To be or not to be' is still debated. The new Oxford edition suggests certain major changes in places like the end of *Measure for Measure*. It was something that obviously happened pragmatically in the theatre.

That is not to say that the general idea of respecting the text and believing that Shakespeare knew what he was doing is not paramount. But believing that your duty is also to hold and take the audience with you, if you find that something is palpably not going to work — maybe it's your fault or perhaps you can't find a way of making it work — and you can think of something that might make it flow a bit better, then I don't think that's so very wicked. It's a solution for the moment.

Bill Alexander An example of that might be the first half of *The Merchant of Venice*, which has a very difficult rhythmical structure. What I did was transpose the first Morocco scene and graft it onto the beginning of the second Morocco scene. So there was just the one scene, which I think is absolutely valid because you just do not want that endless to-ing and fro-ing at that point. The argument against it is that Portia is absent for too long.

John Caird Yes, I think Shakespeare calculated that he could keep the suspense going by bringing in the triple suitors for the caskets, but actually it doesn't hold up.

Bill Alexander We know that some plays are rougher in their structure than others. Some arguably even have other hands in them. In some plays, the early texts differ massively from each other. But I think that *Twelfth Night*, along with *A Midsummer Night's Dream* and *As You Like It*, are among the most perfect plays ever constructed — whereas *Henry VI Part I* isn't!

Terry Hands I was tempted with *The Merchant* to do the same thing, and in the end I didn't. But the danger when we start to talk about restructuring is that we're talking about today's audiences and interests. And because in *Twelfth Night* today the comics take up such a share of an audience's attention, it is that much harder to push home the story of an Orsino and a Viola, or of a Sebastian and an Antonio, which are based purely upon love. My solution was to invent a lot of mobility for Orsino and Viola, by having Orsino ready to go out on a hunt and Viola slapping his boots and striding around because it was cold, and there was snow around. But when John did it, it was very beautifully still: they just sort of sat, and you followed the story. Now that's hard to get today's audiences to follow, because the boy-gets-girl and girl-gets-boy element is not as fashionable as the mechanicals in *Midsummer's Night Dream* or the clowns in *Twelfth Night* or Shylock in *The Merchant*.

Michael Billington This seems to be a fundamental question though — how far one compromises to accommodate the tastes of a modern audience?

Terry Hands I think every age has done it, Michael. If you look at the nineteenth century, you'll find the play is cut down finally to five scenes.

Michael Billington But it's not an argument you would endorse?

Terry Hands No, it isn't, but I understand it.

John Caird We're getting away from the central issue here, which is the issue of transposition of scenes and cutting. It's really a technical problem. You've all mentioned the *Dream*, and the mechanicals being so fascinating. But how many scenes are there in *Antony and Cleopatra*? Over forty? And there are eighteen scenes in *Twelfth Night*, but there are only nine in *A Midsummer*

Night's Dream. Nine scenes out of five acts: it's fantastically compressed, and you couldn't transpose anything, it would be completely impossible.

The thing that you most want to do in the *Dream*, for technical reasons, is to have Bottom waking up before the lovers do, and then going back to Athens, so that you don't have a quick-change problem if you've got the same actor and actress playing Oberon/Titania, and Theseus/Hippolyta. But you mustn't do that, because Bottom has *got* to wake up when everything else is finished. It's the comic echo to what's happened to the lovers. But in the case of *Antony and Cleopatra* it's not at all difficult to transpose scenes or, as John's pointed out, in *Hamlet*, which is a very complex, muddled play structurally. *Twelfth Night* is somewhere between those two extremes. Parts of the play are rhythmically completely sound, but there are also several very, very short scenes stuck in the middle of nowhere.

The 'Pressure Points' of a Play

John Barton You talked, Michael, about compromising according to an audience's taste. I would never define the problem in those terms at all. What obsessively occupies my mind, if I'm doing Shakespeare in a big theatre with a mass audience, is really to make them listen and concentrate rather than to switch on and off in the way that many audiences, especially matinee audiences do. So one of the main things I would think about in any Shakespeare play is: where are the danger points? Where are the tedium points? And what do I do about them?

You can feel it when you watch your first run-through: we're going to lose them there, we're going to lose them there. Sometimes it's to do with the actors, sometimes it's to do with the rhythm and the structure of the play, or the nature of the text. So, what do you do? Well, the first thing you do is rehearse the scene, of course, work with the actors: you go at it that way. Secondly, you invent, as Terry says. You have the actor do something physical or inventive prop-wise, or something that energises and picks it up. But you know that there are areas, I think in every Shakespeare play, however perfectly constructed, that are the tricky areas. I don't think that's a compromise with the audience, because one's duty is not to lose them.

Bill Alexander It's also a question of the technique of the

dramatist in constructing a play that has pressure points — points where the pressure is built in order to wind up either the narrative action or the emotional action and then released. Take the example that's come up in *Twelfth Night* of the first Antonio and Sebastian scene. It's necessary for three reasons. It's necessary simply because you've got to get the characters on. It's necessary, I would argue, because you need to separate the consequences of Malvolio being handed the ring from the consequences of him passing the ring on to Viola. And it's necessary to add an element to the story that's going to pay off later.

Now, the point is that the scene in which Olivia gives the ring and the scene in which Malvolio delivers the ring are wonderful scenes. You could argue that in some terms you *need* a scene that is not so good between them — of course one has to do it absolutely as well as possible, and find its reality, but actually you want to take the time also for anticipation to accumulate. It's a very delicate balance.

Michael Billington What you seem to be saying is that Shakespeare knew extremely well what he was doing there in delaying the pay-off of Olivia giving the ring to Malvolio so that he can pass it on to Viola. It gives you a pause to build up anticipation of another comic scene?

Bill Alexander That's right. But I do think that the first Antonio and Sebastian scenes *are* among the most difficult scenes to do because they have to have an intrinsic interest and credibility, and yet they are necessarily sort of relaxation points. Do you know what I mean?

Terry Hands There's this wonderful thing here. 'I do I know not what', says Olivia, having just played a love scene with Viola, 'and fear to find mine eye too great a flatterer for my mind. Fate show thy force', she demands. And fate promptly does! Onto the stage comes Sebastian.

Bill Alexander It's a wonderfully ironic juxtaposition, and highly calculated.

Michael Billington What I think that scene is also doing is offering us a sort of a prose bridge, isn't it, between two rather lyrical scenes? And the whole play seems to be based on alternations of that kind.

Bill Alexander   You need the prose rhythms.

John Caird   Yes, and of course Shakespeare knew what he was doing in that scene. But it just so happens that Antonio and Sebastian are very small parts compared with the size of the parts that are surrounding them. And you often do have the problem of attention because of the actors that are on stage. It's a fact. Maybe Shakespeare didn't have that problem. Maybe he had crackingly wonderful actors. The other point is that you have a Sebastian who is so unbelievably like Viola when he walks on, you don't have a problem with that scene because the audience is going 'Aah, they're just the same!' Maybe you have to stage that scene as producing Sebastian out of Viola in a way that's very obvious, very clever.

John Barton   The thing I would personally question, which is perhaps heretical, is whether everything in Shakespeare is invariably — conceptually, artistically, and technically — absolutely perfect. Of course generally, ninety per cent of the time, it us: but it is also palpably evident in places that a writer turning out masses of stuff under pressure roughs certain bits here and is carried away by other bits there, or sometimes just bored. Sometimes we do go on, as if we're talking about the Bible. Sometimes it may well be that, as Bill says, an apparent difficulty is valid and useful dramatically, but you do get difficulties in areas where that's not true.

Bill Alexander   Sure. And the question is, at what point do you make the decisions? You decide after you've tested it, usually.

John Barton   Yes, that's right. You decide when you work with the actors — and very often it's the actors who are saying it as much as you.

The Choice of Period

Michael Billington   One of the areas I'd like to bring out, which stems from what we've been talking about in terms of Illyria, design, and so forth, is what costume and period you choose when you're doing *Twelfth Night*. Does it stem inevitably and inexorably from your basic design decisions? Do you keep the play within a broad Renaissance time-scale?

John Caird Yes, it's so richly in the text. That's the difficulty. You can do it in the nineteenth century or whatever, but you do have to fight with swords, and you do have constant allusions to all the bric-a-brac of Elizabethan social life.

Bill Alexander That's right. the question is whether you set yourself more problems than there are anyway by transferring the play — any Shakespeare play — out of context. If your chosen ambience for the production simply adds to those problems, adds to the suspension of disbelief problem and all sorts of other things, then it's simply not worth it, it's a vanity.

John Caird I got very close to the problem because in my first thinking I kept being haunted by the word 'Chekhovian'. I thought, this has got be a Chekhovian production. I used the word all the time, meaning an intensely naturalistic production, set somewhere in the Crimea, you know! And I wanted it to be full of *Three Sisters* costumes and sets.

The problem was the conflict between late nineteenth-century Russian imperial life and the bric-a-brac of Elizabethan life — they are completely different. It just became perverse to have the characters constantly referring to Elizabethan artefacts and ideas and to be imposing on that a system which would actually be very foreign — damaging not just to the comedy of the play but to the whole social fabric of it, the whole emotional feel.

Michael Billington Some Shakespeare comedies take changes of period more easily, don't they — *Much Ado* is the most conspicuous example, perhaps. *Twelfth Night* seems more resistant to changes of period.

Terry Hands I think that a lot of plays are quite damaged by modern dress being very fashionable. It can set up barriers. I don't think there's a simple answer. . . . Of course you can put Messina in a different place, you can put *Merry Wives* in a different place, because they've both got a very strong social context and therefore you can relocate or update them provided it doesn't get you into a muddle. But I think what we tend to do at the RSC is to take a costume roughly near a period but to alter its aesthetic. Now the aesthetic of the Elizabethan costume was a very slender male leg. We don't actually do that any more by putting pumps on: what we do is turn it into a modern aesthetic which is a strong leg — that is, there's boots, and they go up to the knee or they go up to the

thigh or whatever. It is actually quite radically altered. An Elizabethan probably wouldn't even recognize it, but an audience comes in and is able to adapt to the reality of the world you present. I think you can present them with a world where everybody wears silk pyjamas, provided the realities all around are consistent. Provided it's real to that place and time, the audience will settle into it. But when somebody comes on with a sub-machine gun, you are in trouble.

John Caird   You do have a significant problem in *Twelfth Night* — it's called 'crossed gartering'. If Malvolio's living in a world where crossed gartering has not been worn for three hundred years, then he's patently completely loony when he walks on. His decision to wear cross-garters has got to come out of there being a possibility that that would be a good idea.

Bill Alexander   Absolutely. But that depends what you're after. In a production like Cheek By Jowl's, which used a style of merrily eclectic modern dress, an audience who had enjoyed it would say, 'Well, what on earth does John Caird mean, saying there's a problem with crossed gartering? You get round it in an imaginative way that is part of that modern eclecticism.'

John Caird   It's the solution of giving Bottom a red nose instead of an ass's head. That's the same principle.

John Barton   I think John and Bill have put their finger on it. There are a lot of elements in it, and in the end you have got to apply common sense, as John has done. The whole question of anachronism is there in the text anyway, like Elizabethan costume references in Roman plays. Shakespeare didn't bother about it. One only bothers about it in terms of 'Will it work with the audience today?'

You started this bit of the conversation off by saying, 'After you've done the set, what do you do about the costumes?' Of course, you may have solved it by deciding on the period of the costumes before you do the set. It may be that that is the more crucial decision. But it comes down to four choices. Do you go for historical accuracy — which is the norm for a history play or a Roman play? Do you go strictly Elizabethan, which today has a feeling of pedantry and tightness and costuminess, rather than realness for us? Do you go for modern dress, which has easy dividends with obvious dangers, and can sometimes be wonderful

but can sometimes distort the play? Or do you go for something 'timeless'? Now timelessness can mean the most abstract and invented of costumes, like the Noguchi *Lear*. That's one solution. But there's also the solution which I suppose between us we use a great deal, and that's probably the solution I took with *Twelfth Night* as far as I can remember, which is that you keep the Elizabethan feel because it would be perverse not to, but you do it suggestively and loosely, not heavily and in great detail, so the actor is comfortable and the audience don't feel he's in fancy dress. Then when somebody *is* in fancy dress like yellow garters it means something.

John Caird   I would add one other element, John. Something we all have to think about is the fact that a girl is going to dress up as a boy. So you tend to look for an adjustment of the costume which will enable two sexes to come on and not immediately betray themselves. If they've both got tights on their legs it's perfectly obvious which is which.

John Barton   I've personally gone with the feeling that if the anachronisms textually were too many and great, updating wasn't worth it, but if it involved the minimum of them, it was okay. That was my thinking, maybe wrongly, when I did a nineteenth-century, military *Othello*. The curious thing was that the nature of the *Othello* text meant that in the course of the whole play, where I was being as strict to the text as possible, I think I only changed two words — one of them was the change of 'galleys' to 'fleet'. But there weren't the continual references to swords and stuff that there are in other plays. Therefore there wasn't much textual anachronism even if the general idea was a bad one. On the other hand, when Bill did a very textually anachronistic *Merry Wives* he had a unifying concept that meant you didn't worry about it. It's something you have to solve not philosophically, but in terms of a given play.

John Caird   Where you have a play that is dealing with timeless, philosophical and political notions, modern dress is fine, because Shakespeare himself was writing plays and having them performed in modern dress, as it were — *Julius Caesar* being done in modern dress rather than Roman. But I think the danger of modern dress productions isn't just in trying to find ways of fighting with swords in three-piece suits: presumably if something desperately unimaginative happens, they all chance to have knives in their

31

socks or something. The difficulty is on the obverse side of the coin — you keep wondering why they aren't using all the paraphernalia of twentieth-century life which goes with the modern dress.

That seems to me to be something that directors who are always using modern dress duck. If you do start using all the paraphernalia of twentieth-century life which wasn't around when the play was written you start, if it's a comedy, getting all your laughs off the text, and that plays havoc with the natural rhythms of the piece. Or, if it's a serious work, the audience becomes obsessed with wondering what is the next thing that these actors are going to do which is going to make it relevant for today.

Michael Billington   Can we come back to *Twelfth Night*? I just wondered, Bill, having chosen your specifically Greek island setting, was there ever a moment when you wanted to take the kind of path you had with *The Merry Wives*? One could conceive a *Twelfth Night* set on a gay island like Mikonos where the genders would be more easily confused. . . .

Bill Alexander   Tony Sher said exactly that on the first day of rehearsals. He said, 'With this set you could walk on in jeans and T-shirt.' And that's absolutely right. But one of the reasons I chose that set was because it was actually timeless. Those whitewashed buildings were the same, arguably, in the sixteenth century as they are in the twentieth century, and so were both familiar and yet appropriate to the period. The position I took about dress in my production of *Twelfth Night* was that it should be Elizabethan Illyrian: therefore it's Greek-Yugoslav dress of that period, which is very different from Elizabethan — very beautiful, and actually much freer and looser and more natural. I felt that worked very well.

Michael Billington   What was the argument against using the jeans and T-shirts?

Bill Alexander   It limits it. You start cross-referencing every-thing in the play against the pertinency of the modern context.

Michael Billington   But *Twelfth Night* is a play about sexual confusion, confusion of sexual identity, and you could see that happening on a modern Greek island, couldn't you, where the sexes dress in very similar fashion?

32

Bill Alexander You could indeed. But you don't have bear baiting, you don't have that attitude to madness, you don't have the possibility of someone being put in a dark room and tortured by someone else. You don't have a duke with that particular set of references — the fact that his country is going to the dogs while he, obsessively, thinks about one love affair.

John Caird Attitudes to virginity, attitudes to sex are also part of it.

Bill Alexander You don't have the same attitude to virginity, you don't have the same attitude towards the safety of the central character. Because one of the narrative difficulties of *Twelfth Night* is actually coming to terms with precisely why Viola needs to disguise herself. And you have to accept the convention that girls were in great danger in those times if they went around in skirts and didn't have a bloke to look after them.

John Caird If it's modern dress, why doesn't she go to the consulate?

Bill Alexander Precisely. That's why I think you are probably safer with a kind of merry eclecticism which cocks a snook at all those problems, and allows you to create a stage world in which anything can happen.

Terry Hands If you set the play on a modern Greek island, then obviously Malvolio would have to come on, not in crossed garters but in hippy clothes, like a flower child wearing a lot of beads, and there would be a social context which you would have to accommodate. The problem is, at the end of that road lies 'A tank, a tank — my kingdom for a tank!'

What we are talking about also, though, is a form of sophistication. I very much dislike the Jonathan Miller solution to *The Merchant of Venice*, when Olivier played Shylock, because the necessities of nineteenth-century costume and the period he put it in meant that Shylock appeared on the stage as an investment banker. That is really not what he is. And it was all switched into a different kind of social structure. I believe the best solution I've seen to this conundrum was the one hinted at by Deborah Warner in her recent *King John* at Stratford. Now her people were basically wearing modern dress, but they added bits of armour, rather like the Elizabethans would have done. They had a coat and

they had a sword, they had all those things that are actually necessary, and I think that worked. Probably with *Twelfth Night* you could do something similar, or you could keep it with a modern aesthetic but close to its own times, so that you can accept that crossed garters are part of an older system of wooing and courtship dress which, used by Malvolio, is rather ridiculous.

Michael Billington   What I was trying to pin down was really whether *Twelfth Night* had so many specifically Elizabethan properties, references, and values in it that it does in the end resist too much in the way of updating.

John Caird   It does.

The Social Structure of the Play

John Barton   Terry's used the key phrase, which is not 'anachronistic' or 'period' but 'what is socially right', which is slightly different and cuts across a lot of what we're saying. That's the test: firstly, what would be socially acceptable in the context of the play, and secondly, what socially reflects the feeling of the play? Like when I popped *Much Ado* into the British Raj, it didn't actually distort anything much in the play: it did actually fit it. The social definition of *Twelfth Night* is important because it's to do with a household. It socially matters from that point of view, so if you start to put it somewhere else you distort the social sense, therefore you come back to the Elizabethan. I think that would be the way one's thinking would go: some form of Elizabethan solution would be preferred by a process of elimination rather than because one has any great feeling it has just *got* to be Elizabethan.

John Caird   It's not a purist thing. I've just opened the text at one of the comedy scenes and it says:

> SIR TOBY: Dost thou think because thou art virtuous there should be no more cakes and ale?
> FESTE: Yes, by St. Anne, and ginger shall be hot in the mouth, too.
> SIR TOBY: Thou art in the right. Go, Sir. Rub your chin with crumbs. A stoop of wine, Maria.
> MALVOLIO: Mistress Mary, if you prize my Lady's favour at

anything more than contempt you would not give means for this uncivil rule. She shall know of it by this hand.

MARIA: Go shake your ears.

SIR ANDREW: Were as good a deed as to drink when a man's a-hungry to challenge him the field and then to break promise with him and make a fool of him.

There's four or five things in there that refer directly to Elizabethan behaviour and social presence.

Terry Hands Yes, but even that bit you've just read, for instance, could be eighteenth century. I can't remember whose, but I've seen a kind of Beau Brummell *Twelfth Night* where they had their swords and they had boots. . . .

Bill Alexander Sure. But then you think, if there are fewer suspension of disbelief problems if you only transfer it by a century or so, what actually gets added by doing that? For precisely the reasons that it's easier to do, it is also more questionable. And the further you take it towards modern times the more you can defend the point of it, but the weaker the credibility becomes.

Michael Billington I don't think the world of Beau Brummell is any more accessible to us than that of Elizabethan England.

Terry Hands It is in the sense that it's a more modern physical line of costuming, and it follows a modern aesthetic. But I think John's point is absolutely the key — that you have such strong social structures in *Twelfth Night,* on which the play depends: there's the Lady of the Manor, Olivia; her steward; the old landed aristocracy of Sir Toby Belch; Ague-Cheek as an older version of Slender from *The Merry Wives,* with land and money; an Orsino who is infatuated — and the sort of world where you have a fool who is going to entertain everybody. The closer you get to the modern day, the harder that is, whereas in the eighteenth century, and even perhaps down to the Edwardian era, you could almost get away with it.

Bill Alexander How can you have Maria saying to Feste, 'Where the hell have you been? You'll find yourself hung.' He is a paid fool. You transfer it to the twentieth century and, okay, you turn him into some kind of drop-out, a deadbeat hippy that's paid

to stay around. But the amount of explaining you have to do about that choice, which is all extra-textual, seems completely unjustifiable, because the evening becomes about the production, not about the play. And so the effect is that you have an absolutely schizophrenic time — on the one hand you are listening to the play, and on the other hand you are following the lines of the production. The two do not meet and so your attention is divided and unfocused throughout.

Michael Billington   What you seem to be concluding is that Illyria can take many different physical styles on the stage, but in the end you have to show some Elizabethan base to it?

Bill Alexander   I think it is more quintessentially Elizabethan than a lot of the plays, yes.

John Barton   I would like to add one point, which is that as far as Shakespeare and the Elizabethans were concerned they would have been baffled at our conversation, because their convention was that they wore modern dress, although they put togas on to play Roman plays and helmets for histories. The problem would never have occurred to them for a moment. Until the masques began and Inigo Jones started designing costumes.

About the modern dress question, where I think it could possibly work for *Twelfth Night* is to make it vaguely Edwardian — a form of modern dress that is palpably not of the late twentieth century yet is not too heavily Victorian either, and that you don't actually think about too much because it is the Elizabethan convention in modern terms. That, very often, is what solves it.

John Caird   Because the social classes in the Victorian era and the Edwardian era were still delineated by what they wore. That's a very important issue for us. I think it's also important in terms of whether or not you use Elizabethan costume, because a modern audience is no longer aware of the codes which would have been very clear to an Elizabethan audience as to what the costumes meant. What is the difference between a duke and an earl? What is the difference between an earl and a cardinal out of religious garb? They would have known right away. I think that we do as a matter of course what both Terry and John have suggested we do anyway, which is that we take the Elizabethan era and, for all sorts of reasons, don't do it accurately. The interesting thing about late

Victorian and Edwardian is that it is the period which is closest to us in which social distinctions were still absolutely obvious — where a cardinal was a cardinal, a bishop was a bishop, a prime minister was a prime minister. . . .

Bill Alexander   And it allows you to get into trousers, which everyone's easy with.

John Caird   It gets much easier with trousers. Yet swords were still worn at times because we were still a militaristic and imperial nation. There's so many things that are handy. But it is an easy option in some ways, and there is always the danger — the pitfall which Bill pointed out — which is that you are doing something in period which is somehow parallel to the text, not congruent with it.

Viola: Passive or Volatile?

Michael Billington   I would suggest we might talk a bit about Viola now. One thing that strikes me is how attitudes to Viola seem to be changing all the time. When I first went to the theatre, on the whole the character was treated romantically. What seems to have happened over the last twenty-five years or so is that the character's humour, self-awareness, self-mockery, are all coming out much more strongly. I suppose it started with Dorothy Tutin in 1958. I remember her as the first cheeky and mischievous Viola that I ever saw. But I wonder if that is how all of you would tend to interpret the character now? Not as a purely romantic character but as someone who is compact with irony, a certain amount of self-mockery, a certain amount of self-deflation. I think there are one or two speeches in the play that indicate this. The soliloquy she has after the ring has been sent back by Olivia seems to be crucial in how you play and interpret Viola. But do you all see her as a character who is far more than straight romantic heroine?

John Caird   That's the most touching thing about her, I think, that she is able to speak wryly and objectively about the awful situation that she's in, even while she's in it. That's what is so achingly horrible for her in the great Orsino/Viola scenes: that right at the crux — at the moment when Orsino is being most masculine and seemingly obtuse about his feelings for her — she is able to describe this poor girl who sits like Patience on a

monument, smiling at grief, as if she was describing somebody else. It shows extraordinary objectivity and wryness. In the scene with Feste there is a great deal of self-humour, and during all the Olivia scenes, too.

Terry Hands I would agree with that. It is a fascinating role because it does seem to me she is the most inactive heroine in Shakespeare. That is to say, everything happens *to* her. If you compare the two famous trouser parts, Rosalind dresses up as Ganymede, who is a sexually active person (Jove as the lover), whereas Viola says 'I'll be an eunuch', which is something between the two. And even Malvolio says 'somebody between a boy and man, as a squash is before 'tis a peascod'. There is a deliberate choice for Viola, which is part of the ambiguity of the role and of the play, when she decides not quite to be a woman and not quite to be a man, and certainly not to be active. It's passive, it's the eunuch role.

Every situation she gets into, time or some other person has to resolve it. Unlike, say, Rosalind, who really sorts out Orlando and tells him all about women, she just puts in these lovely little touches with Orsino to try and correct his fantasy view of women and show that they can love just as much as men. But there's no real teaching beyond that, and every scene that she's in, somebody's having a go at her. Olivia absolutely hurls herself at her, Malvolio takes exception to her, Belch bullies her. It makes her immensely sympathetic and, I think, a kind of still centre in the play. The one person with whom she really finds her wit is at ease is Feste, oddly enough, in that lovely scene at the beginning of the second half.

John Caird Depending on where you put the interval . . .

Terry Hands Yes. But when people disguise themselves and dress up, the choice of the role they are going to play is very important. And in her case, as I say, it makes her a wonderfully still centre and wonderfully passive.

Michael Billington Do you, John, see Viola as a still centre?

John Barton Well, not quite. I agree that she's relatively passive if you compare her with Rosalind or Portia, but I think that, if you are asking for a definition of her, all I can think of are the contradictions and the conflicts. I would put it the other way

round — she is put into situations which she has to deal with and she can be very strong and positive about them, like 'Yet, a barful strife. Whoe'er I woo, myself would be his wife.' That is a conflict. And then she goes and does the job, and she's not passive a bit when she encounters Olivia. It brings out her wit and sense of humour which is wry and rueful and wistful, but also attacking and punchy as against Olivia.

I would look at Viola in terms of contrasts and contradictions rather than labels. Certainly she's not straightforward, certainly she can be wryly humorous, but she can also be attackingly humorous. She can put on a confident act, like when she breezes back to Olivia, gets egg on her face, gets involved in the duel with Sir Andrew, and panics. There's a volatility about her, I think, rather than a passivity. I would put it more in those terms.

Michael Billington   But she does shrug a bit, doesn't she, as Terry indicated, saying 'Oh, this is too hard a knot for me to untie. What can I do?'

Terry Hands   I think John's right when he says that I'm using the word 'passive' a little too easily. What I meant is that they come at her. But wouldn't you also say, John, that if one takes the kind of sexual uncertainty of a young girl, she is given one of the most amazing experiences, which is what normally only eunuchs get — she can be in the male locker-room and find out what the fellers are thinking about, and how they express it. And then she can go off to a woman and find out what women do when they woo men. Most women never learn what other women do when they pull a bloke, and she's actually able to. I find it offensively witty. Her curiosity is astonishing. In the Olivia scene, she could leave, but she chooses to stay.

John Barton   I think that's very well said, and I agree. The point is that she has serious situations to react to and her reactions are very various. You have just talked of two. They can go to the degree of panic and feminine timidity she shows over the duel. They can be quite strong and passionate, as when Orsino threatens to kill her. What I am saying is that, to me, what is wonderful about the character is its diversity. I hate the idea of a straight Viola or a comic Viola or a romantic Viola.

John Caird   There's a huge streak of naivety as well, isn't there, in that when faced with a problem, an emotional difficulty, she

will tackle it head-on, even if she does it in code. She hates to hear injustice or inaccuracy or wilfulness. She has to attack those with the wonderful brand of naive righteousness that she has. And there's another strain in her, which is very, very difficult to define for an actress playing the part, which is that she's shipwrecked. Within a few minutes of being shipwrecked she learns that her brother has died, and by the end of the scene she has decided not to dress up as a boy and a eunuch, but to dress up as her brother. And in terms of the dramaturgical structure of the play, nothing can happen for her until her brother is returned from the dead. As soon as that happens, something is released for her, she herself becomes active again.

Terry Hands   But isn't that the choice that's made for her by Shakespeare?

John Caird   Well, it's partly made for her by Shakespeare, but it's something the actress can't ignore. There's something deep in the psychology of a twin, when the other twin dies, which would make her want to keep that twin alive by acting out his life as well as her own life. That's never said, it's never spoken about, but it's done, and it's what makes that moment so unutterably moving, when she hears Antonio talking about Sebastian at the end of the duel scene: her defences completely disappear as she realises that all her fondest wishes could come true at the same time.

Terry Hands   But it gives her the choice, then, of being a woman. Up to that point she's had to be a boy *and* a girl, she's been both. The brother turns up, which means she doesn't have to be a boy any more, she can be a girl. But that stops her being a eunuch.

Viola: Limited by Goodness?

Michael Billington   In very practical directorial terms, how do you encourage an actress to discover this opal-like quality that Viola has?

Bill Alexander   One of the interesting things about the character is the way in which she is limited by her own goodness, limited in terms of her actions. She says, 'Oh, damn. What a shame. I want to be his wife.' The audience originally watching that would have

then seen the character go through a whole set of situations in which she always has the choice to reveal herself.

It's very interesting, John, you raising the point about her brother, and her not being able to release it until the end. I think that is a metaphysical point in the play — but the practical point is that she is constant, she is so good that she cannot face taking the liberty of making everyone around her seem ridiculous, even though she sees, as Terry pointed out, wooing from both points of view. The audience are always being asked, what is she going to do, how far is she going to take it? Is she really going to let this guy sit next to her, mooning about love, and not actually drop some little hint about it? All the women in the audience are thinking 'Well, if I were in her position . . .'.

John Caird   Not all the women in the audience. . . .

Bill Alexander   Having been round to Olivia, and being herself an intelligent and witty person, she could start offering a few hints to Orsino — you know, 'Actually you should see her without her make-up.' The fact that she plays the part she's lumbered herself with, never trying to use it for any ulterior purpose, never trying to exploit the possibilities, becomes a wonderful image of how in our human affairs absolute goodness is constantly doing itself down, constantly losing out. While the people who don't go quite by those moral absolutes are the people who tend to win. And that's what makes Viola so appealing as a character. But I absolutely agree with everything that John has said, that she can be quite passionate and she can be passive. Her role is largely passive because that is what she self-selects.

Terry Hands   Yes, but not just self-selects. I would go along with you even further in the sense that, unlike Portia or Rosalind, she's got into an impossible situation. The guy she's in love with vehemently wants to marry somebody else and sends her off to fix it. That's really what I meant by 'passive' — she doesn't, as you say, trick it, wreck it, spoil it, or do anything wrong. She says, 'Time will sort this out. I am just going to be in there learning and discovering things.' She plays at being a woman with Orsino, she plays at being a boy with Olivia. Both scenes should be really quite sexual.

Bill Alexander   That's right, but it's not just the learning and playing. It is actually being perfect in moral terms, because the

man she's in love with loves someone else and, instead of trying to manipulate him out of that, she rigorously and enthusiastically tries to endorse his passion for Olivia rather than subverting it.

John Caird   But she does subvert it.

Bill Alexander   Not with Orsino.

John Caird   Well, she says to Orsino, 'What if she cannot love you?'

Bill Alexander   Right. But that is not subverting it: it is actually trying to rescue Orsino from something that will destroy him, not to get something for herself out of it.

John Caird   I take the point, but I think you're designating her actions as purely good in that illustration. She is certainly self-sacrificial when it comes to the climax in Act V — she would rather be killed by Orsino than remain with Olivia. It's a very moot point, but in the pressure of that moment she would rather go with the man who would do violence to her. But I think that this represents a real streak in a lot of people, and this is why audiences find that scene so touching, both in its sexual and its emotional passivity. Nearly everybody in the world has been in a position where they have loved somebody and not been able to say so, or not even been able to admit it to themselves, or been in a situation where they are in love with somebody who is patently in love with somebody else and sharing the secret. It's archetypal, I think, that situation.

The Problem of Viola's First Scene

John Barton   I find the whole of this very, very difficult. These psychological analyses of what's going on in Viola are very shrewd, very apt, but I'd like to pick up on John's point about the concentration of what actually happens in that short first scene with the sea captain. I know what we're talking about here is really the kind of conversation that comes up in the rehearsal room with the actress playing Viola who has these problems, and who says, 'How the hell if I'm just coming out of the sea, do I dress up as a boy at the end of the scene?' 'Why don't I just tell him who I am?' It comes up pragmatically from the player as much as it does

from the directorial concept. That happens with any play of Shakespeare's. What I always find so difficult is that I believe that needful and very likely truthful psychological analysis to be humanly true, but I don't believe it was necessarily present in any depth in Shakespeare's consciousness.

Having generalised about it, though, I think I can be specific about this particular scene of Viola's arrival. It has to be resolved in a way that is right for the director and the production, but primarily for the actress who's playing it, because it is very difficult for her to make that series of choices in a short time. I don't remember in any detail how one discussed the scene or did it, but I do remember conceptually how it had to be handled. If you tried to make it psychological, or if you *only* made it psychological, you just created more problems for yourself — and so I really went for the feeling of fairytale and dream and strangeness, and of her coming out of the sea like Aphrodite coming out of the waves of mist, so that she didn't know quite where she was. And I said that the most important of her lines in the scene was, 'What country, friends, is this?' And the reply, 'This is Illyria, lady,' had to trigger, 'I don't know where I am. I don't know what's going to happen to me. I don't know what my situation is, and I don't know what Illyria is.' By playing the scene on that note of wonder, and as if the sea captain was almost inducting her into a fairytale, it set up a feeling that anything might happen.

Michael Billington But are you implying that one can actually delve psychologically too closely into some of Shakespeare's characters, or Viola's specifically?

John Barton I am saying that actors always will do that, and that there is problem for a director in Shakespeare about how to keep the balance between the poetic and the naturalistic elements.

Bill Alexander Can I make the opposite point to that? I don't agree with the premise that the further you look the harder it gets, that pursuing realism gets you deeper and deeper into trouble. I do accept there is a problem, a storytelling problem, about why she decides to do what she does, but that is a problem related to the context in which you choose to do it. It is more of a problem if you set the play in 1980 than it is if you set it in 1600. It becomes less of a problem the further you go back in history. But, you see, for me you can absolutely explain that first scene in realistic terms, in terms of the human psychology of trauma. In the first

scene you discover something about the nature of the character through seeing the way she reacts to an incredibly traumatic event. Now, the choice you've got is how much the decision is in the nature of the character, and how much in the nature of that character's reaction to being shipwrecked. I don't think it's necessary to imagine Illyria as a sort of generalised state of dream. . . .

John Barton That's not the point I was making. I am not saying that it's wicked to work at it purely realistically, and I'm not necessarily saying you get yourself into trouble. What you *are* doing is going down a certain road of definition that's also going to define the nature of the performance and the production. All I am raising is the difficulty of reconciling that question with the more difficult question of unlocking the poetic side of the play, which we have not talked about yet at all. And I am saying I find what you have both been saying very stimulating because to me it poses that terribly difficult question.

John Caird There's one thing about that scene which is very difficult to explain in naturalistic terms. First you get that trauma at the beginning, with the captain saying that perhaps the brother has survived, and Viola hoping it's true. 'Mine own escape unfoldeth to my hope, Whereto thy speech serves for authority, The like of him.' Then you get a crashing gear-change. It goes on:

> VIOLA: Knowest thou this country?
> CAPTAIN: Ay, madam, well, for I was bred and born
>   Not three hours travel from this very place.
> VIOLA: Who governs here?
> CAPTAIN: A noble Duke, in nature as in name.
> VIOLA: What is his name?
> CAPTAIN: Orsino.
> VIOLA: Orsino . . . I have heard my father name him.
>   He was a bachelor then.

That is the content of an almost completely different scene — it could be three scenes later, when Viola has recovered from her trauma and is starting to take an interest in things around her.

Bill Alexander I absolutely disagree. The nature of those changes tell us something about the character.

John Barton What John is pointing out, surely, is that Shakespeare has written a scene which is not just the exploration of what a girl says when she has just been through the trauma of a shipwreck.

Bill Alexander That is true of any ten lines in the entire canon.

Michael Billington If I understand this correctly, there seems to be a disagreement about how much you accept the element of fable in a Shakespeare comedy, and John's point is that even if it is a fable, to act it you still have to examine it logically.

John Barton What I am saying, Bill, is that I think you are misinterpreting it still. Is there anything in what I am saying that doesn't marry up with what you're saying? Because it comes back to me that I did analyse the scene in story terms, in realistic terms, in exactly the way that you have been doing.

Terry Hands I am sure the way we can meld the two views together is to agree that there is always in any Shakespeare scene a progress. If you get banged on the head, the first thing you say is, 'Where am I?' and then your eyes slowly focus and you get up, and then you remember why you took that sea voyage in the first place and what was most on your mind at the time. That line, as John says, is terribly important. We discover that the man is a bachelor, then in comes a beautiful girl who says, 'I heard he was a bachelor.' Of all the things to say! She could have said, 'I heard he was tall, dark, and handsome,' or, 'I heard he was a bit of a bastard.' But no: 'He was a bachelor then' — that is, he is probably still marriageable.

John Caird It is a laugh line.

Bill Alexander It is at one level, if one stresses the unconscious irony. At another level it is a line that is saying, 'The most important thing about Orsino at this moment is that the guy never married.'

Terry Hands This is picking up on what John would call fable or dream, and on what we would simply call metaphor or poetic realisation. Obviously there is going to be a philosophy behind this somewhere, and the philosophy is only a way of trying to explain the frightfully complex lives everybody lives. The next

thing after that is not that Viola says to the sea captain, 'Take me to this Orsino's court dressed as a woman and tell him the story of my shipwreck.' I mean, if I was shipwrecked, I wouldn't say first off, 'Hang on, I'm going to find my sister's dress,' and whip off down the road. I would be saying, 'I have had a terrible time, Duke Orsino, please give me another boat and send me back.' But what we get is that traditional Elizabethan fascination with the idea that if men and women are going to get anywhere at all, they have got to come together spiritually before they get together physically. And the only way to make sure that the spiritual gets a chance is to cover up the physical — so they put on breeches. And she *does* get to learn about him and he does get to learn about her by that means.

Bill Alexander   So in a sense her reaction is fabulous rather than realistic.

Terry Hands   What I am saying is that each step within it is both a fabulous extension of the metaphor, and in terms of real life and psychology can still work.

   Can I say one last thing about Olivia falling for Viola as the young boy? We see that in every day life all the time — like fourteen-year-old girls used to go for the Osmonds, that slightly plastic, slightly feminine kind of boy. It is the day they put up the poster of the Rolling Stones that you start getting worried, because that is the moment they are going to take sex seriously. Olivia graduates from the Osmonds to the real thing. The psychology is still sound.

Antonio, Sebastian, and Sexual Ambiguity

Michael Billington   Can I ask a general question which arises from this, which is how far you can apply this Stanislavskian type of realism to Shakespeare's characters?

John Caird   I was going to come precisely to that question, but via another question which I think everything we have been talking about begs. In the original production of this play, the boy playing Viola by the end of that first scene is merely taking off the dress which he is wearing for the one scene and getting into his normal garb. He is preparing himself for a play-long journey in which the sexual ambiguity of every scene is pro-

foundly tied up with the fact that it is a boy who is playing the part and not a girl.

Of course the original audience would have been used to this, and of course a lot of people in that audience would not think it strange at all. But so far we have only dealt rather obliquely with the relationship between Antonio and Sebastian. And we are talking there about a very ambiguously written relationship that may or not have been fully homosexual in one way or another. Now it is very difficult for a director and a group of actors to make concrete statements about this in rehearsal. We know that one of the characters in that relationship, the young boy Sebastian, is the twin of the girl who would have been played by a boy in the original production. We cannot get away from the remarkable sexual ambiguity of that situation. You might choose to ignore it, but if you have a scene where a boy dressed up as a girl plays a scene with a boy dressed up as girl dressed up as a boy, and it is a love scene, and then the boy dressed up as a girl goes back and declares herself to be in love with a man, you would not as a member of an audience be unaware of what was going on. Certainly with Shakespeare writing it you would be aware of what was going on.

What that takes me to, picking up on Terry's point about sexual ambiguity, is this Renaissance obsession with the way that people complete themselves. It is something I alluded to when describing the way that Viola keeps her brother alive. In exactly the same way it is the Rosalind story, the Imogen story. Viola puts on men's clothes and behaves like a boy, she finds out what life is like in both camps, and by the end of the play she is more sexually complete than she was before. The male and the female have been married in her.

Sebastian is going through a similar sort of journey. He is having a relationship of one sort or another with a man in which his masculinity is made passive. I think in many ways your reactions were instant and dismissive: 'Folly. Not worth proceeding with.' And in rehearsal there is indeed very little one can say on the subject to an actress playing Viola — it is pretty pointless to say, 'Well, if you were a boy living in the sixteenth century this would all mean much more.' But you can't ignore it: you've got to study it before you can say it's unnecessary.

Terry Hands One can respond to that in several ways. If you watch the Japanese classical theatre and the female impersonators there, the impersonation is so total, and is intended to be so total,

that what you see on the stage *is* a woman. Even if one goes back to one's old school play, which I did about fifteen years ago, and you watch the little fourth-former come on with his voice still unbroken playing the girl, even with amateurs the illusion is complete. With a dress on the difference between a young boy and a young girl is not that great.

What I am saying is, that it was so clear for Shakespeare's audience that it was a girl on stage who then became a boy that it is not worth thinking of the sexual ambiguity of that moment. More so in *Twelfth Night*, where if you've actually got the Olivia scene between two boys — Olivia and Viola — and you've got the Orsino scene between two boys, and we are to be made aware of their boyness, you actually lose the sense of specialness about the Sebastian-Antonio relationship, which is a very real . . .

John Caird   But you are ignoring the central issue here: it isn't a Japanese travesty.

Terry Hands   It was in Elizabethan times.

John Caird   No. It may have been to the Elizabethans, but only when the boy playing the girl was playing the girl throughout the play. Here we are dealing with a play where, as soon as possible, by the end of the second scene, the boy playing the girl is back playing a boy again. That is not a normal travesty role.

Convention — or Complication?

Michael Billington   Can I steer us towards how this applies to modern productions, and how you as directors have highlighted the sexual strangeness of *Twelfth Night*? There seem to be two or three key moments when that comes through in most productions — usually when Viola or Cesario is sitting at the feet of Orsino, and he starts to look at her with a sort of fixation, and you wonder, 'Are they going to kiss, or what?' In your production, Terry, I can remember, in the scene between Olivia and Viola, Olivia was extraordinarily sexually aggressive towards Viola, and it was almost as though she was about to rape her. Forgetting Elizabethan conventions for the moment, how far do you think you should bring out the sexual peculiarity of this play?

Terry Hands   I believe it is important, but I wouldn't trace it

back to the Elizabethans. I would simply say that I do believe that if you take a sexually passive role, say that of the eunuch, and you have a very young girl playing the role, and a woman makes that kind of very direct approach — like, you know, 'Tie me to a stake' — there must be two kinds of curiosity. One kind is, 'Is this how women behave?' Because otherwise mostly people learn it off the cinema don't they, how women and men behave, or if they are twelve or thirteen years old they are going to see it on the telly. And then there is the peculiarity of whether or not this is the way to go, and Viola makes a decision that it isn't. In the case of being with Orsino, it's not the girl's problem any more, it's the man's problem — the actor's problem of playing it.

I agree that we don't have quite the same approach to the older man and the younger one which Elizabethans seem to have had in aristocratic circles — of being attracted by a mind and by a presence and not knowing quite why — but you can play the sense of bewilderment in Orsino: 'Why am I feeling this curious sense of attraction? I am supposed to be a fellow.' One of the key things about the theatre, I think, is that you can play uncertainty and bewilderment. Yet it is one of the things people often leave out. I always say to actors, 'If you don't know what to do, play that.' It is utterly compelling.

Michael Billington John, did you try to bring out the sexual ambiguity?

John Barton I tend to agree with Terry against John. But I do think that it is the Elizabethan tradition that one has got to start out from. I am convinced that it was like what Terry describes in schools — that as it happened the entire time in all the plays, the audience viewed it as the norm. The device of a girl dressing up as a boy is very frequent in the whole of Elizabethan drama, and it has often been pointed out that it must have been used among other things because of the situation of boy players. I do not believe that it ever crossed Shakespeare's or the audience's mind that there was any necessary sexual ambiguity unless the text said so.

The only time in the whole of Shakespeare where something very peculiar does happen in this respect is in the Epilogue to *As You Like It*, because there you get today the situation where you have a girl, an actress, playing a boy playing a girl who pretends to be a boy who pretends to be a girl who admits she's a boy in the Epilogue: you get a complication-factor of six. Now you can't

ignore that, because it is in the text. Shakespeare in the Epilogue actually points out the paradox. And Cleopatra does it about a boy squeaking with greatness. But if Shakespeare *doesn't* do it, it means there is no special significance, as in this instance. What is significant is surely what Terry said, which is that the actor cast as Orsino has to play on the ambiguity.

Michael Billington But it is built into the dramatic situation. In the Elizabethan theatre, Orsino would have been played by a mature actor, and his relationship was with the boy playing Cesario-Viola. There are already ambiguities built into that situation.

John Barton We are constructing a problem which is false to Elizabethan thinking, muddling to an actor or actress, and a red herring.

Michael Billington But my original question was how it affects you as directors, now.

John Barton And I am saying that, having said all that, it doesn't affect me.

John Caird John, what are the great breeches parts in Elizabethan drama before Shakespeare? Name one.

John Barton Well, all the Peele plays, all the Lyly plays.

Terry Hands *Dido and Aeneas* is one of them.

John Caird I think this is a very crucial point, because it has to do with whether or not Shakespeare is doing something essentially cheeky and experimental in the way he is casting his own plays. What you have to explore in any scene between Orsino and Viola is a scene between a man and a girl dressed up as a boy. You can't go any further than that or ask the actors to do anything more than that. What I am suggesting is that there are different reverberations for us today, because of the lack of that extra remove of sexuality for the whole play, but that it is terribly difficult for us to know what they are. I am absolutely certain that they *are* different.

Terry Hands John, can I ask, if you are looking at a play which has so many varieties of love and indeed of sexuality as *Twelfth*

Night, if Shakespeare had been wanting the girl-boy thing to be played upon, would he not have actually have *limited* the variety? I agree with John Barton that in this particular play he was simply accepting the convention that this was a girl. If he had had a girl player for the part he would have used one. That's why I think when we come to it as modern directors we can play it straight off the basis of the text.

But again, it comes down to casting. You have got to go *young* for some of these Shakespearean roles. My experience of doing, say, *The Merchant of Venice*, *As You Like It*, and *Twelfth Night* is that on the whole, apart from Portia maybe, the femininity of the actress seems to be released by the male costume rather than suppressed by it, and that every performance I have seen where, say, a Rosalind has spent the entire play being butch, the production has died. The women actually become more themselves in male attire. It is the men who have the problem and, more often than not, are troubled by something. When it comes to the crunch, and there's the revelation that it is a girl after all, they discover that they have actually fallen in love with a person, as a friend, and now the sexuality follows — which is very consistent with the philosophy of the times and the values of the times. We don't have those values, but they did.

John Caird I agree with you. It is not something that I would ever ask an actor to play on. Even if I had a boy playing Viola, I wouldn't want him to play on the fact that he was a boy playing a girl. As John says, it is not in the text, it is not in the lines. But it is in the atmosphere of the play, somehow, and I can't ignore it. It haunts me.

John Barton To answer the question, 'What does one do about it in *Twelfth Night*?' I would simply say that I would let the vibrations between Orsino and Viola be taken very far, possibly farther than usual — his sense of something strange, her sense of longing and fear. Those should be played to the full.

Bill Alexander I agree with that, and I would go further. The point about the convention that we inherit, in so far as it affects us, is that I think it's wrong to ask, 'Okay, so Viola is going to be acting the part of Cesario. What sort of person does she decide to make Cesario?' That, I think, is a red herring: the point is, she plays herself. The convention is absolute: because she is in trousers and short hair, no-one for a moment doubts that she is a

51

boy. From that moment onwards you learn about Viola, what she's like, and her particular situation.

John Caird   There is a very interesting fact, that I never realised until the very first preview when I heard some Americans in the audience saying how much they were enjoying the girl playing Cesario. They were obviously new to the play, and hadn't looked very carefully at the programme — but, sure enough, the name Viola is not mentioned until Act V, Scene i, when Sebastian says,

> Were you a woman, as the rest goes ever,
> I should my tears let fall upon your cheek,
> And say, 'Thrice welcome, drowned Viola'.

And that, I think, is a fascinating fact about the way Shakespeare wrote: he wanted you to think that this poor shipwrecked girl who calls herself Cesario was in love with Sebastian, and in the end you find out that she has got a girl's name and it helps you forget. It is a brilliant sleight of hand.

John Barton   It goes further, doesn't it? She loses her name because of what has happened to her: the name's been wrecked. Shakespeare gives her an ambiguous name suggesting both violation and the vial of harmony. You can make a great deal out of the word 'Viola' coming where it does in Act V.

The Comic Chemistry of Olivia

Michael Billington   Can I bring us on to the character of Olivia? The interesting question seems to me how far she goes in self-mockery. It seems to me there is a tendency for her to be almost amused by her own discovery of her sexuality — intrigued, puzzled, whatever, by the discovery of her attraction to Viola/Cesario. Is that right?

Terry Hands   I think it is very comedic, a form of high comedy like Kay Kendall excelled in — exhibiting a kind of excitement at being wicked, and actually taking the lead at coming out of mourning, not having Malvolio around her neck all the time, and being her own mistress, not having her brother around the place, the fact that she is suddenly free. Now, that excitement generates comedy and humour. It's not so much self-knowing as self-

mocking. There is a moment at the end when she has become so wicked, I think, she finally sees Sebastian and Cesario standing side by side, and more or less says, 'Golly. Two.'

Bill Alexander   And the fact that you can accept her making that leap from one to the other is wonderfully comic, and why I absolutely agree that casting her as an old contralto is wrong. She's got to be a young girl. The irony is that she says that she's going to walk around the cloister for seven years, but it's really saying, 'Will you please piss off and stop sending messages. She doesn't like you.' And she gets trapped in the literalism of that by Malvolio, who is in there saying, 'It's a very good idea. I think you *should* do it for seven years.'

John Caird   It is a very adolescent thing to do.

Bill Alexander   Absolutely. It is an adolescent reaction to grief. It's also the best excuse to stop Orsino sending things round any more. It is revealed for what it is as soon as she meets Viola. She starts behaving completely differently.

Terry Hands   Surely the key to Olivia is that you have got to cast a comedienne. If you don't, you are into problems, because it is something in the ring of the line, the flick of the line, that makes that comedy release itself.

John Caird   The thing that you have got to get right about Olivia is that she is very young. Her brother has just died and her relationship with Orsino hasn't even gone as far as, 'You bore me, I don't fancy you,' because we know it is not as simple as that. I think she is terrified of what she does. She is terrified of being colonised, taken over, grabbed, raped, removed, before she has become anybody. And, as Terry said earlier — his point about the young Donny Osmond — she can go on the front foot. She can make a fool of herself without actually losing that much. In the end, if Cesario finally says no, she can enjoy her grief, that it has all gone wrong, that she didn't get the man she wanted. That can be part of her growing up process.

Michael Billington Do you agree about the comedic aspect, John? I thought you were wrinkling your brow?

John Barton   I think that the question of the comedic is a

difficult one. I don't in any way disagree with it, but it seems to me that there are two completely different ways in which you can take the part. I know that, when I did it, I reacted against the language simply because of the dazzling comic performance that Gerry McEwan had given for Peter Hall in 1958. I thought that was of its kind definitive, and I musn't do it on this occasion. Whether or not I would do it on another occasion I don't know, so I don't find that a disagreement. But I think that it is part of the overall chemistry of what you are trying to do, and that it can be taken either way. I went, maybe wrongly, for what you describe and what Terry described as a very young girl coming out of her shell, and I emphasised her vulnerability and that she has got hurt and that she has lost the confidence that she started life with. That was my particular solution, which I think is valid to the text, but I don't think it is definitive at all and I don't think what Terry says is wrong

The only thing we've scarcely mentioned, and it's a very important decision isn't it, is the opening situation of her grief for her brother. Is it an affectation — is it that she's just bored and an alibi — or is she truly grieving? That is a vital question which can have many answers, because the evidence is not there. You can construct your own.

Terry Hands   That takes me back again to the point we were making about Viola, about her not actually *doing* anything. She has that amazing willow-cabin speech but she doesn't actually *build* a willow-cabin. The person who does all the acting, the person who runs her own life and makes her own decisions, is actually Olivia. She is the one who says, 'I am going to have *this* young man, not that one. I am going to put my uncle in his place. I am going to sort out the marriage. I'm going to get the priest together. I'm even going to face up to Orsino at the end.'

John Caird   But surely Shakespeare is saying, look what happens to a household which is run by a woman when she is completely out for what she can get, just below the surface of what she's after. Mayhem! Total bloody mayhem! Because she's stopped noticing what's going on. She's stopped controlling the house.

Terry Hands   It is not entirely her fault. It's that her steward has just gone bonkers.

John Caird   No, but it is a constant theme in Shakespeare, isn't

it? And it brings us back to this sexual theme, the idea of people growing up when they become sexually complete, the feminine and masculine coming together — either between two people, or in one person to make up a whole person, or a whole estate, a whole play, a complete reconciliation.

Michael Billington Doesn't Shakespeare always criticise people who lock themselves up or threaten to mew themselves away? Always the world gets its revenge. And it does, obviously, with Olivia.

Terry Hands But look at the difference between Olivia and Helena in *All's Well*, who's got the whole world against her, but off she goes to find and get Bertram. And look at Portia, going back to make sure she gets her Bassanio, and spending a whole act getting him. Olivia fulfils the behaviour patterns of the Helenas and the Rosalinds, and Viola is left therefore to play a more passive role. She makes the great speeches about willow-cabins but she waits for things to happen.

John Barton One of the crucial lines to focus on, that you can take in many ways, is Olivia's 'I do I know not what'. It is potentially, and often actually, a horrific laugh line. That seems to be a perfectly right solution. It can be the embarrassment that she's been going over the top and betraying herself in her advances to Viola. But it can be to do with going on a journey where she doesn't know what is happening to her, though at the beginning of the play she thought she had. It can be . . . not a comment on or a reaction to what is happening, but an opening up into a new adventure. It is absolutely crucial in the interpretation of the part of Olivia both forwards and backwards. What do you do with that line, why you do or do not focus on that line, triggers all those questions which to me embrace most of what we've been saying. There are a number of key lines in *Twelfth Night* like that — Malvolio's 'I'll be revenged on the whole pack of you', where how you actually react conditions mighty things back down the evening.

John Caird What you have said reminds me of a very important strain in the play. Olivia also says, 'I do I know not what and fear to find mine eye too great a flatterer for my mind. Fate show thy force.' It follows straight on from Viola saying, 'Time, thou must untangle this, not I.' And Malvolio says, 'Jove is the doer of this,

not I.' And Antonio says something very similar. All the major characters at one point or another appeal to some outside force, in that way. So it's not just Viola who is passive. Nearly everybody in the play puts themselves in a passive situation relative to the hugeness of their own feeling that 'This has got to happen. I am being pushed into this. I am not in control of this. This is a passion and an emotion I am incapable of acting against. I have got to let it happen and only Time or Fate or Jove or whoever can sort it out for me.'

Terry Hands   It takes us back to that curious sense you always have, right through to the wind and the rain, that there's some sort of extraordinary cycle going on.

John Caird   Yes. There's somebody out there doing it all for you.

Terry Hands   Compare that with, say, Helena's 'The remedies oft in ourselves do lie which we ascribe to heaven.' That is a completely different ethos being explored.

Sir Toby and Sir Andrew

Michael Billington   From what you are saying it seems to me that the tendency is rightly to find the comedy that underlies the romance in *Twelfth Night*, and see both Viola and Olivia from a comedic point of view. Conversely, there is a tendency to find a greater degree of brutality in the comic side of the play. Can we talk about that in relation to Sir Toby and Sir Andrew? My observation is that, production by production, their relationship has been getting more and more savage until it reached the point in Bill's recent production where it was frankly sadistic or sado-masochistic — Sir Toby enjoys manipulation and Sir Andrew seems almost to enjoy receiving it and to come back willingly for more. Is that how you perceive the relationship going over the years — and how much further it can go?

Bill Alexander   Yes, I think Sir Toby is a frankly sadistic individual. Like everything, that goes back to the context, and how you set the play and what period you set it in. In the twentieth century, comparing ourselves to the Elizabethans, we are astonished by their relative lack of squeamishness — the fact that

mad people wandering around the streets tended to get bricks chucked at them by perfectly normal citizens. So in that sense I think Sir Toby represents a classic, red-necked, cock-fighting, bear-bating, stone-throwing Elizabethan who ruthlessly manipulates a daffy person because he wants to get money out of him. That sadism is there and has to be shown. I don't think softening it enhances the comedy or the romance or the charm of the play, although the tendency is to want to soften things like that, in the same way that people have a tendency to want to soften the fact that the Christians are rabidly anti-Jewish in *The Merchant of Venice*.

It was a harsher society. Shakespeare faced that, it is there in the plays. They had strong stomachs, they laughed at things violent in a way we don't, and Shakespeare in his plays is often testing his society and accusing it of taking things too far because he was probably a greater humanist than most people around, maybe than most people in his circle.

Michael Billington What struck me as unusual about the relationship between Roger Allam and David Bradley in your production was Sir Andrew's hunger to be whipped and beaten and exploited. There was one particular bit of business I remember at the end of one of the drinking scenes, when Sir Toby urges Sir Andrew to carry on drinking and burn some sack, and Sir Andrew says, no, no, he must go back to his little cubicle, and totters off, only to come back some ten seconds later like some poor lap-dog. Could you be saying that people like that are just born to be exploited?

Bill Alexander It wasn't so much that. It was just that one of the things I like about Sir Andrew is that he represents the most weak-willed side of humanity. He is not really capable of saying no to anyone. He is *ill* with drink, and Sir Toby says, 'Come on — let's go and drink some more.' And Andrew says, 'No, I really have got to go to bed now.' And then he can't: he can't deny Sir Toby at any point. Toby's sadism lies in knowing that he's found someone who's got some money, and who can't deny him anything.

For me it makes it more savage, because it means it is the very opposite of caring about someone. If Sir Andrew were a stronger-willed person and Toby really had to work at manipulating him, the balance of sympathies would be completely different. But all he has to do is say a couple of lines, and the most he has to work at it is when Ague-Cheek decides to go because he has seen Olivia

kissing the hand of Viola, they do have to spend a minute convincing him that he mustn't go. But other than that, the poignancy of the relationship is the ease with which this powerful, charismatic, and very violent man manipulates him. I hate the sense of a jolly Sir Toby.

John Caird I agree, there is nothing jolly about Sir Toby at all, but I think there is another side to it. He is vicious almost to the point of being sadistic at times, but he is also a very sad man, and you have to ask about people who are vicious, *why* are they vicious. A lot of the time there is something evil and negative in them that is a reaction against something that's happened to them. What you also have to understand about Toby is that he couldn't exist on his own: he *needs* people like Andrew, and not just to dun money out of them. He needs an audience, he needs to be appreciated. Toby and Andrew are a real pair. He needs somebody to laugh at his jokes, to give him a good feeling of self-esteem: he only finally turns on Andrew when he's got Maria, when he's decided to give up the struggle and get married. But he also needs Maria. He needs Olivia's approbation. He needs people around him to approve of him and to validate him at all times. His sadism and his pursuit of Malvolio have got to be seen in that light.

Michael Billington Talking of the interdependence, someone reviewing Bill's production invoked Beckett's Didi and Gogo. Is that relevant?

Bill Alexander Yes, I think so. And it is a fact that Sir Toby doesn't have to put himself out one little jot. Remember in my production when Sir Toby says of the departing Maria, 'She is a beagle. A beagle truly bred.' And Andrew says, 'I was adored once, too,' and then just opens his mouth to begin to tell him about it, but Toby says, 'Come on. Let's go back to the tavern.' He's not a giving person, Sir Toby, but I think that Sir Andrew is the sort of person that knows he is being taken for a ride.

John Caird There is so much life in Toby. The other side of Toby Belch is what is the opposite of Malvolio. It is the man who says, 'Come on. Just because you are like you are doesn't mean there won't be cakes and ales. We will not put up with this deadly atmosphere. We're going to celebrate. We're going to live.'

Terry Hands I would agree with Bill about the basic definition

of Sir Toby's character, but I think that we have got to remember that we are in the realm of comedy and not in the realm of tragedy. There are awful moments of cruelty in *Twelfth Night*, some really horrid ones that run right through, and they are not just of Sir Toby's making. You come to the moment at the very, very end where he finds he's fucked up on all fronts. He's found himself married that morning to somebody he could have gone to bed with anyway, and he's lost out with Olivia. He's had his head split, everything's gone wrong. It has always seemed that the tremendous cruelty of that moment was verbal. You have got to be a tiny bit careful because there is a similar relationship in a tragedy — between Iago and Roderigo, and there it is given an absolutely tragic ending. In the comedy it has the same weight, but it is just . . . deflected, I think, by fatigue at that point.

Bill Alexander   Deflected from what?

Terry Hands   From being entirely tragic. Where sometimes one gets an overstatement these days, picking up Michael's point, is on the very last moment where finally Sir Toby says, 'Piss off.'

Bill Alexander   I don't quite see the point you are making. That is the cruellest moment in their relationship, and therefore the most tragic, when Toby says, 'Aren't you dull?' and lets him have it. There's no softening that.

Terry Hands   No, what I'm saying is, it doesn't need to go beyond the actual words of the lines.

John Caird   In one sense it is the cruellest moment because it is the last moment.

John Barton   I think the sado-masochistic label is a dangerous one, because it implies psychopathology, which is not present in this comedy. It is more a description of two temperaments that are rather suited to a sado-masochistic relationship, but in a more generous sense, as John is implying. I don't think there is anything sick about it — or there shouldn't be. If I had to define it, I would do something I rarely do, I would actually make a direct historical comparison that makes a lot of sense to me. The temperamental relationship, which may or may not be of psychological dependence, is very well summed up in Johnson and Boswell — a man who is a bully, who loves putting his comrade down, is adored by

that comrade. They need each other tremendously. The great man makes jokes and uses the other fellow, is absolutely brutal to him, and Boswell loves it.

Michael Billington Presumably that is why you made Sir Andrew Scottish?

Terry Hands Can I take up this point about cruelty and darkness in the comedies, and indeed the comedy in the tragedies. We all were concerned at one period about the way that the comedies were being sanitised, and so we went for what we felt was the robust nature of Shakespearean society. There was also a feeling that if you want a complete meal, you mix the savoury with the sweet. There was a recent production of *As You Like It* in the West End where all the dark elements were cut, absolutely erased: there were no brutish stings, no cuckoldry soliloquy, no throwing out of the brother, no killing of the deer. All cut, just got rid of. But back in the 'sixties we were actually trying to put the whole play together so that you didn't just get the pudding, you also got the savoury. Where the problem comes for directors is trying to get the balance right — but I don't think the balance is too difficult in *Twelfth Night*. In *Much Ado* it is harder, a much more delicate balance to strike.

The Inheritance of Tradition

Michael Billington Could I raise a question about directing plays like *Twelfth Night*, which come around quite frequently? Bill has pushed the Sir Toby-Sir Andrew relation pretty much as far as it's likely to go in terms of pain. What does the next director do? Does he then withdraw and take it back to a gentler relationship?

John Caird No. You don't make your decisions based on other people's productions.

Michael Billington But you can't ignore what's been done in the past?

John Caird If you think that an element in the last production was all right, then you do something like that. If you thought it was wrong, then you don't. You make your own decisions based on the text rather on than previous productions.

Terry Hands I think John's absolutely right. But one does feel that one inherits a tradition from all those other productions, and you try and add to it. So if you see a production that is so complete that you feel you cannot add to it, you don't do it. I can't at the moment do *A Midsummer Night's Dream*, because I happened to be there on the first night of the Brook production and got blown away. When I came to do *Twelfth Night*, I didn't do a production in opposition to John's: what I did do was absorb a lot of John's. It's a case of absorbing and inheriting a tradition, and a lot of insights that people have had . But, in one or two areas, I thought, 'Now I'm not quite sure that you took the right choice there. I would like to see if I can contribute a little to that area.'

I can remember at one point in Clifford Williams's production of *Twelfth Night*, Trevor Nunn said to me at the end of the show, 'That piece of business ought to become traditional.' It was a piece of business where they were all talking and laughing in the garden, Maria was going to write the letter, and she talks about the colour yellow and says, 'And it's a colour she abhors.' And the whole group looked around and roared with laughter as they gradually became aware that Ague-Cheek was dressed entirely in yellow. And there was this sense of the man who always gets things wrong. There is a kind of a living tradition to which I think one tries to contribute.

John Barton Whether a production is reactive or not will differ from production to production. For me, in the case of *Twelfth Night*, Peter Hall had done what I felt to be a definitive production, and I said to Trevor, 'I will never go near the play. I don't want to do it.' But he pressed and insisted that I should do it. I then had to say to myself that I couldn't help but make comparisons, and indeed said to myself a lot of what Terry's just been saying. In certain areas, it would be stupid to reject something that was palpably right, and not just the theatrical tradition. There would be certain areas where maybe I could find something that hadn't been found before. And, of course, when I went into rehearsal the question of those traditions came up hugely with this particular play — especially in the case of Donald Sinden, who had read up every bit of business that everybody had ever done.

John Caird All Malvolios do that.

John Barton All Malvolios do it. He had done his research,

decided which bits he thought were right, and invented some new ones. And I spent my time talking about carrying on the tradition and saying, 'I entirely agree that you can't do that bit any other way, but that bit is perverse and has nothing to do with the text.'

Bill Alexander One bit of traditional business that particularly bugged me was that classic thing on 'When thou readest this, revolve.' You expect every Malvolio to spin round, or half turn, or turn the letter upside down, and all the rest of it. Of course it's as wrong as playing a line you don't understand, or you don't think the audience can understand, in a way that shows it's incomprehensible. To do any business on that line other than what that word means is abhorrent, because it is an abortion of the word. The man Malvolio knows what that word means. It just means think about it. Having said that, that's what Tony did!

John Caird That's like the John Woodvine bit of business, where he'd got a long thin mirror, and in order to fit his smile in he distorted his features accordingly.

John Barton At that point I think I only persuaded Donald to do nothing by saying that he'd get a better laugh if he thought about it for a long time.

Michael Billington And he didn't revolve?

John Barton He settled for that. It took a lot of negotiation.

Terry Hands But, John, you've now hit upon another thing which is part of this, because we're none of us saying that as soon as we get hold of a Shakespeare play we feel we've got to do something new with it. But we do come up against this problem of the audience's expectations. *They* know the plays. It's very strange sometimes, when you get audiences in and they know the line and it's coming up. It's not just the ones who mouth Hamlet to you and say, 'The rest is silence' before Hamlet does, if he isn't quick.

John Caird John, you had the problem of having Donald doing all that research. I had the problem of my Malvolio, Emrys James, having played Feste in your production. He came to my very first rehearsal with a complete performance, which he had created while standing on the stage watching Donald all those years ago. That was a real problem.

I once did react to a previous production — my own previous production of *Twelfth Night* for another theatre company, a small repertory company. I had made a lot of design decisions and casting decisions which were dubious. There weren't even enough people to double all the parts, so I was hamstrung about the casting, and I had a miserable time because I found that within two weeks of starting rehearsals, everything that I had decided on was wrong because the play was much deeper and broader and humanistic and reverberative than I had ever properly thought out. And I knew I had to do a completely different production one day. So I was reacting to my own work. But I certainly would never, not in my wildest dreams, do a production which was some sort of response, like Lendl hitting back McEnroe's serve.

Michael Billington I was just getting at the issue of how the next director handles insights into characters which seem to work, whether he absorbs them or rejects them.

John Barton There are a number of times where I have done a production, as it were, as a correction to something I did before, but to me the reaction is simply a stimulus. I find the alternative much more difficult — when you have to do a play you don't know how to do. That is much more difficult, because there is no trigger.

John Caird I find the biggest stimulus is watching a play that I feel is being produced very poorly, because then I switch off the production and just listen to the text. As a director, I find that a terrific stimulus — just sitting in the theatre listening to an imaginary production unfold. Like listening to the radio.

Feste — Fool or Clown?

Michael Billington We've hardly mentioned Feste yet, though in production he's often felt to set the mood of the play. First of all, what is Feste within the play? What is the key line about him? Is it that he is a corrupter of words?

John Caird Not a fool, a corrupter of words.

Michael Billington Do you think that is a key to understanding him?

John Caird It's one of them. But I'd like to ask whether we believe in the academic theory concerning the lines of Viola that you've already mentioned, Terry: 'Thou shalt present me as an eunuch to him, for I can sing and speak to him many sorts of music.' There is a theory that there is an earlier text of *Twelfth Night* which we no longer have, and perhaps even an earlier draft that was never performed, where those lines would have been realised — the boy playing Viola would also have played Feste, and sang the songs that Feste sings, and so become a very much more distanced character. Both characters go from court to court. Feste is in the box tree later with the others. But the theory goes that when the boy playing Viola's voice broke, and another boy took over who couldn't sing, Shakespeare took the opportunity to rewrite the play, also inventing a completely new character called Fabian half way through, because Feste was now singing Viola's songs and could not be the sort of character who was overseeing the gulling of Malvolio. It's a very compelling academic argument.

John Barton Hang on there, John, because it is one of the few textual questions which has been fairly well answered, hasn't it? It is probably true that something like that happened, and that, as with many textual cruxes in Shakespeare, evidence of older versions comes through. That goes right through the cannon, but in the case of *Twelfth Night* it isn't any practical problem, because the text we have has replaced it by giving Feste a scene where we have 'Call the fellow. Prithee sing; pay him for singing.' Therefore you don't actually have a practical problem.

John Caird I'm not suggesting that it's a problem. I am suggesting that it gives us an insight into what Shakespeare intends Feste to be and, indeed, what Shakespeare intends Viola to be.

Michael Billington And what does Shakespeare intend Feste to be?

Terry Hands I could answer it, if I can have first go, and then be corrected. There's certainly ample evidence of Shakespeare revising things and probably making them better. And there are bound to be tag ends left around because of the whole process of presenting the play. I think what we're left with, in the case of Feste, is that his songs are so important in their natural philosophy

1. 'If music be the food of love...' Richard Pasco as Orsino, in the 1969 John Barton production, captivated by his own languorous romanticism.

2. The drinking-scene (1969) with Bill Fraser as Sir Toby, Emrys James as Feste, and Barrie Ingham as Sir Andrew. Christopher Morley's set, with its slatted floor, curlicued screen and candles, evokes Illyria with minimal resources.

3. A deck-chaired Malvolio (1969) with Donald Sinden inspired by the Sutherland portrait of Maugham. The simple box-tree enables Fabian (Peter Geddis), Sir Toby (Bill Fraser) and Sir Andrew (Barrie Ingham) to stay in close attendance.

4. *Judi Dench as Viola (1969) with, in J.C. Trewin's words, 'an enchanted dream-like quality and an appealing break in her voice'.*

5. 'Nor wit nor reason can my passion hide.' An ardent Olivia (Kate Nicholls) presses her attentions on a disturbed Viola (Cherie Lunghi) in Terry Hands's 1979 production.

6. Daffodils begin to peer and branches to blossom in Terry Hands's winter-into-spring production: Cherie Lunghi (Viola), Gareth Thomas (Orsino), John Matshikiza (Curio), Kate Nicholls (Olivia), Geoffrey Hutchings (Feste).

7. *An ardent lady's maid of a Maria (Gemma Jones) looks on in rapture at a sottish Sir Toby (John Thaw) in John Caird's 1983 revival.*

8. Robin Don's set (1983) is dominated by a giant, gnarled tree. In the foreground Christopher Neame (Antonio), Daniel Massey (Sir Andrew), John Thaw (Sir Toby).

9. All boys together? An understandably perturbed Viola (Zoë Wanamaker), a self-absorbed Orsino (Miles Anderson) in the 1983 revival.

10. 'This is Illyria, lady.' Kit Surrey's geographically precise Greek Island set for Bill Alexander's 1987 revival with Viola (Harriet Walter) and an inquisitive Sea Captain (Richard Conway).

11. An apprehensive Sir Andrew (David Bradley), a younger-than-usual, domineering Sir Toby (Roger Allam) in the 1987 production.

12. *Antony Sher's bulging-eyed Malvolio, tethered to a stake by a halter, is driven out of his wits in the Bill Alexander version: Bruce Alexander as a quietly tormenting Feste.*

and their natural wisdom because they are nearly always corrective — they nearly always point out the reality behind the fantasy. In 'The Wind and the Rain', for example, he does the seven ages of man.

Michael Billington   He expresses the wisdom of the play . . .

Terry Hands   And he also presents a kind of very wry . . . I was going to say loving, not properly loving, but natural philosophy: 'Youth is a stuff that will not endure.' And we've got the three of them trying to be still young, and they're not. In the final song he says, 'Once when I was a little boy, I grew up, and I did this and then there was still the wind and the rain and that's the way the human cycle goes.' Which is why I've never enjoyed Festes who were too passionate, too active, too aggressive, too involved. They need to help the story along, comment on the story — and then keep reminding us that it will all happen again.

I feel that Feste is ageless, timeless — like the sunny candle going from here to there. He can take words and show them as fashion and what their real meaning is. He turns them inside out like a cheveril glove. But he can play the actual fool if he wants to. And that's why, in a way, all the best Festes, for me, have been sexless in the right sense — I mean, not sexual participants in the play, as opposed to everybody else, and played by actors with that young-old quality.

Michael Billington   Is Feste middle-aged?

Terry Hands   I think so, but I would rather say timeless. It's like Merlin. I mean, you don't think of Merlin being young or old: you think he's eternal. We talked about people like, say, the late Emrys James or Geoffrey Hutchings: and they had that wonderful young-old quality that is never quite one or the other. They're sort of commenting. I think the songs are astonishingly important. Feste is the kind of man who says, 'I don't care. Let her hang me. But she needs me at this moment to make her realise what is *natural*. And it is not natural to mew yourself up for seven years.'

Bill Alexander   Yes, very good. I think that the important thing about Feste is that he is the professional comedian within the play. Like any good comedian, he is paid to present a view of life that's knowing and satirical, and helps other people see themselves better. One of the interesting things about *Twelfth Night* is that he

doesn't do that a great deal: but then I suppose you could say that's true of professional fools in Shakespeare. The important balance in the play is the Feste-versus-Malvolio one — the professional comedian against the *idiote* figure, the natural buffoon. Feste is the man who, by being a clever and perceptive man, makes fools of others, while Malvolio is the man who makes a fool of himself because he's not perceptive, because he doesn't see and he doesn't understand.

Terry Hands   The difference between the clown and the fool.

Bill Alexander   Yes, in the line of the idiot, like Parolles, the accidental or the natural fool. And I think that what connects Feste in human terms to the rest of the play — because it's very easy to see him as someone who stands back and judges everyone's actions and surveys things — is that he doesn't ever forget what Malvolio says about him: that he's not funny. That's the greatest insult that a professional comedian can be paid. He carries it with him right through the play, and punishes Malvolio for it in the Sir Topaz scene by being absolutely unremitting in what he's being required to do. He reminds him of it at the end of the play, and it's quite shocking to realise that that character has carried that bitterness and resentment along with him — but it's also good, because it balances the character, it makes him a vulnerable person who gets upset and carries resentments, as well as conveying his objective view of human behaviour.

Michael Billington   So it's a long-delayed revenge comedy in which Feste gets his own back on Malvolio?

John Caird   I think there is an element of that. But, as I said earlier, what Feste is saying to Malvolio is, 'Do you remember, you who were so pompous, you asked, why laugh at such a barren rascal? Now look at what's happened. Now look who the joke's on. Thus, the whirligig of *time* brings in its revenges. I didn't.' Feste doesn't actually *do* anything.

Michael Billington   Time is the ultimate arbiter.

John Caird   Yes. Once Feste's been humiliated, he puts the boot in, but he's not an active participant in Malvolio's humiliation.

Terry Hands   There are two ways of tackling Feste's final lines.

One can interpret them as: 'I've carried this burning anger and resentment, and finally my revenge has come,' and a vicious line can flick out of the mouth. Or there's the person who says, 'Do you remember when we began this play? You see what happens if you take up those kind of positions of cruelty or lack of caring or insensitivity. Time works its way out. Be kind.' If he's central in my terms or the way you're talking, the key idea is that 'Time will do it. So be careful of these poses, be careful of trying to change the cycle.' I've seen it done as revenge, and it always worries me slightly. I'm not saying I'm right and you're wrong, Bill: I'm just saying that it always worries me. I always feel that Feste really is simply pointing out that spring will come again, the cycle will continue.

Michael Billington John Barton, why did you choose Feste as the key to the play?

John Barton I think Terry describes Feste very well. It's as dangerous with him as with any of the characters to define him as an either-or, either dark or light, either funny or sad. He's a classic example of the mixture. There is a danger in Bill's definition, which seems to thin out the character slightly by defining him too narrowly for the complexities of the part, and indeed of the play. One needs to keep remembering here our well-established knowledge that the part was written for Robert Armin, at the time Tarleton had just retired, and when Shakespeare turned from the professional hearty clown to the melancholy professional clown, who was funny in a different way from the extrovert Tarleton.

We asked ourselves earlier, is there any key line about a character or a play, and I suppose that there were two key lines that I took which resonated for me about the part. The first was, 'And thus the whirligig of time brings in his revenges.' To me, the word that needs focusing on there is actually 'whirligig': it's not too solemn, it's saying, 'Don't take revenge and time, those two cosmic Shakespearean words, too heavily here.' And that suggests to me the vital Shakespearean balance. The other line that I felt tied up the whole part is Feste's 'Pleasure will be paid one time or another.' Which is light, wry, dangerous, accepting.

John Caird John, it's so depressing that you take that as a key line of the play!

John Barton No, a key to the *part*, I said.

The Songs and the Singer

Michael Billington Can I ask another basic question about Feste? How good a singer should he be? It always strikes me that if he's too musical then it actually destroys the point. And if there's something slightly abrasive about his singing, then the songs and lyrics have a greater power.

Terry Hands There is the danger of the modern composer. The lines themselves are lyrically very straight, and the trouble is that if you get them dressed up too much you don't get the message — that's a problem with *Much Ado*, too, isn't it, John? In the garden, just before the gulling, there's an extraordinary song to tell them all about the fickleness of men, and by the time you get a lot of music on top, you've completely lost the meaning.

Bill Alexander I think it should be a Leonard Cohen type of singer, myself — someone who uses the voice to convey lyrics.

John Caird But you can't get away from the most obvious fact that you pointed out, John: that this play was probably the first to be written for Armin rather than Tarleton. And if it's got more songs in it than any other Shakespeare play, then it must be because Armin had a marvellous voice.

John Barton But what *kind* of marvellous voice?

John Caird I toyed for a long time with the idea, and actually got quite far down the road towards asking Peter Pears to play the part. He's a fine actor, Peter Pears, and would have sung it with exactly that sort of gratingness we're talking about. I felt that the songs were also very beautiful, and they should have something both beautiful and rough about the way that they're sung.

Michael Billington But on the whole, isn't the best and clearest rendition of the lyrics what it's all about?

John Caird Possibly so, but then why a song? Why not a beautiful speech in iambic pentameters? If a song is a song, it's got to be sung by somebody with a decent voice. There's nothing more horrible in the theatre, whether it's musical theatre or straight theatre, than listening to somebody singing off-key.

Terry Hands   But John, you must admit we do occasionally get overdressed with our songs and our music.

Bill Alexander   I had no doubt in my production that I wanted the songs sung unaccompanied. Every time I see a Feste produce a guitar or lute to accompany himself, or some accompaniment comes from the wings, I shrivel up. He's a man who can just stand there and start singing. He provides music and he has a pleasant voice, but it's a vehicle for the words.

John Caird   But other characters say that he's got a marvellous voice.

John Barton   I think that a question about him which is worth raising is, 'Where is he socially? What are his class and background?'

Michael Billington   Are the answers in the play?

John Barton   There aren't any official answers. It could be that he's a courtly clown, or it could be that he's a peasant clown. But I think it is rather an important decision to take that affects the tone of the whole production.

Michael Billington   Which direction did you steer in?

John Barton   I went for the peasant — that he was somebody who had made it by his wits and earned money by his wits, but is not on the social level of anybody else in the play. As he was rather special, they took him in, but it was something risky that he was doing, being inside that aristocratic network.

Terry Hands   Who's that famous illustrator of Shakespeare, John, who did the most wonderful illustrations to *Twelfth Night*, where he seems, in every single illustration, to get the play right?

John Barton   Arthur Rackham?

Terry Hands   Arthur Rackham. In his drawings there it seems to me it's just the kind of Feste you're talking about — almost like a peasant. Equally, he might be a tramp.

Bill Alexander   I think if you met him, you really would wonder

what class he was. He could be a hobo tramp. He could be a guy who's just wandered in from somewhere, maybe from another country.

John Caird   He could be a fallen gentleman.

Bill Alexander   Absolutely. He could be an ex-law student, of many years ago.

John Caird   I think there's more than a key line, there's a key speech about Feste, which does highlight this thing about the change in practice from a broad comic fool to a courtly fool: and Feste and the Fool in *Lear* are very similar types. But the key speech is that after the scene with Viola, when this fellow is wise enough to play the fool, Shakespeare decides to give Viola an apology for Feste. It's interesting he felt that to be necessary — that he wanted one of his characters to point out to the audience that Feste has a lot of wisdom in him, in spite of the fact that he's just a clown. And it makes one wonder whether or not the audience were quite ready for it, whether perhaps Shakespeare was somehow insuring himself. And what Viola actually says tells you an awful lot about his sense of humour and what he's up to.

John Barton   I raise the question of Feste's social status not because I think in this case there's any proof one way or the other, but because it's a choice that's bound to come up in the casting and it's a choice that's going to affect the chemistry of the group of people playing *Twelfth Night*. You can't take characters entirely one by one, because what they are must be in relation to what the others are. And the way that Feste is cast and played depends very much on getting the right balance with Toby, Ague-Cheek, and Malvolio.

Michael Billington   And he's of a generation with them.

John Barton   I think so, yes.

Fitting the Music to the Mood

Michael Billington   By extension, can we turn to the music in *Twelfth Night*? There's no Shakespeare play that has more music, is there? Or more songs? What as directors do you do about this?

Do you go and hire a composer, who will write you a score, or do you look for traditional airs and melodies for the songs?

John Caird Well, I did both. I got Ilona Secacz to write a new score for the songs 'O Mistress Mine' and 'Come Away Death'. But I told her when we started that I didn't think 'The Wind and the Rain' should be newly composed — that there was something about that song at the end of that play that was essentially just somebody singing a traditional folk song. In fact there's a great deal of doubt whether Shakespeare had a hand in writing it, or whether it was a traditional song sung by Armin stuck on at the end of the play. I felt it was right it should be the only point in the evening when traditional music was heard.

Bill Alexander Yes. I didn't have a composer on my production because I wanted to use all the early music that was available for it. I wanted to keep the music very simple, and I felt that in a play that has so many songs and in which music plays such an important part, there ought not to be any other music that goes 'around' it. So there was no music covering the scene changes, no music other than when someone sang, and that was unaccompanied — except the playing of the music in Orsino's court, which had to be there because it's commented on. So I used the original setting for 'O Mistress Mine', which I think is so beautiful.

Michael Billington If memory serves correctly, John, you actually began your *Twelfth Night* by having music playing as the curtain rose. As we came into the theatre, there was music playing and Orsino listening. The play was saturated in music before a word had been spoken.

John Barton As I remember, the main music cue, or rather sound cue, was the sea, which I had continually at certain moments, and it came up on the scene changes. That's the only difference from Bill. I did, now I remember, have guitarists playing, and Orsino just sitting there brooding before the curtain went up: but it was very muted because it was crossed with the sound of the sea, and the sea was more dominant than the lute. I think we found it helped Orsino into the mood — 'If music be the food of love play on' being the first line of the play, it meant music had been playing and I didn't have to do any entrances and exits. I suppose that must have been the logic. But it was always in relation to the sea.

Like Bill, I wanted all the traditional stuff, though some of it comes from a slightly later date. And I'd also said, 'Look, it seems to me that all the songs and lyrics are in some way uncourtly, more primitive, and that's the musical style.' That's another reason why I wanted a roughish singer. But there is a great problem with 'Come away Death', where there isn't anything. We actually tried out *six* versions before I bought the final, brilliant one that Guy Woolfenden composed and which was tremendous.

John Caird It's just that the lyric is a bit courtly, that's the problem

John Barton Well, talking more about it, that indeed leads to the interpretive problem of how you do it. It was the lyric that I worked on by far the most, in terms of how it should be *acted*. And I took it that the first verse was more peasant-like, very straight and simple; but the second verse is more courtly, and I got Feste to sing it as a parody of the lovesick mood of Orsino, and he did it behind Orsino's back, with Viola knowing that he was doing it, so it was very ambiguous. Actually, he did it as an insult that Orsino thought was beautiful. I'm not saying that's necessarily right, but that was an example of how we tried to think through the music and the text together.

Orsino: Setting the Tone

Michael Billington Bill, can I come back to the question of character? You were the odd man out when I asked about the character who dictated the mood. You said Orsino. Why Orsino?

Bill Alexander Well, it depends what you mean by 'dictating the mood'. I feel that I had the most problematic time over casting Orsino. I do think it's a key decision, whether you play him older or younger: if you make him younger, round about the same age as, or just a few years older than, Viola, it becomes one kind of play; if you make him an older man it becomes very much more about a young girl falling for a mature man, and so many shades within the play are tied up with that.

It's even more important than how old Malvolio is or how old Feste is, or how old Sir Toby is, because although Orsino doesn't actually have much to do, it's vital to our belief in the viability of that love relationship at the end when it has to happen — when

Orsino has to decide whether to accept that this person has turned out to be a girl, and how much subconsciously he intuits about that person's femininity, and how much he falls in love with her before having to say, 'I take you as my wife.' On those sorts of things the balance between realism and myth in the play really depends. That's why I found it a particularly important bit of casting.

John Caird The thing about Orsino is that you want to have somebody very authoritative for the part, because he sets the tone. Whether or not he's at the centre of the play is another matter, but he certainly sets the tone. It's a very difficult part because it's got three scenes that make a good continuum with one another, and then a huge gap, and then the final scene. So you need a really strong, major actor to play that part. You've got to feel there's somebody . . . dangerous, that there's a danger coming from him — that he could suddenly start duking it and put his foot down and demand. You must feel that that danger is real, right up until the last moment of the play.

Michael Billington He might kill Cesario . . .

John Caird Yes, he could kill Cesario and insist that his version of the truth should be the one that the play ends on. It's an interesting play, in that Olivia falls in love with somebody and ends up with somebody else, and Orsino falls in love with somebody and ends up with somebody else. It's not exactly a classic happy-ending story is it? It's a difficult, very ambiguous part to play, because you've got to be very strong and authoritative, yet you are in a sense the butt of a very big joke.

Bill Alexander Completely at the mercy of a very big joke.

John Caird You've got to be big-hearted about the way you play it.

John Barton I think it is an absolutely crucial piece of casting in the play, equal in importance to the more obviously major parts, in that the play will never work fully without that danger and weight in it. I completely agree with Bill about that. I suppose that must be one of the reasons why I had him sitting there brooding for a long time before the play began — because I knew he was going to disappear for such a long time, yet he's got to have the same weight in the play as all the other parts. And I think that's one of

the huge problems about doing the play. Because if you don't, he just becomes wet, and that trivialises Viola's feelings and the whole chemistry of the evening is affected.

Michael Billington That's interesting, because surely the tendency *is* slightly to send him up these days. . . .

Terry Hands But I think the interesting thing is that both of you, Bill and John, chose people who were rather noble and dignified but very gentle. I go along with your thinking, but the two that I chose were Gareth Thomas and Francois Beaulieu, who were more kind of powerful. The problem is that when you get on to the chamber plays, and you've only got a very small number of people, the casting has got to be perfect.

I don't really believe that Orsino will finally set the tone for the whole thing — I believe Feste will, because he's in everybody's scenes, he touches everybody's scenes. But nonetheless, if your Olivia isn't quite comic enough, or your Viola isn't quite ambiguous enough, or your Toby Belch doesn't give you quite that tremendous engine-room drive, you are in deep trouble. It's almost like type-casting, where you've got to find the ones who after a long period of rehearsal nonetheless still have it within their type-range to cope with the role. It's the huge difficulty of plays like *Twelfth Night*. When you do the great orchestral pieces — not the chamber pieces like this, but the orchestral pieces — you can have a far greater variance without damage.

Michael Billington The parallel with Chekhov is coming back again in that you've got to have a small team of stars all perfectly cast . . .

John Caird There is no part that drives the play. We talk about Toby Belch as the engine-room of the play. But if the other elements weren't there he'd have nothing to motor. There's no sense in which he is the lead.

John Barton I agree with what Terry has said. I had a very good major actor playing Orsino, but he was gentle and, even in that case, it was not how I would ideally have cast have it. I would agree that if there'd been a bull with a dangerous, anarchic quality about him in the company at the time, that would have been how it should have been done.

Malvolio: the Social Status of the Steward

Michael Billington   Although we have talked about Malvolio, I don't think we have suggested what Malvolio's place is in the social world of the play. Is it easily identifiable, easily recognisable?

Bill Alexander   Yes, I think it is. We have several clues to go on. When I did my production, I spent some time doing research into the structure of an Elizabethan household and finding out exactly what the steward was in that context. I was interested to discover that he was a far more important figure than I had thought, far more than just a glorified butler. He was a very highly trained, highly educated person, responsible for all aspects of the house, gardens, and land. He was often a very erudite person, a very well-educated person, and probably an expert huntsman and expert archer. He had to have a very good economic sense in that he ran and organised the books. You could well imagine how he was key figure in a large Elizabethan household.

It's the importance of his role that gives the character its interest and ambivalence in dramatic literature, I think. When Malvolio says to himself, musingly, 'The lady of the Strachey married the yeoman of the wardrobe,' he may be quoting a slightly ridiculous topical example, but unless you take the aspiration of Malvolio as a realisable one then I think you undermine the comedy of the play and make it purely fantastical and farcical. The fact that it is an outrageous thought to Sir Toby that Malvolio should aspire to marry Olivia is neither here nor there — that tells you something about Sir Toby, not about the reality of what Malvolio wants for himself.

If you don't accept that it is a possible social movement, as it indeed *was* in the Elizabethan period, which was a time of great social mobility, then you simply have to come to the conclusion that the man is completely mad, in which case the *driving* of him mad or nearly mad loses its complexity, the play becomes thinner and more obvious. There was a play written only a decade or so later about a steward marrying a duchess — *The Duchess of Malfi*. It says a lot about the changeability of society and the way people were relating to that — the way people could be offended by it if they were aristocrats, but its possibility nonetheless.

We know other things about Malvolio, of course. We know that he is a man without a sense of humour, but a man who is

nevertheless called upon to express his opinion all the time. We have to remember that he is invited into the play by Olivia. 'What do you think, Malvolio?' she says. Part of what that tells us is that it begins to define Olivia's job of keeping the discordant elements of the household in some sort of equilibrium. 'Ignore Malvolio too much,' you can hear her thinking, 'and he will only get worse and worse and more isolated.' She wants to bring him in. But we know he is an unremittingly unforgiving man in terms of people he doesn't like and doesn't approve of, and when Maria says of him later in the play, 'Marry, sometimes he's a kind of puritan,' I think that is one of the most revealing things about him.

He is often portrayed as *the* puritan — as opposed to the free-wheeling, life-loving Sir Toby — but I think the point is that he is indeed a 'kind of puritan,' and when Maria goes on to say, 'The devil he is a puritan, or anything other than a time-server, an affectioned ass, someone who can't state without book,' the implication is he will be *anything* that he thinks will advance him, but his pose is the pose of a puritan because that's what, for him, gives him his own sense of authority, dignity, and purpose within the household.

You do have to keep reminding yourself what an absolutely crucial element the real puritans were in the society of the time. Another forty years and they were running the country. Therefore, the idea of a man who regards his status as steward in the household as being terribly important is crucial. If it wasn't for Malvolio, probably the place would be in total chaos. If it was just left to Sir Toby to bring back his drunken friends, completely overrun Olivia, and carry on an affair with Maria, who is presumably meant to be another responsible person within the household, things would fall apart. Like Malvolio or not, and most people in the play do not, the place would be a shambles without him. Presumably also, he is serving some very good purpose in keeping at a distance the messengers that keep coming from Orsino, who are not wanted.

You then have to look at the adverse side of that — how he *uses* his position, how he is keeping Olivia to himself, how he is enjoying the state of mourning that is being imposed, and may even have encouraged the notion of seven years with the veil, of walking round the cloisters. But the thing I am really trying to get at is that he thinks of himself as important because he *is* important, and the analysis that must then go on is about how as a personality he is nevertheless out of balance, and has a blinkered view of himself and what he can achieve.

Michael Billington   That's a fascinating analysis. But I wonder how easy is it in a modern production, Terry, to convey the importance of Malvolio within the household? Not many productions, these days, present us with a household and a chain of servants, and Malvolio is often seen almost in isolation, isn't he?

Terry Hands   I don't think it's a problem. You can usually set it up in the costuming and behaviour patterns at the beginning of the play. I agree with everything that Bill said, because it informs the social context, the fact that he is an NCO and they are officers, as it were, and therefore his aspirations are towards that kind of marriage. There is a function within that society that is so clear that any audience would understand it, even if they did not know about the Elizabethan background. I think his age is between the older level of Belch, Ague-Cheek, and Feste, and the youngsters. He comes sort of midway. This is one of those men who is going to take over in the Commonwealth period, and Shakespeare keeps hinting at that — *Merry Wives of Windsor* is another example — and keeps letting us know that this new generation, because of trade, because of their abilities, are going to take over. You can show that in context, and you could do a production which was in a complete Elizabethan household, in which you would very quickly see how it all worked. I also agree with Bill that the seven years' mourning might very well be Malvolio's idea, because if Olivia is fourteen, which she is probably meant to be in Shakespeare's terms, twenty-one is about the right moment for marriage, and he's running it.

But there is a poetic as well as a social context, which tells just as clear a story, which is that if it is 'la nuit des rois', the night of the kings when they came and brought the gifts — that is, *Twelfth Night* — there is also a figure who is stopping the revelry and trying to bring things back to order, but in a comic way, because he never really wins. He stops the party, but there is still a rebellion simmering on into the night. We have that nostalgic feeling, and you get the old boys wandering off with their bottles.

His double function surely is that he is the most proper, the most organised character, and as such I find him quite sympathetic. But he is also a bore and pompous, and it's lovely to laugh at pompous people. In the first half of the play his comedy is entirely in his language, it's not in any way in business and should not be. I am convinced of that because of the way he phrases, the way he times his speeches. This kind of character is quite common in Elizabethan literature — think of William Prynne and *Satiro-*

77

mastix — and he's the sort of person we still see around. Who is that terrible Belfast fellow . . . ?

Michael Billington   You mean Ian Paisley?

Terry Hands   Yes, Paisley. You know, there's that same extraordinary sense of arrogance. A sergeant-major in the army, he knows more than any of the officers, but he has to call them 'Sir'. All those things fit very well. But what we discover about Malvolio is that he is a reactive comic in the first half of the play, in the sense that everything *happens to* him, and he responds — like when Olivia says, 'Run, run, run, run,' after Cesario, and he says, 'Madam I will', and the idea of him running after anybody becomes, in itself, very funny.

I think most Malvolios go wrong by trying to cram the part with business in the first half. Now his function is to go absolutely mad, and we know there are character reasons for this because we see him on his own in the garden. In *As You Like It* Rosalind says, 'Love is merely a madness, it deserves a dark house and a dungeon as madmen do', and here the only reason it doesn't work is because the whippers are in love too — I mean, they're as mad as everybody else. This *is* very midsummer madness.

The comic explosion of the role is when the moment comes for him, too, to be caught up in the madness of love, and in terms of the poetic context that is Shakespeare's constant message: it's like the blades of grass getting through the concrete. Roger Michell came in yesterday and said that his entire car had been wrecked by a mouse, and I said, 'How absolutely wonderful. This is terribly Shakespearean. How did it happen?' He's got this Chevrolet, or something, where the whole gearing of the pistons and everything comes off a band in the front of the motor, and the mouse went in and ate it, so all his pistons misfired and functioned wrong and blew the engine apart. Now he has an entire engine to be rebuilt because of one mouse. He said the interesting thing was, looking through his insurance policy, he discovered he is insured against mice. That to me is the thing behind Malvolio: no matter how perfectly he fulfils a social function — a 'mal-volio', ill-wisher, or restrictive function — Shakespeare has provided the blade of grass or the life force, and it is his change which gears the mechanism of the play.

Michael Billington   John, on the subject of the social context, is that something that has to be implied in the production of *Twelfth*

Night, or is it something that you have to clarify — Malvolio's place in the household?

John Barton   I would tend to make the decision based on who was playing the part, and one would evolve the social background around that particular temperament and personality. I think all that Bill says about the nature and importance of a steward is absolutely correct, but it is actually more ambiguous than that. At one extreme a steward could be a knight. I lived for years in a house which had been owned by an Elizabethan knight who was the steward of Leicester of Kenilworth, and himself a big landowner. On the other hand, I bet you if you analysed all the Elizabethan and Jacobean plays which have stewards in them you would find some very lowly stewards. Dramatists make stewards what they want to make them in a given play. So one could argue against Bill textually, because of the insistence on 'Art any more than a steward,' and the fact that the other two are knights, so social inferiority is implied in that group for the purposes of that play. But it's very healthy to assert that stewards are important, so I feel a bit ambiguous about it, and would come round to it in terms of talking it out with whoever was playing it. They would need the social background more than I would!

Malvolio: What Kind of a Character?

Terry Hands   Talking about the actor involved, when you, John, had Donald Sinden, what Donald wonderfully managed to convey in that production was a man who was so determined to be more lordly than the lords that he even had an accent that was posher than theirs. He could let it drop or he could put it on. Everything about him was self-created.

John Barton   That's right, and I utterly believed in that. But if it had been another actor it would have been something quite different. That's all I am saying.

Bill Alexander   It's later in that scene that Sir Toby says to him, 'Art any more than a steward,' and suddenly that brings us up against that social fact. Yes, he is their social inferior, however important a steward he is. It is the question of how his sense of self-importance fits in with his actual hierarchical position. But *he* talks to *them* in very strong terms: 'Masters, are you mad, or what

79

are you, that you gabble like tinkers at this time of the night?' The language is very strong: he accuses them of gabbling like tinkers, which from a steward to a lord is very extreme language.

What I suggested to both John Carlisle and Tony Sher about Malvolio is that he is not a good handler of people, but he tries to be and even thinks he is. When he first speaks and is asked what he thinks of Feste, he says, 'I marvel your Ladyship can take delight in such a barren rascal. I saw him put down the other day by an ordinary fool, one who has no more brains than a stone.' Now, in my view, Malvolio is trying to be funny but is failing to be funny, because he doesn't have an innate sense of humour or an innate sense of how you can put someone down in a way that is both effective and actually gives you more status in relationship to other people.

The same sort of thing is true when he comes down and says, 'My masters . . .'. That's the first thing he says, 'My masters.' He admits the social difference. 'Are you mad that you gabble like tinkers at this time of the night?' He is trying to portray them in a sort of jokey way. You've got to see him accepting the relativity of his status to them, while at the same time showing that in his own head he thinks he is above them. What you can't portray is someone coming down saying, 'What the fuck's going on here? Who the fuck are you?' That is inconceivable. So it's finding the sense of humour that Malvolio *thinks* he has but actually fails to have that's the key.

Terry Hands Could I challenge that? I would disagree about Malvolio and the sense of humour, even that he is trying to show one. I would challenge it without any dogma, but simply to offer another view which is that the fascinating thing about the character is that he is a *passionate* man, who therefore needs to make extraordinary efforts right from the word go to control his own passions. He is a man of great fantasies, of great dreaming. He sits up in his little room and plans out extraordinary life stories for himself connected with Olivia, who is now on her own and is very dependent upon him . . . the lady of the Strachey and the yeoman of the wardrobe. Whenever he needs to give his opinion in those early scenes, instead of just simply saying, 'I think Feste is a bore — get rid of him,' there is that slow, measured control. And when he comes out in the middle of the night, he has to play it like you or I would play it — we've just been dragged out of bed by this appalling noise and our sleep's been ruined. He's trying to control his anger. To call them 'tinkers' shows a tremendous

passion which he then tries to sit on. The fascination of the role is that this passion is only just beneath the surface, and once it's actually let off the leash, his behaviour becomes more ludicrous, more irrational, more extraordinary than anything we have seen anybody else do in the whole play.

John Barton   What you have both said shows that it is a part that you can push in many ways, and in some ways I might dispute those particular interpretations. The point I would make, the feeling I have about it, is really a quite different one. The part is different in kind from the other characters in the play, and actually it is dangerous to get too complicated about it. I think it is basically a Jonsonian humours part, like a misfit in a Chekhov play. Malvolio's obsessiveness, his one trackness, his blinkered limits, say to me 'Jonson' more than 'Shakespeare'. So I think that any solution shouldn't be too complex, because the mechanism of the play, however it's interpreted, is that if a fine actor comes on and plays Malvolio you do always get a sense of an eruption into the play of something that's a bit different in kind and style.

Terry Hands   That's very true.

Michael Billington   Bill Alexander, do you want to pick up on either of those points?

Bill Alexander   Both points, John's first. I know exactly what John means about the part being like a Jonsonian part in the middle of a Shakespeare play. I would just question the usefulness of stressing that, because the danger with Malvolio is precisely that he *will* seem to be in a different style from the rest of the play. Of course, the fact is that in life there are some people who are more extremely obsessed and bound by their humours and their objectives than other people, but you have got to be terribly careful that Malvolio doesn't seem to be coming from a different dramatic heritage, but that you explain him as a personality within that household.

John Barton   I think there is a real distinction here between the need for exploration in depth in rehearsal, and what Michael asked us originally, which was about our conception of Malvolio. I remember thinking when I was studying the play that it is a different kind of part, and actually I can see it could be played in many, many different ways. And whereas with some of the

characters I wanted really to push them in one or other direction, I was very aware that it was vital to make Malvolio real and specific — but the possibilities were more open-ended.

Bill Alexander I don't disagree with that. But can I now pick up on Terry's point? I don't disagree that he is a passionate man, but I think that is very open to interpretation. A word like 'tinkers' comes out because Malvolio really does think they are gabbling like tinkers, but he is trying to find a way of saying it that can be received by them. Terry says, there he is having been woken up in the middle of the night and he comes down in a terrible rage about it. Well, maybe, maybe not. I think the internal evidence of the scene is that it's not him that's been woken up by the noise but Olivia that has woken *him* up, and asked him to go down and sort it out. It is not his choice. He says, 'My lady bids me tell you that you are very welcome to be here if you clean your act up. Otherwise you have got to go.' It's not him that is saying it, it's Olivia.

Now that tells us something about Olivia, and it tells us something about Malvolio. Malvolio is *not* someone who instinctively steps over the bounds and comes screaming down the stairs saying they're keeping him awake. He recognises his stewardship. He does it because Olivia has told him to do it. Olivia doesn't come down herself because it would be extremely undignified: she is a woman and she just can't handle it. It is a little description of the network of tensions in the household. You could argue, of course, that Malvolio is making it up, that *he* has been woken up, but my view of Shakespeare is that he doesn't usually write like that. Characters nearly always speak the truth about what has happened to them and about why they're there.

Terry Hands The only thing I would come back on has to do with a slightly different area, and that is the degree of insult intended. If you say to a duke and the landed gentry, 'You are like a tinker,' it was the lowest of the low, because the tinkers were regarded as the male equivalent of whores and pimps, and I therefore think it was quite a heavy insult.

The thing I'd like to bring us back to is that question of what you have to do in terms of the modern audience. Supposing you are doing it in Japan or whatever, do you have to create a social household that they will understand? If, finally, you have got an audience that knows nothing about it, the one thing that is true of the play at all times is that it's a love story. I rather agree with

John: there are these humours characters — Belch, Ague-Cheek, Malvolio, Feste — with rather curious names, and then there are the characters in the central plot with human names — Antonio, Sebastian, Cesario, Orsino, and so on. But the structure of the play right from the beginning, is that everybody is chasing this woman called Olivia. Right in the centre of the play there is this extraordinary competition as to who is going to get her. Will it be Orsino? Will it be Belch, by being the favourite uncle? Is it going to be Ague-Cheek, or even Malvolio, who dreams of being the man? And the person who does get her is Cesario, who doesn't want her and who is a girl anyway, which is wonderfully Shakespearean.

So the whole structure of the play, if you knew nothing about anything else, is people squabbling and fighting for the hand, or at least the approval of Olivia. Olivia is in the centre. So even if we knew nothing about Elizabethan society, the moment we got Malvolio on stage we'd see he was putting up blocks against anybody else getting to Olivia. He pushes aside Feste, and he is extremely upset that there is a ring being sent to Cesario, to the point where he leaves it on the floor rather than actually handing it over. And he is trying to push Toby and Ague-Cheek out of her care. Whatever means he is using, the actual mechanism in front of your eyes is that there is this man, who is close to her, and who is doing his damnedest to stop anybody else getting anywhere near her.

Michael Billington   I wonder if there has been a tendency in post-war productions of *Twelfth Night* for Malvolio to assume an ever greater importance, almost to displace the love interest from the centre of the play? John said Malvolio changes depending on who is playing him — and the tendency is for the leading actor in any generation to want to play Malvolio. Now is there any danger that we are becoming preoccupied with Malvolio in modern productions and maybe unbalancing this very delicately structured play?

John Barton   That's always been the theatrical tradition, hasn't it? If you go through eighteenth- or nineteenth-century cast lists, it's Malvolio's part that has the big actor in.

Terry Hands   Wasn't it Burbage's role?

John Caird   Pepys described going to the play, and he said he

thought it was one of the silliest plays he had ever seen and that it was all about the steward falling in love with the widow.

Bill Alexander Some of the earliest diary references called the play *Malvolio*.

John Caird It is a problem. You are right to call it a problem, but it is a problem initiated by the playwright, and it is very difficult to get round it because any actor reading the play isn't going to see any other part as the leading part.

Terry Hands Yes, but I would argue that it doesn't unbalance the play, and didn't do so even when it was played by Larry Olivier. *Twelfth Night* is a play about love and ends up with marriages of various kinds. If the Malvolio is linked to that part of the story, the love story, then the play holds together. If, on the other hand, we start to do a production which is actually about stewards in households and Elizabethans and puritans, then the play will go crazy — and will fall apart. If we make it a political play, or even a play about Viola, it will go wrong. But if it's a love story where they are all pursuing Olivia, and then Olivia makes *her* choice, which is what pulls in Viola and Sebastian to the story, then it will work out.

Look at the first two scenes — they're hardly scenes, they're prologues. The first announces Orsino, the second announces Viola, we know they are going to be got together. So that is the plot. Then in the world they go into, everybody's chasing Olivia. If we're told that, I don't think Malvolio does break it. The way he can destroy the play is if the actor says, 'I've been told that in four centuries of playing this is the funniest part in the play and I'm going to be funnier than anybody else.' Then it goes wrong.

John Caird Or, 'I am going to be funny by doing the same thing that all my predecessors did at this moment in the plot.' That's the other problem, because everybody who plays Malvolio has usually played some other part in the play before, and has worked out how he would play Malvolio if he ever got the chance.

Maria and the Matter of Marriage

Michael Billington Can we move on to the character of Maria, who we haven't mentioned at all, yet who seems to be a very

interesting and ambiguous character, and who again is part of the household? First, I am interested to know how you define Maria's status in that household. Where, precisely, does she fit in? And secondly, do we perhaps overlook the fact that it is Maria who actually instigates the whole plot against Malvolio? She is the arch manipulator, it seems to me, and by implication an extremely strong woman.

John Barton The personal maid to the lady of the house is very important, but, as with Malvolio, the dramatist in any given play decides on its relative importance. There is nothing grand about Maria, which is why it is perfectly legitimate when she is often played in a soubrettish manner. That's a valid way of doing it, although not one I agree with. The way you take Maria is one of the big interpretive choices because it is open-ended: it's not textually defined how old she is or what she is at all. You can get dividends out of an old Belch marrying a young Maria, or you can go the way I did which was to make them both as old as possible and pretty well past it, so that it was a doomed marriage. Both actually fit the text.

I agree with you about her importance as the instigator of the plot, and of course what we've been saying is that the whole group of characters have in a sense an equal importance. Terry said how vital Olivia is. Orsino we agreed was maybe one of the most important characters. But we could now argue it about Maria. Really, Maria is the part that most easily goes wrong in a sort of glib, jolly tradition, and really needs looking at hard. It's to do with how you cast it in relation to the other people, and with making decisions about social status, but I don't think in practice they work out that powerfully because she is pretty well silent in the first scene with Olivia, and thereafter she's on escapade.

Michael Billington John Caird, how did you tackle this problem of her status and her age?

John Caird Well, I cast Gemma Jones, and it was one of those very happy accidents that happen to one sometimes in the theatre that uncovered an enormous richness in the part. John's right about the age, I don't think that is particularly important. I also don't think, as John says, that her class is important these days. But what *is* crucial is that she is a dependent, and that she is far too witty and intelligent and resourceful to be happy about being a dependent. So she has a lot to gain by marrying out of that.

The crucial scene for Maria is the point at which the three men are carousing and Malvolio comes in and attempts to stop them. Then Belch makes a major decision. Rather than just snipe at Malvolio, he squares up to him and actually insults him openly in a way that perhaps he has never done before. He goes up to him and says, 'Art any more than a steward? Dost thou think that because thou art virtuous there shall be no more cakes and ale?' He really takes him on, and makes it even more of a face-off by saying, 'Go, rub your chain with crumbs.' Then he turns to Maria and says, 'Maria. A stoup of wine!' In other words, he puts Maria in a position of having to decide whether or not she is going to go on playing it quiet and getting on with everybody in the house, or whether she is with him, Toby. In other words, 'Now is the moment when you make your choice between me and a quiet life.'

And Maria turns to Malvolio and says, 'Go shake your ears.' From that moment she has decided, 'I am on Belch's side and I am going to do everything I can to make the festival side of this play work out.' And thereafter every bit of resourcefulness, every bit of cleverness, every artifice, every piece of information she has ever picked up about human nature and what goes on in the household, is going to be important to her and for her collaborators.

Bill Alexander That moment is actually quite crucial. It is the pivotal moment of the whole action, after which she initiates the plan against Malvolio. And you're absolutely right to say that 'Maria. A stoup of wine!' is a challenge to her about which way she is going to go. After all, she is the one who has come down and said, 'For God's sake, shut up. Olivia's awake, Malvolio's on his way, you are going to get us all kicked out.' She has been playing it both ways. And the interesting thing about the text after that is that Malvolio anticipates Maria's response and, before she can reply, he says, 'Mistress Mary,' and turns to her: 'if you priz'd my Lady's favour at anything more than contempt, you would not give means for this uncivil rule,' counterchallenging the 'stoup of wine'. 'Go, shake your ears,' John, is actually after Malvolio has exited. And I think that that is key. You can play it so that she shouts it after him, intending to be heard.

John Caird It's your choice, isn't it? I don't believe the exit is textual: it's an editor's exit, not a Shakespeare exit.

Michael Billington So she might be saying it to his face, or after he is long departed?

Bill Alexander Anyway, the key thing is that it becomes one of those moments, whether she says it to Malvolio, or under her breath, or after he's gone. The blokes have sounded off about it — well, the ones who are going to, the other two have just been cowering in the corner waiting for it all to blow over — but you get the feeling Sir Toby has blown himself out of the whole thing. He is most likely if anything else happens to say, 'Well, fuck it, let's all go down the road to an all-night bar. We'll carry on insulting Malvolio from a distance.' The fact that Maria says, 'I've got an idea. I know how to get back at him,' is crucial because it shows that she wants to make a movement towards Sir Toby that is going to bind him more closely to her. She needs at that point to initiate something for her own reasons.

From what you say about her being a dependent and not wanting to be, there's no question that she's got her eye on Sir Toby as a way out of that situation. She is a gold-digger in that sense. But the detailed nature of the plot that she comes up with, and the malevolency of it, really illustrates just how much she hates being the person she is in that household. It is very vicious, very vindictive. And even at the point where, later in the play, Fabian backs off and says, 'We'll make him mad indeed,' when he sees how terribly the plot is gripping and how in danger it is of turning Malvolio's brain, she says, 'The house will be the quieter.' She never goes back, even in the madhouse scene when Sir Toby says, 'We have had enough of this. I am ready to quit.' She doesn't.

John Caird You know the person who is most like Maria in all the rest of English literature is Jane Austen. She was in exactly that situation and kept writing people in that situation. In her novels there is always the gentlewoman-dependent who has to swallow her pride and has to put up with hypocrisy in others, and who invents a sort of awful satirical commentary on their behaviour which goes parallel to what everybody else is doing.

Bill Alexander Absolutely. And I think the crucial thing in all this is that it is very dangerous to the balance of the play to portray Maria as a jolly, happy, bubbly, dumpy, inoffensive sort of person. She is actually someone with a lot of spiked spunk and edge to her.

John Caird And she must be somebody who is doing this just the once. If she is jolly, you get the impression that, oh, Maria's

always playing these funny jokes and that life is a bit of a laugh . . .

Bill Alexander   Quite. It is a turning-point in the action and it's a turning-point in all their lives.

Michael Billington   John Caird used the word 'witty', which seems exactly right. It is Maria who gives that lightning character assessment of Malvolio, 'the devil a puritan that he is.' She sums him up very accurately in eight lines. And then, immediately afterwards, she is the one, of course, who conceives the plot of the letter and the gulling. She seems very shrewd, very sharp and acerbic, as you say.

The Problem of Intention

John Barton   I think that behind this discussion there lurks an obvious question that could come up with almost any character in Shakespeare, which is, 'How much of the data is definable as certain and how much is open-ended?' It would be perfectly possible to put up an alternative hypothesis which is very different but complementary. It certainly was my feeling that Maria is ageing, insecure, downtrodden, treated very badly by Malvolio and Belch, and slightly scared. And I think that what I am saying is entirely in the text, but it's also entirely ignorable. It seems to me a good character about whom we might raise a basic question when we look at the play: what can we be sure about regarding Shakespeare's intentions? What is consistent with the text but unprovable? And what is open-ended? All the time one is juggling with those three balls.

Bill Alexander   And what is downright wrong?

John Barton   Oh, indeed.

Michael Billington   In resolving the open-endedness you have frequently mentioned, does it nearly always come down to who is playing what?

John Barton   It does, I think. I always feel a complete split between what I may think about the play and what I come to feel about it when it is in rehearsal with given actors. One tries to bring

the two together, but sometimes one doesn't. Sometimes one goes their way, sometimes not.

Michael Billington But you make a choice, don't you? You cast Elizabeth Spriggs as Maria: that was your choice, you were saying something about Maria in your casting.

John Barton When I did *Twelfth Night*, the view of Maria was very much mine, but there would be very many other cases where what emerged in rehearsal was very different from what I had felt when I cast it, or what I thought I was after.

John Caird In the case of Elizabeth Spriggs, she could have played it in fifty different ways, because she is that sort of actress.

John Barton In that particular case, I remember she very much went along with what I went after, but in other cases that might not be so.

Terry Hands But, John, this is taking us back to something you said at the outset. I said, glibly, that once you have done your casting you have done your play. If you choose a twenty-one-year-old soubrette, you've done it, there ain't nothing more you can do. You can put a wig or anything you like on her, but you've wrecked it. And we've all done that at some point. We end up after two weeks' rehearsal feeling, 'Oh, no — we've chosen the wrong person.' I would agree with both Johns in the sense that that age of actress, that kind of social standing, and that kind of being-on-the-shelf feeling is crucial to the role, and both times I went for the middle-aged Maria.

Coming back to the love stories, we are talking about somebody making a last bid, and she is after Sir Toby. Everything she does is to get his approval, and she does get his approval. On whether you play 'Go, shake your ears' to Malvolio's face or not, I don't think she would, because the one person he can fire is her. I suspect that is something you mutter after somebody has gone. Watching that scene, nobody else takes him on — Feste doesn't, Ague-Cheek doesn't, and I don't believe Maria does. Only Toby does, because Toby is the only one who really would not and could not suffer.

The other side of my point about all the men chasing Olivia is: what do the other women in the show do? Well, one turns herself into a man, so she gets to be chasing Olivia as well. And there's

only only one left, Maria. You don't need any other ladies-in-waiting, there's none written into a cast of, what, fourteen people. You've just got Maria, and her one bid is for Sir Toby.

Michael Billington   Why is it her last chance, exactly? Is there any textual evidence for that?

John Caird   I think 'only' is the word we should be using.

Terry Hands   But who else is there for her to become involved with? Possibly a Malvolio. There certainly isn't any love lost between them, but I do think she goes for Sir Toby, and of course she gets him, though the marriage scene we talked about is very cruel. But one of the things you have to accept with Shakespeare is that he is less hypocritical than we are, the elements of cruelty he takes as part of nature and life. He doesn't blame the wolf for eating the lamb, it's what wolves do. In the same way, I don't see any viciousness between Feste and Malvolio, or between any of the characters except Maria and Malvolio — and there there is an extraordinary area of cruelty, which is unplayable if you are a twenty-one-year-old soubrette.

John Caird   I agree. But it's important, isn't it, that Toby is her only chance? The parallel again with Jane Austen is obvious, or George Eliot. You are in a very small community, or in a country house, and there is only one person who is remotely of your social standing — or preferably, in terms of a woman wanting to marry a man, a little bit above your social standing, so you can better yourself. You can't just marry anybody, and of course there is an element of gold-digging to it, as Bill says, but it's not just that: once you've decided that this is your only chance, it is extremely easy to fall in love with someone, because you persuade yourself that that's what you ought to do. And Shakespeare makes it very clear that the emotional relevance of having Maria in the play is to do with Sir Toby. Her first encounter is with him — they have a little scene together in which she attempts to persuade Toby to moderate his behaviour as a way of achieving some sort of liaison with him. And, as we have just said, when that proves to be impossible, because he's much further gone than that, she decides to take the other course: 'If you are not going to moderate your behaviour, I will have to change mine.'

Michael Billington   I remember, Bill, in your production you

had Maria and Sir Toby actually making love and about to go to bed while Malvolio was being taunted. The implication to me was that they were getting sexually excited by the cruelty and the torture of Malvolio. Was that what you intended to convey?

Bill Alexander Yes. But, you won't find that in the text, even if you go back to the third bad quarto . . .

John Caird That's based on, 'Come Maria to my table'?

Bill Alexander Sure, it all starts from that point. I wanted a youngish, active, ruthless, powerful Sir Toby to drive the play. I did not want an aging, very weighty sort of Sir Toby. Therefore I wanted a Maria who would fit that man. You could argue about how young I cast Maria — I actually thought of her as someone in her late twenties or early thirties, but attractive. Pippa Guard played her. And given the nature of those two people in the play, it seemed inconceivable to me that they shouldn't be having a relationship. What the hell are they waiting for? I mean, it's Liberty Hall around there anyway, so I saw the objective in Maria's case as towards marriage, not towards having a boy-friend. They are an item, Sir Toby and Maria, and her being his item is part of the social confusion and disruption of the household. That was my idea.

There's one key moment when Sir Toby comes on burping, and saying, 'Cesario's at the gate. A plague on these pickled herrings,' and then he slurps off, having contributed absolutely nothing to the problem of Orsino and his messengers. And Maria is not given anything else in the scene, so I had him take her by the hand and drag her off into the shadows right under Olivia's nose — because Sir Toby's behaviour is always right under Olivia's nose, giving her two fingers the whole time. So it seemed to me absolutely clear that they were having a sexual relationship.

It also struck me that there is tremendous cruelty in what they do to Malvolio. I don't think you can avoid that. If you try to, you make the pain and the love and the balance of humour in the play rather pointless — the play develops a soft centre. The comedy becomes a meaningless game if it's just a jolly come-uppance for Malvolio: it's not, it's viciously cruel, what they do, and part of cruelty is an excitement at seeing people suffer. Remember we are talking about a society that got excitement through seeing suffering. People didn't just enjoy bear-baiting for the sport, they found it funny that the bear was being tortured, they laughed at it.

Michael Billington But the implication was of sexual excitement in your production?

Bill Alexander I wanted to take it to the limits. I believed that Toby, on hearing what was going on down there, and on being close to the Maria who had created that entertainment for him, even though he OD's on it towards the end, would be making love to Maria. Because they can't see what's going on, and therefore they were doing what came naturally to them.

John Caird Your view would be, Bill, that in saying that he's bored and wants rid of it, he is actually telling a lie in order to cover for this outrageous behaviour.

Bill Alexander No. I think that it's too easy in a modern way to look at that line of Sir Toby's and say, 'Oh, he's having a kind of conversion here. He realises he's gone too far.' Actually, what he's realising is what Maria warned him of ages ago: if he's not careful, he will be out on his ear, and he doesn't want that. 'I am too far in offence with my niece to carry this sport to the upshot.' He actually stops because of that: there is no evidence in the text of remorse, no evidence whatever.

John Caird Not remorse. I think boredom is closer to it.

John Barton I just remembered something that I had forgotten — I did the play so long ago it is lost in the mists of time. But I do remember this question of the sexual relationship, and actually I did what Bill is saying — I did have a very seedy implication that they screwed every now and then in a not very satisfactory manner. At the end of the drinking scene, she went towards Toby and he just pushed her away brutally and said, 'It's too late to go to bed now,' and she was very hurt. That went with the way Liz Spriggs was playing the part, but it was an invention that came out of what we worked out. I never had much on-stage snogging, but that was the basis of the relationship that we went for — that she'd been screwed by him, and although he was pretty indifferent to her, she wanted to get married if she could.

Terry Hands Where I would disagree with Bill quite categorically is that I think I don't believe that there is sexual excitement between the two at any point. It seems to me that the actual taunting of Malvolio is the biggest prize she can give Sir

Toby. It is the downfall of his major enemy, it's like her dowry. I would also add that Toby all the way through is still trying for the favour of Olivia. I don't think he has got his two fingers up to Olivia ever. All the way through he is trying to take over Malvolio's job, even by going to the gate and saying this guy is coming in. He then bullies Cesario in the garden and tries to make him look small, and organises duels. Everything is about seeking Olivia's favour, and when finally he realises he just isn't going to get it, he accepts the Maria push, and by the end of the play it is one of the saddest relationships in it.

Michael Billington I'm slightly bewildered by your argument that everything Sir Toby does is geared to getting Olivia's favour, because after all everything he does would actually antagonise her, wouldn't it? He comes in drunk every night, he insults her steward, and he does a succession of things, surely, guaranteed to put him out of favour with Olivia.

Terry Hands Well, yes and no, in the sense that he is, just like Malvolio, utterly belligerent to anybody who comes too close to her, certainly Cesario, and certainly Malvolio himself. He knows that Cesario is her favourite and therefore he knows that he is in danger of going too far, and he does go too far. And finally she herself turns round to him and says, 'You're a barbarian, you're rude. Get out of my sight. I can't stand you.' And she does it in full view of everybody else. The humiliation, the downfall of Sir Toby, is terrifying, the pain and the wound of it in front of a lot of of people.

John Caird The difficult thing in trying to describe any of the characters being loyal to Olivia is that if they had any self-knowledge or any ability to analyse others, they would realise that they didn't know who they were being loyal to — because Olivia is behaving in a completely erratic way. Toby, to start with, has a vested interest in being loyal to Maria because he is trying to fob Andrew off on her, to keep Andrew sweet and get more money out of him. If he kept his eyes open and was less plastered all the time, he would recognise that the very last person he should be antagonising is this chap whom she spends hours having intimate conversations with, and he shouldn't be surprised when he gets a wigging for beating him up.

Terry Hands But John, surely one of the things we keep

missing out is the conflict over who is going to run that world of the play. We have got a very young woman in the centre and a number of people trying to get on her side to run that world — Orsino's going to take it over, Malvolio wants to take it over, and I believe Sir Toby does also. There is a Falstaffian side to him just as there is a Hal side to Olivia, in the sense that he's the surrogate father figure, and he's going to run England when Hal gets the crown. And there's the Lord Chief Justice figure, too. But whoever's going to run this world is going to run it through her. If Malvolio is going to, it is going to be through marriage. If Sir Toby is going to run it, it is because he is a relative, and it will be like Falstaff hoping to run England through Hal. Now that battle goes on until finally Hal turns round to Falstaff and says, 'I'm sorry, old man. Piss off. You're not what I want.' And in the same way the point comes in the play where Olivia turns round to Sir Toby and says, 'Go. That's it. I don't want you.'

The Role of Sebastian

Michael Billington   Can we turn now to Sebastian? Do you think there is anything more to Sebastian than a plot convenience? Viola has to have a twin — is that all Sebastian is?

John Barton   I think it's a very good example of where Shakespeare hasn't bothered to write much of a character, he has written a function. As I said earlier, Sebastian's first scene is boringly expository. He has got two or three good lines about his grief for his sister's death, but the rest of it is terribly po-faced: he just becomes a plot mechanism. He doesn't have a love scene with Olivia because the play's getting on at that point — it is only necessary that they get married. He has a moment recognising his sister, but even that is really her moment rather than his.

Maybe Shakespeare had to economise because he had so many rich characters! I think any tackling of Sebastian, apart from the height problems with Viola, lies in the casting, which is the crux to the whole thing. Then you hope for the best, and find what relationship you can with Antonio — because he has his two main scenes with Antonio, not with Olivia or Viola, so any conversation about Sebastian must equally be to do with Antonio.

Michael Billington   I can't remember — did you play Antonio as 'in love' with Sebastian?

John Barton No. I think that is a very open question. It has become normal and usual and obvious to play Antonio as sexually in love with Sebastian, but it is not certain. Usually, in Elizabethan and Jacobean plays, if homosexual love is a strong presence it is made very clear in the text, as with Gaveston in Marlowe's *Edward II*. There are plenty of plays where there is great love between fellow and fellow where it isn't clear at all. You just have to make that decision.

Terry Hands The key word is 'sexual'. In both my productions I played Antonio as very much in love with Sebastian, just as that other Antonio is in love with Bassanio in *The Merchant in Venice*. But it's a question of how 'sexual' that is. When it was a sexual relationship, as with Gaveston, that was made very clear and was usually highly disapproved of: there was a great sense of unease. But there was an acceptance — or seems to have been an acceptance, provided it doesn't become too possessive — of the love affair which is to do with a complete emotional commitment to a beloved young man.

We're in a play which is about doomed relationships as well as one that is going to be successful. It's a wonderful mirror to the Orsino-Cesario relationship, and I certainly don't find the first Sebastian scene boring — it's a breath of fresh air which allows us just to rest from the plots, but also enables us to see doom very clearly in front of our eyes and to relate that to the other love stories in the play.

John Barton I certainly didn't think it was a sexually-realised relationship, but that it was more platonic and very deep. The older man and the younger man who loved each other — it's a common Elizabethan phenomenon, though it's not fashionable today.

John Caird It can't possibly be sexual, because the whole point of the Antonio sub-plot is that, when he believes Sebastian has betrayed him, he isn't remotely concerned with sexual betrayal. He is not worried in the final scene about sexual jealousy. What he is in despair about is that he has been betrayed spiritually.

Michael Billington And by Sebastian's ingratitude.

John Caird Yes. He deserves gratitude, friendship, filial love — all the most pure things. In other words, he has built Sebastian into

something of an idol, and that is one of the most powerful forms of love there is. But if you make it sexual, which in the past ten years it has been, then you diminish the other much more important aspects of the play that surround it.

To go back to your previous point, Michael, I think that Sebastian is a nasty problem for an actor because in one respect he *is* just a plot function. But it is a paradoxical problem, because in another respect the first two scenes are dull precisely because he *doesn't* have a plot function: his only function is to be exposed as the twin of Viola. He doesn't have an action — or rather, his action is, 'Let's go and look around the town,' which is a very feeble thing to be doing in a play.

If Shakespeare had decided to give him an action, he would have had to involve him somehow in Orsino's court, and therefore would have had to spend a lot more time with mistaken identity in that world, rather than using all his mistaken-identity plot in the Olivia world. It is peculiar and difficult to explain to an actor why Sebastian doesn't seek out the man that he must have heard of, just as Viola has heard of him, roll up at court, and get himself sorted out, kitted up with another ship, and back home again.

Lover — or Lookalike?

Michael Billington How important is it, Bill, that Viola and Sebastian do actually look alike? Does it matter if they are of different heights, don't look in the least like twins, or is it just a device that the audience is prepared to accept?

Bill Alexander It is more a question of what you, the director, are prepared to accept in terms of the level of acting you get. The more alike they can be the better, that goes without saying, and yet the audience have to be very easily aware of which one they are looking at. The paradox is that it couldn't work if you didn't know it was Sebastian walking onto the stage.

John Caird Jan Kott thinks the play will only work when Viola is played by a boy, and by the same actor as Sebastian. In his so-called great essay on the play, he says something like, 'You would have to get over the final scene by some technical means.' That's the scene where they spend a fair amount of time talking to each other. What those 'technical means' might be he doesn't specify.

Michael Billington Do you regard that as nonsense?

John Caird Well, I think if Shakespeare had wanted it, which is what Jan Kott implies, he wouldn't have written the last scene like that.

Michael Billington But these days directors quite often have one person playing two roles, and then the actors have to meet. It is a soluble problem.

John Caird You could use a double in the final scene.

John Barton It's soluble in some plays and places, not in others.

Michael Billington Not in *Twelfth Night*?

John Caird The reason it's not a good idea in *Twelfth Night* is that a lot of the delight the audience takes in the mistaken identity plot is that *they* know which twin is which, and they are suspending their disbelief and allowing themselves to imagine a world in which other people don't know which is which.

Bill Alexander Can I pick up on a point John was making about the action of Sebastian within the play? The first scene between Antonio and Sebastian is very difficult because Sebastian is recounting something that basically you already know — he is just introducing himself to the audience. But that in itself can be a pleasure — you see this brother of Viola's who is admired, and who looks very like her and yet is clearly different from her, and you get a sense of anticipation about what it is all going to lead to. He *is* provided with an action because he does, John, actually say he's going to do what you advised him to do: he says, 'I am bound for the court of Count Orsino.'

John Caird But he doesn't go there!

Bill Alexander He doesn't go there because Antonio catches up with him and they decide to spend some time sightseeing. You don't get the feeling that he's got much of a drive towards the court of Orsino . . .

John Caird He's not very good at getting there, is he? He's got three months to do it!

97

Bill Alexander   He's very ambivalent about it because, on the one hand, he doesn't want to tell Antonio where he is going, and then he *does* tell him where he is going. He says, 'I can't say where I am going,' in fact he appears not to have made up his mind, and then, seeing Antonio looking like that about it, he says, 'I'm going to find Orsino.' Shakespeare is heightening the anticipation: you're meant to think, 'God, he's going to Orsino's too — he's going to bump into Viola there, and Orsino will mistake him for Viola', and so on.

Where you stop the character being boring is in how you portray the little idiosyncrasies of brother and sister — the things they have in common, the things they do alike, the way they express themselves alike. That's where the charm of it resides. You have got to see that one is a man and one is a girl all the time. Therein also lies the charm of how they are so similar, and yet their similarities manifest themselves differently in a girl and a boy. The agony is that the guys who could play Sebastian really well just don't look enough like the girls who you are going to cast as Viola, and therefore you don't cast them.

John Barton   John has put his finger on it. It is always a danger sign in Shakespeare when a character says, 'Shall'st go behold the wonders of the town?' It means he doesn't know what to do with them at that point, he's got to get them off and there isn't a plot-point to be made.

John Caird   But Shakespeare comes clean on the subject. He tips a wink to those who know a bit about playwriting. By 'Have him stay at the Elephant', which is in South London near where the Globe Theatre was, he is really saying, 'Look I know this isn't much of a plot and I am just throwing that to you chaps and we'll get on with the next bit.'

Bill Alexander   We're in Illyria, but there's an Elephant.

John Barton   What we haven't perhaps stressed enough is that the similarity or acceptable similarity of Viola and Sebastian is very important from the point of view of the audience. I think that if they are of a different height or palpably not twins, it is disturbing to the beholder.

John Caird   Because they think the other people who are making the mistake must be complete idiots.

John Barton   And I think that by far the greatest difficulty I had in casting *Twelfth Night* was finding somebody to play Sebastian opposite Judi Dench, because of her being little. I had auditions, auditions, auditions, and auditions.

John Caird   Michael Williams wasn't available?

John Barton   He wasn't available at the time, no. So it was the biggest problem of casting, to make it credible — not only to find somebody like her, but somebody acceptable. And I think that making Sebastian interesting is only achievable if once in a miraculous blue moon you have a fine, major actor playing it. I once saw Sebastian work because he was played by Ian Holm, who made it a major part. That is the only way you can solve it.

Terry Hands   I was very lucky in France. I had a boy, Francis Huster, who subsequently became very famous as Lorenzaccio and Hamlet and God knows what, and who happened to look like Ludmilla Mikael. They have got to be as alike as peas in a pod, as close as you can, although I do take Bill's point that the real fascination is allowing us to see the differences or the similarities in behaviour that they have. Because they are twins, they have a similar way of scratching their necks, or whatever it is. Building that up for two characters can be wonderful. But I also think we are undervaluing the need for Scene vi to come where it does.

Michael Billington   The first time Sebastian appears . . .

Terry Hands   Yes. Right from the word go — the first scene, the second scene, the first time we see Olivia, and all the rest of it — the action is very heightened, very poetic, the very quintessence of situations, and a fairy-tale as well. Then in come two people, as often happens, who remind us that there is also a world with places called the Elephant, and where you can go and see the sights — that there is a *natural* world existing as well. It's the same use Shakespeare makes of Bianca in *Othello*, to come in and remind us that there is life going on elsewhere. He hasn't bothered to show it up till them

Modern productions tend to feel they have to show that world from the word go. But Shakespeare waits until that scene, and then he says, 'Remember, there is another world. These people are very heightened, they are very special. *This* is the normal world — just put it back into focus. And now we'll go on with the play.'

Bill Alexander That's absolutely dead right. And the difference between a great playwright and an average jobbing playwright is that a great playwright can take something that he knows he needs, a functional element, and make something of it in itself, so that you don't recognise it as a functional element. It is the job of the director to bring that out.

John Caird Can I say something else about the twins, because, apart from anything else, they pose a fascinating technical problem. At least, it starts as a technical problem, to do with how you get two people, a boy and a girl, very like each other, the same height and all the rest of it. But it ends as an imaginative problem — or rather a perceptive problem from the point of view of the audience. What do they perceive those two people to be like?

Our dear friend and colleague Adrian Noble directed this play in Japan, and when he first went over he discovered it had never been performed there before. And he asked the producers why, and they said, 'Because here we can never find two people similar enough to play Sebastian and Viola.' Now, if you think about that for a moment it seems preposterous. But if you look at it more deeply it is absolutely true in Japan. I've worked there, with a cast of entirely mongoloid-featured people with black hair, and because everybody is of a certain similar cast of features, with identical hair colour and often of very similar height, the general trend is that you pay much more attention to facial detail in finding differences between two people that you would do in the West, where you've got a very tall person, or a very blonde person, or somebody with red hair or a great big grey beard, or whatever distinctive feature it may be.

Therefore in Japan they were taking an actor and an actress for Viola and Sebastian, sticking them in a couple of wigs, and saying they still looked completely different — because they are so used to delineating people by facial features. We can take people who are actually very dissimilar and give them both red wigs and say, 'Oh, yes, they are twins.' It is a matter of the collective perception of the audience as much as it is to do with any actual similarity between the actors.

Finding a Function for Fabian

Michael Billington Bill, you were talking about Shakespeare's genius as a playwright, and about that balance of the real and the

poetic. Would you say that the character of Fabian is proof of Shakespeare's genius as a playwright, or of his occasional incompetence? Suddenly, half way through *Twelfth Night*, a totally unexplained character called Fabian joins the action and becomes part of the plot against Malvolio. Who is Fabian? Where has he come from? Why is he there?

Bill Alexander   My own view is that Shakespeare did have to introduce another character, because he wanted to hold Feste back for the climactic dark-house scene. He doesn't want to expend the energy of the character Feste in the whole letter bit, and it's interesting that Feste begins to drop himself out of the action at the time the plot against Malvolio gets created. He says nothing, you are not even sure when he exits in the midnight-revels scene — he's very prominent at the beginning of the scene, but once Malvolio comes on he fades out. We know that he has his own personal axe to grind with Malvolio, and he amazingly reminds us of it at the very end of the play: 'But do you remember, Sir? Why laugh you at such a barren rascal?'

I just think that Shakespeare wants to preserve the nuclear energy of that character for a much more important function when it comes to the dark house. And the route that Toby, Andrew, and Maria take in the letter-scene needs another element in it. I can understand it perfectly in terms of character. You can't quite see what Feste would actually do in all that, what he'd have to say about it: it's not part of his mentality, it's not his kind of humour. When he's presented with this guy who everyone thinks is mad and who's in the clink, right, then he can click into gear, and his philosophic and wry nature can come out and make something of it. But you can't see him stuck up in a box-tree with the others, passing the time of day and laughing at that. So Shakespeare needed another character.

Michael Billington   But does Shakespeare forget to give Fabian a character on top of a function?

Terry Hands   I don't know. It is a very vexed point, and all of us as directors have worried about it. I agree with Bill that you do need the extra character, because Feste does not get involved, does not initiate any cruelties, none at all. And I don't believe that he is particularly vicious in the prison scene, because he takes on his role as Sir Topaz, which is a nonsense role. It's a scene where we watch other people's cruelty coming to its climax.

101

Fabian however, can get involved. He is in the duel. He is needed for the plot in the letter-scene, in the box-tree scene. He is needed in the duel-scene, and he's also needed at the very end of the play to help bring out the truth. So what would he be? I stumbled upon a solution more by accident than design when I was working with the Comédie Française. I thought, well, he ought to be a groom — belong in the stables, the animal world of the play, which would also be part of the household. And I thought that he must be old — he's part of that other group, of the Maria, Belch, Ague-Cheek group. Now I had an actor who was about four feet eleven, and adored by the French public, called George Chamaras. He looked very old — like a walnut, like somebody who had been a jockey when he was young. But he'd grown old, like Fabian. And now people like Malvolio are making Fabian's life hell, as they are trying to make everybody else's life hell.

All I can report is that it worked. Now, I'm not saying that's the only way, of course, but, coming back to one's casting, it actually recreated the world of the bear-baiting, of the Slenders from *Merry Wives*, of the Belchs who are close to the world of the fairs, the horses, the dogs. They talk about the dogs, Fabian talks about horses, he talks about the animal world. And we gave him gaiters, and it sort of fitted in. Yes, I think he *has* primarily got a plot function, he stops Feste having to become involved in any active way with any of the plots against Malvolio — but if you get the right casting within the age group, he fits into the territory.

Michael Billington What advice can you give to the actor playing Fabian? Terry talks about investing the character with a life and a background, but there's not a lot to go on, is there?

John Barton I would look at it the other way round, and ask, 'Why is he there at all? Would it be possible to do the play without him being there?' Then you can begin to find out why he *is* there, if you see what I mean. Terry's absolutely right, you can't do the duel-scene, the letter-scene, without another person. So that's why he is there, and you have got to look first at the function, at *why* Shakespeare has put him in at that particular point. I think it's also to energise a group and a plot which needs a lot of setting up. Belch does this terrific amount of talking, as we've said, and to have a back-up fellow is obviously a playing help in energising the scene.

Having said that, what advice can one give to the actor? In casting terms, you have to find somebody very individual. Terry

had a very old actor, I had a black actor. If you've got somebody who is palpably different and new, then you build the character through that, but it's also one of those parts that actors are not especially passionate to play, so you have to do the best you can.

Terry Hands   The other thing I think about Fabian is that his presence is crucial in illuminating why Feste is this curiously non-active person. Even when he gets to the last scene and Olivia says, 'Read the letter,' Feste quite deliberately fucks it up, and they have to take it away from him and give it to Fabian. What I am saying is that it is crucial that you have this oddly inactive Feste.

Bill Alexander   A non-participant character, someone who won't play the games. I'd like to say one final thing about Fabian, and that is that you have got to invent something for him in terms of his function in the household, and the solution I came to was to make him a kind of under-steward to Malvolio. I think it helps to do what I did, which is to introduce him silently into the earlier scenes: for instance, when Olivia and Malvolio first appear, he was clearly one down the pecking order from Malvolio — he did what Malvolio told him to physically, and he hung around and was dressed in a way that suggested a sort of second-in-command. That's pure invention, but it gives him a potential aspiration, and also a relationship to Malvolio — a reason why he should join in a plot against Malvolio — you know, 'He got me out of favour with my lady about a bear-baiting he had here.' Here is someone who is training to be a steward, and who is organising bear-baitings. It gives him a role within that world.

Michael Billington   John, have you anything to add to that?

John Caird   No, I think Fabian has been exhausted.

Translating the Verse — and the Emotions

Michael Billington   I wanted to talk to you about how your view of the play had changed from one production to another, or through the various stages a production might go through. I suppose, Terry, in one way you had the most radical experience because you did the play first of all in Paris with the Comédie Française, and then in Stratford. Did your vision of the play and of its practicalities change between the two productions?

Terry Hands   No, on the contrary. I made mistakes in Stratford in 1979 that I didn't make in Paris in 1976. I had stumbled, more accidentally than anything, onto what seems to me to have been the right balance of age and youth in France, and thought in Stratford I could use a younger Ague-Cheek with impunity, but I discovered it didn't work that way — not because the actor was bad, the actor was wonderful. The one area I tried to improve on in Stratford was Olivia, whom I thought should be much younger. I needed a comedienne, that sort of Kay Kendall comedienne, and I had a girl who by the end of the season was really excellent, but not at the beginning. It was very difficult also to buck tradition. it always is. If you are doing a production where you challenge a tradition you have got an uphill battle the first time you do it. Supposing you were to cast Beatrice and Benedick young, say the age of Romeo and Juliet: you've got a mountain to climb, because tradition is against you. And to choose a genuinely youthful Olivia who was really excitable and a high comedienne was a challenge. I think that it was right to try, but it was a battle.

But the real mistake I made in Stratford was in getting the balance of the age and weight wrong. I had a Toby who was the right age but wasn't the right energy, and I had an Ague-Cheek who was the right talent but the wrong age. And I had the Olivia who was absolutely the right age but didn't have the technical brio until later in the season. But I would stand by what I accidentally stumbled on in France — though partly guided by John Barton's production and the influence that had had on me.

Michael Billington   One point about the Paris production. You all talked earlier about the Englishness of the atmosphere, this paradoxical Englishness in Illyria. How easy was that to convey in Paris?

Terry Hands   It wasn't easy! I had a very good cast, an exceptionally good cast of really superb actors. But what conveys the Englishness of it, I think, is an English set of emotions, at least this was what we found. Two things, briefly. One is the text, the rhythms of the text. French is a non-tonic language and has to work off the phrase: you can build rhythms into it, but the alexandrine is their norm and we felt, because it was a lyrical play, we would use the alexandrine. And we did six or seven weeks of rehearsal, and the play was utterly dead. I then had to come back to England for ten days, and I said to the translator, 'While I'm away, please change the entire text into iambics from top to

bottom,' which he did. And when I got back we rehearsed a new text for the last two weeks of rehearsal.

John Caird   Other than the prose scenes?

Terry Hands   Yes, but to get back to the ten-syllable line and the five feet for the verse — then the whole thing lifted and came off the page and suddenly started to work. It was quite extraordinary. The translator was the same guy with whom I had done *Richard III*, so he knew what to do.

The second thing was that the play is replete with what I call 'English emotions'. That is to say, emotions which the French don't normally use, such as wryness, ruefulness — wry smiles, rueful grins, that sort of unpositive ambiguity of response. Let's take those two, the wry smile and the rueful grin. They are untranslatable into French as phrases. They are simply not emotions that they use. If you cannot describe an emotion, you don't have it. There are two ways of acquiring emotions: one is to have and find the phrase for it, and the other is to hear a phrase as a child, and then discover what it is.

Michael Billington   So Feste could not be wry, for example?

Terry Hands   No, it just wasn't there. And if you were Viola, you couldn't do a rueful grin as you made yet another mistake. So we started to find ways to introduce into the playing those aspects of the emotion which would be communicable, that they could understand. By building up the passionate, vibrant, secure, sure way that the French have of playing, it began to work. They are very clear cut, black and white, which is why they are wonderful in something like *Richard III*, which is a kind of drumming play — but dreadful in Chekhov, which of course is entirely to be sifted through: they haven't got all the language and the emotions for it.

What came off in the French *Twelfth Night* was a sense of Englishness — but they translated it, if you like, as part of the poetic context and the fairy-tale story. The social context they understood immediately: they had no problem with that at all. They knew exactly where Malvolio fitted, what the old gentry were about, what the passion of the young people was about. And they were ahead of an English audience in responding to the idea in the play of the madness of love. The French make a difference between *passion*, which is what Shakespeare would call

madness or the fire in *Romeo and Juliet*, and *l'amour*, which is love. In a sense, Suffolk in *Henry VI Part II* is *passion*, and Henry's feeling for Margaret is *amour*. We have only the one word. They have got more and better words, much more sifted and precise. *Amitié amoureuse* is quite different from *amour*, which is quite different from *passion*.

All that — and, as I've said, quintessentially the play is a succession of love stories — they were much better equipped for. Similarly, the audience in Paris is much more interested in Romeo than Mercutio, who is a bore to them. Romeo is the guy they are interested in. It is the opposite in England. When French audiences see *A Midsummer Night's Dream*, they want to watch the lovers, and we want to watch the mechanicals. If you take an English audience going to *Twelfth Night*, they want to see what Malvolio gets up to and what Feste does, and what happens in the night scenes. The French wanted to know what happened between Orsino and Viola. So the actual balance of the play was infinitely better. And although my actress was a little bit old for Olivia, she could play the fecklessness, which they found totally proper.

One of the other differences over there had to do with France being essentially a Catholic society. The favourite actress on a French stage, the part the actress has to play to earn her spurs, is Agnes in *L'Ecole des femmes*, and therefore their favourite kind of actress on stage is the daughter-figure, which Viola wonderfully is, and Olivia wonderfully is. In England, it's the tomboy, it's the mistress or the potential mistress — the puritan society looking for something else. So I think that Shakespeare's basic story in the play stood a better chance in France than it did in England.

John Caird It's surprising he wasn't French, really. . . . I have spoken to a man, a German, who said that Shakespeare sounded much better in German than in English, and that he should always be done in German — that if Shakespeare had known the German language he would have written in it.

Michael Billington The Germans call him *unser Shakespeare*, don't they?

Terry Hands Yes, they do — and they do more productions, too.

The Comedy of the Yellow Stockings

Michael Billington John Barton, your famous production of *Twelfth Night* went through various manifestations, didn't it, over three seasons, with shifts of casts from production to production, or version to version. Did you see your *Twelfth Night* as something that was constantly changing and evolving? Were you bringing new ideas into it as it went from season to season?

John Barton No, I don't think in that particular case I was, but it changed a lot according to who was playing. Major cast changes made it very different, because the same thinking would come out quite differently with a different actor, but I don't think I changed the basic concept, which on other occasions with other plays I have certainly done.

Michael Billington So it didn't get mellower with time or lighter with time? Or did it simply depend on the chemistry of the actors?

John Barton I don't remember rethinking it. It felt different when there were major cast changes, but quite a number of the actors — Viola, Malvolio, Olivia, Feste — were the same throughout, so it didn't affect the chemistry as much as I've known on other occasions.

Michael Billington Earlier some of you said you wished you could go back and direct another *Twelfth Night*. Do you share that feeling, John, and if so, do you have any ideas as to what your view of the play would be now?

John Barton I don't think I do have any urge to go back to that particular play. Odd bits of thinking on it were wrong, but I wouldn't change my basic concept.

Michael Billington Bill, your production moved, as most RSC productions do, from Stratford to London, but it also underwent major cast changes, didn't it? Malvolio was taken over by John Carlisle from Tony Sher, for example. Did the production change in consequence — did you want it to change?

Bill Alexander Well, yes. Tony played Malvolio in Stratford,

and John Carlisle in London. It was Tony's decision to leave: he wasn't happy with what he'd done or what we'd done, and when John took over he was naturally reticent, as actors always are about taking over a big part from someone else, but he was thrilled with the idea of taking on Malvolio, because it wasn't the sort of part he'd played before. So we were able to explore new aspects of the character and make new discoveries about the way it was integrated or not integrated.

We began, I remember, by talking about the integration of the character within the play, and we were able to go over that territory in new ways which I found very stimulating and refreshing. I think John's performance was excellent: it raised very interesting questions, though, about the kind of actor you want playing Malvolio. I do think it is an extremely difficult part to cast, for a lot of the reasons John gave earlier about the traditions associated with it and the reasons an actor goes for it, and I don't think that either bit of casting was quite right — or, more importantly, that I handled them quite right. There is a tremendous temptation for the climactic comic scene in the play, when Malvolio does finally enter in the yellow stockings, to be absolutely bravura and hysterically funny, which an actor of Tony's type can make it. The question is at what expense to the balance of the play that happens.

It *was* hysterically funny. We could barely get through the rehearsals, because everyone was in such stitches. They used to accumulate from all over the building to watch that scene, because Tony's approach to it, as with so much of his work, was to grab it by the reins and drive it forward, taking Malvolio into almost surrealistic dimensions of comedy and of performance. And I had to turn a different switch in my brain for that performance: whenever the scene began, I would put down my notebook, suspend my critical judgement, and just fall about laughing with the rest of the audience. Then I would say, 'Hah, that's all over now. Let's get back to the work.'

John is not that kind of actor, and I didn't want him to be. I realised there was a danger of what Tony was doing unbalancing the play, as there always is with a Malvolio, and yet I always missed those two minutes of completely outrageous comedy. Now maybe its okay that you can in a sense take a stylistic break at times, deliberately to do something completely different, as you can with the Porter's scene in *Macbeth* — have him come through the audience, talking to the audience, and suddenly you're in a different genre of performance altogether. I wouldn't argue that as

a defence of Malvolio in the Stratford production because that wasn't my intention, and therefore I think I wasn't fully in control of it as a device, and I don't think ultimately it's truthful. I'm going round the houses, aren't I, to say I don't think I ever got that element in the play right, either with Tony or with John, through neither of their faults.

Michael Billington   What you are saying though, interestingly, is that a comic scene in a play can get out of control and become *too* funny, or maybe make it difficult for the scene that follows?

Bill Alexander   It's not the scene that gets too funny, it's the actor who gets too funny. Can we just concentrate on that scene for a moment, the yellow-stockings scene, because I think we must all have something to say about it. You can base the comedy of the scene on the storehouse of expectation there is behind it, and you can play it for its physical outrageousness so that it is high farce. You don't hear much of the text if you do it like that, because the audience is laughing too much. Now I actually think that it *is* an incredibly funny bit of text, and ideally ought to be played for that because of all the misapprehensions, the non-sequiturs, the simple misunderstandings about what's going on.

Michael Billington   'Will you go to bed, Malvolio?' You mean lines like that?

Bill Alexander   Wonderful verbal comedy. He's quoting things that she has no knowledge of, she keeps trying to understand what he's saying, he assumes her reticence is to do with her not wanting Maria to hear him talking to her like that. It is a brilliantly intricate bit of verbal comedy, which was what we worked on in London, and I don't think we quite got it.

John Caird   What you are putting your finger on is something vital. The great temptation with Malvolio is that because the actor knows that what is coming is not just one but two of the most climactically funny scenes in Shakespeare — the letter scene and the yellow-stockings scene — he is tempted to start playing the character funny the first time he comes on. Actually, paradoxically, the letter scene and the yellow-stockings scene are only truly funny off the text if Malvolio is a completely serious character in the first few scenes.

Malvolio's comedy in the first two or three scenes he's in is not based on anything physical: what few laughs he has are to do with verbal wit, playing off other people's inconsistencies, or the wit of observation. He says some very funny things — some neatly turned, elegantly phrased things — but what you have to steer every actor who plays Malvolio towards is stuffing the shirt as it were, so that the stuffed shirt can then be ripped apart in the great comic scenes. That is a very hard thing to get an actor to concentrate on, and I don't think one should ever castigate a comic actor for falling foul of it. Especially playing Malvolio, who is a very isolated character, it's more than an easy trap to fall into. Actors need directors precisely to point out that kind of pitfall.

Michael Billington Did your own view of the play change as you worked on it over the two seasons — or, indeed, since that earlier production you mentioned?

John Caird Well, the earlier production was for Contact Theatre in Manchester, and it was the first time I had ever directed a Shakespeare play. I was every bit as confident, nay hubristic, as you'd expect a very young director about to direct his first Shakespeare play to be. And I made some quite classic errors in setting it up, in that I based the whole production on Leslie Hotson's book, *The First Night of Twelfth Night*. I set it as if in Middle Temple Hall, I created what I thought was a completely actor-proof — even audience-proof — conceptual production, and within the first two days of rehearsal I realised that I was on a hiding to nothing. There were richnesses I was uncovering in the play in rehearsal which my production could not possibly capitalise on, and which I had never suspected were there.

So my second production, at Stratford, was the result of a somewhat Damascan experience, having done what I thought was a very shallow production originally. And that Damascan experience has mightily affected the way I now approach all Shakespeare. It has given me my roots, I suppose, as to how I investigate the text.

The Laughter and the Pain

Michael Billington Your Stratford production was widely perceived as being unusually dark, stressing the sombre aspects of the play. Was that a reaction against what you had done before?

John Caird   No. I think every production of *Twelfth Night* is received by the critics as being unusually dark! They are always comparing it to a production they have never actually seen which is the jolly production that hasn't bothered to look into the play — unless, of course, they had seen my first production. It is one of those things that critics often say — you know, 'Sir Toby Belch is played unusually brutally.' They say that about every Sir Toby Belch. It is like saying, 'Isn't it wonderful that at last King Lear isn't being played as a doddery old man.' He hasn't been played as a doddery old man for fifty years.

Michael Billington   I would challenge you on that as a worker in the field. I saw a recent *Twelfth Night* directed by Kenneth Branagh at Riverside Studios, where Sir Toby *was* played as a jolly, Pickwickian figure. There is a tradition of harmless Sir Tobys. . . .

John Caird   Not at the RSC.

Terry Hands   Michael, can I come in on this? John's remark has got a lot of truth in it, because not all, but a great many of our critics have grown up, as we have, with some knowledge of theatre in the 'fifties and so on, when indeed you did cut out the darker elements of Shakespeare's plays. The point that we've always tried to make at the RSC, though I think it has been true of good productions anywhere, is that with Shakespeare you have got to bring the two things together, the cruelty as well as the kindness, the darker element as well as the lighter element. It is true that just recently there has been a resurgence of the tradition of removing the darker elements, like the production of *As You Like It* I mentioned earlier. Now that was fine, in that it still made for a good evening's theatre, but the principle of removing the darker elements was something that was current in the 'fifties and has not been happening again in this country until very recently. So there is truth in what you are both saying.

John Caird   I should answer the question seriously rather than mischievously. You're right, it was seen as very dark, and it was intended to be, because when I studied the play, especially having directed it before and feeling that I hadn't even begun to understand its darker side, I didn't find very much to laugh about in it, though there are some wonderfully comic scenes in the centre. So I did what I have done ever since with comedies: I said

to myself, 'I will investigate this play seriously. It's written with serious intention by the playwright, and if I investigate it seriously and get all the scenes right, and I've got actors who have got comic skills, it will be funny. If it isn't funny, it is because it isn't supposed to be funny. What I mustn't do is try to give it a sort of generalised feeling of being light and airy and of how we are all going to have a good evening.'

All of Shakespeare's comedies have got that quality of seriousness and darkness about them, but I think *Twelfth Night* is more considerably dark than almost any. We talked about this earlier: there is, if you examine the language of the play, an extraordinary prevalence of imagery to do with death, plague, pestilence, and hanging. It's not by accident that that's there. The play is about the sea in many respects, and the undertow is there: the waves are falling on the beach in a lyrical, majestic way, but the undertow can easily pull you out into the deeps.

Terry Hands Wouldn't it also be fair to say, John, that it's the pain of love that is constantly part of it? 'Patience on a monument smiling at grief.' If you compare the play with *As You Like It*, which is so upbeat and fizzy, it's much darker.

John Caird It's much darker than *As You Like It*, it's true. Pain is very much part of it.

Terry Hands I think John deserves credit for courageously taking the play into an exploration of its darker side. But going back to what we were saying just now about Malvolio getting out of hand — it is as wrong to cut the darker element as it would be to cut the sunny element, and there is a hugely sunny element as well. Probably, in just those two amazing scenes, you are talking about a violin cadenza in the middle of a concerto: now at one point in history the violinists did their own cadenza, which meant they showed off their own technique, and that is the danger for the modern Malvolios. The great composers spotted this happening and said, 'Christ, this has got nothing to do with my concerto,' and they started writing the cadenzas as well. Now I do believe that Shakespeare *wrote* that cadenza — therefore it can be a tremendous bravura display, but it mustn't lose touch with the rest of the play.

John Caird You have used the word that is absolutely crucial to those comic Malvolio scenes, the word 'pain'. If you create a

Malvolio who is merely a laughing stock as far as the audience is concerned, none of his pain is central to the message of the play, which is that love can be horribly difficult and the cause of badness, and can force people up against the darker side of their emotional lives. If Malvolio is played properly, seriously, while you are laughing at his discomfort with the yellow stockings and the letter, you are also feeling, 'You poor man, you are going to suffer most horribly because of this.' And it's the duality of an audience's feelings for Malvolio that is most interesting, and in the end makes them laugh loudest and most honestly at the really funny moments, while at the same time allowing them to retain their humanity and their sense of the humanity of the play.

Terry Hands   Can we not also say, though, that all comedy is cruel? The moment you analyse what comedy is — the banana skin, the trousers falling down — it is all based on humiliation or discomfort. Any joke is quintessentially a form of defamation or cruelty. But another area which we mustn't forget — though I think sometimes it makes RSC work pedantic — is this idea that there is *no* display element and these are not actors. The great thinking about Shakespeare is that he constantly reminds you that these are actors performing a play, and you are an audience watching them. Even in the middle of, say, *Julius Caesar*, when they have just killed Caesar, they turn round and say, 'Yes, people will be doing this in lots of different languages, and still not get it right.'There's a constant awareness that those two things are there, and perhaps when we were young directors we tended to deny the display element which an audience still demands.

A phenomenon I have just noticed this year (1988) in Stratford which I am sure is to do with the huge push at the moment on television and in film, is the growth among audiences of a quite patent liking for actor-display. I was there when John Wood in the previews of *The Tempest* launched into 'Ye elves', and took it through magically, and at the end of it the audience applauded. John Wood came off stage in despair. We were having supper that night, and he said, 'What's gone wrong? I've wrecked the play.' And all the younger actors were saying, 'John, what are you doing? It makes everything we are doing look silly, just like an opera. Can't you make it real?' So he and Nick changed the beginning of the next scene-change, and it killed the applause. And I said to them, being old and wizened, 'No, no. Never stop an audience applauding if they want to, because that's the bargain of coming to the theatre.' So they left it as it had been.

During the *Plantagenets* trilogy, Ralph Fiennes as Henry VI launched into the great *Part II* speech that ends up 'Gloucester he is none,' which is asking who is the traitor in this kingdom. Ralph has a very fine voice, and he handled the speech superbly, and the audience broke into applause. There is this awareness that you can be in the play and out of the play, and that there are moments when display is required. Now I think the two great key Malvolio scenes are a case in point, the point being simply that, while we have got to keep the display within the terms of the writer, we mustn't deny it. That's the medium we're involved in.

John Caird Very good. In *Nicholas Nickleby* the audience used to applaud when Squeers was beaten by Nicholas — David Edgar always described it as a horribly tribal moment. But Malvolio never does enough. He is never so nasty that the audience would ever applaud him being tortured, and there is an absolute difference between Shakespeare's view of the world, where nobody deserves that sort of pain, and Dickens's view of the world, where some people do deserve every bit of it. I agree with you, Terry: if an audience wants to applaud, damn it, you should be so lucky.

Unlocking the Play

Michael Billington For practical reasons, presumably a lot of people who are going to direct the plays or act in the plays will read this volume, and I think it would be interesting to talk about your personal methods as directors of unlocking plays. When we've mentioned academic critics, it's been rather scathingly. Jan Kott got it in the boot, and obviously Hotson's theories didn't work in practice. Of all the ways to unlock plays, or find the key to a play in production, is the academic scripture any use — is scholarly commentary any help or not? John Barton, can I start with you? Does it work with *Twelfth Night*?

John Barton I personally think it depends entirely on the play, though normally I don't use it. I just read and read and read the play. But now and then I have read a lot of criticism, when there's been a particular reason. I remember I read up a lot on *Measure for Measure* and *Troilus*, but I much prefer just to seep myself in the play, and such reading as I do is textual — you know, finding out about stage directions, which is a point that has been raised.

I think that, as you can interpret any Shakespeare play a million ways, it is interesting to read anything about them, but you only need that stimulus if you feel stuck or if there is an area you don't know about.

Michael Billington   Is social history of interest or relevance?

John Barton   Well, it may be. Again, it depends on the play. If the play is a mythical one you probably don't want to read social history. If you want to find out what Nietzsche says for a given reason, you look it up. But when you say critical reading, what do you mean by it? Do you mean literary criticism, a rationalisation of the play in depth, do you mean textual criticism, or do you mean historical and social stuff? It could be that reading history books is more useful, it could be that to read some modern psychological work would be. There aren't any rules.

Michael Billington   With *Twelfth Night* we were talking earlier about the structure of an Elizabethan household. Is that kind of knowledge necessary if you are directing the play?

John Barton   I think it would be a very personal matter. My own personal thing is to read the play, read the play, read the play, and then research or look up something if I feel stuck or don't know, rather than to start out with the research. On *Twelfth Night* I don't think I did any reading, except for the play itself.

Michael Billington   Out of that saturation in the text comes some vision of what the play could be, should be?

John Barton   Yes. I find that really to get to know the text and all the things that go on in it and refer to each other is the best and only way.

Michael Billington   John Caird, we've been talking a lot about the specific problems *Twelfth Night* poses: this mysterious balance of elements,   a number of characters, any one of whom can became the prominent figure in the play, characters whose ages can be anything from twenty to fifty, more or less. How did you unlock *Twelfth Night* — apart, of course, from undoing what you did in Manchester . . .?

John Caird   The two academic critics we mentioned, Leslie

Hotson and Jan Kott, are both unhappy examples. It was I who was very wrong to base a production on Hotson's perfectly reasonable academic suppositions. Whether they are right or wrong is irrelevant in production, and he would probably be very surprised that anybody would be silly enough to do what I did. Equally, I think it's dangerous to take somebody whose approach to Shakespeare is only academic, and attempt to write into their essay or dissertation some finite proposals for a practical production. An academic approach to the text and a rehearsal approach to the text are bound to be two very different things.

How did I unlock the play? Well I started by doing what John says he does, and which I do with every play, which is to read it — fifty times, a hundred times, I don't know. Again and again and again. Until I know it so familiarly that if I've missed anything it's not for want of looking. I think as a director one has to go into rehearsal armed with an absolute familiarity with the text in the same way that a conductor would have to be armed with an absolute familiarity with the score before he or she could conduct a Beethoven symphony. You can't suddenly come across Bar 25 in the Slow Movement of Beethoven's Seventh and not realise there's a diminished seventh chord in it — you've got to know that before you lift up your baton.

Having said that, once I have achieved as nearly as I can a real familiarity and expertise with the text, I then try to wear that technique as lightly as I can — because having got into rehearsal one mustn't be too categorical, and one certainly mustn't be academic when it comes to working with the actors. So what I then try to do, in the first two weeks of rehearsal in a Shakespeare play, is to use the actors as tools to expose as much more of the text through character analysis as one possibly can.

The other thing that I suppose I do more and more in my work is to insist that every actor is present at all the major rehearsals. One of the ways of avoiding the sort of difficulties over, for instance, the playing of Malvolio that we've been talking about is for the whole company to be *aware* of all the possible meanings within the play, whether or not those meanings are within the scenes that they happen to be performing in.

It is becoming increasingly crucial, for me, to get a whole company feeling that they are representing the writer rather than just representing themselves or even representing my view of the play. I infinitely prefer the actors to feel that *they* are the purveyors of the writer's message to the audience without any intermediary. I am not suggesting that I think I am unnecessary in

116

any way, but that at some point I should be able to withdraw from the actor/audience/writer relationship, and for my withdrawal not to be noticed.

Michael Billington   John Barton was saying that there is no one way to unlock a play. It all depends upon the work. Terry, can you recall what methods of entry you used for *Twelfth Night*?

Terry Hands   I have a different approach to John's. I am not saying that it is right or wrong, but over twenty-five years I have become quite a passionate and voracious reader, and therefore go through hundreds of written commentaries. I have to say that ninety-nine out of each hundred I find useless, and I think the basic school of English Shakespeare scholarship, in the area of critical commentary, is not helpful in the theatre, because you are asking critics to be directors and actors, and that is not part of their training.

I think that where scholarship is useful is in the textual area — the New Arden editions in particular. I have been very grateful for the textual knitting and pointing out that they have done. That is basically a scholarly job, and you need a lot of hours in the day to do it, and they do it very well. Commentary I don't find helpful, because that is opinion, and often ill-informed opinion. I know people don't agree with me, but I am quite passionate about it: it is not based on an understanding of human beings or of the world. They write from and for where they live — university to university to university, from one hallowed chamber to another. You very rarely find academics who go round the world on a bicycle as Shakespeare somehow did in his plays.

John Barton   Academics are *always* going round on bicycles.

Discovering Shakespeare's World

Terry Hands   What I did discover — but this is only for me — was that I did need to know the history. I did need to know the social background, how Shakespeare's society was organised and how it had developed — not necessarily to ape it or imitate it on the stage, but to understand what Shakespeare had in mind. I think that to try to do the *Henry VI* plays without knowing the effect that Henry VII had created — who was as close to Shakespeare as Victoria is to us — is very difficult.

Michael Billington   Can I pin you down on *Twelfth Night*? What would be the relevant social or historical research?

Terry Hands   The relevant area would be the social system, the changing face of England, the population growth — Tawney was very useful on this obviously, in among of lot of writers — the expectations in that world, the new mercantile push, the political climate. But I would like to go into another area which is that, once you have done all that (and you can go on doing it forever), what is interesting is the perception of the English as seen by other people at the time — how were we regarded, what were the social habits? You know, did people shake hands or did they kiss? It doesn't mean to say that we have to ape the behaviour, but at least to know what it was, what Shakespeare would have had in his mind.

Now there are two areas which I think are extremely neglected. One was the way the Elizabethans thought. We have talked today about cruelty. Now we were talking about it as *our* approach to cruelty, *our* approach to society. We have been through the Victorians. We have been through all kinds of curious things. But it is the Elizabethans we have to understand. What were their philosophies? What governed their life? What were their values? What would they have written in the newspapers if they had had newspapers? And I kept feeling that there was a different process of thought in Shakespeare that I didn't quite know about until — and I know John Barton is going to jump up and down in alarm at this — I stumbled on a book by Frances Yates called *The Art of Memory*, which I found the most valuable book on Shakespeare I had ever read, although she hardly refers to him. It actually led me into Elizabethan ways of thinking and the associative processes, as opposed to the linear processes that we are involved with, and into the values that they believed in and were trying to live by. So I am a strong Yatesian. I found her *Theatre of the World*, besides her *Art of Memory*, utterly wonderful.

Modern sociology — the works of people like Ardrey — and psychology can also be tremendously helpful. Also the philosophy of the period, and looking at Botticelli and Michaelangelo, and the neoplatonism of the time, and the fact that so much work at that time was allegorical. I believe in looking at Shakespeare's sources, because I want to know why he *changed* his sources, which will help me discern what his purpose was in making the changes.

The other thing I used to do in the first ten years of my Shakespeare work — but less now because I have a bit more

experience — was rigorously to analyse the text. I read *Merry Wives* many times, and I came away with the belief it was all about hunting, since that was the predominant imagery. But then I analysed it into every single word on the page, which I added up — every single word, from 'the', 'a', everything — to see what was going on in Shakespeare's head. And I found that the dominant imagery was domestic: sausages, carpets, and all the rest of it. Because I was a young man to whom domesticity had no interest whatsoever, I didn't perceive that until I did the analysis. What I saw, because I was young and excitable, were falcons and herons and birds for the bush and dogs.

So I do feel that the analysis system — what did they think, the sources, the history, the background, what the meaning of a word was — is vital. If you take a word like 'melancholy', it has become debased today into a generalised sense of sadness. In those days it was a violent, passionate emotion which even had its own uniform at one point, so you knew somebody was a melancholy man and you didn't sit next to him in the pub because you might end up in a fight. Now the devaluing of words that has happened today, and the different interpretations that a word is given, you can only understand if you go back to their ways of thinking.

I suppose working on five productions in French or German or whatever has also been very helpful, because it has helped me understand what is there in the translation. When you have done all that, you bring it to the rehearsal and you offer it like an encyclopedia, from which the actors can pick up the bits which are useful to them. As you see, I am speaking passionately about this. It is an area that we lose at our peril. What we are coming up against at the moment is the modern response, which will end up with just as empty Shakespeare productions in the twentieth century, with its cosmetic approach, as the nineteenth century did with its repressed approach. I believe we ought to go back to, 'What did they think?'

John Caird I know you are passionate about this, Terry, and I think all of us would say that we would want to do textual research and study the period, and all the rest of it, but I don't think you can stress too much the point you began by making, which is that two different directors could do exactly the same research and come away with two completely opposite conclusions.

Terry Hands You are absolutely right, John, and how this

119

affects *Twelfth Night* is that if you are aware of the social structure and the political structure, the way they thought, what value they placed upon love, why they would put on a man's costume in order to release the spiritual relationship between two people before it turned to the physical . . . well, you get a completely different view of why people put on trousers. Now, it's up to you whether you want to use what you have researched, but it seems to me that as directors our job is not authorial: it is to get into the head of the writer, to the point of trying to sense his subconscious if you can, which is why I say the analysis of every single word can be of use. That is not to be authorial — it is to say, if that is what was coming out of the period, does it give me an insight into why that person does this at this point and that at that point?

What Kinds of Research?

Michael Billington You've all given eloquent confessional statements about your directorial methods and credo. What I am still trying to get at, and it is a very hard question to answer with this particularly difficult play and its particularly elusive mixture of ingredients, is, how does one get to the heart of it? Does one do it through the kind of character analysis to which we've given a lot of time, or is it something much more intuitive? Bill Alexander, can you remember what your method of entry into *Twelfth Night*, your way of unlocking the play, was?

Bill Alexander Yes, I think so. Let me begin by saying that I agree with just about everything Terry has been saying. I can't conceive of not trying to find out more and more and more about the context of Shakespeare's society and its ways of thought. It is simply nonsensical not to continue throughout your career to discover as much about that as possible. Now, I just do it habitually as part of my life. So, in that sense, the more of Shakespeare's plays you do, the more that basic research blends itself into a perception of the world within which his plays were framed. I think it is particularly important if, for some instinctive reason, you have a drive to change the social context of the play and set it at another time, in another place: then your research on the period in which he actually wrote has almost to be doubled in order that what you do on stage is set off against what you know — is, in a sense, trying to find another way of bringing it home to an audience

Specifically in *Twelfth Night*, yes, I think you do need to know things about the structure of an Elizabethan household, the social hierarchies and the process of upward mobility, and yes, you have to know what the Elizabethans meant by love. But I think ultimately one's inroad and insight into a play comes from an examination of oneself and one's own life, and what one wants to say about the unchangeable aspects of life at any time in history. Now for *that* you have to do research into yourself, and, through that, research into the lives of the actors who are playing the parts, in order to find a corollary for the events of the play — to find the explanations for actions which are parallel to the social and historical explanations, but are rediscovered generation after generation.

Therefore a lot of my rehearsal period was about people's experiences of love, of madness — or when they thought they had been going mad or were in love — as much as what it was like to be a young girl in the situation of Olivia or Viola. And then you have to make the imaginative leaps into the areas of the play which we find the most difficult, like how do you accept the fact that Viola is dressed as a boy. You have to look for the nearest equivalencies, to discover why it shouldn't have been such a hard pill for the Elizabethans to swallow. I don't think one can ever get a Shakespeare play right unless it triggers some very personal responses: but then you have to decide how much you allow those personal responses to colour what you do, and how much you repress them.

Michael Billington   John Barton, do you agree with that?

John Barton   Yes, I agree with an enormous amount of it, but I think one needs to redefine it through your question. You started by asking me whether I did research for *Twelfth Night*, and I said I didn't. Terry, on the other hand, took us through an eloquent description of his forms of preparation for all Shakespeare's plays, which is a bit different. I think, for instance, that Terry's technique of counting up the words is one way of getting into the author's mind that has been helpful for him: reading the play many times might be another, studying the imagery might be a third. There are many ways. We have actually widened the conversation here to the feed-in to preparing to do *any* Shakespeare play. It's not so much a matter of 'academic readings' of the play but deep research into certain elements — maybe social, maybe something else — for each specific play. That is one form of work.

121

Deep textual exploration, using the Arden or however one does it, is something else which I don't myself put under the heading of academic reading: that's part of my homework for knowing my way about the play, which is rather a different thing. The voracious reading is absolutely vital, but it takes different forms with different people, doesn't it? I never had problems about the 'melancholy' in *Twelfth Night*, because I had found out about melancholy on some earlier occasion, I had looked it up, discovered examples of its varying uses down the ages. It seems to me that we are slightly confusing research and preparation.

Bill Alexander   I think that's right. Sometimes in my period of preparation for a play, I have got so fascinated with the research material, with something I've wanted to follow up because I've thought it must be relevant — like, say, the economic situation of Jews in seventeenth-century Europe when I was researching *The Merchant of Venice* — that I find that I have spent three days getting incredibly well-educated, but I haven't even read the play for three days. All the time you have got to be disciplining yourself, saying, 'How is this helping me ultimately to do a better production?'

There has got to be a certain amount of self-censorship in the research. I find it terribly difficult, because one gets so interested in things that you have got to be able to tell yourself when to stop, when it is actually taking you away from the point. The other thing I wanted to say is that, in estimating how much time you've got to prepare something, I find I sometimes undervalue the amount of time I should spend on the actual text. That's just a confession, because I think you can research and research, but if you read the play three more times you would find the answers to the things you are researching.

Terry Hands   Except, except. The point to stop researching is the last performance, because there will always be things you will discover when you are doing the play. I am not so sure about the self-discipline. It is necessary in that there is a time-scale, but let's consider something like the first line of *Twelfth Night* — 'If music be the food of love, play on.' Why is Shakespeare beginning with the subjunctive, why is he beginning with the uncertainty of 'if', what is the Elizabethan attitude to music and what it represents, and what do they mean by 'food', or indeed by 'love'? Then if you get on to words like 'fantasy', like 'high fantastical', how did they understand those?

To tell a simpler and sillier and funnier story, I made what I thought was an academic discovery — well, I still think I made it — when I was working in France on *Twelfth Night*. You remember Quinapalus? 'For what says Quinapalus?' says Feste to Malvolio in the prison scene. Now all academic editors say this is obviously some reference which we have since lost. Nobody knows who Quinapalus was. They know who Archimedes and Plato were, all that lot, but they don't know who Quinapalus was, or maybe Shakespeare invented him. My French actor, knowing none of this, pronounced it, of course, in French, 'For what says, qui n'a pas lu' — 'who has not read.' In a play which has got a lot of French tags, suddenly it leaps out at you. 'For what says he who has not read?'

So I wrote to T. W. Craik, who had edited the New Arden edition of the play, and told him the little story, and said, look, I have just stumbled upon this, and if you revise your Arden edition of *Twelfth Night* I just wondered if it might be of interest to you. He wrote back and said, 'Shakespeare very rarely, if ever, uses French in his plays and I think this is unhelpful.' I wrote back and said 'What about *Henry V*', and 'What about Sir Toby in *Twelfth Night* using French, and all the rest of it?' And I got another letter back saying, 'This kind of complexity of the French language was still not known to Shakespeare and I think it should be left as it is.'

Michael Billington   So that was the end of your discovery?

Terry Hands   That was the end of my discovery as far as Mr. Craik was concerned, but let's get it on the record now!

John Caird   I think it's a marvellous idea, and when you told me about it long after I had put on *Twelfth Night*, I kicked myself for not having noticed it. But, Michael, we should answer your question. John pointed out that it was difficult, but I think we have all said in our various ways that we believe in deep research, in familiarising ourselves with the text so that we are in one way or another experts on it. The far more difficult problem is to have the self-discipline and the expertise to know whether or not your research is manifesting itself in the performances of the actors. Because you can sit in wonderful directorial self-delusion, believing that all your research and all your intelligence and all your intuitive instinct about the play must be crystal clear to an audience, but because your actors haven't appreciated what you're

on about, and how to interpret what you are saying, you might as well not have done any of it.

So I come back to my initial statement that there comes a point where you have to put your research on the back-burner and say, 'Whatever it is I have found out about this play is of value if it is not only said to the actors but truly understood, and if they then find a way of manifesting what I have discovered in their performances.' That takes a fair dose of humility to go along with all the extravagant academic arrogance you need to have made the decisions in the first place.

Terry Hands   But, John, surely you have been in these situations where you take an actor who is in a Jacobean play, playing a melancholy man, and if the part is not working you say to him, 'You are making him a sad man. You have misunderstood the use of the word melancholy.' At that moment your research is of tremendous help to the actor.

John Caird   Of course.

Terry Hands   Well, if you take the word 'sweet' in Shakespeare, which has that little extra sexual connotation which it doesn't have for us today, the actor has immediately got a slightly different playing line than they had when they first used the word.

John Caird   Terry, then you have to go on to the next step, which is: 'I am now convinced that my actor has understood what I am doing. But has the *audience* got any clue what we are on about, me and my actors? Is the difference between the accepted twentieth-century usage of a word and the Elizabethan usage made manifest for the audience? Or, worse still, are we so busy *demonstrating* the difference between those two words that we are unbalancing the line or the moment in favour of an explanation, rather than in favour of a natural mode of delivery?'

Terry Hands   That is the danger, but equally it is just what we have been talking about in the way of presenting Shakespeare. Part of the process of doing the plays is clothing the words with their old emotional or demonstrative meanings, so that they become clear — it's trying to bring the language back to life again.

John Caird   And sometimes you can only hope it's coming across.

Bill Alexander You do bring it back to life. But what you're up against is the terrible situation where you tell Jaques, 'Melancholy doesn't mean that, it actually means angry and aggressive', and then the audience spends the entire time saying, 'He doesn't seem to be behaving like the melancholy man we're told he is.' On the other hand, you can take something like Gratiano's description of Antonio in *The Merchant of Venice*, which is clearly also a description of a melancholy man, but isn't so banged on about as it is with Jaques. As soon as you realise that Antonio is actually a very active character, a very aggressive character, you improve the quality of some scenes tremendously. Because the tendency for us in modern England is to be very back-foot about our sentiments.

Terry Hands I don't think you've got a problem with the public, I really don't. But you very often have a problem with the press. Most of the public who go to the theatre want to have a good time and they have bought their ticket for that end.

Michael Billington So do most critics . . .

Terry Hands What you are up against is that the public are open to what the play is going to do for them, and will put the pieces together as they go along. What you are bound to be fighting with the press is the tradition of past productions. And, please, this is not an attack in any way — it is not even a criticism of criticism, but just saying that it is part of that rich dialogue that you have with an audience when they come in.

We've spoken about very overt words, but it's not even just that. It is a question, too, of event. Certain events happen on stage which had a very philosophical meaning to an Elizabethan, and which you must try to find a modern relevance for. I don't see that that's difficult.

Realism and Fable

Michael Billington Can I bring us on to one final area, which is what seems to be the theme that's run through the whole discussion but hasn't been resolved, probably can't be resolved — namely the tension between the naturalistic element in *Twelfth Night* and the poetic, fabulous, magic element. We've all agree that both ingredients are there, and are juxtaposed scene by scene and even within the scenes. Again in purely practical terms, how

does one cope with that problem, which seems to be stronger in *Twelfth Night* than in any other Shakespeare play? In the end, even if one calls a scene poetic in its impact, does it still have to be directed from a naturalistic viewpoint? Do you still have to ask the fundamental questions about what the motivation is, what the drive behind the scene is, what the purpose of the character is?

John Barton This is at once a frightfully simple, basic question and a frightfully difficult one that shouldn't be difficult. I think that, without any doubt, because of the tradition that we inherit, and, because of the way actors work, one *has* to root a play in the motivation of the characters, and one has to tap naturalistic devices to a greater or lesser extent. The problem comes in deciding what the hell you mean by 'poetic', because it means one thing to some people, something quite different to others. The term can be offensive to some actors, frightening to others. What is difficult — and sometimes I feel I have come near to solving it, but more often not — is how to achieve a marriage of the two: because I believe that in any true Shakespearean, whether an actor or director or Shakespeare himself, the dichotomy between the two should not exist, and only exists now because of the habit of mind of the working tradition we apply to most plays that we do.

Now, if there's a very expressionist play, or a very absurdist play, or a play that in some other way is palpably not naturalistic, that is not so difficult. Actors can recognise it. What is so difficult in Shakespeare is that the two are continually intermixed, and very much so in a play like *Twelfth Night*. It came up when Bill and I were talking earlier about Viola's arrival in Illyria, that I basically agreed with all that Bill was saying but he thought I was maybe saying something that I wasn't. What he said was absolutely right — that to make that scene real and alive you have to go at it through situation, unfolding the story from one speech to another psychologically. But what I am saying is that that alone won't give everything that Shakespeare is asking for. And what is very, very difficult for many actors is, having gone about it in that way, to find the key that unlocks the magical or fabulous element.

I am defining the problem, not giving an answer. It haunts me. Sometimes I think I have failed dismally with it. I don't believe at the moment there *is* any certain answer, because each actor ticks a bit differently, sometimes misunderstands it a bit differently. Their roots affect them differently.

Michael Billington Can you, and should you, with a play like

Twelfth Night, construct a past history of the characters as you can do, say, with Chekhov? It is almost obligatory in Chekhov.

John Barton Well, I think you can, but it's dangerous. You have to be aware, and the actors have to be aware, that it may be something that pleases and satisfies them but doesn't mean anything to the audience — which doesn't make it bad, but maybe delusive, in the way that John has described the bringing of research into the rehearsal room. Often you get an actor who is convinced he's cracked something by working out who his grandmother was, but it is a purely subjective thing to him.

Michael Billington Terry, how do you think the director achieves this curious balance between what we are calling the naturalistic and the magical?

Terry Hands They are very difficult words, aren't they? We are to some extent playing with semantics here.

Michael Billington Well, we know what we mean by those words.

Terry Hands Yes, I think we do. I think that any part, any role that an actor plays has to be a reorganisation of the truthful pattern of their own emotions to any given event. Now, when I say reorganisation of a pattern, I mean that, if you smile when it's a nice day and you scowl when it's a rainy day, the scowl is real and the smile is real. If you apply that smile the other way round, because that is what the character does, it is still your reality but the pattern is different.

We tend to recognise each other anyway through patterns of behaviour. We don't know each other: all we do is recognise certain patterns of emotion. Now Shakespeare is always telling a story, but at each moment in the story he does not demand that it be consistent throughout — rather like a music-hall bill, which will give us a sad song followed by a funny sketch, followed by some clowning followed by a bit of a play. I don't think it worries him that there should be a consistent, *Coronation Street* sort of background to everything, but each moment, like a stone in a mosaic, does have to have its own element of complete purity, although later, at the end of the play, we will step back and look at the picture the mosaic is creating. An image I often use with actors is *pointillisme* — if the moment is pure red emotionally give me a

little red dot, and if it's pure white give me a little white dot, but don't give me a generalised pink. That is what you get in Chekhov so often, whereas what Shakespeare gives us is the absolute purity of emotion for that moment, and we need not question it.

What I am saying is, you link it all up on, firstly, the emotional truth of the moment, like 'I have known what it is to give suck': at that moment, not necessarily a scene before or three scenes afterwards, she knew what it was to give suck, that is, she suckled her baby. At that moment the emotional intensity of the moment requires that truth. That's the fun thing.

The second thing is the volatility, the speed of change of the emotions. Shakespeare's characters are ninety-nine times out of a hundred far more intelligent than we are, and much quicker in their emotional responses — actually, I believe that we are too, but we have allowed behaviourism and our environment and so-called national temperament to quieten us down. So you can say, 'I am happy,' as I have just said, and clap your hands, or you can say, 'I am happy,' and go into a tribal happiness dance, given the circumstances. What you are judging in rehearsal is what degree of revelation and fulfilment of that emotion on that line or that word you are prepared to do. It is a question of turning on a sixpence, which is an image we use all the time: the speed of the change I believe is what provides the energy of Shakespeare.

What links what you are calling the poetic and the naturalistic is that the truth you want an actor to have is not the truth of behaviour, it is the truth of emotion, and the speed of the change is what will put it into a Shakespeare story. Where it goes wrong is when we overlay an entire show or an entire part with what I call the Chekhov syndrome, where you mix your colours and they become one generalised blur. The thing about Shakespeare is the absolute volatility of the people, and in my opinion that is more real to human nature than what has become sophisticatedly traditional in terms of stage performance.

Michael Billington That's very clear, but, John Caird, to follow up what Terry has been saying, that volatility seems to me more evident in *Twelfth Night* than anywhere else, because of the lightning speed of mood change within a scene. How does one cope with that as a director?

John Caird I agree with a lot of what John and Terry have said, although this idea that you can somehow get to the truth of a part by appealing to the experience of the actor troubles me, I have to

say. I think that is only sometimes true. What I often find more fruitful than looking at the personal life of an actor, who after all has a rather unusual personal life compared with most normal people, is the imagination. Now the imagination of a great actor is a far more fruitful area in terms of the richness and discovery of human truth than personal experience is.

I don't know whether actors are more self-deluding than other artists, they probably aren't, but as with all artists there is a large area of fantasy in their lives — using fantasy, perhaps, in the old-fashioned Shakespearean sense. When it comes to marrying the naturalistic with the poetic, or the naturalistic with the non-naturalistic — the naturalistic with the mad in the case of *Twelfth Night*, which I suppose is what you are getting at — I think that the question you are asking is the most fundamental and difficult one in acting Shakespeare's plays. If you look at a Shakespeare text and you find great riches in it and great variety and great detail, you have to assume that since he put it there he wants to see it on stage, otherwise he wouldn't have bothered. Equally, if he has written great stretches of epic poetry, lines of great lyrical beauty, he also wants to see those realised. If you start from both those premises, the question then is, how do you inspire an actor or a company of actors to achieve that symbiosis?

The first thing I think you have to do with a group of actors is to point out to them that, although Shakespeare's characters are motivated by naturalistic human needs — in almost every case if you look at the text long enough you *will* find evidence for the motivation of each character — it is no less true to say that no Shakespearean character expresses himself or herself as Elizabethan people would have talked in real life. So you have to bridge that paradox. People didn't use heightened poetic language in everyday speech in Elizabethan times any more than we use heightened poetic language in everyday speech. There were just as many people who were repetitive and bland or monosyllabic in their conversation as we are today.

Michael Billington   Are you saying that you have to acknowledge the artificiality of Shakespearean speech?

John Caird   You have to accept, while investigating all the naturalism and all the motivation, that every character is speaking in a heightened and poetic manner. But if you allow an actor to deliver his lines *as if* he were speaking in a heightened and poetic manner, you will lard the naturalism with a gloss of artiness

through which you won't be able to see the naturalism. What you have to do is get the actors to use the poetry they have been given — to explore the imagery, to cross-refer the images where they need to be cross-referred, to use rhyme, to obey the rhythms of the text — and having done all that work, then to use it and speak their lines in a way that would suggest that they are in a world which is completely natural and consistent with their interlocutor or interlocutors on stage. They must also seem to be behaving completely naturally as human beings, in ways that make people in the audience feel that they are looking at their own lives.

Poetry as Truth to Emotions

Michael Billington Right. Bill, you in a sense provoked this because of that idea you offered earlier on, that Viola must have been travelling from Marseilles to Venice, which was something that had never occurred to me before.

Bill Alexander It is spurious. It's no wonder it had never occurred to you before.

Michael Billington But, seriously, is that the kind of question one asks of all the characters? Where have they come from? Where are they going to? Who are they?

Bill Alexander It's extremely useful to ask those questions and to answer them, and if you have to make up answers, that's fine. I think the actress playing Viola *should* know where she had been heading for on the boat, not that that will ever be manifest to an audience — it's just part of the process of the actor feeling complete within the part and knowing what they are doing. But to address myself to the fundamental question about naturalism and poetry in the speaking of Shakespeare, I agree with nearly everything that my three colleagues have said. I agree particularly about the notions of consistency of style and vocabulary, the nature of speech between a group of people, the acceptance that this is the way these people speak to each other and express themselves to each other. But I don't think you can absolutely have meant, John, that their culture was just the same as ours, and that they spoke just like we do. I'm sure it was a more verbal culture. Printing was less widespread, fewer people could read, the handing down of stories was by word of mouth.

John Caird Show me your evidence that they were more verbal with each other. Show me the tape recordings. Have you read any transcripts of trials in the last few years? They are exactly the same.

Bill Alexander My contention is, unproven, that they were a more verbal culture, that they talked more than we did, therefore that they had a greater sense of words than we do. Even gravediggers. I think that the route from naturalism to poetry lies through an analysis within each character of what they are trying to express, how they are trying to explain what they feel to another person. The words are there because the characters want to explain how they feel. They don't do it, as we tend in the twentieth century, by saying the opposite of what we mean in order to tell our partner or friend how we feel. They did it by being as explicit as they could about how they felt.

It is interesting that the word 'rhetoric' these days has tended to become pejorative, whereas in Elizabethan times it was the very opposite — it was one of the main skills you learned, how to express yourself, how to make yourself absolutely clear. Now that, in my view, leads us from truth to poetry, because if you express how you feel truthfully you are being beautiful in a sense, mentally beautiful to that other person. And that will tend to be even more the case if you are a character in the hands of a great poet. Take what we have talked of as a poetic speech, the willow-cabin speech. It is poetic only because it is that character's absolute and heartfelt definition of what they would do, of how they would wish to be. The essence of the poetry lies in answering the question: 'What would you do?' says Olivia. 'I'd make me a willow cabin at your gate,' says Viola. And if you experience the detail of what she is saying and believe she would do that, then you become both truthful and poetic. That way you unlock the poetry of the play.

Terry Hands I would very much agree with that, and I think a word we could use as well is 'emotional'. Shakespeare's plays are about emotional situations, and you don't need to know you were on a particular boat except to make yourself feel comfy. That willow-cabin speech is a marvellous example because somebody is trying to reveal to *themselves* as well as to the other person what their emotion would be, and the total truth of that will create an emotional realism that the audience will accept. I am very chary of drawing upon an actor's experiences in Shakespeare, where there

131

are a whole load of emotions that a lot of young actors have never experienced. That's why we explore the Sonnets with them, because we want to acquaint them with those areas, and secondly because society builds its own beliefs.

To give you one example. Nearly every English actress who has played Lady Anne in *Richard III* has said to me, 'Why does she spit at him when he says, 'Get married'? Why doesn't she spit at him when he says, 'Go to your bed'?' Now in France the actress had no trouble at all with this, and I said, 'Why do you have no trouble with this? You know, all my English actresses do.' And she said, 'Well, I suppose you could go to bed with him, but *marry* him? Jesus!' There was a totally different kind of social response. I am frightened by the American system of 'My character wouldn't say this.'

Michael Billington   As if the character existed before the word.

Bill Alexander   'Then you're playing the wrong part,' is the answer.

Terry Hands   'Then you're playing the wrong part.' The pre-scene exploration is a terrible problem. The scene exists, and you recognise your role at the end of the rehearsal period, not at the beginning of the rehearsal period. The rehearsal period is a discovery to find who you are, not to come to and tell us who you are.

Bill Alexander   That's right. And the actor who attempts to colonise Shakespeare by saying, 'I feel I know what this character is about' is no better. The reply is, 'It's not your fucking character, it's Shakespeare's character, the guy who wrote it. He created it, you're the interpreter of it.'

John Caird   But I'm astonished to find that you should both think that Shakespeare was a very observant version of Harold Pinter — sitting on top of the Elizabethan Elephant omnibus and jotting down all the fantastic poetic things people were saying to each other. It seems to me a slightly diminishing attitude to Shakespeare's language.

Bill Alexander   I did not say that, John. I am not implying that people went round talking in sonnets or iambic pentameters all the time. Of course they didn't.

132

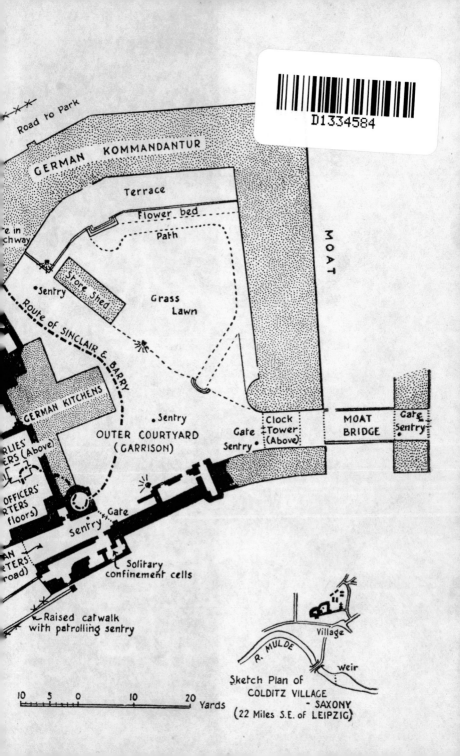

Road to park

GERMAN KOMMANDANTUR

Terrace

Flower bed

Path

re in
chway

Store Shed

•Sentry

Grass
Lawn

Route of SINCLAIR & BARRY

MOAT

GERMAN KITCHENS

•Sentry

OUTER COURTYARD
(GARRISON)

Gate
Sentry •

Clock
Tower
(Above)

MOAT
BRIDGE

Gate
Sentry
•

RLIES'
RS (Above)

OFFICERS'
RTERS
floors)

Gate

AN
TERS
road)

Sentry

Solitary
confinement cells

Raised catwalk
with patrolling sentry

10 5 0   10   20
Yards

R. MULDE

Village

weir

Sketch Plan of
COLDITZ VILLAGE
- SAXONY
(22 Miles S.E. of LEIPZIG)

THE LATTER DAYS

THE
LATTER DAYS

by

P. R. Reid, M.B.E., M.C.

LONDON
HODDER & STOUGHTON

First printed - 1953

MADE AND PRINTED IN GREAT BRITAIN FOR
HODDER AND STOUGHTON LTD., LONDON, BY
WYMAN & SONS LIMITED, LONDON, READING AND FAKENHAM

TO

MICHAEL, DIANA,

CHRISTOPHER AND CHRISTINA

ACKNOWLEDGMENTS

MY principle collaborators in the work of collecting the material for this book have been Captain 'Dick' Howe, M.B.E., M.C., formerly of the Royal Tank Regiment and Captain 'Lulu' Lawton of the Duke of Wellington's. Major Harry Elliott of the Irish Guards has been a close third. Without them this book would not have been written. It is a happy coincidence that Dick and Harry should have been my colleagues on one of the first escapes from a German Prison Camp in the last war—early in September, 1940!

John Watton, who went through the war at Colditz, has contributed the cover and the illustrations. He can bring the written word to life. His sense of atmosphere, his detail and his memory have always astonished me.

From Holland I have had unstinted, generous help from Captain G. W. T. Dames of the Royal Netherlands Indies Army. I could not have written of the Dutch without him. From France I have had the help of General Le Brigant through his well-known work, "Les Indomptables," the French classic on the Fortress Prison, and of Père Yves Congar, who has written a memorable epitaph to the Frenchmen who never returned, in his book, "Leur Resistance".

Mr. John K. Lichtblau, the well-known American critic and newspaper correspondent, has helped me to follow up trails in the U.S.A. and Major V. Dluznievski, now living in England, has traced for me many obscure details concerning the remnants of the Polish Contingent of Colditz.

Herr Hans Pfeiffer has been my link with Germany, and in a frank, friendly manner has given me the German point of view.

Returning to Britain, I acknowledge with gratitude—and pleasure, because they are still very much alive—the help of many ex-Colditz men : Alan Campbell who has contributed poetry and notes of his legal battles with the German High Command, Rupert Barry and Peter Storie Pugh for their scrap books of the war and their notes, Geoffrey Wardle and his wife and children for an enjoyable evening in which the glider was rebuilt in fantasy, Peter Tunstall, Kenneth Lee, Padre Ellison Platt for the use of his sermon and his song, Edmund Hannay and Mike Harvey.

I wish to acknowledge my indebtedness to *The Times* and to

the *Sunday Express* for the reproduction of extracts from editions of May, 1945, and to the publishers of "Detour", a book from the Falcon Press, which contains an interesting series of war reminiscences and much about Colditz. This book has often helped me over questions of history, in particular with regard to the names of officers and to dates of occurrences.

Jack Best sent me the original glider plans and most useful technical notes all the way from Kenya. Lorne Welch and his wife have, together, rechecked those plans in order to confirm, once more, that the machine could take the air.

Lastly, to those who criticized the roughs of this book, in particular my wife and Mr. H. R. Chapman, C.B.E., I owe a great deal, and to my wife especially, who slaved through the late and early hours typing the manuscript, I am irrevocably indebted.

I have not exhausted the list of those who have helped to make this story a reality in print. I cannot forget the succulent meals with which Nanny—Miss Freda Back—kept body and soul together during the long sessions. More names spring to mind as I write : General Giebel, Colonel Guy German, Kenneth Lockwood, Roger Madin . . . I ask them all to accept my thanks and only hope that the story will do justice to their efforts.

Possingworth,   P. R. REID
   Sussex.
September, 1953.

CONTENTS

LIST OF ILLUSTRATIONS

PROLOGUE

I HAVE often been asked the question : "Why did the Germans put up with so much from the Allied P.O.Ws. in Colditz? From the stories told, one is almost sorry for the Germans—the prisoners gave them such a h—— of a time"! In order to answer this question, I wrote—some years after the late war—to the only contact that I could trace among the German personalities of those days. Herr Hans Pfeiffer, the German interpreter at Oflag IVC, Colditz, was, happily, still in the land of the living, safe in the western zone of Germany. Colditz, by the way, is in the Eastern Zone, behind the Iron Curtain. Pfeiffer's reply to my letter was written in good English and this is what he said:

"You ask for my impressions of Colditz. I think our treatment of you was correct. Of course it was your 'verdammte Pflicht und Schuldigkeit' as officers to escape, if you could, and it was like-wise our 'damned duty' to prevent your doing so. That some of you did actually manage to get away under such difficult circum-stances could only arouse the admiration of 'your friends the enemy', but I think your own book shows that such a collection of 'enfants terribles' as yourselves could not be handled with kid gloves. 'Nichts für ungut!'—no offence meant."

The Germans looked upon the prisoners as "their friends, the enemy." It was a curious friendship, but I can see what Herr Pfeiffer means. It was of the kind that springs from respect, that might easily have sprung up, for instance, between the Desert Rats and Rommel's hardened campaigners, if circumstances had ever presented the opportunity.

Colditz was the prison to which Allied officers were sent after trying to escape from Germany. (Towards the end of the war there was not room in the camp for them all and some, who should have been there, never had the dubious honour of residence within its walls!) The initial spark of defiance thus shown in captivity, and registered by transfer to Colditz produced the reaction mentioned by Herr Pfeiffer.

In Colditz itself, however, the spirit of defiance blossomed. In the tropical atmosphere of the prison, where 'the heat' was turned

on by the prisoners, this spirit thrived. The germ of admiration planted in the minds of the warders grew to a personal respect as they came into daily contact with men who would stand no bullying and who showed by their actions that the weapons in the warders' hands were not conclusive arguments as to the conduct of affairs in the prison.

The result was a *modus vivendi*, 'comparatively' neutral as opposed to hostile. The Colditz prisoners received, on the whole, what might be termed manly treatment.

Pfeiffer apologetically explains that the prisoners could not be handled with kid gloves. What he is referring to are, largely, the conditions over which he and his fellow junior officers had little control; the cramped and stifling life in the camp. The German High Command was so intent on keeping the P.O.W.s inside— with a force of guards outnumbering the prisoners—that excesses in the laying down of prison orders were inevitable. Within these limits, the Germans were almost compelled to use the kid glove.

The prisoners were hostages—that became apparent after a couple of years. If the war was to take a wrong turning for Hitler and his entourage, the prisoners of Colditz would be held up to ransom. Perhaps the emergence of this fact caused the Germans to treat the prisoners warily. A dead hostage is no use at all. Of course, he could be replaced—but there would be undesirable repercussions. So, it was worth their while to be tolerant within reason, on the principle that it is better not to tempt fate by baiting a spirited, if not dangerous animal, even though it may be, apparently, securely caged.

Where the Germans failed, was in their excess of zeal to keep the P.O.W.s in prison. Their efficiency reached regrettable heights when they refused, during the lengthening years, to remove sick prisoners and, more particularly, the unfortunate ones who went 'round the bend'. It was inevitable that in the confined atmosphere of Colditz there would be mental suffering among men whose very presence in the camp testified to their deep-seated yearning for freedom. There were several who became mentally unbalanced, even suicidal. They should have been removed. They were a menace to themselves and to the mental balance of their fellow prisoners. They had to be looked after tirelessly. They had to be guarded by men who could sense the danger to themselves, as if they were nursing patients suffering from an infectious disease.

One officer who had delusions and who, thank God, has completely recovered, described his feeling to me recently in this way:

"After this failure to escape, I was so disgusted that I took to studying and research. Shortly after 'D' Day, I got some peculiar delusions—a long story in themselves. I got the impression that we were all drugged and under semi-hypnosis which was the reason the Germans caught every attempt to escape. One day I saw the Castle burning and could see the flames and the smoke and the beams crashing down. Of course, my fellow prisoners got so thoroughly scared that they got Dickie (the doctor) to give me an injection of morphia and put me in a cell."

The desire to escape was paramount among the men of Colditz. They were of all nationalities fighting on the Allied side ; Englishmen, Scotsmen and Irishmen from Britain and every corner of the Commonwealth—Canada, Australia, New Zealand and Africa. There were Poles and Yugoslavs, Dutchmen from the Netherland East Indies as well as from Holland, Frenchmen from the African colonies as well as the mother country and, long before the end, there were Americans too.

Naturally, under conditions in which everybody was trying to escape there was a serious danger that plans would overlap, if not conflict. An Englishman building a tunnel was in danger of meeting a Frenchman digging from another direction!

Each nationality had its Escape Officer ; a man placed in charge of escape affairs, who was made aware of the plans of the other nationalities, who prevented congestion along the lines and initiated an orderly roster with his colleagues. The result often went like this :

"Sorry, old chap, a Frenchman (or a Dutchman or an Englishman, etc.) has already registered that plan. You'll have to wait three months when it's due to come off. If it's not blown sky high after that, I'll see you're entered on the list for the next go, by the same route."

The reader can well understand that the position of Escape Officer was a most important and ticklish one. The holder, of necessity, had to have the implicit trust of his fellow officers. It was axiomatic that he was excluded from escaping himself ; no little sacrifice for a man, who, by his nature and experience—even before his promotion to the post—possessed all the qualifications for making a successful getaway.

While on this point, I am reminded of another which I must place before the reader. Some who have read "The Colditz Story" have said to me : "Surely the remark you made about so much

having to be left unsaid was merely intended to intrigue the reader by introducing an air of mystery?"

May I be forgiven for repeating again that much interesting and exciting material has, necessarily, in the conditions of the world to-day, to be omitted. If the reader feels, on occasion, that he would like to know more than he is told, I hope he will remember this point.

Apart from this, there is, nevertheless, enough material to fill another book. I have had to pick and choose. I must, therefore, ask for the indulgence of the reader if, occasionally, I pass lightly over certain events and mention casually characters that have 'gone before'. I cannot hope to achieve the finesse of Sherlock Holmes who was wont to say, cryptically: ". . . You will notice, my dear Watson, a distinct resemblance here, to the case of the Dasker-ville Diamonds. . . ." I feel sure the reader will understand that, although this story should be sufficient unto itself, it is, at the same time, the second in a series.

It is with deep regret that I have had to sacrifice a 'her' on the altar of truth. Neither would it be honest to the fair to withhold from them—or the men—the fact that there are no female characters in the story. On page 132 I have done my best. It was the nearest a woman ever approached to the forbidding portals of the Castle. Even so, she wasted no time. I can only lean on a good precedent in order to bolster up my failure to make good the omissions of history. Surely I cannot go far wrong in emulating a drama without a heroine that once held the stages of the world for record breaking runs—none other than "Journeys End".

With this introduction, may I usher the reader into the auditorium, where the overture is about to begin. . . .

PART I

1942

OVERTURE

THIS book is the story of a castle in Saxony during those years of the second World War between November, 1942, and April, 1945. It covers only a fleeting moment in the history of the Castle as measured by the life span of hewn stone and oak timbers. There must have been many periods, as the scrolls of the centuries unrolled, when the *tempo* of man's activity within its walls rose to dramatic heights; but, probably, none was more dramatic than the short interval in which this story of human endeavour unfolds itself.

Not that the interval was short for the actors who then walked upon the Colditz stage. It is short in retrospect. The passage of time is registered physically and mechanically in minutes and hours by the clock. A year may sear itself upon the soul of a man so deeply that it becomes a lifetime or it may pass so refreshingly over him that it is gone like a gay summer's day. Man measures time by happiness or sorrow, by tranquillity or torture. The one is past and gone so quickly that it is seldom seized and savoured. The other turns the hours into days, and the weeks into years, and can turn man's nature into unrecognisable shapes.

During the period of which I write, Colditz Castle was the *Sonderlager* or *Straflager* of Germany. It was the stronghold where Allied prisoners of war who had dared to break their chains were incarcerated. It was the cage in which were shut the birds that longed to be free! that beat their wings unceasingly against the bars. In such conditions birds do not usually survive long. It says something for the resilient spirit of man that those Allied prisoners, the inveterate escapers, who were sent to Colditz mostly survived the ordeal.

For such men, much more than for others, the hours were days and the weeks were years. They were men of action by nature and they lived a long time the torture of forced inactivity. They were prisoners expiating no other crime than the unselfish service of their country.

Taking stock of the situation at Colditz in the bleak winter of 1942, entails, first and foremost, taking stock of the escaping situation.

The escape-proof castle of the 1914–18 war had been made to look like a riddled target. Holes had been made everywhere—metaphorically and literally—in its impregnable walls.

By the end of 1942, the British prisoners' contingent had risen to eighty strong. Officers from the three services and from every country of the Commonwealth, they had all committed offences against Hitler's Reich. About ninety per cent. of them had escaped at least once from other camps. There were three Padres : the Reverends Ellison Platt, Heard and Hobling, who had made themselves such nuisances elsewhere, clamouring for Christian treatment for their flocks, that the German High Command considered Colditz the only appropriate place for them. Here, at least, their clamours would not penetrate the thick walls of the fortress.

Seventy three "officer-attempts" to escape had been registered so far. The term "officer-attempt" was used in the statistics so as to be able to register each attempt of each officer. Thus, seventy three officer-attempts does not mean that seventy three officers out of the eighty tried to escape. That figure was probably nearer forty than eighty, but as several of the forty attempted two or three times they were given their individual totals on the escape record and the total of the whole column—so to speak—added up to seventy three. It was not often that a Senior British Officer had an opportunity to escape but Colonel Guy German was not omitted from an early attempt which would have left the camp devoid of the entire British contingent!

Out of the total recorded, twenty-two officers had succeeded in getting clear of the camp. They were "gone away", as it was termed. The number included five Dutch officers taking part in British escape attempts. The statistic, however, that the camp was most proud of, and which has never been equalled by any P.O.W. camp in Germany, was the number of succeessful escapes. Officers' home-runs into neutral or friendly territory totalled no less than eleven out of the twenty-two—fifty per cent.!

The fortunate eleven were: Airey Neave and Tony Luteyn; Bill Fowler and Van Doorninck; the two E.R.A.'s, Wally Hammond and Tubby Lister; Brian Paddon; Ronnie Littledale, Billie Stephens, Hank Wardle and the author.

Coming next to the Dutch contingent, which numbered sixty at the end of 1942, the equivalent records were approximately as follows (excluding the Dutchmen above mentioned): officer-attempts about thirty, gone-aways ten, and home-runs six.

The French contingent numbered one hundred and fifty, including a batch of fifty Jewish French officers who, with rare exceptions, did not interest themselves in escaping. Frankly, the latter realised that recapture, for them, meant extermination; in prisoner jargon a "Klimtin", and their lives were probably safer in Colditz than in France.

French officer-attempts numbered somewhere in the region of twenty to thirty—I cannot recollect them more exactly. Gone-aways numbered about ten and home-runs amounted to at least four.

The Polish contingent had left during the year. They had numbered eighty strong and had been at Colditz from the beginning of the war. They were already there when I arrived in November, 1940. They had no successful home-runs that I remember. Tragic, indeed, it is to recollect that they had no homeland that they could make for. When they succeeded in breaking out of the Castle they headed for Switzerland, Sweden or France, leaving their homes and loved ones further than ever behind them. Half a dozen had "gone-aways" to their credit, but, though some of them reached the Swiss frontier they were caught and the record showed no "home-runs" to neutral territory from Colditz for this company. Nevertheless, after leaving Colditz, two at least escaped from a camp further east in Germany and made their way to France and England. They were: Felix Jablonowski and Tony Karpf. The former, an International lawyer and University lecturer, has recently gone to America to seek his fortune and a new life ; while Karpf, happily married, has settled in Glasgow.

Airey Neave was the first Englishman to reach England from Colditz via Switzerland, France and Spain.* That was in May, 1942. Paddon followed closely at his heels—in time, though by another route—Sweden.

So much for the record up to the Autumn of 1942, but what were the prospects for the future? Conditions were undoubtedly becoming more difficult. Within the Castle the roll-calls for prisoners settled down to a regular four *Appells* every day. The times at which the *Appells* occurred were, however, by no means regular. The factory siren which had recently been installed would shriek its warning at odd hours of the day, in the grey light of dawn or in the night hours. The parade started five minutes after the siren's moans had subsided. Our men, wherever they were working at their nefarious activities, had only one compensation. In the deepest shaft or the longest tunnel, the siren could

* Neave has written the story in his book, *They Have Their Exits*.

be heard and tools downed at once. Nevertheless, the five minutes
tolerance gave little time for sealing entrances and cleaning up.
It was always a close thing and wearing on the nerves. The fact
that there were four *Appells* every twenty-four hours also broke
up the working shifts, impaired efficiency and slowed progress
considerably.

It was inevitable, too, that, as time went on, escape routes out
of the Castle would become fewer and fewer. The Castle, as already
mentioned, presented to the escaper by 1943 the picture of a target
riddled with holes, but unfortunately, at this stage, behind every
hole stood a sentry. The garrison outnumbered the prisoners.
Catwalks had been erected providing an unhindered view into
all the nooks and crannies in the battlements. They hung suspended
like window-cleaner's cradles; they stood on long poles clinging,
sometimes perilously, to walls, like builders' scaffolds supported
from narrow ledges in the cliff sides. Wherever a prisoner had
escaped, there new and forbidding rolls of concertina wire were
stretched. Jerries hung out of skylights with machine-guns beside
them surveying roof ridges, slopes and gutters.

Sound detectors were being installed everywhere. The exits
through the thinner walls being nearly exhausted, men were
digging deeper into the formidably heavy foundations of the older
structure of the Castle.

Colditz, like many other ancient buildings, was not one castle but
many castles; built and ruined, rebuilt and ruined again by wars and
weather, by time and usage. Thus, although some of the senior
prisoners' quarters and probably the interior decoration of the
Castle chapel was attributable to architects and builders working
to the orders of Augustus the Strong, king of Poland and elector
of Saxony from 1694 to 1733, the garrison quarters around the
outer courtyard were of eighteenth and early nineteenth century
design. Returning within the Keep however, most of the archi-
tecture and the building construction bore witness of a *Schloss*
built in earlier days during the sixteenth century. In these medieval
halls and casemates the junior officers lived. When the tunnellers
among them began delving downwards they came upon yet
earlier foundations of a castle destroyed, apparently, in the Hussite
Wars of the fifteenth century. In fact, it can be vouched with
assurance that almost as long as man existed in those parts, and
wished to defend himself against his enemies, he must have
built himself an eyrie on the easily defendable, towering rock
promontory of Colditz.

The searchlights increased in number dispelling the last shadow which might shelter a lurking form on its desperate route to freedom.

Then there were the Alsatian dogs. They had not increased in number, as far as was known, but they were worked harder. Patrols, with or without the Alsatians, had become frequent and were the more dangerous as they became more irregular, touring the Castle at unpredictable intervals of time.

It was also natural that the prisoners and the guards should learn more and more of each others' habits and methods. As the scales were from the first weighted in favour of the guards they held an advantage which told more heavily as the years passed. The training of sentries for the work at Colditz became more scientific. They were instructed in all the known tricks and wiles of the prisoners; warned again and again of what they might expect; their duty stations changed often to prevent staleness dulling the edge of their preparedness. They toured, regularly, the escapers' museum in the garrison Headquarters, carrying away mental pictures of the escaper's art, his tools, his keys, his maps, papers, clothing and his false uniforms, his trap doors and his camouflage. The prisoners' ingenuity was stretched to limits which only the story in its unfolding can adequately describe.

The prisoners were becoming physically weak. Even the most robust men could not stand up indefinitely to the meagre diet. Albeit that Red Cross food was available there was never enough. Men were always hungry and could only bloat themselves with unappetising mealy potatoes and stomach-revolting turnips and swedes. Alternatively they took to their beds for long periods of the day, preserving thereby what little energy their nutrition gave them.

The spirit was unconquered but the flesh was weak. The change in physical condition came imperceptibly and, as each suffered alike, a prisoner did not appreciate the alteration taking place within himself, or his companions around him. A form of evolution was going on within the Castle walls and a different kind of human being was coming into existence : a scrawny individual with a skin and bone physique seriously lacking in vitamins. Mentally, the prisoner who kept himself occupied was none the worse for his captivity. On the contrary, in many cases, the enforced life of the ascetic sharpened the wits and enlarged the horizon of the mind. The age old secret of the hermit was manifestly revealed; men's minds and souls were purified by the mortification of the body.

Unfortunately, a man cannot escape from a fortress by mind alone. He has to drag his body with him. Although the escaper's wits were sharpened and his mind as clear as a bell, his body, in 1942, could not perform the feats it did in 1940 unless scourged by the driving force of a powerful will.

So much for conditions within the fortress, but what of the great outside? The huge face of Germany lay for hundreds of miles in all directions around the Castle embedded in the very heart of the *Reich*. To the men incarcerated in the camp the changing circumstances outside were mostly a closed book. Every tit-bit of information gleaned was treasured and recorded for possible exploitation but so much was unknown. Although the Colditz techniques for the production of false papers were highly skilled, though false identities could be faithfully reproduced which would pass muster under known conditions outside the camp at a given date, these very conditions were altering rapidly for the worse and changes were unpredictable.

The change that was coming over Germany is well illustrated by the two largest breakouts of the war from camps other than Colditz. Jumping ahead in time for a moment, on the night of August 3rd–4th, 1943, sixty-five British officers escaped by tunnel from Oflag VIIB at Eichstatt, in Bavaria. It was a beautifully engineered escape, but not one of the officers made the home run. Apart from the fact that the majority of them were ill equipped both as to civilian clothing and as to identity papers, according to the best standards, they under-estimated the reaction of the Germans to their escape. The latter, during the winter of 1942–43, were beginning to feel the flail of Allied heavy bombing; of our great aircraft sweeps over their territory. They were organising their Home Guard feverishly. It was known as the *Landwache*. The *Hitler Jugend* was also mobilised, and children of tender age were not excluded from routine duties and from lessons upon how to recognise and how to capture enemy airmen. Thus, it was not a far cry to transfer their activities, at short notice, to the recapture of escaped prisoners. When large numbers escaped together, the organisation required would be no different to that which came into play after a heavy aerial bombardment.

Reports have it that after the Eichstatt escape no less than sixty thousand of the *Landwache* were in action within twenty-four hours, searching for the escapers. It was not an escape that paid dividends. Undoubtedly, of course, it gave the Germans 'a

packet' of trouble—that was a good thing. It harassed them and because of that alone it was probably worth while. But it is also argued that it gave the *Landwache* a good field day—impromptu manœuvres—which made them more efficient later on against our airmen parachuting in Germany and trying hard to evade capture. The escape failed on points of strategy rather than in the tactics of its execution.

Practically the same results were achieved, only with far worse consequences, by another, and the last, large British breakout recorded during World War II. This was the disastrous escape of seventy-six officers from Stalag Luft III. The escape occurred on the 24th of March, 1944.* Three made home-runs. Fifty, out of the seventy-six who escaped, were murdered by the Gestapo. Such a breakout may have been thought good for morale, but no visible uplift in escaping morale was noticeable according to subsequent accounts.

The mass escape was the ideal form that escaping could take from 1940 up to the end of 1942.

A superb escape and—though it is always a matter of opinion —probably the finest British escape of the whole war is another illustration of the point. It was known as the "Warburg wire job" and it occurred on the 29th of August, 1942—within the early period of the war. Forty-three officers escaped, in one minute, over the wire barricades of Warburg prison camp with home-made storming ladders. It would be of interest to establish who provided the inspiration and leadership of this escape. He deserves a decoration. David Walker and Pat Campbell-Preston, both of the 1st Battalion the Black Watch, had something to do with it. J. E. Hamilton-Baillie, Royal Engineers, designed the ladders. Again the accoutrement and clothing for the outside part of the attempt was incomplete. Nevertheless, three officers in battle dress made their way to France and subsequently a home-run to England. It is doubtful if they would have succeeded (in battle dress) a year later.

By 1943, a regime had come to an end and even if a great tunnel was built and completed with a good outfall beyond the camp confines, experience—bitter experience—encourages the thought that such a tunnel might have been better employed otherwise than as means for a mass break out. If a transport plane had been laid on from England at a rendezvous to take the men off —that would have been another matter.

* See *The Great Escape*, by Paul Brickhill.

It is only too easy to criticise after the event—and nobody could wish to detract from such magnificent escapes as those above mentioned. This said, there can be no harm in going over an exercise performed, to draw out the lessons for the future, provide food for thought and encourage the fertile imagination. The mind can exercise itself in fields of interest, not to say of entertainment, by posing a few questions. "What might have happened if . . .?

What would have happened if ten officers had escaped instead of seventy-six? They would have been very well equipped—for they would have had the equipment of the sixty remaining behind to draw upon to fill any gaps in their own make up. The most eligible team would be chosen for the attempt, and every advantage would be concentrated in the team to go. Once outside the wire—and once the alarm was given—what might the German reactions be? Ten British officers have escaped. Turn out the local *Landwache*, say two hundred strong; search the locality; send out descriptions and photos; alert all railway security police and report the escape to Corps Headquarters. Now, consider the escape of seventy-six officers. This is serious. It cannot be kept from the General Staff, nor from Himmler, nor even from Hitler, and what is the result? *Landwache* alerted in their thousands—nearly a hundred against each one, and the consequent chances of escape reduced to about the same ratio; the Gestapo sleuths placed hot on the scent, and the revengeful spirits of the maniac leaders of the country roused to anger: fifty of our finest officers murdered!

If only ten men had moved out, how many might have made home-runs? Judging by Colditz statistics the number might have been as high as five. It would be reasonable to say two or three.

The discussion does not end there. What is the effect on the morale of those who stay behind; firstly, upon the whole prison contingent amounting to hundreds of officers; secondly upon the sixty-six standing down, who have had a more personal stake in the escape attempt?

Are the hundreds jealous they were not included in the escape? No! They could not be. Are the sixty-six? A few maybe, but the majority are more pleased at the result, feeling they have contributed to the achievement. Their enthusiasm is whetted. Encouragement at the sight of success ensues and morale is lifted. "Nothing succeeds like success" applies forcibly to escaping.

What is the reaction of the hundreds to the success of the few? Morale is naturally improved. Quite the contrary is the result when many men go out and they all come back or when a large proportion of them are shot.

One question has been begged throughout. What is the reaction when only ten men go out where seventy-six might have gone and when ten men return? This is when the fur begins to fly and recrimination, in the confined atmosphere of a crowded camp, quickly takes on the aspects of a revolt. Among the sixty-six feeling, naturally, runs high. Why were they not all allowed to "have a bang at it"? Herein lies the difficulty of decision, and he has a strong character who makes the unpopular decision and sticks to it. The mass break out is the easier course to adopt. Is it the right one?

By way of a corollary, and a sop to Cerberus, the man who makes the difficult decision can partially insure himself by seeing that the tunnel is properly sealed at entrance and exit after the 'ten' have gone, with a view to a second ten departing after the first hue and cry has died down. The chance of this ever being possible is a minimum, but it provides a safety valve and parries the worst fomentations aroused by disappointment.

Lastly, the value of a home-run is not to be underestimated. Airey Neave and Brian Paddon, returning to England in 1942, were among the pioneers, lecturing our forces training at home upon escape techniques as being developed in Colditz at the time. Their advice on the theory and practice of 'evasion' and their encouragement of our thousands, flying regularly over enemy territory, was an inspiration. They, and those who followed closely after them, helped materially in the success of the 'evasion' campaign which resulted in so many Allied airmen, parachuted from crippled aircraft, returning home safely by devious routes, each with a story of adventure and courage in adversity.

Even the unlucky ones who were captured and thrown into prison camps had some consolation. Their numbers swelled to large proportions from 1942 onwards as our planes, in increasing avenging swarms, traversed the disintegrating enemy cities, while more and more hatred belched upwards in screaming steel and rending explosive. Unlike the early prisoners they were not lost souls, unbefriended and unaided. They arrived in camp knowing what to expect and what was expected of them. After the first terrible depression they had hope to buoy them up. They knew they had friends, both in England and in the prison camps who would

help them to escape if possible. Moreover, the camps were well provided with the practical means to assist them.

The scene was darkening over Colditz. Men gradually realised that the difficulties were multiplying and the hazards of escape more problematical and dangerous as the days dragged on their infinitely slow and tedious procession. Around the cobbled courtyard of the inner *Schloss* the clack-clack-clack of wooden clogs wearing themselves out on the stones was interminable in the daylight hours; it bore into the head like the drops of water in a Chinese torture. It was a motif ever recurring in the symphony being played within the fortress.

There was only one silver lining for the escaper. German Army morale was on the decline and it was becoming noticeable among the camp guards.

It was possible, by slow degrees, to set up a black market, in fact many black markets. Racketeering in the produce of this illicit trade gradually became rife until it was eventually scandalous and the German profiteers were seen to be gaining.

The matter was taken in hand so that an orderly influx of escape paraphernalia took precedence over private cupidity and escapers, harassed by the infinite difficulties of escaping from the Castle, had the comfort, at least, of knowing that, once out, they could hardly be better equipped for the journey across enemy territory.

The overture continues. The cymbals and the kettle drums have had their turn. What of the undertones, the huge background in front of which the violins will play? What say the trombones, the bass drums and the deep throated cellos?

November, 1942, opened with the final phases of the Battle of Alamein which Winston Churchill describes as "the turning of the hinge of Fate," adding, "It may almost be said, 'Before Alamein we never had a victory. After Alamein we never had a defeat'."

Guns boomed from the Atlantic on the North African shore. The American amphibious invasion began at Casablanca on November 8th, and in the Mediterranean, around Oran and Algiers on the same day. Stalingrad was relieved at the end of January, 1943, with the capture of Field Marshal Paulus and the survivors of twenty-one German Divisions. Churchill was anxious to open the second front in Europe in 1943, and Stalin was likewise pressing for it. The British were losing an enormous tonnage of shipping every week in the Atlantic. The drain of this life blood still had to be stopped. It was one of Hitler's few remaining trump cards. The

war leaders argued the pros and cons; Churchill met the Turks at Adana. The latter would not be hurried into the war on the Allied side. Hitler put all his efforts into a Tunisian campaign. The requirements for the successful completion of the Allied North African operation "Torch" sealed the doom of another operation called "Round up".

The prayers and hopes of thousands of Allied prisoners all over Europe were centred on an Allied landing on the Continent—the opening of the Second Front—in 1943.

Although they did not know it by that name, "Round up" was what they prayed for.

The Colditz inmates were by this stage of the war well equipped for the wireless reception of news from the Western Allies. They had, at the same time, by the continous application of carefully aimed shafts of ridicule, silenced the German loudspeakers in the camp. The Germans no longer tried to switch on their news bulletins. Instead they set about dismantling the loudspeakers in the various quarters. Alas! they were too late. When the electricians took down the instruments all they retrieved were hollow shells. The works had been removed in good time and were already in the service of the Crown instead of the Corporal.

The great march of events in the latter half of the war was not lost to the prisoners. Indeed, the majority lived for the news. It was a soul assuaging consolation to the many who knew, in their hearts, that they would never make home-runs. Let the violins speak.

A seeding of players in the escape tournament began to take place. It was a voluntary affair, and brave men stepped out of the queue of their own accord. They did not speak of it.

There was no dramatic renunciation of rights; there were no recriminations. They dropped from the life-line around the over-crowded escaping life-boat and, with resignation, allowed the great ocean of world events to swallow them. They drowned their personal ambitions and drifted, each one alone with his own soul awaiting the end. The end lay over the horizon and the sky was lowering.

To these men, suspended in the boundless sea of time the broadcast news bulletins were essential for mental well-being and sanity. News was like oil poured on the waves; a protecting calm amidst the storm that threatened the balance of their minds, that was never far away, that could descend with the elemental force of a whirlwind. Sometimes, indeed, the news appeared as a mirage, deceiving them horribly, but, at least, the omissions and the veils

drawn over adverse situations coming from the Western trans-
mitters were as nothing compared with the great hoax that was
played upon the German people by their wireless broadcasters.
If the Allies did not tell all the truth, at least they avoided lying.
So, for our men, there was always hope as opposed to the
revengeful bitterness that grows from deliberate deception.

CHAPTER II

ESCAPE FEVER

NEWS of the success of the escape of Ronnie Littledale, Billie
Stephens, Hank Wardle and the author, and of their safe arrival
in Switzerland soon filtered through the censor's net. Four gone-
aways and four home-runs! it was great news, putting the British
contingent well ahead of the other nationalities in the friendly
rivalry for the lead in home-runs. Many men, whose hopes of an
ultimate successful escape had almost vanished, imbibed new
strength and determination. A wave of enthusiasm like a gust of
fresh air swept through the Castle.

Dick Howe, of the Royal Tank Regiment, and officer in charge
of Escape, was overwhelmed with new schemes and the resurrec-
tions of old ones. Activity became feverish and it was clear that
the Jerries were in for a difficult time. The latter soon scented
trouble ahead and the German security team hardly slept at night.
Hauptman Priem and Oberlieutenant Püpcke, Hauptman Eggers
and the deadbeat Hauptman Lange, Oberstabsfeldwebel (Regimental Sergeant-major) Gephard and his Gefreiter (Corporal),
known as the *fouine* or ferret or Dickson Hawk, took turns at
making the rounds. P.O.W. 'stooging' systems had to be double
shifted to cope with the new circumstances. Hardly an officer was
free from some duty or other.

For some unaccountable reason the word stooge, in prison
jargon, had two totally different meanings, depending entirely on
the context in which the term was used. 'Stooging' in the above
case implied the P.O.W. 'look-out' organisation instituted to warn
prisoners of Germans approaching on the prowl, 'snooping' as
it was called. On the other hand, a stooge could be a person planted
by the Germans in the camp to report on the prisoners' nefarious
activities.

As the German security net became more closely drawn and the sentry layout more dense, it was brought home to the prisoners that escapes of almost any kind would have to rely on split-second timing. The old leisurely days were disappearing. This change implied long hours of stooging by an escape team and the plotting of enemy movements for weeks on end in order to discover the loop-holes in their defence system.

Dick, thirty-two years old, had won his M.C. at Calais in 1940. He was standing the strain of the difficult job of Escape Officer remarkably well. To any outsider, he looked sallow, hollow cheeked and terribly thin, but that was normality in Colditz and passed without comment. His good humour remained his greatest friend. Demands on his time were heavy. What kept him always on top of a situation was an obstinate refusal to be flustered either by contrary events or by contrairy people.

Rupert Barry and Mike Sinclair teamed up. They were a formidable pair and would take a lot of stopping. They were given what was known as the theatre shaft job.

Rupert, of the Ox and Bucks Light Infantry, tall, dark and handsome with his big brown moustache and smouldering eyes, had been one of the first escapers in Germany. He, Peter Allan and the author, out of a tunnel at Oflag VIIC, near Salzburg, were half way to Yugoslavia when recaught in September, 1940. At Colditz, Rupert's luck had not been good. Two tunnels on which he worked did not succeed in putting him outside the wire, although the first was completed without discovery.

Mike, of the 60th Rifles, had been free in Poland for a long time, and then in a Gestapo prison for a while before he reached Colditz. He had escaped once from the Castle only to be recaptured in Cologne. He was, by now, a fluent German speaker. He was a few years younger than Rupert—about twenty-six. His red hair and his audacity had earned him the title among the Germans of ' Das Rote Fuchs '—the Red Fox. Of medium build, tough, with a resolute freckled countenance, his life was devoted to escaping, and his determination was as valuable as a hundred ton battering ram matched against the walls of Colditz.

Mike and Rupert reorganised an old twenty-four hour watching roster, which had been started many months before, on what was known as the air shaft or light well situated in the middle of the theatre block, where, also, the senior officers were housed.

The theatre itself was on the third or top floor of this block, and the square light well was surrounded by a corridor on three sides

which separated it from the theatre. A locked door gave onto the corridor, which was lighted from barred windows overlooking the well. The door was the only normal means of entry. There was no staircase. The twenty-four-hour watch was maintained in this corridor.

At the bottom of the well, fifty feet below, were doors leading into various German kitchen and canteen quarters. Thick walls, on the other hand, separated it from the prisoners' quarters at ground level. Needless to say, a sentry stood at the bottom of the well throughout the twenty-four hours.

After a fortnight's watching it was possible to confine stooging activity to some twelve hours, not consecutive, during the day; the other twelve hours being ruled out as impossible for escape purposes.

One early winter evening, as the light was beginning to fade, rehearsals of a forthcoming show were in full swing bringing many officers of all nationalities into the theatre. It was a time of activity. An orchestra was practising; the scene painters were at work; stage managers, producers, actors and staff milled around, all providing admirable camouflage for the movement of shifts of stooges through the locked door into the corridor beside the well.

The old piano clanged out its tinny tunes. Sounds of hammering and scene shifting mingled with the hubbub of voices rising and falling. Dick Howe busied himself around the stage followed by his Dutch stage lighting assistant, Lieutenant Beetes. The dreadful piano worried Dick. He mused over that dream piano—the new Bechstein Concert Grand—that had arrived one day, months ago now, in the courtyard. Workmen had toiled for hours hoisting it up the narrow staircase and had demolished a wall in the theatre in order to install it. Then the workmen's civilian coats, thrown off in the heat of the moment, had vanished. The contents of pockets reappeared mysteriously, but the coats were never found. An ultimatum from the Commandant; stubborn silence from the prisoners; and the Bechstein Grand retraced its journey down the stairs and disappeared again outside the prison gateway.

There were no less than four orchestras now; all of them suffering from the curious version of the chromatic scale reproduced by this rickety, upright cupboard-full of tangled wires.

There was the Symphony Orchestra conducted by a Dutchman, First Lieutenant Bajetto; the Theatre Orchestra with Jimmy Yule as composer, orchestrator and pianist; the Dance Band with John Wilkins as band leader; and finally the Hawaian Orchestra composed principally of Dutch colonial officers.

Dick Howe

"What a difference it would make!" Dick sighed to himself. Then a flicker of a smile appeared at the corners of his mouth, and, as he stood in the middle of the stage by the footlights, surveying a scene, just completed, his thoughts were not on the set he was supposed to be examining. He was wondering if he could not, after all, spirit the Bechstein Concert Grand back into the theatre.

His mind was far away when a tug at his sleeve from the auditorium pulled him back to earth. He turned to see Vandy, the irrepressible Dutchman, plotter of a hundred escapes, smiling broadly as usual, looking up at him.

"I haf made a fine hole," said Vandy in a suppressed voice, "come qvick and see, my two escapers are preparing now to go."

"Fast work, Vandy," said Dick jumping down over the footlights, "I know this theatre pretty intimately and haven't noticed any rat-holes recently."

"Ach no! Dick—you vould not see. I haf been vorking for a veek and you know my plaster camouflage!"

Vandy led him to the dressing-room at the right of the stage. There in the corner was a gaping hole with all the paraphernalia of camouflage strewn around.

"Why!" exclaimed Dick, "you're using Neave's old route."

"Qvite right, it is the same. This hole—qvick! bend down and look along it—you see—it is in the roof of the causevay over the main gate. My men can now reach the guardhouse. They are putting on the German uniforms at this moment in my qvarters. They vill be here very soon. It is a blitz."

"But," said Dick incredulously, "the Jerries blocked up that route some time ago."

"Yes," replied Vandy unshaken, "but my men haf seen Germans recently through the windows of the causevay. Where there is an entrance there must be an outrance."

"Hm!" said Dick, "I'd better get our stooges out from the corridor pretty quick. Thanks for telling me, Vandy, but give me a little more notice next time."

Vandy was full of glee. There was nothing he liked more than surprising people. He was revelling in the joke he was about to play on the Jerries and missed the note of anxiety in Dick's voice. They retraced their steps into the theatre as Vandy studied his watch and signalled to a Dutch stooge at the door leading to the stairs.

At the same moment, Rupert Barry appeared from the direction of the light well. Dick beckoned him over.

"You're in the nick of time, Rupert. Vandy has a blitz on."

They were near the orchestra which had started running over the opening bars of Chopin's Polonaise and the piano was making a noise like a broken down zither in Dick's ear.

"What did you say?" shouted Rupert. "The band has a blitz on?"

Dick took Rupert's arm and they moved away among the chairs of the auditorium. "I said Vandy has a blitz on. He's got two Dutchmen coming up here any moment." Dick pointed to Vandy and his theatre stooge in close conversation some yards from the theatre door.

"They're going over into the guardhouse. They're dressing as Jerries. There may be trouble. You'd better get our stooge out from the corridor. Who's in there now?"

"Peter Storie Pugh," said Rupert.

They were both looking towards the door as he spoke. Hardly were the words out of his mouth when the balloon went up.

The unmistakable figure of Priem appeared framed in the doorway, a dark outline in the gathering dusk. Vandy's stooge had been caught off his guard.

Priem took a few steps into the room. From behind him stepped Gephard who made for the electric switches, and the next moment the theatre was flooded in light. A posse of Goons followed closely at Gephard's heels. The music of the orchestra tailed off to nothing as Priem grated out his orders. Hammering continued in the wings of the stage. The scene builders went on with their work—oblivious of the unrehearsed drama taking place in front. Goons were suddenly everywhere. Vandy made for the door of the staircase, but a sentry barred the way with his rifle across the jambs.

Dick noticed that Rupert had glided away in the direction of the door to the corridor. The situation was tricky. He vaulted on to the stage and collided with Scarlet O'Hara who had just emerged from the wings. Scarlet had heard the familiar guttural shouts as he was in the midst of mixing up some scenery paint for his own use. Dick whispered to him.

"Quick! Scarlet, go and help Rupert. He needs some diversion. He's got his stooge in the corridor and must get him out."

Scarlet, the Canadian Tank Lieutenant, whose complexion had earned him his name, saw the situation immediately and muttering to himself, "These B———— Huns again, never let you alone for a minute, the blasted Kartoffels." He faded into the milling crowd of actors, scene shifters, instrumentalists and German soldiery.

The Jerries knew what they were going for. Vandy's hole must

have been discovered from the German side. They made for the dressing-room and herded everybody off the stage into the auditorium as Priem and Gephard held a conference. They were discussing what action to take. Vandy's blitz had shaken them.

"Will they hold everyone in the theatre and search them all?" Dick wondered to himself. It was a normal procedure. The room would be cleared, one by one the officers would be searched, and finally the Jerries would search the premises and the corridor. He stood leaning against the rickety piano and could see Rupert and Scarlet in deep conversation in the far corner. Lulu Lawton, the black-haired Yorkshireman from the Duke of Wellington's Regiment, Dick's second in command, was weaving his way through the crowd towards him. In the distance Dick also spied Harry Elliott, a captain of the Irish Guards, who waged a private war against the Germans.

As Lulu approached Dick said casually, "I wonder what brought Harry into the theatre. He never comes up here if he can help it. And to choose to-day! It'll be worth listening to what he has to say about the Jerries upsetting his routine. Look, he's arguing with the Jerry on the door now, swearing at him like a trooper."

"He came up to get some more yellow paint for his jaundice set-up," explained Lulu. "He's going before the medical board any day now."

Priem had apparently made up his mind what to do. He mounted the stage and addressed the assembled mixed bag of officers of all nationalities:

"*Meine Herren*," and he continued in German with sarcasm, "I am confident that not all the officers here present intended to escape through the hole I have just found. I shall not inflict unnecessary punishment on you by insisting that you remove all your clothes for searching. You will leave the theatre one by one. My under-officers will feel through your uniforms and in your pockets. I must find the instruments with which the hole has been made, and the culprit. The theatre will probably be closed, but I shall report first to the Commandant. Will you begin to leave the theatre at once and one at a time."

Dick looked anxiously towards the corridor, He could not see Rupert or Scarlet; only a huddle of French and English officers around the locked door. Obviously a scrum was being organised—but the top of the door was clear of their heads and if it was opened it would be plainly visible. Dick thought hard. A long queue had already formed by the theatre exit where several soldiers now stood

while Gephard and two Gefreiters—the *fouine* and another—quickly ran their hands over officers' clothing, occasionally feeling inside a pocket. The search was cursory. One by one the queue was diminishing. He noted through the open door of the dressing-room that a sentry had been posted in front of the hole. The soldiery was all occupied. Priem was the danger.

Dick deliberately avoided the queue and approached Priem who was standing at the top of the stage steps surveying the scene before him. Dick suddenly had the inspiration he was waiting for. Looking up at Priem from the bottom of the steps he said in German:

"Herr Hauptman, I wish to ask you a question about the theatre's requirements."

"*Ach so*, what is it, Herr Hauptman Ho-ve?" said Priem descending to his level and losing his commanding view of the corridor entrance. He always pronounced Howe as two syllables, 'Ho-ve'.

Dick drew him over to the piano and winking at Lulu who was leaning on it, he began:

"The British, Herr Hauptman, have collected a big reserve of *Lagermarks* (prison money), which, together with subscriptions promised from other nationalities, we have calculated is large enough to buy a cinema organ for the theatre. You see, our theatre committee does not want a piano any more. This one here . . ." and Dick struck a few discordant notes on the keyboard of the upright . . . "is *Kaput*, as you know well."

"You cannot afford an organ, Herr Hauptman!" said Priem raising his eyebrows and smirking incredulously.

"Oh yes we can! If you will come with me to our Senior Officer's room downstairs I can ask him to show you the figures."

"But Herr Hauptman Hove you do not require an organ—you need a piano." There was horror in his voice. The shaft had struck home.

"*Nein, nein*, Herr Hauptman Priem," interrupted Dick, "we are not interested in pianos any more, everybody wants to have a fine Wurlitzer organ. The protecting power will support our demand for one because this piano here is finished. We can say you refused to give us a new piano, months ago, when we asked for it."

Looking past Priem, Dick caught a glimpse of Rupert and Scarlet, and then to his relief, as the screening crowd dispersed to take up their positions in the fast dwindling queue at the exit, he noticed the figure of Peter Storie Pugh.

Priem began to walk towards the exit as well, and Dick and Lulu followed. Dick said:

"Herr Hauptman Priem, would you like to see the accounts showing our reserve of *Lagermarks?*"

"*Nein,*" replied Priem, "I believe you." He turned away to speak to his Oberstabfeldwebel, Gephard, and Dick turned to Lulu.

"If that doesn't bring the Bechstein Concert Grand back I reckon we'd better start saving for the Wurlitzer! I have a hunch though, that the old Commandant won't want to have a grand piano left on his hands."

The theatre emptied. Vandy had long since disappeared. Dick, Lulu and Rupert were the last to be "frisked". As they departed the spare Goons were already dispersing throughout the theatre rummaging in the corners and Gephard approached the corridor door with the key in his hand. . . .

In the courtyard below, Vandy was waiting for Dick.

"All is not finished, Dick, I haf a plan. You must distract the sentry who stands at the hole please."

Dick looked at him and burst out laughing, then beside Vandy he saw two bulky looking Dutch officers. He knew them well and knew too that their bulk was not natural. There was no stopping Vandy. Weakly he said:

"Hold your horses, Vandy, Priem's still up there with his posse of Goons. Do you want me to distract them all?"

"No, Dick, vait till they haf gone. Here they come—look! ve must count them," and facing the theatre block doorway he counted, "vone, two, tree, vor, vive . . ." and then finally, "Fouine, Gephard, Priem. That is all except vone," and, as the procession of Jerries filed out of the gate, Vandy sent one of his men to check if they had locked the theatre door. They had not.

"Ve are in luck, Dick! You see, you are not suspect in the theatre; you haf much vork there, you can distract the stupid German. Then I vill send my two men through the hole."

Almost wearily, Dick turned back, asking Lulu to help him do the distraction. It was dark by now outside. They climbed the stairs again and entered the lighted theatre. They pretended to go about their work, talking and laughing. Vandy quietly hid his two escapers in the wings beside the stage door leading down to the dressing room and then joined Dick and Lulu.

"Ve vill go to the dressing room by the other door and attract the sentry to us," he whispered.

After playing a few bars on the piano and banging some chairs about, the three of them filed into the dressing room from the auditorium, apparently discussing heatedly the seating accommodation, the price of tickets, the timing of the various sets and finally in surprise. . . .

"Why the hell is the sentry here?"

Dick asked him what he was supposed to be doing and offered him a cigarette. The sentry took it with a *"Danke"* and hid it in his tunic pocket, pointing out the large hole behind him which they all pretended to see for the first time.

Vandy chipped in with his good German and soon a political discussion was under weigh. The two of them eased around the sentry and Lulu started to look fixedly out of a window near the door by which they had entered. The floodlights came on with a searing flash. Suddenly he pointed and said, "Look! look!" excitedly. Dick rushed to the window and Vandy almost lifted the sentry forward. Nothing doing! The sentry stood rock-like.

The political conversation continued, with Vandy on one side of him, Dick on the other and both edging gradually towards the door in close animated discussion. Lulu, still by the window, interposed some comments at long range in halting German. Vandy and Dick feigned misunderstanding; they shuffled towards him; they enveigled the German to ask him questions. Lulu's German became more halting and less audible. Vandy became the interpreter and courier between them; standing halfway, he tried to draw them together. The sentry would not budge. Vandy was impatient at the best of times. He was working himself up and was on the point of giving the sentry a direct order to stand aside. He left the dressing room with a growl and a wink, scowling at the sentry behind his back.

Dick and Lulu continued valiantly. More cigarettes passed hands and were lit. The sentry would not smoke. Lulu, who was nearest the door, sniffed.

"What've you got in your lighter, Dick?" he said suddenly and sniffed again.

"German lighter fuel," said Dick, "why? Does it smell like eau-de-Cologne?" Then he, in turn, sniffed. There was no mistaking that smell for German lighter fuel and it was getting stronger. "Why!" Dick exclaimed, "it's brown paper—no, it's scenery paint —no! it's both."

Then he smelt wood burning and rushed from the room followed closely by Lulu. As they turned the corner they saw Vandy circling

round a blaze in the middle of the floor of the auditorium, which he was fanning violently with a large sheet of cardboard. He turned to shout *"Feuer"* and, at the same time, piled more wood shavings, brown paper and bits of canvas, which he had collected, on to the flames. A thick blue cloud billowed upwards as Dick and Lulu took up the cry, *"Feuer! Feuer!"*.

Vandy rushed back to the dressing room shouting to the sentry: *"Achtung! Feuer! Feuer! Schnell! 'raus schnell! Sie werden verbrannt wenn Sie hier bleiben.* You will be burnt alive!"

The theatre filled with smoke as more paper was applied. Again Vandy dashed to the dressing room door, gesticulating violently, and shouted to the sentry to follow him.

The sentry would not budge.

Defeated at last, Vandy threw up his hands, "It is no use, the stupid fellow vould rather burn to death."

With that the three of them set about putting the fire out. Then, joined by the two Dutchmen from the wings, they all fled from the theatre leaving a smouldering heap on the floor. As they descended the stairs, smoke was billowing from the high windows, showing up ominously in the searchlight beams, and Germans could be heard shouting *"Feuer! Feuer!"* from the guardhouse outside.

Extraordinary to relate, the theatre was not closed and, the next day, the prison gates opened wide to allow the passage of a heavy lorry carrying the Bechstein Concert Grand piano. Amid a greater ovation than any pianist who ever pressed its keys could hope to hear, the piano was manhandled off the lorry and began its second panting, puffing journey up the narrow staircase to the theatre.

CHAPTER III

THE LIGHT WELL

THE stooging in the theatre light well was progressing satisfactorily and without too much disturbance. But the results coming from the graphs plotted did not give cause for optimism. After a month of watching over the most favourable sections of the twenty-four hours, a two-minute blind spot stood out as a regular feature of the graph shortly after 2 p.m. every day. It coincided with a change of guard. The bottom of the light well

remained void of German humanity for these two minutes. They did not necessarily occur at exactly the same time every day. One day the two-minute gap might be at 2.10 p.m., another day at 2.12 p.m., and even sometimes as late as 2.15 p.m. On an average, 2.10 p.m. was the psychological moment.

The escape was decided upon, and the German uniforms were put in hand for Rupert and Mike. These consisted of fatigue overalls which were the standard dress of Germans working in the kitchens and, when off duty, eating or drinking in their canteens. At the bottom of the well, doors led off in various directions into a maze of German kitchens, sculleries, store rooms, bakeries and canteens. A corridor eventually led to a staircase, down one flight of stairs and out into the German Kommandantur courtyard.

Our two escapers were to descend by rope from one of the theatre corridor windows, a distance of fifty feet to the bottom of the well, and find their way out to the German courtyard. Once there, they had a choice of two routes, depending on the positions of the various gateway guards which were not accurately predictable. The better route, probably, would be that usually taken by the prisoners when marched under guard for their daily recreation of one hour in the park. Once in the park, the escapers could make for a secluded spot near the football enclosure, climb the barbed wire fence abutting the twelve-foot wall surrounding the park, using it as a ladder to help them to the top.

There would be little activity in the German barracks about fifty yards away at this time of day, and they could hope to scale the wall unseen. In addition, although the trees in the park were leafless, the branches provided a good screen at fifty yards, especially as the football enclosure was at a level lower than the barracks.

Preparations for the escape were nearing completion. The German overalls were ready; the civilian clothing to be worn underneath had been fitted and checked. Identity papers were in order; maps, compasses and money provided. Bos'n Crisp, R.N., who, with a few assistants, manufactured all the ropes required for escapes, had made a stout sixty-foot length, fully tested for strength.

The time had come for Dick to start work on the bars of the light well window. The escape would be carried out within a few days.

With Lulu Lawton to assist him and a team of stooges in action led by Grismond Davies-Scourfield, a Lieutenant of the King's Royal Rifles, Dick repaired to the theatre. They entered the forbidden corridor by a small lattice window in the theatre wall instead of by the usual door. This window was conveniently placed

for the escape, being situated in an angle of wall not directly facing the theatre exit. Although officially sealed, opening and closing it presented little difficulty, and it faced the barred corridor window from which the descent was to be made.

Crawling through the lattice window, Dick and Lulu surprised two young Frenchmen who were peering downwards into the light well from one of the corridor windows.

"Hello! Hello!" Dick greeted them with mock gaiety, "can I help you?"

"*Non merci*," replied the Frenchmen.

Dick continued sarcastically, "You're in a forbidden zone here. I shall report this to the Germans," and then taking them to task, "What if I'd been a German—where are your stooges?"

"We have no stooges," was the answer.

"How often have you been here?"

"A few times. We intend to escape from here to-morrow. We have been observing. We think we can descend easily into the well with a rope after cutting the bars."

At this news both Dick and Lulu nearly exploded. The Frenchmen's approach, however, was so naïve that Dick recovered himself in time to burst out laughing instead.

"You b—— fools," he said, "how long have you been in Colditz?"

"Oh! a long time now."

"In that case you ought to know better than to carry on the damn silly way you're doing. Does Colonel Le Brigand know what you're up to?"

"No!"

"Then why the hell not!" said Dick, "it's about damn well time some of you gay young dogs realised that there is a Senior French officer in the camp, and that when he orders you to keep him informed of your escaping activities he means it. Get out of here quick." Turning to Lulu he added, "We'd better all get out quick and seal up. What a b—— awful mess!"

Outside in the theatre, Dick and Lulu explained to the Frenchmen that they had very nearly ruined an escape which had been in preparation for months. The Frenchmen, unfortunately, did not take kindly to the explanation. The more they realised how inept they had been, the more their pride was wounded. They insisted on their right to escape by the light well if and when they wanted to. The matter ended with both sides saying they would refer it to their respective Commanding Officers.

"For crying out loud!" said Lulu, as they both wended their way back to the British quarters, joined by Grismond on the way. "Months of hard work and a first class scheme, and those two nitwits come along to break it up. I've always liked the French, but, my godfathers! the crass stupid way they sometimes behave makes me wonder if they've any brains in their heads at all. Discipline! Great Cæser's ghost—and they all did two years military service before the war! They're crazy!"

Lulu, the staid Yorkshireman, could not contain himself. Grismond could make no sense of it all, and Dick walked back to the quarters in glum silence. At the bottom of the stairs he said to Grismond:

"Go and fetch Rupert and Mike—tell 'em there's a hitch and will they come along straight away to the C.O.'s room. You come along too. Lulu! let's go, we've got to have a showdown and the sooner the better."

There was a showdown, and when the sheafs of graph paper were produced showing the months of patient stooging that had been done in order to establish a two minutes safe period in the light well, the Frenchmen at last climbed down.

The curious attitude of the French towards their C.O.— towards any C.O.—was always a matter of mystery to the British. Their Commanding Officer in Colditz was one of the finest Frenchmen imaginable. Yet a large number of French officers felt no compunction in carrying on their own escape schemes without telling a soul, although it was a recognised rule of the camp, that the respective Senior Officers should be informed so that they could compare notes, avoid messing up each others plans and prevent chaos.

Frankly, some of the French were insubordinate. Presumably, they thought that, so long as they told nobody, at least their security was good. On the other hand, the Senior Officers of the army of a defeated nation did not feel in a position to enforce strict military discipline under prison conditions.

This state of affairs, fortunately, seldom displayed itself openly and, apart from one or two high spots such as the light well debacle, the French chain of Command in the camp was respected.

The French had to give way, but their stupidity in the execution of the project was made up for by their astuteness in seizing an opportunity.

"If two can escape by the well, surely four can, without much

more difficulty?" they queried, adding, "and if four can get out, there is more hope of at least one or two making home."

Dick and the C.O., and Rupert and Mike chewed over this proposition for a while. Finally, it was agreed:

"Yes, all right. Four will go. An Englishman with a Frenchman—in two pairs." With that the pact was concluded and the escape was on. The British were not satisfied, but, at least, they were magnanimous. Extra risk was involved inside the camp; once outside, four heads were always better than two and, after all, the "entent Cordiale" was being toasted daily in the camp!

German overalls were provided for the Frenchmen. Civilian clothes, paper and other paraphernalia they supplied from their own sources.

Dick and Lulu found themselves once more, some days later, mounting the stairs to the theatre on their way to cut and prepare the window bars ready for the descent.

Grismond's stooging was excellent. Nowadays, in the Castle it could not afford to be anything less. The Germans were jittery and their movements had to be watched with extreme caution.

The bar cutting was not so difficult, but it took time. The window being high above ground and overlooking a well about thirty feet square, Jerries at the bottom could not see anything going on inside the window sill. Kitchen noises and the continual hubbub of movement served to drown the tell-tale sound of sawing. Dick and Lulu cut the bars successfully, replacing the loose pieces with patent sleeves manufactured by Scarlet O'Hara. These provided a perfect camouflage against observation. The bars could even stand gentle shaking, but would not survive the violent tug of a brawny Goon. If the bars were tapped, of course, they would not ring true.

Zero hour for the descent was ten minutes past two in the afternoon on November the 20th, 1942. This is where the next snag arose. An *Appell* was, more usually than not, held at two o'clock!

Appells, when properly organised, and provided there were no unforeseen hitches, could be called to attention as the German officers appeared, and dismissed again within eight minutes. Such an *Appell* was indeed a rare occurrence. The German officer had to appear dead on time, and each contingent had to be warned to behave in exemplary manner. The French were the largest group, but as two of their own number were escaping, order and co-operation could be expected from them.

There was always the haunting fear of an unknown spy inside the camp. Sometimes, as in this case, the best that could be done to combat the possibility of such treachery was not to give the traitor enough time to 'put his spanner in the works'. Only at the last minute were officers, gathering for the *Appell*, warned to behave amenably and cut the *Appell* time to a minimum.

The afternoon arrived. Everything was prepared. The rope was concealed under the bed of Duggie Bader, the Air Force ace. His room was one of the nearest to the theatre. A vaulting horse, normally housed in the theatre, was close to the lattice window and would take the strain on the rope. Rupert, Mike and the two Frenchmen were dressed for the occasion: first, civilian clothes, then over them the German fatigue overalls, and on top of everything, army overcoats and trousers.

Rupert and Mike were both seasoned escapers. For that reason, their feelings as the crucial moment arrived, were more like those of an experienced bomb disposal officer about to begin an operation than anything else. Panic at the thought of the approaching danger, at the prospect of possibly being 'written off,' was gone. With it went the worst symptom of physical nausea which, in earlier days, brought on vomiting. There was an outward coolness, which was deceptive. The fear, which came from knowledge of the odds, lay less heavily upon the stomach. The anguish was in the conscious mind instead of in the subconscious—the entrails. There was little nervous reaction, no visible shaking.

The suffering of the conscious mind is a stage ahead. It is fearful of overconfidence. It must remember the lessons of experience. It must not forget. The beginner has no experience to forget. His fear is of the unknown. Curiously enough, escaping is one of those adventures in which experience counts a great deal. Only the seasoned escaper knows it.

Compare a tame animal with a wild animal. They are as chalk and cheese. An experienced escaper is a tame animal that has learnt something of the wiles of a wild one.

The experienced escaper feels a heavy responsibility lying at his own door. He knows how to succeed and, if he fails, it is probably his fault. The odds are his own making. He knows he cannot blame 'bad luck' any more. The beginner does not know the odds, they are not of his own making. He is lucky or unlucky and until he has passed the stage of blaming failure on bad luck he is not a seasoned escaper. The experienced bomb disposal officer knows this too. If he is blown sky high it is because he made

a blunder, though in conditions fraught with terrifying danger for the uninitiated.

The *Appell* sounded at 1.55 p.m. and the prisoners gathered in the courtyard. Obedient to whispered commands, ranks were formed in an orderly manner and in record time. As two p.m. struck Oberlieutenant Püpcke, tall, in his well-fitting grey artillery uniform and highly polished jack boots, walked quickly through the gate.

"True to form," thought Dick, and he winked at Mike and Rupert forming up not far away.

The *Appell* went off without a hitch except for the ominous arrival of the Abwehr (security) officer, Hauptman Eggers, in the middle of the proceedings. As the prisoners had nowadays come to expect, the Jerries were not far behind them. Eggers knew that something was in the wind, but evidently had few clues.

The parade was dismissed. Dick and Lulu made for the entrance to the theatre block as nonchalantly yet as quickly as possible.

Eggers deliberately headed for them and buttonholed Dick. With a slow calculated pronunciation he rasped out in English:

"Well, Captain Howe, and where are you going?" There was suspicion in his manner and sarcasm in his voice.

"I'm going with Captain Lawton to do some boxing in the theatre. Why do you ask?"

Eggers ignored Dick's question and said slowly, looking Dick straight in the eye, "I thought Captain Lawton was a great friend of yours. Why do you want to box him?"

"This is terrible," thought Dick, holding his gaze. The precious seconds were ticking away. He replied:

"We can have a good fight and still remain friends."

"Very remarkable! very remarkable!" commented Eggers dryly, nodding his head. He moved out of earshot, and Lulu said, as they both marched into the theatre block:

"Let's call it off for to-day. He's up to something."

"No, we go on," said Dick. "He'll have to be damn quick now to catch us and I'd much rather see him in our courtyard than waiting on the German side for our chaps to come out."

They hurried up the stairs and into the theatre to find the four escapers ready and the stooging in action. Davis-Scourfield was in charge, already giving the running commentary of Goon movements reported by signals from his staff.

"Eggers in courtyard—Dixon Hawk in sick-bay—two snoops at entrance to French quarters . . ." he reported slowly translating

the signs given to him, like a bookie's mate taking his cues from the semaphore men on a race course.

Lulu secured the rope to the leg of the vaulting horse and passed it through the lattice window. Dick and Lulu then scrambled through into the corridor. The four escapers were already waiting.

"We're running late," said Dick looking at his watch, "it's ten past."

He opened the air-shaft window and listened. The next moment he was removing the sleeves and the bars. One look down the well was enough. Out went the rope, and Mike Sinclair started to descend. He seemed to be ages going down. Grismond's voice came from the theatre.

"Eggers has entered theatre block . . . he's coming up the stairs to the first floor. . . ."

Without further ado Dick and Lulu picked up the first Frenchman and threw him out of the window shouting, "*Allez, vite!*"

There was a violent jerk on the rope as the Frenchman's slack was taken up. Grismond's voice could be heard:

"Eggers on way up to second floor."

"Get the rope away, Lulu," Dick shouted, and to Rupert and the waiting Frenchman, "run for it, vamoose *vite!*" He was already sealing up the window bars and applying the camouflage.

"Eggers coming up the last flight to theatre," came through steady as a rock from Grismond.

"You must come out," said Lulu hoarsely, as Dick applied the finishing touches to the bars. Dick made a running dive through the lattice window and as Lulu locked it quietly, Dick picked himself up and gave him an almighty clout in the solar plexus.

Eggers walked into the theatre.

What he saw was a first class rough house. On the floor of the theatre auditorium with chairs flying in all directions, an irate Yorkshireman made it plain to the world that the Christian beatitude of turning the other cheek did not apply where he came from.

This might have been enough for Eggers, but, to his perplexity was added bewilderment, as the French chapel choir, which had foregathered for a practice at the other end of the theatre, entoned the opening lines of a dignified "Kyrie Eleison."

Eggers pulled himself together. He was accompanied by two snoops before whom he had to keep up appearances. His sly eyes roved the theatre quickly, then, with a sudden movement, he unlocked the door into the forbidden corridor.

Dick and Lulu stopped fighting and innocently pressed forward towards the door to see what Eggers was up to. One of the snoops tried some of the window bars but missed the ones that had been out. The procession retraced its steps. Eggers relocked the door and turned to continue his tour of inspection. Spying the two Englishmen, he grinned at them, then, shaking his head as he departed, he quoted, "Mad dogs and Englishmen . . ."

The stooges reported that Mike and the Frenchman had walked casually out of the German courtyard by the deep archway leading to the park. Turning to the right, they had walked downhill, then through a wooden gateway on the left hand side, down the steep winding path to the bridge over a stream which bounded one side of the park and they were lost to view.

Half an hour passed without any alarms. It could be safely concluded that the two had succeeded in leaving the camp.

Dick had little time to congratulate himself on this achievement. The next problem loomed up like a black cloud. Rupert and the second Frenchman had not been able to go. Dick was determined that Rupert should not be disappointed. He felt his reputation was involved. If he could "fix" three *Appells*, and provided neither of the first two escapers were re-caught, it should be possible to repeat the escape. It would have to be done the next day at the same time or never.

He decided to try a method of fixing the *Appell* which had not, to his knowledge, been used at Colditz before. It was known as the "Rabbit" method. He had heard of its use elsewhere, but in Colditz it was thought generally that there were too many sentries present to allow of its success. He conferred with the French adjutant and called Lieutenant Gigue of the French Foreign Legion to his rescue. It was agreed that both contingents would adopt the same system and conceal one absence each at the next three *Appells*.

Bruce, "the medium sized man," the indefatigable and ever willing young R.A.F. officer, who stood about five feet one inch in his socks, would be Dick's rabbit. The operation required the co-operation of a large number of officers.

With the help of Rupert and Lulu, Dick rounded up thirty of the tallest British available and in a secluded corner of a dormitory, his audience lolling on the beds and seated on the floor, Dick called for attention and began:

"We managed to get Mike away this afternoon with a Frenchman, but it was a near thing. Eggers was hot on the trail—so hot

The Rabbit

in fact, that Rupert who was the next to go couldn't make it. If we can fox the next three *Appells*, one to-night, and two to-morrow, we should be able to send Rupert out immediately after the 2 p.m. roll call. This is why I want you fellows to help. I'll have to grade you for height first. So will you please all stand up in line facing me as if on *Appell*."

With some jostling and banter a line was formed, then re-shuffled, so that the tallest was at one end and the smallest at the other.

"Now," said Dick, "I think the quickest way to get what I want is for you to number off. Squad," he shouted with mock seriousness, "from the left, number!" This was followed by "even numbers, two paces backward, march!"

Having obtained two similar rows of fifteen men each, he explained:

"We've now got to re-shuffle each line so that it looks fairly natural, but I'd like the tallest in the middle of each line."

This was done and Dick continued:

"Will each of you please note your positions carefully, that is, the man on each side of you. Got it? Good, now let's break up and try a rehearsal."

The team broke up and when Dick said, "Form up!" the two lines reformed without a hitch.

"That's fine. Now, for heaven's sake, remember your positions carefully. A lot depends on it. The next step is this: your two lines are to form the middle portion of the second and third ranks of the parade turn out. There will be half a dozen officers on your right flank in each row; there will be a complete rank of chaps in front of you. Those left over will tag themselves on to the left flank. Now this is where Bruce comes in." He shepherded Bruce to the right of the front rank.

"As soon as the Jerries have counted Bruce's file of three, and have passed on towards your left, Bruce will duck and run between your two ranks to the left hand end of your front rank. Let's try it, Bruce."

Bruce ducked down between the two rows and reappeared in a few seconds at the far end.

"O.K.," said Dick.

Rupert, who was watching carefully, butted in, "Dick, both ranks had better form up pretty close. I could see Bruce easily between their legs."

Dick agreed. "You'd better all wear overcoats on the *Appell*,

it's cold enough, and form up close," he said, and to Bruce, "carry an R.A.F. cap with you on *Appell*. Don't wear it to begin with, but when you reappear, have it on your head with the peak well down. Last man on the left of the front rank: remember, on the actual *Appell*, to keep a gap on your left just sufficient for Bruce to fill in."

The parade reformed from scratch with Bruce in position, hat in hand.

"Now I'm the Jerry officer and there's a complete rank in front of you. Rupert, see how it goes as I do the counting."

Dick started to count the files in the German fashion and as he passed three files from Bruce, the latter glided out of sight and was in his new position, with his hat pulled well down over his eyes, long before Dick reached him.

"That'll do," said Rupert.

Dick then gave some final cautions and the party broke up.

The rabbit method was more foolproof the bigger the number on parade. The French were a hundred and eighty strong by now compared with the British eighty, and little difficulty was expected with their contingent. This was the kind of game which appealed strongly to the French mentality.

The evening *Appell* and the next morning *Appell* went off serenely. The French, noticing what was happening, thought it a great joke. For Dick, there was the satisfying feeling of an operation going according to schedule, but behind it was always a haunting misgiving—the stool-pigeon; the unknown traitor who might be in their midst, who had his own secret method of transmitting information to the Germans within the prison, and who could ruin the best of schemes.

The midday *Appell* assembled as usual. Dick, Rupert and Lulu formed up at the end of the rear rank. From here they could witness the rabbit performing. To their right they could see the French forming up. Nothing looked unusual. The parade came to attention and Lieutenant Püpcke entered the courtyard on time. He was always punctual. The counting began. As it passed Bruce, he could be seen stiffening for the "off." He bent his head down, looking at his feet, and as the counting reached the fourth file beyond him he seemed to slip to the earth and in a second was diving along the closely formed corridor between the two rear ranks. He reappeared, if anything rather suddenly, in his new position.

As Püpcke reached the end of the counting, a sentry near the

canteen door came smartly to attention and left his post at the double. He halted in front of the German Sergeant Major, and spoke hurriedly to him. The Sergeant Major saluted Püpcke, and spoke to him. Together they accosted the sentry and a consultation took place. This was the signal for the prisoners to start barracking and shuffling their feet to register impatience. The sentry had obviously seen something. He was the one nearest to the point where Bruce reappeared. Püpcke, however, did not appear convinced. Turning away from him, he ordered the parade to dismiss.

Dick and Rupert had little time to congratulate themselves on their good fortune. In less than a minute they were in the theatre where the drill was laid on as before. Rupert, calm and collected, not showing a trace of the excitement seething within him, took up his position in the corridor and his French colleague soon stood beside him. He, too, was behaving himself well. He could hardly be excited with the coolness all around him. The operation worked like clockwork. Dick gave no orders. The men who were on this job were old hands.

The rope went over the sill; the bars came away and Rupert was outside. As he dropped down Dick whispered hoarsely after him, "Good luck, Rupert! Remember they can't shoot a British officer."

Grismond Davis-Scourfield's voice could be heard as yesterday, but to-day there was a ring of optimism in his reports:

"Püpcke walking out of courtyard through main gate . . . Gephard talking to Dixon Hawk in centre . . . two snoops at sick bay entrance . . . all clear in theatre block. . . ."

The Frenchman followed Rupert and as the rope slackened it was whipped up and removed immediately to its permanent hiding place. The camouflage replaced and the windows closed, the whole team quickly dispersed. Dick and Lulu transferred their activities to genuine theatrical preparations on the stage and awaited the reports of the stooges watching the progress of the escapers.

Ten minutes later, small, ginger-headed Peter Storie Pugh bounced into the theatre.

"They've been caught, Dick," he said, "at the gateway down to the park."

"What the hell!" exclaimed Dick. "How were they caught there? There's no sentry."

"Quite, but there was when Rupert and his Frog got there. He appeared from nowhere and stopped them."

"What happened?"

"I couldn't see much for the trees, but there was quite a lot of

talking before he made them put their hands up. Then they were marched back to the Kommandantur."

"Somebody's been quick off the mark this time if you ask me. That's Eggers' work all right—but what gets me is that he should know when our men were going and the direction they'd take."

"I'm afraid it's the old story, Dick—a traitor in the camp," said Peter. "This always happens when too many people get to know an escape's coming off. The whole camp knew about the escape to-day."

"You're probably right, Peter, but we'll never know for certain. A stool-pigeon would certainly account for Egger's behaviour yesterday. But we were one step ahead luckily. Eggers wouldn't have known any more than his informer, who could only tell him an escape was likely in the afternoon and that we should be watched closely."

"But to-day," Peter interrupted, "he'd know a lot more. You can't stop people talking. He'd know about everything—except probably the actual light well."

"A damn shame!" said Dick. He was boiling with suppressed anger. He was sure in his own mind that an informer was at work, and he was impotent to trace him. The whole camp would have to be treated as suspect.

A Polish informer had been found—it was old history now—but he had been found by the Poles themselves. Dick might be able to set some sleuths at work among the British, but nothing could ever be done about the French—that was the trouble—it was his Achilles heel.

Scarlet O'Hara walked into the theatre. He had been watching the German courtyard.

"They're caught," he said grinning broadly.

"Thanks for the news," said Dick. "I can't see anything funny in it. What's the joke?"

"They were marched into the Kommandantur about ten minutes ago, from the park. I stayed put to see what happened. They've just been marched out again and they're off down to the town jail, dressed in their underpants, with their hands up and four Goons trailing 'em."

"I bet Rupert's cold, his pants always remind me of a piece of wire netting," said Dick. He was thinking, "Thank God two are out anyway—not as depressing as it could be."

Lulu had joined the group. Peter and Scarlet were recounting their stories again. Dick changed the subject.

"I don't think the 'Rabbit' will work again in a hurry. We'd better lay up a couple of ghosts while we have the chance. That means three absent from the British ranks next *Appell*. The Jerries may call one any time now."

Lulu said, "I think Monty Bissell's our man for that. He's got the best hide-out in the camp."

"Let's get cracking," said Dick with sudden energy in his voice. He disappeared through the theatre door, and down the stairs two at a time, followed by the others.

They found Monty in the prisoners' mess room and a hurried consultation took place. Monty had recently embarked on a tunnel scheme in the Chapel, under the pulpit. The entrance was cleverly concealed by a slab of marble forming one of the steps up to it. There was already ample space in the tunnel for the concealment of a couple of bodies which, it was now agreed, should be permanently housed there. Volunteers were quickly called for from among Monty's tunnelling team, and two were elected for the job. They went straight to the Chapel and were walled in.

The *Appell* siren began to moan.

On a previous escape attempt Dick had put away no less than six ghosts. It had been too much for the Jerries to swallow. Besides, the ghosts were not superlatively well hidden, and were all, eventually, discovered. On this occasion Dick decided to compromise with two ghosts.

What was the purpose of a ghost? It was this: after a 'gone-away' escape the chances of success of the escaper increased tremendously the further he was from the Camp. The area of search to be covered by the Germans increased, mathematically, by the square of the increased distance away.

Thus it was of the utmost importance to give an escaper the longest start possible by concealing his absence on *Appells* as long as possible; for this purpose ghosts were created.

In this particular instance, as the two 'gone-aways'—Mike Sinclair and his French colleague—had a good twenty-four hours' start, Dick considered it unnecessary to conceal their absence any longer. On the contrary, it was now more important to think of the future. The two ghosts in the Chapel would 'fill in' on *Appells* after the next escape, whenever that might be.

German sentries entered the courtyard and took up their positions for the roll call. Their officers appeared. The parade came to attention. The count was taken. Four officers were missing.

Messengers were dispatched to the Kommandantur. After a long delay they returned. The parade was dismissed.

Dick now had two cards up his sleeve.

*   *   *   *   *

Optimism ran high after Mike's escape. He was known to be heading for Switzerland, towards the hitherto almost foolproof secret Colditz frontier-crossing route.

Then after five days came the news of his recapture. The Germans were never slow to announce the recapture of an escaper: in fact, it was by the absence of such announcements that the successes were counted. An almost audible groan went up from the whole camp. He carried the hopes of so many and bore personal messages with him to so many loved ones waiting patiently at home in England for their husbands and their sons.

Within ten days Mike was back in the Castle, in a solitary confinement cell. His story came through.

When he and his French companion had walked through the German kitchens from the theatre light well, they found their way down the stairs and into the German courtyard without mishap. One quick glance had been enough for Mike to assure him of the direction to take. The gateway to the park lay open. There did not appear to be anyone on duty there. Without a word the two men, in their German overalls, passed the courtyard sentry, heading for the gate. Through this they walked and on down the hill, turning through the next gate to the left of the roadway and then down further along the steep, wide path into the park, over the bridge.

Within ten minutes they had climbed the park wall and were free. Mike parted company from his companion *en route* and in two days he was in Singen. The Frenchman made for the city of Leipzig where there were many French workmen and where, also, a convoy of lorries started for France, at regular intervals, with supplies for the occupation troops. Mike was re-caught near Singen. His was the story becoming menacingly common these days; an air raid had started a round-up for parachuted airmen. Thousands of civilians were out on the manhunt. He was picked up by a patrol within half a mile of freedom and three days out from Colditz. The Frenchman was already in the cells on his return; his contacts in Leipzig had failed him.

Mike was not allowed to communicate with anyone during his stay 'in the cooler', which lasted six weeks. He was left alone with

his thoughts, disconsolate and dejected, to brood upon his failure, 'so near and yet so far . . .' Mike would take himself to task seriously. He had a strongly developed conscience and an unswerving devotion to duty. A feeling that he had let down his fellow prisoners would not leave him at peace. At twenty-six he could stand a fair amount of loneliness and introspection without ill effect, but—six weeks was a long spell and, besides, Mike had taken more than his share of punishment with the Gestapo in Poland.

Resolution was the healing salve that would conquer the putrifying poison of morbidity. He would try again. He would not give up; that was certain.

PART II

1943

RADIO NEWS

DURING the autumn of 1942, Dick Howe had entered into private negotiations with a French clique which possessed one of the two wireless sets in Colditz. A second group of French headed by Lieutenant Gigue owned the other. The first set had been smuggled into the prison with the arrival of a batch of Frenchmen from a camp where they had had considerable contact with the outer world, mainly through orderlies and French workmen in the town and countryside. Gigue's set had been smuggled into the camp in parts hidden in thirty-five parcels, received over a period of months, from France.

The British had no set of their own and a purchase was arranged. Dick had been Escape Officer for some months by then. From the many contacts he had and the many rather morbid impressions he picked up, he saw, only too clearly, the value of possessing such a link with the outside world. He was preparing the hide for it when a hitch occurred. The proposed purchase became widely known among the French contingent; their senior officers were told of the transaction and were prevailed upon to stop it. Feeling, among the French, ran on the lines that as they were likely to be moved at any time—which was true—they would probably be separated into groups for different destinations and would need both sets. After all, they argued, Frenchmen had gone to much trouble to obtain them, so, why should they dispose of one? They even argued that as British morale was higher than theirs they had more need of the boost given by allied news broadcasts. Of course, as long as they remained in Colditz, the British would continue to use translations of their bulletins. Dick retired from the scene.

Lieutenant Gigue came from the south of France and had spent most of his life in Marseilles. He had the typical French accent of the region which differs from normal French, enunciated between the lips and teeth. The tongue plays a great part in producing the Marseilles accent by giving the impression of always sticking to the palate a split second too long.

Gigue carried a huge scar across his cheek and neck. His hair and eyebrows were jet black and his skin a deep suntanned brown.

A pair of mischievously flashing dark eyes and a ready grin completed an appearance of good-humoured energy. His movements were unbelievably quick and he had the knack of changing his position without being thought to have moved at all. It was a most curious and even eerie propensity. If it had not struck so many different officers at different times, the likelihood is that each one would have thought he had had an hallucination or was just suffering from prison slow-wittedness. But after about a year or so, when men repeatedly found themselves talking to thin air where they had thought they saw Gigue a moment before, the matter became one of public interest. It was even advanced that possibly Gigue was endowed with occult powers. Certainly it was most disconcerting for Englishmen to be found talking out loud to themselves in French in the middle of the courtyard; Gigue understood no English. He moved without a sound wherever he went.

Marseilles is not so far from Corsica. It is said that Napoleon had the cat-like propensity of walking, not on his toes and heels, but somewhere in between. Nor was Gigue unlike a Corsican bandit in that he had a faithful company of followers who, in all escaping ventures, appeared to understand his every mood and interpreted his unspoken wishes with unfailing accuracy. Gigue's heart was made of gold and the English had no better friend among the French contingent. Long before the French left Colditz, Dick Howe and Gigue had become close collaborators and the friendship between them paid dividends.

One spring-like day in February, 1943, Dick careered down the spiral staircase from the French quarters out into the courtyard and nearly bumped into Colonel Guy German who was taking his morning constitutional.

The sun just climbed high enough at midday to peep over the steep roofs of Colditz and send a few shimmering sunbeams to scatter the shadows that ruled unchallenged in the yard during the long and dreary winter months.

There was a glow in Dick's heart and triumph in his voice as he spoke to his senior officer.

"Good morning, Colonel."

"Good morning, Dick."

"I've got good news for you, sir."

"What is it? You sound excited. Coming from you that means it must be very good."

"The French are going as you know."

"Yes, they're going very soon, I think. Colonel le Brigand has told me. He has it on good authority from his own stooges. Incidentally, he's also told me the move is to make room for British. You remember the rumours we heard of the big breakout from Warburg? Well, the British are reported to be coming from Warburg—at least some of them. So the rumour may have been true."

"Well, sir, my bit of news concerns a wireless set."

"Ah, ha! are the French coming round then? We don't want a repetition of the last effort. There was some bad feeling over that—you remember?"

"Yes, I remember well. But this time they want to present it to us."

"In that case it must be given through the Senior French Officer so that we know where we stand. I'm afraid I'll have to insist on that point."

"I think that's all laid on. Gigue tells me that he has the agreement of Colonel Le Brigand to leave one of his sets behind. You see Gigue has two now. He's damn decent about the whole business. He can claim that the sets have been obtained entirely through his efforts and he is pressing his claim and the right to dispose of the set as he likes. He says there'll be practically no opposition from the French quarters. They've two other sets now which will travel with them."

"Of course, Dick, there's our own set on the way. . . ."

"Yes, but . . . it's not here yet and may never reach us. Gigue knows about it too, and says his C.O. knows it."

"Very well! It looks as if we can accept with a clear conscience."

"Colonel Le Brigand will be speaking to you about it soon."

Dick was about to turn away when his senior recalled him.

"One moment, Dick, that's not the end of the matter. What about the use of the set? Have you thought about that? First of all there's the maintenance, then there's the stooging and the recording, and we'll have to decide on reception times and the best wave lengths and produce the best news bulletins possible."

"Yes, I've thought about it," said Dick, and the slightest trace of weariness crept into his voice. He knew what was coming. The Colonel was thinking. He had, when in thought, the unusual habit of raising his eyebrows and wrinkling his forehead. They walked together round the yard—now in shadow, now in sunlight. The Colonel always walked briskly. He had a robust physique and was still tough in spite of the years of weakening. His was a forceful character that stood no nonsense from Germans or anybody else.

He could be frighteningly abrupt. To those in whom he placed his confidence he was a towering pillar of strength. He could scent out weakness like a bloodhound after his quarry, and he wasted no time. He was the ideal Commanding Officer in a difficult situation.

It was his regular exercise hour and the circle he walked never varied, though the direction in which he walked it changed unpredictably. Dick walked beside him as they speeded round in clockwise direction. The Colonel, as if to jolt his thoughts, stopped suddenly and reversed direction. Dick was well trained in his habits, and had caught him up again in a yard.

The Colonel had been ruminating and now he spoke as if unwillingly:

"I see no way out of it. You are our best wireless engineer. I daren't put the machine in anyone else's hands. It's much too valuable—our only link with reality in fact. If it broke down it would be like cutting an artery. Yes, Dick, I'm afraid it means more work for you."

"I know that."

"What you must do, at least, is to try and relieve yourself of all the news routine, and arrange the security so that you're free of that responsibility. Pass it over to someone else."

"Lulu Lawton?" queried Dick who had already given thought to the problem of stooging.

"Yes, by all means."

"Gigue has shown me the works," Dick continued, "and they're first class. We have absolutely nothing to teach that crew. I must hand it to Gigue. I can understand why the Jerries have never found it."

"Well, it's up to you, Dick, or rather to the man you appoint for stooging and camouflage to see that the Jerries continue not to find it. If they do—it'll look bad and we'll have only ourselves to blame."

Early in 1943 Gigue had received a second brand-new receiving set in another round of thirty-five parcels from France. They were smuggled, as usual, out of the German parcel office before the Germans ever set about examining the day's parcel delivery. The French were consequently happy to leave the British one of their three sets before they departed from Colditz.

There was no need even for the British to construct their own wireless hide. They took over the French set in its stronghold, lock, stock, and barrel. It says much for the ingenuity of Gigue

and his French colleagues that, although towards the end of the war the Germans knew the British had a set in action they never found it. They searched until they were blue in the face without success. Eventually our prisoners made no concealment of the news bulletins which were read publicly at the evening meal. The war situation was discussed openly with the Germans; their arguments contraverted and their alleged facts and figures contradicted.

As to the situation of the receiver, it was concealed in the eave of the steep sloping roof above the French quarters—which became British on the departure of the French.

When a roof is forty feet high from gutter to ridge, it can be appreciated that at least two floors may be built inside it having dormer windows and comparatively high ceilings. The floor area of rooms within the roof becomes reduced at each level upwards, not only because the two sides of the roof are approaching each other, but usually because a vertical wall is built around the sides of the rooms so that the inmates do not have the impression they are living in a tent. This vertical wall, in the case of rooms at Colditz, was about five feet high and concealed behind it a small triangular space bounded by the three sides; slanting roof, vertical wall and horizontal ceiling of the room below. Actually the architectural features were slightly more complicated than this description implies. The triangular space had to be enlarged out of the seven-foot-thick walls. Within it the wireless installation was set up, complete with electric light, switch gear for the receiver, earphones, a table and two chairs for the operator and the shorthand writer acting as news-recording telegraphist. Beside it, a second cavity was enlarged to provide a hide for contraband.

Entry to these secret apartments was made from the attic which formed the apex of the roof itself.

*　　　*　　　*　　　*　　　*

Jim Rogers, the mining engineer from South Africa, could not have lived long without the news. The progress of the war could be foretold by the tilt of his broad moustache. This had grown from nothing at the time of his capture. Jim had once been a burly, tough six footer but the lengthening war was telling on him. He seemed to grow smaller. As his stature shrank and his body grew thin, his moustache alone waxed in splendour. His strength, like that of Goliath, was going into his hair. Where Goliath had wielded a club, Jim wielded his guitar.

C

Before ever the B.B.C. news bulletins became an organised part of the daily schedule, Jim had developed his own system of news summaries, which he recited daily, with infinite relish, to the whole British contingent assembled for their meagre evening repast. What Jim really needed was a huge beef steak in front of him, but alas! as that dream dish never materialised, the best that he could do was to whet his appetite with words. He revelled in his phrases and smacked his lips over his metaphors. His war appreciations were full of meat, peppered with doubtful facts, heavily salted with assumptions and blanketed with the opaque rosy coloured sauce of optimism. His prognostications were sweet fruit to the easily gullible, enriched as they were with the cream of the latest rumours. The "Old Horse" as he was affectionately called, really had very little information to go on. His principal source was the meagre French bulletins which were often garbled with news coming from Vichy. In addition, he had the German press and the hearsay of the latest prisoner arrival from another camp.

As a writer may use a true story for the basis of his novel, so Jim used the news. He would come rushing into the common room just before the midday meal, eyes glistening, a lock of straight hair falling over his forehead, and his moustache quivering with excitement.

"Great news to-day, boys! Great news! I've just got it all straight from the horse's mouth—a chap just in from Marlag Nord—he's in the delousing shed. He was on that Dieppe raid some time ago —won't say any more now—keep it all for to-night—managed to get the whole story at last—it's terrific. It'll shake you."

"Aw, you don't say!" would come from Don Donaldson, the Canadian, often called 'the Weasel,' who had once climbed into the cockpit of a German Messerschmidt, but could not find the starter.

"Come on, Horse! don't hold back."

Jim would then become as close as an oyster, "Awfully sorry, old chap, but simply mustn't jump the gun—besides I might give the wrong impression—got to draw the right conclusions, you know—that means some thinking—there's big strategy behind this."

It was a cat and mouse game. Don and Jim's other messmates would feign indifference. At lunch time, over the table, surrounded by eight glum officers, silence would reign. After ten minutes, with the meal practically finished and not a word spoken, Jim would realise an opportunity was slipping from him. Bursting to tell his story and thoroughly put out at the lethargy of his companions,

he could not hold out any longer. In an offended tone he would blurt out:

"My God! I think you fellows are a lot of bums! Nothing to talk about—no interest in the war—I can't understand chaps not taking an interest in world events . . . terrific things going on."

There would be a pause as Don would drag out the comedy. It was like teasing a big Newfoundland dog which was your greatest friend. Jim knew he was being teased. But his nature could not be suppressed. When Don judged he had wrung the last ounce of patience out of him, he would say again:

"Aw, now Jim you're playing with us! We just can't wait to hear about Dieppe straight from the Old Horse's mouth. Just give us a hint."

So Jim would unbend, and gathering the "chaps" around him, with their heads all bent close together over the table, he would tell them in a hoarse whisper:

"The Allies have the whole invasion buttoned up. It's coming any day now. Dieppe was terrific strategy—I've worked it out. It was all a hoax to make the Jerries think that we'd think that invasion was hopeless and so ease up on coastal defence. No more now chaps, but I'll give you the whole works to-night. Keep it dark—I want to shake everyone. Damn good for morale."

And indeed it was. Jim was our camp Goebbels—but he did a much better job than that despicable propagandist, probably because he just could not have told a lie if he had tried. He was, by nature, a good story teller. He was a spider who could weave a tantalising web to enveigle even the most suspicious fly. Once in his net, he wrapped his listeners up in a pleasantly soft cotton wool of optimism and hope which, curiously through all the years of despair, became a wonderful protection against the lengthening shadows; the misery of the polar extremes of the unknown and of reality. He was a magician who, by pretending not to be able to deceive his audience, by even encouraging their laughter and their ridicule at his naïvety in the lesser tricks of his trade, cast over them the greater spell at which he aimed; succeeding with genius, so that they were completely unaware of what he had done to them. There is no doubt he kept hope high and courage strong even in the darkest days. He was the Knight of the Silver Lining.

As with Dieppe, so it had been with the loss of the two great battleships, with Singapore and the retreats in the Libyan desert.

When Singapore fell, the French were terribly upset. The Poles were full of sympathy, and the Dutch were calm but silent. The British treated it as if one of their favourite football teams had been beaten, and as if the coming defeat had been known beforehand because the star forward line had been changed.

The fact was that the British contingent had been cushioned for the coming fall for some time by the Old Horse and a confederate, Colonel Kimber. The French came to our quarters with

Jim Rogers

long glum faces wringing their hands as soon as the news was confirmed. The war in the east was over for them. They could see the Japanese hordes in the Mediterranean. They did not come to condole, but rather to join the British in a common act of despair. Singapore appeared to them, to be for the British what Dunkerque had been for themselves. They found their allies in good spirits and were dumbfounded.

Colonel Kimber had worked on the defences of Singapore before the war. He had, even in those days, fumed at the pigheadedness of men who installed enormous guns with a traverse that covered attack from the sea, but gave no protection whatever in the direction of the Causeway.

By the time Singapore fell it was old news to the British, and Jim passed over it lightly:

"Singapore has gone, but I told you all about that three weeks ago, so there's no need to bother about it now. It merely serves to bear out the accuracy of my forecasts."

Loud cheers interrupted him and French guests, who were present, sat with mouths agape at the spectacle of British officers cheering the news of the fall of Singapore. It is not without reason that Europeans speak seriously of "mad Englishmen".

When the cheering, catcalls and whistling died down Jim continued his summary of the news of the day.

When he had finished, and the clatter of plates and hum of voices had resumed its normal cacophony, as if to emphasise the complete indifference of the British to a huge catastrophe, Don Donaldson's Canadian drawl would intervene:

"Come on, Old Horse! tell us a good story."

Jim had quite a fund of them and they grew longer and more elaborate with every telling.

"Well, chaps! when I was mining in Yugoslavia some queer things happened to me—you just wouldn't believe them. D'you know there was a princess out there and guess what she did?"

"No! What?"

"Well, you just wouldn't believe it."

"Aw, you don't say! Come on, Old Horse, tell us all about it."

And Jim would tell the story how, once, when prospecting in the mountains of Yugoslavia, his camp had been visited by a Royal party. They were entertained lavishly by Jim's mining team and the "Slebovitza" flowed freely. A beautiful princess became quite incapable of retracing her steps, after the party, down the rocky gorges to the mountain road, where the cars and retinue attended. Jim and a mate formed a comfortable chair for her with their four hands interlaced, and seated upon them she slept peacefully as they carried her down the stony path.

"What happened then, Jim?"

"Her little head was against my shoulder." He paused.

"Go on, Horse!"

"I slipped on a rock. It gave the princess an awful jolt and she promptly pee'd into my hand."

THE FRENCH TUNNEL

THE French had been digging a tunnel for eight months. It looked as if there might be a race between the tunnellers and the Germans; the former to finish the tunnel and escape before the latter moved them all from the camp. A small party of French had already left for Oflag IVD.

The French architects of the tunnel consisted originally of a team of nine officers who constituted themselves the "Société Anonyme du Tunnel de Colditz". To make sure that it was "anonyme" the tunnellers had no chief. "Liberté, Egalité, Fraternité" was the motto they lived up to. They were: Jean Brejoux, a professor of German; Edgar Barras, the strong man and the champion French 'stool-ball'* player; Bernard Cazaumayou, the weight lifter; Roger Madin, an engineer who was the tunnel electrician; Paillé, French Sappers and Miners; Jean Chaudrut, the chief stooge; Georges Diedler, from the Vosges; Jean Gambero, the astute Parisian; and Léonce Godfrin, from the Ardennes.

The conception of the tunnel was curious, yet typical. The French are a logical. race. They had read in the German press that the Leipzig Fair was to be held in spite of the war. Leipzig was only twenty-two miles away. It would provide wonderful cover for the escape of a large body of prisoners. Leipzig would be full to overflowing with visitors, coming from all parts and speaking many languages. The only way, it seemed, to dispatch a large body of prisoners to Leipzig was by tunnel—but not the whole way by tunnel; that opened the discussion of the next problem. Again, the French decided where they would like their tunnel to debouch so as to provide a safe get-away. From there they worked backwards into the Castle to see where the entrance should be. Alas! none of the French quarters touched ground level; underneath them on the ground floor were rooms occupied by Germans during the daylight hours; the sick-ward, the parcels office and Gephard's office. Once more, logic saved the day. "If we can't start at the bottom," they said, "let's start at the top." And that was what they did.

* Described in *The Colditz Story*.

The clock tower provided them with a means of access to the cellar. The clock had not worked for years and the weights, with their long chains, had also been removed, leaving empty cylindrical sleeves which extended from the clock down to the ground floor. There were small cubby holes, presumably inspection chambers, giving access to the sleeves at each floor level. The cubby holes had long ago been bricked up by the Jerries.

A heavily barred steel door on the top landing of the French quarters, at fourth floor level, was the first object of attack. It led to the clock room. With men like Gigue and Roger Madin in the camp, the padlocks, mortice locks and cruciform locks securing the door were soon provided with keys. Once in the clock room, a camouflaged opening was constructed in the floor and in the ceiling below, which let the Frenchmen down into the cubby hole on the third floor. They could have descended through the sleeves, but these were a tight squeeze for any adult, being only sixteen inches in diameter, and coming up again would have been difficult. They constructed ladders instead, piercing holes in each cubby hole floor down to ground level. Here the first serious tunnelling began. It consisted of a vertical shaft through the stones and mortar of the arched roof of the Castle cellar.

Once in the cellar, which, of course, was subject to examination by German patrols, the Frenchmen had the choice of digging in any direction they wished. Having already chosen their direction—they started breaking out a hole, four feet from the ground, in the wall facing the chapel.

The cellar contained a stock of old Hungarian wine reposing in bottles under a layer of dust—a serious temptation to the French. They only weakened once, according to their own admission. That was the night when they examined the cellar from end to end in search of a secret passage or other ready made exit from the camp. They were unsuccessful. Momentarily depressed at the prospect of months of tunnelling, they "won" four bottles of wine.

Having made an entrance door on pivots like a safe door, out of the original stones from the wall, they continued, digging a horizontal tunnel behind it, through the heavy foundation which supported the dividing wall between the chapel and the spiral staircase to the French quarters. This continued for a distance of fifteen feet.

Once under the chapel, they dug a vertical shaft upwards for a distance of nine feet until they met the beams of the chapel

floor. Progressing under the floor they searched for the entrance
to a crypt, but found none.

The team realised, at last, that there was no short cut and that
they would have to continue the tunnel until they were outside
the wire. They decided to increase the number of shareholders in
the Tunnelling Company. They had been working by day and
night for two months and were ready to welcome new blood.

The S.A.T.C. obtained its recruits without difficulty. Many
eyes had watched with envy the guarded movements and mysterious
disappearances of the founder members and had noted the surreptitious washing of the dirty sweat-stained underclothing of
the Société Anonyme. The Company increased from nine in
number to thirty. Tunnelling continued in three shifts throughout
the twenty-four hours. The spirits of the French rose as yard
after yard of tunnel opened in front of them.

When the tunnel was nearing completion in the early days of
1943 Gigue, who was, by then, a long standing member of the
Company, and Madin, who had been one of the original members,
offered to take Dick on a conducted tour of the premises. It was
January, and they were hoping to break soon. When that took
place the British would never have an opportunity of seeing the
work they had carried out, and they were genuinely proud of their
tunnel.

"You know," said Dick, gladly accepting their invitation,
"we've heard you digging away for months, and of course, your
own people have too. Haven't you been running a tremendous
risk all this time? The Germans must know well enough that a
tunnel's in progress."

It was a fact that at all hours of the day, but more especially at
night when the Castle was wrapped in the silence of sleep, tunnelling could be heard. The sound was definable as high up as the
third floor of the Castle above the chapel, where some of the
British lived, and it even kept light sleepers awake. It could be
compared to the regular, consecutive landing of high explosive
shells over the hills some miles away. There was a gentle con-
cussion which appeared to come from various directions, carried
by the air, the walls, the floor and even the ceiling. The dull,
heavy thuds struck the ear from all sides. Eventually, it was
possible, by continued careful listening, to eliminate echoes and
secondary sound waves, and to establish with some certainty where
the sounds emanated from. Indeed, the Germans must have done
this by now.

"The Jerries may know it well enough," said Gigue in French, "but as long as they can find no entrance we are safe."

"But the Germans will persevere. . . ."

"Come with us this evening and you shall see why they will not find the entrance," replied Gigue. "We are on the night shift and you will spend it with us."

They met again after the last *Appell* of the day. Dick had finished his supper and was prepared for a night's vigil. Lulu would make up a dummy in his bed. He had been warned to put on plenty of warm clothing.

The Castle was in darkness, except where the reflection from the searchlights glowed. Dick mounted the French staircase with his two friends. They reached the attics at the fourth floor. From the landing, to the left was the Ghetto where the French Jewish officers lived; to the right were attics, locked and uninhabited.

Gigue looked at his watch. It was 9.30 p.m. If all went well there would be no further *Appells* until 7 a.m. the next morning.

They waited for the remainder of the shift workers to appear. It was to be a "removal" shift. Tons of debris from a week of tunnelling had to be cleared away that night. While they were waiting Gigue explained to Dick in French:

"We have been lucky to find a good place for the debris of the tunnel. When we go through the steel door over there," he said pointing, "you will see a ladder leading to a skylight in the roof. Outside on the roof within a distance of two metres there is a window in the gable of the attic above your English bedroom, the one over the chapel. It has bars which we can remove and replace. In this attic we have found plenty of space for hundreds of tons of rubble between the slanting roof and the partition walls." Gigue flashed a sly grin at Dick as he caught his puzzled expression. Dick asked:

"But how do you pass the rubble from the skylight into the attic?"

"*Eh bien!* A man sits on the roof outside the skylight. He passes the sacks from one man on the ladder to another inside the attic."

"So that is why you do this at night?"

"Yes, indeed. If it was done in the day our man could be seen from the town and the countryside. At night he is in a dark shadow cast beyond the searchlight beams."

"He must get damned cold up there," said Dick. "Why, it's freezing hard."

"He freezes to begin with. But when he has lifted sacks weighing twenty-five kilos for half an hour, he is not cold any more."

The *équipe*, as the French always called their team, had, by now, all arrived. There were twenty energetic Frenchmen milling around them on the small landing. Dick was aghast at the crowd. Gigue and Madin, receiving the "all clear" signal from their stooges, began work on the locks. Within a matter of minutes the steel door opened and the whole *équipe* was soon safely inside the clock tower. The door was locked behind them. Everybody seemed to know what to do. At signals from Gigue, who stood near the door keeping contact with a stooge outside, the team set to work. The secret trap door in the floor was disclosed, and bodies disappeared downwards through the hole. A ladder was hoisted from below and propped against a skylight window which Dick saw for the first time. Around it gathered half a dozen Frenchmen ready to go out on the roof. If there was an alarm this section of the team would have to leave the clock tower. Jerries might enter and search the room. Those who descended would have the trap door sealed above them and would remain hidden unless they had to come out because of an *Appell*.

Gigue handed over his post to a colleague and invited Dick to descend the ladder. Madin had already disappeared below. Gigue followed and the trap door was closed above them. In the small chambers at successive levels, men were changing into their tunnelling kit. Dick noted a gaudy variety of designs and colours in woollen vests, pants and stockings which the Frenchmen donned, layer upon layer. It was evidently going to be cold. Some of them wore tin helmets, and, as if answering his unspoken question, Gigue said to Dick: "Put on this English Tommy's helmet. It's the only English one we have and it's right that you should wear it. When my friends start shifting the rocks you may need it."

They were soon ready to descend to the lower regions. They stood for a moment surveying each other laughingly.

"You look like an old Roman warrior," said Dick, "with that helmet on."

Gigue indeed looked like something out of a nightmare classic. He wore gaily coloured stockings and knee-pads, a pair of dirty dark blue shorts over several pairs of pants and a bright red thick woollen sweater drawn in at the waist by a broad leather belt with a brass buckle.

Dick looked no less peculiar. From the plimsolls on his feet two pairs of long woollen pants stretched up to his waist, while,

over them, a pair of white rugger shorts covered his buttocks. Three short sleeved vests clothed his chest and the tin hat crowned his head. He looked like Tommy Atkins after a bomb had blown off his uniform. Gigue said:

"You need not laugh at me. Laugh at yourself. You remind me of an English General going to have his bath in the trenches."

They climbed down the next ladder, one after the other, and carried on downwards, passing, at each floor level, through a small room packed to the ceiling with loose stones and rubble until there was scarcely sufficient room to manœuvre.

"You are now at ground level," said Gigue. "The team is about to start work—we shall watch it from here for a moment." As he spoke a blue and white check sack the size of a laundry bag, rose through a hole in the floor. Dick recognised the pattern of the standard German palliasse cover used throughout the camp.

The sack was seized by a Frenchman, standing over the hole, who checked and tightened the cord which closed it at the top, and then lifted it into a cradle made of rope with a heavy steel hook attached. Dick lifted the sack himself, out of interest, and estimated that it weighed half a hundredweight. The cradle, with the sack in it, was hooked to a loop on an endless rope that disappeared upwards through the two round sleeves which had housed the clock chains and weights. The Frenchman pressed an electric button beside him. The cradle started to move upwards and was greedily swallowed by the mouth of the sleeve above Dick's head.

"An endless rope lift?" queried Dick.

"Yes," said Gigue, "we use the original pulleys and a reduction gear from the clock at the top. It makes the work much easier for our men."

Another sack rose through the hole in the floor, was hooked to the lift and began its ascent to the attic.

"How much debris do you move in a night?" asked Dick.

"We can move nearly one ton per hour," replied Gigue. "We shall work to-night for seven hours. If you stop for long you catch cold. So we carry on continuously."

Dick said he could well understand it. He was already feeling the chill of a strong draught coming up through the hole in the floor. The clock tower was acting like a chimney.

"Let us go down further while the way is clear," said Gigue.

They dropped through the hole feeling for the ladder beneath them. Dick went carefully downwards in a narrow shaft for a few feet, then found himself again in the open. Descending further he

landed on the floor of the Castle cellar. A closely shaded electric light was focused on the ladder to direct the worker mounting it with a heavy sack on his shoulder. Beyond the light was impenetrable darkness. Dick looked around him wonderingly.

"Where do we go from here?" he asked Gigue quietly.

"Wait, a sack is coming," Gigue whispered as if that explained everything.

Dick heard a rumble that seemed to come towards him out of nowhere. Gradually his eyes became more accustomed to the dark and he could see a rectangular glow of light, bright at the edges, which appeared to shine out of a wall at eye level some yards away. Then the rumbling stopped, shadows moved across the glow and suddenly a bright square patch of light showed in the wall. A Frenchman passed him and began to climb the ladder with a sack on his shoulders.

"This is the entrance to the tunnel," said Gigue in an undertone. "The noise you heard was a sack moving along on the sled. We can now go forward." He beckoned Dick to follow.

They approached the hole in the wall. Dick looked along the tunnel. It was a little higher than it was broad; about two feet four inches by two feet in section. It had been hacked through stones and mortar and he began to understand the sounds he had heard for so many months. "There's certainly no need for any shoring or timbering here," he mused.

An electric bulb burned brightly at the far end which was five yards away. The walls of the tunnel gleamed white with light reflected from stone surfaces polished by the frequent rubbing of passing bodies.

Dick stepped on to a large block of wood placed on the floor under the entrance. Then he noticed the heavy door which shut the tunnel. It was a complete section of wall, a foot thick, which had been built inside a wooden casing. A long piece of steel, three quarters of an inch in diameter, acting as a pivot, ran vertically through one end of it. The lower end of the pivot rested on a steel plate hollowed out to receive it. The plate was concreted into the floor of the tunnel. The upper end of the pivot passed through a hole in another steel plate concreted into the roof of the tunnel.

Dick recognised something familiar about the design and asked Gigue:

"Who made the door?"

"I did," was the reply. "I saw Van den Heuvel's door after the

Jerries had found his secret room—you remember?—and I copied it."

Dick remembered. It had been impossible to find Van den Heuvel's door, sealed. The irregular edges of the present door were obviously carefully set to fit into crevices in the wall as a pattern fits into a mould. Putty, cobwebs and dust completed the camouflage which would defy minute investigation.

Dick was lost in admiration at the work when he heard Gigue calling from the far end of the tunnel.

"*Dépêche-toi*, Dick. Another sack is coming."

Dick hoisted himself into the hole and crawled to the far end. A rope, made of bed sheets resembling those produced by Bos'n Crisp, ran the length of the tunnel between well polished tracks of wood at each side. These, Dick realised, carried the sled with the sacks of rubble.

"Here," said Gigue, "we have buried the largest stone of all. We have had them of many sizes, but the one upon which you are kneeling weighs about one hundred and fifty kilos."

"Did it bother you!" said Dick mockingly.

"Yes, it was at the top of the shaft which you see over you."

Dick looked upwards. Above him in the glare of another electric bulb was a vertical shaft, some nine feet in height. Their breath, forming clouds of vapour, rose upwards into it. Dick asked:

"How did you get rid of the stone?"

"Flynn's bar was the answer," said Gigue. "You know that he is the only Englishman with a place promised on this tunnel. Well, if he had not stolen the bar from a lorry in the courtyard, I don't think we would ever have passed that rock. I will show you the bar later. We use it all the time. Barras and Cazaumayou worked upon the stone. It could easily have killed them, for it was as big as the shaft. They made a hole here to receive it. Then they worked underneath it for days, loosening it. It was touch and go. Finally they needed a long bar so that they could free it and escape from underneath it as it fell. At that point Flynn produced his bar. The stone fell one night while they worked, here, where you are. It shook the building. They escaped in time. Afterwards our work was simplified. You know, we had reached the floor of the chapel. Now follow me up the shaft."

Dick climbed upwards after Gigue on a skeleton timber scaffolding that had been erected inside the shaft. Below stood a helmeted Frenchman whom he left with a grin saying, "*Excusez-moi si je tombe sur votre tête.*"

At the top Gigue disappeared again. Dick thought of Alice in Wonderland. Then he reached the top, looked over and reflected that he was not so far wrong. Gigue was lying in front of him completely blocking the view. Not a ray of light penetrated past him. He was struggling and panting as he moved forward. Dick waited patiently at the top of the shaft thinking. "They won't shift a ton this hour. We've put paid to that."

All transport of sacks had ceased. Beside him was a rope suspended from a wooden pulley above his head. The tackle carried the sacks down the shaft.

The puffing and blowing continued, growing more distant. Then Dick heard a "Pssht!" and looked forward. Gigue's head appeared round a corner a long way off.

"Come quickly, Dick, you are occupying the place of one of our men who must handle the sacks."

Dick had already realised this.

Now it was his turn to push and squeeze, to twist and turn, to sweat and rest, wondering if he would ever see again the light of day. He squirmed himself forward eight yards under what was the floor of the chapel between heavy oak timbers which had been sawn through. At last he found himself in a large space, deeper than before, about two feet, but almost a living room in other respects— about six feet square, in fact. Here Dick collapsed to recover his breath while a gentle rumble told him that the sacks had started moving again along the tunnel corridors.

"How did you get past those timbers?" asked Dick.

"They nearly finished us," said Gigue. "They are of oak, only six hundred years old, and forty centimetres square. We had to cut through seven of them, each twice, and our saws were made of German table knives!"

Dick felt the sweat clammy around his waist. He suddenly thought of something and asked Gigue:

"Did your fellows cut those seven beams in this freezing cold without getting pneumonia?"

"It was worse than that, Dick. It was very cold lying on those blocks of granite out there, you know, but they were not even allowed to catch a cold! We are under the chapel floor and a German in the church would think it funny if he suddenly heard a cough coming from the dead underneath his feet. We have had stooges always in the chapel when we worked underneath. They warned us if a Jerry came in."

"Pious chaps, I suppose," said Dick.

"Oh, yes! they were very pious. They held a retreat which lasted for months. One after the other, for two hours each, they came to the chapel and prayed for our success. If a German came— well, you know, as we say, it is not prayer alone but good deeds also that count, so our friends did the good deed. They banged on the floor as they knelt, with their toes. There was not even a sneeze from the dead below after that."

"I suppose we are near your heading now?" Dick asked.

"No, we are not half-way," replied Gigue. "We are underneath the sacristy. You see the switchboard in the corner. That is where the electricity is branched off from the main chapel supply. Ah! here is Roger. He will explain all to you."

Madin's head appeared through a large hole in the floor of the tunnel some yards away. His pink face, appearing out of the ground, reminded Dick of a ferret. He had a long nose that looked as if it could smell out anything. His angular forehead was surmounted by a wispy crop of fair hair and he wore thick lensed glasses. His teeth were conspicuously undershot so that his huge triangular-shaped chin protruded outwards giving the impression of complete separation from the remainder of his physiognomy. He smiled on the least provocation and, when he did so, the sparkle in his eyes, enlarged by the spectacles, emanated humour and good temper as a fire radiates warmth.

"Hello, Dick!" he said pulling himself up higher out of the hole. "How do you like our tunnel? Not so bad, eh? Do you approve of it? I have just been checking the electric wiring."

Gigue said to Madin:

"Roger, will you tell Dick all about the electrical installation. I shall leave you—I must go forward to the digging face. Come along later, when you are ready. Au revoir."

He disappeared into the hole leaving Madin in charge.

"I must tell you how we obtained electricity for the tunnel," said Madin grinning above his large chin. "We should never have had it without the aid of our Curé Jeanjean. You know that the chapel is closed after the morning service. Jeanjean protested he could not continue the spiritual instruction of his converts unless he was allowed to teach in the sacristy. He obtained permission for two hours a day. I was his principal convert! I worked on the wiring, and whenever a German came near the sacristy I was on my knees beside the curé praying hard or listening to his exhortations."

Roger was lying on his stomach, with his head resting in his

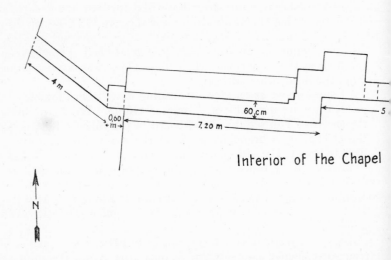

60 cm

7.20 m

0,60 m

4 m

5

Interior of the Chapel

N

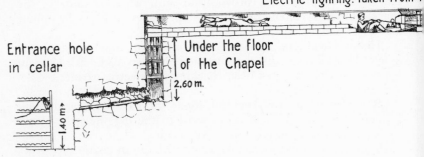

Electric lighting: taken from t

Entrance hole
in cellar

Under the floor
of the Chapel

2,60 m.

1.40 m

THE FRENCH TUNNEL

This drawing has been traced from the original Plans made by the Ger
after the discovery of the Tunnel. The Plans were kept in the Escape Museum
German Komandantur. When Colditz was relieved the Museum was found
P.O.W. and Rupert Barry procured the originals.

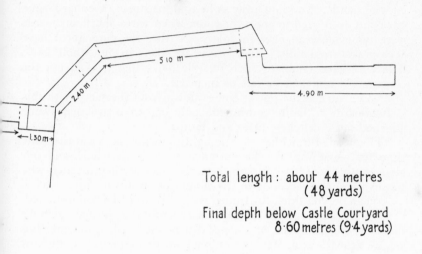

5·10 m

2·40 m

4·90 m

1·30 m

Total length: about 44 metres
(48 yards)

Final depth below Castle Courtyard
8·60 metres (9·4 yards)

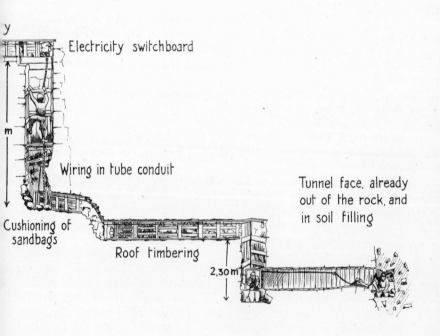

y

Electricity switchboard

m

Wiring in tube conduit

Cushioning of
sandbags

Roof timbering

Tunnel face, already
out of the rock, and
in soil filling

2·30 m

cupped hands, chuckling away as he told his story: "Gephard came once and even tried to enter the room when wires and floor boards were lying loose all over the place. Neither the curé nor I have ever prayed so loudly, either before or since, in our whole lives. The curé gave Gephard such terrible looks that he had not the courage to enter and he left us in peace."

"Now, you see the power comes down from the sacristy to this switchboard," Madin continued, pointing to a wooden frame adorned with switches, fuses and lamps.

"The whole tunnel has electric lighting which serves at the same time for signalling. At the entrance there is a switch, and our stooges up above pass messages to the man at the entrance who passes them to everybody in the tunnel by means of this switch."

"When do you think the tunnel will be ready?" Dick questioned.

"We are working very hard to finish before the Germans remove us. You will take over, of course, if it is not finished in time. But we are near the end. We have only about fifteen metres to dig now in loose subsoil. You know how long the tunnel is?"

"No," said Dick.

"It is over forty metres long including the vertical shafts. The latter total up to eleven metres. The one in the corner over there which you will go down in a moment is the deepest, it is six and a half metres. We had to go underneath the main foundations of the Castle."

Dick was shivering again. The cold was intense. Movement was the only means of keeping warm.

"Take me down the mine, Roger," he said, "before I freeze to death here. You've been working but I haven't."

"Come along then," said Madin, leading the way. "After the next sack we will go."

A rope and pulley tackle was suspended over the hole and every few minutes a sack, appearing as if from nowhere, was unhooked by a worker who transferred it to the waiting sled. Empty sacks were also making their appearance from the other direction, heading towards the working face.

"Be careful to place your feet firmly in the prepared footholds," said Madin as he disappeared. Dick followed. The shaft was well lit and was about three feet square. It was lined with a timber framework, and a rope, attached at intervals to the frames, served to steady the climber. Dick descended warily, using the easily recognised, well worn footholds on the frames where the rock had been hollowed out so that the toes could take a good bite. A fall

here would be dangerous. When he reached the bottom Dick looked up. The top seemed to be miles above him. A sack full of stones was swinging in mid air half-way up the shaft. Dick turned to Madin:

"I see now why you all wear tin hats. I wouldn't like to get a rock on my head from twenty feet, not to mention a half hundred-weight sack."

The Frenchman who was hauling on the tackle grinned. He understood enough English to know what Dick was talking about. He remarked in French:

"*Je ne permet à personne d'enlever les sacs sauf celui qui est là haut. J'ai plein confiance en lui!*"

Dick nodded expressively looking upwards. He was wondering what it would feel like to walk in the open air again. Here in the bowels of the earth, surrounded by tons upon tons of rock, a sudden fear gripped him. He wanted to breathe freely and expand his chest but was cramped and confined by the forbidding walls closing in upon him from every side.

"Good God!" he thought. "I'm getting claustrophobia."

In spite of himself the thoughts recurred. "One fall of rock would be enough; we could never get out. The air in here would only last half an hour with all these bodies around. A self-made tomb in just the right place," he muttered, "underneath the chapel."

He followed the tunnel forward. Madin had vanished. He soon saw why. There was a staircase ahead of him. He had to squirm himself round so that he lay on his stomach with his feet facing downhill. He descended steps, cut out of the layers of stratified rock, until he reached a new level five feet lower. Here he turned himself round again and crawled forward on his hands and knees. The tunnel was now of more spacious dimensions and he could kneel almost upright on the floor. Tunnellers could pass one another, and half a dozen men were hard at work filling sacks with rubble which was piled to the roof at one side as far as Dick could see. Madin was a long way ahead beckoning to him. Then he disappeared again.

Dick followed as quickly as he could, greeting the Frenchmen one after the other. They were working at top pressure filling the blue and white check sacks as fast as they could, then tying them with cords already sewn into the tops and stacking them ready for departure. They were dripping with perspiration and Dick asked one of them:

"Why don't you take off your shirts?"

"*C'est dangereux*," came the reply, "*aussitôt qu'on arrète, même pour un instant, on attraperait froid si on n'est pas bien habillé.*"

Dick arrived at the end and found himself looking down another shaft. He counted. "That's the third shaft in this tunnel," he thought, "not counting the clock tower. The place is just a rabbit warren."

A large square wooden tub rose up towards him from the depths, hoisted by another pulley tackle. As it came to the surface the Frenchman next to him unhitched it, emptied it to the side of the tunnel, hooked it on again, and the tub descended. Not a word was spoken. Unseen hands worked the lift from below. The operation had become mechanical.

Dick followed the tub, descending carefully one foot at a time. This shaft was not so deep, about eight feet, Dick estimated. He could see that he was nearing the working face. Rubble, earth and large rocks were cluttering up the passage, making progress difficult. Three men were at work filling wooden boxes as fast as they could, while a fourth carried them and emptied them into the tub on the lift. Dick passed them, caught up with Madin, and looked beyond him.

There was Gigue hard at work on the tunnel face in front. He was digging in comparatively loose earth and rock with a short-handled spade. It was coming away easily and he was working so fast that there were not enough wooden boxes to keep him supplied and he was piling earth up behind him, leaving it to his mates to clear away.

Gigue turned a sweating countenance towards them and flashed a broad smile at Dick. He wiped his face with a piece of towelling, "What do you think now, Dick? If we can get enough timber for the roof we shall finish in a week. The digging is easy, but it is dangerous too, without supports. It could easily fall in."

"I'm lost in admiration," Dick replied facetiously, "but not only in admiration. I've been up and down, backwards and forwards so often I'm lost in any other way you like to think."

"You see the tunnel just behind you. It's completely timbered— floor, walls and roof—you notice? Well, we had to do that. It is the most dangerous section of all. It is under very old foundations which are loose. There are some big stones above and there is not much holding them."

"Thanks for telling me. I shall move faster next time," said Dick feelingly. "Where exactly are we?"

"We are outside the wire and approaching the side of the

valley which drops down to the stream in the wood. We should surface in about twelve metres."

"You deserve to have a break after all this," said Dick. "I've never seen a tunnel like it."

Gigue was patting affectionately a steel bar an inch and a half thick and four feet long. "Flynn's bar," he said, "The most useful tool we have."

At that moment the lights went out.

"Great Cæsar's ghost," said Dick, "what happens now?"

The lights flashed on again. Then "off" and "on" a second time.

"That means there is a German patrol in the courtyard," explained Madin. As he said the words, the lights blinked three times in quick succession then went out completely.

"Danger! Stop work! remain quiet!" whispered Madin. "The Jerries must be heading either for the chapel or for the cellar, probably the chapel. They suspect the chapel very much. They have heard our digging but cannot trace it. All they know is that it is in this region. I suppose their instruments cannot get close enough. We are very deep here.　　"

They sat huddled in total darkness at the end of the tunnel for ten minutes waiting for the "all clear". Dick was catching cold rapidly. Madin, beside him, was shivering. The lights suddenly went on again. Everybody breathed a sigh of relief but remained motionless. The lights might signal again. They remained steady and bright. After a further minute, the tunnellers started moving, stretching cramped limbs, blowing on their hands, massaging and rubbing.

Work was resumed at full pressure. Dick looked at his watch and gasped as he realised how quickly time had passed. It was three a.m.

Madin now took over from Gigue at the working face, and Gigue said to Dick:

"Come back with me to the sacristy junction. There is more room there. We are in the way here if we are not working. We can eat something up there and relax for a moment."

They both set off, Gigue going first. Dick followed closely, looking upwards now and then through the cracks between the boards—bed-boards, of course, he noted, almost subconsciously —to see whether any large rock was about to tear through the timber crushing him to pulp in its fall. They passed the danger zone and retraced their steps to the "junction" as they had come.

Dick breathed a sigh of relief as they reached it. He was warm again from climbing and crawling, and he was feeling hungry. He had come provided for this. Seated with his back against one of the heavy chapel timbers, he removed a bright yellow handkerchief, that had once been khaki, from the pocket of his rugger shorts, and, unfolding it gently, revealed a thick sandwich composed of two slices of German bread enclosing a slab of Canadian cheese.

Gigue was not slow to follow him. His equally cumbersome sandwich, however, did not contain cheese but a thick, strongly smelling paste. They munched in silence for a while. Then Dick's curiosity made him ask, "What's that high smelling paste you've got, Gigue?"

"It's home-made *foie gras*," said Gigue. "I make it out of everything that's left. It smell's good, doesn't it?"

"I'm not so sure," Dick replied. "If it tastes as it smells, I think it should make excellent manure."

"You don't know what's good," said Gigue.

Together they sat for a while, each wrapped in his own thoughts. Dick was reflecting upon the extraordinary twist of fate that could bring about the present situation; a Londoner, and a Frenchman from Marseilles a thousand miles away, sitting side by side eating sandwiches in a burrow underneath the floor of a fifteenth century chapel in a medieval castle in the middle of Germany. How would it end, this great upheaval of mankind all over the world? Would he ever come out of it alive? Dick questioned and, as always, reached the usual conclusion: "Probably not. The Nazis will see to it—the lousy bunch of gangsters."

In spite of the cold he began to feel drowsy. The rumble of the sleds and the pulleys was monotonous and the sacks passed interminably before his eyes. Gigue was already asleep. Dick dozed fitfully, shifting uncomfortably now and then, growing steadily stiffer with cold and cramp. At one point he awoke and noticed Gigue had gone. Then dozed again, as he thought, for five minutes. . . .

Madin was shaking him.

"Wake up, Dick, it's time to go," he said. "Follow me."

The shift had ended, and the tunnellers were filing past, one after the other, on their hands and knees. Madin and Dick joined the queue.

At six-thirty a.m. Dick found himself, once more, out on the landing at the top of the French staircase. It was all so strange. He felt as if he had been living for months in the tunnel and he

had to pull himself together to realise where he was. In Gigue's dormitory he was given a mug of hot coffee. He drank it quickly, lay back on an empty bed and fell fast asleep.

Three days later the fate of the tunnel hung in the balance. According to the French, one of their own men, who had gone to Oflag IV.D, had talked too loudly or too openly about a French tunnel at Colditz which started on the top floor. The Germans were after it in earnest. Search followed upon search. Work on the tunnel had to cease completely with only five more yards to dig, to finish it. The situation was ominous.

Then there was peace for three days. Work started again—cautiously. But the Germans had not finished. Gephard made a surprise attack. He probed the long weight sleeves in the clock tower, he could see nothing as he flashed his torch down into the darkness, but there were men below. He sent a messenger out to the Kommandantur by the hand of the sentry who was with him. Had he heard a movement? A cough maybe?

Within ten minutes several Goons appeared with a small boy amongst them. A coil of rope was produced. The boy, a fair haired young Teuton, pale and tembling with fright, suffered the rope to be tied around his waist. He was led to one of the sleeves. With promises and blandishments he was encouraged to descend. He was lowered slowly through the sleeve into the blackness below. In his hand he carried a torch which he aimed at the floor beneath him. As he landed he flashed the torch around him and screamed in terror.

"*Hilfe! Hilfe! Es gibt Leute!*"

There were three Frenchmen in the chamber. Gephard was occupying the only exit. The Frenchmen knew of a last desperate way out. At one corner of the chamber, a comparatively thin wall, nine inches thick, separated them from a bathroom used by patients from the sick ward.

As the terrified youth, sobbing with fright and shouting, "Hilfe", was hauled up again through the sleeve, the Frenchmen attacked the dividing wall with crowbars like demons and, in five minutes, had battered a hole through it. The noise they made was deafening, yet the Germans above them were so occupied with the youth that, when they awoke to reality and sent search parties in frantic haste to locate the new hole being pierced with all the publicity of a battery of pneumatic drills, they were too late. The birds had flown.

A Belgian army Major, Baron Lindkerke, was peacefully reading

a book, lying in his bath, when the earthquake started. The wall beside him began to pulsate and heave. Long cracks appeared, accompanied by earsplitting crashes from the other side. A brick shot out of the wall into the bath, landing on his stomach. "It was time," he thought, "to evacuate. Something was under pressure at the other side and an explosion would occur at any moment."

He rose from the bath and reached for his towel. Plaster was flying in all directions, and brickbats were leaping outwards splashing into the bath around him. A jagged hole suddenly appeared. Iron bars flayed the opening, enlarging it. As he stepped from the bath, a head and shoulders came through the opening. Then a half naked body scrambled over the bath on to the floor, bespattered, sweatstained and dirty. Another body followed and then a third, more bulky than the others. It had difficulty in squeezing through and fell into the bath.

Major Linkerke picked up his belongings and rushed from the room shouting: "*Mon Dieu! Mon Dieu! c'est le comble!*" Which translated means, "My God! My God! this is the end!"

Soon the whole Kommandantur was alerted. Squads of workmen appeared with crowbars, pick-axes and sledge hammers. The chambers at each successive floor were broken into and the finger of fate pointed ever downwards to the cellar.

For a time the French hoped that the Germans would not find the tunnel entrance in the cellar; but alas! the scent was now too strong. The Germans were hot on the trail. The cellar was combed from end to end. Every inch of wall was sounded. No camouflage could stand up to German thoroughness indefinitely.

The next day the news came through: "They've found it!" That was all that was said. With those few words disappeared the hopes of more than a hundred Frenchmen. So many dreams smashed, so much yearning for the sunny lands of France; so many wives who would never hear the sound of a familiar voice on the threshold; so many hours, days, and months of dangerous toil, for nothing.

And through it all came the voice of the French conscience: "Was it our own fault? Was our stooging at fault? Were we too confident?" Like the masters of the Titanic, they had thought their ship could not founder.

THE PARCEL OFFICE

THE French were still leaving. Throughout the Spring of 1943 the rumour persisted. They were repeatedly warned they were going. One day it was, "*Nous partons demain*,"—the next day it was, "*Non! pas aujourd'hui, mais dans une semaine—certes—par nos tuyeaux l'information est toujours juste*."

They packed and unpacked many times; their *couvertures*, and rucksacks, their *valises* and portmanteaux, their *pousettes*— push chairs and prams. Some were glad to go, looking forward to the move as a relief from the overpowering walls of Colditz. Many of the French Jews saw the writing on the wall and were, quite legitimately, not so keen. Men like Gigue and Madin would leave with mixed feelings. They would have more opportunities in another camp—but not the same atmosphere. . . .

A dead Goon was found in the parcel office one morning. There was a bullet wound in his chest and his revolver lay beside him. The Germans said he had committed suicide. The question they never answered was: "What was he doing in there, locked up for the night amongst the parcels belonging to the prisoners?"

The dead German was removed from the parcel office without ceremony and hurried out of the courtyard. Few prisoners were about at the time. The Germans chose their moment. The mystery was never solved and the reader, with this outline before him, knows as much as at least ninety-nine out of each hundred prisoners at Colditz. The odd ones are not talking. . . . The author is not one of them.

The office was naturally a focus of interest among the prisoners and many would have liked to have access to it. The entrance, however, gave straight on to the courtyard and on to the beats of two sentries placed there day and night.

During 1942, the British had been greatly troubled by the installation of an X-ray machine in the parcel office. Most valuable contraband material was lost, which, incidentally, never came in Red Cross parcels at any time throughout the whole war. The contents of other parcels, if in the least suspected, were passed across the X-ray screen which showed up secret cavities or metallic objects. The British quarters were a long way from

the parcel office, and nothing much could be done about it. A burglar alarm in the guardhouse, wired from each of the two locks on the entrance door warned the Germans of any tampering. They installed it so secretly that the fact was not known for a long time. The Germans were obviously taking no risks.

Parcels were normally opened on a long counter behind a grill: suspected items were submitted to X-ray and then the contents passed to the recipient through the grill, which was opened for the operation and shut again immediately afterwards. The opening and shutting of the grill for every parcel was an unmitigated nuisance. The German N.C.O.s on parcel duty agreed with the prisoners on this point and occasionally became lax.

Some days after the dead Goon had been removed, the British were drawing parcels. Lulu was "Parcels Officer" at the time. He had been planted there because contraband was expected. Bill Fowler, who had escaped from Colditz in September 1942 was, by this time, in France. Lulu's official duty as Parcels Officer was to be present at the opening of all parcels—a witness for the defence. The job was intriguing for the first twenty parcels or so and thereafter became steadily more boring until, at the end of a fortnight, "one grew a beard" as the French would say.

John Hyde-Thompson stood in the parcel queue on this particular day because the parcel list, posted on the notice board outside the office, had his name upon it. He arrived in front of the open grill. An N.C.O., known as "Nichtwar!" because of his irritating habit of ending every sentence with this ejaculation and who had the local reputation of being a Gestapo man, searched among the stack for John's parcel. It was unearthed and opened on the counter in front of him. Lulu stood beside him. His thoughts at that moment were in the Yorkshire Dales.

As the seals were broken and the maltreated cardboard cover burst asunder, there was a clatter of steel on the counter which brought Lulu's reverie to an end as conclusively as might a clap of thunder. John Hyde-Thompson was expecting warm woolly underwear and some good books. Lulu was not expecting the consignment which was on the counter at that particular moment. Wires had crossed somewhere.

He was not going to be outdone, however. Before the grill could be slapped down, he enfolded the parcel in his arms and was careering out of the office door as an astonished Goon held aloft a brand new pair of wire cutters, screaming, " *Halt! Halt!*" and struggling with the pistol in his holster.

Lulu was too quick for them all. He tore across the courtyard, as German banknotes fell like autumn leaves in his wake. Not a shot was fired. Up the spiral stairs he ran and collapsed at the top of seventy steps, shouting for help. Willing hands took over, and the contents were distributed and hidden within a few minutes —long before the pursuing riot squad was able to mount the stairs and seal the doorways into the various quarters.

Lulu Lawton

The spectacle in the courtyard after the meteoric passage of Lulu was out of the dream world of a prisoner in a high fever. The two sentries in the yard stood transfixed. They had never, in their whole careers as soldiers and P.O.W. guards, been given instructions as to what to do when German banknotes rain like confetti around prisoners of war, whose principal aim in life is to have enough money to travel as fast as possible out of Germany.

The notes were like manna from heaven. Prisoners, who had, one second before, been ambling aimlessly around the yard in their clogs and khaki overcoats, did not take long to realise, unlike the sentry, that they had witnessed a miracle and had suddenly become the chosen people. As Lulu disappeared through the staircase doorway there was a rush, and before the sentries could gather their wits together there was not a note to be seen.

A search followed, but nothing was found. The Germans were disillusioned. So many searches had yielded so little that searching had become a disheartening pastime. Since Priem's nocturnal visit in 1941 when his hatchet, tearing some floor boards asunder, had impaled a trilby hat concealed underneath, the Germans had had no luck. But the initial search after this episode would not be the end of the matter. A report would go eventually to the Gestapo. The Castle was heading for another ransacking, of this there was no doubt.

Lulu Lawton was removed from his post and sentenced to a month's solitary confinement. The contraband parcel contained everything that an escaper dreamt of, from wire cutters, files and dyes to cameras and photographic materials.

This kind of bull in the china shop operation, however, frankly disgusted Gigue. He had an advantage, of course, in that he lived in the French quarters over the parcel office, but, to be perfectly honest, he returned the compliment the British had paid his countrymen in connection with the theatre light well escape—with interest. As a parting gift before he left, in addition to the secret wireless set, he bequeathed to Dick his method of entering the parcel office.

Gigue had spirited seventy parcels out of the parcels office for his two wireless sets alone. He had caused no rumpus, no publicity, and had lost nothing.

First of all, he manufactured his own cruciform keys for the two parcel office locks. The cruciform lock is roughly equivalent to four different Yale locks rolled into one. While the office was open and in use, he had searched for, and discovered, the carefully concealed wiring of the burglar alarm system. This travelled, at one stage, along the ceiling under an electric light tube conduit. Gigue made a careful survey. Any civil engineer would have been proud of his work. Under the floorboards of his own quarters, he pierced a minute hole through the plaster of the ceiling below, immediately over the alarm wires. He then tapped the wires and, manufacturing his own switch, he placed it in the circuit. He could thus control the burglar alarm system at will.

The method of operating his switch was equally ingenious. The switch was fixed under the floor boards which were replaced permanently and made to look as if they had not been touched for fifty years. A hole, about one eighth of an inch in diameter, was pierced through the board directly over the switch, which was then operated through the board by employing a long thin

electrician's screwdriver. When camouflaged, it was impossible
for anyone to find this hole unless he possessed the secret of the
measurements from two recognisable points in the floor.

Gigue's method of entering the canteen was simple enough
when carried out with a first class team. It consisted of providing
distraction for the two courtyard sentries, while Gigue manipulated the keys with the help of two assistants at the parcel
office door.

Dick initiated a team of his own into the secrets of the parcel
office, and, when the French left in the summer of 1943 this team
carried on successfully until the end of the war. The British had
no further trouble in removing such parcels as they required, at
will.

Dick's key assistant, in both senses of the word, was Vincent
or 'Bush' Parker, an Australian and a Flight Lieutenant in the
R.A.F. He might equally well have been called "Fingers" Parker
for his wits and his hands were as quick as lightning. He learnt
to handle locks with consummate skill. Bush was a colourful
character, which makes it worth digressing to shine the spotlight
upon him. Colditz would not have been quite what it was if Bush
had not been there, and his activities throw a revealing sidelight
upon the life of the prison.

Bush was well knit and strong, a good athlete and an outstanding
stool-ball player. Though not more than five feet seven inches tall,
he was handsome with the features of a young Adonis and a winning smile which showed off his fine teeth. Black wavy hair crowned
his classic shaped head. He had a charming manner which must
have made him the complete lady killer in those happy far off days
when ' Bush' was a Battle of Britain Spitfire pilot.

All that he could exert his charm on now was the sour, sensible
Oberstabsfeldwebel Gephard from whom he could wheedle more
of the rationed coal than anyone else in the camp. Gephard thought
the world of him and the coal came in handy. Bush was one of
the three directors of the British Distillery Monopoly, which
developed by the natural process of free enterprise, unhindered
by anti-cartel laws and appreciated by the drinking public because
of the excellent service rendered.

Bush was definitely talented. He was an amateur card sharper
of the highest professional standing!

One evening Dick sat in, as sixth player, in a regular poker
school of five. The other players were "Rex" Harrison of the

Green Howards, head escape tailor, six foot two in his socks, an indefatigable worker for the escapes of others and unfailingly good humoured; "Bag" Dickenson, a Bomber pilot in the R.A.F., second director of the British Distilling Monopoly; "Bush" Parker; Teddy Barton, the camp theatrical producer; and Scarlet O'Hara making up the sixth.

After a quarter of an hour's desultory play, Bush whispered to Dick:

"Watch this one carefully," as he started to deal.

Dick found himself, after the deal, with the Ace, King, Queen of hearts and two nondescript cards. The pool was opened with four players, Bush and Teddy Barton throwing in their hands.

Dick was watching Bush. He asked for two cards. Picking them up he found he had the knave and ten of hearts. A Royal straight flush—unbeatable !

Bag Dickenson drew two cards, Rex drew two and Scarlet three. The bidding started with Rex making the running. Dick tagged along and Scarlet soon fell out. When the "raises" reached a hundred *Marks* (about £7) a time, Bag looked worried and said to Rex, "I warn you, I've got a power house."

Neither of them seemed interested in Dick who stayed in, and the bidding continued. Finally, coming to the fore, Dick raised another hundred, whereupon Bag said, "I'll see you."

But Rex was not satisfied. He began another raising spree—two hundred Marks this time—putting three hundred into the pool.

A few onlookers had gathered round the table. There were nearly two thousand *Lagermarks* in the pool. This was worth £140 which in Colditz, was no mean kitty on a single hand.

Dick and Bag called a truce and "saw" Rex who laid down on the table three aces and two kings.

"You're daft," said Bag, "raising like that on a full house. I've got fours," and he put down four nines. He had drawn a nine and another to fill three nines.

Bag could see the *Lagermarks* already in his wallet—and began to pick them up when Rex asked casually:

"What did you have, Dick?"

Dick replied by firmly removing Bag's hand from the pile of notes saying, "Just hold everything chaps for one moment. I think you'd like to see this," and he laid down his "Royal"!

All the prisoners in the room gathered around the table to see the hands as the immediate onlookers announced jubilantly to the world, "Boys, come and look! Dick's drawn a Royal Straight Flush!"

Bush and Dick roared with laughter as they saw the look of utter disappointment on Bag's face, and Rex sat back, stunned.

Bush spent much of his time teasing Bag and this occasion was a high-light. When he had pulled his leg enough about his four nines power house, Bush and Dick revealed the conspiracy and all the cash was refunded.

Not for one moment throughout the dealing and playing of the hand had the players suspected anything and Dick, who tried hard to see how Bush manipulated the cards, was none the wiser.

Dick could rest with an easy mind, assured that the parcel office keys were in good hands.

The others of the parcel office team were 'Mike' Harvey, a Lieutenant of the Royal Navy, Lulu Lawton, 'Checko,' the Black Marketeer, two stooges and Dick. They started the habit of sitting on the office steps to read and chat, so that, eventually, when the French left, sentries would be accustomed to seeing Englishmen seated where, formerly, Frenchmen had had the priority. The team-work was interchangeable among the four assistants who distracted the two courtyard sentries, warned against patrols, and passed the "all clear" to Bush and Dick at the door. Bush performed the opening and closing ceremony. Dick slipped inside to seek out the parcel to be smuggled. The relocking of the door was carried out in the same manner as the opening and the complete operation usually required not less than an hour, giving Dick twenty minutes inside the office.

CHAPTER VII

ATMOSPHERE

AN atmosphere can cling to a building just as cobwebs to its walls. It is intangible but it is there. In the years to come, man will, doubtlessly, invent instruments of such finesse that they will be able to pick up sound waves emitted in a room centuries before. The voices of great men of the past will be recaptured by detectors of microscopic accuracy, magnified and broadcast.

If man can measure the amount of heat radiated by a candle at a distance of a mile, if he can prise open the oyster of the atom,

it is only a matter of time before he will hear the voices of the past talking in the present.

Dogs have been known to return home hundreds of miles across country; pigeons fly homeward across the seas. Animals can smell what man cannot smell, and hear sounds that man cannot hear.

The human brain is found to emit wireles waves; if it can emit surely it can receive.

The scientific explanation of the working of the refined senses, of instincts, and of the brain, is writ large inside a deep scientific tome of which this generation is now opening the introductory pages.

Certain of man's senses have been dulled. One of them is the ability to appreciate consciously the proximity of fellow beings in the present, not to mention out of the past, without the aid of the simpler senses which remain man's standby—sight and hearing and the nervous system.

Yet, dulled as the senses have been, something remains; an inchoate attribute by which man can sense vaguely what he commonly calls "atmosphere". Undoubtedly, much that provides the reaction in human beings which is often loosely termed the sixth sense, comes into the brain subconsciously through the other senses. The eyes, particularly, will take in much more than is consciously registered by the brain and will perform unconscious permutations and combinations with memories much like a calculating machine. The answer is then handed over to the conscious mind which registers "an atmosphere". At the same time, almost certainly, this other indefinable attribute reacts within the brain.

Colditz had an atmosphere. Naturally a castle that had stood for centuries would. But it was not the atmosphere of antiquity, of the passage of history within its walls that struck every new arrival upon entering the courtyard.

Colditz had more recently been a lunatic asylum. There was a weird, bleak and depressing air about the place which struck the newcomer so forcibly that he knew, without being told, that the Castle must have been filled at one time by a great sadness.

It was not the place to encourage a sane outlook upon life. The high, dun coloured walls surrounding the tiny cobbled yard; the barred windows—even those opening on to the yard were barred; the steep roofs which hung precipitously overhead; the endless clack-clack of wooden sabots; the cacophony of voices in different languages and musical instruments in different keys, were not calculated to breed contentment or resignation. As a lunatic

asylum it had never been a sanatorium where insanity might hope to be cured. It could only have been a home for incurables and a dungeon for the violent.

Into this prison the Germans threw the men who, of all the prisoners of war in Germany, were the most likely to chafe and strain and pine under the stifling confinement of its oppressive walls. Those who had found resignation were not for Colditz. Those who had broken their chains and would continue to do so, filtered into the Castle.

Colditz was a fruitful breeding ground for frustration and might easily become a prison full of mentally unbalanced men.

How easily it might happen is illustrated by the proportionately large number of officers who actually became unbalanced. The development of the malady could be seen and the symptoms usually followed a regular course. The process was known as "going round the bend". It started, commonly, with a passion for classical music, often followed by a demoniacal lust for physical training, after which the particular form of "unbalance" of the individual developed—plain for all to see.

In one, it would be sheer violence and the officer became a danger to his fellows, but even more so to the Germans. A sentry was the "red rag to a bull", and the demented prisoner would have to be held down by friends to stop him from hurling crockery, bottles, anything that came to hand, at the victim of his 'hate' complex. In another, it would take a suicidal turn. These two forms were the most trying for the community. The Germans were appallingly slow in taking action to remove the sufferers to a proper house of treatment and in the intervening months, a constant guard had to be maintained by the prisoners themselves which wore down resistance to a malady that almost became infectious.

Other forms of unbalance were as innocent as they were amusing, but their general affect was not to fortify the sanity of the other prisoners.

One would become eternally sullen and develop a baleful glare. It was disconcerting to a man, sometimes consciously aware of his own liability to "go round the bend", to be fixed by this stony and hypnotic gaze. Thoughts of the fabled "Old Man of the Sea" mingled with an uncontrollable desire to run. The glassy eyes could change their expression from mild to murderous without a flicker.

One officer of this type retained a devilish sense of humour,

D

concentrating on the German sentries in the courtyard. He would approach one of them stealthily and fix him with his stare. The sentry was not aware of the attack until he turned and faced him. For a full minute their eyes met as the satanic hypnotist scowled at him. Then, with no warning, the insane one suddenly leapt high into the air and the unnerved Jerry jumped equally high in sheer terror. The lunatic then walked off, quite unconcerned. Eventually, the sentries grew accustomed to this treatment. When they did, our man ceased to plague them.

Another "leg-puller" type made a habit of puffing smoke from a filthy home-made cheroot in the faces of the same unfortunate sentries. Having done so, he flicked the ash off his cigar on to the cobbles in front of the sentry, then produced a dustpan and brush from behind his back, swept up the offending ash and marched off to the dustbins.

A soulful, melancholy type used to play the guitar for hours in the bathroom, seated on a stool with his head inside an empty suitcase. This officer was once removed to a hospital where he displayed remarkably good sense by denuding the hospital garden, in one night, of a good crop of ripening tomatoes.

Yet another type gave up washing and became so filthy that he was not allowed to eat at table. He sat cross-legged all day long on the top of a seven foot cupboard, occasionally eating from a bowl a nauseating mixture of his own concoction consisting of egg-powder and an inedible semi-dried vegetable, a German issue, called "Rabbi" which the prisoners normally used for stuffing pillows and mattresses.

The Germans did nothing about the "wackys" unless they were violent, and then only after several years. Others, they picked out, like the guitarist, as if they were picking an apple out of a basketful. There was no logic in their methods. One officer, who was not mad, pretended to be so following medical advice as to symptoms and behaviour. The "fake" lunatic, after nearly a year, became discouraged and returned to normal. The attempt was known only to Dick Howe and a doctor. The community, as a whole, considered him a genuine "round the bend" and were encouraged at the sight of a recovery.

Then there was the religious maniac of the proselytising variety who unlocked the staircase door in the dead of night and sallied forth into the lamplit courtyard where only the sentries monotonously paced their beat. Dressed in a flowing sackcloth robe and holding aloft a large wooden cross of his own manufacture, he

recalled the world to prayer in loud, ringing tones, chastising the
stolid sentries with his tongue, accusing them of dreadful sins and
demanding their immediate submission and repentance.

*   *   *   *   *

Each prisoner had his own personal struggle and suffered his
own fears. In the silence of the night, in fitful sleep, they rose
uncontrolled to take on grotesque proportions. Waking from
dreams of long unending tunnels, of the search for an opening
that never appeared, tearing at stones with bare hands, lying prone
in the clammy earth amidst worms and maggots, queer thoughts
came uninvited. Waking from a nightmare race, thrashing the
blankets, cursing, sweating and gasping for breath, fleeing for life,
always uphill, with the Jerries close behind; hearing their shouts
merge into the *crescendoes* of the proselytising preacher in the
echoing courtyard, then melt away into silence; no! not peaceful
silence, but another sound, travelling upwards through the windows, along the searchlight beams, the pad—pad—pad of the
enemy—a sentry on his beat; at such a time men wondered if
they were sane. The preacher in the yard might be funny no
longer, the joke had lost its savour. Lying awake on his straw
palliasse in the eerie half light a prisoner could see himself swaying
on the tight rope of sanity, could visualise himself bearing down
on the sentries with a cross or sitting like a buddha on the top of a
cupboard.

Such moments were the testing time and much depended on the
prisoner's reaction. A sense of humour was a healing balm of in-
calculable worth. If a man could laugh at the vision of himself
seated cross-legged on top of a cupboard, it was as if he tore himself clear of the encircling tentacles of a strangling octopus. He
promptly slept and woke up refreshed in the morning. If he did
not laugh a red light glowed threateningly before him. Soon he
would not dream his nightmares. They would begin to occupy the
stage of his conscious, wakeful mind. He would rise in the morning
nervous, irritable and depressed. That way lay danger.

Of all the qualities that make for sanity in such surroundings a
sense of humour stands paramount. Thank God there was no lack
of it at Colditz! It was small wonder that men returned in spirit to
their boyhood days and took refuge in the antics of a schoolboy.
What can be saner than a schoolboy!

The masters had guns instead of canes and might use them; the
antics had a steely edge to their humorous side, but that way,

nevertheless, lay sanity. The majority of the prisoners of Colditz instinctively found comfort and solace in the carefree, day to day psychological outlook of the schoolboy. It was another of the many secrets that the Castle held; a secret that the prisoners did not whisper about, for the simple reason that they were unaware of it.

CHAPTER VIII

THE COCOA 'V'

IN spite of a few deceptive spring-like days in February, winter took a firm grip upon the Castle in the early months of 1943; it was proving to be worse than the last. It was the winter of Fate for the Germans in Russia: the siege of Stalingrad.

There was less coal for the prisoners; fewer bed boards that could be removed with safety from beds for fire wood. Relief from perpetual shivering was only obtained by retiring under the blankets. Rations deteriorated further. The most plentiful food consisted of sugar beet residue, dyed red and brought into the camp in barrels labelled, "*Nur für Kriegsgefangener*"—only for P.O.W.s. It was issued as a jam ration and was uneatable.

In these conditions of cold and hunger the German Commandant decided to alleviate the lot of the P.O.W.s by purchasing a luxuriously complete and up to date equipment for the barber's shop. The finance was provided by what was known as "The Commandant's Fund", which depended, for its revenue, on canteen profits.

One frosty morning, a decorator's van arrived, accompanied by a representative of the contractors, a civilian plumber, a fitter and four sentries. Such an exciting intrusion was a gala occasion for the prisoners. To look upon civilians, to see a civilian lorry, why! if a prisoner were to put his fingers in his ears so that he did not hear the clack-clack of wooden clogs nor the guttural sound of German voices; if he half closed his eyes so that he saw nothing beyond the lorry—neither the field grey nor the khaki around him; and if only he could stop shivering, why! he could imagine himself standing on the pavement in Regent Street beside a lorry drawn up at the kerb; a real live motor vehicle—a delivery van. Such a phenomenon was only seen in Colditz once a year, if that.

Enough of day-dreaming. There was work to do. The four sentries would require a considerable amount of skilful distraction. That merely meant a little more exercise for the talents of men like Scarlet O'Hara, Rex Harrison, Bush Parker, Peter Storie Pugh and Scorgie Price.

While the contractor and his men disappeared for a moment into the barber's shop. Rex and Peter, looking like Mut and Jeff—Peter was not much taller than "the medium sized man"—on their way to commit a burglary, set about deflating one of the back tyres. They did not succeed because they were not meant to. Instead they started a loud argument in bad German with the two near side guards protesting that they were only interested in the type of tyre and the shape of the wheel, which, they maintained with significant gestures, was not round. This brought the other two sentries over to the near side of the car which was the signal for redoubled angry protestations while, on the off side Scarlet removed the road maps from under the driver's seat and Bush Parker disappeared with the tools. It was on an occasion similar to this, a year before, that "Errol" Flynn, a Flying officer in the R.A.F., had "won" the four-foot long crowbar which earned him a place on the fated French tunnel.

The contractor's men reappeared as Peter and Rex concluded their harangue and walked away exuding an aura of righteous indignation.

The workmen opened the van and began to off-load a highly polished adjustable barber's chair. Scarlet, returning to the scene, noted a hydraulic jack reposing on the floor of the van not far from the doors. The two sentries on normal duty in the yard stationed on the near side of the lorry, could see the open van doors. Rex and Peter were sent off to distract them, while Bush Parker and Scorgie Price took over the two sentries at the rear of the van.

The secret of the operation is synchronisation. It is impossible to distract a person and to keep an eye on three or four other people as well. It is difficult enough to look at one person out of the corner of an eye while concentrating upon a second, the sentry. Scarlet only has to watch one of the other four, namely Bush Parker nearby. Bush cannot see Scorgie at the far side of the van but only has to watch Rex, Rex watches Scorgie, Scorgie watches Peter, and Peter watches Scarlet. The circle is complete.

Peter, furthest away from the scene, starts the action upon a signal from Scarlet who then turns his gaze on Bush. Peter, facing

so that he can see Scarlet, stops in front of his sentry who is momentarily standing at ease and begins talking to him mockingly about Stalingrad. The sentry is not supposed to talk, is confused and turns to march away which is what is required. Peter follows him still talking. Scorgie has now started work upon his sentry. He has a book in his hand. He is looking at a funny picture and roaring with laughter. His sentry can only half see the picture and is tortured with curiosity. Rex has seen the effect of Scorgie's effort and busies himself beside his sentry whittling a curiously shaped piece of wood. The sentry is intrigued. Bush then comes into action by showing his sentry a card trick. Scarlet vaults quickly into the van, seizes the jack, jumps off and walks casually away with it under his coat. This action is completed in five seconds. Peter has seen Scarlet walk off and retires. The others follow.

Later, when the balloon goes up, the sentries will all swear they never took their eyes off the van.

Having removed the jack, handle and all, Scarlet now contemplated "winning" a wheel. He needed a heavy fly wheel for a lathe he was manufacturing. The rubber tyre and tube would always come in useful. The wheel brace was among the tools already taken. An offside back wheel would give his stooges an opportunity of practising their art upon the two sentries on the off side of the van.

The wheel nuts are loosened first. They are very resistant. A new distraction has to be brought into action at five minute intervals for each nut. The whole operation will take well over half an hour. . . .

The German contractor's representative, in a "natty" suit, long green heavy tweed overcoat with a strap at the back and a dark green homberger hat, was busy supervising the unloading and transporting of his equipment into the room which was to be transformed into the palatial barber's shop. He did not become aware of the gradual disintegration of his lorry for some time. Then, suddenly, he missed the jack which he had seen not half an hour before. He gave tongue in no ordinary manner. He screamed with anger and his invective was aimed, mostly and quite rightly, at the German guards. He demanded that the security officer be fetched at once. Scarlet had to give up his task of wheel removing—with the job only half done. Four of the five nuts holding one rear wheel had been removed. Nobody noticed it. Scarlet thought it might be tactless to point out the fact.

"It would be more reasonable," he said, "if the Goonery let me finish the job. Then they would notice the wheel missing and put on the spare which is chained inside the van. It would save the back axle anyway," he continued. "I hate to think what's going to happen after a few hundred yards running."

Sadly Scarlet returned to the British quarters carrying under his coat three bricks on to which he was going to lower the brake drum. He had no intention of leaving the jack.

Hauptman Eggers was apparently not available. Instead Hauptman (Rittmeister) Lange, another security officer, arrived on the scene with another sentry. He and the irate civilian retired to the *Evidenz Zimmer*—the interview room—which had just been swept out for the day. The civilian, taking off his green homberger, put it on a table near the half open window. He did not remove his coat as it was too cold. The sentry stood at the door. A heated discussion took place. Rex Harrison took the opportunity to remove the hat with the aid of a long piece of wire passed through the bars of the window.

The civilian was gradually mollified by promises from Hauptman Lange that a search would be conducted and restitution made. He turned to pick up his hat and leave the room. He stood with mouth agape for several seconds, then raised his clenched fists above his head and turned his goggling eyes heavenwards.

"*Was ist es?*" asked Lange innocently.

"*Mein Hut! Mein Hut!*" screamed the German, stamping his foot in a fury. "*Es war bestimmt hier—Donnerwetter—eine neue Schweinerei! Mein Hut ist jetzt verschwunden. Ich bin in einem Verücktenanstalt gekommen.*" He stormed out of the *Evidenz Zimmer*, shouting for his driver to come immediately and take him out of the madhouse while the lorry still had four wheels and an engine. The dramatic irony of his own remark was lost upon him.

By implication the solitary nut and bolt must have held the rear wheel for at least two days, because the workmen returned, albeit on foot, in the afternoon and all the next day to complete the installation. If the wheel had come off—the prisoners argued with reason—they would not have returned at all.

*   *   *   *   *

The big search was well overdue and everybody looked to his hide carefully and with some anxiety. It came, one morning as the first snow of the year began to fall. The Germans made the fatal mistake of "letting slip" to the British, before the first *Appell*,

that they were to leave the Camp for a day's outing. That was enough and every possible precaution was taken. The whole contingent, now nearly one hundred strong, marched off after seven a.m. *Appell*, across the causeway of the Castle and down into the town. They were accompanied by a guard of one hundred Goons and half-a-dozen Alsatian dogs.

The walk was greatly appreciated by the contingent although it lasted only ten minutes, hardly enough to warm up the body, ending on arrival at a building called the *Schutzenhaus*. Upon entering the building after a roll call in the yard outside, the prisoners were delighted to see signs of a festive occasion. There, at one end of the *Schutzenhaus* hall, stood a large canopied platform. It was already adorned with decorations and a long rosary of coloured electric bulbs. Outside the snow continued to fall gently.

Although some officers had set out with the intention of making a break, the weather was not propitious. The overpowering company of guards who took up their positions around the building did not serve to dispel that impression. Still, there was one vague possibility which was hawked around the hall by Dick Howe. The British were settling down for the day. Groups gathered around the few tables, and, on the floor in the corners, blankets were spread. Cards were produced, chess was soon in progress, Red Cross food appeared and the air grew heavy with tobacco smoke. Someone obtained permission to boil water in an adjoining scullery and tea was served. With all this luxury in new surroundings Dick found only one officer sufficiently enthusiastic to attempt an escape which had the remotest chance of success. Captain Geoffrey Munro Pemberton How, R.A.S.C.—alias Pembum—was prepared to have a go in spite of the fact that he had just received a new pipe from England; a treasure which would have kept him happy, even in Colditz, for many a long day. Pembum was renowned, among other things, for his voice which resembled that of a corn crake. Added to this, he spoke in staccato monosyllables. He had a ruddy face with a ruddier nose and, being somewhat older than the average at Colditz, he was looked upon kindly, as might be an uncle. Pembum wore, over his uniform, a British-warm which was a colour that could pass as civilian attire; like his pipe, it was brand new.

In the late afternoon, the order to return to the Castle was given. The British paraded in front of the *Schutzenhaus* over a predetermined spot, a manhole cover in the yard. The snow had almost ceased and was melting into a slush on the ground.

It says something for Pembum that even when the manhole cover was opened and a revolting slime revealed, his courage did not desert him. Down he went in a second, and the cover was closed on top of him.

The parade count was fixed. All went well and the company marched out of the yard, turning left along the road. Dick looked back as the column wheeled and was shocked to see a conspicuous cloud of smoke rising around the manhole cover.

"The blighter's smoking his damned pipe," he thought.

There were so many Goons in the yard that it was impossible the cloud would remain unnoticed for long. Within a few seconds and with the yard still in sight, the company was halted. An *Unteroffizier* returned, at the double, to the yard as one of the sentries at the rear, shouting a warning, called for assistance. The *Unteroffizier* lifted the manhole cover, saw Pembum, dropped it again and then jumped up and down on the cover several times whooping like a Red Indian war dancer.

Only the rear of the column saw Pembum removed and led off ignominiously, his brand new overcoat dripping with the grey brown filth from the walls of the manhole and his head bespattered with droppings from the underside of the manhole lid, the result of the pounding of the *Unteroffizier*.

Dick accused Pembum, on his return from a month in the cooler, of succumbing to temptation by smoking his pipe in the manhole. Pembum denied it and explained that the smoke was condensation in the cold atmosphere of the manhole rising with the air heated by his body. His explanation was correct, but in spite of protestations of innocence he took a long time to live down the jibe that he had sold an escape for a pipe of 'baccy.

The procession returned to the camp, but not empty handed. The *Schutzenhaus* platform had lost its rosary of coloured lamps and the *Schutzenhaus* itself was the poorer by a dozen electric lamp bulbs, several electric fittings and switches, some yards of cable, a useful length of lead pipe from the lavatories and some linoleum from the floor, window curtains of a good neutral tint, half a dozen chairs which had been converted into small firewood and, finally, the four legs sawn off a table and made into presentable logs, while the table top remained, leaning neatly against a wall.

The Germans discovered all these losses later in the evening,

but they were by then disheartened. An exhaustive search of the British premises had been carried out over a period of eight hours that day, and the Germans had only some useless contraband— chicken feed—to show for their hard work. The quarters looked as if a bomb had burst in them, furniture and belongings lay in shambles all over the floors. The Dutch reported that immediately after the British contingent had left the camp with their escort, another company of a hundred Goons had marched into the courtyard headed by four bloated-looking Gestapo officers. They had filed up the stairs into the British rooms where heavy thuds and rumbles continued all day which Vandy described as "like the noise of many vindmills all turning round at vonce."

To consider a further search at that moment for electric light fittings and other paraphernalia, though admittedly enough to stock a reasonably sized jumble sale, was out of the question.

Where was the contraband hidden? The type and dimensions of hiding places varied enormously. The beams across the ceiling of one of the larger rooms were supported by simply designed cornices protruding from the vertical wall face. These plinths were of stone and mortar covered with plaster. The architect had omitted one, perhaps with his thoughts on the evil eye. Lulu Lawton, who was officer in charge of "Hides", made good the architect's omission and the evil eye winked. The false cornice, with its trap door always repainted with plaster of paris and sprinkled with cobweb mixture after use, survived the war without a tremor. Other places, of course, had to be found for articles such as the hydraulic jack. Take a good look at a lavatory pan!

The French must have had the impression that the Germans were weary that night and would not be on the alert. Their notion was a good one. Two of their number, Edouard Desbat and Jean Caillaud, decided to attempt an escape over the roofs of Colditz, which they had been planning for some time. Snow lay on the ground though it was melting on the roofs. It would make the climb more difficult but there were signs of a mist coming up which was exactly what they wanted.

After the last *Appell* at 9 p.m. the British retired to their bunks and most of them were soon asleep.

Shots rang out in the stillness. Men stirred and turned over; some sat up. Scarlet O'Hara was heard to remark, "Coo! Did you hear that? Three grosse coup de fusil!"

More shots followed.

Blackout blinds were raised.* Lights went on in courtyard windows like patches in the quilt of night. Windows opened. There were shouts, orders, jeers, counter orders and laughter. Windows shut again, blinds were lowered and the lights went out, one by one.

Only two Frenchmen, one, clinging by means of a lightning conductor to the vertical face of a chimney breast eighty feet from the ground, the other, perched on a roof ledge close at hand, knew what the shouting was about.

Desbat, hanging perilously from the conductor, knew it because he was being shot at, and Caillaud was taking the strain on the safety cord linking the two of them, ready to save his friend if he fell, wounded by the German attack.

Their objective was the outer end of a roof ridge, from which they could descend two hundred feet in comparative darkness clear of the encircling wire and the ring of guards. The mist had failed them. They still might have succeeded, relying on the supposition that sentries seldom look skywards, and upon the fact that the chimney breast was in half-light, reflected from floodlight striking an adjacent building.

A loose piece of mortar was Desbat's downfall. His foot dislodged it, and it fell with a crash to the ground near a sentry in the outer courtyard. The sentry looked upwards. Desbat saw him out of the corner of an eye. He did not move. The German, accustomed to the glare of the lights, could see nothing at first. He called another sentry. Together they peered, shading their eyes, trying to pierce the gloom. They saw Desbat.

Shouts of "halt" were followed by three shots which loosened bricks around Desbat's head sending dust and splinters flying into his face. He yelled, *"Schiessen Sie nicht, ich ergebe mich"*— "Don't shoot, I give myself up" several times.

The guard was turned out. In spite of his yells which could be heard clearly below, fifteen more shots were fired at him. They may well have been warning shots, but the nearest hit the brickwork only three inches from his head and the volley was unnerving to say the least of it.

The alarm having been given, the sentries inside the prisoners'

---

* Although the outside of the Castle was floodlit, prison orders were to the effect that blinds must be drawn. It was a precautionary measure in the event of air raids, when the floodlights were always extinguished. The order was, needless to say, flagrantly disobeyed.

courtyard caught sight of Caillaud on his ledge and covered him, ordering him to descend.

The Jerries might have been tired early in the evening. They might justifiably have been in high spirits later in the evening at the recapture of two escapers. But they were ill at ease, jittery, uncertain of themselves and trigger-happy by midnight.

There was an atmosphere of "Macbeth" abroad. Men slept restlessly. Dogs barked in the distance and would not settle down. The familiar tread of the sentries in the courtyard was not audible. They moved like ghosts in the snow, silent and unearthly. It was a night for witchcraft. Indeed Priem was plotting. With a mug of Schnapps beside him, he sat brooding in his office in the Kommandantur. He would have a revenge on the British after his own style.

At two a.m. he ordered an *Appell* for the British P.O.W.s. His heavy-booted Huns came striding through the dormitories, switching on the lights and shouting, "*Aufstehen—Appell! Sofort! Schnell!*" hardly giving the officers time to don overcoats over their pyjamas and stuff cigarettes and food into their pockets, before being herded without ceremony into the courtyard, now thickly carpeted with snow. They were met by a posse of Goons with their guns in the rabbiting position. This meant the Jerries were ready for trouble.

Priem himself appeared while the rooms were being cleared by his men. The floors were still littered with the debris from the search of the day before. Officers in pyjamas and Goons, tripping over their guns, were milling around the beds and tables in a glorious congestion of confused humanity. The Goons were shouting and the prisoners were all talking at once.

Harry Elliott, still lying in his bunk, yelled across the gangway to Dick, "What the hell's happening?"

Dick, struggling with one leg in his trousers, replied above the din. "Priem's on the warpath again."

Harry said, "Ask him what the devil he thinks he's doing."

"Ask him yourself," shouted Dick.

Harry jumped out of bed and strode off, in his pyjamas, in search of Priem. He found him on the staircase and said:

"Captain Priem, what the hell do you think you're doing? Go away and leave us alone."

Priem, saluting with mocking humour, replied, "Hauptman Elliott, please go down to the courtyard."

"You go to hell!" said Harry, "I'm going to do a pee," and

with that he marched back into the quarters and headed for the *Abort*. Harry relieved himself and returned to bed.

In the meantime, one of the German rifles had been stolen. The tempo of movement and the clamour redoubled. Guards charged around the rooms searching in the beds and under them for the missing weapon. Priem was sent for. He arrived as the scene reached a climax of pantomime chaos. He could not make himself heard. The more rebellious prisoners, who had not yet descended to the yard, were chanting all the songs they could think of at the top of their voices. Strains of the "Siegfried Line" mingled with "B—— and the same to you." Suddenly, Priem spotted the rifle inside an officer's pyjama leg. There was a mad rush of Goonery. The officer was completely smothered and then almost carried bodily out of the room under *"Strengen arrest."* Jeers, whistles and catcalls rose to a deafening crescendo. The Germans were losing control and began to manhandle the prisoners towards the staircase with the usual, *"Los! Los! Schnell! Los!"*

Priem now took it into his head to visit the Dutch, living on the floor above. He mounted the stairs followed by a squad of Goons and, also, a party of British in pyjamas and overcoats; led by Rupert Barry, determined not to miss the fun. Sleepy Dutchmen rose on their elbows and blinked with astonishment at the incredible procession as it burst into their quarters. Priem was greeted with roars of laughter on all sides. Beside himself, he ordered the Dutchmen out of their beds, then turned to his soldiery and saw the cause of the laughter: a pyjama column of twenty Englishmen in attendance on the Germans, chatting innocently, grinning, waving to friends and generally awaiting developments. He emitted a bellow and went for Rupert, thumping him on the chest with his fists and screaming between the punctuating blows, *"Gott verdamnte Englischer Schweinhund!"*

His squad were meanwhile pulling the blankets off the Dutchmen and turning them out of bed. Priem could not hold all the English. He was gripping Rupert with his two fists clenched over handfuls of pyjama and overcoat. The others mingled with the Dutch and the hubbub increased.

Within seconds the scene in the Dutch quarters became a repetition of the act in progress on the floor below. The shouting and singing, wafted up the stairwell, was soon drowned by a chorus upstairs.

Priem countermanded his order, screaming at the top of his

voice that the Dutch should return to bed. But, by now, they were all awake, enjoying the fun and had no intention of doing so. Priem sent in his men to force them and a steeplechase began around the clusters of bunks. The Dutch and British were indistinguishable in their night attire and the hide and seek continued fruitlessly until Priem, in despair, called his men off, and left the prisoners to sort themselves out.

Down in the courtyard everybody was singing. Blackout blinds were going up again and faces looked down upon the rioters below.

The *Appell* had been extended to the senior British officers from the theatre block. They descended, sleepily, one by one. The S.B.O., Lieutenant Colonel Stayner of the Dorsetshires, know as "Daddy" because of his grey hair and gentle, fatherly manner, walked into the yard. He looked frail and tired. He stopped for a moment under the lamp near the doorway, surveying the unruly mob before him, his tall, thin frame silhouetted against the darkness beyond. Wisps of hair straying from under his fore and aft cap, were caught by a swirling gust of wind which sent a myriad snowflakes pirouetting. He heaved a tired sigh, shrugged his shoulders and took up his accustomed place for the *Appell*, resigned to a long session in the cold.

The French and Dutch began booing from the windows as Priem appeared on the steps outside the entrance to the British staircase. Priem held up his hand, waving at the windows and shouting orders that nobody could hear.

His N.C.O.s must have understood him. They gesticulated warningly up at the windows as the rifles of the sentries came up to the shoulder. The French and Dutch wisely retired. There was a momentary expectant lull. David Hunter, a Lieutenant of the Royal Marines, could not resist the temptation. He yelled, "*Feuer*", and a salvo of shots echoed through the yard, as bullets flew into the night or embedded themselves in the walls. Slates rattled to the eaves.

Daddy Stayner remonstrated half-heartedly, "Hunter, don't do that again, you're aggravating the Germans."

He knew his junior officers well enough. He had no intention of attempting seriously to call for order. In fact, he was beginning to enjoy the fun.

A sly smile played about his mouth as he watched the German N.C.O.s, led by Gephard and the ferret, running around the yard demanding of the sentries, "Who gave the order to fire?"

Priem ordered the S.B.O. to command his men to form ranks for an *Appell*. Daddy Stayner maintained a stubborn ignorance of the German language and called for the British interpreter.

Flight Lieutenant "Bricky" Forbes, R.A.F., the interpreter, was nowhere to be found. He had a Balaclava helmet well over his face and was determined to remain incognito. A German interpreter was sent for.

At this point a blackout curtain in the British quarters went up, and Harry Elliott poked his head out as far as he could to see the fun. Priem saw him and exploded. He bellowed orders at Gephard who headed up the stairs at the double with two sentries. He returned in five minutes without Harry. Harry was back at the window.

From behind the blinds in the windows of the French quarters a plainsong choir could be heard chanting. The voices rose and fell in monastic rhythm.

The French were intoning their usual litany:

"Où sont les Allemands?"

"Les Allemands sont dans la merde."

"Qu'ils y restent."

"Ils surnagent."

"Enfoncez-les."

"Jusqu'aux oreilles."

Gephard reported to Priem:

"Hauptman Elliott says he is too ill to parade in the snow."

Harry, it may be remembered, was cultivating a chronic jaundice at this period of his captivity.

"Escort him downstairs to the doctor's dispensary," ordered Priem. "He will parade in there."

Gephard clicked his heels, saluted and disappeared upstairs again at the double.

Bedlam continued in the courtyard. The prisoners were still singing and shuffling around in a turmoil of movement like a bubbling cauldron, with the legitimate excuse that they were trying to keep warm.

The monotonous chant of the French inside their building provided a background of continuous sound like seas breaking on a distant shore.

A German security officer appeared, accompanied by an elderly, wizened little German corporal who was to act as interpreter. The latter had obviously just been dragged out of his bed and was

half asleep. What he saw on entering the yard made him blink, wondering if he was still dreaming.

Priem was at his wits' end. If he threatened again with the rifles of his men, a machiavellian voice would shout *"Feuer"*, and he would be ultimately responsible if men were killed or wounded. He had lost the substance of power for a failing shadow—his voice.

Harry descended the stairs under escort and was greeted with vociferous cheering. He was led to the dispensary and locked in.

The Germans conferred with Colonel Stayner, then turned and faced the mob. The S.B.O. raised his hand, motioning for attention. Almost miraculously a lull descended on the unruly mob.

The intoning of the French could now be clearly heard and the quavering sound of Harry's voice—he did not see the S.B.O. from the dispensary—wafted into the yard rendering, to the tune of "Mademoiselle from Armentières", an extempore composition:

> "...
> The Huns were hanged, one by one, parley-vouz,
> The Huns were hanged, one by one,
> Every b—— mother's son,'
> Inky, stinky Hitler too."

The S.B.O. continued to demand silence as a wave of laughter threatened to bring new disorders in its wake. For a moment there was silence.

The German interpreter uttered in ringing tones his first words: "All British are warned to mutiny."

They were his last.

A roar of applause greeted the announcement. Priem threw up his arms in despair, giving up the unequal fight. He turned to the S.B.O. and spoke to him.

Colonel Stayner turned towards the prisoners, "Parade dismiss!" he shouted as loudly as he could. The order was greeted with wild cheers and the British broke up in high spirits. They had won a signal victory.

Gradually they filed back to their quarters under the sullen gaze of the bewildered sentries.

The courtyard emptied and the sound of voices dropped to a distant murmur issuing from the turret staircase door. The guards faced each other across the yard waiting for the order to "fall in".

On the snow in front of them, where the British had stood a few moments before, was an enormous dark brown 'V'. An enterprising spirit had thought it worth the expenditure of iron rations—a tin of Bournville cocoa!

CHAPTER IX

FRANZ JOSEF

INTROSPECTION had little place in Colditz. On rare occasions a prisoner became interested in psychology. As a rule he went on—"round the bend". Psychological studies, in fact, could be dubbed a third form of the initial symptoms of the disease; the other two being, as already mentioned, the inordinate passion for classical music and the untiring cult of the body—physical jerks.

The majority of the Colditz inmates seemed to prefer the more simple variety of self-examination; an occasional examination of the conscience. After all, it had the prestige of a few thousand years of beneficent usage, whereas the modern version achieved, in prison, sometimes startling, sometimes comic, but never satisfying results. The difference between modern psychological introspection and the Christian examination of conscience was described by a wag at Colditz as the difference between a Futurist nightmare and a Michelangelo masterpiece; only the canvas and paint were common to both, as the mind of man to the two forms of mental approach.

A new British escape scheme was afoot. There was little time, opportunity or inclination for the self-indulgence of morbidity. The project was big: it would involve the breakout of a large party. As usual it started in a small way.

One bright morning in April, 1943, Dick Howe was looking vacantly down from a window in the British dayroom at the sentries below. He was joined by 'Monty' Bissell, a six-foot Irishman who was a curious mixture of two temperaments. He had the temperament and the physique of a prize fighter and his bones must have been made of case-hardened steel. He had no fat on him whatever. Yet, although he was as thin as a rake, his weight remained well over fourteen stone. He charged everywhere with his head down, like a bull. He could not walk slowly, with

the result that he frequently bumped into people. It was like being hit by a shunting engine. He had black hair which fell over his forehead and a long face with a beak of a nose and hawk-like eyes. When he laughed, which he did at the most incongruous moments, accompanied by a loud snort and a satanic jerk of the head backwards, his mouth opened, revealing several yawning gaps where once had been a fine row of teeth. Boxing had done that for him.

Monty had the soul of a poet. He would quote Shakespeare and Yeats—in equal mouthfuls—lovingly, with the tenderness and complete unselfconsciousness of one to whom the music and the meaning of the words were ineffably majestic, imposing and intuitive.

Monty leaned on the window sill beside Dick. Neither spoke for some time. Then Monty recited with his huge hand on Dick's shoulder:

> "I've looked too long at life through a window
> And seen too often the freedom I crave.
> Yes, I've looked far too long at life through barred windows,
> But I'll look much longer at death from my grave."

"Not bad, not bad, hah! What do you think, Dick? I got it from Black Campbell. Didn't know he was a poet, did you? Ha! Hm!"

A long pause intervened. Dick was in a reverie. Monty might have been on the moon, but his heavy hand came down again with a resounding thud on Dick's shoulder.

"What's all the thought about, Dick? Listen to this!" and he intoned with almost fierce intensity:

> "Come
> Close your eyes, see the graph of expression
> Traced by the pencil of Modernity,
> Watch those steep ascents and sheer declines
> Marking the course of enthusiasm
> Whose fire consumes itself and Phœnix-like
> Creates once more the spark of quick desire.
> These jagged peaks must needs record some trend.
> Dizzy heights and abysmal nothingness
> Can cancel out: but nothing cancels out.
> In Time all that does not move is stiller
> Than the still. We must progress or perish,
> And being able must progress yet more
> Else perish sooner. Man as yet unborn
> Has all but solved the mystery of birth.

This Science cannot aimlessly suffice,
For one must know the 'I' to know the all.
To know this 'I' each age has creased the brow,
But ours of all the ages sets small store
Against the value of this seed of hope.
Philosophies, Religions, Mysteries,
Give way to stark Reality . . ."

"That's Humanity! Huh! not bad, eh! for a caged bird! Black Campbell again."

Dick replied without looking up.

"I was thinking that, if we could change a sufficient number of the sentries on one side of the Castle, we could let out a large number of chaps through a prepared window and nobody would be the wiser."

"Eh? What's all that?" queried Monty, taken aback, "I was talking about Humanity."

"Were you?" said Dick and leaning again on the sill with his chin cupped in his hands he continued his reverie.

Monty did not go away. Instead, he elbowed Dick over to give him room so that he, too, could cup his chin and stare out of the window—out and then down. Thus they both remained, silent and absorbed in their own thoughts for a long time. Then Dick drifted away and Monty was left alone.

That was how the escape attempt started.

*   *   *   *   *

At the end of April, Monty Bissell and Mike Sinclair could be seen frequently walking together around the cobbled yard in deep conversation. Mike was back in prison circulation again after his long spell in solitary. He was looking, it seemed, paler than before, but then he had red hair and the sunless winter was only just beginning to recede before the onslaught of Spring.

Now, as they strode around the yard, Monty displayed, at times, great agitation, flinging his arms wide, slapping Mike on the back and walking at a pace that often brought his companion to a trot. Mike was of medium build, just about the same height as one of the German Guard Commanders, who was known in the Castle as Franz Josef.

Franz Josef was indeed the subject of their subdued discussion as they tore around the yard. It was not long before they button-holed Dick.

One evening after the five o'clock *Appell* they approached him.

"Dick," said Mike, "we want to have a chat with you. Would

you spare Monty and me half an hour in a quiet corner some-where?"

"Come along to my room. We can sit on the beds. There's nobody there and we've got lots of time before supper."

They climbed the long spiral flight of steps to the room, where, in a secluded corner, well away from the door, was Dick's bunk. Nearby were the two-tier bunks occupied by Lulu Lawton, Rupert Barry and Harry Elliott. The room was long and the ceiling high but the windows were in deep casements which kept out much of the light. They sat or lay on the beds as the shadows slowly deepened in the evening light.

Mike began:

"Monty has an idea for an escape which, at first sight, appears pretty crazy, but we've talked about it a lot and I, for one, think it can be done. Roughly—without going into details—it's this; I dress up as Franz Josef and with two others, dressed as German guards, we get out of a certain window at the psychological moment. I relieve the guard below our old quarters, the ones that are empty. There are two sentries; the chap on the cat-walk and the fellow at the barbed wire gate. I send the real guards back to the guardhouse and my two men take over. Then, having the keys of the gate and having possession of that side of the Castle, you can send out a batch of say twenty chaps—more if you like— through another prepared window and the whole lot of us clear out as fast as we can."

"Hm!" said Dick lying back in his bed and appearing to examine intently the canvas palliasse and the bed boards of the bunk above him. "I see, Monty, you haven't been idle!"

"Eh! What! No! by Gad! I've been working up this scheme ever since you mentioned the idea, weeks ago. I think it's terrific —a cinch—I can't sleep at night for thinking about it. All we need are two more German speakers—three German uniforms— Teddy Barton fixes up Mike to look like Franz Josef—we cut the bars on two windows—the guards are relieved and off we all go—first class railway tickets to Blighty." A torrent of words flowed from Monty as he stood up excitedly and enacted the escape with his long arms.

"All right, Monty. That's all right, old boy. Sit down now and let's have a few details, quietly. First of all, this is how I see it. We'll have to do a long period of watching so that we know exactly what motions Franz Josef will go through on the particular evening assuming it will be in the evening—of the escape. Then, we must

also do a lot of stooging so that we know which sentries will go on the posts we're going to relieve—we want dumb ones." He paused for a moment, thinking, then continued:

"We've not only got to make three uniforms complete, and mighty good ones—better than we've ever made before—but we shall have to make two rifles and a revolver in its holster for Franz Josef—also the two bayonet scabbards. Changing the guard means plenty of time for the Jerries to notice the uniforms and the lights may be on. Anyway, it's not at all like a couple of chaps, in uniform, marching past a sentry, in a hurry. That's how I see it. The answer is stooging—hours and hours of it, and the best uniforms we've ever made. Apart from that I'd like to see how Mike makes up as Franz Josef; and lastly which windows do you propose to work from?"

There was a moment's silence before Mike spoke:

"We'll show you the windows now if you'll come with us. I think Teddy Barton can fix me up as Franz Josef. I've asked him about it already and he's fairly confident about it. I'm the right height."

"You'll have to examine old Franz with a microscope for a couple of weeks at least, to pick up all his mannerisms. You've got to be word perfect," Dick interrupted.

"Yes, I know," continued Mike. "Have you any ideas for my two Goons?"

Dick thought for a second, "Where do you come in all this, Monty? You'll never pass as a weedy little tich of a sentry."

"No! I'm going to lead the storming party out of the second window," announced Monty with gusto. "What a show it's going to be! Hah!" and he threw his head back with a devilish grin.

"I thought, maybe, John Hyde Thompson could be one of my guards," said Mike. "He speaks German well enough. I hadn't fixed on another yet."

"All right," said Dick rising slowly from the bed, "let's go and have a look at the windows. The idea's crazy all right, but if everything is word perfect—well—who knows! We must think about your guards and I'll talk to the C.O. about it."

They walked downstairs, across the now darkening courtyard and into the sick bay corridor. Monty led the way into the sick ward itself and they stood, huddled together, by a window. Monty then explained, in subdued tones, that this window was 'blind' from the sentries at night unless one of them walked the full length of his beat, and he could be expected to stand still for part

of his duty period. Dick checked up and thought there was something in what Monty said. Two or three officers could be let down quickly out of this window, and, provided they were suitably dressed, they could walk away, round a corner, towards the next sentry without causing suspicion. The bars, of course, would have to be very carefully dealt with.

They continued their tour of inspection, to the window where it was proposed to let out the main body. This was on the park side of the Castle. The window was in quarters now vacated and in darkness, in which the British had once lived. Keys were employed to make an entry and here, beside the second window, Monty and Mike pointed out the two German sentries who would be involved in the escape.

One of the two sentries was stationed on a high catwalk surveying a long frontage of the Castle. The second sentry was posted at the barbed wire gate, for the keys of which he was responsible, and which opened on to the roadway leading downhill towards the park and the German barracks. The gate was also next to the deep tunnel-like archway leading into the Kommandantur courtyard; the one through which Mike and the Frenchman had sortied not many months earlier.

With the window bars prepared, if these two sentries could be relieved by ours, the way was clear for a rope descent by a large party.

The scheme was daring to say the least of it.

Dick put the wheels of his organisation into action. Another 'Mike', namely Michael Harvey, R.N., one of the parcel office team already mentioned, kept a regular stooging roster on call for such eventualities. Dick arranged with Mike to put his roster at the disposal of Monty whom he charged with the task of obtaining sufficient data to be able to forecast with certainty, *three days* ahead of any given date, when Franz Josef would be on duty as Commander of the Guard; to map out his complete circuit and the frequency of his rounds with the time intervals between posts; the exact hours of evening guard changes; the times required for guards to regain the guardhouse from different posts, (*a*) if walking direct and alone, and (*b*) if in a squad on the circuit. The posts taken up by respective Goons were to be noted and particular Goons seeded out, leaving only dumb-looking ones in the running, whose tours of duty on the catwalk and the gate were to be graphed with accuracy. It was a job the team were accustomed to, but it would necessitate at least a month of concentrated effort.

Dick required the *three days'* grace to provide ample time for

completing the cutting of the bars of the two windows concerned. This was an operation which called for the greatest patience and for much experience. The work demanded such delicacy of touch that only saws made of razor blades could be used. The sick bay window would be comparatively simple, but the window opening in front of the sentry on the cat-walk was an extremely ticklish job. The escape depended on the success of both cutting operations, and the awkward point was that they would be the last part of the scheme to be completed. This work was put into the hands of Lulu Lawton and Bricky Forbes.

Two thirty foot lengths of rope were required. They were ordered from the marine department, Bos'n Crisp in other words. So much to begin with, but it was only a beginning.

Rex Harrison of the Green Howards, blond, six foot two, with a long curling moustache, even tempered and patient, would have to produce three perfect German uniforms, one for a Sergeant. He no longer had Bill Fowler to help him expertly with the embroidery and cloth insignias, but there were other willing hands to fill the gap. 'Andy', Major W. F. Anderson, R.E., and Scarlet O'Hara were commissioned to produce two German rifles, two bayonet scabbards and a holster complete with revolver, and Scarlet was to deal also with the foundry work for buttons, badges, medals and belt clasps.

Finally, the principal actor in the whole drama had to be coached and transformed into the mirror image of Franz Josef.

The elderly and somewhat stout N.C.O. who was to be given a twin brother was not called Franz Josef for nothing. He was a living impersonation of Franz Josef, Emperor of Austria, King of Hungary and of Bohemia; ruddy complexion, puffy cheeks, grey hair, portly bearing and an enormous Franz Josef moustache which covered half of his face. Provided this could be faithfully copied it would, in itself, provide a magnificent mask.

Teddy Barton was one of the theatre past-masters. Besides producing shows and acting in them, he had the professional touch when it came to 'make-up'. His 'girls' on the stage had at once been the delight and the despair of theatre audiences. His male efforts could not have been bettered by Madame Tussaud. He and his principal aide, Alan Cheetham, manufactured fourteen Franz Josef moustaches before they were satisfied with their handywork. The face, hair, and even the hands, were practised upon with like thoroughness.

Teddy Barton, Mike Sinclair and Alan Cheetham studied

Franz Josef's gestures, facial expressions, manner of speech accent and intonation for a month on end. Franz Josef was dogged every time he entered the courtyard. He was engaged in long futile conversations while, unknowingly, he was scrutinised microscopically by three pairs of eyes that took note of every muscle he moved, every cough and splutter, every smile and grimace he made. Mike rehearsed, was criticised and rehearsed again and again, until he lived in the rôle of Franz Josef.

His moment was approaching. Two sentries had been chosen to accompany him. They were John Hyde Thompson and Lancelot Pope. Both were good German speakers. They rehearsed with Mike the German words of command, and practised all the movements of guard changing according to the German routine. It was Pope's second effort of this kind. He had once marched out of Eichstatt prison with 'Teddy' Broomhall (Lt.-Col. R.E.), posing as a German General.

It was decided to prepare a first wave of twenty men to make the rope descent from the old British quarters immediately the guard had been relieved and was out of sight.

The factor, limiting the number in the wave, was the time it would take the first German sentry relieved, to march back to the guardhouse and report to his N.C.O., the real Franz Josef—Franz Josef I. Then the balloon would go up. This interval of time was checked repeatedly as a minimum of three and a half minutes and an almost certain maximum of four and and a half minutes. Twenty men would, in this space of time, be able to drop down the rope and be well on the road to the park. If there was no violent reaction by the time the twentieth had descended the rope, more officers were ready to follow, but responsibility rested with their leaders not to lessen, in any way, by their action, the chances of the first wave. There might be German reactions other than from the guardhouse and much nearer the scene of the escape. Late departures might cause suspicion or an escaper might even be seen on the rope. This would shorten the start of the first twenty which, in all conscience, was short enough!

An escape of this calibre involved the co-operation of about fifty officers in its preparation. In addition to the month of preparation before the day of the escape, there had been the months of earlier work put in by the artists and the printers reproducing the maps, identity papers and passes carried by the officers who were to make the attempt. These personal credentials were now brought up to date and officially stamped. German money was

issued. Each escaper, of course, had to produce his own civilian attire. In this task he was assisted by the expert advice and practical help of the tailors.

The team had gathered for briefing several times and at the final meeting, Dick wound up, with a wry smile:

"I'm sure you'll have an exciting time and plenty of fun. You can rely on it, there'll be some shooting, but keep your nerve and go on running. You know the password 'they can't shoot a British officer!' We have the advantage of darkness. Make for the three points indicated for climbing the Park wall, splitting up into your respective groups. And remember, once you're out, we don't want to see your ugly faces here again."

The main body was to make straight for the park at the double, followed closely by Mike—Franz Josef II and his two sentries. If a stray Goon appeared they were to keep running. Franz Josef II would give the impression of chasing the party and would intercept any such stray Goons and order them to run in the opposite direction, towards the Castle, with instructions to raise the alarm.

The revolver and the rifles were nearing completion. Scarlet spent hours trailing the sentries in the courtyard holding sometimes a long piece of string, sometimes a ruler in his hand. When a sentry was stationary, Scarlet approached him casually from behind, then surreptitiously measured a particular section of the rifle. "Andy" prepared the plans. Each measurement was recorded, the ruler providing the details in fractions of an inch. Then they set to work and made the dummies. The result was perfection. The rifles could pass close inspection in daylight. Contours, colours, shape and sheen were all correct. Only the weight would have given them away. Rifle straps were made to match. The revolver and holster followed the same high standard.

"D" day had to be fixed. Careful examination and discussion of the reports of Monty and Mike Harvey, resulting from their exhaustive stooging, settled the date, which was to be the 19th of May, and the hour was to be—immediately after the nine p.m. *Appell*. Franz Josef I would be the guard commander on that day and a particularly dumb-looking Goon was calculated to be on duty at the gate.

Among those remaining behind were Lulu Lawton, Dick's second in command, Bricky Forbes, Bush Parker who was to release the Franz Josef II party from the sick ward, and the stooging team for the event under the command of Mike Harvey. Monty headed the main escaping party.

Signalling was to be done by flashlight. It was laid on as a two-way code between three lookout points; one, at a window on the floor above the sick ward in charge of Bush Parker, with communication to the sick ward by tapping on a water pipe; a second, with the main body in the old British quarters; and the third overlooking the German guardhouse.

The most delicate operation in the whole scheme now had to be accomplished. The bars of the two windows in the different parts of the Castle had to be cut. Complete concentration and devotion to the job in hand was essential. Months of work and the desperate hopes of many men were at stake. Failure would involve much bitterness. For this reason, Dick chose the two men in whose conscientiousness the whole British contingent had confidence. It could be said with conviction that if they failed to do the job, no other officer would have succeeded.

One window was 'comparatively' simple. The second window was in direct floodlight. 'Comparatively' is a relative term. In other circumstances the cutting might have been deemed very difficult, but, as bar cutting had, by now, become a stock in trade of the Colditz convicts, only the cutting of bars in full floodlight with a sentry immediately below attracted comment and a mild compliment from those who knew what was involved; the ear of a gazelle, a hand of iron controlled by a thread of silk, a heart of ice, a brain, calm as a mill-pond and as quick to react as a trout flashing in the stream. During the five years Colditz was used as a prison, in World War II, the operation of cutting a bar in full floodlight was performed successfully only three times.

The bar cutting was accomplished successfully and camouflaged.

May the 19th arrived. The day passed slowly. There was suppressed activity everywhere, concealed by an overall air of casualness. The men taking part in the attempt were not beginners. What worried most of them more than anything else was the short start. If the first stage—the relieving of the guard—came off, that, in itself, would be tremendously exciting, but the real fun would start when twenty P.O.W.s were out, the first with perhaps a three minute start, and the last with less than a thirty second start, in front of the pursuing enemy. The hounds would be in full cry. Colditz had never known such an attempt before and the consequences were unknown.

Monty, six foot of heavyweight boxer, strode around the quarters all day like a rhino in search of a muddy pool in the Sahara.

Mike remained outwardly calm while the turmoil of nervous

anticipation was inwardly tearing at his entrails and gripping his throat.

Dick spent his time checking up on everybody's instructions, amplifying them, where necessary, to cover every possible hitch or misunderstanding. The escape was the largest and most daring so far attempted from Colditz. If it succeeded, it would make history. If it failed, "Well!" thought Dick, "it'll still make a good story!" He watched the final rehearsal of the guard-changing squad and thought they were word perfect. Franz Josef II could have walked out of the Castle with ease.

The hours dragged heavily towards the 9 p.m. *Appell*. Those in the escaping team lay on their bunks, trying to sleep. They yawned and stretched themselves nervously finding no relief for the tension around the heart or the nausea threatening the stomach, for the hot flush or the cold sweat. Then, when everybody least expected it, the siren began to wail. The show was on.

The *Appell* went off normally. Immediately afterwards, Bush Parker and the guard relieving party—Mike, John Hyde Thompson and Lance Pope—faded off towards the sick ward. The second stooging contingent disappeared to their respective posts on the upper floor overlooking the guardhouse. The main escaping party with its stooges, led by Dick, Bricky Forbes, Lulu and Mike Harvey and followed by the members of the second escaping wave— altogether thirty-five strong—passed silently through locked doors into the dark unoccupied rooms of the old British quarters.

Dick looked down on to the sentry path below. "The ivory-headed Goon's at his post on the gateway—so far so good," he whispered.

Sounds of life in the Castle died down. Soon a deathly stillness reigned. Thirty-five men waited for the warning signals.

The first message came through:

"Franz Josef returned to guardhouse," Mike Harvey reported in an undertone. Then came, "All quiet in German Kommandantur."

That was the signal for Bush to act and release Franz Josef II and his party through the window, down the rope, on to the sentry path.

A silence, vibrant with tension, followed. Then, suddenly, Mike Harvey spoke in hoarse excited tones:

"Our guard party on their way—past first sentry."

A moment later, Dick, Lulu, Monty and Bricky Forbes, crouching near the window, heard the crunch of marching feet on the path and a loud heel click as a sentry, out of sight, saluted the passing

patrol. Then they came into view, round the corner of the building
This was the crucial moment.

Franz Josef II followed by his two guards walked to the gate
and spoke to the dumb sentry in German:

"*Sie werden Ihre wach zu diesem Posten übergeben. Gehen Sie
sofort zurück an den Wachtraum, einige Gefangener sind verfluchtet.
Man hat Sie notig.*"

Lance Pope took up his post beside the gate. Franz Josef II
mounted the ladder to the cat walk and repeated his orders to the
second sentry who started to descend. John Hyde Thompson took
over his post.

"My God!" whispered Dick, in a dripping perspiration, "it's
going to work. Get ready!"

The cat-walk sentry had reached the ground and was marching
off. Then Dick noticed the gate sentry had not followed. Franz
Josef II was talking to him. Dick could hear the gist of it through
the open window and repeated it to the others.

"The sentry says he's under orders not to move. Mike's demanded the keys. The sentry's handed them over . . . but he
won't move. What the hell! . . . Mike ought to go. He's wasting
time. The three of them can make it. He's getting annoyed with
the sentry . . . he's told him to get back to the guardhouse. No!
. . . it's no good . . . the dumb bastard won't budge . . . why
the devil won't he move? Mike's getting really angry with him . . .
this is awful. He's got to go! He's got to go! Mike's shouting at
him." Dick was in a frenzy. "Good God! this is the end. The time's
nearly up."

Mike was having a desperate duel with the ivory-headed Goon
and the precious seconds were slipping away. He was thinking
of the main party—he was determined that the main party should
escape at all costs. He had cast his dice—it was to be all or nothing.
He was sacrificing himself to win the larger prize.

As soon as he started to raise his voice Dick's stomach began to
sink. The game was a losing one. He wanted to shout at Mike to
make a run for it, but dared not interfere with Mike's battle. He
was impotent, helpless, swearing and almost weeping with a foreboding of terrible failure. The scheme within a hair's breadth of
success, was going wrong. Mike might possibly have disarmed the
offending sentry but it was too late for violence now with less than
half a minute's start. If he had been disarmed at the very beginning it might have been different, but who would have done that
when persuasion was the obvious first course. Alas! persuasion

Mike Sinclair and the ivory-headed Goon

meant time and the precious minutes had flown. Four minutes had gone. It was nearly hopeless now.

The two British sentries stood their ground. John Hyde Thompson was solemnly pacing his beat up and down the cat-walk.

Mike's voice rose to a typical Franz Josef scream of rage. Even as he shouted, there were sounds of hurrying feet and discordant voices shouting in the distance. A dozen Goons came through the archway near the gate, running fast with their bayonets fixed. At their rear, panting hard and bellowing commands, ran Franz Josef I. The game was almost up, but Mike was determined to play it to the end. He would challenge his rival; let the Germans choose between them. Franz Josef II outbellowed Franz Josef I and countermanded his orders. A scene of frenzied confusion ensued, in which the Germans obeyed first one and then the other—turned down the hill and then reversed—looked towards Franz Josef I and listened to Franz Josef II, seeing, yet not believing that Franz Josef had suddenly split into two violently opposed personalities.

The German sentry who had been relieved, was prominent. He was yelling at his rival, pointing upwards and dancing with excitement, completely out of control. His substitute stood quietly at his post on the catwalk looking down innocently upon the chaos below.

N.C.O.s ran backwards and forwards in a panic, waving their revolvers. They were no longer certain of the allegiance of the men they commanded. Lance Pope had mingled with the Germans and Dick could not distinguish him. In the alternate searing floodlight and darkness around the searchlights men who were dressed alike, looked alike.

Mass hysteria broke out. A German voice began screaming: "Armed mutiny! Armed mutiny!" which was taken up by a chorus, waving rifles in the air.

A shot rang out.

One of the Franz Josefs swayed and sank to his knees. A confused mob of soldiers gathered round him, all talking at once.

"They've shot Mike—I think it's Mike—I can't be sure," said Dick, turning to the men around him, "I can't see what's happening."

The panic and the hubbub continued for a moment, then subsided. Lance Pope was in the middle of the mob of Germans. John Hyde Thompson was being pushed down the ladder of the cat-walk with a revolver in his back.

Dick spotted the Franz Josef on the ground. "It's Mike all right. I'm sure of it."

Monty at the window was shaking with rage, thumping one fist into the other and shouting, "Let me get at 'em! Let me get at 'em."

"The bastards!" said Dick, then turning to the waiting men, "they'll be in our quarters in a minute. Everybody clear out! Lulu see to the bars. Mike, signal to the others to return to quarters."

Then after a pause and another look through the window as Lulu carefully reset the bars: "They've left Mike on the ground. My God! The filthy swines aren't even attending to him!"

Dick and Lulu did not see the end. The *Appell* siren was moaning and Germans were already in the courtyard. They had to leave the premises in haste, removing traces and locking up behind them.

For nearly ten minutes, Mike was left lying on the ground, bleeding profusely from a wound in the chest. His Franz Josef moustache had been torn off his face. A squad of Goons was standing by, evidently waiting for orders.

An N.C.O. appeared and Mike was picked up. He was semi-conscious—fainting from loss of blood. They carried him away to the Kommandantur.

In the courtyard feeling among the prisoners was running high. Many thought that Mike had been killed. There were struggles on the British staircase. David Hunter, shouting "Deutsche Mörder" at the top of his voice and resisting arrest was hustled off between four Goons with rifles and fixed bayonets in the rabbiting position, and thrown into a cell in his pyjamas.

Monty Bissell spotted the Goon whom he thought had shot Mike. Shaking his fist in his face, he confronted him with *"Kaltblütiger Mörderer! Deutscher Mörderer! Deutscher Schweinhund!"* He was promptly surrounded by another four Goons who manhandled him across the courtyard and pushed him into another cell.

There were fifty Goons in the yard waiting for the *Appell*, with their bayonets fixed and rifles at the hip. Priem had evidently learnt his lesson and was taking no chances. The guards were in an ugly mood. They had tasted blood. The atmosphere glowed hot and red with sparks that might start a nasty conflagration.

Oberst Pravitt, the German Commandant of the Camp, hurried into the yard. He spoke to the S.B.O. who called the prisoners to attention and announced amidst a frozen silence:

"Lieutenant Sinclair is wounded but out of danger."

Mike's time had not yet come.

UPLIFT

THE kitchen stove in the British quarters was naturally a centre of activity around which life hummed all day long and all night too. Then the distillers were at work. During the daylight hours a former Merchant Navy Engineer officer, Lieutenant Ernest Champion, R.N.R., more widely known as Ernie, constituted himself, like an Arabian genie, the guardian of the stove. He knew all about cooking as it should be done at Colditz because "Bertie" Boustead, an ardent amateur, asked him, one day, when he had some pale looking potato rissoles on the fire, "How do you know when these are done?"

Ernie, who was sitting beside the stove, told him.

"When they're brown they're burning, and when they're black they're finished."

Lieutenant John R. Boustead was a thin six foot length of Seaforth Highlander, who had been taken prisoner in June, 1940. He possessed unfailing good humour and, at the same time, somewhat hazy ideas about the mundane matters of everyday living. He was, at first, welcomed with great enthusiasm into the cooks' circle. They saw in his desire to cook a descent from an Olympian detachment.

Ernie was naturally anxious to help him so that when he saw Bertie, early one morning, stirring hot water in a small saucepan on the stove he asked him, "What are you stirring it for?"

To which Bertie replied with the enthusiasm of a pupil who was at last benefiting from his cooking course, "To prevent it burning, of course, you ass."

But Bertie never lived down the reputation he earned as a cook when he approached Ernie with a sizzling frying-pan in which an egg gaily cavorted from side to side. The shell was brown in patches, black in spots and cracked all over. He said:

"Ernie! I can't seem to get this egg to fry properly. Can you help me?"

The kitchen stove would have told some soul shattering stories if it could have spoken. One scandal which leaked out, fortunately after the dish concerned had been greedily consumed and appreciatively digested, concerned a delicious curry. The chef was

Derby Curtis, a Captain of the Royal Marines. When his curry was only half cooked it took fire without warning. With consummate aplomb, which was only witnessed by a few onlookers, he lifted the frying-pan quickly off the stove, put it on the floor and stamped out the flames with his heavy booted feet. He then wiped his boots off carefully on the edge of the frying-pan and continued to cook the curry.

In the evenings, when all meals were concluded, the stove was taken over by the distillers.

The origin and early development of this industry dates from the year 1941.* In 1943, however, an efficiently run firm grew from small beginnings and eventually mastered all competition and became a monopoly. The head of the concern was a Dutchman, A. Van Rood, a Flight Lieutenant in the R.A.F., who had been studying medicine in England when the war broke out. He joined the R.A.F. and, as a fighter pilot, was shot down over St. Omer in 1942. Van Rood was a good-looking blond type and was born to be more than a doctor because he was an authority on every subject known to man. His opinions were definite on them all and he did not hesitate to expound his views at any hour of the day or night, when given a cue and an audience, in a loud voice in any one of the four languages—Dutch, English, French or German—which his audience might care to choose because he was fluent in them all. He became a skilful brewer and was the chemist, as well as a Director, of the Company. Scarlet O'Hara christened him "Good Time Charlie Goonstein" after the Damon Runyan character who ran a speakeasy off Broadway. The name stuck.

His brother Directors were Bush Parker who acted as the fuel contractor for the combine, and Bag or 'Ming' Dickenson. The latter came from Bristol, was also a Flight Lieutenant in the R.A.F., and before the war had been an engineer working for the firm of Rotol Ltd. He was shot down on a bombing raid over Germany. He liked to escape in an impromptu manner, on the impulse and alone. His best effort from Colditz was from the solitary confinement cells in the town. Returning from exercise, he stepped behind a door—it sounds so easy—and, while the guards marched upstairs to the cells, he marched downstairs, out, into the town, dressed as he was, in mixed khaki and R.A.F. blue. Reaching Chemnitz, he thought himself conspicuous, so casually left his purloined bicycle at the kerb and entered the best hotel in the city. He walked into the lounge and over to a nice collection of coats hanging on a stand.

* See *The Colditz Story*.

E

He chose the best fitting one and walked out. Alas! The owner was not far behind him and that was the end of Bag's outing.

He was tall and thin, with a fair complexion and his temperament was essentially placid. He could not be ruffled—hence his alternative nickname, 'Ming.' When Bush was not hauling coal, playing cards or tasting liquor he was teasing the old Bag, but, in three years at Colditz he never succeeded in rousing him. Bag's placidity extended to his clothing. He disbelieved in the old adage, "A stitch in time . . ." With a fatalism reminiscent of the East, when a button fell off, a shoe lace broke or a seam came apart, his shrug expressed the spirit enshrined in the words, "Ins' Allah"— "Allah's will be done!" His equanimity reached distressing extremes when his bed caught fire as he lay on it. This happened frequently because he had a habit of dozing off in the afternoon with a lighted cigarette in his mouth. Scarlet O'Hara, who slept next to him, kept a bucket of water under his bed for the sole purpose of extinguishing Bag's fires—he may also have been tempted to use it sometimes when there was no fire. Bag would come to, soaked to the skin, while the acrid smell of burning hair mixed with smouldering straw and canvas dispersed itself through the room. Bag would stretch his long frame and rise slowly from the bed to say, between yawns, "Thanks, Scarlet, old boy, but try and keep the water off my feet. You've soaked my only good pair of socks."

Bag was the Distilling Engineer. He was ever producing bigger and better stills at the expense of the Castle plumbing system. At other times he manufactured keys and tools of all kinds, beautifully finished and correctly tempered or case-hardened, out of pieces removed from iron bedsteads in the senior officers' quarters.

The three Directors ran their business on a barter basis and always had stock in hand to satisfy demands. An official exchange value, with a margin of profit, was placed on both sugar and raisins, and a given quantity of alcohol of any desired flavour handed over the counter for a given quantity of the two raw materials.

Flavour and colouring were the fruit of careful experiments under the direction of the Chemist. Very passable imitations could be purchased of gin, rum, crème de menthe and whisky.

Apart from the concentrated spirits, Good Time Charlie Goonstein and his mates displayed ingenuity in finding a use for the barrels upon barrels of almost uneatable "jam" supplied by the Germans which littered the canteen and the camp kitchen. This was the stuff, already mentioned, made of sugar beet waste, dyed

red, and distributed to prison camps all over Germany in barrels marked '*Nur für Kriegsgefangener*'.

The distillers transformed half a dozen casks into vats, where the "jam" fermented, giving off a foul smell. The ferment was distilled to produce "Jam-Alc". Van Rood really deserved his nickname for this "speak-easy" alcohol. It tasted of old rubber tyres. The Company conscientiously tried to improve its quality, but, experiment how they would, even after three distillations, "Jam-Alc" still tasted of rubber.

In spite of this gastronomic disability it had a ready sale, at a low rate of exchange—for instance, three bottles of Jam-Alc for a bucket of coal—among a clientele who seemed able to stomach it without immediate undue ill effects. One gay party, however, which began on Boxing Day, 1943, as a fancy dress party, continued until February 29th, 1944. Undoubtedly Jam-Alc played a part in the celebration of such a happy and glorious anniversary as the fourth New Year spent in a Nazi prison.

Coming round from it, after a debauch, was unpleasant. So much so that the sufferer was tempted to return to the comatose condition, rather than face the horrors of the no man's land which lay between him and sobriety. Jam-Alc then became known as "the needle" after the hypodermic variety. One reveller spent New Year's Day sprawled on the floor with his head in a lavatory pan. The cisterns had been arranged to flush automatically as soon as they filled. Every time a cold douch of water poured over his head, he raised himself a few inches on one elbow to splutter, "Thanks ver' much, old boy–ver' kind of you," then dropped his head again, ready for the next two gallons.

*   *   *   *   *

As 1943 dragged out its endless repetition of daylight and darkness and as the significance of the capitulation of Stalingrad slowly sank into the reactionary recesses of the Teutonic mind, German morale became noticeably poorer. Like the weeds which show themselves when a soil is badly cared for, so the German temperament sprouted corruptive practices when the selective weed-killer of propaganda lost its force and hold upon the people.

Nineteen forty-three saw the birth and growth of the corruption of the Colditz guards. In 1944, it grew to such proportions and involved such a large quantity of the consumable Red Cross foodstuffs, cigarettes and tobacco that even a casual observer could deduce that

the prisoners were not obtaining value for money. There was under-cutting, throat cutting, Dutch auctioning and blackmail. There were rings, cabals, cartels, subsidiaries, commodity monopolies, short and long term contracts and financing houses.

In the midst of this tumultuous sea rode "Checko" in an un-sinkable boat. Flight Lieutenant Ceñek Chalupka, R.A.F., was, metaphorically, made of cork. In the hey-day of Neville Chamberlain he flew for his country—Czechoslovakia. After Munich he flew for Poland; after Warsaw he made his way to France; and after Paris he flew for England. He was decorated by every nation for which he fought.

He was tall, dark and handsome and full of vitality. He spoke English with a catching accent in a manner that would rival Maurice Chevalier. How the women must have fallen for him!

He was the only prisoner in Colditz who could claim to have kissed a girl while imprisoned there. It happened in 1944. Checko was escorted to the dentist in the town for treatment. One look passed between him and the pretty German receptionist. It was enough. The next day she contrived to deliver to the camp a muffler Checko had "inadvertently" left behind! She persuaded the Guard Commander to send for Checko to come to the prison gates. There, through a tiny grill in the massive oak, no bigger than the palm of a man's hand, the muffler and Cupid's dart passed simultaneously, and a pair of rosy lips presented themselves for their reward.

Checko was an adopted godson of Eric Linklater. Indeed, his was a character that would fit admirably into this famous author's portrait gallery; puckish, virile, humorous, dynamic, uproarious and explosive. Checko, in the course of 1943, flooded the Colditz market with maps, files and hack-saw blades; dye stuffs, photo-graphic materials and coloured inks; stamps, identity papers and time tables; tools of every description, paints, plaster, cement and chemicals. He had rivals and he had difficulties. Racketeering among the French—until they left—was reaching alarming dimen-sions, and, whereas he concentrated as far as he could on the accessories of escape, he was up against firms that worked only for the bodily comforts of prisoners. Extra food and fresh food, eggs, butter, cheese, vegetables and fruit, commanded high prices and threatened, at times, to run him out of business. For a while he sailed with the wind, keeping his head, and gathered allies to his cause until public opinion in the camp was eventually roused and came to the rescue of those seeking escape, as opposed to luxury.

All this, however, did not happen in a day. Not until December, 1944, did order develop out of chaos. David Sterling, the tall Scotsman whose exploits as the Commander of the Long Range Desert group are written in war history, was detailed by the S.B.O. to co-ordinate and to regulate the Black Market activities of Colditz. Prices came down with a crash, distribution became orderly and goods remained plentiful. In addition, by way of bonus with every exchange, "pieces" of Military intelligence were collected. When these were all put together they solved the jigsaw puzzle of the local German Command; the division of responsibility between Wehrmacht, Gestapo and Landwehr, the pressure groups and personalities, the weight of weapons and military supplies and the local forces that could be deployed. But this is jumping ahead in time and sequence. . . .

Returning to the spring and early summer of 1943, when racketeering was still in its infancy and the Goons were not demoralised, one of the principal aims of the Colditz convicts was, naturally, to try to demoralise by every means possible. Goon baiting is a self-explanatory term. It meant simply baiting the Goons. This activity, like distilling, gained impetus and attained dizzy heights in 1943.

There were few officers at Colditz who had not, at one time or another, faced court-martial charges. There was, generally speaking throughout the war, at least one officer languishing in a solitary confinement cell under sentence of death.

Appeals took a long time and the first appeal was not usually successful.

No death sentence was, in fact, carried out from Colditz, but this did not lessen the heavy toll of suffering inflicted on the unfortunate ones imprisoned for years, alone with their thoughts and with the shadow of the shroud spreading over them. To die or not to die—that was their question. It was worse than knowing the final outcome because, during the eternity of months, there was hope manacled to frustration and utter impotence on the part of the prisoner to help himself. It is one thing, for instance, to struggle madly against death in the depths of the sea, but it must be a far worse agony to lie, pinioned and helpless, in the depths in a submarine, dependent on the help of others that may never come or which may, when it comes, be ineffectual.

The situation in which some of the prisoners thus found themselves became almost intolerable. They were spirited men of fine character, expiating no crime and the strain told heavily on their

nerves. Some indeed were insane before they were finally reprieved. As far as is known, they have recovered.

Goon baiting was not therefore a pastime to be undertaken lightly. A little surreptitious baiting here and there was always good fun and the risks attached to it added to the excitement. But there were some who attached a more serious view to this side of prison life. Goon baiting was a weapon—of some potentiality in the prison "cold war." If wielded systematically and with perseverance, in a campaign extending over several consecutive months, its effect on the morale of the German garrison could be gauged. There were results. It paid dividends.

The waging of this cold war involved risks. The danger of a court-martial death sentence, with its accompanying anguish, was always real and proximate. In the heat of an argument with a German officer, the laying of a restraining hand upon the officer's sleeve was interpreted as "a personal attack", punishable with death; the raising of an accusing finger close to his face became an insult, a menace; and if it touched his face it was "an attack" punishable with death.

Happily for the prisoners, there was Lieutenant Alan Campbell, R.A., known as "Black" Campbell. He had been training for the Bar before the war and devoted himself at Colditz to the defence in court-martial charges brought by the German High Command. Black, the heavy eyebrowed, black-haired sleuth with the hawk-like nose, gave the German legal pundits no relaxation. When Black himself relaxed, it was to play the piano and write poetry. He had escaped from Tittmoning in broad daylight by climbing over the wire, while twenty-six assistants diverted the sentries armed with machine-guns.

The Germans would not supply him with a copy of their Army Code. He arranged for one to be ghosted out of the Kommandantur. He burnt the midnight oil over this frightening document, written in the heaviest of legal German, a language which, even in its simplest phraseology, lends itself to alternative translations. German is a tortuous language. Its meaning can be twisted and Black learnt, in time, to make good use of this flexible faculty. He quoted, for the benefit of the German barrister defending, usually a Dr. Naumann, passages of the Code which the Germans omitted to mention and he shook their confidence by his ability to beat them at their own game of weighting interpretations of text in their favour.

Altogether, he defended forty-two court-martial cases, including

thirteen in which the charge was high treason and the sentence death; the plaintiffs being Czech officers flying for the R.A.F. He saved them on a point of International Law. It should be of interest to many and to legal circles in particular to read, one day, the story of his long, arduous battle of wits against the German High Command. He fought to ensure that a prisoner had access to his legal advisers in order to prepare his defence. At one period of the war, the number of acquittals he secured on account of his incisive verbal duelling, so incensed the Germans at Colditz that they packed him off to another camp—Spangenburg. Within six months he had been caught under a bridge at night, on his way out of his new prison. Sentries shot at him with the aid of spot-lights and he was only saved by feigning death. He was returned to Colditz.

Among the many colourful characters he defended was Flying Officer Peter Tunstall, R.A.F., who, in the course of his sojourn in Germany, underwent five courts-martial with an endless round of appeals and re-trials and paid the price of four hundred and fifteen days of solitary confinement for his convictions with regard to escaping and to the value of Goon baiting. His last sentence of nine months, for "insulting the German nation," was awarded too late for him to carry it out. "Pete," a Hampton bomber pilot, was of medium build, fair, with good features and pale blue eyes that had a warning light. His mouth had a humorous curl that could also convey defiance.

In one court-martial, Pete was offered honourable acquittal if he would state that there had been a misunderstanding between himself and the German N.C.O. concerned. The case was one of assault with his index finger! Pete refused to make the statement, adding that the N.C.O., witness for the prosecution, was lying. A re-trial was ordered and took place at Leipzig. The N.C.O. fainted during cross-examination. Pete quickly seized a carafe of water off the judge's desk and administered it to him, asking the judge, a German general, not to press the poor fellow too hard with awkward questions. Although the prosecution attempted to tamper with the written evidence of defending British witnesses, the court awarded an acquittal. The only spur that drove the Germans to show a semblance of justice was the existence of the protecting power—Switzerland—and the threat of "Nach dem Krieg! After the war!" Black insisted on handing all his briefs to the Protecting Power representatives, when they visited the camp towards the end of the war.

Scorgie Price, one of the said British witnesses, went to Leipzig with intentions far removed from the simple resolution to see that justice was done. He went with the idea of making a break. Although the opportunity never presented itself and the expedition was, as far as he was concerned, a failure, it is worth recording what he did.

He wore a standard army officer's service dress uniform on which had been sewn sky-blue, silver embroidered épaulettes; sky blue collar badges and two, broad, sky-blue, silver embellished stripes down the trouser legs. Rex Harrison and Scarlet O'Hara had gone "all out" to produce a "variety show" costume. A Frenchman had given him flamboyant, gilded aiguillettes to which he added red tassels. His service dress cap was adorned with silver and blue edging. Over this exotic uniform he wore a simple khaki overcoat.

The German Regimental Sergeant Major, in command of a heavy guard accompanying the court-martial party, looked askance at what little of the uniform he noticed under the bottom of the overcoat and on Scorgie Price's head. But it was too late to remonstrate. Scorgie had timed matters carefully. The team had to catch a train at the station a mile from the camp. Senior German Staff Officers would be waiting impatiently at Leipzig. Lieutenant Price was a principal witness in the trial. Besides, the Sergeant Major was assured that British officers always attended important functions in full dress uniform—if they possessed it. Lieutenant Price's uniform was the correct ceremonial dress of his regiment, the Gordon Highlanders. The Sergeant Major could check it, if he liked, but there was the train to catch. . . .

The most important parts of Scorgie's outfit were not visible even when he removed his overcoat. They consisted of the credentials of a high ranking Hungarian officer on a tour of inspection of frontier patrols. The *pièce de résistance* was a letter of introduction, beautifully forged, completed with the embossed crest of the German Foreign Office and signed by none less than Baron von Neurath, German Ambassador to Hungary.

The cortège returned from Leipzig with mixed feelings. The acquittal of Peter Tunstall was a victory but the return of Scorgie Price was a defeat. Scarlet O'Hara ruefully conceded where his allegiance lay, when he was heard to remark disconsolately, addressing his question to the heavens, "Is there no justice in this God-forsaken country!"

*   *   *   *

It must have been the advent of the horse-drawn fire brigade which put ideas into the heads of some of the Goon baiters. The German Commandant decided to hold a fire practice in the Castle courtyard. It was a ludicrous performance consisting merely of the entry into the yard, at a hearse-like pace, of a hearse-like fire engine drawn by two chestnut horses which looked as if they had pulled gun carriages in the First World War. Hoses were uncoiled. Orders were issued to shut all windows, whereupon weak jets of water rose towards the second floor while the firemen were soaked to the skin by cascading jets which spouted in all directions from the leaking canvas coils.

The rehearsal was quickly terminated. Amid hoots and jeers the fire engine retired. The prisoners could, obviously, seek no succour in that direction if a fire broke out. The fact that all windows were barred was a little discomforting—but thoughts of fire soon disappeared—ousted by rival and more congenial thoughts of the possibilities of water.

Peter Tunstall was among the first to use the water weapon. An identification parade was in progress in the courtyard, one morning, in the chilly early hours, after a major escape. The Dutch were lining up before a table at which sat Hauptman Eggers —security officer, the official German interpreter, and a feldwebel behind a tall pile of files, card index forms, paper, pencils, ink, pens and blotting paper. A bucket of water was poured from a window high up in the wall, behind the seated officials. It drenched the Jerries and left the table a slippery mess of ink pools and sodden paper. Unfortunately for Peter, Hauptman Priem was also in the courtyard and caught a sidelong view of the face of the culprit. He was "clapped into jug" and, later, produced for court-martial on charges of: assaulting a superior in the course of his duty; causing a superior to take cover; causing confusion on a roll call parade, and breaking a prison camp rule prohibiting the throwing of water out of windows.

A sentence of two months' solitary—to run concurrently, did not prevent him from doing it again. On the second occasion he used an oversize water bomb. It was high summer and the German Camp Commandant appeared in a spotless white duck uniform, followed by five Germans in the brown uniforms of Nazi politicians, with massive leather belts encircling their paunches, their left arms swathed in broad, red armbands carrying the black Swastika in a white circle. Their shoulders, collars and hats were festooned with tinsel braid like Christmas trees. They were Gauleiters from Leipzig and Chemnitz.

The *Gefreiter* called "Auntie" ran ahead of them, up the British staircase, and burst into the mess room. Prisoners were having their tea and his shouts of "Achtung! Achtung!" were received with the usual compliment of "raspberries" and rude remarks. Tea continued and his more frenzied "Achtungs" were ignored. The Commandant walked in at the head of his procession. He had expected everyone to be standing glassily at attention. Instead he had to wait three minutes; the time it took for the more ardent tea drinkers to note his presence "officially."

Benches and chairs scraped, mugs and plates clattered and men rose slowly to their feet wiping their mouths and blowing their noses with large khaki handkerchiefs in a studied display of insolence of finely calculated duration.

The Gauleiters raised their arms in the Nazi salute with their arms bent—Hitler fashion. The salute was returned by the members of one table including Scorgie Price and Peter Tunstall in a manner which appeared to please the Gauleiters. The prisoners saluted with a variation of the "V" sign in which the fingers were closed instead of open and the thumb facing inwards. The Gauleiters, happy to think that their importance was appreciated, saluted again, and the salute was acknowledged again but with greater vigour. As the procession passed between the rows of men standing to at their tables, the cue was taken up and prisoners everywhere gave the new salute, which was acknowledged punctiliously at every turn by the Gauleiters.

They turned, retraced their steps, saluting and being saluted, beaming with smiles at their pleasant welcome and finally left the quarters.

A water bomb just missed them as they emerged from the British doorway, but spattered the Commandant's duck uniform all over with mud. He shouted for the guard, hurried his visitors through the gates and returned alone. A posse, despatched upstairs at the double to find the culprit, was not quick enough. Pete was learning; nothing could be pinned on him. The Commandant left the courtyard followed by cries of "*Kellner! Bringen Sie mir ein whisky soda!*"

His exit signalled the arrival of the riot squad. Windows were ordered to be closed; rifles were levelled upwards at those delaying to comply with the shouted commands. Scarlet O'Hara, sleeping peacefully beside an open window, awoke from a siesta in time to hear the tail-end of the shouting. Poking his head out as far as the bars he cautioned the squad: "*Scheissen Sie nicht*, my good men,

scheissen Sie nicht!"—all to no avail. A bullet zipped through the opening and he closed the window from a kneeling position cursing the ill manners of the "uncouth b—— Huns." The word he had pronounced was *scheissen*, not *schiessen*.

The Commandant never appeared again in his white duck uniform.

* * * * *

International games of stoolball between the British and other nationalities had not been popular in the early years of the war. The game had no rules and no referee and the Continentals were frankly not attuned to such a form of competition.

Then the camp had decided, in 1942, to hold an Olympic games. Stoolball was not included in the competitions. The Olympics were a great success and it was thought, generally, a pity that stoolball had not been included.

The upshot was that some British officers conferred together, invented a few rules and produced a referee. British teams were pitted against one another, and the rules modified until they dovetailed with the circumstances and surroundings of the game. Then they were codified and published.

Once more the game was to become international. By that time, however, the Poles had gone, but the French started practice matches of their own with a British referee. Teams consisted of seven a side; scrums were broken up after a few minutes if there were signs of a deadlock and the ball thrown into the air; as before, the ball had to be bounced every three steps or passed in any direction.

A team was composed of three forwards, one half back, two full backs and a stoolie.

International matches soon became a monthly feature, and heavy betting took place on the results. For the British, the three forwards were chosen from Peter Storie Pugh, Checko, Dick Howe, Colin McKenzie and Howard Gee; the half backs from Allan Cheetham, Bush Parker and Peter Allan; the two full backs from Lulu Lawton, Willie Elstob and Sydney Hall—a Channel Islander, lumberjack and strong man of Colditz who, with one arm, once lifted an Australian orderly, Archer—a grandfather in the 1914–18 war, by his coat collar and hung him on a peg. The stoolie was usually Bill Goldfinch. Rupert Barry was the recognised international referee. The French team always included Edgar Barras and André Almeras.

The last international match of all, just before the French left

Colditz in the early summer of 1943, was the most exciting game ever held in the courtyard. The whole camp, and a large number of Goons, turned out to watch it. The game resulted in a draw at four all. The Jerry spectators were as excited as the rest, some yelling for the British, others for the French.

Although stoolball was the excuse for a "rough-house," played in a cobble stone courtyard, nobody hurt himself seriously; Checko is recorded to have once broken a finger during a dive for the stool over the top of a large scrum.

When the French left, enthusiasm for the game waned, it was gradually replaced by basketball—known in Colditz as "dolley-ball." It lacked the verve and the rough and tumble excitement of stoolball but was very fast. Bill Scott, a Canadian captured in the Dieppe raid, had represented Canada at basketball in Olympics before the war. He undertook coaching and was the moving spirit in popularising the game. A league was formed. It provided scope for the laying of odds, which the camp bookies, principally Hector Christie and "Screwie" Wright, were not slow to appreciate.

The bars on the courtyard windows saved them from breakage by wide flung balls during the more hectic moments of stoolball, but the Gothic chapel windows were only protected by wire netting which was not tough enough for the job. They were consequently often broken. The Germans did nothing about it, preferring to replace the broken panes on rare occasions rather than go to the expense of stronger screens.

One day, shortly after the French farewell international stool-ball match, the courtyard gate opened to allow the entry of a little man in grey overalls, known as Willie, carrying a long ladder and accompanied by the usual sentry to look after him.

Peter Tunstall happened to be ambling across the courtyard at the time. He was rather at a loss to know what to do with himself since the Franz Josef escape attempt in which he had been one of the participants. The weather was fine and warm. Spring had turned to summer and some prisoners had even started sun-bathing in the square of sunlight that carpeted the yard at noon.

Pete's normal relaxation, "Goon baiting," also seemed to have "hit a low" since the climax of the water bombing. He was on the verge of one of those vacuums in a prisoner's life when several months may pass in a procession of painfully slow days, at the end of which the prisoner, waking up, cannot account for the passage of time. There are no signposts and he appears to have been dreaming through a long, fitful slumber.

Pete sat down absent-mindedly on the stone steps near the canteen and idly watched Willie, an ordinary little workman, carrying a wooden rule, who now slowly climbed his long ladder which he had leant against the wall beside one of the chapel windows. Absent-mindedly Pete's gaze turned to the sentry who stood nearby.

"They're all alike," he muttered to himself, "can't pick out one in a hundred—wonder who thought of the name 'Goons'—just what they are."

Little Willie took measurements, climbed slowly down the ladder again, spoke to the sentry, and walked off towards the courtyard gate.

Peter saw him disappear, wondering vaguely why he had gone away. "Suppose he's gone to fetch the glass." Then his eye roamed once more towards the sentry. The latter was standing stolidly on guard five yards from the ladder and facing the courtyard.

The reaction of a well-trained "Kriegie" was instantaneous. Peter rose; the vacuum had filled. There was a glint in his eye. He returned hurriedly to the British quarters and buttonholed the Weasel (Don Donaldson), who in turn shouted towards a far corner of the almost empty room.

"Heh!—come over here, you browned-off eagle—I want to talk to you—quick."

Bag Dickenson yawned and slowly rose from a bed in the corner. "Are you addressing me?" he queried, tucking his shirt into his trousers as he walked over. He sat on a bed opposite the other two. "You've upset my sleep quota, you rocky mountain buzzard."

. . . A few minutes later they descended together to the courtyard where they separated.

Don sat down on the cobbles. There was nothing unusual about that. He sat near the sentry, upright, against a wall and facing him. He started playing with his hands. Looking wide-eyed into the sky, he made his hands climb Jacobs' ladders; he played churches and people and the preacher in the pulpit; he made his hands into mice which chased each other all over his body, behind his back, round his neck, under his shirt and up his trouser legs; he counted his fingers and started all over again. He not only attracted the gaze of the sentry but that of a small group of mildly amused spectators whom he had to motion away so that the Goon's view was not obstructed.

In the meantime, Peter Tunstall and Bag Dickenson removed the ladder which they carried into the porch at the bottom of the British staircase, behind the sentry's back. They started to climb the spiral steps but found that the twenty-five foot ladder would not circumvent the curves.

Peter Tunstall and Bag Dickenson remove the ladder

It became securely wedged. There was only one solution which did not require much thought. While the browned-off eagle fetched a saw (made out of a gramophone spring) from his tool kit, which was the best in Colditz, Pete returned to the courtyard and signalled the Weasel to carry on. This was asking for something because Don was not prepared for a long solo act. Pete could see his mind turning over as his eyeballs rolled, following the juggling motion of his hands. He left him to it and went back to the staircase, where Bag and he were soon engaged in an argument as to

how much of the ladder should be sawn off. Bag was playing for safety while Pete insisted on running it close. They compromised at five feet from one end.

It took ten minutes to saw through both legs of the ladder, which they did to the accompaniment of generally encouraging, but sometimes very rude, remarks from passers-by navigating the obstruction on the stairs.

Pete was wondering what the Weasel was doing and how soon Willie might return. He was delighted to see, when he descended to the courtyard with a five-foot length of ladder under his arm, that the little fellow had not yet come back and that the Weasel's knot of spectators had grown. Don was finding great difficulty in clearing a view for the sentry who was genuinely intrigued by his efforts to scratch his left ear with his right foot.

Pete leaned the five foot length of ladder where the twenty-five foot one had previously reposed and retired to a distance to view the effect. At that moment little Willie was let into the courtyard again, carrying a large square pane of glass carefully in his arms. Don, seeing that his act was no longer required, stood up with a final handspring and walked off hurriedly to the French quarters. The knot of idlers was dispersing when the new focus of attention presented itself. The sentry and little Willie stood, side by side, gazing incredulously, with jaws dropped, at a transformation of which Lewis Carroll might have been proud.

The prisoners started to laugh. The sentry shook his head slowly from side to side and Willie looked up and down the chapel wall. They faced each other and Willie asked, "*Was ist gefallen?*" A crowd was gathering and the laughter was growing. The sentry answered, shrugging his shoulders and looking frightened as if he had seen a ghost. "*Ich weiss nicht. Es war hier bestimmt. Gibt es ein Poltergeist vielleicht?*"

Little Willie laid the pane of glass against the wall, took out a large handkerchief, mopped his brow and blew his nose to recover his composure. It was not easy. There were faces now at almost every window, and laughter was echoing round the courtyard. He and the sentry were the only figures on the stage, playing before a large audience.

He approached the five-foot ladder, picked it up, turned it over and adjusted it under his arm. The sentry, crestfallen, picked up the glass, fell in behind him and, in single file, they marched forlornly across the courtyard through a gangway formed between cheering prisoners.

THE FLYING DUTCHMEN

ON June 7th, 1943, the Dutch contingent received orders to pack up and leave at twelve hours notice. This did not perturb them as they had known of the move for a week through information passed inside the camp. Their contraband was safely stowed in prepared suitcases. One Dutchman packed his suitcase for the last time at Colditz. He had packed it every morning and unpacked it again every night for two years.

The Dutch were bound for Stanislau, in Poland. Their departure would mean the end of a long chapter in the story of Oflag IVC; a story of close collaboration with the British, of unfailing understanding and generosity, of courage and good humour. They would be missed everywhere in the camp. The smartest "turn out" on parade, and in chapel; their divine contempt of the Germans; the Hawaian orchestra would be no more; Vandy's inimitable personality would disappear from the Castle and only his ghost would haunt the corridors in the minds of the men who remained. Soon, even those memories would fade, but, for all who knew Vandy and his Dutchmen well, they can never fade entirely. A pleasant aura surrounds them to this day, and an honoured place remains for them in those inner recesses of the mind where narrow distinctions fade but a deep impression rests. As the tracks left by a stream of vehicles which pass along a sandy road twist and intertwine and eventually merge into two great ruts, so the mind recollects an episode, a chapter, an era that has long since passed.

The whole camp turned out to see them off.

"We'll miss you, Vandy," said Dick.

"I'm *rather* sorry to go," replied Vandy, who was obviously deeply moved. "Ve may haf a chance to escape on the vay. I haf many men prepared. Good-bye, Dick. Ve had good times together. In Colditz ve haf shown those Huns how to behave themselves."

"Yes!" said Dick, "it's funny isn't it, how well they've behaved in Colditz considering the hell we give them."

"Ach! Dick that is the secret. You must alvays give them hell. If you do not you are finished. The Hun, he vill sit on you and sqvash you and bully you to death, unless you bully him. He only understands that. I was in camps before I came to Colditz. There

I saw vot happened. Germans despised the prisoners and gave them hell. Here it was othervise. You vere all brave men—you had proved it—and you gave them hell from the virst days. So, they respect you and are afraid to bully. It is a simple qvestion of domination by vorce of the character. Do not vorget! Good-bye, Dick . . . and . . . Gott bless England! . . ."

Vandy

So, the irrepressible Vandy, the officer in charge of all the Dutch escapes but never of his own, departed.

Hardly had Vandy left the courtyard with his men, to be searched in the Kommandantur before entraining, than he gave expression to his deep convictions with regard to the Germans. His large suitcase was a maze of secret pockets, and had a false bottom filled with escaping contraband. The Germans took from the open suitcase an army overcoat, the collar of which Vandy had altered and dyed for civilian purposes. Speaking German fluently and with

a fine colloquial vocabulary, equal to that of any *Wehrmacht*
sergeant major, he seethed with indignation, mounted a stool and
harangued the whole room. He would not move without his coat.
He would lie on the floor and they would have to carry him. How
right Vandy was! The Germans knew that he would lie on the
floor. They knew that bayonets would not move him. It was
"vorce of character" all right. The major in charge gave in and
his men were sufficiently subdued by Vandy's oratory and by his
determination, not to look further into his belongings.

The fifty-eight Dutchmen voyaged for four days in two old-
fashioned railway coaches, crammed together like sardines. The
Colditz guards, numbering thirty-three, under the command of a
Hauptman, stood at the windows of the compartments and along
the corridor. The windows were plastered with barbed wire. On
the evening of the second day, near Feschen on the Polish border,
while water bottles were being filled at a stop, Baron van Lynden,
a cavalry lieutenant and an aide-de-camp of Queen Wilhelmina,
escaped. He was soon missed, and the German Captain of the
Guard, stopping the train at Krakau, refused to continue further
without guard reinforcements from the local garrison. Twenty
more guards were piled into the coaches on the third evening and
remained with them until they reached Lemberg (Lwow). The
party reached their destination, without further incident, at the
end of the fourth day.

Stanislau is an industrial town in the province of Galicia, in
the South East of Poland. The camp to which they were conducted
was two miles from the railway station. It had once been an
Austrian cavalry barracks and later a Polish prison. On their
arrival at the station they were met by a German officer with a
bicycle. The Colditz Hauptman flatly refused to escort the prisoners
to the camp without adequate supervision; thirty-three guards
were not enough. Again, reinforcements arrived from the prison.
The fifty-seven Dutchmen were then marched, in four squads at
intervals, surrounded by a total of fifty-six guards and eight
N.C.O.s and led by two officers, along the Adolf Hitler Strasse,
the main street of Stanislau. Silent, sympathetic Poles, clustered
on the pavements in small groups to watch them pass. They
arrived at the camp singing patriotic Dutch songs and were delighted to see Dutch faces at the windows to greet them. They
were all officers and cadets of the Dutch forces who had remained
in Holland on a bogus *parole* at the beginning of the war. In
May, 1942, one hundred of them had been shot for underground

activities and about two thousand had been transported to Stanislau. Their morale was not good, but the influence of men like
Vandy changed the atmosphere of the prison within a matter of
weeks.

Vandy had his showdown with the Prussian Abwehr officer of
Stanislau immediately on arrival. The latter was showing off in
front of the Captain and the guards from Colditz and began
browbeating the prisoners. He "went for" a lieutenant in Vandy's
platoon and "caught a packet" himself for addressing a junior
officer in a squad under the command of a more senior officer.
Vandy took the opportunity, with righteous indignation on his
side, to explode with anger and concluded by appealing in German
to the Colditz Hauptman who was handing over his assignment.
The Colditz sentries thoroughly enjoyed the situation.

"Herr Hauptman, is it not your experience from Colditz that
we prisoners have always behaved with correctness and decorum
because the German officers have treated the prisoners in the
same manner?"

The Hauptman could only answer "Yes", although he was
still smarting under the loss of one of his prisoner contingent.

This collusion left the Stanislau Abwehr officer at a loss. Vandy
believed in attacking from the start and never letting go, once he
had the advantage.

To emphasise the contempt in which the Dutchmen held the
Germans of Stanislau, and the Abwehr officer in particular, three
of the Colditz party escaped from the first floor of the building
within an hour of arrival. The windows overlooked a drop of
twenty feet and beyond that a garden and the highway to Hungary.
The drop was, nevertheless, too much for two of the three who
twisted their ankles in the fall. A window collapsed with a crash
of splintering glass at the psychological moment and gave the
alarm. Otherwise all the Dutchmen would have disappeared
within ten minutes.

The two men with twisted ankles were recaught immediately,
but the third, Van Lingen, was free several days before he was
recaptured in the Carpathian mountains, having asked for food
at the farm of a *Volksdeutscher*, by mistake.

Van Lynden, who had escaped from the train, was recaught
after some days at Görlitz, and returned, at first, to Colditz much
to the amusement of the inmates. He remained in the cells for a
week before removal to Stanislau.

Vandy was soon recognised in the camp as "Escape Chief."

Among the younger officers, and especially the cadets who had been incarcerated in 1942, there was a feeling that they had been duped, by their seniors in Holland, into betraying their country by giving their *parole*. They had little confidence left in those around them. The advent of the Colditz diehards caused a spiritual rejuvenation among them, and the blood of patriots began to course, once more, through their veins.

The camp was separated into two halves; the officers being kept apart from the cadets (aspirants). Vandy placed one of his most trusted cadets, Aak Hageman, in charge of escape matters in their barracks. The morale of the whole camp rose steadily throughout the summer and autumn of 1943.

On November 30th, three more Dutchmen escaped. One, travelling alone, made his way to Hungary and later to London. The other two, former Colditz men, Charles Douw van der Krap and Fritz E. Kruimink, nicknamed Beer by the English, reached Warsaw, where they disappeared into Bor Komorowski's underground. Beer was eventually despatched to Paris where he fought with the French Resistance and took part in the relief of Paris.

Van der Krap and an Englishman were stopped by a German sentry, one evening, on a bridge over the Vistula in Warsaw. He demanded their papers. While he was examining Douw's, the Englishman gave him a right to the jaw which sent him over the balustrade, into the river and through the ice. The next day the Germans found the body under the ice and Douw's papers lying nearby. The Poles thought it was time he moved. With typical *sang froid* they sent him as a fireman on the engine of a German military train which carried him back to Holland. Van der Krap took part in the Battle of Arnhem and was rescued with the few survivors of the Airborne Division who were helped back to the Allied lines.

Then came the "big move" on January the 10th, 11th and 12th, 1944. It was public knowledge when it came and was, in fact, considered to be rather late in the day as the Germans in Stanislau were terrified of a Russian advance long before January. This time the move was to a huge camp at Neu Brandenburg in Mecklenburg, a hundred miles north of Berlin, housing Americans, French, Poles and Serbs in different compounds.

Vandy and his second in command, Lieutenant Dames, made the escape preparations and gave Hageman the assistance he needed to organise the cadets. In general, the intention was not to make a break on the journey unless a reasonable opportunity

presented itself; the new camp was reputed to have good possibilities. However, before leaving Stanislau, there were several escape schemes on hand, to be put into immediate action.

Vandy and Dames first concealed twelve men under the floor of their theatre auditorium. Secondly, they equipped six others to re-enact the escape of Douw and Beer in 1943, which had depended on the help of Yugoslavian orderlies. Four of the six were Colditz men, the fifth non-Colditz, and the sixth, a Dutch Rear Admiral. Thirdly, among the cadets, four men, of whom two from Colditz, were also concealed in the camp before departure.

The move was organised by the Germans, in three batches, one on each of the three consecutive days.

The cadets departed on the first day. Before leaving, the Abwehr officer made a speech. He said that it was no use trying to escape because: (*a*) it was mid-winter with snow everywhere, (*b*) their boots would be removed on the train, and (*c*) he had transported thirty thousand Italians from Italy without a single escape. This incredibly tactless approach was enough for the cadets.

When they arrived at Neu Brandenburg there were sixty-eight missing. Many more had escaped but had been recaptured at various stations and put on the train again. A German sentry, who spent hours shooting at the cadets as they escaped, said afterwards that the men leaving the train reminded him of a game of Tiddlywinks.

On the second day the Senior officers left. One escaped on the way to the station and hid in a culvert. He was seen by a guard who fired twice into the culvert, wounding him seriously. He was transported back to the Stanislau camp.

On the journey, the same guard shot and killed another Dutchman who had made a hole through the floor of his wagon and lay between the tracks waiting for the train to move off after a stop in the open country.

A third officer jumped the train, fell and remained unconscious on the tracks. A train, passing in the other direction, cut off both his legs. In addition, forty-four others escaped.

The next day, the third batch, including the Colditz group, travelled. Thirty escaped. On the way, the third train, like a trawl net, picked up those recaptured after escaping from the first two trains. The Dutchman who had lost his legs was taken on board. His case was given up as hopeless by German doctors,

but a Dutch surgeon attended him in Neu Brandenburg, day and night for a week, and saved his life.

The move was a major disaster for the Germans. When they counted up the totals at the end of three days, one hundred and fifty prisoners were missing.

A special alarm was broadcast covering Germany and Poland. Hitler was advised of the escape and Himmler's minions were set to their work of extermination. The code name for the order was known to the Gestapo as the the order "*Stufe Drei*".

It was many a day before Vandy could add up the final score of this escape. It went somewhat like this:

1. The twelve who were hidden in the theatre had to give themselves up after a week as the camp remained fully guarded though empty. They followed the main body to Neu Brandenburg.

2. Of the six who escaped (including the admiral) two, the Admiral and Diederik Baron van Lijnden (ex-Colditz) reached Roumania with identity papers and exit and entry visas supplied to Vandy through his wife from the Dutch underground. They were freed by the Russians and sent to England. The other three (ex-Colditz), including Captain Veenendaal, R.N.I.A., and Lieutenant Donkers, R.N.I.A., reached the Dutch border where they were trapped. The sixth was recaught on the Czecho-Slovak frontier. They were all later forwarded to Neu Brandenburg.

3. Of the four cadets who hid in Stanislau before the move: one reached Hungary, was released by the Russians and found his way to England; one was recaught and sent back to Stanislau where he disappeared, and two ex-Colditz men, Hans von Seydlitz, Kurzbach, and Aire Ligtermoet escaped to Russia, where they were imprisoned along with Germans. Ligtermoet, who died in Odessa in 1947, was awarded a posthumous decoration. Von Seydlitz is still missing.

4. Ten officers including the officer wounded in the culvert and the cadet from 3 above were submitted to "*Stufe Drei*", and one officer was shot dead under the train.

5. In spite of the snow on the Carpathian mountains and the absence of boots on their feet, seven men reached Hungary.

6. Three more arrived safely in Holland and two reached Switzerland via Vienna.

Totalling up: one hundred and sixty-four men attempted to

escape, of whom fifteen made home-runs, eleven were murdered, one had his legs cut off, two died in Russian prisons, and one hundred and thirty-seven were recaptured.

*　　　*　　　*　　　*　　　*

Within eight days of arriving at Neu Brandenburg, on January 22nd, the first escape, organised by Vandy and Dames, took place. Twelve men, seven of them from Colditz, disappeared from the camp. One, ex-Colditz, named Fraser, reached England via Sweden; one is missing; one was executed, and the remainder returned to Neu Brandenburg.

These men were incorrigible.

A new block of eleven solitary confinement cells had to be constructed beside the old, rotten, timber frame Barracks in which they were housed in this camp. The cells remained fully occupied into the autumn of 1944.

In September, 1944, many of the older officers were moved to a camp at Tittmoning, not far from Salzburg in Austria, owing to the damp, unhealthy conditions existing in Neu Brandenburg.

The record of Vandy's sixty-four officers and cadets, mostly of the Dutch East Indies Forces, who were sent from Holland in 1940 to Colditz via another camp—Juliusburg, is here set down.

Thirteen made home-runs; two others reached Russia, one is dead, one missing; and, in addition, this company can lay claim to twenty-six "gone-aways."

CHAPTER XII

ROUNDABOUT

THE summer was in full course when the French, at last, after several false starts, received orders to pack in preparation for a move. They were going north-eastward to Lübeck where the Poles had gone. The move was to include the Belgians but left behind, temporarily, a second batch of eighty French for whom there was no room on the first train. The second batch also included a few de Gaullist Frenchmen who, eventually, remained permanently.

Shortly after the departure of the main French body, sixty-five British Officers arrived from Oflag VII.B, Eichstatt. This raised the total of the British contingent to about one hundred and sixty souls.

The Eichstatt mob, as they were sometimes called, comprised the men who had broken out of their camp by tunnel on the night of the 3rd–4th June.

The tunnel was well engineered and was about forty-five yards long. Unfortunately, none of the sixty-five who escaped made the home-run.

After completing their bout of confinement, during which three made another break, they were despatched to Colditz in several parties. The three who made the second break were Gordon Rolfe, D.S.O. (Major, Royal Canadian Signals), Bill (Dopey) Miller (Lieutenant, Royal Canadian Engineers) and Douglas Moir (Lieutenant, Royal Tank Regiment). They did not travel far and soon turned up at Colditz.

Among those who arrived from Eichstatt were: Mike Edwards (Lieutenant, R.W. Fusiliers), George Drew (Lieutenant, North-umberland Regiment), Charles Forester (Lieutenant, Rifle Brigade), Bill Scott, M.C. (Lieutenant, Essex Scottish, Canada), John Pen-man, M.C. (Lieutenant, Argyll and Sutherland Highlanders) and Lieutenant-Colonel C. C. I. Merrit, V.C. (South Saskatchewan Regiment). Captains, the Lord Arundell of Wardour (Wiltshire Regiment) and the Earl of Hopetoun (Lothian and Border Horse), were also Eichstatt tunnellers who trickled into Colditz.

Others who arrived at about this period were Charlie Upham, V.C. and bar, the New Zealander, Tony Rolt, the motor-racing driver, and Michael Burn, M.C., *The Times* reporter who had been captured at St. Nazaire.

The opportunity offered by the move of a large party was not lost upon the old hands in the camp. When the Poles had left in 1942, Bertie Boustead had changed places with Count Felix Jablonowski.

Bertie Boustead was tall and thin and exchanged with Felix Jablonowski who was of small build. Boustead knew no Polish but learnt off by heart his Polish prison number. During the departure proceedings, each time the name Jablonowski was called, he stepped forward and, in reply to whatever the German interpreter asked him in Polish, he said, "*Piench shedem sheish yeshem*" which was Felix' prison number—5678. It did not matter what the interpreter asked. He always obtained the same answer.

The Germans made a habit of asking for the prisoners' numbers so that Bertie managed to "get away with it" on the final parade and again in Lübeck, the camp to which he was sent with the Poles.

After a week, Bertie's name was called out at *Appell*. The Germans wanted some information about a parcel addressed to Jablonowski. The interpreter asked in Polish, "What are the contents of the parcel?"

Bertie replied, "*Piench shedem sheish yeshem*." The interpreter asked him a second and a third time, but always received the same answer: "*Piench shedem sheish yeshem*." The comedy could not last long. The Germans checked up on Jablonowski's particulars and Bertie had "had it".

At Colditz, Felix was soon busy answering a string of awkward questions in atrocious English. He was "rumbled" and an exchange of prisoners took place causing the Goons much annoyance. Neither Felix nor Bertie managed to escape on the journey, which was the purpose of the whole subterfuge, owing to the number of guards employed—an N.C.O. and two sentries to each prisoner.

This exchange had now passed into history. The only memory which remained vivid was that of Felix Jablonowski sitting up in his bunk on his first morning in the British quarters wearing a hair-net. He had to be told that the practice might make him conspicuous.

When the Eichstatt British arrived, Dick immediately prepared an exchange with some of the French still at Colditz who were due to leave any day. The faces of the "old lags" were too well known to the Germans, but some of the "new boys" might be exchanged successfully.

Lieutenant Cazamayou and two other Frenchmen quickly responded to the idea and three promising-looking British officers among the new arrivals were picked out. They were Lieutenant T. M. Barratt, The Black Watch (R.M.R.) of Canada, commonly known as Jo-Jo the Dog Faced Boy, who took the place of Cazamayou, and Lieutenant D. K. Hamilton, R.A., and Lieutenant C. E. Sandback, Cheshire Yeomanry.

These three left Colditz with the last French contingent. They had no opportunities for escaping *en route*. They arrived at Lübeck, where there was a huge French camp, and were soon lost in the crowd. They began reconnoitring for an escape. It was high summer —July. The weather was fine and dry, most suitable for a long trek across country but, within four days, Hamilton and Sandback were

unearthed, evidently from the Colditz end. The discovery would have come about through photograph identity checks on the Eichstatt men in Colditz, which were due in any case.

Peter Barratt, however, appeared to have a respite. He knew it would not be for long, so he arranged with one of his French colleagues from Colditz to make a further exchange if his name was called. The next day it was. Sous-Lieutenant Diedler presented himself as Lieutenant Barrett, and was whisked back to Colditz with Hamilton and Sandback.

Barratt was caught a few days later leaving the Lübeck camp under a pile of sacks in a cart. He was escorted to the Kommandantur, where he gave his name as Diedler and was marched off to the cells.

The next morning he was cross-examined about his attempted escape, and the German-French interpreter began to think he was dealing with a moron.   Barratt knew well enough how to say, "*La plume de ma tante*," but his French lessons at school had not provided for the present contingency.

He was soon unmasked.

The Germans were confronted with a problem. They had already disposed of a Lieutenant Barratt under the alias of Lieutenant Cazamayou. Now they had a second Lieutenant Barratt under the alias of sous-Lieutenant Diedler. They even began to have misgivings as to the seriousness of the name Diedler. It had an ironic, Anglo-Saxon ring. They unravelled the mystery eventually, but it annoyed them considerably, just as it amused the Frenchmen at Lübeck, to know that the prisoners were playing with them.

*   *   *   *   *

The companionship of men like Gigue and Madin, of the French stoolball players, and the French language teachers was badly missed in Colditz, but their memory was kept alive by the wireless set the French left behind them. Dick took over the control of the secret studio. Lulu Lawton and Hector Christie, together, organised the stooging teams required for the periods of news reception and the routine camouflaging of the secret entrance to the studio.

Michael Burn, adept at shorthand, became the first news reporter. He was known as "The Scribe".

The operation of entering or leaving the studio took five minutes. Stooges were posted on each of the four floors of the building, two more in the courtyard and one at the entrance to the upper attics

where the studio was concealed. The last stooge held the key and was responsible for the door through which passed the operator —Dick, the scribe—Mike, and the camouflage-man—Lulu. The three crossed two more attics. Lulu went to work at a point where the roof beams and the attic floor joined. Floor-boards were removed, then a sawn length of timber joist, then a four-inch depth of under-floor rubble and, finally, more boards. The operator and scribe descended into the studio. Lulu replaced all camouflaging as he worked, and then retired. The heavy layer of dust over everything in the attic was a great bugbear and necessitated careful treatment. A knocking signal at the end of fifteen or twenty minutes warned the stooges that the news reception was over. The process would be repeated to extract the two officers from the studio. Mike then retired to a quiet nook, enlarged on his shorthand notes and prepared his bulletin. When this was ready he called together his assistant news reporters from their various quarters and copies were made from his original.

As the Allied pressure increased from 1944 onwards, news bulletins were demanded ever more frequently and the work became too much for one team to carry out efficiently. The studio operation, in fact, was carried out so frequently that the danger of over-confidence or staleness on the job became very real. The team consisted of no less than eleven officers. Dick decided to institute a second team. He trained Jimmy Yules as operator. Jim Rogers, who had begun studying shorthand furiously as soon as he saw his principal joy in life being taken from him by a news reporter who was proficient in this art, was appointed scribe of the new team, to his intense satisfaction. Norman Forbes undertook the camouflage work, Hector Christie trained a second team of stooges.

In the event of being trapped in the attics or studio, two methods of escape were available, depending on where the Germans were.

When the French tunnel had been discovered, the ropes which had been used by the French for the disposal of their tunnel debris were removed, leaving the long cylindrical sleeves from the top of the tower to ground floor empty. There was access to the sleeves from the attic.

In effect, the radio team of three had a fast-descending lift at their service. A piece of iron plate reposed over the sleeves at each floor level. If an alarm was given when all three were in the attic above the studio, they waited until the last moment, in case of false alarms. As soon as they heard the German keys in the attic lock (and having checked that the iron plates were in place!), they

dropped, one after the other, down the cylindrical sleeves, using their arms and thighs as brakes. An exit was, nowadays, conveniently provided by the Germans two floors below—they used it for inspection purposes. All three could, thus, descend two floors in a matter of seconds and sortie by the exit into their own quarters. The safe descent of the sleeves required practice, because, if the braking was not sufficient, the body accelerated downwards and a heavy fall could result. Of course, if the iron plates were not over the holes there was the prospect of a vertiginous descent, out of control, to the ground floor.

If the operator and scribe were ever to be actually trapped in the studio there was a last line of retreat. The studio reposed, partly over the solid outside wall, partly over the ceiling of the (now) British quarters. The joists and ceiling lathes were exposed in the studio and the latter could be broken in an emergency simply by jumping on them. The operators would then fall into the room below. In the event of surprise, they could, at least, save the wireless set by the emergency exit. Fortunately, this method of evacuating the studio never had to be used. The sleeve self-propelled lift, on the other hand, was frequently employed as the Germans made surprise searches of the attics. Although its existence was known, the whereabouts of the wireless set remained a secret from the Germans until the end of the war.

The electric power for the receiving set was tapped from the Castle mains. The supply was 220 volts d.c., that is, direct current. The set was manufactured to work on 110 volts d.c., and a dropping resistance had, therefore, to be employed in the circuit. The mains supply was switched off by the Germans at night, but this obstacle was circumvented by tapping the positive lead, using it as supply, and by earthing the negative lead to a lightning conductor.

All went well until the R.A.F. and the U.S.A.A.F. set about obliterating the power stations. Then, for long periods, there was no power at all.

The prisoners had to have their news. Dick and the scribes were in a quandary.

Officers used to mess together in groups of between seven and ten, depending upon how many could be conveniently seated around the various-sized kitchen tables which were provided. A group seldom remained more than a few months together. The petty exasperations that pass in everyday life were liable to accumulate, to combine and become distorted into grotesque catastrophes, causing major upheavals in the stifling conditions of the prison.

One group alone is known to have remained constant throughout the war. Its members were Padre "Dicky" Heard, Harry Elliott, Kenneth Lockwood and Dick Howe. They formed a durable nucleus at their mess table around which others gyrated, sometimes attracted, sometimes repelled. It was to be expected that the variety of topics of conversation was gradually exhausted as the war continued until, among the old guard when at table, there was scarcely any object in conversing. It was as if each could read the mind of the other.

Even mannerisms were so well known that their subconscious motivation was understood. Questions could be answered before they were asked. When Dick Howe stroked his nose he was given a cigarette, because that was what he would have asked for in a few seconds' time. If Harry twirled his moustache with one hand and stared momentarily into space, his table companions sat back, wondering which of his many funny stories Harry was about to tell. If he stroked his moustache with both hands, the question was, "Which Goon has got your back up this time, Harry?" because, indeed, that was what he was going to disclose. When Padre Heard coughed gently twice, it meant he wanted "A pinch of salt, please," and he was given it, usually, before the words came to his lips. When he gazed fixedly out of a nearby window overlooking the chapel it was understood by his colleagues that his remarks, in a few minutes' time, would concern the chapel organ and he would relate how the Germans never repaired the bellows nor the missing keys and stops.

The association of ideas—the sequence of thoughts that fill up the mental activity of man is like the pathway in a labyrinth. New openings and new paths appear at every turn, tempting the mind to travel along them. Concentration is, presumably, the art of not being deflected, or of consciously noting the deflection so as not to take the wrong path a second time.

Dick Howe was certainly not concentrating when he sat, one day, at the mess table mentally bemoaning another power cut that had ruined the whole day's news bulletins. He was staring vacantly in the direction of Dicky Heard who, in turn, was staring fixedly out of the window. Dick was suddenly thinking about organs and then about bellows, then about electric motors and then generators. At this point there must have been a short circuit somewhere in his mind because Dick jumped as if he had been electrocuted and banged the board in front of him with his fist. "I've got it!" was all he said and left the table.

He repaired to the chapel, mounted the miniature spiral staircase that led to the choir loft and examined the electric motor that worked the bellows that worked the organ.

"If the Jerries won't repair the bellows," he thought, "we may as well, at least, make use of the motor."

Electricity supplied to an electric motor turns it. If an electric motor is turned by other means it can supply electricity. Upon

The Treadmill

this simple principle Colditz wireless news reception was made independent of a mains supply of current. The prisoners built their own power station!

Dick "borrowed" the organ motor. It was wired into a closed circuit through the ordinary wiring of the camp in such a way as to feed the radio. The motor, when required, was produced from a hiding-place and bolted on to a firm platform. Bos'n Crisp provided a rope pulley belt, fifty feet long, which fitted the "V" section rim of the motor pulley. A large wooden, collapsible, driving-wheel

was manufactured. It was five feet in diameter, made in three segments, bolted together, and it was mounted on trunnions attached
to a cupboard which was lain flat on the floor in the dormitory.
When not in use, the cupboard resumed the vertical and the wheel
was dismantled. The trunnions and wheel segments were transformed into shelves, angle-pieces, back boards and loose, nondescript pieces of wood.

The wheel was known as the treadmill and it amply deserved
the name, because the reduction gear ratio to the generator pulley
was, as might be expected, not sufficient to provide the generator
speed necessary for the current required, without immense exertion
on the part of relays of the camp's strong men. The power plant
worked well. The background interference of the unsmoothed
current was noticeable, though not disturbing. Its volume depended on the steadiness of the output which depended, in turn,
on the freshness of the slaves.

After severe bombing raids the slave-gang, consisting of men
such as Checko, Charles Lockett and Mike Edwards, was called
out for work on the treadmill in order to provide the camp with
the "news" and the Radio Parson's bulletins, precious links with
the outside world and with reality. What would the Radio Parson
think! What might have been his thoughts had he known, as he
came over the air, that men were sweating at a home-made treadmill to turn a chapel organ motor in order to feed a wireless set
so that they could hear the gospel he was preaching! Could he have
heard the swearing and the groaning of the perspiring slaves!
Could he have seen the glow of the tell-tell lamp in the parallel
circuit as it rose and fell, accompanied by the voice of the foreman
of the slave-gang—now cautioning "Slower!" then urging, "Faster!
Faster!" and ending with, "Steady at that speed!" as the intensity
of light indicated the strength of current being produced.

There were several reasons why the men in Colditz went to such
pains to ensure that no news bulletin was ever missed, but it may
be revealing to mention one reason in particular. It was imperative
that no report of the capture or surrender of any town to the Allies
should be overlooked. Large sums of money were involved for the
lucky holders of winning tickets in the continuously running
"Town Falling" sweepstake.

WALLY AND TUBBY

NEWS concerning the men who escaped successfully from Colditz in 1941 and 1942 trickled into the camp slowly and was sketchy when it arrived, to say the least of it. Nevertheless, when it came, it boosted the prisoners' morale considerably. A first wave of elation started about a week after an escape, when, with the continued absence of the escapers and glum reactions from the Germans upon questioning by the S.B.O. as to their whereabouts, it was reasonably safe to assume that the men were out of enemy territory, provided they had not been killed *en route.*

Reliable confirmation arrived by various routes : sometimes a picture postcard slipped through the censor's net, written in a disguised hand from a fictitious character, but leaving no uncertainty in the mind of the recipient as to the meaning of the seemingly innocuous phrases in the text.

Hank Wardle, often called Murgatroyd by Rupert Barry, had thus written to him from Switzerland in November, 1942:

"We are having a holiday here (in Switzerland) and are sorry you are not with us. Give our dear love to your friend Dick. Love from

Harriette and Phyllis Murgatroyd."

"Harriette" and "Phyllis" with the H. and P. heavily emphasised, were obvious cover-names for Hank and Pat.

The successful exits of Colditz escapers leaked into the camp during the spring and summer of 1943. Details of the escapes never reached the prisoners, and the stories which they would have given much to hear were left untold until years later.

On the other hand, inaccurate reports, rumours and half-truths became rife, sometimes even leading men astray by causing them to concentrate their efforts on doomed escape routes. For instance, one conclusion reached by some of the Colditz escapers in 1943 and 1944, was an unfortunate one, though deduced from a sound premise; sound, in that, as the rate of outflow of escapers from Switzerland across German-occupied France to Spain and England

from November, 1942, onwards, was woefully slow, men argued it was better to seek other frontiers ; unfortunate, in that other frontiers presented all the problems of the unknown, whereas, in Colditz, there reposed the secret of a well-documented frontier crossing into Switzerland, which had proved successful on repeated occasions.

Bill Fowler reached Switzerland safely in the early hours of September 13th, 1942. He reached Spain on January 30th, 1943, and was in England on March 27th, over six months from the time of his arrival in neutral territory. Billie Stephens took even longer. He arrived in Switzerland in October, 1942, and landed in England a year and eight months later. Men who escaped to Sweden were back in England in a matter of days, but, along the escape routes from the camps to Sweden, the casualties could be counted in tens, if not in hundreds. The old adage, "Better safe than sorry," was applicable in so far as safety can ever be held to apply to escaping: "Slow but sure" suffers from the same inexactitude. Perhaps "Better slow than sorry" is the answer.

Although the escapades of Wally Hammond and Tubby Lister, free in Germany like a couple of Don Quixotes, took place in December, 1942, titbits of information concerning their adventures reached Colditz only by the summer of 1943.

Going back a little in time, what happened was this:

One day, at the end of November, 1942, Wally asked Dick Howe what he thought was the best remaining way of escaping from the Castle and Dick's reply was of crystal clarity. He answered, dryly, "The best way, Wally, is through the main gate." Dick's accompanying grin conveyed an ironical twist to his dryness.

Wally and Tubby were both Engine-room Artificers. The former had been rescued by his captors from the Submarine H.M.S/M. *Shark*, on July 6th, 1940, and the latter from H.M.S/M. *Seal*, in May, 1940. Wally was small in build with a barrel chest. He dressed neatly and gave a clear-cut impression. His features stood out distinctly against a sallow complexion of uniform tint from his neck to his deep-furrowed forehead. His eyes were sharp and watchful, like those of a bird. Tubby was very much his opposite: taller, much heavier and inclined to run easily to fat, with a rosy complexion, a big nose and a casual air. He would accept life as he found it, with one proviso—that he never lost an opportunity of improving his lot if it came his way. But he would not go out of his way to find it. Wally provided the initial driving-force and, once roused, Tubby displayed all the ingenuity of a sleuth.

F

They made a formal application to the German Camp Commandant to be removed from Colditz and to be sent to their rightful camp—they were not officers; they were chief petty officers. Dick engineered a demand from the S.B.O. to the Commandant to the effect that the officers objected to their presence in the camp. An interview took place. They expressed the opinion that they did not want to live with officers.

The Commandant's dictum was:

"You escaped with them—you must live with them."

To which Wally replied, "The only reason we escaped was because we had nothing to do."

In parenthesis, they had been caught in Hamburg with a number of Naval officers tunnelling their way out of another camp—Marlag Nord.

"Are you prepared to work for Germany?" asked the Commandant.

"Yes," was the answer.

A few weeks passed. Then, at an hour's notice, they were given the order to move. They were ready: completely equipped by Dick with papers made out for Flemish Engineer Collaborators, money and a mental picture of the Swiss frontier crossing. They survived the search before departure by the means prescribed at Colditz, which is better left unmentioned. Accompanied by three guards, they set off for a troops' camp at Lamsdorf.

At Leipzig main station they supplied the buffet attendant with Red Cross tea while she, a war-worn blonde, provided the boiling water. Prisoners and guards sat down together to enjoy a brew of good, strong English "cha". The combined charm and carefree friendliness of the two E.R.A.s was difficult to resist. The Goons, returning hospitality, bought a round of beer. Cigarettes were offered by the prisoners.

The buffet was crammed with German uniformed men of different ranks and services. Many were intrigued, stopping for a moment to gaze upon the unaccustomed sight of men in khaki and field grey, chatting together round a table in jovial conviviality. Wally was enjoying himself. Unaccustomed to the sound and movement of a busy hub of life, he sat, for a moment, surveying appreciatively the scene before him. He noticed a very old man threading his way amongst the crowd, picking up cigarette butts from the floor and out of the ash-trays on the tables. He wore the medals of the 1914–18 war.

As he approached the table where the prisoners and their escorts were now busy over tall glasses of lager, Wally pushed a newly

opened packet of Player's cigarettes, which lay at his elbow, in his direction. The German veteran raised his eyes, poignant with the sadness of a long disillusionment, to look at his benefactor, clad in the uniform of the enemy. Grasping the cigarettes, he came smartly to attention and saluted Wally Hammond. The echo of his heel-click sounded painfully loud in a room where the hum of conversation had suddenly ceased. Eyes turned incredulously towards the scene of an act of treason. But the veteran profited by the pause and disappeared from the restaurant before a movement was made to accost him.

The two prisoners arrived in the R.A.F. section of Lamsdorf prison just at the moment when the P.O.W.s were having their hands tied behind their backs with Red Cross string, in retaliation for the tying of German prisoners taken by our Commando raiders on the Channel Islands. They were thrown into the same compound and suffered the same fate. Thus they remained from seven a.m. to nine p.m. daily, with an hour's freedom for lunch.

Within a week, however, early in December, 1942, Wally and Tubby succeeded, with the help of a Regimental Sergeant Major named Sheriff, in having themselves drafted to a working party in the gasworks at Breslau. One hundred British P.O.W.s were working there, but none had as yet, according to report, escaped.

When they reached Breslau, Wally and Tubby carefully studied the route they travelled—by tram—to the works. Their plans were maturing. They had gathered some useful information about the possibilities of making a break from the gasworks. They were handed over by the Germans to the N.C.O. in charge of the working party, Sergeant Brown, and, wasting no time, they began sounding him to find out his reactions.

He was the right type, as far as they were concerned; enthusiastic, anxious to help and thoroughly knowledgeable as to the routine of the works. He advised them to lie low for a few days and to study the lie of the land while he set about procuring some necessary articles of civilian clothing and equipment for them. In the meantime he allotted them the task of shifting coal from one dump to a second, which was within the reach of an electrically powered rail-mounted grab engaged in loading it into railway trucks. They began their first day of toil amidst the hum of industry. The gasworks was a maze of railway sidings. Shunting engines whistled and belched smoke and vapour, marshalling the clattering wagons. White puffs of escaping steam rose from a hundred points around and above the grime-covered brick buildings.

Every time an engine passed near Wally and Tubby, the electric leads of the grab crane were across the tracks. During the first day's work, to the accompaniment of sparks and sheets of flame, they were mangled out of all possible service.

The evening saw a small heap of coal shifted six yards. During the second day the heap was shifted another six yards in a direction at right angles to the first move; the crane was out of commission. On the third day the heap was moved a further six yards again at ninety degrees and, on the fourth day, the coal was returned to its original location by this indefatigable team of coal hauliers. Before the fourth day's work was over, an old poverty stricken couple appeared with a cart drawn by a starving horse. They were old age pensioners, allowed to appear at regularly defined intervals to remove dross, the only fuel permitted them for heating their homes. Wally and Tubby took charge of the horse. No foreman was in sight. They halted the cart between their coal heap and an extensive pile of dross nearby and loaded the cart with coal. The aged couple stood by, looking on appreciatively, but with fear in their glances. When the cart was full and the coal covered with a layer of dross to pass inspection, they proffered surreptitiously, a packet of German cigarettes which the two prisoners accepted. They would be useful camouflage on the forthcoming journey.

The cart trundled away.

Towards the end of the week, after loading the remains of the coal on to a wagon, they were instructed to tidy up, collect the remaining coal dust together with a lot of rubbish in the vicinity and shovel it on to the existing pile of dross. On Saturday, December the 12th, 1942, before knocking off work, they carved out of the slack a long mound representing a newly filled grave. A cross made of two pieces of wood nailed together was placed at the head and in large letters in the coal dust, plain for the world to see, was inscribed "ADOLF, R.I.P."

They planned to move that night. Wally describes their preparations in these words:

"For a Colditz incumbent the getaway was a cakewalk; the filing of a few bars, the cutting of a few wires, the timing of a few patrols, obtaining some civilian attire, and we were ready.

"With the help of Sergeant Brown and two soldiers I gathered together a pair of large brown and grey check flannel trousers, a dark grey jacket and a fawn raincoat with the initials F. L. inside which I could not remove, so I added

a P. to make it P. F. L. as the name I was travelling under was Pierre Lebrun. I also wore one of those caps that grandfather wore, very small, with a button in the centre. Tubby had a dark blue pair of trousers, a heavy woollen jacket and a Trilby hat that had been folded and hidden for years. All the steam in the world would not remove the creases. Later, the rain and sleet improved it. But his coat was the funny piece, a despatch rider's windjacket, treated with boot polish. If it was not a Savile Row fit it nevertheless kept the rain out. Tubby carried his toilet gear, boot brushes and food in a small suitcase and I contented myself with a large size briefcase, in which I carried, amongst other things, needles and cotton and a small bottle of concentrated cough medicine: the latter in case I might get my smoker's cough at an awkward moment.

"We both smoked pipes, of German meerschaum design. Our pouches were filled with Bulwark Strong underneath and covered with a layer of mixed French and German tobacco. We also flaunted the German cigarettes."

But Wally and Tubby had not reckoned with a stooge. On Saturday night, for the first time in two years, a Goon sentry was placed on their projected route. They were undaunted. Packing away their civilian kit, they let it be known widely that the show was off until Sunday night. At the same time they resolved to try an alternative route during the early part of the next day, Sunday. They volunteered for the routine chore of washing out the Sunday dinner soup cauldrons. Quietly they collected their escape equipment and hid it in the cauldrons. They carried these to the washhouse which had an exit into the gasworks proper. They changed their clothes in the washhouse, walked into the works and left again through the manager's garden. They encountered little difficulty and there were no alarms. Taking a tram to the railway station, they bought tickets for Dresden, their first hop, to regain the Colditz escape route, and by nine-forty p.m. were trundling towards freedom. Wally's papers were signed by Willy Wants, after the variety artist! They were stopped and questioned on two occasions but their papers carried them through. Once a police officer retained their papers an unusually long time and their anxiety grew acute. Then the officer returned to them and apologised, saying he had to be on the look-out for escaped P.O.W.s. He added reassuringly that he had caught two the previous day. Wally accepted his apologies and expressed the

hope that he would catch a few more before long. "They are a *verdammte* nuisance to the honest hardworking citizen," he said feelingly, in German, as they parted.

They reached Dresden, and then Nüremberg, travelling standing all the way in packed railway coaches throughout Sunday night and Monday. *En route*, at Chemnitz, a sympathetic German soldier bought them each a glass of beer. From Nüremberg their journey continued during another night and day towards Ulm. They were on tenterhooks, because Ulm was the death trap for many a Colditz escaper before them. It was to be avoided if at all possible, yet, like Rome, all roads seem to lead there. They found, arriving at nine p.m. on Tuesday evening, that there was no connection for Rottweil until the next morning. They were stuck in Ulm for the night.

They had to make a decision quickly. To remain in or near the station was suicidal. The weather could scarcely have been worse. Sleet had been driving against the carriage windows as they drew into the station; the temperature was now below freezing and a high wind was blowing snowy gusts into the booking hall. It was no night to spend out in the countryside. Besides, Ulm was a big industrial town. They would spend most of the night walking to the country and, to find a sheltered hiding place where they would not freeze to death was, virtually, impossible in the darkness. Walking anywhere after midnight was dangerous. Police patrols would stop marauders abroad in the late and early hours. They had to find cover somehow and quickly. A cinema was no solution. There was only one answer.

As they hesitated for a moment under the archway at the main entrance to the station, peering into the snow-laden blackout beyond, Wally said in an undertone:

"How about it, Tubby? We're in it now up to our necks. We can't stay here."

"The only sensible place to be to-night is in a warm bed, my feet don't belong to me any more. Our papers are pretty damn good. Why not try a cheap hotel?"

"Our German lingo's not good enough."

"Yes it is. You've managed fine so far, and aren't we Flemish anyway!"

Wally turned to a passer-by.

"*Bitte gibt es ein guter Hotel neben bei—aber billig?*"

"*Ja wohl!*" replied the stranger, "*zwei Minuten von hier, links daoben es gibt das Bahnhof Hotel. Es is nicht teuer.*"

"*Danke schön*," said Wally as the stranger disappeared into the darkness.

They followed, pressing against the wind and holding on to their hats. They turned left, crossed the road and proceeded slowly looking at the doorways one by one until they they saw the sign of the Bahnhof Hotel faintly outlined above them.

"Here it is," said Wally, "it's all or nothing now. Once inside, if the Jerries examine our papers and don't like 'em they'll catch us with our pants down—good and proper—in our beds, as like as not."

"It's a fair risk," said Tubby, "my feet say so!"

"O.K. Here goes!"

They pushed through two pairs of heavily curtained swing doors and found themselves in a long hall furnished in Victorian style with plenty of gilt. A lounge opened out to the right and a staircase ascended at the far end. On the left were the offices, the cashier's desk and the Hall Porter's lobby. The whole place needed repainting, but there was an air of cleanliness about the floors and furniture.

The weather outside was an excuse for the two men to remain muffled up, concealing their shabby suits. Wally asked for a room in his elementary German and a well-dressed man behind the cashier's desk asked in perfect English:

"Do you speak English? I see that you are not German. Perhaps you understand English?"

Wally was completely taken aback. He was on the point of saying, "Yes, of course," when his wits returned to him. "Just a leetle, speak veery slow, please. I can understand Eenglish a little better than German. Ven you speak fast I understand not."

"Tell—me—exactly—what—you—want," pronounced the man behind the counter slowly and distinctly. He spoke in an educated manner with an air of authority. Wally accepted him as the manager, which he was.

"*Ach!* that ees good. Vee weesh one small room with two—*zwei* beds—vone great bed eef not, yes?"

"Yes, I can give you a room with two beds."

"How much, please?"

"Seven marks fifty with fifteen per cent. *Ablösung*."

"Vee shall take it," said Wally relieved. At eight marks to the pound he had expected the price would be higher.

"Fill in these forms, please," said the manager, politely. "Here

your name, here your occupation, your nationality, where you come from, where you go to; and your reason for travelling."

"Vee are Ingineers—diesel—nationality Flamsche, go to Rottweil, vee come from Stuttgart. Vee haf important reparations to do in Rottweil." Wally reamed it out slowly in pidgin English as he wrote his particulars down.

He noticed Tubby spelling "Engineer" with an "E" in the English way and nudged him meaningly, pointing with his pen to the word on his own form. Tubby dropped a blot of ink on the "E" and started again with an "I" in the continental fashion.

The manager looked up the railway timetable and confirmed that their Rottweil train left at ten a.m. the next morning. Being Flemish workmen, though not understanding a word of that language, Wally and Tubby felt it appropriate to exchange a few broken sentences in Maltese which they knew in a scrappy fashion. This made a good impression on the manager who smiled and said:

"I will give you room fifty-two. Let me have your papers, please."

They handed in their identity papers which were pinned to the forms they had completed and they were escorted upstairs. The lift was not in use. Two comfortable beds in a warm cosy room greeted them.

"Do you wish for anything to eat or drink?" asked their conductor.

"Noting, *Danke*," replied Wally—with Tubby echoing the words a split second after him. As the door closed, Tubby went to a basin in the corner and turned the taps. After a minute he exclaimed, "Hot water by G——!" and began stripping off his boots and socks as fast as he could.

Within ten minutes they were fast asleep, tucked into their beds between clean sheets enjoying more luxury than they had ever had since they left their submarine base in 1940.

They awoke next morning thoroughly refreshed but with hunger gnawing at their vitals. They had not eaten for nearly forty-eight hours. It was now Wednesday morning. Tubby produced German bread, margarine and sugar from his suitcase and they sat up in their beds chewing in silence. The evening before, they had not felt so hungry. That was the effects of weariness after the severe nervous tension. Fatigue alone, if sufficiently intense, can suppress the pangs of hunger. Two major primitive forces seem incapable of taking possession of the human frame both at once. One or

the other is uppermost and claims the whole consciousness until it is satisfied. The hackneyed expression tired *and* hungry is inaccurate unless the sufferer is neither very tired nor very hungry.

As the pangs of hunger ebbed, nervous anticipation began to assert itself. Their pulses quickened as thoughts came unchallenged and their hearts pounded. Wally expressed their mutual anxiety:

"Do you think we'll ever get our *Ausweises* back?"

"They're probably examining them with magnifying glasses at the police station at this moment," said Tubby with nervous jocularity. "If they're not downstairs I'm not waiting for them."

"We'll never get far without 'em," said Wally. He jumped out of bed and went to the window pulling back the curtains. Outside the snow had turned to sleet again and the roofs were glassy grey under a sombre sky.

They shaved and dressed hurriedly and packed their belongings.

"All set?" asked Wally, opening the door of the bedroom. Tubby nodded. Then they noticed a beautifully polished pair of military high boots reposing outside a door on the opposite side of the corridor.

The anxiety of the moment faded into the background and a gleam of devilment came into Tubby's eyes. He glanced at Wally and met his gaze.

"No! not that," whispered Wally. "Just plain water. Fill the chamber pot." Tubby was back in the room in a twinkling, filling his bedside pot with water from the basin tap.

"Steady!" said Wally, as Tubby appeared again with the brimming pot, "don't spill it near our door for hell's sake."

Gently, they tipped the water into the boots.

"Not enough," said Wally, "Quick another!"

The corridor was empty. No sound issued from the other side of the door. Quickly another pot-full was tipped into the thirsty boots filling them, and a faint trickle of water appeared from underneath the soles. They closed their own door quietly and walked downstairs. It was eight forty-five a.m.

At the cash desk, Wally asked for the bill and the identity papers. The manager was obviously short of staff. He was in his shirt sleeves and had been cleaning the lounge, but his grey hair was carefully brushed and he had shaved. He asked if they had had a good night and "Will you not have breakfast?"

"Vee haf no coupons," said Wally biting his lip and feeling he would like to run straight out through the swing doors.

"You must have some coffee then—*erzatz* coffee. It is very

cold out this morning," said the manager almost forcing them towards a small table in an alcove of the lounge. They sat down. Then, suddenly, rose in their seats ready to take off. A German officer was coming down the stairs and he was not wearing jack boots. . . .

He passed them with a *"Guten Morgen"* and did not stop at the desk. Wally and Tubby relapsed into their chairs, sighing audibly.

"What the hell made you do it?" whispered Wally hoarsely.

"It was your idea," said Tubby, "you distinctly said water!"

"My godfathers! now we've got to sit here for half an hour drinking filthy coffee." Wally grimaced and resigned himself to fate. What they had done could not be undone. Their papers were not yet forthcoming. The *erzatz* coffee seemed to be waiting for the acorns to grow and, at any moment, screams of rage would issue from the stair well. They fidgeted uneasily in their chairs.

After an agonising wait of ten minutes the coffee arrived in two large, steaming mugs. More sighs were followed by subdued curses. The coffee was far too hot.

"We've got to drink some of the blasted stuff," said Wally eyeing the staircase. Tubby promptly poured most of his mug into a flower pot of aspidistras where it formed a cloud of vapour around the plant.

"For crying out loud!" said Wally, pouring half the contents of his mug into Tubby's empty one. "Let's get out of here quick before the place blows up."

Together they vacated the alcove and approached the desk again.

"Tank you, *Danke schön*," said Wally to the manager, now seated behind his desk. "Ze bill, if you please. Vee must hurry."

"But your train does not go until ten o'clock, you have plenty of time!" said the manager with exasperating accuracy.

"If you please, vee vish to buy zom tings bevore," Wally replied with painful care. He was hypnotised by the stairs and could not keep his eyes away. He spoke now, deliberately facing the staircase, ready to turn about and run at the first bellow from above. "Hurry please, and do not vorget the *Ausweis*, *bitte*," he murmured as beads of perspiration appeared on his forehead. Almost in a trance he noticed Tubby edging towards the swing doors.

At last the bill was ready. Wally fumbled—much too nervously, he thought—for the German notes in his wallet. He paid the bill; still no shouts from the direction of the staircase.

"The *Ausweis* please?" he questioned. He could see them nowhere on the desk.

"*Ach* yes! of course, forgive me. Here they are," said the manager apologetically, bringing them out from under a counter.

"Good-bye! *Aufwiedersehen!* Tank you!" Wally said clutching the two papers with soaring relief registering on his countenance. "I 'ope vee shall kome again zoon to visit Ulm."

Tubby repeated "Good-bye, tank you!" and opened the swing doors.

Outside, they both gasped as heavy sighs filled their lungs with cold air. They quickly disappeared into the crowd hurrying towards the station. They muffled their coats around them as they scurried along, and the first streaks of a storm of sleet carried on a biting wind, stung their faces.

In the shelter of the station they paused for a moment to recover their breath and their composure.

"Phew! we're well out of that," said Wally.

"I 'ope the R.A.F. vill kome again zoon to visit Ulm," mimicked Tubby grinning. "Vone German officer kan use his boots to put out ze fires *nichtwar*! I'd give a lot to go back and see the fun, wouldn't you?"

"Sorry, Tubby, we've not got time—let's telephone the manager from Switzerland instead. Come on! we've got to get the tickets to Rottweil. There may be a queue. The train goes in half an hour," said Wally, and they headed for the booking office.

There was a queue and they waited nervously for fifteen minutes before their turn came. Wally did not wait to be asked for his *ausweis*; he pushed it in front of the girl issuing the tickets saying, "*Zwei mal, dritte klasse, Rottweil bitte*," and tendered his Reichmarks at the same time. The tickets and change appeared without a word.

They hurried off to the train and found the platform without difficulty. Finding a "Raucher" (smoking) third class carriage, they climbed in and were soon smoking their pipes with evident satisfaction and more at ease than they had felt since they awoke that morning. Several other passengers entered the carriage just before the train departed.

As it gathered speed, leaving the grey windswept atmosphere of Ulm behind, Wally noticed that one middle aged unprepossessing female passenger was obsessed with Tubby's despatch rider coat. Tubby had finished his pipe and was feigning sleep. Wally saw her curiosity growing and spreading as she gazed up at his

crumpled hat, then studied, it seemed, the texture of his coat, and continued downwards to his boots. There was only one answer to this. Wally stared at her—long and intently—with his sharp eyes. It was not long before she became visibly self-conscious. He continued the grilling until she was so confused that she forgot

Wally stared at her—long and intently

all about Tubby. He kept it up until she reached her destination half an hour later. She left the carriage blushing crimson as she stumbled over Wally's feet to reach the door, still followed by his burning and pseudo-lecherous gaze.

They arrived at Tüttlingen at four p.m. where they broke off their journey to Rottweil. This was the Colditz route as followed by the author and others from the Castle before them. Tüttlingen was only fifteen miles from the Swiss frontier, whereas Rottweil,

reached by another line, changing at Tüttlingen, was much further away, and for that very reason a less suspicious town to be heading for. A wait for the Rottweil connection gave passengers a legitimate excuse to leave the station. Wally and Tubby took the precaution of drinking water from a cast iron fountain in the station before they walked past the barrier showing their tickets.

Before they had walked half a mile, they encountered a police patrol. They were ready. The officer questioned them and searched their wallets, their pockets and Wally's brief-case, all the time with one hand on his pistol. He said:

"*Warum fahren Sie nicht nach Rottweil?*"

"*Wir warten auf dem Zug nach Rottweil um sechs Uhr fünf und dreizig,*" answered Wally. "*Wir sind seit zwei Tage im Zug—wir machen yetzt eine kleine spaziergang. Können wir irgendwo ein Bier kaufen?*"

Wally continued volubly. His German vocabulary soon exhausting itself, he carried on in broken German with words of Maltese, pidgin English and some French thrown in. He and his mate were going home to Belgium for Christmas when the order came for the rush, breakdown job at Rottweil. If the police officer did not believe them he only had to telephone the *Arbeitsführer* (works foreman) at Rottweil. They would be quite happy if the police officer could put them up for the night, provided he 'phoned the *Arbeitsführer*.

The officer was slightly taken aback by this frontal attack. He said simply, "*Komm,*" and they set off together, not as a party of prisoners with their gaoler, but amicably, side by side. After twenty minutes they reached a large house standing back from the road. They followed the officer inside and discovered that they were in a "pub."

There were a dozen country folk and two soldiers in the saloon and the officer told one of the latter to keep an eye on the two strangers while he went to the telephone. The officer was calling their bluff. They looked around casually but with their eye on the door. A "getaway" might be managed, but Wally had plenty of fight in him still. He could continue to bluff in spite of the 'phone call. Within five minutes the officer returned; handed them back their papers; led them outside and told them how to find their way back to Tüttlingen station.

Wally said in German, "But we have had our walk. Now it is time we had a drink."

"*Ach so!*" replied the officer, "then go back and have your beer

and return to the station afterwards. *Gute Nacht*," and he left them standing at the pub doorway.

Tubby and Wally looked at each other. A sly smile spread over Wally's face and Tubby winked. They re-entered the pub and ordered beer. They drank one each quickly and ordered seconds. The other occupants of the bar were friendly and talkative. A large flabby looking man with a bald head and staring pale blue eyes approached them asking, "*Sind Sie Flamisch?*"

"*Ja vohl!*" they answered with mock gusto.

The large man then recounted what seemed to be a long story in a language they had never heard before in their lives. At last Wally and Tubby were listening to the throaty tones of the language of their adopted birthplace! So this was Flemish they thought and exchanged bewildered glances. They were definitely "up against it."

The large man stopped, smiled jovially and fixed them with his glassy eyes. For a second there was stony silence. Then, with one accord, Wally and Tubby started to laugh. They laughed loud and long—not forgetting to drink their beer between guffaws. The large man began to laugh too. This gave them a chance to stop. When he ceased, they began again. Their beer finished, they put down their empty glasses and, still roaring with laughter, they shouted "*Gute Nacht! Gute Nacht!*" to the Flemish linguist and the assembled company and backed out of the room as quickly as propriety allowed.

"Phew! Lumme!" said Tubby, as they stepped outside, "that was a near one. Who would have expected to hear that lingo on the Swiss frontier. Do you think it really was Flemish? Perhaps he was having us on and that's what all the joke was about!"

"He was speaking Flemish all right or perhaps Dutch. I could pick up a word here and there," said Wally, and added as an afterthought, "that was two near ones, not one! You've forgotten about the policeman and the 'phoney telephone!"

"He seemed quite happy about it. We must be expected at Rottweil after all! What was your next move going to be, Wally? I was ready for the door, if he'd come back looking glum."

"If he'd come back suspicious," Wally answered, "I would've told him to 'phone again and let me speak to the *Arbeitsführer* about the Diesel breakdown job. That would've stumped him long enough for us to think up the next one."

They walked quickly, continuing along the road they had come, then, approaching some woods, they left the road, skirting along the fringe of the trees. They travelled by compass all that night

and the next, making very slow progress across country, and lying up in the daytime in dense woods. In the early hours, after the second night's tramp, in spite of the walking, they began to feel the cold. They were stopping frequently to check their direction and at such moments the sweat on their bodies chilled and made them shiver. They came upon a woodman's hut. The door was locked. By climbing on to the low roof and removing a few tiles they were able to drop inside. They made ready to spend the day there with suitable precautions. Wally detached the lock on the door and held it shut with a piece of string while Tubby cut out knots in the pine wood boards of the walls with his jack-knife providing spy holes in all directions.

They found some boards in a corner, spread them out on the floor over the damp earth and slept fitfully until morning. From dawn onwards they took turns at the spy hole watch. They were in a clearing and would make a run for it if anyone approached the cabin.

During the day they reviewed their trek of the previous night, established their position with a fair degree of accuracy and made plans for the frontier crossing. At midday they ate the last of their food. They suffered badly from thirst and during a rainstorm they tried to collect water in a bowl under the hole they had made in the roof. The rain did not last long, but they captured a few drops which they lapped up like dogs. It no more than moistened their tongues.

Not a soul approached the cabin all day. At dusk they departed leaving a five mark note under the broken lock which they placed carefully in a tool cupboard in the hut. They walked, at first, due west along a railway line in the forest until they reached open country. Then they turned south, skirting the trees for an hour before hearing the sound of traffic using the road they were heading for. They lay down near it and began timing patrols.

At this point, about five miles west of Singen the road passed within half a mile of the frontier. Across the road were fields inclined to be marshy, and the bottom of a wooded hill sloping towards the east beyond the fields was their target. A deviation of two hundred yards to the right or left of the bee line from where the men lay to the edge of the wooded hill would find them back in Germany and probably into the arms of a sentry.

By midnight they were ready for the "off." The moon was shining brightly and had been helpful so far. Now, for the last lap, it would be a hindrance. It would help others to see them when they least wanted to be visible. There was a low ground mist on

the other hand which would be useful if they chose to drop suddenly at an alarm.

They waited for a motor cycle patrol to pass with flashing headlamps, counted three minutes and crossed the road. Wally went about twenty yards in front of Tubby. They timed the crossing well, as a large cloud began to cover the face of the moon. They carried jack-knives in their sleeves. After twenty-five minutes of fast going, with the mist enveloping them up to their waists, they approached the trees at the bottom of the hill. Suddenly a torch was flashed on Wally before he had time to drop, and there was a shout, "Halt! *Wer geht da!*" He approached the sentry in a round-about way. Tubby had dropped and had not been seen. Wally forced the sentry to turn with him as he advanced until his back was facing the direction where Tubby lay. The moon re-appeared bathing the scene in an unearthly light. The sentry had not unslung his rifle. It was a good omen. Then Wally distinguished the outline of his Tyrolean style cap, and his buttons gleamed showing up the Swiss cross. He looked beyond the sentry and saw the form of Tubby appearing out of the ground mist. He was much nearer than expected and Wally caught the glint of his knife as he moved noiselessly like a shadow. "Stop! Tubby, for God's sake!" he shouted over the guard's shoulder, "he's Swiss."

Tubby masked his knife and fell on the astonished sentry's neck as he turned. Keyed at one moment to the pitch of killing his enemy, Tubby was so overcome at the next that he found himself hugging the sentry shouting, "Swiss, Swiss, good old Swiss!" The sentry accepted the greeting good humouredly. He spoke a little English and contented himself with establishing that they were prisoners of war who had escaped, accepting their statements at face value. He shouted to another sentry in the darkness of the woods and then escorted them, talking cheerfully all the way, to the village of Ramsen. They were handed over to the Commander of the guard post who promptly produced bowls of soup and sent them to bed with four army blankets each in the "off duty doss-down." The time was two a.m. on Saturday, the 19th of December.

They arrived in Berne for Christmas and for a reunion party that will be long remembered by the participants. The others were: Ronnie Littledale, Billie Stephens, Hank Wardle, Bill Fowler and the author, all ex-Colditz inmates who had escaped during the autumn.

*   *   *   *   *

The Colditz group in Switzerland was growing into a colony. The escapers were packed off by the Military Attaché for a time to Montreux, then to Wengen and later to Saanenmöser in the Bernese Oberland. They all learnt to ski on the comparatively deserted slopes, first of the Kleine Scheidegg and then of the Hornberg and in a matter of two months had regained much of their former strength and energy.

The invasion of North Africa in November, 1942, by the Allies and the subsequent entry of the Germans and Italians into Vichy France upset all the recognised ways of travelling to Spain. With the Germans present, new and much more clandestine "tourist" routes had to be organised.

Bill Fowler and Ronnie Littledale were the first of the colony to leave. They crossed the Swiss frontier into France on January 25th, 1943. Bill set down his record of the journey to Gibraltar on his arrival in England and it is reproduced here as he wrote it— a straightforward account fresh with vigour and the simplicity of understatement which was so typical of this fine airman who, as his companion Ronnie too, was to meet his end before the war was over.

"On the 25th of January, 1943, Ronnie Littledale and I went to Geneva, where we were given French identity cards and introduced to a Belgian called Jacques. We were told that our journey must be left entirely to him.

"We were taken then by car a short distance, to a point near the French frontier, west of Annemasse. Here we waited in a yard while Jacques made a reconnaissance. In a few minutes he came back and told us to follow him, so we walked till we came to a small stream, where we were joined by a French girl about twenty years old. We crossed the stream, which was shallow, and were helped out of the water on the other side by a French customs official in uniform. We waited hidden behind a wall for a few minutes, and then Jacques led us down a deserted road into Annemasse village. He took us to a house where we dried our clothes, had some food and met a man in a ski-ing suit, who, Jacques told me, would be our guide for the next part of the journey. He and the French girl left us.

"We went to bed and very early next morning, with our new guide, we walked to a garage, passing some Italian soldiers on the way. The guide left us here, arranging with a man to drive us in a car to La Roche, where we arrived at

eight a.m., and went to a hotel. We slept most of the day in a corner of the lounge, interrupting our dozing to eat a good lunch, at which our guide rejoined us.

"At four p.m. he led us to the railway station, where he gave us a hundred francs each and told us to book separately to Chambery. We boarded the train—arriving at Chambery at about 9 p.m., where we changed. The guide bought tickets to Perpignan, where we arrived after an all night journey, at 9 a.m. on the 27th of January. We took a tram to the Hotel St. Antoine. We spent the 27th and the 28th very quietly in the hotel, only going out once to have our photographs taken for our fake identity papers in the back room of a small shop close by.

"On the 29th of January our guide handed us over to a Spaniard and then departed. We took a bus to Elne, arriving there in the evening. The Spaniard insisted on our buying our own tickets and sitting separately in different parts of the bus. At Elne we met a French boy about nineteen years old who said he was coming with us.

"Darkness descended upon us as we walked along the railway line southwards and crossed the River Tech by the railway bridge. We continued across fields until after an hour's trek the guide said he was lost. I directed him towards the south by the stars and we eventually came to a goat track which the guide said he recognised. We followed this and arriving at a cave, we lay down and slept for some hours. At 6 a.m. the following morning (30th January) we set off again. We marched the whole day, reaching the La Junqueras-Fiquaras road at 4 p.m., and, while crossing it, we were arrested by Spanish soldiers who were patrolling the district in a lorry picking up the numerous refugees in the neighbourhood. They seemed familiar with this routine and were not even armed.

"The lorry took us to La Junqueras, where we were locked into a cell. We were not searched. Later we were interrogated in French by a Spanish officer who said he supposed we were Canadians. We told him we were British officers who had been captured in France (following our instructions). I gave the name of John Parsons, while Ronnie gave his name as Bighill (opposite of Littledale). The military authorities then handed us over to the jurisdiction of the civil police.

"Our guide was put into a separate cell, and the police telephoned to Madrid about him. They found out that he

had been a Red in the Civil War and beat him up properly in the next room apologising afterwards to us for the nuisance caused, saying that the man was a 'Red murderer' and deserved all the treatment he got. While waiting in the cell, we burnt our papers. The police searched us and questioned us again. The Chief of Police promised to treat us well and to send us to a hotel. He asked us what we thought of General Franco and what was our opinion of the Bolshevists. We said we thought Franco was a grand fellow and that we admired the Russians, who were our Allies. At every opportunity we demanded permission to see the British Consul and always received the answer, *Mañana*.

"On the 1st of February we were marched off to a central prison in Fiqueras, where our heads were shaven and we were inoculated under dirty, unhygienic conditions (I was tenth in line for the same needle), and thrown into the filthiest gaol I have ever seen in my life, and I have seen quite a few! All that has been written in the war about Spanish prisons is correct. We were jammed in with fourteen other men; some of them criminals, mostly Spanish, and two of them awaiting death sentences, in a disgusting, dirty hole, measuring four yards by two. In this cell we spent twenty-three days without blankets or even straw, sleeping on the damp stone floor huddled together like sardines and crawling with vermin. The only window was bricked up leaving a six-inch aperture, and as it was mid-winter long hours were spent in total darkness. The cold was intense. For all natural functions, a pail was placed in the middle of the cell and removed once every twenty-four hours. It made the atmosphere so foul that prisoners were sick intermittently all day long. Two men died during our incarceration and their bodies remained propped up in the corner for two days before the guards removed them. A tureen of gruel a day was all the food we were given. The only hope of maintaining life was to pool valuables and to buy, at exorbitant prices, extra food from the guards. My only asset, a wrist watch, went.

"We were visited, once, by a representative from the British Consulate, and, as a result, on the 22nd of February, a Spanish army sergeant conducted us to Barcelona, where we reported to the British Consul and were sent off to a hotel.

"We were given civilian clothes and stayed there till the 18th of March, when I parted company with Ronnie.

"A Spanish air force officer took me to Alhama de Aragon, where I met several men of the R.A.F. and U.S.A.A.F. We were well treated here, and, on the 24th of March, I set off with six R.A.F. personnel, mostly Canadians, to Madrid; and thence to Seville, where we spent the night. The next day we motored to Gibraltar, stopping on the way at one of the principal sherry towns, where the British Consul, a Spaniard, happened to be a wine merchant. He conducted us over his cellars. We sampled varieties copiously and, on our departure, he presented each one with a bottle of sherry 'for the road.' One of the Canadians admired the Madonna lilies in his front garden so the Consul pressed an enormous bunch on him. The sherry lasted us as far as La Linea, on the north side of the neutral zone separating Spain from Gibraltar. Here the Canadian with the lilies climbed on the bonnet of the car, swearing he would kiss the first British citizen he met in Gibraltar. At the north gate of Gibraltar, a sentry challenged the convoy, whereupon the Canadian climbed unsteadily from his perch, solemnly kissed the sentry on the cheek and presented him with the huge bunch of lilies. The party were escorted to the guard room, led by the Canadian. The sentry, carrying his rifle under one arm and the madonnas in the other, followed. He seemed to regard the incident as an everyday occurrence, evidently accustomed to the arrival of service 'tourists' from captivity."

CHAPTER XIV

THE GHOSTS

DICK HOWE, in his capacity of Escape Officer, played an important rôle in the black days of Colditz, in the darkness before the dawn. Always encouraging, never despairing, he fostered, cajoled and counselled.

*　　　*　　　*　　　*　　　*

When Scarlet O'Hara was allotted a bed in the first floor quarters over the parcels office where the French had formally resided, he browsed around the rooms for several days and then took to measuring. What he carried out was a miniature trigonometrical

survey. It was certainly three dimensional and soon wound itself up around the spiral of the staircase in the turret leading up to his dormitory.

Between the first floor and the ground floor, beside the spiral, he calculated there was an uncharted space sealed off from all directions. He set to work and in a matter of six weeks of patient toil he had worked through a couple of feet of masonry and found his secret chamber. He quite expected to find some treasure, hidden there centuries before, but there was nothing. Dick helped him to build a camouflaged entrance weighing a hundredweight and turning on pivots like the French tunnel entrance.

Then Dick left Scarlet to his own devices, to choose his own team of workers and carry on with the job. "The Job," of course, was tunnelling downwards through the stone, mortar and concrete of the massive staircase foundations.

The point in favour of Scarlet's scheme was that he could tunnel in almost any direction. The Germans might hear his sledge hammer at work—in fact they did—but for a long time they could not find his working.

His team consisted of senior officers, none below the rank of major, which accounts for the title conjured up by Don Donaldson. "Crown Deep" was the name and it stuck like glue.

Tunnelling continued for many weeks. The dull thuds of hammer blows reverberated up the stairs, rivalling the sounds of heavy excavation that used to emanate months earlier from the nearby French tunnel. The Jerries listened and probed and searched in vain.

Scarlet approached Dick periodically.

"I want you to come and have a look at the working," he would say, and both of them would descend through the hinged opening into his chamber. Scarlet would light up his lamp.

"I've been driving a heading in this direction, see?" and he would point to a depression in the foundations about the size of a small hip bath. "That represents three blasted weeks work! It's heading in a good direction, out between Gephard's office and the chapel. It starts off fine and dandy and then it gets tougher and tougher. It leads you up the garden path good and proper and lets you down good and proper."

Both the scene and the occasion were familiar to Dick and he would look wistfully round the chamber at the other holes. One after the other, as his gaze travelled round, he recollected Scarlet's grumbling phrases. Grudging defeat, painful susceptibility at his

own impotence, dogged refusal to accept fate, and a nonchalant sarcasm that veiled the suffering.

"And where do I go from here?" Scarlet would ask pathetically, kicking the rubble under his feet in a fruitless gesture as he followed Dick's gaze.

"Why not try heading inside towards the courtyard, you might pick up the drains again," or "Have a go over there towards Monty's hole. He's heading for the old French tunnel and two different entrances would have many advantages."

Dick's counsel always encouraged Scarlet to start off again and the familiar thud of his working would waft up the medieval turret once more. It was a reassuring sound to the men who climbed, daily, up and down the winding stairs. Comments passed from mouth to mouth.

"Crown Deep's at work again."

"Yes, never heard it last week. Couldn't think what was different about the place."

"Life's not the same without it!"

"It's like a heart. When it stops throbbing, there's a death in the house."

The Germans were bound to react violently eventually. Their sound recorders must have been working overtime. Crown Deep never had a real chance. As they could not find the entrance, in desperation, one day, they brought in their own team of navvys and set to work on the staircase. Their action savours of the rival mining operations that were carried out between the German and Allied trenches during the First World War. In this case, fortunately, Scarlet had no high explosive or he would certainly have used it. The Germans wielded their pickaxes, sledge hammers and wedges and discovered his concealed chamber. Crown Deep passed into the catalogue of Colditz failures. Only the name survived; an epitaph without a grave.

*   *   *   *   *

It is one thing to be incarcerated alone in a stone cell like the Count of Monte Christo; to have only bare hands with which to hammer against the walls and finger nails with which to scrape away the mortar. To have company in such a situation is another matter. It is a mixed blessing.

Prisoners can commiserate together, they may also grow to hate each other. They can help one another and they may be wildly jealous of each other. There can be order or anarchy; an

outstanding character can seize the helm and hold the course; moral weakness and the absence of leadership breed bad blood and lasting enmity. The elemental forces in man's nature are scarcely veiled; they lie under a veneer of civilised custom which grows tenuous. They can burst into fury as a spark becomes a roaring furnace. All the physical constituents, the infinite monotony; all the mental anguish, the panoply of tyranny and the atmosphere for revolt, are present.

The stage was set for heroism or violence in the stifled community life which existed behind the walls of Colditz. The majority of the inmates lived for escape. The decision, for most of them, taken long ago, was irrevocable. It was too late now to turn back. There was no road behind them. Instead, if they turned, beneath them was a yawning chasm. They stood giddily on the brink. It was the pit of despair threatening to engulf them in a mad, suicidal fall. Scarlet O'Hara's Crown Deep was an instance of men beating their fists against walls of solid rock. Monty Bissell's hole was another, and the glider, in a different sense was, probably, the last. Here was resolution for its own sake. This way lay sanity for active, courageous men who were determined not to look back.

A few, very few, attained Nirvana; they deliberately faced the yawning chasm, gritted their teeth, steadied their swaying minds, clung to the edge and slowly stepped backwards into tranquillity and resignation.

*   *   *   *   *

The ghosts were in a bad way. In spite of all the tender care that Monty Bissell expended on them they were definitely wasting away. Like a mother hen looking after its chicks, Monty saw they were fed and kept warm before he ever thought about himself. But their trouble was disturbing. It was not so much physical, as mental. Their morale was at rock bottom.

Not that their chains were heavy. They did not have long sessions of clanking; on the contrary they were quiet ghosts. Their job was to be silent and to be inconspicuous. In fact, they were not supposed to appear at all. Naturally, under such conditions the morale of any ghost could be expected to go to pieces.

The reader will remember that the ghosts, two of them, were hidden in Monty's hole in the Chapel. Their appearance or disappearance—take your choice—had coincided with the escape of Rupert Barry and his French companion down the theatre light well in November, 1942. Dick had decided, on that occasion, to

be reasonable as to the number. Volunteers were called for and Jack Best and Mike Harvey had been chosen.

Monty Bissell, at the time, was busy digging a tunnel under the steps leading to the pulpit.

Jack Best thought that, by becoming a ghost and going to ground, he would be free to help Monty and to work to his heart's content, and Mike Harvey thought so too.

Monty looked after them well. They were his first, and almost continuous, charge to the exclusion of other activities. He attended to their every need, brought them their food and all the titbits he could muster. He saw that they were warm, regaled them with news of the activities of the camp and of events taking place in the world outside. The ghosts for their part repaid Monty's care and attention by tunnelling quietly and leisurely forward.

They had a few tins of Red Cross food laid in as a reserve, but Monty thought it would be a good idea to lay in a stock of staple diet for them as well. Bread would go mouldy in a day. There was nothing else save potatoes; they were better than nothing and, thought Monty, they would prevent starvation. Thus, if the chapel was closed by way of a reprisal for some "offence against the Reich" for a month or longer, the ghosts would survive long enough for Dick and Monty to evolve a plan to extract them and at the same time obviate their disclosure. Dick thought this a wise precaution and set about obtaining the potatoes.

He went to the mess kitchen in the British quarters one Sunday afternoon to find Goldman, the cockney Jew orderly. Goldman was there, seated at the kitchen table, poring over a letter he was writing home. His blond, curly hair fell over his forehead and a pencil protruded from the corner of his mouth. The table was littered with postcards and letters, on paper of many different colours.

"Goldman," Dick said, "I want to talk to you."

"Yes, Captain 'Owe," said Goldman standing up and transferring the pencil from his mouth to behind his ear.

"Could you scrounge me a small sack of potatoes?" Dick continued, "I want them for the ghosts. They must be absolutely sound—no bad ones—because they may have to last some time."

"Why, Captain 'Owe, that ain't so difficult, and you know I'd do anything for you anyway. Come along wiv' me. De Jerry cook and me, we're pals. 'E's comin' to visit me after the war an' see de family."

They descended the stairs to the courtyard and headed for the cookhouse. The door was locked. It was two o'clock and a

Jack Best

Sunday. Cooking for the day was finished. Goldman was not deterred. He opened a small serving hatch near the door, stretched his arm through and slipped the lock of the door on the inside. Dick and Goldman walked into the kitchen and shut the door quietly after them.

Silence reigned in the deserted cookhouse, but from around a corner, in an alcove, wafted a sound of gentle snoring. The German cook corporal was sprawled over a desk fast asleep, with his head on his folded arms. Goldman crept over to him, then bawled at the top of his voice, "*Achtung!*"

The German N.C.O. came to his feet as if a thousand volts had been shorted across his terminals and stood rigidly at attention before Goldman's cheery "Wat yer, cookie!" brought him to his senses and relaxed his galvanised frame. Goldman grinned airily at him. "That's right, cookie, you can stand at ease now, but don't go to sleep on dooty again, see!"

The German, a comparatively young man, retired from the Russian front on account of wounds, was, rather naturally, in a surly mood. He and Goldman wrangled for several minutes. Finally the grumbling ended with Goldman showing the corporal all the photos of his family in Hackney, in return for which extraordinary favour, the Jerry felt it his bounden duty to hand over thirty pounds of potatoes. Goldman and Dick turned to leave the cookhouse with the sack hidden under a jacket. The German, as docile as a lamb, accompanied them to the door and closed it politely after them.

"You see 'ow it is, Captain 'Owe. It gets you anyfink you want."

"What does?" asked Dick.

"Charm," replied Goldman. "It's charm wat does it."

The ghosts now had their reserve of cooked potatoes.

Three weeks of confinement in a black hole under a chapel are not warranted to lift morale and the ghosts, in spite of Monty's nursing, began to wilt. The atmosphere was not of the best, either physically on account of the curious smell which could hardly be described as the odour of sanctity, or spiritually, because of the indefinable proximity of the dead. The dead had died many, many years ago, but their spirits seemed not far removed from their decayed coffins under the chapel floor. It was ironical that the ghosts should be so affected by the company of their elders, if not their betters. The fact is the chapel was "plain spooky", in the dead of night.

After three weeks it had become obvious that the ghosts should be relieved of the strain and given some fresh air. The excitement and hubbub of the light well escape had died by Christmas, 1942, and it was considered safe to let them out of close hiding provided they were protected by stooges from being seen face to face by a German who might recognise them.

The French tunnel was discovered within two months of their taking up residence. Work had to cease completely for a time. Then they began once more in a new direction with a view to connecting up with the French tunnel and making use of it again.

Sound detectors were known to be installed all around the Chapel. They had to proceed at a snail's pace.

By the summer of 1943 work on the Chapel tunnel had to stop. Monty and his ghosts had reached the French tunnel, but the Germans had laid a trap. Sound detectors must have been left hidden in it. Every time the British tunnellers entered it the Germans appeared to know, and a squad would enter the Chapel, search it and leave a sentry posted there for twenty-four hours (relieved, of course, periodically). Progress came to a standstill.

Grismond Davies-Scourfield made a break during the summer. He was "gone away" for seventeen days before recapture at the Dutch frontier. His story cannot be told here, but during his absence Mike Harvey stood in for him on *Appells*, with the result that when the German Commandant was informed by long distance telephone of the recapture of a Colditz prisoner he replied, "It can't be so. We had an *Appell* two hours ago and the count was correct."

Mike promptly went back into close hiding until the tangle was sorted out!

For the period of less restricted confinement, Monty, still looking after his brood like a mother hen, instituted the stooging system that made it safe for his chicks to sortie at all times, except, of course, during roll calls when they went to ground again. He had a team of stooges working for him, including Keith Milne, known as the "City Slicker," one of the most charming, unassuming and gentle characters it is possible to imagine, and handsome, dark-haired and black moustached into the bargain. Be that as it may, he was noticed late one evening at his look-out post by Lulu Lawton.

"What are you up to, Slick?" he asked.

"Stooging for Monty's ghosts," came the reply.

Lulu said nothing, but it was eleven o'clock and he suspected

something. He searched high and low for Monty and could not find him. Then he happened to pass Monty's bed and there he was, tucked up nicely, fast asleep, with only his forelock showing. Lulu shook him.

"Huh! . . . Hm! . . . Oh! . . . What? No! What the hell do you think you're doing?"

"What time did the ghosts go to ground?" asked Lulu.

"Hours ago. Has anything happened? Are they all right?"

"What time did you put them away?"

"Six o'clock. Why? What the devil's up with you anyway, Lulu?"

"Nothing, nothing at all, Monty! only the City Slicker's going to be a bit browned off."

"By the holy Saint Patrick!" shouted Monty, leaping from his bed. "I forgot to lay him off." He looked at his watch, "That's five hours ago," and he rushed in his pyjamas to release the faithful sentinel.

Stooging hit a low spot at that moment, but Monty could be said at least to have erred on the right side. Stooging also had its high spots and reached a peak in Dick's plan for the escape of Bush Parker and Mike Harvey.

The Australian airman and the English sailor had a notion that a door in the wall of the Castle halfway down the first causeway led somewhere. The door was marked *"Luftschutzraum"*—air-raid shelter, and was being used fairly frequently these days for its allotted purpose. Although it was impossible to estimate with certitude—as the door was not visible from the prisoner's windows, frequent observation during air raids gave the impression that there was a second way—in or out—of this air-raid shelter.

Bush Parker was determined to find out and he wisely chose Mike Harvey as his partner for the attempt. Mike, being a ghost, was at the top of the escape roster.

Together they buttonholed Dick about it.

"Mike and I," he said, "have been watching the causeway during air raids now for a couple of months and we are as certain as we can be that there is a second entrance to the *Luftschutzraum*."

"How do you make that out?"

"We've counted the bodies going in and then the bodies coming out. They never agree."

"H'm, where have you watched from?"

"From the window in the *Saalhaus* (theatre block) on the

second floor which overlooks the causeway and is immediately above the air-raid shelter entrance."

"But you can't see the door from there," said Dick.

"No, I admit that, but by looking downwards from the top of the window there's only about a yard of the causeway which is blind. We can't be absolutely certain but we're nearly certain. If there's a second exit, it's beyond the sentry on the second gate. Once past this gate we have a good chance of bluffing our way past the others. It's worth a try, Dick, if you'll O.K. the idea and help us."

"Wait a minute, now, what's the rest of the plan?"

"Well, Mike and I drop from our *Saalhaus* window by rope right in front of the door. I can bring some keys which I know will open it. I've studied the lock carefully every time we've walked by the door, going down to the park. We get into the cellar, kit and all and find our way out."

"With three sentries looking at you all the time!" commented Dick.

"No!" replied Bush. "Only two for certain. The third would not worry us very much if properly stooged."

"I reckon all three will have to be properly stooged. It's just about impossible, Bush. Look! where have you got to put your stooges to cover the beats of the three of them? . . . you see? They have to be miles apart in different rooms. So you'll need a string of supplementary stooges to pass on the signals. That means seconds wasted and I can see right now this is a job of split seconds. You're in the direct beam of searchlights all the time."

"Once I can get into the air-raid shelter doorway," interrupted Bush, "I've got some deep shadow to help me. It's about nine inches inside the wall face. If I hug one side I might get away with it for a few minutes while I open the door."

"That's a fair risk I agree," said Dick, "but the stooging is the trouble. You'll need all the stooging in any case while you cut the window bars. That'll take you ages. No! you go away, Bush, and have another think about it. I will too."

Dick kept his promise and produced what he christened "The electric stooge". Five stooging posts were necessary to follow the movements of the three sentries directly concerned and also stray patrols. Dick manufactured five "make and break" press button switches. These he fixed at the five stooging posts, connecting them all in series through the Castle wiring along with a

tell-tale shaded lamp installed at the corner of the window where the "job" was to be performed. When all buttons were pressed down the light went on. This signal meant work could proceed. If one stooge only saw danger, he released his button and work stopped instantaneously.

The cutting of the window bars by Bricky Forbes took many days of the most patient labour. Absolute silence was essential. The saw used was made, as usual, of razor blades. By the time the window was ready, however, the even more hazardous operation of letting the two bodies down in the full searchlight glare within the vision and easy hearing of the three sentries, one only fifteen yards away, could be tackled with some confidence.

Incredible as it may seem Dick and his colleagues succeeded in letting Bush and Mike down to the causeway where Bush picked the air-raid shelter lock. As he did so a sentry saw Mike, fired at him, missed, and ran to the alarm bell. Bush and Mike disappeared through the door, which was not solid but made of wooden slats. As a posse of Goons dashed out from the guard-house, Bush put his hand through the slats, relocked the door and removed his key. The two men disappeared down a long flight of stone steps into the recesses of the air-raid shelter.

The Jerries searched the area for an hour, but never thought of unlocking the door of the air-raid shelter. However, Bush and Mike were unlucky. There was not a second exit. They were in a cul-de-sac. The escape was, to all intents and purposes, from the moment of that discovery, doomed. Although dressed in German fatigue overalls, they would have to walk out of the air-raid shelter doorway into the glare of searchlights and in full view of three sentries. Not only that, they had, within ten yards, to ask one of the sentries to open a locked gate, which required a password. If an air raid had occurred while they were in the shelter they might have had a chance, but they could not budget for an air raid in advance, and that night there was none. The two men therefore remained hidden in the shelter until the next day. They then tried to pass the sentries, but were trapped. . . .

Months of difficult work for nothing; the escape was a failure and a complete anticlimax.

The same evening over their supper, Dick's table were holding an inquest on the escape. Harry Elliott said it reminded him of a story that his uncle George used to tell. Twirling one end of his moustache, he began:

"This old Uncle of mine, you see, lived for a long time in

India, Uncle George was his name. He always talked about snakes
as serpents, and he had a habit of telling stories without any
point at all. There was one story of his in particular which we, as
children, always loved, and we could always be certain of getting
it by asking him; 'When you were in India, Uncle George, did
you ever see any snakes?' to which he would reply, 'Serpents,
my boy, serpents! Well as a matter of fact I did see one, very
close too. When I was in Poona and your Uncle Edward was
staying with me, we were walking together in the compound
when we saw a serpent of the species *cobra de capello* coming
towards us. It came to within a few feet of us and then disappeared
down a hole.

"'I clapped my hands and the servants came running. I ordered
chairs to be brought and had them placed one on either side of
the hole. Your Uncle Edward sat in one chair and I sat in the
other, and though we waited there for several hours, we never
saw the creature again'."

The ghosts had doubles. Mike Harvey's double was Lieutenant
Bartlett (Royal Tank Regiment), who looked rather like him. As
soon as Mike was caught he posed as Bartlett and Bartlett went
into hiding. Unfortunately, when Mike set off to the solitary confinement cells the German sergeant in charge looked at him closely
and said, "You are not Bartlett!"

He could not make out who the stranger was, but he put him in
the cells, nevertheless, for safety. It took the Germans two days to
sift out the mess this time. A security officer came to Mike's cell
with his correct papers and that was the end of Mike as a ghost.

Jack Best carried on.

CHAPTER XV

THE TERRACE

DICK was sunbathing on one of the rare occasions when he
found time to do so and during that short period of the
day when the sun stared almost vertically downwards into the
deep pit of the courtyard. It was sultry August weather. Roughly
a third of the yard reflected the dazzling white glare of the sunlight,
while the shadows deepened to black around the sides.

He lay on a blanket stretched over the cobbles, naked, except,

for a pair of pants, and was deeply engrossed in "Gone With the Wind" His eyes followed the printed words and his thoughts soared on the magic carpet of fiction, upwards and outwards, far beyond the walls, beyond the horizons. Over the blessed gardens of oblivion he floated happily setting his course towards the mountains of the past. What a Godsend books were; like cool water upon the fevered brow; like the caress of a loved one!

Dick was brought back to earth through the sudden covering of his open page by a blanket which descended seemingly from nowhere. He looked up.

"Sorry, Dick," came a cheerful voice as the blanket was whisked away and spread more carefully beside Dick's own. It was Gordon Rolfe, the Canadian. The sunlit patch of cobbles in the courtyard was filling up with bodies. Soon no cobbles would be visible as row upon row of sunbathers formed up for an early afternoon siesta.

"Getting like Coney Island around here," said Rolfe.

"Palm Beach!" protested Dick. "Put on your rose tinted spectacles—look at those two lovelies—just flown in from Hollywood this morning." Dick nodded towards two particularly skinny, angular, almost nude figures wending their rickety way amongst the recumbent forms.

Rolfe grinned and sat down cross legged on his blanket.

"Dick," he said, "how about you taking me for a Cook's tour around the Castle. It'll save me a hell of a lot of time. I'm trying to find a way out the same as everyone else, but if I can build on your knowledge I might, with a new pair of eyes, hit on something that hasn't yet been thought of."

Dick thought for a moment before replying.

Among the Eichstatt tunnellers there were many outstanding escapers, men who had broken bounds more than once before but who had not made the home-run. Gordon Rolfe and Dopey Miller; Frank Weldon of the R.H.A. and J. Hamilton-Baillie, R.E., the two leading tunnellers of Eichstatt; others like Hugo Ironside and Douglas Moir of the Royal Tank Regiment, and Tom Stallard; Phil Pardoe and Tony Rolt of the Rifle Brigade.

Dick said, "The Old Lags have looked out of the same windows for so long that they've got permanent squints. I'll take you round all right with pleasure, but if it's to be a Cook's tour how about half a dozen of you new chaps coming along together?"

Dick mentioned some of the names he had thought of.

Gordon Rolfe agreed:

"I'll get hold of them, Dick; they'll be only too glad. What's

the best sort of time? We don't want to look like a bunch of tourists."

"Oh, sometime in the evening is probably best. How about after the five o'clock *Appell*?"

"I'll fix it—sorry for interrupting your reading." Rolfe sprawled over his blanket and Dick returned to the realms of the Southern States and the times of the Civil War.

They met again in the cool of the early evening after the roll call. Rolfe had gathered quite a party, including Dopey Miller and Tony Rolt. He led them, first of all, once the *Appell* guards and N.C.O.s had retired, through the doorway opening from the cobbled yard into the corridor leading to the sick ward. He walked over to a small window in the north wall of the ward beside a round turret at the north-west corner of the Castle, and beckoned the others to look out and downwards, pointing:

"Have a look down there," he began. "Through this window— you can see where the bars have been repaired—Bush Parker did his stuff with Mike Sinclair, Hyde Thompson and Lance Pope in the Franz Josef escape. . . ." He went on, describing to them how the escape had been engineered. He told them how Mike had hung on, trying to get the second sentry to move, how the two Franz Josefs had faced each other and how Mike had been wounded. At the end Rolfe asked:

"Why didn't Mike make a break with his two men—he should have, don't you think—instead of hanging on?"

"Many people have asked that question," said Dick, "to be quite candid I've taken the can back for it. I left the final decision to Mike himself instead of giving him a specific instruction to quit at the slightest sign of obstruction. What some chaps argued afterwards was that, knowing Mike, I should also have known that he just wasn't the type who would quit and I should, therefore, have given him an order."

Walking back once more into the corridor he pointed to Gep-hard's office and they looked through the window at the end of the corridor down on the sentry footpath. "Six men went out there to the right, from the building known as the clothes store, starting off with a hole underneath Gephard's desk. They were dressed as German N.C.O.'s and Polish orderlies. Two of them—Bill Fowler and a Dutchman—got to Switzerland. Underneath where we're standing is the cellar where the French tunnel started; it ran under the chapel towards your right heading for the park."

They returned to the courtyard. Dick stopped outside the

G

doorway, looking up at the clock tower. "The French used the tower," he explained. "Their entrance was at the top and they hid fifty tons of stone and rubble in the attics mostly over the chapel. In the chapel at the moment," he went on, "there is a working, run by Monty Bissel. We're hiding the ghosts in it. Don't do any snooping in there without letting me know first."

The party walked casually across the courtyard and into the dentist's room on the east side of the Castle. Dick gathered them once more at a window and pointed out through the bars. "You see that buttress over there to the right. Well, it's hollow—it was a medieval lavatory. Vandy and half a dozen Dutch and British got down to the bottom of it from the third floor. It was on rock. They tried tunnelling but were caught. Just round the corner, beyond the buttress and above us, is the window where we had the team ready to go out if the Franz Josef bluff had worked." He led them through several small low-ceilinged rooms, unlocking two doors on the way with his master key.

They found themselves in the barber's shop. "Under this floor there is still a whacking great hole left by Pat Reid. The Jerries have never found it. If anyone has ideas for starting up work again here, they're welcome. There are several snags but nothing is impossible. You might have a think about it." He led them next to the canteen in the south-east corner.

"This area's vulnerable," he explained, "and may give you something to think about. We had a tunnel here in 1941 which led out under the canteen window and under the grass lawn beyond. Fourteen of us were caught. Several efforts have been made by Poles and Frenchmen to get out of the window—unsuccessful. Up above, there's a sealed room which we reached by a snow tunnel. It connects with the German quarters. On another occasion a team got into their quarters through a hole in the German lavatories which backed on to one of our dormitories. There's hope of doing something up above on the roof—it might be possible to have another crack at breaking through the gable of the Kommandantur and entering the German attics . . . let's go and have a look at the cookhouse."

Germans and orderlies were still at work and they could not approach the windows overlooking the German courtyard to the south. Dick contented himself by standing inside the doorway and explaining:

"This is where Reid, Ronnie Littledale, Hank Wardle and Stephens got out into the courtyard, then over the sentry's beat

into the Kommandantur and out to the moat and away; four home-runs. Above the kitchen, Frenchmen have tried the roofs and chimney stacks, so has Peter Storie Pugh. It might be tried again, but it's not a cake walk. Don Thom and Donaldson have had one shot also along the lean-to roof just under the stacks—you've got to be an acrobat to get there because it's an overhanging roof, though nearly flat, once you're on it."

Someone asked 'out of the blue': "Why don't you ever try to escape yourself, Dick?"

"I suppose because I'm a b—— fool," was the response, "but you can't do my job and try to escape as well. The two just don't add up. I know everybody's plans. It would be too easy to pinch someone else's idea and use it myself. Even if I had an idea of my own—nobody would believe me. I might have retired some time ago and asked someone else to take on the job—but now—at least I can't do it until you fellows are well stuck in. Then one of you might take over."

In the courtyard again, he showed them the de-lousing shed. "In one corner of the shed," he said, "there's a tunnel shaft—it was found by the Jerries but the working has been used again. The Poles, before they left, made a tunnel, from their quarters over the canteen—which were once ours, too; joining up with the drains. The drains run just beside that corner of the de-louser and they linked up. They continued outside the courtyard, under the main gate. The escape is in hand at the moment and Duggie Bader's in charge of it. He could do with help—it's a stinking job—every cut festers."

They next trooped upstairs to the theatre where Dick told his audience the story of the light well escape. Then pointing to the stage, he said:

"Four men got out from under the stage—Airey Neave was one. They went through a narrow corridor, over the main gate, into the German guardhouse and walked downstairs and out—in German uniforms, of course. Two made home-runs to Switzerland. A couple of Poles also got into the guardhouse from the building opposite this theatre block, by walking along a four inch ledge, forty feet above the cobbles. They made too much row climbing down their rope on the outside. A Jerry officer popped his head out of a window. They were only then about a hundred feet above the rocks at the bottom, hanging on to the rope. The Jerry pointed a pistol at them and shouted 'Hands up!' I'm told the Poles laughed so much they nearly let go."

Looking downwards from one of the theatre windows facing due west he showed the group where Bush Parker had dropped in the searchlight beams on to the causeway. Finally, the tour ended in the British quarters overlooking the terrace which also faced westward and were situated just to the south of the turret where Dick had begun.

"Some weeks ago," he told them, "Don Thom took the bull by the horns. He's an Olympic diver, incidentally. He's as tough as nails and a bundle of springs. I think he was browned off by all the effort we put into Bush Parker's escape which fizzled out. We've got another job on hand at the moment, too, and I'd ask you chaps to leave this area alone until it's over. If I tell you of Don Thom's effort you'll see that we're up against a very tough proposition."

"Have you a large scale plan of the Castle?" Gordon Rolfe asked. "I'd like to study it for a while to get my bearings."

"Yes, there is a plan," said Dick, "it's a series of plans really. It gives the state of the buildings from about the seventeenth century onwards as a matter of fact. The one thing I can't tell you is how we got it. I'll show it to any of you who want to examine it. Lulu Lawton will get it out of its hide after dinner."

"What happened to Don Thom?" Tony Rolt asked.

The group had relaxed. Some were lolling on the beds, others were looking out of the window down upon the terrace. The bars prevented them from having a clear view directly below them. Nobody was in a hurry.

"Don Thom's escape was a Douglas Fairbanks showpiece," Dick began. "Don first of all earned himself a month in the cooler —that was easy. Then, during the hour's exercise on the terrace you're looking at below you, he just leapt for it. It's the most daring escape recorded here and more death defying even than the Park escape of Mairesse Lebrun, the French cavalry officer. Mairesse at least had the assistance of one other officer and was exercising in the park under vigilance. There have been many escapes from the Park, incidentally, which you'll hear about. Don Thom dared four sentries in broad daylight, one of them—you can see from that window—with a machine gun. I know exactly how he must have felt because I'd never have the guts or suicidal courage—call it what you like—to do it myself.

"The men in the cooler inside the Castle are usually taken out under guard to the terrace through the guardhouse itself. They came out through that small doorway at the south end. The

terrace wall drops, from the outer balustrade, forty feet to the garden below. The far edge of the garden is protected by the low parapet wall which you can see, and by the nine-foot barbed wire fence. On the far side there's a precipitous drop which descends into a welter of rocks and concertina wire about fifty feet below. The cliff then levels out into the back yards of a few houses alongside the road which borders the river.

"Bag Dickenson, Van Rood and Don were all doing solitary together. One morning, the same as any other as far as solitaries are concerned, the three of them were escorted for their daily exercise, one sentry in front, one behind—regular daily routine—through the courtyard gate, into the guardhouse, down a few curving steps, and out on to the terrace.

"A sentry went first, and Bag next, through the little doorway into the open air. Don Thom was third. As he passed the door, he took off his jacket, dropped it in the corner, and vaulted the parapet; a clear forty foot drop—just like that! Don's tough, but still, forty feet is not the kind of jump to be contemplated when rifles and machine guns are going to open on you as soon as you land. As he dropped, he gripped the bars of two windows, one under the other, to break his fall. You can't see the windows from here, they're below the terrace in the guardhouse wall. He was seen by four sentries, including the one following Van Rood, and the fifth—the sentry in front of Bag—turned round when his mate shouted. Five sentries tried to hit him as he ran. Bag and Van Rood jitterbugged into their two sentries on the terrace and managed to upset their aim. But a machine gun post in a pagoda and two other sentries opened fire without hindrance.

"Don Thom ran to the fence. He probably saved his life by turning to the right when common-sense dictated he should go to the left. He scaled the nine foot wire with the bullets whizzing around him. He was forced to slow up by the climb. Then he dropped out of sight down the cliff below; hit or unscathed nobody could tell. He wasn't yet out of danger. Two sentries, who could still see him, potted away. He must have been moving fast at the bottom, tearing his way through a weak point in the concertina wire. But he couldn't make it. His clothes were ripped to pieces and he got tangled up; he had to put up his hands and they stopped firing. The nearest bullet took a piece out of his scalp."

There was a long pause when Dick finished the story. Then Tony Rolt asked:

"Did you say, Dick, that another escape was being planned from the terrace?"

"Yes, Mike Sinclair and Jack Best are going to have a crack, at dusk though, not in broad daylight. They have to start inside the Castle, of course. The only other way to get out on to the terrace is to do what Don Thom did and that means a daylight job."

There was a long silence. It was broken by the sound of a raucous voice in the corridor shouting: "Cha up! Cha up!" As if waking from a dream, the men rose and ambled out silently one by one to the mess room.

*   *   *   *   *

Jack Best, of the R.A.F.V.R., the boy from Stowe, the Empire builder with a farm in Kenya, was becoming desperate. He had been a ghost for almost a year. The tables were turning upon him and he was beginning to look like a haunted man. Jack, at thirty years of age, had the patience of Job. It was the reason why he had been accepted when he volunteered for the unenviable task of becoming a ghost. But it was plain that the job was beginning to tell on his health. Don Donaldson had, not without reason, christened him the "unfledged eagle". Now his downy feathers were drooping; his hair was looking thin and bedraggled, ready to fall out in a high wind. His long beak of a nose was losing flesh. The bridge was standing our prominently and the tip would soon meet his chin as his mouth receded. His dark eyes, with the fire of the eagle within, were more sunken than ever, and looked like two coals burning into his skull. His tall angular frame was hunched. The protruding shoulders and arms looked as if they should sprout feathers at any moment.

The only way by which he could break the vicious circle in which he found himself and retain his self respect was by escaping, because he was no longer officially recognised as a prisoner. He had escaped, but into another prison inside the prison instead of outside. If and when he escaped properly, another officer could take up his ghostly manacles. If he made a home-run the arithmetic would, in his case, be simplified; it would have caught up with him. From the German point of view, the sum would add up correctly. But if he was re-caught the Germans would have to use algebra, beginning with "let X be the officer who escaped in November, 1942. . . ." If Best was re-captured after some days

of freedom there was one series of possible solutions. If he was caught at the camp, there were other solutions, including the possibility that he was entering the Castle—gun-running—a possibility not so far-fetched as it might appear at first.

Although Jack had a tremendous sense of humour, he lived on his nerves. He had seen the funny side of living like a mole underground at Sagan—Stalag Luft III—while he tunnelled himself and his friend, Bill Goldfinch, outside the wire to mark up a "gone-away" and earn them both a place at Colditz. He could still see the funny side of being a ghost—up to a point, but, by November, 1943, the joke was wearing thin.

Mike Sinclair was planning his next escape. A duel of wits of his own conception was to take place on an old battle-ground : the terrace where Don Thom had sailed gaily over the parapet as if he had been performing in the high jump at his annual school sports.

Mike selected Jack Best as his partner for the break.

The time at which the perimeter searchlights were switched on was tabulated and graphed as a matter of routine. What Mike was looking for was a short blind interval at dusk; blind in two senses: firstly, on account of the approaching gloom and, secondly, coinciding with a change of the guards, taking them from their points of vantage. He posed the problem to Dick Howe and indicated when he thought the short interval of time might occur.

Regularly, over a period of four months, Dick, Lulu Lawton and Mike watched the changing of the guard in the terrace area; in the pagoda; on the cat walk; in the garden (an orchard), and in the corner turret. Jack Best could not help them in this, being a ghost!

A machine-gun sentry post, an outsize crows-nest, situated on an elevated scaffolding, reached by a ladder, in the garden beneath the terrace, commanded the whole wall face of the prison on that side, including the outer wall of the German guardhouse. It was known as a "Pagoda," and was manned day and night. Another type of scaffold, providing a long elevated corridor with timber balustrades, was known as a "catwalk." One such was built close to the outer wall of the guardhouse where the garden narrowed, and at one end it jutted out over the precipice below. The sentry post at ground level in the garden and the machine-gun post in the turret under the prison walls was only manned at nightfall, when it became difficult for the machine-gun post in the pagoda to command the walls fully, owing to deep shadows cast by the

searchlights at certain angles. The garden sentry also replaced a sentry on the terrace itself, who was useless at night, standing directly in the glare of the searchlight.

The turret sentry and the garden sentry came on duty at the nearest regular guard change coinciding with nightfall. With this pinpoint of knowledge, culled by simple observation, Mike Sinclair opened an oyster.

The first essential that the three watchers deduced, was that, between the time when the pagoda sentry at dusk left his post and was replaced and the first turret sentry had gained his position, there was a blind spot of sixty seconds duration. The second essential for the escape was the seasonal advent of a period when the searchlights, governed, as was discovered, by a routine schedule depending mainly on the time of year and hardly at all upon the state of the light on any particular day, were switched on just after a regular guard change. "Just after" was the important point, so that the sixty seconds coincided with the maximum darkness possible. Not until the end of November, 1943, were all the conditions favourable for the attempt to take place.

Sixty seconds! Perhaps seventy seconds. Perhaps only fifty! Dick, Mike and Lulu were not prepared to argue over ten seconds either way. The job to be performed was one that would require the services, under peace-time conditions, of a team of workmen for a day with long ladders and several tool kits; an industrial safety inspector, and a merger of Lloyds insurance brokers. Mike Sinclair and Jack Best, dispensing with the anomalies of peace, reckoned to do the job in sixty seconds.

The bars of a window in the British quarters on the second floor of the Castle, thirty feet above the terrace, had to be cut by way of an opening gambit. This was done in the same manner as for the Franz Josef attempt.

Bo'sn Crisp prepared no less than ninety feet of the best rope he had ever made from strips cut out of the blue check cotton sleeping bags and tested at every splice.

The civilian clothing, the maps, the money, the home-made compasses and the identity papers were forged with minute accuracy.

Mike Sinclair selected his wire-cutters. He preferred the pair made by Bill Goldfinch to the factory-made pair smuggled into the camp.

The four of them discussed the launching ramp.

"You'd better use the long table," said Dick, "and give it a

thorough rub down with sand-paper. The long one will take the two of you lying flat, end to end, and you can be shot straight through the window opening, holding on to the rope."

Mike said, with a curious air of finality, "I want you two, Dick and Lulu, to do the launching, nobody else. I don't want anyone else to do it."

"Mike will go out first," Dick explained, "with the wire-cutters strapped to his leg. When he's dropped to the terrace he takes the rope end with him and jumps over the balustrade, Don Thom fashion. Now, Jack, if you don't hustle after Mike, you'll find yourself suspended in mid-air over the terrace when he takes the rope with him over the second drop. Everything's got to move together. Lulu, you must let the rope out as fast as Mike needs it, but keep it fairly taut all the time. Jack, you've simply got to be on the terrace by the time Mike goes over, so you must slide down the rope following Mike like streak lightning down a moving escalator. Get me?"

Jack intervened. "What about the brief-case and the second length of rope all attached to the end of the main rope?"

"When you've finished with the main rope, that is, after the second drop, unhitch them both—they'll be on a slip-knot—and carry on. Now, Lulu, this is where you come in. As soon as the tension is off the main rope you must haul in like mad! Jack, don't forget to keep a firm hold on the rope or you'll find your food and kit disappearing upwards. Let go only when everything is clear. After that the rest is up to you and we can't do much more for you."

When the two escapers reached the bottom of the second drop they would have to run thirty yards diagonally across the garden, cut a gap in the barbed-wire perimeter fence, tie the second rope to a post and drop down the rocky cliff below, a matter of fifty feet. This was the cliff over which Don Thom had thrown himself, clinging to jutting crags as he hurtled down in broad daylight with rifles blazing at him. On the new assault, Mike and Jack hoped to tie their rope and disappear over the edge before they were seen. To this end, of course, silence was invaluable.

At the bottom of the cliff they had concertina barbed-wire to deal with before they were finally "gone-away."

*   *   *   *   *

The stage is set for the escape of sixty seconds. It is a cold afternoon at the end of November, 1943, with sleet and a biting

wind which augurs well for a murky evening. The day wears on. The two bars of the window have been cut by Bricky Forbes and Bill Goldfinch. The stooges are placed as the gloom of evening begins to creep over the Castle and their intercommunicating code system is checked. The signal, "all clear," will come from the accordion of the master stooge at a window directly above that at which the operation is about to take place. Dick will give the final order, "go". . . .

Zero hour has arrived and zero minute will soon be here. The wind has dropped, which is a pity. Mike and Jack will need all the self-control they can muster to avoid making a noise and giving the alarm on the last lap.

In the dormitory there is silence as the shadows deepen. Along the smooth table the two escapers lie. Jack Best is dead still. Mike is fidgety. The cutters strapped to his leg are uncomfortable. They may give trouble. Dick is readjusting them.

High up in a corner, sitting on the top of a wardrobe, is John Watton, the camp artist, with his drawing-board, pencils and chalks. He is working furiously in the gathering dusk. his hand and brain alive to the terrific tension as he tries to translate the suspense of the moment on to the flat medium of paper. He stares downwards. His eyes gleam in the fading light and his hand circles upon the paper.

"Three minutes to go," says Dick, in a hushed voice, "providing the sentries behave themselves. Keep dead calm. Remember it's a cinch. Go quietly as you dròp and move."

The two men lie still, stiffening against the fierce heave that will project them along the table out into the twilight one after the other, like rockets from a launching ramp; that will shoot them out of the window in a headlong swoop which they must check before landing. The rope is laid out straight beside and behind them. Mike holds it coiled around his right arm.

All the actors on the stage who may approach the window have blackened faces, and the two escapers, in addition, wear long dark stockings over their shoes. Their two forms lie stretched, like beasts on a sacrificial altar, ready for the moment when the high priest will raise his arm aloft and pronounce the words of doom.

"One minute to go," Dick intones in a low voice, clear for all to hear in the grim silence.

Two strong men stand rigid beside the window, waiting, ready to grip the bars and twist them out of the way at the signal. The whites of their eyes flash out of their blackened faces.

Derek Gill and Mike Harvey stand by the rope, to pay it out, to prevent it tangling and to take the weight of the descending bodies.

Dick and Lulu, the priests, stand over the table while Dick leans towards the window, listening intently, peering downwards.

Mike is jittery. He is complaining the cutters are too tight around his leg. Almost like a child, he is whispering to Dick, "They're too tight! They're too tight! I must have them looser —help me quickly—looser—quick—— No! Dick, there's no time now. It's too late. There's not enough time, stop."

The accordion starts to play.

—Go!

Dick looks at his watch and raises his arm, counting audibly, "Four—three—two—one," and then drops it at "go!"

The two strong men at the bars clench their teeth and heave with the strength of devils, twisting the bars inwards and sideways in a slow, quivering movement fraught with the tautness of muscles and the wracking of sinews. Hell breaks loose. The spirit of action like an unholy demon takes possession of the room.

Lulu and Dick grip Mike bodily, one on either side, and hurl him through the window feet first. He shoots horizontally outwards. Another tremendous heave and Jack Best slides forward, rockets out

and disappears from view. Gill and Harvey feel the rope tearing through their hands. They let it out to the first marker knot, lean back, take the strain with the rope twisted round their forearms. There is a tremendous jerk, followed by a thump. The rope holds. The two are down on the terrace, thirty feet below.

The rope pays out again, uncoiling like a cobra, weaving, snatching and turning, as Mike races across the terrace.

Dick, at the window, raises his arm again in signal. Gill and Harvey take the strain once more on the rope. Mike and Jack are over the terrace and dropping down the second forty-foot descent.

The guardhouse door is opening. A shaft of light breaks through the gloom along the terrace. A German N.C.O. walks out, advancing slowly along the terrace. He seems momentarily blind.

"They must free the rope!" hisses Dick. " Good God, he can see it! It's straight in front of him. For Pete's sake, Derek! heave it in, heave like mad!"

As he speaks the light blue rope slackens. The German leans on the balustrade. He looks over the parapet. At that instant the rope whistles past him, upwards, not a yard away. He has heard something; he whips out his revolver, but seems not to have seen the rope. He shouts: "*Hallo! Hallo!*" There is no answer.

A scurry above, as the rope is hauled through the window, makes the German look upwards for a moment, puzzled. Then he turns towards the garden as a distinct "ping" is heard from the direction of the wire below. Another loud "ping" and the German shouts again, "*Hallo! Hallo! Was ist es?*" and peers into the shadows below, shading his eyes with his hand, and with his revolver cocked.

Mike has crossed the garden and is cutting the wires underneath the pagoda where the new sentry has taken up his position. Mike appears to take no notice of the guard who has come out on to the terrace. He has not seen him. The sentry above him answers the N.C.O.: "*Ich weiss nicht.*"

Jack is in the shadow under the terrace wall. He can see the German above him and dares not move. He cannot warn Mike. A third "ping" is heard clearly by Dick and Lulu in the window high above.

The German walks slowly along the terrace near the parapet, looking outwards. The night sentry in the garden has reached his post and is standing fifteen yards away. This is Jack's chance; he creeps to the end of the wall and then across the garden among the fruit trees and the deeper shadows to where Mike has already fixed the rope for the last drop. Mike drops over. Jack follows, but

lies on the edge of the drop, trying to close the wire gap behind him. He looks up and sees the German on the terrace staring straight towards him with his pistol at the ready. That is enough. He drops out of sight, sliding down the rope over rocks and bushes, fifty feet, to the bottom. The N.C.O. turns slowly away.

There is more barbed-wire below—coils upon coils of it.

"We can't get through there," whispered Mike hoarsely; "we must crawl along to the end."

They do so, slipping and stumbling on the steep incline, ripping their clothes on the wire at every move until they reach a narrow path.

Here Mike tackles the wire again. "Ping! Ping! Ping!" Bill Goldfinch's home-made, five-to-one lever wire-cutters do their work. They crawl through.

But a woman in a nearby cottage has heard the scrambling and comes to the window, looking out. "*Was ist los?*"

Silence! as the two men lie prone, their hearts pounding, she moves away and they are off again.

They are dripping with sweat, winded and breathing painfully. Their civilian clothes are badly torn. Seventy seconds ago they were prisoners in the impregnable fortress. Now they are free. . . .

*　　*　　*　　*　　*

As they moved off into the countryside at a slow trot, Dick stood motionless at the window high up in the Castle.

The German N.C.O. had returned to the guardhouse, walking slowly with hesitant steps, frequently turning round, obviously worried and uncomprehending.

Dick gazed outwards over the fast darkening countryside, out into the gloom towards the river where he knew his two men were heading. He was tingling all over with nervous elation. Then, as he peered, he felt his legs weaken under him and he gripped the window sill to steady himself. Gall rose in his throat and a sudden revulsion turned his stomach. His eyes misted over. He closed them quickly, gripping the sill tightly. The nausea continued for a couple of minutes as he fought against the urge to vomit. . . . The crisis passed slowly and he opened his eyes.

The searchlights came on with a blinding flash around the Castle and all beyond turned as black as pitch.

"They've gone away! They're safe by now!" said Dick thickly, turning to Lulu and the others, and mopping his blackened brow

with the flicker of a smile spreading over his face. There was silence again. He glanced at his companions, noting at once he was not the only one whose stomach had turned over. After the fever of the past two minutes they were stunned. For a few seconds they had all been escaping with the two who had disappeared. Now they stood, silent, wondering, almost inexplicably, why they had not gone, why they were still in the room within the oppressive walls. There were no words that they could say.

Watton climbed down from his perch, shaking with the excitement of the action. "Fantastic, simply fantastic!" he shouted, waving his drawing-block wildly around his head.

"I'm glad you like it," said Lulu drily. "I'll appreciate a signed copy of the result, if you don't mind."

Dick said simply, talking to them all, "Thanks for a pretty piece of team work. You've made escaping history to-night—I think." And, as they went about clearing away the signs of the escape, Dick turned once more to the window, staring out into the blackness beyond the searchlight beams.

He stood, motionless, with the reflection from the blazing arcs outside accentuating his worn, haggard features, still streaked with black theatre paint; the strong chin, the drawn lines of the skin and the sunken eyes. His thoughts had suddenly been turned inwards. He was trying to answer the question that had flashed through all their minds when they stood silent and perplexed a few moments before. "Why were they still there? Why had others gone?" There seemed to be no general answer. "Many are called, but few are chosen," he thought, "might not be far off the mark."

It was more than a question of plain guts. For this kind of escaping a man required a will of iron and a calculating, cold-blooded courage that was not commonly found. There was a deep sense of duty behind it all, too—but that applied to all of them.

"All over the world," Dick thought, "men are fighting and falling. To be impotent—a prisoner—helpless and unable to help, is a degrading state, hard to bear."

At least these men were doing something. They could hold up their heads and keep their self-respect. They were thinking of the future and not necessarily of their own. They had not Milton's excuse. "They also serve who only stand and wait" was not for them. They were not blind.

For several minutes Dick stood at the window, then, turning slowly, he came out of his reverie.

"I thought Mike was a bit jittery to-night, not quite his usual self," he said to Luke. "I wonder why the Goon chose to come out on to the terrace at that precise moment?"

"Most inconsiderate of him," was Lulu's comment as they walked out of the room together.

CHAPTER XVI

CHINA TEA

TONY ROLT was one of the sixty-five Eichstatt tunnellers. From the day they had arrived, in July, 1943, these tunnellers had been known as "the new boys." The name clung to them and, the English being a conservative race, they were still new boys at the end of the war, by which time they had been indistinguishable from their blood-brothers, "the old lags," for nearly two years.

In self-defence the "new boys" invented "the men of spirit" —a term which they applied to any and sundry among the "old lags" who, either by innuendo or direct attack, tried to inculcate in them a sense of inferiority. They were not to be browbeaten and the sarcasm behind the appellation had its effect.

Undertones and rumblings, disturbances from the intrusion into Colditz, echoed around the camp and slowly died away. Like the spilling of one lake into another when the weir gates are raised, the two waters clashed, shot up in spray, sent waves dashing to the shore, swirled in eddies, rippled, merged and gradually subsided into one, still, homogeneous pool, deeper than before.

The new boys were under a disadvantage: the disadvantage suffered by all new boys throughout the world. They did not know the ropes, they did not know the old boys, they were in strange surroundings and sometimes at a loss—humiliating, under any circumstances. But they brought with them some new ideas which the old boys eventually acknowledged—grudgingly to begin with —and later with enthusiasm. The scorpion's lash of "the new boys" lost its sting.

Tony Rolt was one among the many whom the old boys would have liked to claim towards the end of the war, as one of the "men of spirit." This term also, like an old, well-worn, ugly pair of shoes, became "cosy" from long usage.

Rolt, in his early twenties, was an amateur motor-racing driver who had achieved fame before the war. He was a lieutenant of the

Rifle Brigade. He was tall, dark and clean-shaven, almost stream-lined, like one of his cars, and he had a serious yet lively nature ; at one and the same time, painstaking yet bubbling with enthusiasm.

He could not drive a delicate, highly-tuned racing car out of Colditz, even a heavy tank would not have gone far. He used to lie for hours on his bunk, exasperated by the frustration, stung by his own impotence and goaded to action by the blackness of the escaping outlook. He wondered how some highly technical *flair* could be brought to bear on escaping; there was any amount of scientific talent in Colditz. It was clear to him that only the most desperate action would succeed in these days. The last two escapes which had put British prisoners outside the perimeter wire were cases in point. When men were taking to leaping over forty-foot walls in broad daylight, braving the machine-guns, rocketing out of windows attached to ropes, weaving between sentries in mad, second-splitting escapes, it was time to be original, and in a big way. To Rolt's way of thinking there was no hope of success for anything in the least mundane. The Jerries had all that taped, tied up and sealed irrevocably.

He brought together and crystallised the gleanings of weeks of cogitation one day in December, 1943. He sat brooding over a morning cup of acorn coffee, made palatable with powdered milk and a saccharin tablet.

Rumours were abroad that Mike and Jack Best had been re-captured. Pessimism was on the prowl again, looking for victims.

He spoke first to Bill Goldfinch, who was sitting opposite to him munching a piece of German sawdust-bread thinly coated with the remains of a Canadian Red Cross butter ration.

"Quite a tribute, I thought, the way Mike Sinclair took your home-made wire-cutters in preference to the factory-made variety. You're a bit of a wizard with your hands, Bill. Where did you learn it?"

It was not a coincidence that he should be talking to Bill Goldfinch. It was part of his thinking—this morning, it seemed, everything had come to a head. Bill Goldfinch was sitting there. The time was ripe.

Bill was speaking.

"There's nothing to it, Tony. I just got the habit of tinkering when I was a kid, ever since the family went out to Rhodesia. My old man was an engineer. I suppose that had something to do with it. He sent me to work in the Salisbury City Council engineering department. I'm not happy unless my hands are at work."

"What made you join the R.A.F.?" Rolt asked.

"I got mad keen on flying and aircraft design. That sent me into the R.A.F.V.R. when I was twenty-one. It must have been about 1938. That's how I'm here now. I got called up when war started and was trapped in the Greek evacuation. My Sunderland flying boat crashed at Kalamata. If I hadn't been spitting blood I'd've been evacuated. Instead they operated on me—found nothing wrong—only mouth bleeding. But before my operation wound healed I was a prisoner. I met up with Jack Best in the hospital."

As he listened, Tony was thinking, "This is the man all right. I'm sure he'll do it. . . . I bet he will." Aloud he said, "Bill, I've got an idea. I'm going to tell you something that'll make you think I'm going round the bend. I'm not though—not yet."

"Go ahead, I'm listening," said Bill quietly, in a reassuring voice. He was like that, reassuring, with a touch of kindliness. His fair complexion, his mousy hair and his pale blue eyes, made up a picture of an unassuming, even shy nature. His inner strength, the peculiar tough fibre which has nothing to do with physical strength, but a lot to do with mental equanimity, only made itself felt after long contact with his personality. He was the type of man who would survive alone in a lifeboat after weeks of exposure, long after all the other occupants had gone overboard.

"I'm not an engineer, you see, Bill," Rolt continued, "but I know enough about mechanics and, I think also, enough about aerodynamics to imagine that what I'm thinking about is not complete nonsense.

"I seriously think a glider could be built that would be able to take off from one of the roofs of this castle. Don't think me crazy yet—listen—let me finish. I've been thinking about this idea for months. There's a long roof overlooking the river—the one over the old French quarters. It's so high that the ridge is completely out of sight from all the sentries below. In fact, you can only see the ridge if you go down into the town or away, over the river. Look!" Here Rolt produced a piece of paper from his pocket. He unfolded it and spread it before Bill Goldfinch.

"You see—there's a cross-section of the castle to scale with the sentries at their posts. Their lines of vision run from the roof gutters straight up, skywards. They can't see anywhere near the roof ridge. We could make a flat launching ramp like a saddle, built in sections, to sit on the roof ridge. It's twenty yards long."

"You mean," interrupted Bill, who was becoming curiously

excited in spite of himself. "You mean, the glider would be catapulted then?"

"Yes, that's it. I've already got some ideas for the catapult, but let me finish. The glider would have to be built in parts, with dismountable wings. I don't know how many persons it could take. That's where you would begin to come into the picture. What do you think, Bill? I can't do this myself, but with one, or even two, professionals, I'm sure a glider can be built. I'll do all the donkey-work, everything I can possibly do, but I don't know enough about aerodynamics, and I'm not a highly skilled craftsman."

"A glider isn't so very hard to build, you know," said Bill, becoming involved and beginning to fall for the idea. "What it requires is tremendous patience. I only wish Jack Best was around. He's just the man for this. He's got the patience of Job. A glider consists of literally thousands of parts, all the same—like the wings of a bird—thousands of feathers all the same shape. If I made a few prototype parts and some templates, you could carry on."

"Does that mean you'll seriously think about the idea?" asked Tony.

"Yes," said Bill, "I'll think about it," and that was all Tony Rolt could extract from him at that sitting.

During the next two weeks Rolt continued to badger Bill Goldfinch until he had the latter sitting down in front of a home-made drawing-board with pencils, paper, rulers and rubber. From that moment Bill Goldfinch was lost. He found himself starting upon a course which would lead him he knew not where, but quite likely to a "sticky end." He was at the top of a steep hill, sitting astride an infernal machine of his own making, without brakes— or engine. He was gaining momentum, out of control, and the end of the hill was just round the corner.

*   *   *   *   *

While the new boys were still new, it goes without saying that they had their legs pulled.

Harry Elliott was recounting to a few of the newcomers, sometime after their arrival, the history of the several continental contingents which had come and gone from Colditz. He talked glowingly of the Poles; humorously of the French and Belgians, warmly of the Dutch, and, to make sure that he lost nothing in effect, he reminded his listeners of the Yugoslavian officers, the Indian doctor and the North Africans, and introduced them forth-

with to a Bedouin sheik who was, at the time, a resident in Colditz. Nobody quite knew, and least of all the Bedouin himself, how he had filtered down to Colditz. He had been mixed up in some mêlée in North Africa and had been captured. Nobody understood what he said, and he could not understand what anybody else said. One misunderstanding led to another, until, the smiling sheik, with the features of an Orient King and the character of a humorist in perpetual adversity, arrived at Colditz, where it seemed he would not have much opportunity to strike his tent or silently fade away.

"What a collection of nationalities!" exclaimed one new boy in respectful admiration. "What a pity there are no Chinese!" said another with a slight hint of sarcasm.

It was enough for Harry. He would shake them.

"Oh! but haven't you met the Chinese naval officer?" he said.

"No! Where is he? Do introduce us. This is terrific!" The hint of sarcasm had gone. Now there was only astonishment and unconcealed wonder.

The Chinese naval officer was in the sick bay, explained Harry. He was not very well but he would try and arrange an introduction for the next day.

Harry lived in the sick quarters himself at that time. He was working hard at his own escape plans. His jaundice had given place to duodenal ulcers. These were having marital complications with a genuine form of arthritis, which he was nursing successfully into a galloping paralysis. He had, unfortunately, failed to discover an appropriate disease that was highly infectious—one which would help him back to England quickly and not into a "Klim tin".

Two Dutch Colonial officers, one of them a naval lieutenant, had remained behind in the sick ward long after the main Dutch contingent had departed. They occupied beds near Harry. He confided to them that he was committed to produce a Chinese naval officer on the following day. They agreed to carry it off with him. The Dutch naval Lieutenant was sallow-skinned with an Asiatic type of head and definitely oriental eyes, which, of course, accounts for the mental vision that had goaded Harry on. This Dutchman would be the Chinese officer; the other Dutchman, Steenhouwer by name, would be his interpreter. They would speak "Chinese"—in reality Malay, and hope none of the British would understand.

Harry returned to the charge next day, telling the new boys

that his Chinese naval officer friend was feeling well enough to pay an official call on the British in their quarters. He suggested after tea that day as an appropriate time and explained that the Chinese officer could, of course, only speak Chinese, but that, fortunately, a Dutch officer in the sick ward knew a smattering of that language and had kindly offered to act as interpreter.

Tea-time arrived. The senior ranking officer of the quarters, Captain Lord Arundell, posted himself near the door as he heard the visitors mounting the stairs. There were thirty officers scattered around the large room, some sleeping, others reading, smoking or studying, others seated round the tables chatting over empty tea-mugs. They had been warned of the arrival of the visitor. Harry entered the room first and spoke to John Arundell, who called the room to attention, announcing the arrival of " a representative of our brave Allies, the Chinese." Harry whispered his name as the Chinaman and his interpreter came through the door and Arundell repeated in ringing tones: "Lieutenant Yo Hun Sin of the Chinese Navy." Arundell stood his ground, while the Chinese Lieutenant advanced, bowing towards him and towards the company in turn. He was wearing a dark blue naval uniform with brass buttons and anchor insignia. An exchange of greetings took place— the Dutch officer interpreting in Malay for the benefit of Arundell.

The occupants of the room began to lose interest. A hum of conversation arose. Arundell called for silence. Attention turned towards the party again, and the Chinese officer gabbled a few sentences of Malay, in a sing-song voice, at the assembled company. Steenhouwer, the 'interpreter,' translated:

"The Chinese officer sends greetings and wishes of long life to his English friends."

Then the Chinese officer bowed slowly and stiffly down to his waist. The Dutchman followed suit, but not quite so far and a few of the Englishmen, rather self-consciously, thought they had better do something, so they bowed too.

Arundell said: "Please give our greetings to the Chinese officer and say we are glad to welcome him as representing our staunch Ally."

Steenhouwer translated. There were more bows and then some handshakes also, for good measure. The Chinaman spoke further phrases, which were interpreted as:

"Great honour to be fighting as Ally of British people, China

and England, together, are invincible and will win war, perhaps, after many years."

This piece of laconic Chinese realism, rather shaking to British P.O.W.s, was received with pained smiles.

The Chinese naval officer was introduced to Captain Lord Arundell by Harry Elliott (extreme right)

John Arundell then asked the visiting party to join him at his table. Cigarettes were produced. Officers began to gather around, and the interpreter was inundated with questions.

"Ask him if he knows Chiang Kai-shek."

Malay sentences passed between the two; then beams and smiles and much nodding of heads.

"In case you do not know, Chiang Kai-shek is a great General," was the reply.

"Good Godfathers! what does he think we are!" was the English reaction.

"I say, ask him if they've got heavy tanks in China."

More sentences in Malay, then out came the answer:

"Yes they have got very heavy tanks in China."

"Ask him have they finished the Burma road yet?"

"Where was he taken prisoner?"

"How is the Chinese Navy doing?"

"How did he get to Germany?" Questions were reeled off and the two were hard put to it, to keep up with their Malay.

The answers were repeated into the crowd who had gathered in the background.

"I say, did you hear that, they *have* got heavy tanks in China."

"The Burma road is nearly finished."

"He blew up a Jap warship and then got blown up himself."

"The Chinese Navy has a secret weapon."

There was a pause and the Chinese officer seized the opportunity to rise to take leave. He spoke some more words in Malay. The interpreter recorded faithfully: "The Chinese Naval Lieutenant wishes, before departure, to sing his National Anthem."

Unfortunately, many of the prisoners, by this time, were back at their private occupations. John Arundell had to call for order again—banging on the table.

The Chinaman was standing with his hat on his head, looking very solemn.

An awkward moment of embarrassment followed; the British not knowing whether to stand or remain seated, to put their hats on or stand at attention without them.

The Chinese officer began in a pale, quavering voice, snatches from a Malay fisherman's song that he happened to know.

The British stood stiffly to attention and, when the Chinaman saluted at the conclusion, they acknowledged the salute—a little sheepishly.

Someone said: "Hadn't we better sing 'God Save the King'?"

With doubtful enthusiasm and some self-consciousness officers persevered with the lines, and finished the anthem with a major effort.

The Chinaman now bowed in all directions, moving backwards slowly towards the door, followed by his cortège who had to edge out sideways, so as not to get in front of his bows.

The door closed behind them, and the curtain dropped upon the incident until the next day when the new boys spent the morning telling the old boys what the Chinese Naval officer had told them. "They've got heavy tanks in China. Got it out of that Chinese Naval officer—decent type, I thought," and the old lags would say:

"What Chinese officer? We've got 'em all colours, but take me to a Chinese!"

Then someone began to smell a rat and soon the story was all over the camp. The new boys took a few days to live it down. The man who enjoyed it most, of course, was Harry, who laughs to this day when he talks of it.

*　　　*　　　*　　　*

Harry Elliott may have had an even earlier cue for his practical joke about the Chinese Naval officer. In fact, he was not the first in the Chinese field and the Colditz story would not be complete without the episode (it happened in 1942) of the British officer who taught Chinese to a Pole for several months.

Cyril Lewthwaite, of the Royal Warwicks, was an unforgettable character. He hailed from Bromwich and was one of the first escapers of the war. On a solo effort from Laufen, Oflag VII.C, in October, 1940, he escaped in the middle of the pig-swill cart. On reaching the off-loading place, Cyril rose out of the swill with a scream as he received, in the fleshy part of his leg, the full force of a sharp fork aimed at a recalcitrant heap of rotting potatoes under which he grudgingly reposed. Within a matter of minutes he had the whole village of Laufen chasing him in full cry. He ran gamely in two senses of the word, and then found himself cornered in a sharp bend of the river Salzach. He took to the water in the style of Walter Scott's stag with the hounds baying behind him, but, unlike the stag and coming from the Midlands, he had forgotten in his youth to learn to swim. He was soon up to his chin and going deeper. At this tragic point he was recaptured and marched back to the prison. He was escorted by the whole village in a pitchfork procession in which, as the chief object of veneration, he made a sorry spectacle, dripping from head to foot, filthy, with the slime of half a ton of pig swill upon him and smelling to high heaven as he slopped along the village street accompanied by the

jeers, hoots and screams of a population that had nearly tasted blood.

When Cyril arrived in Colditz, he became involved in languages. He had only one language to sell, that was English. He wanted to learn French, German, Italian and perhaps Russian also. He could, of course, select a different teacher for each language he required, and teach them, each in turn, English. But English bored him stiff. He could speak it, but he could not, for the life of him, explain how he spoke it or why. He would have preferred Latin for that. His best French friend had already another English teacher. It was all rather difficult until he found the way out. Then it was plain sailing. He was talking, one day, to a Polish officer who was a barrister. The Pole recounted a story in which a Chinese business man had fared very badly at the hands of the Polish law-courts because nobody in the country understood Chinese. The Polish barrister spoke French well. Cyril seized upon this and suggested filling the gap in the Polish legal fence by teaching his friend Chinese. The Polish barrister took the bait, hook, line and sinker; gave up teaching French to his other pupils and agreed to concentrate on Cyril alone, in exchange for Cyril's Chinese.

Cyril did not know a word of Chinese but he was undaunted. He started his lessons quite simply on classical lines. He outlined the notions of Chinese declensions; he said there were twenty, thinking that would give him plenty of breathing space. He spoke of the various tenses and emphasised that the Chinese, living as they do without much reference to time, and the passage of history, spoke of everything in the present tense unless it was about a thousand years old in which case it went into various forms of imperfect, ultimately ending in the perfect past. As for the future, unless it would take place after a thousand years it was also in the present. This paved the way for Cyril. He was able to explain with graphic illustrations why it was that the Chinese always spoke that peculiar tongue known as pidgin English. He would then quote an old story he knew, about a Chinaman who fumed at a railway station cloakroom attendant searching for his luggage, screaming as his train left without him: "Pretty damn seldom how my bag go. She no fly. You no fit keep station than God's sake." He would explain, "You see, everything is in the present tense unless it's very, very old."

He continued with conjugations and thought it wise to have lots of those too, Chinese being an ancient language.

He started the Pole off with a Chinese version of amo, amas, amat. It was! Mo, mao, maoto, pronounced in a decidedly oriental manner. Cyril thought he ought to change the meaning, so "mo" meant, "I eat" and so on. He gave him a few other simple verbs to learn as well.

To increase his vocabulary, as the declensions, Cyril said, were so complicated, he would teach him the first declension and with the nouns of other declensions he would permit his pupil, for the time being, to speak pidgin Chinese. It would increase his "word power" rapidly. He gave him the equivalent of "mensa, mensa, mensam . . . ." to study.

It went like this:

Soya, soya, soyo. . . . It meant, a bean.

I eat a bean: mo soyo. The Pole made progress. In fact, he was much too quick, because Cyril found that, instead of learning any French, he spent his homework hours trying to keep up with his frighteningly assiduous pupil. He struggled on for several weeks until, one early morning, when he was on mess orderly duty, as he queued up in the grisly dawn outside the German kitchen, wooden clogs on his feet, his head swathed in a long balaclava, bare legs showing beneath his dressing gown, a tattered French khaki cloak, he suddenly heard a voice beside him.

"Hokito tao yen yosh inko?"

He knew the voice only too well. He could bear it no longer. Besides he did not know what on earth the man was saying, and to be caught out like this, at an early hour, was just the last straw —speaking Chinese in his underpants! Cyril prided himself on his military turn-out, and rightly so. In the normal light of day, he was one of the smartest looking officers in the camp.

"Yoshinka yen?" continued the voice solicitously. "Mao cha pani undu yoyo." It was the "yoyo" that finally choked Cyril. He remembered teaching some quite fantastic participles, which ended with yoyo, weeks before. Only a prodigy could have remembered its meaning now. With a weary sigh he pulled himself together and looking his pupil in the eye, he said solemnly, placing his hand over his stomach;

"Mo chu la beri-beri suyu."

To which his pupil replied, "Munchi sunya! munchi sunya!"

Between them there was a bond of perfect mutual comprehension. Cyril fled upstairs and his pupil gazed touchingly after him before returning to the copybook over which he diligently pored.

That was the last Chinese lesson Cyril ever gave.

THE WRITING ON THE WALL

WHEN Mike Sinclair and Jack Best had escaped over the parapets, Dick Howe had no ghost to cover the absence of Sinclair at the evening *Appell*. He laid on the 'rabbit' instead. An air-raid that night also gave Dick the opportunity to repair the window bars while the searchlights were extinguished. He expected that the Germans would notice the hole in the wire and the dangling rope in the morning. His fears proved groundless. The hole, hidden under the structure of the pagoda, remained undiscovered for two days.

Upon the discovery, Lieutenant Barnes, who was Jack Best's double, went into hiding. At the *Sonder*—i.e. special—*Appell*, Mike Sinclair and Barnes were declared to be absent.

At this point there were no more volunteers to undertake the unhealthy job of being ghosts. Jack Best had been haunting the Castle for just one year!

Mike Sinclair was missing. The *"Rote Fuchs"* had escaped again! Military and Gestapo telephone lines began to hum. Heads began to swim and a special inquiry was set up. The German Commandant appeared before the High Command at Leipzig, where he had to make the ignominious confession that he did not know when the escape had taken place.

The two escapers had ended up their hair raising descent of the east cliff wall, on that fateful evening, with their clothes ripped to pieces by the barbed wire. They found a small path at the bottom of the cliff, and followed it. In the friendly darkness of a wood, half an hour later, they sat down to repair their damaged clothing, threading their needles by the light of a burning cigarette.

Three days later they were captured by civil police in the small town of Reine, twenty-two miles from the Dutch frontier.

On this occasion they had not headed for Switzerland. The trouble was that men who escaped to Switzerland had been filtering much too slowly out of that country, with the result that escapers were tempted to try other routes with the chance of a quicker re-patriation to England. Knowing the Colditz route by heart, they should have had a much better chance of crossing safely into neutral territory. It was a pity they were biased by information which,

though correct at the time, should not have been allowed to outweigh their better chance of freedom.

An astute police officer at Reine thought he recognised Mike from a photograph published in a police broadsheet circulated daily throughout Germany. At the same time he did not like the look of Best; "not Germanic enough," he said later. The police officer arrested them both while they were walking together along the main street of the town.

The two men were escorted back to Colditz guarded by an N.C.O. and four soldiers—a small tribute to the esteem in which they were held.

The German High Command were in a quandary. The Red Fox had escaped at an unknown date. Positive evidence as to the Fox's presence in the camp went back several weeks. They were bewildered and angry. All they knew was that there was a large hole in the perimeter wire and that, in the hours of darkness, prisoners might have used it as a rabbit run. How many had gone out? How many had come in? Nobody really knew. The Colditz inmates were playing hide and seek with them. The High Command had to consider the possibility that the Allied secret service might be at work, that the wire had been cut from the outside—nobody had been seen cutting it inside—and that prisoners were being removed or exchanged 'ad lib'. The Commandant was made to look very foolish, and his senior officers let him feel the whip of their scorn. The Germans were convinced that the British were up to no good. Mike was a dangerous man, known to have had contacts in Poland before he came to Colditz. A veritable underground movement was forming under their noses. They could not keep the scandal away from the Gestapo, who, as far as the prisoners' intelligence service could estimate, took charge of Colditz men, recaptured while escaping, from that day forward.

Jack Best, immediately upon recapture, knew his part and posed as Barnes. On his return to the Castle he was allowed back into the camp pending his sentence. The question then arose: should Barnes or Jack continue as the ghost? Jack thought he himself should because Barnes, at least, could then remain Barnes, though he would have to do a month's solitary for Jack! Jack, on the other hand, would always be in difficulties roaming the camp as Barnes. However, it was decided the other way.

The Doctor Jekyll and Mr. Hyde comedy continued for several days. But the Germans, under the prodding of the Gestapo, were forced to probe the mystery of the Red Fox's escape.

They must have reflected upon the case of Mike Harvey and his double.

A long drawn-out identity parade was held at which Jack appeared as Barnes, but the Germans pondered a long time over his record sheet. They suspected he was not the man whose photo was before them, but they let him go.

The next day they pounced again. Jack was removed and his finger prints were taken. They were not those opposite the name of Barnes!

The game was up. Jack continued to bluff until he saw that the Germans suspected he was Flight Lieutenant J. Best. They were awaiting his records which had gone to Berlin when Jack confessed his real identity.

The end of this story is that Jack was sentenced to a month's solitary for escaping and to a further month for . . . "being absent from one thousand, three hundred and twenty-six *Appells*, including three Gestapo *Appells*."

Lastly, Dick found out, months later, how it was that a German N.C.O. had opened the guardhouse door and walked out on to the terrace at the same moment as Mike and Jack dropped from the parapet. Jack, climbing over the balustrading, had accidentally pressed an alarm bell button which had immediately summoned the N.C.O. to the very spot where the escape was taking place!

PART III

1944

THE YANKEES ARE HERE

AMERICANS were trickling into Colditz in 1944.
Colonel Florimond Duke of the U.S. Army was taken
prisoner in Hungary. He had been parachuted into that country
on a special mission and had, after some weeks of activity, been
captured by the Gestapo. He was treated according to the Gestapo
routine, travelled in chains to Colditz, and was released into the
Castle more dead than alive. A brave man, who fought in the
U.S. Air Force in the First World War, nothing could keep him
away from the hazards of the Second, and he 'stuck his neck
right out'. He was handsome with a dark brown military moustache, stood over six feet in height and was a quiet retiring individual, with a consoling personality. In civilian life he was the
advertising manager of the magazine "Time".

A member of Colonel Duke's team who ended up at Colditz
was Captain Alfred Suarez of the U.S. Army Engineers, commonly
known as 'Al. He was another who loved adventure and, being
originally of Spanish descent, he had volunteered and fought for
the Government Forces during the Spanish Civil War in the
thirties. After this episode, it came about as a natural sequel to
his career, that he found himself parachuted into Hungary. He
was a gay daredevil with a great sense of humour.

Another member of Duke's team was Colonel W. H. Schaefer,
U.S. Army, who was less lucky than his two colleagues. Although
he reached Colditz, he was kept there in solitary confinement
pending court-martial. He was sentenced to death and remained
isolated while appeals were made continuously on his behalf up
to the time of the liberation of the Castle. This happy event saved
his life.

None of these Americans had any opportunity to escape. For
Schaefer, even the most recalcitrant Colditz convict would have
admitted there was not a hope. As for Duke and Suarez, there
was another very good reason why they should not 'stick their
necks out' any further than they had already done. Their necks
were, metaphorically, hanging on to their bodies only by the
thread of sufferance. A queer twist of the Gestapo mind had

saved them from extermination. Even these brave men realised that they had had their day.

*　　*　　*　　*　　*

The "Prominente" were a class of prisoner set apart by the German High Command for special treatment in Colditz. They consisted of prisoners who had connections with important personages on the Allied side by virtue of birth, or of fame, either their own or that of antecedents. By the same token they possessed special value for the Germans. It became plain to all, as the war progressed in favour of the Allies, that they would ultimately be used by Hitler as hostages and this is, in fact, what Hitler, through his lieutenant, Himmler, attempted to do when the time of the great holocaust approached.

Such prisoners were not maltreated. On the contrary they were allotted small cell-like single bedrooms giving them some privacy and elementary comfort. But they were most closely guarded. During the day they could mix with the other prisoners. At each roll-call they were counted separately. At ten o'clock each evening they were escorted from the general quarters to their rooms by special sentries and locked in.

A guard was maintained outside their cells all night. They were only released again at breakfast time in the morning. The door of each cell had a shuttered spy-hole fitted in it, and the sentry patrolled regularly throughout the night, flashing a torch through the open shutter to see that the prisoner was up to no mischief.

There was Giles Romilly, Winston Churchill's nephew. A young man with a misleadingly sulky expression because he was unfailingly cheerful with a kind disposition. A wave of dark hair flopped over his forehead; he had strong features and he had heavy lidded blue eyes and was small and stockily built. He had left England with the Narvik expedition in 1940, as a newspaper correspondent and had been captured by the Germans. He tried, once, to escape from Colditz, without success. At the end of the war he tried again and succeeded, but more of that anon.

Captain the Master of Elphinstone, a nephew of Her Majesty the Queen (now the Queen Mother), arrived in Colditz in 1944. He had been captured near Dunkirk in 1940.

Other Prominentes who arrived earlier from Eichstatt, most of

them having escaped from its famous tunnel, were: Captain the Lord Arundell of Wardour, Wiltshire Regiment (already mentioned); Captain Lord Haig, son of the Field-Marshal; and Lieutenant Lord Lascelles, nephew of King George VI; Captain Michael Alexander, cousin of Field-Marshal Alexander; Captain The Earl of Hopetoun, Lothian and Border Horse (already mentioned), a son of the Marquis of Linlithgow; and Lieutenant Max Duhamel, a relative of Winston Churchill.

Charlie Hopetoun was one of the three star theatrical producers of Colditz. He produced " Gaslight " by Douglas Hamilton in October, 1944, which played to overflowing houses in the Colditz theatre and, later, he wrote a play which received quite an ovation.

While on the subject of theatrical productions, which became an important part of camp life in 1944, it is worth recording the versatility of Dick Howe who found, in conditions of semi-starvation, the energy and the time to carry through major theatrical productions, run the escape nerve centre and control the wireless news service of the camp.

Dick produced "George and Margaret," which had run in England before the war, in June, 1944, and "Jupiter Laughs" by A. J. Cronin in November of that year.

The third outstanding producer, and the peer of the trio, was Teddy Barton. He produced "Pygmalion", in February, 1943; "Rope" in January, 1944; "Duke in Darkness" in March, 1944; and "Blythe Spirit", in April, 1944, with Hector Christie of the Gordon Highlanders, acting superbly the part of Madame Acarti. Other leading lady parts were excellently performed by Alan Cheetham, a Lieutenant of the Fleet Air Arm. In May, the theatre was closed by way of reprisal for an offence against the Germans; in June, 1944, Teddy produced "The Man Who Came to Dinner". "Hay Fever" and "To-night at 8.30" followed, and several Noel Coward compositions occupied the theatre until the end of 1944, when productions ceased.

The scenery for the theatre was painted mostly by the master hands of John Watton and Roger Marchand on newspaper glued to wooden frames. Roger Marchand was a French Canadian who had somewhere in his travels picked up a 'Bowery' accent. He was asked one day what he was painting and his reply was, "A'm paintin' a scene for dat guy, Ot'ello."

Dresses were manufactured out of crêpe paper. There was plenty of Leichner make-up provided by the German Y.M.C.A. A carpenter's tool kit was accepted, on *parole*, but the prisoners

H

soon dispensed with it, preferring to use illicitly manufactured tools, equally good.

Hugo Ironside was invariably stage manager. The electricians were: a Dutchman, Lieutenant Beetes and later Lulu Lawton, who performed wonders in lighting effects. And the litany would not be complete without mentioning the manufacture of stage props., such as a highly polished concert grand piano for "George and Margaret", an ugly looking brass festooned coffin for "The Man Who Came to Dinner", out of old Red Cross boxes by Hugo Ironside, Mike Edwards and George Drew.

The superior productions of 1944, were a far cry from the early days when a handful of British gathered together in their quarters on Christmas Day, 1940, to hear Padre Platt sing:

> "Any old iron, any old iron, any any any old iron!
> You look sweet, talk about a treat!
> You look a dapper from your napper to your feet,
> Dressed in style with the same old tile
> And your father's old green tie on,
> And I wouldn't give you tuppence for your
> Old watch chain.
> It's iron, old iron!"

Let it be said that our popular padre sang it with an unforgettable éclat. His false teeth took off from his mouth at the crescendo enunciation of the finale "Tuppence" and clattered to the floor amidst roars of laughter from the boorish audience.

The possibility of a general reprisal on the camp theatre was always uppermost in the minds of the theatre actionaries. Until the curtain rose on the opening night, nobody could ever be sure a production would take place; there was so much clandestine activity in progress that might be unearthed at any moment, and the closing of the theatre was always among the first acts of retribution carried out by the Jerries.

A cinema show once came to Colditz, but only once; that was in 1943. Scarlet O'Hara remarked loudly after the performance, and in the close hearing of Hauptman Eggers who understood English well, "If that's the b—— sort of film the Jerries put up with, no wonder they're losing the war."

His remark closed the theatre for a month and no more films came to Colditz.

No "privilege" lasted long. Two games of Rugby took place on the Colditz village green in the winter of 1943/44. On two occasions in the summer of 1944, a batch of prisoners was escorted down

to the river for a bathe. On one occasion a party of officers went to the cinema in the village. These outings constituted "privileges". They were all *"parole* jobs", that is to say, prisoners had to sign a promise not to make an attempt to escape during the excursions.

Privileges were extremely rare. Suspicion was mutual. On the one hand, the Jerries thought that frequent repetition would ultimately prove to the advantage of prospecting escapers. On the other, *parole* savoured of the thin end of the blackmail wedge and the Colditz inmates were nothing if not diehard. The number of prisoners willing to sign *parole* passes dwindled remarkably after the first outing.

Douglas Bader, the air ace, indulged in a different kind of *parole*. He demanded *parole* walks on the grounds of his inability to exercise properly in the Castle precincts owing to his physical disability; namely, that of having both legs missing. The very ludicrousness of a legless man demanding *parole* walks is reminiscent of the defiance of this great airman.

During the summer and autumn of 1944, he had his way. He gave his *parole*—promising not to make any attempt to escape or even to make preparations to this end. What he did not promise to eschew was the continuation, outside the camp, of the cold war campaign which he relentlessly carried on against the Germans inside the camp. He would continue to break German morale by every means in his power.

So, insisting that he had to be accompanied on his walks, in case his tin legs gave trouble on the hills, he usually obtained permission for Dick Howe or another to go with him. Together they would load themselves with Red Cross food. With internal trouser pockets elongated to their ankles and filled to the brim and with their chests bursting outwards, they would set off to demoralise the country folk with food and luxuries they had not seen for five years; English and American cigarettes and pipe tobacco, chocolate, tinned meat and ham from the four corners of the earth. Bader and Dick gave generously, asking for little in return; a few eggs, maybe, or fruit or lettuce. They naturally started this campaign on the accompanying sentries. When they had the latter in their pay by the simple process of bribery followed by blackmail, the way was clear for the major offensive. At first lone farms were visited, then the attack approached the fringes of the town of Colditz itself. The enemy fell like ninepins for the subtle, tempting baits. German morale in the countryside bent under the attack.

MUTINY

AS early as the autumn of 1941, Harry Elliott had studiously learnt the symptoms of a common and unnerving stomach trouble—duodenal ulcers, and had applied carefully the lessons he learnt. He complained of pains. He lost weight. He had warning prior to being weighed, so he started off with bags, full of sand, hanging down inside his pyjama trouser legs, supported at his waist. Thereafter he lost weight regularly by off-loading a few pounds of sand at a time. He painted the skin round his eyes with a mixture of carbon and yellow ochre so regularly that it became ingrained and would not come off with washing. Harrowing pains and the loss of two stone in weight succeeded in sending him to a hospital, Elsterhorst, in February, 1942. Here he found two stalwart Indian doctors captured in Cyrenaika in 1941 who "fixed" blood in his various medical samples. All was ready for a breakout with his Belgian confederate, Lieutenant Le Jeune, when the night before the "off", the latter's civilian clothing was found.

The Germans were nothing if not radical and, knowing the Colditz reputation, they acted judiciously. The whole Colditz contingent at Elsterhorst was returned, lock, stock and barrel, under heavy guard by the 4.30 a.m. train the next morning, to their natural home.

Harry lay low for a while, then started a chronic jaundice. By 1943, Harry's back began to trouble him; the result of a fall when he was trying to escape in France, after his capture in 1940. Arthritis set in and showed on X-ray plates, but Harry had cooked his goose, as far as hospitalisation was concerned. Nobody would take any notice of his serious and troubling complaint. He was becoming a cripple.

"If the Goons won't swallow it one way, they'll jolly well have to swallow it another way," thought Harry. He decided to start up his duodenal ulcers again. This time he had to travel far to make the grade. Already as thin as a rake he had to lose two more (sand) stone. After several successive weighings he ran out of sand and still the Jerries would not transfer him. His face was the colour of an ash heap at dawn, but the German doctors were unsympathetic. Harry decided he had to starve. He ate nothing for a week, could scarcely stand upright and the Germans gave in. He returned to Elsterhorst hospital.

There were several English doctors working in the hospital, including a Radiologist, whom Harry made his particular *confident*. The result was some really juicy ulcers on an X-ray plate which had his name attached to it. All this time Harry was suffering the real pangs of arthritis which was turning him into a crippled 'old man of the sea'.

Harry's ulcers flared up and died down in the traditional manner of the really worst type, and the X-ray plates showed the legitimate and pitiable arthritis mingling with cleverly transposed awe inspiring, if not terrifying, ulcers in such a picture of blended medical misery that expert opinion considered he was, at last, ripe to appear before the Mixed Medical Commission.

Harry was returned to Colditz as an incurable case with not long to live and a ticket of recommendation for interview by the Commission.

The Mixed Medical Commission was a body formalised by the Geneva Convention for the examination of sick and wounded Prisoners of War with a view to their repatriation. It was composed of medical officers divided equally between nationals of one belligerent power and nationals of the Protecting Power of the other belligerent. The Mixed Medical Commission which, at intervals, toured around Germany consisted of two German doctors and two Swiss doctors. Doctor von Erlach was the best known of the Swiss delegates. Although the war had been going on for over four years, the Commission had never been allowed to put its nose inside the gates of Colditz.

Now, in May, 1944, the miracle happened and the new Senior British Officer, Colonel Tod, was informed of the forthcoming visit of the Commission to the *Sonderlager* of Germany. Germany was surely losing the war! Colonel Tod had recently taken over as S.B.O. from Tubby Broomhall of the R.E.s, who in turn had taken over from Daddy Stayner in 1943.

Harry realised it was all or nothing. The Commission was due next day. He and another officer, Kit Silverwood-Cope, who had thrombosis in one leg, spent the night walking up and down the circular staircase leading to their quarters— a matter of eighty six steps—at twenty minute intervals. They were still alive when the sun rose and took to their beds in the sick ward as bona fide stretcher cases.

Unfortunately this was not the last ditch. The Gestapo had the final word. Silverwood-Cope had been loose, too long for the Gestapo's liking, in Poland, after an escape and knew much that they

would like to know. They had already submitted him to torture in a Warsaw prison without success but were not courageous enough to go the 'whole hog'. At the same time, in the camp records, he had a red flag opposite his name: '*Deutchfeindlich*'—an enemy of the Reich. It was almost certain they would not let him go.

The other cases submitted for examination included: Major Miles Reid, an M.C. of the First World War; Lieutenant 'Skipper' Barnet; 'Errol' Flynn and Dan Halifax of the R.A.F.; in addition, two French de Gaullist officers. De Gaullists, captured fighting in various parts of Europe, were now arriving in Colditz replenishing the French fire which had added much to the spirit of the prison through the earlier years.

The camp, as a whole, was resigned to the rejection of the case for Silverwood-Cope. But when, at the last minute, the High Command, through the instigation of the Gestapo, began quibbling over the repatriation of the two Frenchmen, they came up against trouble.

The names of those to be examined by the Board for repatriation would be called at the morning *Appell* and the Gestapo decisions would then be known.

The roll call sounded and the officers paraded. After the count had been checked by Hauptman Eggers, Hauptman Priem read out the verdict of his High Command.

Major Miles Reid, Captain Elliott, Lieutenant Barnet, Flying Officer Flynn and Flight Lieutenant Halifax were named, and after that . . . silence. The silence continued, palpitating ominously, fraught with meaning. "*Danke*" shouted Priem in a forced stentorian voice. This was the German signal for the British S.B.O. to dismiss the parade. No order was given. Nobody moved.

Then something happened which under other circumstances would have caused chuckles of laughter in the ranks. But another mood had gripped the waiting men. They had seen the incident, funny but pathetic, often enough. At this moment, its occurence spoke worlds more than any words. An officer, who had gone round the bend and who should have been repatriated long ago, appearing from nowhere, advanced towards the German officer in the middle of the open space in front of the parade. He was dressed in a tattered blue tunic, his bare legs protruded from beneath a dirty pair of khaki shorts and on his feet were old plimsolls. He wore a paper cap of his own design like a French képi on his head. It resembled, vaguely, the headgear of a French Foreign Legionary. A white handkerchief trailed from the back and the hat was coloured red

and grey. Slanting over his left shoulder he carried a long piece of wood—his rifle. He came to attention in front of Priem, saluted smartly with his rifle still at the shoulder, then fumbled in his tunic, produced a piece of paper and handed it solemnly to the German. Priem unfolded it, turned it over and held it open, loosely, in his hand. It was blank on both sides—a helpless, mute appeal. The French Legionary saluted again and marched briskly along the stationary ranks, reviewing the parade before returning to his place in the rear.

"Why was his name not on the list too?" The silence shouted, echoing the unspoken question and, of course, there was no answer. The Germans did not explain their actions in the mad-house of Colditz.

Eggers, speaking in English, addressed Colonel Tod, the S.B.O.: "Parade the walking cases in front at once, Herr Oberst. Stretcher cases will be inspected later."

The tall, grey haired Royal Scots fusilier, standing alone in front of his men, replied coldly: "Herr Hauptman, this action of the German High Command is despicable. It is dishonest, unjust and cowardly. The Frenchmen must go. I will no longer hold myself responsible for the actions of my officers. The parade from this moment is yours. Take it!" and with that he turned about, marched back to the ranks behind him, turned again, and stood at attention —at the right of the line.

Eggers, speaking in English, started to harangue the parade: "British officers, you will remain on parade until those ordered for examination by . . ." His further words were lost as, with one accord, the parade broke up in disorder and men stamped around the courtyard, drowning his voice with the shuffling of boots and the clatter of wooden clogs on the cobbles.

This was mutiny. Priem hurried to the gate and spoke through the grill. Within seconds the riot squad entered the courtyard. The two German officers, surrounded by their men with fixed bayonets and followed by three N.C.O. snoops with revolvers drawn, forged into the crowd before them in search of the bodies. Their scheme was to identify and seize the men approved for interview, take them out of the courtyard by force, bang the gates behind them and leave the prisoners to nurse their wounded feelings in impotence.

The German officers and their snoops peered, now to the left, now to the right, into the sullen faces around them. Suddenly there was a shout and a pointing finger was levelled:

"*Dort ist Oberst Reid, schnell! nehmen Sie ihn fest!*" Four guards

charged at the man, surrounded and held him fast by the arms and shoulders awaiting further orders. "*Sofort zum Kommandantur! Rechts! marsch!*" Reid was frogmarched out of the courtyard, the posse forcing their way with jabbing bayonets through the swarming, obstructing prisoners, shouting as they went, "*Los, los! weg machen! los!*"

The search continued, but the other walking cases could not be found.

The mêlée in the courtyard continued for fifteen minutes. The Swiss members of the Commission were in the *Kommandantur* waiting for the proposed repatriates. They became impatient and demanded to be allowed to see the Senior British Officer. The courtyard was, by now, in an uproar with jeering, booing, catcalls and singing competing for the maximum volume of sound. The Swiss could hear the riot in progress. The Camp Commandant was spotted from a window giving orders outside the gate. He dared not enter. Priem left the courtyard for several minutes, then returned. He sought out Colonel Tod and spoke to him. Tod mounted the steps of the Saalhouse and raised his arms calling for silence. There was an immediate lull. He announced:

"The German Commandant has agreed that the De Gaullists shall go forward for examination."

The whole camp broke into a tremendous cheer. Within a few minutes, the two Frenchmen were produced and, together with the rest of the walking cases who appeared also, as if from nowhere, they were escorted out by the German guards, marching through a lane formed by the cheering mob.

The German capitulation was complete and Allied solidarity, aided by the Swiss Commission outside, had won a memorable victory. The German arrogance of 1941 and 1942 was changing and from this day in May, 1944, onwards, the Prisoners in Colditz began to feel solid ground once more beneath their feet.

The episode was an important turning point. The prisoners knew that Hitler and his minions intended to use them as hostages in the hour of defeat. Here was a gleam of hope. The camp Commandant would have to square his action over the de Gaullists with the Gestapo, but the fact remained he had countermanded their orders, obliged to do so by the combined pressure of the prisoners and a neutral power, and was evidently prepared to cross swords with them. What had been done once for two de Gaullists might be repeated. In the hour of Germany's defeat, the sign post for action pointed towards defiance.

The mixed medical Commission passed for repatriation all those they examined, including Harry. They took one look at him and wrote his name down on the list.

*   *   *   *   *

Most of the repatriates, including Harry, remained in Colditz until July when, one evening, they received orders to pack, and the next morning at 5.30 a.m. in the grey light of dawn they bade farewell to Colditz for ever. The departure arrangements were so sudden that Harry as he walked through the gates thought he was dreaming. It was difficult, almost impossible, to believe that he was, after four years, really on his way home, that he would not wake up and find himself lying on his palliasse inside the walls and the barbed wire. A curious feeling took possession of him. A few heads popped out of windows as they filed out, hands waved and voices shouted good-bye. It was all a dream. He had seen it happen before. He would wake up soon. Another part of him felt suddenly guilty; he was disloyal to the men who were shouting those pathetic good-byes behind the bars; and, more peculiar than anything else, was the sensation of tearing himself away from something that had become a part of him—the Castle itself. Could he be having regrets? Yes! He was feeling sorry. Something was being wrenched from him. He was hugging his chains, and would feel lost without them in the strange world of freedom.

The repatriates marched down to the station with the German guards and, as the dawn came, Harry looked back over his shoulder and upwards to the towering outline of the Castle showing pale and faintly luminous in the first light. Only then did he realise he was not dreaming. A sudden fear gripped him and his skin contracted. He was, indeed, outside the walls but they were reaching out to seize and envelop him again. Now that he could see the Castle's forbidding exterior, the ghostly horror of its greyness, fear came upon him—he wanted to run from the loathsome prison before he was trapped.

The party arrived at the station and boarded the train. Only as it steamed out of the station did Harry begin to feel safe. He was filled with a great exaltation and a surge of revengeful elation; he cursed the Castle, as it faded, growing paler and paler in the morning haze, cursed it again and again in a queer uncontrolled frenzy. . .

He had defeated his bitter enemy, the Castle; he had escaped

from Colditz. Those who remained, facing nearly another year behind the bars, would talk about his exploits and his humour until
the end of the war, and long afterwards too. They would never
forget his 'Battle of the Dry Rot'* which was waged unceasingly
until the day he departed. They would miss his excursions up the
stairs, into the attics, with his faithful band of followers manned
with buckets of water—water which they thereupon poured through
cracks in the floors until the ceilings seeped, dripping upon the
occupants of the rooms below. How the Dutchmen swore when they
returned to their bunks at night to find soaking pillows and blankets
below the weak spots in the ceiling! They never found out where the
water came from. For years they thought it was caused by leaking
water pipes and holes in the roofs. They employed a different staircase, and, consequently, never saw Harry at work. His 'razor
blades in the pigswill' campaign* was over. There would be no more
Chinese officers; no more sand-bags jettisoned along the road of
the years; no more ulcerous landmarks on the patient uphill climb
which eventually led him out of Colditz. He had reached the top of
the hill and looked once more over the sunlit plains of freedom.
He was going home again to his beloved England. He would be
missed back there, behind the grim walls, where a gay heart and
an unquenchable spirit were like sunshine in the early spring.

          *   *   *   *   *

"Dopey" Miller (Lt. W. A. Miller, R.C.E.), a Canadian and a
born escaper, who thought of nothing else all day long, escaped
from Colditz in June, 1944, at the time of the Normandy invasion.
His was a lone effort. The route out of the Castle was the beginning
of that route used by Ronnie Littledale, Billie Stephens, Hank
Wardle and the author in 1942. Dopey and his helpers cut a bar in
the window in the camp kitchen facing the outer courtyard. On a
favourable night, during an air raid, he climbed out of the window, over low roofs and dropped to the ground in a dark corner.
He hid underneath the chassis of a lorry that was parked every
evening in the outer yard. During the daytime, the lorry was used
on haulage work for the camp, in the village and the surrounding
districts.

Early the next morning, the lorry driver started up his engine
and drove out of the camp. Dopey was hanging on, underneath.
There were no alarms at the outer gates.

* Described in *The Colditz Story*.

He was never heard of again. It is assumed that he was recaptured and that the Gestapo submitted him to "*Stufe drei*".

Within the camp, of course, none of this was known or thought of at the time. It was hoped that Dopey had chalked up another "home-run" from the impregnable fortress. As the days passed into months, however, and there was no news of him, uncertainty as to his fate left an uneasy feeling in the minds of those who knew him. He was not the kind of man who would leave the camp in ignorance if he had succeeded in reaching the Allied lines.

CHAPTER XX

THE RED FOX

AS the autumn days of 1944 shortened and the second front in France settled down, the prisoners of Colditz gritted their teeth once more to stand another winter behind the bars, hoping for relief in the spring. The prisoner contingent numbered about two hundred and seventy at this time, of whom two hundred were British, the remainder French de Gaullists and a sprinkling of every other Allied nationality. They had hoped for freedom in the autumn but it was too much to expect and they knew it. An air of sadness and depression spread over the camp: the eternal optimists had little enthusiam left for the victory that was always "next month" and "just around the corner"! They were nearly played out. The winter of 1944–45 was, for Colditz, the grimmest of all the war winters. The incarcerated men had made what little contribution they could to the war effort. They had done everything possible behind the bars and had given of their best. They had pinned down a German battalion. The Landwehr were afraid of them. They had made Colditz a by-word in the offices of the German High Command. The Gestapo loathed the mention of the name.

Patience in the camp was at the sticking point. As runners, reaching the last lap of a marathon, feel their hearts being torn out of their bodies, unable to drag their legs another pace, yet knowing they must still race hundreds of yards before they pass a finishing line which, in the mist of perspiration before their eyes, they despair of ever beholding, so the escapers of Colditz struggled in a motionless marathon of the mind to retain their equilibrium to the end. The last lap was the toughest endurance test of all.

The Red Fox

In such an atmosphere Mike Sinclair decided to try again. His indomitable spirit could not be tamed. He would finish the war in harness. The Red Fox had to be free.

This time he planned a lone and desperate break. Surprise was the essence of it. He would repeat the escape of the Frenchman Pierre Mairesse Lebrun who, in 1941, had been catapulted over the barbed wire fence in the recreation pen in the park beneath the Castle. Mike planned the break alone so that no other man could be blamed if a hand or foot slipped or the timing went wrong. Lebrun had dared the sentries to shoot him, dodging as the bullets whistled past and jumping to safety behind the park wall with a volley as a send off. Dick Howe would not have to take the blame on his broad shoulders this time. He would not have to 'take the can back' as he had done for the Franz Josef affair. Mike was seeing to that. He told nobody.

On September the 25th, 1944, Mike went down to the recreation ground and walked the well-trodden path around the periphery inside the wire with Grismond Scourfield.

In half an hour the guards had settled down. They suspected nothing. This hour of recreation would be the same as the hundreds that had gone before it.

At the most vulnerable point in the wire, Mike stopped suddenly, turned and shook hands with Scourfield. "Good-bye, Grismond," he said quietly. "It's going to be now or never."

He was ashen pale. Even the gigantic courage of his spirit could not conceal from his own brain the awful risk he was about to take. The subconscious reactions of the nerves and cells of his frail body rebelled and would not be controlled. His hand trembled as he grasped surreptitiously the hand of his friend. His whole body seemed to quiver. His eyes alone were steady and bright with the fire of a terrible resolve.

In the next instant he was at the wire, climbing desperately, climbing quickly, spreadeagled in mid-air. To those nearby, his progress seemed painfully slow, yet it was fast for a man mounting those treacherous barbed strands. He had reached the top and was balanced astride the swaying wires when the Germans first saw him. They began shouting: "Halt! Halt!" and again, "*Halt oder ich schiesse*" came echoing down the line of sentries.

He took no notice. Freeing himself from the top strands he jumped down to the ground and stumbled at the nine foot drop. He picked himself up as the first shot rang out. There were shouts again of "Halt!" and then a fourth time "Halt! Halt!" He was

running. The hill was against him. He was not travelling fast. He dodged once, then twice, as two more shots rang out and he ran straight for the outer wall. But the Germans had his range by now and a volley of shots spattered around him. He dodged again. He could still have turned and raised his hands. He was nearing the wall but he was tiring. Another volley echoed among the trees of the park and he fell to his knees and a gasp of horror rose from the men watching behind the wire. Then, slowly, he crumpled forward amongst the autumn leaves.

He lay still as the sentries rushed forward, swooping, on their prey. He did not move when they reached him. A sentry, bending down, turned him over while another quickly opened his shirt and felt with his hand over the heart. He was dead.

The Red Fox had escaped. He had crossed the last frontier and would never be brought back to Colditz again a recaptured, spent, defeated prisoner. He had made a "home-run". He was free.

     *   *   *   *   *

Seven months later, the Castle was relieved and Mike would have been freed—alive. That freedom would not have been of his own making, nor to his own liking. He had reached that stage in the humiliating mental struggle of a prisoner of noble stature when, to desist from trying and to await freedom at the hands of others, would seal his own failure, scar his heart and sear his soul. His duty would have remained unfulfilled.

The sermon that follows was delivered by Padre Platt at the memorial service in the Castle.

"Mike came from an Ulster family living in England. He was at school at Winchester, went up to Cambridge, and joined the 60th just before the war. He fought at Calais, was taken prisoner, was sent to Laufen and then to Poland. There he made his first escape in which he crossed the frontiers of the General Government, Slovakia, Hungary, Yugoslavia and was caught getting into Bulgaria. He tried to escape on the way back through Czechoslovakia, was recaptured, held for a time by the Gestapo, and finally sent on here two and a half years ago.

"Since then his life has been practically one attempt after another to escape. On different occasions he has got as far as Cologne,* the Swiss Frontier, the Dutch Frontier. You know better than any congregation in the world what that means.

* An escape carried out from Colditz early in 1942.

About a hundred of you have got right away from a camp once, only about twenty more than once—let alone a frontier—and this is the 'Escapers' camp.

"He didn't himself take foolhardy risks, but when he went with others and risks were unavoidable he took full share—and more. You remember his escape as Franz Josef. And in his last and riskiest attempt he went alone. Whenever the story of escaping in this war is written, Mike Sinclair's name will be there, high up on the list. And he deserves it because he had qualities that really ultimately matter.

"When he'd made up his mind upon a thing he was absolutely determined to carry it through. He made mistakes, as we all do, but he learnt from them and had a conscience about them. Most people's reaction to failure is to wipe it out of their memories and be comfortable. Mike's was NOT to forget it—and at times it made him very depressed—but to go on trying till he'd made up for it. That is the kind of character that really matters in a soldier—the kind of quality that made Wellington and Sir John Moore great.

"On at least two occasions while he was here, he made escapes that any soldier would be proud of. When he and Jack Best went through the line in the orchard, the scheme—and it was largely Mike's scheme—was about the most brilliant there's been here. It came off, so we took it for granted, but it was a grand piece of work. The other occasion was on his earlier 'Franz Josef' escape, then he was nearly killed by a guard losing his head. Mike took the lead in the preparations and the escape itself—he spent three months on it. With two or three people it was a 'certainty', with the members he agreed to include—well, not likely to succeed. At one stage in the escape it was clear to Mike that to get the main body out was going to be a much more dangerous and difficult job than expected, but that, by forgetting about them, he, Lance and Hyde Thompson could walk out and get clear away. That's a testing moment for a man's character, and we know how unhesitatingly he chose the unselfish way.

"Finally, Mike was a believing Christian, and one who'd known suffering and turned it to use. That's why, although his death is a tragedy for his parents, it isn't just a wasteful tragedy of a life. We say in our Creed that we believe in the Resurrection of the Dead and WE KNOW that Christ's promises are sure. Mike was the kind of man who wouldn't be confident about himself, but we, who knew him, know that he is all right, and that he's

met up with his younger brother, who fell at Anzio, and the countless others who, in their country's service, have gone before us on the way that leads through death, but comes out in a brighter eternal world."

CHAPTER XXI

THE GLIDER

BY the autumn of 1944, the construction of the glider was under weigh in a secret workshop. Assembly had not yet begun but tall piles of wing sections lay carefully stacked and docketed ready for the great day when they would be threaded on to the spars.

Jack Best had long ago been incorporated in the team; a fourth member, stooge Wardle, the submarine officer, had also joined them.

Jack Best had come out of solitary confinement after the terrace escape in the early spring of 1944. By that time, Bill Goldfinch and Tony Rolt had made a little headway with the glider plans. Tony had remembered Bill's remar[k] about how useful Jack Best Jack was only just out of s the horns and proposed he

"It's asking something I probably had a belly-full o and want nothing more tha

"Tell me some more abo

"We've already started n has a lot of drawings and sections and detail part dra I've been working on the plates; but we need help. T need. You're good with yo going to require a lot of w I've got."

"Have you mentioned the scheme to Dick yet?"

"No, I think it's time we did. If you'd agree to join us, that would count with Dick too, and I think he'd see we got all the help possible."

Journal states to-say.

The article, based on a study of the trend of United Kingdom exports recently prepared by Government officials, draws attention to the difficulties of further expansion.

"The volume of total United Kingdom exports has risen substantially since the middle of 1953, but the volume of German exports has risen even faster. It should also be borne in mind that the exports of aircraft, refined petroleum, and arms and ammunition have played a large part in the expansion of our exports over the past twelve months, and we cannot count on sales of these things continuing indefinitely to make up for deficiencies elsewhere."

If those three items were excluded, exports would show little or no increase in volume and a significant decline in value between the years 1952 and 1953.

"Show me the plans and some of the parts you've made," said Jack.

Tony had led him over to the corner of the dormitory where his miniature workshop, consisting of a small table and a cupboard were situated. He spread some engineering drawings out on his bed and showed him bits of wood already taking shape as wing ribs. He had a pot of glue, and a primitive wooden press weighted with bricks.

"How long have you been at this?" asked Jack.

"Over a month."

"You'll never get anywhere at that rate," Jack had said. "It's all too cumbersome. Where do you melt your glue? Where do you hide the parts? You must have a proper workshop—you need space to build a glider. It can't be built on a bed."

"I know that only too well," said Tony. "What about it?"

"Let's have a talk with Dick," said Best. "We need room and a place where we can work undisturbed."

"I'll find Bill Goldfinch, and we'll tackle him together."

So Jack Best had fallen for the scheme and Tony had again won his way.

Bill Goldfinch had been working for a long time on the design when Jack Best joined them. He was beginning to wonder whether the machine would ever materialise or merely remain a dream child—perfect on paper.

Tony's introduction of Jack Best into the scheme gave him new zest and enthusiasm for the work.

Dick was tackled and listened, incredulously at first, and then with growing interest as the three men laid before him the details of the plan. What sounded preposterous to begin with became feasible in Dick's mind as he looked over the drawings and realised that the entire machine would be constructed from wooden bedboards and floorboards, cotton palliasse covers, and a large quantity of glue. Goldfinch and Best were, probably, the two finest craftsmen in the camp. Jack Best had manufactured, years ago, a complete tool kit of tempered chisels, saws, planes, augurs, bits and brace. The two men had infinite patience. They were meticulous and persevering. If anyone would ever succeed, they would, thought Dick, and Tony Rolt could be relied on to whip up the necessary enthusiasm among the stooges and recruit unskilled help when required.

He gathered together the sheaves of paper on which Goldfinch had drawn his stress diagrams and made his aerodynamic calculations.

"Have you checked these," he asked.

"I've been over the figures three times," said Bill, "but they should be checked by someone else. Lorne Welch could do it. He's a gliding expert."

"Right! Get him to run through them carefully and give them back to me afterwards. I'll have a third opinion also, and, if all three agree that it will fly, then go ahead, and we'll find a proper workshop for you.

"I suppose the dumb cluck who wins the toss will have to take off in it?" he remarked as an afterthought.

"The glider is designed to take two passengers," said Goldfinch calmly.

Dick turned to him in astonishment, "Blimey O'Reilly! you'll need some catapult to launch that weight safely!"

"Yes," said Goldfinch, "we'll need a bathful of concrete."

"Go on," Dick chuckled, "what then?"

"As I see it," continued Goldfinch, "we'll fix a pulley at the far end—the launching end—of the runway; you know—the flat tablelike pieces saddled astride the roof ridge. The glider will be pulled forward on its skid by a rope passed around the pulley returning the full length of the runway underneath it, passing over a second pulley at the starting end, and there attached to the weight."

"Do you mean," intervened Dick, "the bath filled with concrete?"

"Yes. The bath will have to be free to fall a distance equal to the length of the runway, that is sixty feet."

"How do you release the rope from the glider?"

"Simple enough. We'll use the same type of automatic release hook as all towed gliders use. It's foolproof. Better still, we could make a light trolley for the glider to sit on and fix the rope to that."

"Provided the glider calculations are O.K. and it's airworthy," said Jack Best, "I'm sure the take off will be all right. Holes will have to be made in all the Castle floors, as far as I can see, down to ground floor level. That should give the full sixty foot drop required for the bath."

"I propose," said Goldfinch, "to use the bath tub, you know the one, on the third floor under the attics. We can suspend it over the holes and let it go when everything's ready. You've got plenty of cement, Dick. Will you let us have enough to mix up and fill the bath?"

"Yes, if you ever get that far," said Dick. "There's tons of sand and gravel and rock up in the attics from the French tunnel. You can mix that with it and make a respectable concrete. Where are you going to build the glider?"

"Ah! now this is where I come in," Tony interrupted. "Jack Best says we've got to have a proper workshop where we can work undisturbed. I'm afraid I agree. Otherwise it'll take years. I've only made a few parts, so far, to Bill's designs and it's taken me ages. It's not so much the actual work, but all the alarms and the hiding of parts and the stooging and so on that wastes the time. If we could fix up our jigs on benches and not have to dismantle them: if we had a permanent stove handy for the glue pot; if the tools did not have to be hidden all the time, then we could get somewhere."

"Well, there you are!" exclaimed Dick. "You've posed the problem that I was just going to raise. What are you going to do about it?"

"I've been thinking about it a lot," said Rolt, "and I have an idea. We might be able to wall off completely a section of the top attic over the chapel without the Jerries being any the wiser. If it was done, say, in one night and made to look exactly like the original wall at the end, they might never notice the shortening of the attic. It's long enough as you know."

"What do you think, Dick?" said Bill and Jack together.

"Quite canny," Dick agreed grinning, tickled at the prospect of the Jerries regularly patrolling the attic with torches to see there was no monkey business going on while a whole workshop was set up under their noses. "The French tunnel debris is going to be put to good use, I see! Let's go and have a look at the attics."

The four of them, together, examined the uppermost attic carefully. The west end of it was ideally situated for the workshop because it abutted the roof ridge above the old French quarters along which it was proposed to launch the glider.

If this end of the attic were sealed off, the machine could then be constructed and assembled where it would be used. When ready for launching, a large hole could be pierced in the west wall just at the level of the roof ridge outside. Unseen by prying eyes, the saddles would be posed and interlocked forming a runway two feet six inches wide; the machine taken through the hole; its wings attached outside; the rope fixed around the pulleys, and the machine would be ready for the "take off".

The attic was long and dark. There was no ceiling; only the timber roof trusses and the boarded floor, and the faintest glimmer of light entering between the layers of tiles.

A properly constructed false wall, built to look like the existing end wall, immediately under one of the trusses would give no clue as to the existence of a space beyond, unless measurements were taken to check the lengths of the floors at different levels.

The four men agreed the idea had a fair chance of success.

"The problem as I see it now," said Dick, "is to get the wall built and camouflaged to look like the old one before a Jerry interrupts us. That means it's got to be done in one night. Can you see it being done?"

"I think so," said Tony Rolt. "If you'll give the O.K., we can get enough volunteers. With about a dozen men working all night it should be possible. We'll make a sketch of the old wall and reproduce it again in three ply and cardboard as near as damn it. We can prepare the wall in sections beforehand."

"That'll do as a foundation," said Dick "What you want after that is to tack canvas on to the wall; you can use the palliasse covers from the beds in one of the unused dormitories and apply a coating of plaster on to the canvas. I'll show you how to prepare it. The French used it on the tunnel doors very successfully. It turns out exactly the right colour when it's dry. To be expected —I guess—as the original plaster was obviously made from local ingredients. You sift out of the tunnel debris a fairly fine grit about one eight of an inch diameter—no more. You mix that with the clay and sand from the tunnel—there's tons of it round the corner —and make a puddle. You smack this on to the canvas about a quarter inch thick and let it set. We'll try a sample out right away and check it. How about the framework for the wall?"

"There's some good floor boarding around here," said Tony. "It's thick stuff—a good seven-eights of an inch and five inches wide, that should do. It's what Bill proposed to use also for the main wing spars of the glider."

"How long are the wings to be?" Dick asked, beginning to pace out the width of the attic.

"Each wing is sixteen feet long and five feet wide," said Bill, "but that includes the aileron—fourteen inches."

"Good," said Dick, "they'll just fit nicely into the width."

"Just a minute—" interrupted Bill, "the fuselage is longer. It's eighteen feet without the tail wing and rudder."

"Well, I make the width thirty feet," said Dick checking again,

"It should be ample, even allowing for dead space where the sloping roof meets the floor."

"That'll do," said Bill, "the tail and rudder are separate and fit on afterwards."

"Good! Now, what about the width of the room—where shall we build the wall. About twenty feet should do you. That brings us. . . ." Dick said breaking off his sentence as he measured again. . . . "That brings us just under the second truss. What do you think?"

"Twenty feet should do, "Bill replied, "if we take too much the rest of the attic will look suspiciously short. We've got to squeeze a bit. We can always break a hole in our own wall to help push the fuselage out, if necessary, on the day."

"The next thing you want is lighting, leave that to me," said Dick. "Lulu Lawton and I can fix up a branch circuit from below. We'll do that when the wall's finished. Now, about getting in and out? How about that corner over there, where the flooring's already off. You could get in by ladder from the lower attic and we could make a trap door. Yes," Dick ruminated, "let's go down below and have a look at that corner."

They left the upper attic, locking the doors as they went and descended to the lower attic which was unoccupied and lit by dormer windows. Dust was everywhere as it had been above, but at least there was daylight, and some pretence at turning the attic into a room had been made. The gable walls and also the low walls beneath the dormer windows had been whitewashed and the ceiling was of plaster.

They walked over to the corner where Dick had suggested making the entrance.

"Yes," he said, "I think this corner will do nicely. There's some plaster already fallen down on to the floor here. That makes the job easier. Jack," he said, turning to Best, "I'll arrange for Lucy Lockett and Andy to make the trap door. You'll have to help. But they'll do the actual trap; they're experts. Fit it so that the laths are cut behind the plaster and show nothing from below. You can support the plaster from above. I'll give you some cement for it. That hole where the plaster's down already will do nicely. It's near enough to the gable wall to lean a short ladder against and a man can climb up, get through and take the ladder with him. You must be damn careful always about this loose plaster lying on the floor. See that it's always left dusty and no footmarks must be left around."

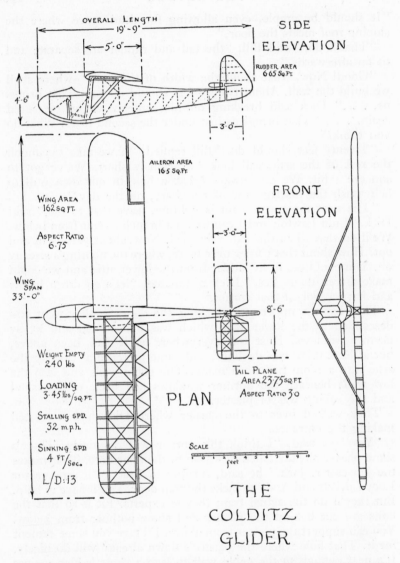

OVERALL LENGTH
19'-9"

5'-0"

SIDE
ELEVATION

RUDDER AREA
6.65 SQ.FT.

4'-6"

3'-0"

AILERON AREA
16.5 SQ.FT.

WING AREA
162 SQ.FT.

ASPECT RATIO
6.75

FRONT
ELEVATION

3'-0"

WING
SPAN
33'-0"

8'-6"

WEIGHT EMPTY
240 lbs

LOADING
3.45 lbs/SQ.FT.

STALLING SPD.
32 m.p.h.

SINKING SPD.
4 FT/Sec.

L/D:13

TAIL PLANE
AREA 23.75 SQ.FT.
ASPECT RATIO 3.0

PLAN

SCALE
0 1 2 3 4 5 6 7 8 9 10
feet

THE
COLDITZ
GLIDER

THE GLIDER PLANS HAVE BEEN COPIED FROM THE ORIGINAL DRAWING MADE
AT COLDITZ AND NOW IN THE POSSESSION OF JACK BEST IN KENYA

A stooge put his head round the door of the attic:
"Jerries in the yard," was all he said.

The four men retraced their steps to the door. As they left,
Jack Best, the last in line, spread a heavy dust mixture over
suspicious marks on the floor with the aid of a small bellows
which he carried for the purpose. It looked like a small beehive
smoker and was effective in action.

In the dormitory below, Dick continued, "If you need any
paint or whitewash, I've got some. You can collect all the cobweb
mixture you like yourselves and also a few pounds of soot and
dust will help. We'll need a hell of a lot to cover the false wall.
When do you think the wall sections could be ready?"

"We can produce them in about a fortnight," said Jack. "There's
a big area to cover and it's all got to be prefab."

"All right then," said Dick, "other things being equal let's
prepare for to-day fortnight—after the last *Appell*. I'll produce a
sample of the plaster beforehand. Then you can get weaving on
producing it in bulk. I can lend you five volunteers and Lulu
and myself, making seven for the building operation; you'll collect
the rest between you. Don't forget the stooges, Tony, I guess
you'll see to that. Provided the design—the calculations and so
on—are checked again and found O.K. the escape is on, as far
as I'm concerned. I wouldn't dream of taking off with you, of
course, but then I was brought up in a Tank and I get scared
moving in anything weighing less than ten ton."

A fortnight later, all through the night, a dozen men worked
furiously with shaded lights to assemble the dummy wall! Screws
were used to fix the framework to the existing roof truss. All
had been carefully measured up beforehand. The prefabricated
sections, covered with a layer of canvas, were then screwed into
their predetermined positions. Towards morning, the plastering
began, with the thick puddle prepared according to Lulu's prescription. It stuck well to the canvas but the droppings created
a problem for the camouflage men who followed. Damp marks
on the floor at the foot of the wall could not be covered easily.

By dawn the wall was finished and professional touches had
been applied. But, as the morning light pierced through the grimy
window panes, they showed up a wall which did not look in the
least like the original. The colour stuck out like a sore thumb.
It was dark brown, uneven, and patchy with sooty streaks. Too
late to do anything now; the team departed to clean up and rest
for an hour before the seven a.m. *Appell*. They were depressed.

Dick felt badly about the result of the night's work but he was sure the cause of the trouble was the moisture. If only the Jerries would keep away for twenty-four hours, he thought—the crisis would be past. He watched the Germans all day with apprehension. Towards evening he breathed more freely and together with Lulu Lawton he paid a visit to the wall. It was already much better in appearance but still damp. Another day would improve it out of all recognition.

During the next day the Germans paid a routine visit to the attics. They must have flashed their torches cursorily. There were no alarms. All that day, Tony Rolt and Jack Best paced the courtyard nervously, longing to mount the stairs every hour to register any toning down in the colour of the wall. But they had to possess their souls in patience—no good could come of too frequent visits. It was wiser to keep away.

Towards the evening, just before dark, Dick and Lulu went to the attic along with the glider team. Stooge Wardle, (the submarine lieutenant), recently added fourth member of the team, who had helped in the wall construction was there. As they opened the door a broad smile showed on Dick's face. The change in the colour of the wall was remarkable. The tint was not yet perfect, but, to anyone who had seen it twenty four hours before, it was clear that it would be perfect in a matter of another twelve hours. The stucco had now turned an old sandy grey, like Sussex or Cotswold stone and would be a lighter colour by the morning. It was almost indistinguishable from the surrounding walls even to those who had worked on it.

Dick turned to Jack Best and said, wryly:

"Jack, you'd better think about fitting that trap-door mighty quick. The ball's over to you and you're holding up the proceedings. Get on to Andy and Lucy. Thanks, Lulu," he added, turning to him, "you've got a better eye for colour than I thought a few hours ago."

" Don't be a damn fool," said Lulu, " anyone in the wool trade knows about allowances for moisture. It's a question of judgment. There's nowt to be afraid of."

"So you concocted that b—— awful mixture!" said Stooge, turning to Lulu. "I thought we'd all been having our legs pulled. Now I must say . . ." he looked at the wall critically, ". . . it's not bad; not bad at all for an amateur job."

"Any more cock from you and I'll make you walk the plank," retorted Lulu cheerfully.

A load had been lifted from their minds. They locked the attic door and returned to their quarters talking animatedly of the next stage in the venture.

The attic was vacated entirely for a week in order to watch Jerry reactions. Patrols unlocked the doors, and controlled the attics almost every day. They noticed nothing unusual. After the week had elapsed Best completed his trap-door and the team took possession of their workshop. The construction of the glider began in earnest.

A work-bench was set up, and tables for the jigs and templates. There were no windows in the workshop, but Dick and Lulu produced electric light. Dick also provided the glue which was melted on a stove, using as fuel a mixture of any kind of fat that could be found, including boot polish. The glue came, mostly, through the channels of Cheko's black market. Racks for the tools soon made their appearance. The four men spent the greater part of every day at their work and continued, sometimes, late into the night. Then they had to use heavily shaded lamps to prevent light showing through cracks between the roof tiles. The myriad component parts of the glider piled higher and higher upon the floor and hung festooned from long pegs on the beams awaiting the final assembly.

Their carpenter's kit consisted of the following principal tools:

A side-framed saw, the handle of beech bedboard, the frame of iron window bars, and the blade of gramophone spring with eight teeth to the inch.

A minute saw for very fine work, with gramophone spring blade, twenty-five teeth to the inch.

A square, made of beech and gramophone spring.

A gauge, made of beech, with a cupboard bolt and a gramophone needle.

A large plane, fourteen and a half inches long with a two-inch blade, bribed from the Goons, the wooden box made of four pieces of beech screwed together.

A small plane, eight and a half inches long, with a blade made from a table knife.

Another plane, five inches long.

Drills for making holes in wood were made of nails; a five-eighths inch drill for metal was obtained by bribery.

And lastly there was a set of keys, including a universal door pick, forged from a bucket handle.

The two wings of the glider were each made up of seventeen

aerofoil section frames or ribs, manufactured out of deal and beech bedboards, which were cut into long strips of cross-section, half an inch by three-eighths of an inch. The ribs were put together in jigs, dovetailed, glued and gussetted where necessary, using three-ply wood stripped down to two-ply, nailed in position. The underside of the wing was flat. The curve on the upper leading edge was reproduced on the aerofoil sections partly by bending the wood strips and partly by making a series of small saw nicks along the outer edge to give pliability.

The aerofoil sections were assembled by threading on to the spars and tacking into position. The main spar of each wing was a solid floorboard eighteen feet long of section five inches by three-quarters of an inch. A secondary spar at the trailing edge of the wing, of section two and a half inches by three-quarters of an inch, provided the surface on to which the ailerons were hinged.

The aileron ribs were of uniform construction from one end to the other; they were fourteen inches wide. Ten ribs and two spars, smaller than those of the main wings, were required for the tail wing, made in one piece, to fix above the rear end of the fuselage.

The fuselage itself was constructed from floorboards cut into strips of section one and a quarter inches by three-quarters of an inch. The two side trusses were curved in both the vertical and horizontal planes and were strapped together at the bottom by short, straight ties and at the top by longer hooped ties, all gussetted where necessary. A raised head-rest, behind the pilot's seat, provided the pillar which supported the wings. Light wooden struts nine feet long were also used underneath the wings. A wide skid of well-planed board shaped like a ski was hinged to the fuselage at the front end. It was also highly polished with french chalk and lead. The top of the fuselage bellied upwards, which gave it a streamlined, airworthy appearance. It was not unlike the body of a Spitfire. The controls—stick, rudder-bar and rudder—were of conventional pattern, lightly constructed. The control wires were made from field telephone wire which the Goons had used for electric lighting in certain rooms.

Prison sleeping bags of blue and white check cotton were employed for the "skinning" of the glider. Wrapped around the leading edge of the wings, they were stretched tightly back to the trailing edge, where they were sewn together. Doping was the next process and, for this, German ration millet was ground fine and boiled in water for four hours, forming a paste. This was applied

hot to the skin. When cool and dry, it produced a smooth, glossy surface, shrinking the fabric at the same time, so that it became as taut as a drum.

Apart from the light two-ply gussets and thin sheet metal capping-pieces used all over the machine, parts requiring greater strength and solidity were made from straps and bars taken from some of the iron bedsteads used by senior officers in the Saalhaus. Such parts were the root fittings, stout metal straps with steel dowels, two at the inside end of each wing-spar, which linked the wings together through the fuselage immediately behind the cockpit.

The four members of the glider team knew that only two of them would eventually take off in it. They agreed not to make the selection until the machine was ready, thereby ensuring that all four would continue to put their whole effort into the labour of construction.

Normally all four of them were in the workshop together: three at work and one stooging. The stooge sat on a cross-beam in the apex of the roof above the heads of those below. He raised a tile, propping it up with a wedge. Through the slot provided he could see a window in the British quarters on the third floor in which a second stooge was posted. The second stooge surveyed the courtyard and the entrance to it. He employed four signals: a white towel which, placed prominently in the window, meant "all clear," a blue towel, which meant "Silence—Goons in the building—stop smoking," a green mustard-pot, which meant "stand by for danger—silence—take precautionary measures to quit workshop," and a larger red-painted metal jar containing salt which meant "quit workshop at once."

The safety of the team depended greatly on the common sense of the window stooge. To quit the workshop, camouflage the entrance and conceal the ladder took a good five minutes. The stooge had to divine when the Germans really meant business such as a snap *Appell* and when they were just snooping, for which the green signal would suffice.

The above stooging system was not enough. Circumstances might arise in which the stooge might not be able to give his signals. This would occur, for instance, if the Germans raided his room and prevented him from acting. A secondary system—another electric stooge—was brought into play if the window stooge failed.

Germans, entering the room in which the stooge worked, had

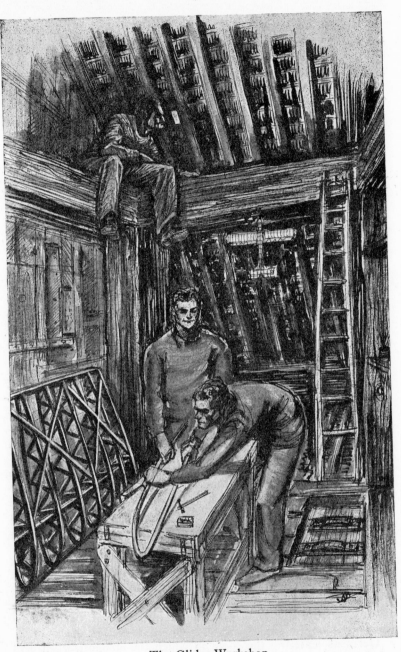

The Glider Workshop

to pass through an ante-chamber. In this lobby sat another stooge. As soon as a Goon entered the lobby he lifted a small piece of iron mostly covered with rubber which lay at his hand, against a corner of the window-sill. The action broke an electric circuit. Upstairs, a long way off, in the glider workshop, a light promptly went out. In case this was not noticed (with other lights on) a long nail fell at the same time from an electromagnet into a tin basin which acted like a gong.

The complete stooging system, organised for work over an extended period of time, involved a personnel, consisting of twelve principal stooges, known as 'the disciples,' with forty assistant stooges.

During the ten months which it took to construct the glider, there were some thirty red alarms—wearing on the nerves, and every day's work included at least one or two "greens". The most nerve-wracking "green" alarm the team experienced occurred when three German N.C.O.'s spent over an hour in the attic. They remained motionless while the Jerries probed the floors and even sounded the false wall, but discovered nothing. Old plaster on walls often sounds hollow! That fact probably saved them. The Jerries were after the hidden wireless set.

Work continued on the components and on the assembly of wings, fuselage, rudder and controls and on the runway saddle boards, pulleys and ropes through the winter of 1944–45. Construction had started seriously in May. The take-off was scheduled for the spring of 1945. By that time, it was estimated that air raids over the Berlin and Leipzig areas of Germany would be sufficiently intensified to provide ample black-out cover at night in which to break out the hole in the outside wall; set up the launching-ramp and take off without being heard by the sentries below or seen by observers farther afield in the village. By the spring, too, the winter floods on the meadows flanking the far side of the river below the Castle should have subsided. They would provide an excellent landing-ground for the glider, over three hundred feet below the launching-ramp and two hundred yards away.

The stage was being set for the greatest escape in history. Would the spring of 1945 see its fruition?

PART IV

1945

THE END APPROACHES

IN January, 1945, the camp held about three hundred British officers from England and every part of the Commonwealth. A recent arrival was Brigadier Davis of the Ulster Rifles, who had been parachuted into Albania. There were the three Americans, the twelve Czech airmen in the R.A.F., some Jugoslav officers, a company of de Gaullist paratroopers from North Africa, and a number, growing daily, of other Free French officers.

Early in February, Prominente began to collect in Colditz from different parts of Germany. Five French Generals arrived from the east led by General Denny. A sixth should have arrived, but was detained and "Klim tinned"—never heard of again.

General Bor-Komorovski, the head of that courageous, almost suicidal, band of Polish patriots who kept the heart of Poland beating throughout the blackest years of the war, arrived, accompanied by five Polish Generals and other Staff Officers. The Warsaw insurrection was the culminating point in the General's underground career. He survived, though war, treachery and murder had threatened to engulf him each day. He possessed hostage value in the eyes of the German leaders, which fact undoubtedly saved his head.

A man of infinite courage and resource, he won the hearts of all who knew him by his simplicity and cheerful friendliness. He was every inch a hero, yet with the modesty of an æsthete, saintly in his detached outlook upon life. His head was partly bald and reminded one of a tonsured monk. Of slender physique, medium in height but wiry, he had direct, searching, hazel eyes under dark eyebrows. A neatly trimmed moustache, beneath an aquiline nose, set off his sensitive nostrils.

In March, twelve hundred French officers were dumped into the prison, six hundred more parked in the village. They had been marched eighty-five miles from their camp east of the Elbe in the face of the Russian advance. Overnight, Colditz became a crowded refugee centre. Men slept everywhere, on straw laid out on the floors. The Castle theatre became a large dormitory choked with human beings. It was calculated that if everybody assembled in the courtyard at once there would be three officers per square

yard of cobbles. The invasion heralded the end of an era—the end of normal camp life. The closing days of the war were at hand.

The French, many of them old friends from the early days of Colditz, were starving and there were a large number of sick and dying hospital cases amongst them. They had had no nourishing food for months. The British took them gradually in hand, sharing food and clothing, while the S.B.O. and the French generals fought with the German Camp Commandant for extra medical attention, which was produced, and for medicines, which never materialised.

Heavy air-raids, centred on the Leuna oil refineries south of Leipzig, became a nightly performance. By day, the tactical Allied air force began to make its appearance.

The tempo of events quickened and the daily wireless News Bulletins issued in the camp showed that the end was approaching.

The race was nearly finished.

It had been described in a German propaganda leaflet, distributed in English to British prisoners and others in Germany, in the following terms, as early as September, 1944:

> "In 1944 they (the Allies) started a grand offensive, and at the same time Stalin, in the east, threw in all he had. It was certainly impressive. But why was this sudden terrific outburst of energy necessary? Why all the hurry?
>
> "Because Churchill knew something. A year and more ago he knew something which most of the Germans at that time had no idea of. Mr. Herbert Morrison knows something about it, too. Remember how he warned the House of Commons recently about the 'Frightful things' which Germany had in store for Britain.
>
> "This vast Allied onslaught against Germany is not a sign of strength. It has been caused by their deadly anxiety and intense panic. They must get to Germany and defeat her before she can use her new weapons.
>
> "Think of a race between two motor-cars. The Allied motor-car, although it has been fitted up with a reserve petrol tank, has now got to go all out. The German machine, which had been left far behind as its juice ran out, has in the meantime filled up again. And it is racing ahead. Its tanks are full with special fuel.
>
> "Germany's victory, the final victory, is not so very far away. . . ."

The German V1's were well known by September, 1944, when this article was published. The V2's were about to start their work of indiscriminate destruction. But Hitler had another secret weapon nearing completion. His scientists were working frantically on the heavy-water bomb—the hydrogen bomb.

Lieutenant John Winant Junior, of the U.S. Army Air Corps arrived in April. Being the son of the American Ambassador to the United Kingdom, the Germans treated him as a Prominente. He had been shot down in a Flying Fortress raid over Munster. A fair-haired young man with steel-blue eyes, and a strong, though sensitive, character, he went to war straight from his university.

Early in April, Dick Howe's wireless communiqués began to speak of General Patton's and General Hodge's armoured spearheads, moving like shafts of lightning and driving deep into enemy territory.

Colonel 'Willie' Tod, the S.B.O. of the camp, came into his own as the man to be relied upon in a crisis. He was recognised as the senior officer of the whole camp and represented all nationalities in their routine dealings with the Germans. He watched the mounting tide of chaos around the Castle with cool detachment, and, having the confidence of his own officers, he was able to handle the Germans with skill. He was all that a soldier should be.

Aged about fifty-four, Willie Tod was a regular officer of the Royal Scots Fusiliers, tall, grey-haired and good looking, with strong features and bright blue eyes.

Dick Howe always remembered a short conversation he had had with him; it must have occurred in 1943. He had lost his son— killed fighting. The news had come to him, a helpless prisoner in Colditz. Dick had said, sympathetically, after some casual conversation:

"I'm sorry, Colonel, about the news you've just had."

Tod replied simply, "It happens to soldiers." There was a moment's pause, then they had continued their discussion.

Almost forgotten, as the tornado of world events swept across the globe and the Allied armies from West and East dashed headlong to meet each other in the heart of the German Reich, the Colditz glider was made ready for flight. Discussion centred around the use to be made of it. Dick had recently been criticised for allowing the building of the glider to proceed. Some senior officers criticised it on the grounds that it was completed too late for use, saying that a better estimate of the time required to build it should

have been made. They were correct in that the glider was finished too late to be of use for an escape, but they were speaking after the event. Others maintained it was a waste of good time and material from the very beginning. The answer to this was a simple one. None of the men even remotely connected with its production regretted what they had done. As for others, did it concern them?

Nobody could foresee when the climax and conclusion of the war would occur. If it had not occurred in the spring of 1945, but months, perhaps even a year later, which was by no means impossible, then the glider would have undoubtedly been launched. Those who built it were prepared to fly in it. They were certain it would take off.

Colonel Tod did not criticise. Even if he had wanted to, the discipline of a soldier forbade the criticism of junior officers who had been allowed to build the glider with the help of his own staff and with his own knowledge. On the contrary, Tod foresaw the possibility of a last and desperate use for the glider and issued his instructions accordingly: "The glider is to be held in reserve in strict secrecy until the Castle is liberated, or until you have further prior instructions from myself or my successor in Command."

On Tuesday, April the tenth, came a new sound; quite different to the familiar "whoof" of bombs which had been falling every night on Leipzig and the Leuna synthetic oil plant not twenty-five miles away. There was the distinct crump of shell bursts, and the evening clouds glowed on the horizon with vivid infected spots as the dusk came down.

Dick found it difficult to throw off the feeling of unreality that surrounded the events taking place. This untoward intrusion into the normality of the camp was deeply upsetting. Here was a routine that it had been sacriligeous to break during five years, now going overboard in a day. *Appells* almost ceased. The S.B.O. was repeatedly in conference with the German Camp Commandant, and not inside the prison, but outside, in the Kommandantur. A world was coming to an end. It was an eerie feeling and unsettling.

There were maniacs at the helm in Berlin. The prisoners of Colditz were hostages. They had known it for a long time. There were so many imponderables in the atmosphere surrounding them and in the kaleidoscopic nightmare of events taking place in Germany. Anything might happen. "Thank God," Dick thought, "there's a cool head looking after our interests. Tod will handle

the situation if anyone can." The same thought was in the minds of many. Their lives were literally in his hands.

Tod had their confidence because their discipline showed it. His responsibility was so much the greater. He must save their lives at all costs and, in these hours, life was being held cheaply by the Germans. An S.S. Division had moved into the village of Colditz overnight. He had information that the remnants (those who had not died of starvation or illness) of four hundred Jewish slave prisoners, in a camp three miles from the town, had been murdered already by the newcomers. Four only survived to tell the tale, having remained hidden under piles of dead until nightfall.

Tod saw clearly that he had to temporise, yet show no weakness. The German Commandant was terrified. His own Wehrmacht High Command had moved to Dresden. Underneath his window were the S.S. and the Gestapo. The mention of the Russians, who were closing in from the east, made him shiver. Hodge's Task Forces from the west were advancing quickly—but how quickly would they reach Colditz? They might be checked. The Commandant would run with the hare and hunt with the hounds as long as he possibly could.

The murder of prisoners on the spot was the first danger. A time might come when it would be advisable for them to make a mass break-out and run for the Allied lines. But there was no front line, properly speaking, at the moment, within two hundred miles. Over that distance, the *Sturmge schutze*—stormtroopers—and the Hitler Youth were running amok, well armed and merciless. Tod was not going to lose half his men that way if he could help it. Then, close at hand, was the S.S. Division in the village and in the surrounding district. The prisoners might not make their escape quick enough to pass even this initial obstacle, and their break-out might precipitate the very mass murder from which they were trying to escape.

The second danger which the S.B.O. had to combat was the removal of the prisoners to the redoubts in which the Nazi fanatics would make their last stand. Hitler's own redoubt was known to be in the Austrian Tyrol around his beloved Berchtesgaden. Here he would bargain for his life and those of his immediate entourage, employing as many Prominente prisoners as he could muster as his hostages. His minions, the S.S. and the Gestapo, would similarly use officer prisoners and even the rank and file, wherever they could seize and hold them in last-ditch defences and mountain fortresses.

Tod's strategy, therefore, was to turn to the best account the value of his men to the Germans as live prisoners; while, at the same time, stalling and delaying any attempt to move them away from the advancing Allied columns.

There was a third danger which Tod had to envisage in connection with which he issued his orders concerning the glider. It was to be a standby in case the Commander of the S.S. troops in the surrounding district had a dangerous brain-wave. He might take over the Castle itself and use it as a stronghold for a last stand on the lines of the siege of the Alcazar in the Spanish Civil War of the thirties. The prisoners would not, in that case, be compelled to move from Colditz, which was the order expected and which Tod was prepared to resist. There was a danger that the Germans, in desperate straits, might turn upon him and say, "All right, if you will not move for us and with us, then we shall move into the Castle and you will remain too, as you so wish it, and as our hostages!"

In this event, the glider could come into its own, to send emissaries from the prisoners, like carrier pigeons, in the hope that they would reach the Allied lines, conveying perhaps vital information at a crucial stage in the siege, or even the plans for a combined assault, from outside and from within.

In the early afternoon of April the tenth a messenger arrived at Colditz from the Wilhelmstrasse, in Berlin, carrying an offer to General Bor Komorowski. The Commandant conveyed to him the instructions of Hitler, to the effect that he should be freed at once along with his staff, who included General Petczynski, his Chief of Staff, and General Chrusciel, Commander of the Warsaw garrison, on condition that they helped Germany to form an underground army to fight against the Russians. It was the third time the offer had been made and, for the third time, General Bor rejected it.

Wednesday, April the eleventh, passed quietly within the Castle. The sentries around the perimeter remained at their posts. In the distance the thunder of battle continued. Ominously, in the foreground beneath the Castle, could be seen feverish preparations for the defence of the town. The bridge across the river Mulde was mined, ready for detonating. Tanks and motorised artillery rattled through the streets to positions in the woods around. Houses on the outskirts were taken over by troops and barricaded for defence.

The unreality of it all continued to obsess the minds of men, like Dick, who had looked down upon the quiet town without ever noticing a change during five and a half weary years. The scene had become so permanent, so indestructible, that nothing could change it; only in their dreams and reveries had the scene ever altered. When they awoke it was always there, the same as before, unchanged.

They had imagined bombs falling on the houses; Allied artillery flashing and shells raining into the town; the rattle of machine-guns then the advance into the streets; British Tommies, armed with hand-grenades and tommy-guns, creeping stealthily or dashing forward from doorway to doorway in the wake of Mark IV tanks. The dreams of years had never materialised. Could it be different now? Why should it be different? The sound of the guns in the distance might fade to-morrow. The Germans would bring up reserves. They would drive wedges into Hodge's advance. The wireless news would alter, at first subtly, letting the listener down very gently, then the Allied retreat would begin. The S.S. would leave Colditz once more . . . to its former peace. The distant rumble of bombing in the great cities would alone remain a reality. That had gone on for so long now, it was part of their lives, but it altered nothing. "To its former peace . . .!" A quiet, like that of the solitary confinement cell, where the thud of the heart, beating in futility, is the loudest noise, would descend again.

Dick shivered at the prospect and his skin crept. If the guns were to retire, now that they were so near, perhaps, real after all; if the "crumps" of exploding shells died away now, it would be much harder for him to live and bear the silence. To raise the hopes of a despairing prisoner, then to drop him back into the slough of despondency, is one of the more refined tortures that mankind has invented.

Dick dared not hope. He lived a suspended existence, numbing his virile senses with a self-imposed stupor.

He slept feverishly that night. The gunfire had ceased and he asked himself repeatedly, "Will it begin again in the morning?" It was always at night that thoughts took their own course and the will was at its weakest. He longed for the reassuring sound of the guns.

Thursday, April the twelfth, dawned. As the prisoners sat at their tables over a breakfast of acorn coffee and German bread,

news came through from the wireless-room, which was continuously manned, that the Americans were at Leuna. They were only twenty-five miles away. A cheer went up at the announcement, and the fears of the night gave way to a reassurance which buoyed the spirit through the daylight hours.

On Thursday, April the twelfth, the defence preparations continued around the village more furiously. Slit trenches could be seen everywhere, thrown up, like mushrooms during the night, in the fields on the higher slopes and bordering the woods. Boys and girls of all ages could be seen at work with spades and pickaxes alongside their elders in uniform. The Germans looked as if they were going to make a serious stand in the country around the Castle.

Keith Milne, the City Slicker, known also as 'the Breed' because he came from Saskatoon, had, in the course of the years, manufactured a couple of good telescopes, making use of spectacle lenses. They were in high demand, more so than Rex Harrison's telescope, the lenses of which had been made by grinding down glass marbles. Scarlet O'Hara swore the Castle would not be relieved until the pearl handles on General Patton's own pair of pistols could be seen through a telescope.

Towards evening, Colonel Tod was called to the Kommandantur. Lance Pope, of Franz Josef fame, accompanied him to interpret in case of difficulty. Oberst Prawitt, tall and emaciated, standing beside his desk in the plainly furnished office, looked at the Commander of his prisoners. There was no softness in the answering glance. Tod stepped forward over the soft pile carpet and took from Prawitt's hand the letter which he held out. It was a letter from Himmler's Headquarters, addressed from Himmler personally, but unsigned. It contained the marching orders for the Prominente. They were to be removed that night to an unknown destination. Two buses would be waiting at the Kommandantur entrance at midnight. Oberst Prawitt would be answerable with his life if any of them escaped.

"This is an outrage, Herr Oberst. The order must be disobeyed," said Tod.

"I cannot. I am under orders, even though I might wish to disobey them," was the reply.

"Our guns are on the horizon and you still have the temerity to dare to carry out this act? Herr Oberst, you must reflect. You will have to answer for the lives of every one of the men on this

list which I see attached to the order," said Tod, flinging the papers on the desk.

"You must also reflect," said Prawitt. He looked very old, tired and haggard, and his white hair was bedraggled. He was no longer master of the situation. He was merely a tool in the hands of men who used the blackmail of life or death to impose their will. "If I overrule this order which has come through the local S.S. Headquarters, they will enter the Castle and see that it is carried out. I shall not even live to see it done. There will be many deaths throughout the camp and still the Prominente will depart. What will you have achieved?"

"Have you no sense of justice, Herr Oberst? If you will not face matters now, you will have to face them later, before an Allied court-martial."

"I would far rather face an Allied court-martial," said the Commandant with a sigh of infinite weariness. He was played out. The future that he saw before him was a violent death, sooner or later, and he preferred it later. The thin thread which held him to life was still precious, old as he was. Time was his only hope and a poor hope at that, but he would try the course that gave him time.

The dangers of the situation presented themselves clearly enough to Tod. If the Commandant would not act, the S.S. would, with bloodshed that might end anywhere. It was not the moment for heroics by unarmed men—unless—and he thought of the last resort, but, looking at the Commandant he could see, almost before he said what was in his mind, that it was useless.

"Will you either hand over the garrison inside the Castle and the armoury to me, or will you, at least, help me to hide or get away the Prominente from here?" he asked.

"It is more than my life is worth. If the men escape they will not get far. It is better to temporise."

"You are certainly not a hero, Herr Oberst!"

"I am old but not yet ready to die in a suicidal attempt to save the enemies of Germany. In fact any such attempt by me will merely precipitate their end."

Tod saw the relentless logic behind his words. They were both confronted with a vicious enemy who valued life at nothing. He too, must play for time. Time alone could save the Prominente.

"What is their destination?" he asked.

"I do not know."

Tod was not sure that he was not lying.

"I insist on knowing their destination," he reiterated.

"I can only do one thing," said the Commandant. "As some of my personnel will accompany them, I can instruct that they bring back here a message from your men. From that, you should know where they have gone."

The conversation was at an end.

The S.B.O. was escorted back to the prison, where he found that extra guards had already been mounted over the quarters of the Prominente. An *Appell* was held just before dusk and the Prominente were then locked into their cells.

Colonel Tod was allowed to speak to them. He told their senior, Captain the Master of Elphinstone, of his conversation with the Commandant, of the position with regard to the Castle and warned him, at all costs, to fight for time, wherever they might find themselves. "The situation is changing hourly and in our favour," he concluded, and then gave them a final word to cheer them, saying: "I've foreseen this eventuality for some time. You will not be deserted. The Swiss Protecting Power Authorities have had specific warning and requests to watch this camp and to follow the movement of any prisoners. They are in close contact with German authorities in Berlin, who are in the know. You will probably be followed by a representative in person or, if not, your movements will be known in their Legation. You are being carefully watched. Good-bye and good luck to all of you."

Nobody else was allowed near them. At eleven-thirty p.m. the order came for them to move. They were roused from their beds and given two hours to dress, pack and make ready. At one-thirty a.m. they were escorted through a lane of guards to two waiting buses. Bor Komorowski was there with twelve of his most senior officers. John Winant appeared. There were seven British: Captain the Master of Elphinstone, Lieutenant Lord Lascelles, Giles Romilly, Captains, Charles Hopetoun, Michael Alexander and Earl Haig and Lieutenant Max du Hamel. The prison windows were crowded with faces. There was a chorus of good-byes! and good lucks! The twenty-one men filed through the gate. Outside two buses were waiting to take them to an unknown destination . . . .

There was really not much difference between those who left and those who remained. They were all going to be hostages; only the Nazi *Herren Raze* believed in classifying them, under the delusion that the Allies would bargain for the lives of men as if they were cattle, pedigree cattle being worth more than others.

As the buses, escorted by a light armoured vehicle, tore out of Colditz and into the night, Giles Romilly, in the British bus, said suddenly, breaking the silence:

"I thought you'd all like to know to-day is Friday, the thirteenth!"

CHAPTER XXIII

HITLER'S LAST REDOUBT

DURING the course of Friday there was a lull within the Castle. Two important items of news, only, came into the camp: one, from the guards returning after taking the Prominente to their destination, the second from the secret wireless receiver. In their wake, the story of Colditz divides naturally into two separate trails, which it were better the reader followed separately to avoid becoming lost. The first trail leads away from the Castle.

A written message was handed to Colonel Tod, signed by Elphinstone, saying the party had arrived safely at the Castle of Königstein on the river Elbe; the same from which General Giraud had escaped to rejoin the Allies earlier in the war. Two of them, he added, Hopetoun and Haig, were seriously ill. They had been ill before they left, as the authorities knew well, and the journey had made their condition worse.

On Saturday, the fourteenth, in the afternoon, the Prominente were moved under heavy guard as before from Königstein, through Czechoslovakia, to Klattau on the borders of Bavaria. There they spent the night. Hopetoun and Haig were left behind at Königstein being too ill to move. The German Commandant had to obtain permission from Berlin to leave them.* The sound of Allied guns could be heard as the two buses and the armoured car left Königstein heading for Hitler's redoubt in the Austrian mountains.

Sunday morning, in bright spring sunshine, the Prominente were moved again. Now they headed towards Austria. As evening drew on, they arrived at Laufen on the river Salzach that divides Austria from Bavaria. They stopped outside the barracks, once

* See Author's note on page 288.

the palace of the Archbishops of Salzburg, and also the prison where the story of Colditz began. The barracks, which, at the beginning of the war, had been Oflag VII.C, was now a civilian internee camp.

Elphinstone as head of the British party refused to disembark. He was suspicious. The camp was not under Wehrmacht control and responsibility for any outrage might be difficult to trace. Where he was, he was definitely under Wehrmacht control, facing an Army Colonel who would pay with his head under Himmler's orders if his prisoners escaped and who would also pay with his head under Allied retribution if they disappeared by other means.

The German Colonel in charge agreed to take them to another camp at Tittmoning, ten miles away, occupied by Dutch officers.

It was nearly dark when they reached Tittmoning. They were marched into the prison, another castle perched on a hill, and in the presence of the German Commandant, were introduced to the Senior Dutch Officers. Giles Romilly could hardly contain himself. Who should he see in the group standing before them but Vandy, grinning all over his face and with the usual devilish twinkle in his eye. Giles was the only one in the British group who had been a contemporary of Vandy in Colditz. The others had all arrived after his departure.

The Commandant of the camp commended the party to the care of the Dutch officers and left them together in order to organise extra precautions amongst the guards. Himmler's orders were clear. German officers responsible for the prisoners, would pay with their lives, if any of the prisoners escaped.

As soon as they were by themselves, Giles approached Vandy and the two men shook hands warmly.

"I am zo glad you haf come here. Ve vill look after you," said Vandy ubiquitously. "How strange to meet you again in such circumstances."

"Tell me how you got to this camp," said Romilly, "and then I'll give you all the news from Colditz."

Vandy looked at him.

"Come with me. Virst you must haf a hot coffee and something to eat."

He led Romilly through the echoing corridors, to a mess room where a meal was in full swing. They sat down together and as Romilly ate hungrily, Vandy went on:

"I vas sent here in January because the Germans thought to

get rid off me. I vas a damn nuisance, they said. I vas *Deutch-feindlich*. They knew I organised all the Dutch escapes and zo they sent me here where there are only old officers and many sick ones—none who vish to escape. Zo they thought, but again they are wrong, vor I haf now some men here ready to escape!" Vandy chuckled with glee. He was looking older and his face was deeply lined but his eye had not lost its sparkle.

Vandy introduced Giles to the officers in the refectory and they talked for some time. Then he escorted him to a dormitory prepared for the five British and the one American Prominente, John Winant. The Polish Generals were entertained by another Dutch officers' mess in a different part of the Castle and slept in a separate dormitory.

The Prominente stayed at Tittmoning for several days.

On Thursday, the nineteenth of April, Vandy had news through the German guards, some of whom were in his pay, that Goebbels and Himmler had been seen in cars, passing through Tittmoning at high speed, in a whirlwind of dust, taking the road to the redoubt built near Hitler's Berchtesgaden. On the same day the Prominente were informed they were to be moved to Laufen. There was little doubt as to the implications of this move. At Laufen, out of the control of the Army, Himmler's thugs would take charge of them.

A secret conference was held at which Vandy produced a plan of campaign. He was nothing if not resourceful, but he was not only resourceful, he was far-sighted. He had a method of escape prepared for two of his own officers which could be used in an emergency such as this. The escape could take place the next day, the twentieth. He proposed that three officers, of whom one should be Romilly who spoke German fluently and the other two, his Dutchmen, should escape by his projected route. But he had not finished. He proposed to wall up the other five (including Winant) in a secret radio room which he had prepared for a clandestine wireless set. They would have food and water for a week, and the Germans would think they had escaped with the three.

The Prominente had only to listen to Vandy for ten minutes, after which they placed themselves entirely in his hands.

The twentieth of April was Hitler's birthday. The escape was

planned for the evening. Romilly was equipped along with Lieutenant André Tieleman and a young officer Cadet, both of whom had come to Tittmoning by mistake, as they were neither elderly, nor decrepit, nor sick, nor dangerous like Vandy.

First of all, the five men were walled into the secret radio room with their food reserves. Then, as the moon rose, Vandy and his assistant for the escape, Captain van den Wall Bake, escorted the three escapers to a doorway in the castle from which, one at a time and with suitable distraction of the sentries by helpers in the castle windows, they were able to quick make a dash into the shadows immediately underneath a pagoda sentry box inside the prison perimeter and beside an eight foot wall, bounding the castle. On the other side of the wall was a seventy foot drop to a water meadow. Vandy had the rope. He climbed carefully up the pagoda framework to the top of the wall and secured the rope firmly to a timber strut. The sentry was ten feet above him, on the platform, inside a glass shelter with a veranda around it. Vandy helped Tieleman to mount and then eased him over the edge for the long descent. Dutchmen, in their mess rooms close by, were playing musical instruments and keeping up a continuous cacophony of laughter, music and singing. Romilly and the Dutch Cadet came next. Romilly lay flat on the top of the wall and gripped the rope. As he lifted one leg to drop over, he hit one of the timber stanchions a resounding whack with his boot. The sentry came out of his pagoda and leaned over the balustrade. He saw two men standing on the wall and a third lying along it. He had left his rifle inside the pagoda. He yelled "Halt!" and ran to fetch it. In that instant Romilly disappeared over the edge and Vandy whispered to van den Wall Bake, "Quick! Quick! on to the wall." Van den Wall Bake had not been seen in the shadows. The next moment he was lying on the top beside Vandy.

The sentry had rung the alarm bell and now dashed on to the veranda again, aiming his rifle over the side at the three men and shouting: "*Hände hoch! Hände hoch!*" The Dutchmen complied as best they could without going over the edge down the seventy foot drop. The guard was turned out, arrived at the double and arrested the three men. The sentry reported he had caught them in the act and had spotted them in time, before anyone had escaped.

They were led before the Commandant, who treated them jocosely, in conformity with the state of the war at that moment. "How silly of you to try to escape now! What is the point?

The war is nearly over. You will be home soon. I have told you that General Eisenhower has issued strict orders by wireless that prisoners are to remain in their camps. They run excessive dangers of being killed by moving about alone in the open country at this time. I suppose you just wished more quickly to see your wives and sweethearts?"

The Commandant was elderly, grey haired and formerly a retired senior ranking army officer. He was not an arrogant personality.

Vandy replied in German.

"Of course, the Commandant has devined our intentions correctly."

"Very well, the matter is closed. I must, according to regulations hold an *Appell*. I am sorry, but, please remember, it is you who have caused this trouble and not me."

The whistles blew and the floodlights were switched on. The Dutch officers assembled, and the Polish Prominente assembled. . . . There was a pause as the German officers, with horror-stricken incredulity, surveyed the ranks before them. Hurriedly and nervously the count was taken. Six Prominente and one Dutch officer were missing. A second count was taken. The result was the same. It was reported to the Commandant in his office. The elderly soldier's hair rose from his scalp. He had thought he would spend the last years of his life quietly and peacefully. Now, in a moment, all had changed and he saw his head in the noose, the gallows below him and felt the sickening drop. No! he thought, as his eyes started from his head, it would not be like that. Instead, he felt the handkerchief round his eyes, he could hear the fire orders and then one rending crackle. . . .

He sat up in his chair behind his desk. His junior officers were awaiting orders. He would have to give them. He would be signing his own death warrant. He must stall. It was his only hope. He ordered his officers to search the camp at once and to continue until he issued further orders.

Searching continued for two days in the camp. Nothing was found. The Commandant had to report and give himself up. He was arrested, summarily court-martialled and sentenced to death. The order of execution remained only to be signed by Himmler, as being the Head of the Organisation which, under Hitler's authority, had issued the original commands. Himmler was not easily accessible. He was already in hiding in the mountains. In the meantime, the search continued desperately, outside the camp. Three thousand

Germans scoured the countryside without avail. The Polish
Prominente were removed to Laufen. On the fifth day, perhaps
information had leaked out, nobody could tell, they began to
search inside the camp again; knocking down walls, removing
floors and attacking the ceilings. Eventually, they came upon the
secret hide and unearthed four British officers and John Winant.

This discovery occurred on Tuesday, the twenty-fourth of April.
What followed is best told by the Master of Elphinstone himself
in a report which was published in *The Times:*

"Under very heavy escort we were taken to the internee
camp at Laufen. Here the German general commanding the
Munich area visited the camp, and in the course of an interview finally gave me his word of honour that we should
remain there until the end of the war—a promise repeated
in the presence of the Swiss Minister by the German Kommandant next day. The latter, however, could, or would,
give no information as to the reason for our detention apart
from all other officer-prisoners, except that it was ordered by
Himmler.

"All remained quiet until the fall of Munich, and then,
with the Americans once more rapidly approaching, the
orders were given that we were to move at once—in spite of
promises given—into the mountains of the Austrian Tryol.
Two officers, an S.S. Colonel and a *Luftwaffe* major—were
sent by Obergruppenführer and General of S.S. Berger to
conduct us. At six-thirty a.m. we entered the transport, with
the colonel, fingering his revolver, watching us, together
with a somewhat sinister-looking blonde woman who accompanied him in his car. This was possibly the most trying of
all the moves, as the whole scene had a gangster-like atmosphere. We drove through Salzburg, past Berchtesgaden,
and finally stopped at a Stalag in a remote valley in the Tyrol.
We were allowed no contact with the prisoners, who included
representatives of most of the allied nations, but were isolated
in the German part of the camp.

"The representative of the Swiss Legation (Protecting Power),
with admirable and very reassuring promptitude, followed
us and visited the Kommandant within a very few hours
of our arrival. Later the Swiss Minister and his staff started
on the series of interviews and discussions with the leading
German Government figures who were in the neighbourhood.

This work, which they carried out with such wonderful patience and success, was of the utmost difficulty, as the leaders were scattered in remote mountain hamlets, and all roads were choked with army vehicles and personnel.

"Finally, S.S. Obergruppenführer Berger, chief among other things, of all prisoner-of-war affairs, agreed to hand us over to the Swiss and allow them to conduct us through the lines. He did this on his own responsibility, and warned the Swiss that other elements in the Government would, if they knew, resist his orders and lay hands on us. He therefore sent to the camp a special guard under an S.S. Colonel, armed with every type of weapon, to guard us against the "other German elements" during this final night of our captivity.

"Berger himself came to visit us and in a long and theatrically declaimed speech reiterated, probably for the last time, many of the well worn phrases of German propaganda together with several revelations of the complete break-up of the German Government and people. He then informed us that owing to this break-up he felt he was no longer in a position to safeguard us properly and had agreed to hand us over to Swiss protection. On leaving, he turned, theatrical to the end, to the German officers in charge of us and, having given his final commands, said: 'Gentlemen, these are probably the last orders I shall give as a high official of the Third German Reich.' We were due to leave at eleven next morning. The Swiss Legation attaché who was to accompany us in his car arrived early, but for more than three rather tantalising hours there was no sign of the German trucks which were to take the party, a fact which caused some anxiety in view of Berger's warnings. At length, however, two other trucks were secured locally, thanks once again to the perseverance of the Swiss attaché, and finally at about five p.m. we set off, each vehicle draped with the Swiss flag, along the densely packed roads. Accompanying us was an S.S. medical officer as personal representative of General Berger.

"At about eleven-thirty p.m. this officer stopped the convoy in a small village in the mountains, saying he had orders from Obergruppenführer Berger to see that we had food and drink in his headquarters here. We entered a house filled with S.S. troops, many of them intoxicated, and were

K

shown into an upstairs room where some food and much drink were laid out. In the middle of the meal the Obergruppenführer himself once more made a theatrical entry, played the expansive if somewhat nerve-strained host, and again poured out a flood of propaganda and explanation. After some time he gave an order to an S.S. adjutant, who handed him a scarlet leather case. After yet another speech he turned to me, as senior of the British-American party, and handed me the case, as 'proof of his good feelings.' Inside was an elaborately ornamented pistol of ivory, brass and enamel, with his own signature engraved across the butt.

"After this strange interlude we set off once more. At dawn we passed successfully through the last German post, and shortly afterwards were halted, to our joy and relief, by American tanks. A few hours later we were most kindly and hospitably welcomed by an American Divisional Headquarters at Innsbrück. It would be difficult indeed for our party adequately to express our gratitude to the Swiss Minister and his staff for all that they did to make this release possible."

The Polish Prominente were released in the same convoy.

It is interesting to note that Colonel Tod's last cheering words to the Prominente before they left Colditz were not said without avail. The Swiss Minister to Germany was on their trail and caught up with them at Laufen on the 25th of April.

Giles Romilly takes up the thread of his own last escape from the castle at Tittmoning in an article he wrote for the *Sunday Express* of May 6th, 1945. He says:

"My legs were dangling over the wall. The drop was seventy feet down to the moon-whitened grass, and it looked terrifying.

"I gripped the rope, let myself forward and began to go down faster than expected.

"I knew I should grip with my feet, but never once managed it. And the rope was tearing my fingers. About halfway I remember thinking 'This parachute should open soon.'

"At the bottom, already down, was the Dutch officer, Lieutenant André Tieleman.

"We tramped down lonely side roads, star-guided. It was a grand night. And it was Hitler's birthday. And we were free; precariously free—but still free.

"That was eleven days ago.

"We were Prominente, and I heard the word in Dachau horror-camp.

"In Dachau there were thirty-two thousand prisoners—and forty Prominente. Two of the 'Proms' were English. One was Lieutenant Colonel McGrath, brought there for refusing to form a 'Free Irish' corps.

"The other, I believe, was Major Stevens, captured on the Dutch frontier by a trick in the first months of the war.

"A few days before the U.S. troops moved in the 'Proms' were moved to Schloss Ita, near Innsbrück in the Tyrol."

The Prominente were, indeed, all moving in the same direction. From camps all over Germany, the great trek had begun to bring Hitler's hostages into his spider's web, cast in the Austrian mountains.

Romilly and Tieleman managed to reach Münich in three days, after some adventures. On one occasion, they were held for questioning at a police station but their papers, prepared by Vandy, were found to be in order. The officer in charge received an urgent telephone message while they were standing in his office, concerning the escape of important prisoners from Tittmoning. He hurried them out of the office immediately, saying he had an urgent assignment and politely wished them a pleasant journey.

In Münich, the two men lived as Germans, quietly and inconspicuously in a cheap hotel, awaiting the American advance. They reported themselves to American Army Headquarters as soon as the latter entered the city during the last week of April. Romilly was back in England by May 2nd.

Vandy had not completed his duty as a soldier, and an ally. Not satisfied with having delayed for five days the execution of Himlers' orders, perhaps saving the lives of the Prominente thereby, he risked his life by leaving the camp in the dead of night as soon as the Americans had entered Tittmoning and contrary to American Army orders. There was a severe curfew in operation. Anyone seen on the streets was liable to be shot at sight. He appeared at American Headquarters where he reported the transfer of the Prominente including John Winant and was able,

moreover, through his own German sources of information to give details as to the route they had taken into the Tyrol from Laufen.

The cataclysm that swept over Germany and Austria in April saved many lives. Communications were severed, the roads were clogged with refugee traffic, and the precious signatures of Hitler's hierarchy were not forthcoming. Hitler committed suicide in the Berlin bunker on April 30th; many executions were stayed and many a happy man to-day owes his continuing life on this globe to a missing black scrawl on a sheet of white paper; among them is the German Commandant of the Dutch Camp at Tittmoning.

CHAPTER XXIV

FINALE: THE RELIEF OF COLDITZ

BACK in the Castle: Friday, the thirteenth of April, an unlucky day for the Prominente, brought good news to Colditz through the secret wireless receiver. Hodge's spearhead, south of Leipzig, was advancing again after a slight check during the day of the twelfth. The Americans were twenty miles away at dawn and, by the evening, they were in the Colditz area, invisible but there, nevertheless. Shells fell in the town as the dusk approached and, in the distance, machine-gun fire could be heard. Desultory firing continued through the night.

The next morning, Saturday the fourteenth, at dawn, the battle for Colditz began. The Allied Air Forces had possession of the sky. An American reconnaissance plane zoomed overhead. A few shells followed, dropping into various parts of the town. The artillery were ranging.

Colonel Tod was called again to the Kommandantur, where Prawitt faced him.

"You are to move the British out of the Castle towards the east under guard. I have orders from Dresden."

This was Tod's chance. Twenty-four hours had just made the difference. The S.S. had their hands full. To-day, they were under attack fighting a battle, and they could not possibly deal with three hundred British prisoners not to mention a thousand Frenchmen. They could not even spare the time to come into the camp and shoot them all. Tod seized the opportunity.

"The British refuse to move," he said. "You will have to turn them out with the bayonet and the British will fight. This is not mutiny. It is self-defence. You are sending them out to their death. Tell Dresden we shall not move."

Tod was recalling another occasion, a long time ago, when the Commandant had shown he was less fearful of his superiors when they were a long way off. Those nearby were heavily engaged which came to the same thing.

The Commandant weakened.

"I shall 'phone my Headquarters," he said, sitting down at his desk and picking up the army field telephone. He spoke to a couple of exchanges in turn, using German code names. Then he was speaking to the General. He reported the position at Colditz, leading up to his interview with Tod, saying, . . . "and the British refuse to move."

There was an explosion from the other end. A guttural German voice was yelling blue murder at the Commandant who held the receiver far away from his ear. Gradually the rasping died down. Oberst Prawitt was at last showing signs of courage. With remarkable calm he addressed his senior:

"I cannot move the prisoners without shooting them and they will then resist. Their Commander will disclaim mutiny on grounds of self-defence. Will you take the responsibility if I use my weapons and prisoners are killed?"

"No!" came the answer, shouted down the telephone.

"Neither will I!" said the Commandant and banged down the receiver. . .

Even the few marker shells dropped into Colditz by the American artillery were having a suprisingly salutary effect on the conduct of affairs within the Castle walls.

The prisoners did not move.

Heavy shelling started in the afternoon and buildings were soon on fire in many quarters. The noise of gunfire increased to a crescendo. To the onlookers in the Castle, no orderly plan appeared to be unfolding. There was only destruction, smoke, flames and noise, the tearing scrunch of shells, the whine of splinters, the acrid smell of burnt explosive and chaos.

Half a dozen shells landed in the Castle, splintering glass everywhere and leaving ragged holes in the roof. Nobody was seriously hurt. Duggie Bader was knocked off his tin legs. The prisoners were ordered to the ground floor.

The Kommandantur fared worse and a dozen shells tore large

gaps in the building, wounding several Germans. Nevertheless, the general shelling appeared to be avoiding the Castle.

In the early afternoon, Colonel Tod had another session with Oberst Prawitt. The Commandant, judging by his appearance, had probably received information, though he did not say so, that the S.S. would not retreat into the Castle and make a stand in it. His face showed immense relief. He was wreathed in smiles and almost fawning on Tod as he told him that he would surrender to him the inside of the Castle on certain conditions: the S.S. were still in the town, and no sign must be given to them that the Castle had been surrendered; no national or other coloured flags to be in evidence; no white flags of surrender to be visible at the windows; appearances to be kept up by leaving the sentries at their posts around the exterior; a guarantee to be given by the S.B.O. that he, Oberst Prawitt, would not be handed over to the Russians.

Tod refused to give any guarantees. He thought for a moment, realising the value and importance of access to the armoury in case of need. He decided to take a risk. He compromised on one point, making a counter proposal. If the interior of the whole Castle were handed over to him, including the armoury, if and when he so desired so that he could move his officers freely within the Kommandantur area, he would instruct them not to show signs of surrender outside the Castle. He added that he would see the Commandant was treated with justice, that was as far as he could go. Tod was becoming master of the situation. He would move his officers about and would obtain arms if he wanted them though already he felt the danger from the S.S. receding. He ran the risk that the Americans might take it into their heads to blow up the Castle not knowing who was inside. He would like to have put out flags. He used his judgment. The shells, he considered, which had entered the Castle were "off target". The Americans were now pouring high explosive into the town. He was sure that they were avoiding the Castle and for no other reason than that they knew there were prisoners inside. Finally, Tod considered it wiser to keep his men within the inner courtyard, unless the situation deteriorated. If the S.S. decided to move into the Castle he was to be informed in time. The Commandant was not treacherous. He himself with a small staff would keep their eye on developments from the Kommandantur.

The Commandant accepted the terms with some alacrity. As Colonel Tod walked back to the prisoners' courtyard to assemble his

staff officers, the first American tanks were spotted on the horizon through Keith Milne's telescopes.

All through the night of the fourteenth to the fifteenth the battle for Colditz continued. There was an electric power cut in the whole district, and the slave gang was hard put to it, to keep the wireless receiver in action. The searchlights went out. Instead, a pale moon suffused the Castle with ghostly luminosity. Its belfries, buttresses and towering walls stood out grimly against the skyline. Unearthly lights and shadows flickered across its surface, cast up from the flames and the smoke in the valley. Like an evil witch, it hovered over the steaming cauldron of the town, applying fuel to the fire underneath as the bright flashes of exploding shells sent dark clouds into the air and new fires licked around the bowl.

Nobody slept much during the night. The moon cast a grey light into the dormitories and the very air seemed feverish. Men tossed and turned, straw palliasses rustled interminably. Explosions shook the buildings and air blast whoofed through the wide open windows, tinkling the panes of glass. The rasp of machine-guns increased as the moonlight faded giving place to a dawn that streaked layers of grey and gold across the sky from the east. The rattle of muskets drew nearer. American light bombers droned overhead and dropped their shattering loads on the railway lines and the roads.

Sunday, the fifteenth of April, saw the culmination of the attack. The weather was fine and the sun shone in a translucent spring sky. American shellfire was heavy all through the morning, yet the Castle was not hit. It was now obviously being carefully preserved. The town was being reduced to a mass of burning timber, rubble and twisted steel.

One of the five French Generals who had recently arrived, General de Boisse, of the French 62nd Division, chose this morning to have his portrait painted in pastelles by the camp artist, John Watton. A jagged white chalk streak on the picture, underneath the General's chin, which he would not allow to be removed, records to this day, the moment when the Germans tried to blow up Colditz bridge.

It was their last despairing effort to delay the Americans before retreating with their tanks, a beaten enemy, towards the south-east.

The blown bridge did not collapse. Piers were damaged but the roadway held, and the Americans were not stopped. By eleven o'clock in the morning their tanks were seen in the village. One

after the other, with long intervals between, they trundled carefully into the main street, splaying out fanwise into secondary roads and lanes as they reached them. Moving warily in front and around the tanks could be seen the mine removal squads and the infantry. The latter, covered by the tanks, advanced from house to house amongst the ruins, breaking in the front doors where they remained standing, and disappearing inside. From the windows, white sheets would appear, one after the other, in token of surrender.

Underneath the walls of the Castle, a tank rounded a street corner, Lying in the gutter, not fifty yards away, a fairhaired Hitler Youth, of scarcely fifteen years, opened up on it with a machine-gun. A woman, probably his mother, screamed at him from an upper window in the house nearby. Another machine-gun crackled angrily, and the boy rolled over. American G.I.s appeared from behind the tank and began taking over the houses, one by one, on either side of the street.

Half an hour later, the gate into the prisoners' courtyard opened, and an American soldier stepped into the spring sunshine in the middle of the yard. A tall, broad-chested G.I. with an open, weatherbeaten countenance, his belt and straps festooned with ammunition clips and grenades, a sub-machine gun in his hand, he stood and, looking upwards, slowly turned around. His gaze toured the full circle of the steep roofs above him, the massive walls, the barred windows and, finally, the cobbles at his feet.

There were many officers in the courtyard at the time. For fully a minute they watched him, incredulously. Some were walking around the yard. They stopped and stared at him blankly. Some were chatting in groups. They ceased talking and looked, quizzically, in his direction. A few, unperturbed by the march of events, were sitting on benches, reading. The sudden silence made them raise their heads. They stared with mouths agape at the strange intruder standing in the sunlight. Faces at the windows remained motionless like wax masks without expression.

Dick Howe saw the G.I. enter. A brainstorm momentarily paralysed the normal currents of his mind. His memory played tricks upon him, and switched, suddenly, to a scene which floated past his inward eye. He saw himself standing on a dusty road outside Calais in 1940, unarmed and a prisoner. A German soldier was passing and he shouted, "*Für Sie das Krieg ist geendet. Wir fahren gegen England, Sie gehen nach Deutschland.*" Now the irony of the words struck him. "For you the war is over." That was five years ago. And the German? He was probably dead long ago.

An officer, standing near the gate, advanced with outstretched hand and shook the hand extended by the American, who grinned at him and said, cheerfully, "Any doughboys here?" The spell was broken.

The blown bridge did not stop the Americans

Suddenly, a mob was rushing towards him, shouting and cheering and struggling madly to reach him, to make sure that he was alive, to touch him and from the touch to know again the miracle of living, to be men in their own right, freed from bondage, outcast

no more, liberated by their Allies and their friends, their faith in God's mercy justified, their patience rewarded, the nobility of mankind vindicated, justice at last accomplished and tyranny once more overcome.

Men wept, unable to restrain themselves. It was not enough that the body was free once more to roam the earth. Feelings, pent up and dammed behind the mounting walls of five successive torturing, introverted years, had to erupt.

They welled up like gushing springs, they overflowed, they burst their banks, they tumbled unhindered and uncontrolled. Frenchmen with tears streaming down their faces kissed each other on both cheeks—the salute of brothers. They kissed the G.I., they kissed everyone within range. The storm of emotion burst. The merciful rain descended. The grey clouds drifted from the horizon of the mind, borne on fresh salt and moisture-laden breezes across the unchained oceans of memory from the far off shores of love. Home and country beckoned, loved ones were waiting. Wives and sweethearts, mothers, fathers, and children never seen, were calling across the gulf of the absent years.

Man was at his finest amidst the grandeur of this moment of liberation. A noble symphony arranged by the Great Composer had reached its thunderous finale and, as the last triumphal chord swelled into the Hymn of Nations, man looked into the face of his Creator turned towards him, a vision of tenderness, mirrored for an instant by the purity of his own unrepressed torrent of joy and thankfulness. At such a moment, mountains move at the behest of man, he has such power in the sight of God.

CHAPTER XXV

CODA: THE CLIFFS OF DOVER

THE celebrations upon the relief of the Castle began in earnest on Sunday afternoon, the fifteenth of April. Food reserves, laid in for a siege, were broken out and the Americans brought wine and beer from the village. Colonel Tod wisely kept the prisoners inside the Castle until the first exuberance at their deliverance had worn off. It was better they should become accustomed in their minds to the idea that they were free before they were actually let loose upon the world. They were, be it remembered, "the men of spirit".

Tod had already organised officers into squads with specific duties and instructions, varying according to the different eventualities that he could foresee. In the circumstances, as no fighting was required of his men, only the squads with technical duties came into action. Before they did so, however, he held a conference with the American officer commanding the troops who had captured the town.

Lieutenant-Colonel Shaughnessy came from Carolina. He spoke with a slow drawl and acted with lightning rapidity. He was not, after all, in command of one of Hodge's most daring spearheads, driving hundreds of miles into enemy territory in advance of the main forces, for nothing. Tried in battle, full of initiative and daring, he was one of the men who shortened the war and saved thousands of lives. A colonel of the 69th American Infantry Division of the U.S. Third Army, he was commanding detachments of his own division, supported by mobile artillery, along with tank units, taken from the American 9th Armoured Division. These together, constituted his Task Force. Among his junior officers was Lieutenant Keny Dodson, the genial and efficient young artillery officer who had commanded the shoot against Colditz.

At the conference, held in the German Kommandantur, Shaughnessy accepted the surrender of the Castle and its garrison. The Commandant and Hauptman Eggers, the Security officer, were arrested. Tod proposed that the P.O.W.s, other than those on special duties, should be kept within the Castle precincts until Tuesday the seventeenth. Shaughnessy agreed this was wise and warned that German suicide parties were still dotted all over the countryside. Tod offered the services of his organised squads to keep the water and electricity supply of Colditz functioning, to look after other essential town services, and to see that repairs were effected as quickly as possible. Shaughnessy accepted, and the British Technical Squads came into action.

Gordon Rolfe left the camp with a party within the hour, to take over the Colditz power station and start it running again. Dick set off with another party to look after the water pumping station. On the way he commandeered a powerful B.M.W. German Army motor-cycle which became "his transport" until he boarded a plane for England. He found the pumping station had not suffered badly from the bombardment. Buildings had been damaged but the sturdy machinery was in working order. Debris alone had to be cleared and the pumps could be started again on power from the heavy oil engines. German staff were already back at the

station when he arrived. The Teutonic passion for work and order could not be denied. Dick found they needed no goading and no supervision, although they did not know how, where or when their next pay packet would materialise. They cleared and cleaned and repaired. The pumps were working again by Sunday evening, supplying water to the town. Water pipes were burst and leaking everywhere. The task of repairing them was tackled by another squad of Royal Engineers.

In the Castle, Americans came and went and stories of the latter days went the rounds. Lieutenant Dodson confessed that the Castle was within an ace of being bombarded by his mobile artillery detachment with high explosive shells followed by phosphorus, when the task force approached Colditz. Standing orders were to flatten anything that showed resistance. Colditz showed resistance, and the best target in the town was the Castle. Dodson's artillery was fanned out and ranging on it when a spotter noticed a flag in one of the windows through his binoculars. It was a French flag. He scanned the Castle more closely and saw a Union Jack. He immediately telephoned Dodson who held his fire and sent word back to headquarters at Hohnbach, a village they had just captured, asking for confirmation as to the nature of the Castle. The answer came through: "Do not repeat not shell Castle which contains P.O.W."

The prison was, in fact, within an ace of being shelled. As far as can be ascertained Hohnbach received the order to preserve the Castle from Hodge's headquarters at about the same time as Dodson asked for confirmation. Be it noted that this occurred some twelve hours before Colonel Tod agreed with the German Commandant not to hang out flags. By then there was evidence indicating that the shelling was deliberately directed away from the Castle.

On Sunday afternoon, the glider was taken from its hiding place. The trap-door in the floor of the workshop was carefully enlarged and the glider parts were lowered into the big attic with the dormer windows. In this empty room the four builders assembled the glider. By five o'clock it was ready. They sealed the trap-door up to the workshop and then opened the main door of the lower attic. Dick experienced the pleasure of sitting in the cockpit and manipulating the controls. "It's a perfect little bird," he said as he waggled the rudder. "I believe I'd be as safe in this as in my old Matilda."

And Lulu Lawton commented sadly, "I'd have given a lot to see the Jerries' reaction when the bathful of concrete landed on the floor after falling sixty feet."

News of the existence of the glider had spread like wild-fire. The

camp had been advised that the glider would be on view and there was a queue already waiting that stretched to the bottom of the spiral staircase. When the door opened the crowd surged forward.

As there were thirteen hundred officers in the camp at the time, the queue continued late into the evening. An American girl, a newspaper correspondent—Lee Carson was her name—had found her way to Colditz and she was escorted to the attic by Duggie Bader. She took photographs. (The glider builders and the author would give much to be able to trace them.)

The glider reposed on its polished skid, a symphony in blue and white check; its wings glossy and taut; its controls sensitive, balanced, easy to the touch; a tropical bird, it looked as if it needed only a gentle breeze to float it easily off the ground. It filled the attic. Its total span from wing tip to wing tip was thirty-three feet. It was a beautiful piece of craftsmanship and astounded all who saw it. Men gasped with wonder and appreciation as they toured around it. The Americans asked:

"Where has it come from? How was it possible to build it under the Germans' noses?" They were told.

Germans, remaining in the camp under Allied orders, to keep it functioning, who saw it too, asked the same questions. The answer was, "You were our guards. You ought to know without being told."

Before the prisoners vacated the Castle the attic was locked up again. Both the glider and the secret workshop may still be there to this day. . . .

Monday the sixteenth was a dog day in which prisoners recovered from the celebrations of Sunday and began to regain their perspective, looking towards new horizons.

On Tuesday, they were allowed the freedom of Colditz, but warned not to venture into the surrounding country which was placed out of bounds. Three Frenchmen who disobeyed the order were recaptured by the Germans and disappeared.

Colonel Shaughnessy was busy, with British and French help, organising preparations for the evacuation of the prisoners. Dick Howe recalls two vivid impressions of that day. The first was that of the Weasel, the City Slicker and Mac (MacColm) holding open house in a villa near the Castle in which three beautiful blonde

German Fraüleins acted as their hostesses serving tea, coffee, drinks and meals throughout the day to all visitors. The second was that of the Distillery Monopoly Directors, Charlie Goonstein Van Rood, Bush Parker and Bag Dickenson, driving around the town in a huge Mercédès Benz touring car.

The town was found to be full of slave workers of both sexes: Poles, French, Czechs, Russians, Rumanians, Yugoslavs, Hungarians and Jews.

On Wednesday, April the eighteenth, the evacuation began.

American trucks, driven by Negro drivers, carried the British contingent a hundred miles to the south-west.

Dick, on his B.M.W., acted as outrider to one of the columns. The convoy was widely spread out for safety, and on the move, the Negroes drove the trucks at full throttle all the time. The leading fifteen-hundredweight truck contained the American officer in charge and Hauptman Püpcke, one of the German officers of Colditz. He knew the roads of the district. The going was danger-ous at times, especially through the woods, where German *Sturm-geschutze* nests—S.S. stormtroopers—still lurked in ambush. Dick, at the behest of the American officer, had the nasty job of recon-noitring a road block which loomed ahead at one stage of the journey. He rode flat out up to it, weaving as he approached. He found it unmanned. Not once, through thirty miles of no-man's land, was the column shot at, though shadows flitted about amongst the trees in the surrounding woods. Strength in numbers seemed to be the explanation.

They arrived, in the late afternoon, at a captured airfield near Chemnitz, called Kaledar, were given a hot meal of American Army rations and bedded down on clean straw for the night.

Early next morning, as Dick stepped out of the hut where they had been sleeping he was accosted by the Major in charge of the airfield.

"I hear you boys are back from five years in prison?" he questioned.

"That's correct," said Dick.

"I guess you're keen to get back home then. I'll see what I can do." He hailed the leading crew of a flight of Dakotas that had just landed.

"Where're you going back to?" he shouted.

The leading officer replied, approaching:

"We're due for Rolle."

"No you're not," said the Major, "you're going to England."

"Suits me!" came the answer.

Within two hours they were boarding the planes. There must have been ten of them because they took the whole British contingent, thirty to a plane. Dick tried to take his B.M.W. with him—it was a beautiful machine. There was nothing doing, he had to leave it behind. He rode around the hutted camp at the edge of the airfield until he saw a G.I. coming out of a workshop. With a roar he rode up behind him, stopped and said:

"Hey! can you ride a motor-bike ?"

"Yea."

"Well," said Dick dismounting, "you've got one."

He hurried off to join his plane and, looking back, saw the G.I., arms akimbo, slowly walking around the machine, with his eyes agog, like an art connoisseur who had just been presented with an old master out of the sky.

The weather was bad and the ceiling was practically zero. In Dick's plane were many of the "Old Contemptibles"—men who had been in Colditz from the very early days: Guy German, Rupert Barry, Scarlet O'Hara, Cyril Lewthwaite, Padre Platt, Don Donaldson, Peter Storie Pugh, Stooge Wardle, Keith Milne and Jim Rogers. The plane cavorted about the sky. Everybody except Don Donaldson was sick. They landed to refuel at Rouen and then crossed the Channel amongst the clouds, almost dropping into the sea at times.

Jim Rogers, who was not as ill as some of the others, went forward to the cockpit and looked ahead into the blank wall of vapour. He asked the Pilot:

"Are we anywhere near Dover?" The plane lurched and sank a hundred feet. The green spuming sea appeared just below them.

"Don't know!" was the reply, "I'm following the guy in front."

Jim scanned the clouds in front without seeing anything. He was rubbing his head ruefully where something hard had hit him when the aircraft bumped.

"Visibility yesterday was nil," said the Pilot. "One of our planes flew head on into the cliffs, "It's better to-day."

Jim went back to the others, seated facing each other on the floor, backs propped up against the bulwarks. They were looking green. The smell of sick was overpowering. Jim was terrified. After five years, to come to a sticky end in the Channel! He longed to see the cliffs of Dover but he did not want to meet them head on. He could see the crash coming. In a daze he heard his own voice:

"We're nearly home, boys. The pilot's terrific. Gives you confidence. He says he's sorry about the weather, but he wants you to see the cliffs of Dover. That's why he's flying low—so you don't miss them." He suddenly halted in his speech as he realised what he had said. Then another thought struck him. "About time I stopped this morale boosting," he said to himself. "The chaps'll have to look after themselves now."

Don Donaldson, the R.A.F. veteran, wedged in a corner near the tail, had been dozing peacefully. He looked up at Jim and then at the rows of green faces around him and said: "Tell 'em a story, Old Horse. They look as if they need cheering up. Tell 'em about the Mandarin's daughter you met in Hong Kong. They've got to get accustomed to having women folk around again."

* When Admiral Doenitz surrendered on May 2nd after the death of Hitler, the Russians, by Allied agreement, occupied Königstein. A week later, the prisoners, including senior staff officers, Dutch, Belgian, French, British and American, were still confined in the Castle. Two Americans escaped to the American lines, forty miles away, and within hours a U.S. armed convoy entered the town and removed the whole prisoner contingent. Hopetoun and Haig were promptly flown to Britain in an ambulance plane. Both men recovered their health slowly.

DRAMATIS PERSONÆ

[The publishers will gladly include in subsequent editions any corrections or additions to these particulars, which have been completed and checked to the best of the author's ability]

Page of First Mention	Surname	Initials or Christian Name	Late War Rank	Regiment or Corps	Nickname or Abbreviated Name	Decorations	Present Rank
225	ALEXANDER A nephew of General Alexander.	Michael	Capt.	D.C.L.I.	Mike		
33	ALLAN	A. M.	2nd-Lieut.	Queen's Own Cameron Highlanders	Peter	M.I.D.	Captain G.S.
139	ALMERAS	André	Lieut.				
119	ANDERSON	W. F.	Major	R.E.	Andy or Oboe-Sport	M.B.E., M.C. and Bar	Colonel
139	ARCHER	L. R.	Spr.	R.A.E., A.I.F.			
152	ARUNDELL, OF WARDOUR	John	Capt. the Lord	Wiltshire Regiment		He was the sixteenth	
	Repatriated. Died in hospital in October, 1944, a few days after landing in England. Baron. He left no heirs and the title is now extinct.						
47	BADER	Douglas R. S.	Wing Commander	R.A.F.	Duggie or Wings	D.S.O. and Bars, D.F.C. and Bar	Group Captain
34	BAJETTO	M. C.					
153	BARATT Now in Canada	T. M.	Lieut.	The Black Watch: R.H.R. (of Canada)	Peter		
218	BARNES		Lieut.	R.N.R.			

Page of First Mention	Surname	Initials or Christian Name	Late War Rank	Regiment or Corps	Nickname or Abbreviated Name	Decorations	Present Rank
230	BARNET	R.	Lieut.	Royal Inniskilling Fusiliers	Skipper		
	Escaped successfully from Colditz in 1944.						
70	BARRAS	Edgar					
33	BARRY	R. R. F. T.	Captain	52nd Light Infantry: The Oxfordshire and Buckinghamshire Light Infantry	Rupert	M.B.E.	Major Now Parachute Regiment
91	BARTLETT	D. E.	Lieut.	R.T.R.		M.C.	
94	BARTON	H. E. E.	Lieut.	R.A.S.C.	Teddy		
33	BEETES	Trevor	Lieut.	R.N.I.A.	Ted		
273	BERGER		General	S.S.			
184	BEST	W.	Fl.-Lieut.	R.A.F.V.R.	Jack	M.B.E.	
	Farming in Kenya						
56	BISSELL	J. B.	Lieut.	R.A.	Monty		
279	de BOISSE		General	French 62nd Division			
128	BOUSTEAD	John R.	Lieut.	Seaforth Highlanders	Bertie		
	Died in London in the summer of 1947.						
70	BREJOUX	Jean					
229	BROOMHALL	W. M.	Lt.-Col.	R.E.	Tubby	O.B.E.	Maj.-Gen.
	S.B.O. at Colditz for a period of the War.						
163	BROWN		Sergeant				
50	BRUCE	Dominic	Fl.-Lt.		The Medium-sized Man		

Page of First Mention	Surname	Initials or Christian Name	Late War Rank	Regiment or Corps	Nickname or Abbreviated Name	Decorations	Present Rank
94	DICKENSON	J. P.	Fl.-Lt.	R.A.F.	Bag or Ming		Fl.-Lt.
70	DIEDLER	Georges			Kenny		
283	DODSON		Lieut.	U.S. Army Artillery			
66	DONALDSON Now in Civil Aviation	M. W.	Fl.-Lt.	R.A.F.	Don or The Weasel		
150	DONKERS		Lieut.	R.N.I.A.			
22	DOORNINCK (Van)		Lt.-Cmdr.	Royal Netherlands Navy	Rip Van Winkle		
148	DOUW-VAN-DER-KRAP Escaped successfully from Germany.	Charles	Lieut.	Royal Netherlands Navy			
152	DREW	G. S.	Lieut.	Northumberland Regiment (58th)	George		
225	DUHAMEL Nephew of Sir Winston Churchill	Max	Lieut.				
223	DUKE	Florimond	Lt.-Col.	U.S. Army			
152	EDWARDS	R. W. (?)	Lieut.	Royal Welsh Fusiliers	Mike		Major
32	EGGERS German Security Officer at Colditz.	Hauptman			Smarmy		
38	ELLIOTT Escaped successfully from Colditz in 1944.	H. A. V.	Captain	Irish Guards	Harry		
224	ELPHINSTONE Nephew of the Queen Mother.	J.	Capt. The Master of		John		Major (Ret.)
39	ELSTOB		Lieut.	R.N.	Willie		

77	FLYNN		F.-O.	R.A.F.	Erroll	
111	FORBES		Fl.-Lt.	R.A.F.	Bricky	
22	FOWLER	H. N.	Fl.-Lt.	R.A.F.	Bill	M.C. Killed while

22 FOWLER. Escaped successfully from Colditz, September, 1942, was promoted to Squadron Leader. test flying in March, 1944.

151	FRASER					
70	GAMBERO	Jean				
139	GEE	Howard		A civilian attached to the Finnish International Brigade		
32	GEPHARD		Oberstabs-feldwebel	German Army	Mussolini	
22	GERMAN	Guy	Lt.-Col.	Royal Leicestershire Regiment		D.S.O., T.D.

22 GERMAN. Senior British Officer at Colditz, 1941–1942.

50	GIGUE	D.	Lieut.	Foreign Legion		
203	GILL	D.	Lieut.	Royal Norfolks		
70	GODFRIN	Léonce			Derek	
139	GOLDFINCH	L. J. E.	Fl.-Lt.	R.A.F.V.R.	Bill	Mentioned in Despatches
184	GOLDMAN	S.	Fusilier	Royal Northumberland Fusiliers	Solly	
148	HAGEMAN	Aak				
225	HAIG		Capt. Lord	Scots Greys		
230	HALIFAX	D.	Fl.-Lt.	R.A.F.	Dan	
139	HALL	Sidney				
153	HAMILTON	D. K.	Lieut.	R.A.		

Page of First Mention	Surname	Initials or Christian Name	Late War Rank	Regiment or Corps	Nickname or Abbreviated Name	Decorations	Present Rank
27	HAMILTON-BAILLIE	J.	Lieut.	R.E.		M.C.	
22	HAMMOND		Engine room Artificer	R.N.	Wally	D.S.M., B.E.M.	
	Escaped successfully to Switzerland in December, 1942. Now with the Iraq Petroleum Company in the Middle East.						
93	HARRISON		Lieut.	Green Howards	Rex		
95	HARVEY	E. M.	Lieut.	R.N.	Mike		Cmdr.
22	HEARD Died in 1952.	R. G.	Chaplain (4th Class)	R.A.Ch.D.	Dicky	M.B.E., M.C.	
36	HEUVEL (van den) Killed in action in Java on June 28th, 1946.		Capt.	Royal Netherlands Indies Army	Vandy		
22	HOBBLING Killed in Germany while still a P.O.W., 1944, as the result of a bombing raid upon his P.O.W. camp.	J. C.	(Rev.) Capt. R.A.Ch.D.		Joe or Hobbles		
152	HOPETOUN (Earl of) Now Marquis of Linlithgow.		Capt.	Lothian and Border Yeomanry	Charlie	M.C.	
104	HOW	Geoffrey Munro Pemberton	Capt.	R.A.S.C.	Pembum		
32	HOWE Awarded the M.B.E. for his work as Escape Officer, Colditz, from 1942 to 1945.	R. H.	Capt.	R.T.S.	Dick	M.B.E., M.C.	
110	HUNTER	David	Lieut.	R.M.		M.C. awarded in Malaya	Major

No.	Name	Rank	Regiment	Nickname	Honours
90	HYDE-THOMPSON R.J. — Died in Uganda in August, 1951.	Lieut.	Durham Light Infantry	John	M.C. Major
192	IRONSIDE Hugo — Nephew of the Field-Marshal.	Lieut.	R.T.R.		
23	JABLONOWSKI F. (Count)	Lieut.	Polish Army (Horse Artillery)	Felix	
79	JEAN-JEAN (Curé) Paul — Vicar of an R.C. Parish in Monte Carlo in 1950.				
23	KARPF Antony	Lieut. (Aspirant)	Polish Army	Fish	
68	KIMBER T.	Major	R.E.	Tom	
148	KOMOROWSKI Tadeusz — Leader of the Polish Army of Liberation, Warsaw, 1944.	General		Bor	
148	KRUIMINK Fritz E. — Escaped successfully from Germany.			Beer	
32	LANGE — German Assistant Security Officer at Colditz.	Rittmeister	German Army (Cavalry)		
225	LASCELLES, LORD George — The present Earl of Harewood.	Lieut.	Grenadier Guards		
38	LAWTON W.T. — Awarded the M.I.D. for his work at Colditz.	Capt.	Duke of Wellington's Regiment.	Lulu	M.I.D.
44	LE BRIGANT — Senior French Officer at Colditz.	Colonel	French Cavalry		General
196	LEBRUN-MAIRESSE Pierre — Escaped successfully from Colditz, July 1st, 1941.	Capt.	French Cavalry		Officer of the Legion of Honour, Croix de Guerre. M.C.
215	LEWTHWAITE Cyril	Capt.	Royal Warwickshire Regiment.	Luthers	M.C.

Page of First Mention	Surname	Initials or Christian Name	Late War Rank	Regiment or Corps	Nickname or Abbreviated Name	Decorations	Present Rank
150	LIGTERMOET	Arie					
	Died in Odessa in 1947 after his escape from Germany.						
147	LINDEN (van) (Baron)	Jap					Major
	An A.D.C. to Prince Bernhardt of the Netherlands.						
87	LINDKERKE (Baron)		Major	Belgian Army			
147	LINGEN (Van)						
22	LISTER		E.R.A.	R.N.	Tubby	D.S.M. B.E.M.	
	Escaped successfully to Switzerland in December, 1942.						
22	LITTLEDALE	R.B.	Major	60th Rifles	Ronnie	D.S.O.	
	Escaped successfully from Colditz in October, 1942. Killed in action in Normandy in August, 1944.						
159	LOCKETT	Charles	Sqdn.-Ldr.	R.A.F.	Lucy		
157	LOCKWOOD	K.	Capt.	The Queen's Royal Regiment	Kenneth or Lockout or the Ear		
22	LUTEYN			R.N.I.A.			
70	MADIN	Roger	Lieut.	French Artillery	Tony		Capt. (Reserve)
225	MARCHAND	A	Lieut.	Fusiliers Mount Royal	Roger		
	A French Canadian.						
285	McCOLM	M. L.	Sq.-Ldr.	R.A.F.	Mac		
	An Australian.						
275	McGRATH		Colonel				
139	McKENZIE	C. D.	Lieut.	Seaforth Highlanders	Colin	M.C.	
152	MERRITT	C. C. I.	Lt.-Col.	South Saskatchewan Regiment	Cecil	V.C.	Major

152	MILLER	W. A.	Lieut.	R.C.E.	Dopey	
	Escaped from Colditz, missing ever since.					
187	MILNE	Keith	Fl.-Lt.	R.A.F.	City Slicker or Slick	
	A Canadian.					
152	MOIR	Douglas N.	Lieut.	R.T.R.	Duggie	
134	NAUMANN (Dr.)	Alexander				
22	NEAVE	Airey	Lieut.	R.A.	Oscar or Tony	D.S.O., O.B.E., M.C., Croix de Guerre, T.D. (with 1st Clasp) — Lt.-Col. (T.A.)
	Now Conservative M.P. for Abingdon					
37	O'HARA	W. L. B.	Lieut.	R.T.R.	Scarlet	
	A Canadian Died in Canada shortly after the war.					
22	PADDON	Brian	Sq.-Ldr.	R.A.F.		D.S.O., D.F.C. — Group Captain
	Escaped successfully from Colditz in 1942.					
70	PAILLE			French Army		
192	PARDOE		Lieut.	K.R.R.C.	Phil	
93	PARKER	Vincent	Fl.-Lt.	R.A.F.	Bush	
	Killed while Test flying.					
152	PENMAN	John	Lieut.	Argyll and Sutherland Highlanders		M.C. — Major
	M.C. awarded in Korea.					
262	PETCZYNSKI	Tadeusz	General	Polish Army of Liberation, Warsaw, 1944		
22	PLATT	J. Ellison	Capt.	R.A.CH.D., attached to 10th London C.C.S.	Platters or The Old Crow	M.B.E.
	Now Methodist Minister at Orpington, Kent.					

Page of First Mention	Surname	Initials or Christian Name	Late War Rank	Regiment or Corps	Nickname or Abbreviated Name	Decorations	Present Rank
120	POPE	Lancelot	Capt.		Lance or Steiny		
127	PRAVITT		Oberst-Lieut.	German Army			
	The German Commandant of Colditz.						
101	PRICE	I. S.	Lieut.	Gordon Highlanders	Scorgie		
32	PRIEM		Hauptman	German Army			
	Died at the end of the war.						
32	PÜPCKE		Hauptman	German Army			
	Owned a chocolate factory in the Russian Zone of Germany and is reported missing.						
230	REID	Miles	Major	Recce Corps		M.C.	
22	REID	P. R.	Capt.	R.A.S.C.	Pat	M.B.E., M.C.	Major
	The author of the present book.						
65	ROGERS	D. J.	Capt.	R.E.	Jim or The Old Horse		
152	ROLFE	Gordon L.	Major	Royal Canadian Signals		D.S.O.	
152	ROLT	A. R.	Lieut.	Rifle Brigade	Tony		Major
	The motor-racing driver.						
224	ROMILLY	Giles		War Correspondent			
	A nephew of Sir Winston Churchill						
129	ROOD (van)	A.	Fl.-Lt.	R.A.F.V.R.	Good-time Charlie Goonstein		
	A Dutchman in the R.A.F.						
153	SANDBACK	C. E.	Lieut.	Cheshire Yeomanry			

No.	Surname	Name	Rank	Regiment	Nickname	Decorations	Later Rank
223	SCHAEFER	W. H.	Colonel	U.S. Army	Bill	M.C.	Major
140	SCOTT	W. H.	Capt.	Essex Scottish, Canada	Gris	M.C.	Lt.-Col.
43	SCOURFIELD	Grismond Davies	Lieut.	60th (K.R.R.C.)			
150	SEYDLITZ (von) —KURZBACH	Hans					
	Missing in Russia.						
283	SHAUGHNESSY		Lt.-Col.	U.S. Army			
163	SHERIFF		R.S.M.				
229	SILVERWOOD-COPE	Christopher H.	Lieut.	Surrey and Sussex Yeomanry R.A.	Kit		
33	SINCLAIR	A. M.	Lieut.	60th Rifles (K.R.R.C.)	Mike	D.S.O.	
	Killed while escaping from Colditz on September 25th, 1944.						
192	STALLARD	T.	Major	D.L.I.	Tom	D.S.O., O.B.E.	Lt.-Col.
110	STAYNER	D. S.	Lt.-Col.	The Dorsetshire Regiment	Daddy		
	Senior British Officer at Colditz for a period of the war.						
211	STEENHAUER			A Dutchman			
22	STEPHENS	W. L.	Lt.-Cmdr.	R.N.V.R.	Billie	D.S.C., V.R.D.	Cmdr.
	Escaped successfully from Colditz in October, 1942.						
133	STIRLING	David	Lt.-Col.	Scots Guards. Long Range Desert Group		D.S.O.	
37	STORIE-PUGH	Peter D.	Lieut.	Queen's Own West Kent Regiment	Puff	M.B.E., M.C., T.D. and Clasp	Major, Cambridgeshire Regiment R.A.
223	SUAREZ	Alfred	Capt.	U.S. Army Engineers	Al		
270	THIELEMAN	André	Lieut.				
195	THOM	D.	Fl.-Lt.	R.A.F.	Don		
	A Canadian in the R.A.F.						

Page of First Mention	Surname	Initials or Christian Name	Late War Rank	Regiment or Corps	Nickname or Abbreviated Name	Decorations	Present Rank
229	TOD	W.	Colonel	Royal Scots Fusiliers	Willie	D.S.O., O.B.E., M.C.	
	Senior British Officer at Colditz towards the end of the war.						
135	TUNSTALL	Peter D.	Fl.-Lt.	R.A.F.	Pete		Sq.-Ldr.
152	UPHAM	C. H.	Capt.	New Zealand Military Forces	Charlie	V.C. and Bar	
150	VEENENDAAL		Capt.				
27	WALKER	David H.	Capt.	Black Watch			
270	WALL BAKE (van den)			R.N.I.A.			
240	WARDLE	Geoffrey	Lieut.	R.N.	Stooge		
22	WARDLE	H. D.	Fl.-Lt.	R.A.F.	Hank	M.C.	
	A Canadian. Escaped successfully from Colditz in October, 1942.						
202	WATTON	J. Fessenden	Lieut.	Border Regiment	John		
	The Artist.						
152	WELD-FORESTER	Charles W.	Lieut.	Rifle Brigade	Charlie		
92	WELDON	F. W. C.	Capt.	R.H.A.	Frank	M.C., M.V.O.	Major
	Now commanding King's Troop R.H.A.						
242	WELCH	Lorne	Fl.-Lt.	R.A.F.	Lorne		
	The gliding expert and instructor.						
34	WILKINS	John	Ldg. Tel.	R.N.			
259	WINANT	John, Jr.	Lieut.	U.S. Army Air Corps			
	An American. Son of the war-time American Ambassador to the U.K.						
140	WRIGHT	Stephen Fitz-herbert	Capt.	9th Lancers	Screwie		
	The race-horse trainer.						
34	YULE	J.	Lieut.	R.C.S.	Jimmy		Major